D1503397

Under the Editorship of

Herold C. Hunt

Charles William Eliot Professor of Education

Harvard University

Educational Administration: Cases and Concepts

CYRIL G. SARGENT · EUGENE L. BELISLE
Harvard University

HOUGHTON MIFFLIN COMPANY
Boston · The Riverside Press Cambridge

Personal and place names in the cases are disguised, except in Cases 12, 16, 26, and 28–30.

The Riverside Press

Cambridge · Massachusetts

Printed in the U.S.A.

TO STUDENTS WHO USE THIS BOOK

May you find in your experience together much more
than we as teachers can give to you

Editor's Introduction

Although educators differ on many problems confronting their profession, they have long been agreed that there is no one right or best method of teaching. The skillful teacher is likely to employ a variety of methods as he seeks to meet the many different conditions of formal and informal study. In recent years the case method, originally developed in other disciplines, has increasingly proved its value in education courses. Though variously used in different fields, the method has several common denominators, and the differences in its application are largely matters of emphasis. Inherent are the appropriate use of theory and the acquisition of factual material and procedural skills, but the core of the method is the use of the description of an actual situation out of which a problem ("case") has developed. The purpose is to encourage and develop in the student not only the necessary competences for dealing with real-life problems, but also the wisdom to see whether and how the problems might have been avoided.

Advocates of the case method suggest that it develops experience in the process of thinking. They point out that the study of a case involves all the steps associated with problem-solving: the recognition and location of the difficulty; the definition of the underlying problem; the arrangement of facts and skills necessary for handling the difficulty; the construction of possible solutions; the testing and elaboration of those that seem best; the verification of conclusions; the obligation to extend the solution into a form of knowledge which will facilitate the solution of other difficulties having similar characteristics and dimensions.

At Harvard University, where much has been done to pioneer the case method in various fields and develop it to a high level of proficiency, the Graduate School of Education has been busily engaged in gathering case materials and working out effective ways of using them. Active in that undertaking have been the authors of this book, Cyril G. Sargent and Eugene L. Belisle. Not only have they given leadership to the careful garnering of data and the subsequent development of the cases on which this text draws so richly, but they have also been responsible for the "Cases and Concepts" courses through which the student is helped to move dynamically between the general and the concrete, the theory and the practice. They are, therefore, pre-eminently qualified to offer a textbook that approaches educational administration and its concepts through the case-study method. It gives me particular pleasure, as their colleague, to write these words of introduction, not only in grateful expression of a friendship that is both professional and personal, but also in recognition of the significant contribution which they have made in this book, and in the endeavors that underlie it, to the field of educational administration.

HEROLD C. HUNT

Preface

This textbook in educational administration had its origin in a program that began in the spring of 1952 at the Graduate School of Education at Harvard University. Earlier, the need for new directions in research and training in educational administration had been expressed in a proposal to the W. K. Kellogg Foundation, and this proposal had led, in September, 1950, to the Cooperative Program in Educational Administration in New England, with the Harvard Graduate School of Education serving as the regional center. By late fall of 1951, enriched by contributions from several fields of administration and from the social sciences as represented on a growing staff, the thinking had become clarified to a degree that justified the test of a new training program. This Administrative Career Program, as it was named, broke sharply with traditional programs of doctorate study in its attempt to prepare for a field of action.

In the past three years a number of variations have been introduced into the original design; but a continuing element of the program has been a sequence referred to as "Cases and Concepts." This book presents some of the cases which have been used in this unit. It also suggests some of the thinking of the authors, as this has evolved over these years of collaboration both on the development of the cases and on the instructional responsibilities of the "Cases and Concepts" unit.

As a result of our close collaboration in this and many other activities, it is impossible and indeed pointless to try to separate the ideas and points of view each of us has contributed. We have, however, gravitated into a mutually satisfying arrangement by which Mr. Sargent tends to assume the major role in the "case" aspect of the program and Mr. Belisle the major role on the "concepts" side. Mr. Sargent insists on acknowledging that Sections Two and Five of this book reflect particularly Mr. Belisle's experience and thinking.

We wish to acknowledge our debt to our colleagues for their stimulation of our thinking during those exciting days when the new Administrative Career Program was being crystallized as a joint undertaking. To each one individually — Alfred D. Simpson; George Flower, now Director of the CEA–Kellogg Project in Canada; Neal Gross; James M. Shipton; and Alfred De Grazia, now at Stanford — we express our appreciation. We are also indebted to Francis Keppel, who, as Dean of the Graduate School of

Education, gave support to the idea — including tangible support in the way of making funds available for the collection of case materials.

We have profited greatly from our discussions with members of the Faculty of the Harvard Graduate School of Business Administration. Dean Stanley Teele, George F. Lombard, John D. Glover, Andrew R. Towl, and Thomas J. Raymond have given generously of their time and interest. Joseph C. Bailey of that Faculty not only met with us but gathered the material for one of our first attempts at a community-focused case.

We are similarly grateful for help given by James Laurits, now President of Newton Junior College.

The staff of the Cooperative Program in Educational Administration at Ohio State University, and especially John A. Ramseyer, Director, have been most cooperative. We have prepared several cases based on their research materials, although these cases are not represented in this collection.

The members of the Center for Field Studies staff (Harvard Graduate School of Education) who participated in the research and writing of the cases given in this book include Faith Halfyard, Norman L. Thoburn, Evelyn I. Banning, William T. Perry, and Russell G. Davis.

We wish especially to express our appreciation to Russell Davis, with whom, for the past two years, we have shared many discussions about the development and presentation of cases and the possibilities for future directions of case research. During the past year he has been responsible for many of the cases which increasingly have seemed to us to reflect our growing experience and, we hope, sophistication in both their production and use.

Our secretaries, Peggy Gleicher, Louise Eckerman, Theresa Kovich, and Dana Cless, have spent many hours typing the manuscript, editing the cases, and proofreading. We are grateful to them for their patience and cooperation.

We wish to acknowledge that the article used as Prologue came to our attention via *Customs and Crises in Communication,* by Irving J. Lee (New York: Harper and Brothers, 1954).

Finally, for permission to use the cases we express our thanks to The President and Fellows of Harvard College, by whom the cases have been copyrighted.

* * * * *

Although he may be largely unaware of the more recent work and experience which underlie this book, it has been made possible in part by the exceptional interest in the development of American public education — and more particularly in the training of administrators and the use of case methods of learning — manifested by James B. Conant, formerly President of Harvard University.

Cyril G. Sargent
Eugene L. Belisle

Cambridge, Massachusetts
April, 1955

Contents

PROLOGUE *In the Laboratory with Agassiz* *

BY SAMUEL H. SCUDDER

IT WAS MORE than fifteen years ago [from 1874] that I entered the laboratory of Professor Agassiz, and told him I had enrolled my name in the Scientific School as a student of natural history. . . .

"When do you wish to begin?" he asked.

"Now," I replied.

This seemed to please him, and with an energetic "Very well!" he reached from a shelf a huge jar of specimens in yellow alcohol.

"Take this fish," said he, "and look at it; we call it a haemulon; by and by I will ask what you have seen." . . .

In ten minutes I had seen all that could be seen in that fish, and started in search of the Professor — who had, however, left the Museum. . . . Half an hour passed — an hour — another hour; the fish began to look loathsome. I turned it over and around; looked it in the face — ghastly; from behind, beneath, above, sideways, at a three-quarters' view — just as ghastly. I was in despair; at an early hour I concluded that lunch was necessary; so, with infinite relief, the fish was carefully replaced in the jar, and for an hour I was free.

On my return, I learned that Professor Agassiz had been at the Museum, but had gone, and would not return for several hours. My fellow-students were too busy to be disturbed by continued conversation. Slowly I drew forth that hideous fish, and with a feeling of desperation again looked at it. I might not use a magnifying-glass; instruments of all kinds were interdicted. My two hands, my two eyes, and the fish: it seemed a most limited field. I pushed my finger down its throat to feel how sharp the teeth were. I began to count the scales in the different rows, until I was convinced that that was nonsense. At last a happy thought struck me — I would draw the fish; and now with surprise I began to discover new features in the creature. Just then the Professor returned.

"That is right," said he; "a pencil is one of the best eyes." . . .

With these encouraging words, he added:

"Well, what is it like?"

He listened attentively to my brief rehearsal of the structure of parts whose names were still unknown to me: the fringed gill-arches and movable operculum; the pores of the head, fleshy lips and lidless eyes; the lateral

* From *Every Saturday,* April 4, 1874, pp. 369–370.

line, the spinous fins and forked tail; the compressed and arched body. When I had finished, he waited as if expecting more, and then, with an air of disappointment:

"You have not looked very carefully; why," he continued more earnestly, "you haven't even seen one of the most conspicuous features of the animal, which is as plainly before your eyes as the fish itself; look again, look again!" and he left me to my misery.

I was piqued; I was mortified. Still more of that wretched fish! But now I set myself to my task with a will, and discovered one new thing after another, until I saw how just the Professor's criticism had been. The afternoon passed quickly; and when, toward its close, the Professor inquired:

"Do you see it yet?"

"No," I replied, "I am certain I do not, but I see how little I saw before."

"That is next best," said he, earnestly, "but I won't hear you now; put away your fish and go home; perhaps you will be ready with a better answer in the morning. I will examine you before you look at the fish."

This was disconcerting. Not only must I think of my fish all night, studying, without the object before me, what this unknown but most visible feature might be; but also, without reviewing my new discoveries, I must give an exact account of them the next day. I had a bad memory; so I walked home by Charles River in a distracted state, with my two perplexities.

The cordial greeting from the Professor the next morning was reassuring; here was a man who seemed to be quite as anxious as I that I should see for myself what he saw.

"Do you perhaps mean," I asked, "that the fish has symmetrical sides with paired organs?"

His thoroughly pleased "Of course! of course!" repaid the wakeful hours of the previous night. After he had discoursed most happily and enthusiastically — as he always did — upon the importance of this point, I ventured to ask what I should do next.

"Oh, look at your fish!" he said, and left me again to my own devices. In a little more than an hour he returned, and heard my new catalogue.

"That is good, that is good!" he repeated; "but that is not all; go on"; and so for three long days he placed that fish before my eyes, forbidding me to look at anything else, or to use any artificial aid. "Look, look, look," was his repeated injunction. . . .

OVERVIEW *Cases and Concepts*

THERE IS a considerable body of writing and comment on the case method as it has long been used in law, in medicine, in some clinical disciplines, and more recently in business administration and public administration. There is, however, much less experience bearing on its application to educational administration, and little of that has yet been reported. Although there is a basic similarity in the idea of a case and its use in each of these fields, there are also some significant distinctions. For this reason, it might be better to think in terms of "case methods" of learning, rather than of "*the* case method." The experience of developing and using cases in educational administration has given rise to some new variants both as to cases and as to ways of using them.

Those who are familiar with case methods in the fields of business administration and public administration will find parts of our presentation to be merely a special footnote to this larger body of writings. We are, however, writing on the assumption that many of our readers are not particularly concerned with the subtleties of case definitions and uses in various professional fields at this time. We therefore select and present definitions of cases and views, their use and values, as we have experienced these in our special field of interest — educational administration.

Despite this somewhat parochial approach, the reader will find presented here a considerable variety both in types of cases and in uses of cases. Our warning that it may be more meaningful to think in terms of "case methods" rather than of "*the* case method" will become clear. For although our approach is not entirely eclectic, we have borrowed or adapted quite liberally from some of the varying and even conflicting thought and experience of other professional fields using case methods.

We present no rigid or definitive answers to such central questions as: What is a case? How is it developed? What values or learnings are anticipated from its use? How is a case used? What is the role of the instructor or the case discussion leader? What kinds of behavior are to be desired or expected within the case discussion group? Finally, how can learning through study of specific situations be effectively related to learning through study of abstract concepts?

In anticipation of a possible feeling, after reading Section One, that the use of cases is complex and uncertain, we offer this thought: It might be just as well to skip Section Two entirely and give case methods a try. In fact, we have placed one case, "The Letter," immediately following this "Overview" in the hope that you will at least *read* this case before proceeding to read and think about some of the things we begin to say in Section One. The best initial guide might be one's own inclinations, whether as teacher or as student, toward ways of using a written account of a concrete administrative situation in an attempt to learn by this method.

This is, after all, the way case methods of learning were invented and developed. It is reported that Langdell, who originated the case method in law, was considered foolish by his academic colleagues when he indicated his belief that this would constitute an adequate approach to the study of law. And we have found ourselves none the worse for venturing to develop and use cases long before we began to feel familiar or comfortable with the many nuances of possible case definition and use.

In short, we suggest that in order to discover what values case methods of learning may have, any particular instructor and group of students may need to limit their advance contemplations of these methods and turn to acquiring some actual experience with them through participating in a series of case analyses and discussions. We would emphasize, however, that a few intermittent case discussions do not constitute an adequate test of the values of this method of instruction, which are essentially cumulative.

Decision as to the way to use a case need not be made at the outset — or ever with absolute finality. Although logicians and psychologists have useful contributions to make with regard to efficient analysis of problems, the analysis and discussion of administrative cases (frequently for the purpose of encouraging the student to deal with the situation "as if" he were one of the administrative actors) may be most productive when the process is not warped to fit one particular theory.

The use of cases inherently involves a sequence of new experiences for the individual student and the discussion group, based on examination of each new case situation. The way in which students use cases and the values which they extract from them change in a sequence of case studies. For those who are willing to look upon education as something of an adventure, cases offer this opportunity *par excellence:* no one — neither instructor nor student — can ever know or predict surely in advance *all* of what may be discovered in the examination of a case. Not infrequently, the focus or insight which is most valuable to many of the students will be unanticipated. If a continued zest for learning is a criterion of good teaching, cases foster good teaching by providing this kind of stimulus. Following those occasions when both of us have attended a class discussion of a case, we have often found ourselves continuing the discussion on leaving the classroom — with somewhat different perceptions and judgments. Only the actual experience of working at a case can bring its potential values to light.

In order to conduct an adequate series of case discussions, a very few simple ingredients are necessary:

1. A number of cases appropriate to the special field and audience. These need to have been subjected to the test of analysis and discussion sufficiently to insure that they will magnetize increasing observation, thought, and feeling vis-à-vis the administrative situation and various actors in it.
2. A concept of learning which at least tolerates the notion that the study of concrete situations may yield significant insights and facets of knowledge which can elude even the most successful attempts to educate through communicating generalizations and presumed norms about administrative situations and behavior.
3. A willingness to try out new methods in pedagogy which others testify to be of some value, and even to experiment a bit.

Whatever readiness there may have been — among teachers and others responsible for educational administration curricula — with respect to conditions 2 and 3, it must be admitted that the satisfaction of condition 1 has until recently proved a major obstacle. The development of suitable cases for advanced instruction in administration is an expensive and time-consuming process. Hence the availability of cases in this field awaited a commitment by some institution of the necessary funds and staff resources.

The decision at Harvard in 1952 to commit its funds to an investment in case development has now led to a decision to make the products of this effort available for use elsewhere. Many institutions and teachers interested in the use of cases for teaching educational administration do not feel justified in making the investment required for a shelf of carefully researched and written cases. Yet they recognize that the case taken "off the top of the head" — that is, based on the rationalized recollection or report of a situation by a former participant — lacks many of the dimensions of "reality." A very few cases wherein a *trained interviewer's account* of an interview reflects one person's recollection may help to develop student skill in drawing inferences about the kinds of rationalization which appear to have accompanied the recall. It is our experience, however, that few of the products of personal reporting or hearsay reporting of situations stand up as cases, in comparison with the more skillfully researched ones, when it comes to the crucial test of analysis and discussion.

This book has been prepared at a relatively early stage of our own experience. Whatever there may be of value in case methods for this field will be more quickly and efficiently brought to a higher stage of maturity, we believe, if other institutions have an opportunity to share in the use of the products and to contribute to the development of these methods. Cases and case methods are capable of being improved through use. It is better for others to discover possible improvements in both the cases and the methods than for us to pursue a goal of perfection — and thereby fall into the fallacy of believing that instruments and processes of education can be milled into final form in just one educational workshop. In almost every way imaginable, case methods can be devastating to an attitude of expertise.

To some, the idea that a case may represent a considerable investment of time, money, and special skills may come as something of a surprise. The problem seems to be to capture administrative situations faithfully enough to awaken, in persons of administrative orientation and experience, an urge to test their mettle in comprehension and handling. In no administrative situation do all of the participants see things in the same way. A case usually reflects differential perceptions of the situation, of the actors, and of the interpersonal relationships. There are different degrees of rapport and empathy among the actors. There are differing value prisms through which the light on the situation passes into the mind of each of the actors. These materials supply the warp and woof of which the dramatic texture of administrative situations is woven. Case research endeavors to reflect this kind of reality. But the quality of the research is not the only factor.

The key lies partly in the nature of the administrative situations represented in the case. The "sport" type of situation not infrequently produces a "strawman" type of case and response; whereas a seemingly more normal and less obviously problem-laden situation may yield unforeseen values in use. Some cases serve as "springboards" into generalizations about issues, norms, or values. A very few cases which may prompt this tendency quite strongly are included in this volume. For the most part, however, we seek to develop cases wherein any discussion of issues and values which moves away from the question of action inherent in the case eventually leads to a return to it.

Cases do not, of course, correspond to the original reality, no matter how faithfully they seek to reflect it. But to the practicing or potential educational administrator, a good case seems to serve as a magnet. All movement away from the case represents attempts to perceive it from new perspectives; the case itself remains the center of attention. Perhaps there is no better definition of a good case in educational administration.

Our experience leaves little doubt in our minds that however theoretically feasible it might be for students of educational administration to learn a great deal about administration by the study of cases drawn from other fields of administration or from education in general, this does not seem to work very well. Orientation appears to affect motivation.

For this reason, the cases used in the Administrative Career Program and represented in this volume have been, with a few exceptions, developed specifically for an audience oriented to educational administration. The exceptions are a very few cases originally developed for use by students in education (as contrasted with educational *administration*) which focused primarily on administrative situations; researchers from the School of Business Administration collaborated with our staff on the development of the "Laketon" cases.

The thirty-six cases in this book have been selected from the shelf of approximately one-hundred-thirty usable cases developed over the last three years by a special staff in case research and writing for educational administration. Parenthetically, it might be mentioned that almost twice that number of possibilities were considered and frequently explored at least to the point of initial contact; further, quite apart from the budgetary considerations which seem to be the general fate of schools of education, a good many cases were abandoned in the course of development, or were rejected after completion, as lacking the requirements or "feel" of satisfactory cases.

All the cases in this book have been used by groups of candidates in educational administration. We have had little experience as yet with their use by other groups, except by persons enrolled as graduate students in our program. Preceding the development of our educational administration cases, we did use cases from other fields in one-week Advanced Administrative Institutes for public school administrators, conducted by the Cooperative Program in Educational Administration in New England. We have had no experience with the use of case methods for in-service training of administrators in specific school systems. If the experience of some industrial and business corporations with the use of cases in executive and management training programs is a criterion, these cases may offer similar possibilities for programs of continuing professional development. Such programs might be conducted both in individual school systems and in state and regional programs where groups of administrators are engaged in professional development.

Although the Administrative Career Program for which these cases were developed aims to prepare for educational administration generally, it does place major emphasis on the superintendency. Hence the cases in this volume reflect a distribution weighted toward problems and situations which directly involve the superintendent. At the same time, many of them revolve around other administrative roles.

With students enrolled in general programs in administrative preparation, the instructor may not want to use all of these cases in any given course. Presumably, however, growth of insight into the superintendency function by any administrator of a school system will improve his awareness of the relations between his own roles, problems, and decisions and those experienced at levels of administration to which he is accountable.

The book is organized in five sections. The reader may choose the order in which he wishes to read and make use of them. Our suggestion would be as follows: After reading the case, "The Letter," which follows this "Overview," and also Section One where certain important aspects of case methods of learning administration are highlighted, proceed directly to the cases themselves in Section Three. Then, after some experience in discussing cases, return to Section Two, in which relationships between case methods and other approaches to learning in administration are more thoroughly pursued.

Section Four, which presents a comparative view of educational administration, may well be read in conjunction with Section Two. Both sections (Two and Four) involve some consideration of the nature of administration; administration is obviously a complex function, and the ideas developed in these sections represent simply an attempt to pursue some of its implications. They therefore tend to cut across the two aspects of study represented by cases on the one hand and concepts on the other.

The concepts, as discussed in Section Five, are basically determined by the students. No definition or assignments of concepts are made by us. After a period of using cases, each student is expected to define for himself one or more areas which he feels would be valuable to explore. We then stand ready to suggest an initial course of reading in consultation with each student. Both the directions and sophistications of choice vary widely at the outset. They at first seem quite highly individualistic; as reports feed back into the classroom, individual directions and choices are increasingly influenced by vectors of value emerging in the group. To a considerable extent, we as instructors serve as relatively nondirective catalysts in the early stages of this reporting and discussion process.

We are, however, concerned with the way in which students organize their experience emerging out of concepts study and draw implications from it, just as we are in the study of cases. We play a part in examining the patterns submitted by students, in working toward the clarification of meanings they have in mind, and in conducting the class sessions devoted to reports and discussions.

In one major respect we might be accused of being highly directive. We have convictions as to the importance of study of concepts. We could probably not conceal these convictions even if we tried to do so. We are not satisfied, however, with success in engendering study of concepts by virtue of exhortation, by purely logical explication, or by the exercise of authority which may become operative merely by disclosure of our bias. If our convictions are justified, if growth toward the effective performance of future roles in educational administration can be enhanced by conceptual enrichment, it seems to us that it should not be necessary to resort to such stimuli. A search for a more satisfying role as teachers of educational administration becomes necessary.

An emphasis on concepts in philosophy, social science, and other fields, in a program of administrator education which also stresses case methods and responsibility for dealing with live problems in a field situation, reflects both a concept of administration and a concept of education for administration.

The aim of these kinds of study and training is to develop behavior, not merely knowledge. It is all too plain, for example, that *knowing about* the kind of leader behavior that is conducive to group productivity, in the light of social science knowledge, is something different from *behaving* in terms of such knowledge.

Some aspects of our program represent endeavors to develop and test administrative behavior by situational learning in which conceptual growth *may* spring from insight into experience. At the same time, we assume that study of concepts *may* increase the potential of behavior more sensitive to the human and social factors in a situation. The problem is how to maximize both kinds of learning by men and women engaged in or oriented toward educational administration.

It is our observation that most persons aspiring to active administrative careers in public education respond somewhat more readily to the challenges of concrete situations and problems, whether live or of the written case variety, than they do to the prospect of study on more abstract levels. Indeed, responsiveness to "situational" problems may be one criterion of the potential administrator, as differentiated from the potential scholar. To a considerable, and probably not yet fully developed degree, we think it is possible to utilize the concrete and the situational as stimuli for explorations into territories of knowledge and thought farther beyond the bounds of professional literature than these students would otherwise go. They thus perceive concepts which give new patterns to the concrete. Such new insights may change the perspectives of men who will be "judges of values and determiners of policy" with respect to the social and philosophical questions and issues which revolve around public education.

Both the concept areas noted in Section Five, particularly those from other than the social sciences, and the ways in which these areas have been selected and explored, are really no more than a report of an effort to find keys to highly motivated study by graduate students oriented toward administration. The results have been encouraging — sometimes beyond our expectation. They lead us to believe that this approach to concepts may be similarly effective in stimulating other students of administration to discover the work of the scholar, the researcher, and the philosopher as of peculiar value to administrators also.

During the first stages of planning the "cases and concepts" sequence, we imagined the possibility of relating specific cases and specific concepts very closely, in a kind of contrapuntal scheme. We imagined a pattern which would move sometimes from a case to the study of related concepts and sometimes from an area of concepts to a case or series of cases. We soon discovered various errors in our idea.

The first of these lay in our assumption about the feasibility of this kind of planning. Numerous concepts may cast significant light on many cases without being particularly obtrusive in any one of them. To attempt, by plan, to relate a particular area of concepts to one or a few cases would involve highly arbitrary and unsatisfactory decisions on our part. A second major disadvantage would be the seeming indication that a particular concept was of little relevance to the cases not selected for association with it.

Conversely, the elements of any single case may point toward numerous concepts. Sometimes, concept areas not apparent on first view of a case may prove to be significant as more searching analysis develops new insights. Our realization of the difficulties, the arbitrariness, and the dangers involved in a neatly packaged series of cases related to concepts and of concepts related to cases led us to abandon our early plans even before we had begun the work of case development.

The first experience we had with a group of administrative candidates in turning to the study of concepts after discussion of cases for several weeks reinforced our convictions that we had been on the right track in abandoning the packaged approach. Some readings were suggested, one of which dealt with a familiar concept treated by the author under the less familiar term of "the conjugate principle." During the next case discussion, someone mentioned an aspect of the case as illustrative of "the conjugate principle." It thereupon apparently became necessary for others to engage in verbal demonstration of their acquaintance with and grasp of this notion, with the result that much of the case remained undiscovered.

We assume that the values of concept-study may have relatively little to do with the extent to which the concepts may subsequently be verbalized in academic language. The important thing is the extent to which the behavior of an administrator in a situation (including the examination of a case) reveals interpretations which are illuminated by concepts included in his mental resources. It may or may not be pertinent — and it frequently is not, in mature administrative behavior — to verbalize the concepts, and particularly to verbalize them in academic language.

It may be objected that unless the student can verbalize the concepts, there is no assurance that he has gained any. We agree that there may be no positive assurance, but if there is evidence of strong motivation for study in an area of concepts, and if the student indicates, in one way or another, that he has, so to speak, a "bear by the tail" and can't let go even if he doesn't know how to manage it at the moment, we tend to assume that some significant learning is under way. We feel that a positive disservice may be done by forcing the student at such a stage to regurgitate the original verbalizations which he may be trying to translate into his own structure. Given some evidence of a student's strong motivation and struggle to metabolize some new kinds of content into nourishment for his particular semantic system, it may be wisdom on the part of the teacher to conclude that he has already played his role as fully and as well as this situation warrants. We feel that under some circumstances further intervention by the teacher may disrupt or even put a stop to what may otherwise already be an irreversible equation compounded of a searching human mind, a beckoning terrain, and time.

We believe that the very drive of administrative students toward the concrete, toward "experience," places the teacher in an important stand-by role; the growth of concrete experience will lead to the need for mental effort to organize and relate this experience. At the point where the student begins to feel this need, guidance may help him cross new thresholds. Without guidance, or with pressures too strong in other directions in the academic atmosphere, these opportunities for significant conceptual development may be lost and the very urge be stillborn. In one way or another, the student will solve the problem of devising a framework of thought in order to relate his content of experience. The teacher can but help him.

CASE A *The Letter*

CARTERTOWN, a city of 86,000 on the northwest perimeter of metropolitan New York, is in the heartland of American suburbia. In 1952, Ralph Robinson was in the fifth year of his superintendency of the Cartertown schools, enrollment 11,638. During Dr. Robinson's superintendency, roughly the post-World War II period, the City of Cartertown had spent over three million dollars for new school buildings and sites. Improvement in the internal functioning of the system had kept pace with the physical growth of the school plants; and Cartertown had progressed from the classification of "good system" to that of "excellent system." The teaching staff had been increased and improved; newer and better auxiliary services, guidance, special teaching, and adult education, had been put into operation. After a bitter struggle through the years 1947 and 1948, the old problem of districting in the Cartertown schools had been settled. In all but unusual cases, a child was assigned to a school solely on the basis of the geographical location of his home.

It was the matter of districting and an exception made in the regulations which brought Mrs. Folson to the office of Dr. Robinson early in the fall of 1952. Dr. Robinson had a pre-audition of the reason for Mrs. Folson's visit long before the lady appeared in the inner office. From the outer office, the voice of Mrs. Folson came loud and clear to Dr. Robinson as he worked at his desk. "I demand to see him — and at once! This is a matter which affects the reputation of the entire school. I . . ."

Dr. Robinson flicked the switch on his intercom phone. "Send the lady in," he instructed his receptionist.

"Yes, sir, her name is Mrs. Folson."

"I know," Dr. Robinson said. "I chanced to overhear her."

Mrs. Folson didn't wait to sit down, but opened her barrage on her way across Dr. Robinson's rather spacious office. "I demand an explanation of the handling of the Bates boy," she said as she stormed toward the superintendent's desk. "Why should the Bates child be assigned to Southard Junior High School? The Bates family lives two blocks further into the Prentice Junior High School district than we do. Yet Robert Bates goes to Southard. William — that's our son — goes to Prentice."

"Well, now," Dr. Robinson murmured, "suppose we sit down, Mrs. Folson. Let me hear about this." He arranged a chair for her in front of the desk, and offered her a cigarette. By the time Mrs. Folson had her cigarette lighted, she appeared somewhat less agitated.

The purpose of her visit was to protest the assignment of Robert Bates, aged 13, to the Southard Junior High School. The Bates family were neighbors of the Folsons. "I play bridge with Henrietta, and Robert Bates and my son William are close friends. This year Robert was suddenly allowed to transfer to Southard. Our house is much nearer to Southard. Yet our son is forced to continue at Prentice. Why?"

"Well, I don't know why," Dr. Robinson admitted. "We have almost twelve thousand children in our schools. But I can certainly find out why." He raised the desk phone: "Martha, will you please get the folder on Robert Bates, aged 13, a student at Southard."

"I can tell you why," Mrs. Folson said angrily. "Henrietta admitted it to me. Her husband fixed it. He has influence in the school department."

"That's not so," Robinson said. "I have to approve all transfers out of district — and I don't know Mr. Bates."

"Why do you suppose we moved out here from the schools nearer the city?" Mrs. Folson asked. "We heard that you had a reputation for fairness in this community."

"We have and we intend to keep it," Robinson told her. "I can assure you of this, Mrs. Folson: whatever the reason the child was transferred, there was no influence used. Either on me or on my staff."

Mrs. Folson said, "I didn't come here to get Robert put back into Prentice. I came to arrange for the transfer of my son to Southard."

"What are your reasons?" Robinson asked. His secretary entered, laid a folder on his desk, and left the room.

"Everyone knows that Southard is better," returned Mrs. Folson. "The building is newer. Their guidance program is the best in the city. Mrs. Trenholm, their director, has spoken to our club. The children have a lot more activities there. Children just seem to like Southard better. My boy turns green with envy at the stories Robert Bates brings home about school."

"I'm afraid you misunderstood me," Dr. Robinson said. "I meant what reason did you have for requesting a transfer to Southard? We don't cross districts except for very special reasons."

"Why, I gave you the reasons! Southard is better. We want the best for our child. And that Bates boy boasted to my son that his father had fixed it with the school department."

"We have close to 2,500 children in our four junior high schools," Dr. Robinson pointed out. "I can't put them all in Southard. It has a top capacity of 1,100."

"Well, you put the Bates boy there. Why not our child too? We live two blocks nearer to Southard than the Bates family. Robert boasted how his father had arranged everything."

Robinson opened the folder and glanced down at it. "The Bates child has a reason," he said after a moment. "A medical reason."

"Why, that is ridiculous! The child is perfectly healthy. What is that reason?"

"I'm sorry, but I can't discuss it with you," Dr. Robinson said. "However, you can take our word for it that the child has a reason. He is presently under the care of a physician."

Mrs. Folson rose abruptly. "You'll hear more of this," she promised grimly. "If there is fraud involved, I can promise you will hear more of it. That child is not under a doctor's care."

"If there is fraud involved," Robinson said, "it is not the fault of the school department. And I'll personally investigate it, Mrs. Folson."

As soon as Mrs. Folson had left the office, Robinson called John Lawrence, principal of Southard Junior High.

"John, I'm checking into the case of Robert Bates, one of your students. We have on file a letter from Gregory Phillips, M.D. The letter is on Dr. Phillips' official stationery. It states that Robert Bates is presently a patient undergoing therapy. It states that Robert Bates has been placed on a special regimen. Phillips requests that Robert Bates be transferred to Southard School. Phillips states, 'I request this inasmuch as Southard is within five blocks of my office where Robert will come for visits two times a week.' Phillips goes on to say that he plans to arrange a special program for the boy at your school while Robert is undergoing therapy. We've just had a lady in here who states that young Bates is not under the care of a physician. She alleges favoritism in the transfer, and wants her son accorded the same privileges."

"I'll check it at once," Lawrence promised. "Clara Trenholm up in the Guidance Office would know about that."

Dr. Robinson called his secretary into his office. "Would you send this letter out to Dr. Gregory Phillips, 168 Orange Street, this city? 'Dear Dr. Phillips: We have on file a letter from you requesting transfer of Robert Bates, aged 13, a student in our schools, to Southard Junior High School. The reason given was that Robert is under your care and on a special regimen. We would like a further statement on the present condition of Robert Bates.' Send it out at once, Martha," he instructed his secretary. "I may be making a mountain out of a mole hill, but I'm not going to let the district war flare up again."

The following morning, Clara Trenholm's report on Robert Bates arrived at Dr. Robinson's office. As far as Miss Trenholm knew, Robert Bates was not undergoing therapy, nor had he since his entrance into Southard. Miss Trenholm kept a record of such matters, and Mrs. Bates had made no mention of it on the school health questionnaire. The child had not been excused from athletics or activities, and there had been no request for an excuse from the family. In fact, the boy carried more activities than usual. Miss Trenholm had talked to Robert Bates, and had tested him upon entrance into school. She had noticed nothing untoward in her interviews with the boy. Furthermore, no person named Dr. Phillips had been in contact with the school principal or guidance office. Miss Trenholm suggested that Dr. Robinson get in touch with Dr. Mabel Parker, director of guidance, to see if there had been any correspondence through her office.

Before Dr. Robinson could talk to the guidance director, he had a telephone call from Mrs. Folson. She apologized for her call of the day before. She said that on consultation with her husband they had decided to drop the matter. She appeared anxious to forget the whole thing.

"Well, that's fine, Mrs. Folson," Dr. Robinson said. "But we are not quite so ready to drop the matter. You've started an allegation of fraud, and I mean to see it through."

"But my husband wants to drop it," Mrs. Folson said. "George Bates is one of his closest friends."

"Well," Dr. Robinson said, "the matter is pretty much in our hands now, Mrs. Folson. We have an obligation to other parents to see the matter through."

As soon as Mrs. Folson had hung up, Robinson called Dr. Mabel Parker, director of guidance for the Cartertown schools. She had no knowledge of the Bates child. A search through the folders revealed no letters from the parents or from Dr. Phillips. "What do you think?" Robinson asked. "I mean, what does it look like to you?"

"I hesitate to say," Dr. Parker answered. "But it does look like a scheme to get the Bates youngster into Southard. Variations on the same theme have been tried before. I'd wait for word from the doctor before deciding." She promised to check further on Robert Bates' records at Prentice.

Three days passed, and there was no word from Dr. Phillips. Superintendent Robinson dispatched a letter to the Bates family requesting information on the present state of Robert's health. Mrs. Bates called in answer to the letter. When informed that Dr. Robinson was not in his office, she said that she would call back. At 1:00 P.M. of the fourth day after Mrs. Folson's visit, Dr. Phillips called the office of the superintendent.

When informed that Dr. Robinson was at lunch, Dr. Phillips said, "All right, I'll leave a message for him. I'm pretty busy. It's about that letter on a child named Bates. My records show that I have not had a patient named Bates under treatment during the past few months. I don't know about before that period." With that Dr. Phillips hung up.

"Didn't he mention his letter?" Dr. Robinson asked the secretary. "No. That's all he said." An attempt to contact Dr. Phillips by phone resulted in the rather cryptic answer that "Doctor is presently engaged."

Robinson called Dr. Parker and described the Phillips call to her. "It sounds pretty cute to me," Robinson said. "He called, knowing I would probably be out to lunch. He didn't send me a letter, and he didn't mention his letter."

"It looks strange," Dr. Mabel Parker agreed. "I remember the child now. Bob is a high-strung, sensitive boy, but he seems to like it up at Southard. Clara Trenholm found the record of her interviews with him. The boy apparently loves it at Southard. We have some information on him from the guidance office back at Prentice. At Prentice, on several occasions, the child was sent out of class for creating a disturbance. The teachers at Prentice say that Bob was restless and indifferent and did not participate in school activities. His marks were pretty far down."

"How is his class work at Southard?" Robinson asked.

"Good. Of course it's too early in the year to have a record of marks. Clara talked to his teachers, and they reported that he was doing well."

"Well," Robinson said, "I don't know what to do. It is fairly apparent that somebody is trying to get away with something. Maybe the father is a friend of Phillips'. Maybe the doctor wrote the letter to oblige a friend. Phillips may have become frightened when we wrote him. They might have thought that with twelve thousand children we weren't going to look into the case of one."

"That's what I meant," Dr. Parker said. "You have twelve thousand youngsters to take care of. I have to think of individuals. You have public relations to worry about."

"I don't think that's such a fair assessment," Robinson said. "It's not just public relations. I have the corporate well-being of all the individuals involved. We've had increasing pressure from parents who want their children in Southard. Last year I had to take nearly eighty youngsters out of that school and put them in Cartwright. What about those children and their parents? Every parent wants the best we have."

"But it is to this child's best interest to stay at Southard," Dr. Parker rejoined. "Possibly the family had a friend who works in Dr. Phillips' office and they wrote the letter on his stationery. I don't know. It really isn't a proper concern of mine."

"It is a concern of mine," Robinson said. "The system was accused of fixing this transfer."

"The boy is in the band there," Dr. Parker said. "He's in two club activities. He was a non-participator at Prentice."

"I make exceptions in districting for three reasons," said Robinson; "one, health; two, safety; three, religious education. Cartertown is getting an increasingly heavy Jewish population, and the parents sometimes ask for a public school assignment near a Hebrew temple school. Do you think it's to the boy's best interest to learn that this is the way things are done?" Robinson asked. "I mean should he learn that you get things this way?"

"We don't know that the child is aware of the situation," Dr. Parker said. "It may be just the parents."

"He boasted to the Folson boy that his father had fixed it. He must know something. I feel I should take some action."

"I wouldn't," Dr. Parker advised. "And I feel pretty strongly in this matter. I'd think of that child. If he gets pulled out and sent back to Prentice, you will undo everything that has been done."

"We'll see," Dr. Robinson promised. He hung up the phone and swiveled around to face the window. Whatever action he might take in the case of the Bates boy, it had to be taken soon. The situation was only one of the twenty or thirty matters of a routine nature which lay on his desk. He had no wish to fan the embers of the old districting fight, and if the Bates situation had come out once it would come out again. Apparently the Bates family were not content to win quietly. While the morals of the Bates family were not Robinson's immediate concern, he did have obligations in the matter of the training of youngsters. Dr. Robinson felt rather strongly about the matter of deceit, and there was no sense deluding himself — he was emotionally involved in any matter which reflected on the school system's reputation for integrity. His building program, and he had not planned to slacken the tempo of it, depended in part on his ability to keep people happy in all sections of the city.

All children could not attend Southard, the newest and best equipped of the four junior high schools; nor could they all attend Prince or Babcock, the two new elementary schools.

On the other hand, there was the well-being of the boy, Robert Bates. The youngster could have been doing some harmless boasting to the Folson boy. Perhaps he had no idea how he had reached Southard. The boy was happy there and progressing in his studies. It would do no great harm to leave him there until the end of the school year. There was further the matter of Dr. Parker who felt strongly that the child should stay. Robinson made it a practice to allow his supervisors almost unlimited scope in matters which affected their departments. He was not sure that the situation warranted going against Dr. Parker's recommendation. In the past he had found it difficult to agree with Mabel Parker's approach to problems, and only recently had she begun to show evidence of trust and confidence in his judgment.

His phone rang and he turned from the window. His secretary said, "Dr. Robinson, Mrs. Bates is on the line." Whatever he was going to do, this was the time to do it.

SECTION ONE

SOME ASPECTS OF ADMINISTRATIVE SITUATIONS AND CASES

Some Aspects of Administrative Situations and Cases

In the "Overview" we indicated that it was by no means essential for instructors and students interested in using cases to do anything more than start using them. We suggested getting some "feel" of cases and their possible uses before making conscious efforts to analyze the pedagogical implications of the method.

Yet if cases offer significant values in preparing the student for educational administration, the most productive use of the method implies, sooner or later, a sharpened consciousness of these potentials and how they might best be attained. This consideration confronts both us, as authors of this book, and you, as readers and users, with a dilemma: How little or how much to write and read, respectively, about the implications and experience of case methods?

We have had to make a decision on our own part with respect to this dilemma. In this book we include a good deal about the case method. Here in Section One we shall explore this somewhat generally; in later sections, more intensively. We have suggested a pattern for the reader to follow, but in the last analysis he will have to make his own decision. That decision will involve his hunches as to possible effects of an early sharpening of his awareness about case methods — and therefore probably of his self-consciousness in the use of them.

How Much to Say About Methods Before Using Them?

This problem has not presented itself so strongly in the fields which have antedated educational administration in their use of cases, for case developments in those fields have been largely pragmatic ones. Not that theory has been absent; case methods had to be at least a vague theoretical idea before they could be adopted consciously for trial in the classroom. But the development in each field appears to have been shaped first by applying the very general notion of "cases" to the particular characteristics of the field — law, medicine, business administration, public administration. New hunches about both the instruments (cases) and their use then appear to have arisen much more largely out of continuing everyday experience than out of any systematic studies — particularly studies which cut across several fields.

As a late arrival on the scene, educational administration has been presented with relatively greater opportunity to examine case method experiences. Case methods are now being used widely enough to result in a considerable awareness of the varieties of these methods, even without really extensive and comprehensive study. Awareness of the special characteristics of educational administration has implied still further variance. The net result has been to give rise to more *theorizing* about the case methods at the present time than earlier. It is necessary to analyze and theorize to a greater extent in trying to decide on some directions for the development and use of cases in a field where they have previously been little used.

We do not for a moment suggest that this process of attempting to analyze the experience and the assumptions underlying the use of cases is peculiar to those interested in educational administration. On the contrary, recent years have witnessed a general increase in this kind of study. Currently there are signs of systematic studies and research in contrast to the earlier more general observations. There is at present, therefore, a climate stimulating more highly conscious and theoretically conceived notions about case methods and their part in pedagogical schemes.[1]

There is another factor which has tended to emphasize the examination of experience in other fields in the course of shaping a program for educational administration. Those involved in education *about education* (and *about the administration* of education) are or ought to be peculiarly concerned with the subject of *pedagogy*. Yet this field has devoted relatively little attention, study, or experiment to case methods. Conditions in this field suggest, however, that it needs to understand more about case methods — and understanding them involves using them, if only in an experimental way.

The present period is one which reflects major ferment, activity, and experimentation in developing educational administrators more effectively. Nationally, the Cooperative Program in Educational Administration has given new directions to thinking on this subject. In one way or another, virtually every school of education which engages in the training of school administrators is reappraising its existing programs and designing new ones.

The foregoing factors all deal with conditions which have influenced the direction of our thinking in such a way as to yield the particular viewpoints which we now have about cases and their use. They do not answer the question we are dealing with, namely, how little or how much to present regarding these viewpoints. We could, of course, have chosen merely to present the cases, which presumably reflect these viewpoints in various ways; to state, but not explain, a few things about them; to suggest something of how they might be used, without any discussion of reasons why. Since there is now a considerable body of writing available about case methods, it would

[1] Case methods are now being used not only in law, medicine, other clinical disciplines, and several fields of administration, but also in undergraduate programs in science, human relations study, and other subjects.

be up to each instructor and student to decide whether or not to consider anything but his own subsequent experience. He could, if he wished, review the current literature, compare reported viewpoints, and thus sharpen his own view of learning by case methods.

Although there has been some tendency on the part of some proponents of the case method to "just use" cases, and only then, if at all, to explore the instrumental properties and values which may be involved, our approach is somewhat different. We believe that the progression of learning from childhood to adulthood involves a widening awareness of the learning process itself. A mature stage of learning involves an *awareness of the relationships* between "what" has been learned, "how" this has been learned, and what some of the ancillary effects on the learner have been.

The task of considering what may or may not be worth while trying to understand about any one of these at any given time is a part of this problem. Obviously something must be known about an instrument, for example, in order to use it productively. A physics student must understand something about a spectroscope in order to understand the spectrum. But he cannot understand all about it without knowing all of the knowledge of physics that went into its invention and development. Trying to learn something, using instruments for such learnings, and understanding the instruments — these aspects of the learning experience cannot be arranged in a neat sequence. The track of learning shifts from one to another aspect or conditions of learning — sense of one's own goals, instruments, data on the subject matter, social elements of the learning situation, methods of work. Awareness and self-awareness grow throughout. Learning becomes increasingly a *self-conscious* process; the results of learning are bound up with increased *awareness of all aspects of the experience.*

In higher education, it is taken for granted that the student is involved in defining the goals of his learning, in shaping the processes and in organizing whatever he experiences. Consideration and selection of content, instruments, and methods are part of this problem. Being a student in higher education means becoming increasingly aware of both resources for learning and their conscious selection and use. This implies growing awareness of one's own values, needs, choices, and achievements at the beginning, throughout, and at the conclusion of a particular learning experience.

The sense of what kind of track may be involved in using case methods will be quite different, depending on whether the student proceeds to "just use" cases or to read what we have to say on the subject. Furthermore, the rationale for cases which we have at this stage will point to a path somewhat different from that which lies in our experience. This rationale will reflect views of administration, of what is involved in learning administration, of implications for the teaching of administration, and, of course, ideas about cases and case methods, which are different from those we had at the outset of this experience. There are changes even in our concept of "what administration is all about" which have been influenced by our development and use of cases. However, these ideas have *evolved;* we are anything but sure what the effect may be of presenting "in a package" at the outset our present outlook to those who are considering a path of study which includes the use of cases.

But we rebel inwardly at the practice of holding "experience" close to one's chest, as if whatever fruits there may be are an esoteric luxury to be withheld from others until they have proved their fitness for membership in a cult by acquiring similar experience "in the raw." We prefer the position which seems to us necessary to sustain the idea of the advance of knowledge, namely, that those engaged in higher education record their experience and convictions for test and criticism. If the users of this book choose to dwell, at an early stage of their own case experience, on many of the views which we project in subsequent pages, they may find some of these notions either unclear or out of keeping with their own views of administration or learning. On the other hand, we have no way of predicting that this will be so. We can merely express the hope that in whatever way this book is used it will prove beneficial to the teaching and learning of educational administration.

What we say about administration will be said to clarify our thinking about those aspects of it which seem to us most germane to the development and uses of cases. Our discussion will start with cases, and cases will remain the ultimate focus, however much we may find ourselves dwelling on notions regarding the nature of administration. Seldom, in the course of these branchings out from the primary focus, will we say: "We are talking about something at the moment which may not appear immediately pertinent to the general topic of cases and their uses. But if you will bear with us, we hope that its relevance will become apparent." But the above may make our intent understood.

Let us now turn to a quite pragmatic problem — that of developing a *shelf* of cases which might provide a range and variety of experience valuable to educational administrators. The very idea of *range* and *variety* rather quickly made it unprofitable to labor at an abstract definition of "a case." Even without any goal of comprehensiveness of coverage, the task initially invited a fairly broad and flexible set of definitions.

To be sure, one common denominator appeared in almost all of the cases we had in mind. This was the idea that each case would be some kind of written or recorded account of *a real situation* in educational administration — although by no means all accounts of real situations would have the qualities felt desirable in cases.

At the outset we did not stop to ask what we meant by "real situations," perhaps because the answer seemed self-evident. We concerned ourselves, rather, with some of the kinds of situations which seemed to us to be most desirable to include in a shelf of cases. We decided to avoid too heavy an emphasis on the "sport" type of case — the highly abnormal or unusual problem. We began also to develop some tentative ways of checking on the distribution of the cases with respect to both problems and persons involved. We concerned ourselves with qualities which we considered desirable in cases, such as the extent to which it might be possible to reflect how various central actors thought and felt rather than merely what they said and did. Subsequently in thinking about the values which might be derived from use of cases, we found it pertinent to think directly about the question: "What do we mean by a real situation or real situations for learning in educational administration?" The answer appears no longer to be the self-evident one that we assumed.

We have, of course, not found "the answer" to the question. But we have found the question well worth exploring, and perhaps necessary to explore quite persistently in order to sharpen our sense of what it is that case methods may contribute to learning administration. For the idea of "real situations," we have indicated, is central to our idea of cases. We must attempt some sort of definition if what we are to say about cases is to make any sense. But what kind of definition can be made of real situations?

The Novelty of Real Situations

Real situations — that is, real-life situations — are always unique. It is axiomatic that no situation is *exactly* like any other.

Each situation contains at least some elements that are quite literally new or novel, in the sense that they have never appeared previously in *precisely* the same context and never will do so again. (The validation of this statement would take us into considerable philosophical discussion; we can arrive at no other conclusion unless we are ready to abandon virtually the whole of scientific knowledge about the universe.)

Of course, many situations appear to be the same as others, so much so that quite careful examination may be necessary to discover the uniqueness lying underneath the similarities. It is also granted that we may often have to act in a situation *as if* it were the same as some other situation with which we are familiar. But if we do so, our action may turn out to be less appropriate than if we were aware of the novel factors.

Now, one basic problem of administration revolves around this fact of the novelty of each situation. Obviously we cannot always undertake to discover the novelties in any situation confronting us. We may have to act without the time required to search out some subtle factor distinguishing a situation from others apparently like it. We constantly have to risk acting inappropriately because of what we do not know about a situation in which we must act.

But at the other extreme, if because of broad resemblances we tend too easily and quickly to class each situation we meet as identical to others with which we are familiar, we increase the likelihood of inappropriate action. The *norms* of experience are important and stand us in good stead. The process of administration involves adapting the norms to the novelty and the novelty to the norms. Unless awareness of norms is balanced with awareness that every situation is different, we may not develop the skills or use the potentially available time to examine and discriminate in the new situation. Yet if we do so, our comprehension of the varieties of experience which are included in the shaping of norms will be richer. This in turn may help us to recognize both the differences and the similarities of situations more skillfully and quickly.

A pertinent incident is reported about the behavior of an administrator who, in addition to possessing skills in administration, has contributed greatly both to thinking about administration and to teaching and learning administration in such a way as to develop these skills. The story is told as follows:[2]

> Some years ago a defunct street railway company was taken over in receivership, and the court placed in charge of the company a very able man, Mr. Wallace B. Donham, skilled not only in finance but experienced in management. Within a week after taking over control he was faced with a strike vote that meant, if issues in dispute could not be settled within approximately five weeks, that some 5,500 men and 950 miles of track would be idle. Immediately Mr. Donham and his advisers began daily meetings with union representatives, who were tense and suspicious. Shortly Mr. Donham was able to present a proposal that was within the resources of the company to pay but did not meet the initial demands of the union. Two more weeks were required to work out details before the plan could be presented to Mr. Mahon, international president of the union. In the first meeting with Mr. Mahon and other union representatives, the plan was outlined, and the tenor of the conference indicated to Mr. Donham that the union would accept.
>
> The next day Mr. Mahon and his delegation filed into Mr. Donham's office where the latter and four of his associates were already waiting. After a pleasantry or two the following conversation took place:
>
> Mr. Donham: Well, Mr. Mahon, what did you decide about the proposed plan?
>
> Mr. Mahon: We have decided to have nothing to do with it. It is a scheme devised to break the union, and we will have nothing whatever to do with it.
>
> Mr. Donham (rising): Thank you, Mr. Mahon. That leaves nothing further for us to discuss.
>
> Mr. Donham left the room immediately, followed by the other company representatives, disturbed by the turn of events and with no idea of what would happen next. Within a matter of hours, however, the union asked for additional conferences, and an agreement written by Mr. Mahon, with the assistance of his lawyer, was signed three days prior to the strike deadline.
>
> The day following a celebration in honor of the agreement, in which both the union and company participated, Mr. Donham interpreted some clauses of the agreement in a way that was favorable to the union and some in a way that was unfavorable. In the meanwhile, Mr. Mahon had left

[2] From F. K. Berrien, *Comments and Cases in Human Relations* (New York: Harper and Brothers, 1951), pp. 50–52.

the scene of dispute for his home office in a distant city. Immediately the local union leaders protested Mr. Donham's unfavorable interpretations, whereupon Mr. Donham urged them to contact Mr. Mahon for his interpretations and report back.

Eight days later the sixteen local union representatives came to Mr. Donham's office and reported: "Mr. Mahon said he didn't understand how a man like you, with your position in the community, could make an agreement on one day and go back on it completely the next day."

Mr. Donham's reply was immediate and with some vigor: "No, Mr. Mahon never said that!"

The faces of the union men dropped momentarily; they exchanged quick glances and then smiled. Their spokesman handed Mr. Donham a letter. "You're right; Mr. Mahon didn't say that; he said this." The letter, in effect, said that Mr. Donham's interpretations had been correct and that he had been generous in his concessions.

From that point on until Mr. Donham left the company, relations with the union were cordial and cooperative. A hostile situation had been converted into one of active collaboration.*

* The facts of this situation were given to the author in conversations with Mr. Donham and from notes on file at the Harvard Graduate School of Business Administration.

This story is cited by Professor Berrien as an illustration of behavior reflecting a response in terms of awareness of the pattern *as a whole* rather than merely of the incident of the moment. Without such an example, a phrase such as "seeing the situation as a whole" might seem to suggest the opposite of being sensitive to the novelty of the situation as it developed *at the moment.* Under such circumstances we tend to respond not to the particular situation but in terms of "others similar to it," that is, in terms of *norm* responses.

But in this situation, Mr. Donham seems to have been simultaneously aware of the previous pattern "as a whole" and of the immediate facet which it now presented to him; he thereby responded with behavior which, almost spontaneously, took both into account. As Professor Berrien comments, "Judgments of this sort are flashes of insight based on information comparable to our instantaneous judgments of distances." Thus seeing the pattern of the situation "as a whole" and being aware of the novelty of the situation at the moment appear to be part of the same process and achievement. Seeking to be aware of the uniqueness of a situation at a given moment need not imply a preoccupation with particularistic details, any more than "seeing a situation as a whole" need mean being aware only of the major or "more obvious" aspects, with the finer elements blurred or dropped out. A high awareness of and skillful responsiveness to both these "dimensions" of administrative situations seems to be involved.

The development of a rich backlog of generalizations about administration and the recognition of the essential novelty of each situation are thus not antagonistic but complementary. When we speak of a backlog of generalizations (derived from numerous situations) we mean *something more than* learning some abstractions which someone else has formulated out of *his* direct experience. To know verbalizations representing significant experience is admittedly a *part* of learning administration.

However, learning the generalizations of scholars or authorities is quite different from having or knowing the experience from which these were derived. And even the latter cannot teach or impart the new that inheres in, and may presumably be found through adequate examination of, *any actual situation.* If administration could be learned *merely* by knowing *generalizations from the experience* of others, or their *reports of specific experience,* or even by having enough administrative *experiences* oneself, the development of training programs would be a much more easy task than it is. But however much may be gained through these three kinds of learning, they are perhaps even worse than useless if they blind the administrator to the essential point that not all these together can give him the most appropriate answer to any particular situation before him. In one sense, their greatest value is negative; they help him to see how a given situation is *unlike* others. They thus set the stage for adapting past experience so as to be more appropriate to the given situation — or, if need be, to invent new actions or new solutions.

The stress we have placed on the novelty and uniqueness of all situations may seem, at first, to run counter to all sorts of requirements for efficient and economical action. "Of course, in an absolute philosophical sense, all situations are 'unique,'" one may say, "but after all, this situation is practically identical with many others, or at least some others."

A very great gain is made, however, when we cease to speak and think in terms of one situation being "identical" with another, or to mean "identical" or "the same" in our minds when we use such phrases as "a similar situation." A habit of differentiating sharply between "similar (in certain respects)" and "identical (the same as)," and of recognizing that only the first of these phrases can apply to administrative situations, almost spontaneously prompts the corollary query: "In what respects is this situation different?"

There are situations in which it may take only a few seconds, perhaps even less, to see a difference, *or to think of a possible one and check by examination.* Or it may take hours and a great deal of imagination and examination. Even when time and economy of action prevent us from perceiving and taking into account the unique factors, recognition that we have not done so will leave us less surprised at the consequences. Awareness of the novelty of situations makes us more ready to respond to realities around us and less ready to be thrown off balance by the unexpected, of which administrators must always anticipate a goodly share.

The novelty of administrative situations is, of course, bound up with the human factors involved. Of all fields of knowledge, those which deal with human behavior are least developed. Human situations contain subtle logics lying beyond the boundaries of our knowledge about the behavior of human beings. In any situation where human action and human relations are involved, the very primer of knowledge recognizes that discernments are at best approximate and always contain some elements of uncertainty. The question of separating out "human factors" from the study of administrative problems will be discussed later. Holding at the moment simply to the idea that any actual administrative situation or problem has human factors mixed up with it, we may say that no matter how much anyone knows, or thinks he knows, about human behavior, every administrative situation offers an opportunity to learn something new. Every new situation offers a new problem in human understanding.

Cases as Reflections of Situations

Although we have as yet perhaps only slightly sharpened what we mean by real situations, we want to turn for a few moments to an idea that may appear to involve a quite contrary notion — that of purely imaginary or fictitious cases. We believe that this seeming diversion may throw a different kind of light on both real situations and their use for case purposes.

If we consider the problem of developing fictitious cases, we find that with the possible exception of the literary genius, the author of such cases cannot escape the dilemma of his own mental system which does not contain "the new" present in any real-life situation. This stands in sharp contrast to what may be reflected in a "real situation" case by a researcher and writer who has adequate skills and training. Given adequate competence, his cases will reflect elements in the situation which may be quite new in his own awareness.

A researcher who has cultivated the outlook and art of being a reflector of the elements of situations can succeed to some extent in incorporating, in his finished case, aspects of these situations which may be no more immediately or precisely explicable to him than to a subsequent reader of the case. This is not to claim that any case can be entirely free of highlights and shadows stemming from the psychological make-up of the particular casewriter.

A case is not the same as "the real situation" portrayed in the case. It is a "real situation as reflected through *a transmitting lens*, in the person of the case researcher and writer." But training and skill can improve the quality of this "lens"; can reduce the extent to which reality is distorted as it passes through the individual as "lens"; can result in less screening out of aspects of situations, and fewer "ghosts" or false images in the projection of the picture.

The skilled case researcher, like the trained social science observer or interviewer, has developed himself as a more highly perfected receiving instrument than most human beings are likely to be unless they have undergone similar training and experience. He thus "picks up" the data of a social situation under study through interviews and observation, mentally recording more of the subtle factors in such a way that he can better reflect the situation onto paper. On the writing side, of course, the case researcher must have some skills not necessarily demanded of the social science researcher; yet he must beware of an overutilization of these skills lest they distort the case in giving it form, style, and life in words.

One difficult problem for a case writer is to avoid trying to "figure out the case" until after it has become a finished product. If he crystallizes conclusions about the case before it is written, he will tend to organize all the elements in terms of an underlying structure which his own thinking has imposed on the situation. The relation of these elements in the original situation may have been different.

The case writer's "logicizing" of the data of the case will then stand as a barrier between the students of the case and the real-life situation; it slants the case toward the explanation that the case writer had in mind.

This suggestion of some of the problems involved in developing cases with some faithfulness will probably also suggest some of the difficulties which emerge in fictitious cases. The first difficulty is that they may tend to be neat, nicely ordered, and "flat." They lack the subtleties which a "good" case writer will reflect from the situations he has investigated. The fact that they are contrived usually means that a consciously constructed rationale and plot is first designed; the human and other data of the case are then hung on the framework, like clothes on a mannequin. The persons in such cases tend to be stereotyped underneath the surface, even though bedecked with differences of behavior or language.

Suppose, however, that someone endeavoring to construct a wholly fictitious case is aware that these kinds of deficiency may appear in his finished product. He is aware that real-life situations, more often than not, contain elements whose place in the design of the situation is by no means readily clear or finally certain. He knows that human beings are not composed of pure reason only and that human relationships involve more than classical logics.

His effort to build "more realistic" fictitious cases may then take the direction of attempting to incorporate some "illogical" or "puzzling" features into the otherwise neat order of the case which he has conceived. But these deliberate and contrived variations do not yield the qualities of real situations. The uncertainties of real life probably do not emerge in quite the same way. Presumably the puzzling or less explicable relationships of *real* situations are not the work of some master contriver eager to throw us off the track of the main design.

A more optimistic explanation of the presence of some slightly unusual or at first seemingly inconsistent elements inherent in most problems of human relationships would be that these are merely expressions of the partial ignorance which we bring to any new human situation. Growth of knowledge may reduce, but never eliminate, such ignorance — as long as life changes and yields situations that are new.

To note the two directions of almost inevitable defect in fictitious cases is not, however, to imply that cases too neatly ordered or with too obviously contrived inconsistencies might not be substantially improved by exceptionally imaginative and able writers. For these are basic problems in the creation of fiction. They are solved to a greater or lesser degree according to the creative powers and skills of different writers. It is not unlikely that persons of considerable talent as novelists, short-story writers, or dramatists might produce some excellent fictitious cases about some kinds of situations. In fact, Professor Irving Lee at Northwestern University, who teaches communications, human relations, and semantics by case methods, has found some short stories which serve as very good cases indeed.[3]

Although it would be scarcely feasible to consider employing creative literary artists to dream up cases in educational administration, it is of some value to consider what may lie behind the observation that *exceptional* works of fiction do illuminate real-life situations.

Exceptional writers of fiction have indicated that sometimes they do not know the outcome or the characters of their works, except as the plots and the persons emerge in the process of writing. In some of Charles Dickens' novels, for example, the over-all framework was frequently not clear to him until the successive characters appeared in his mind, as the novel developed. The interaction of these (to him) real persons unfolded the ultimate plot or story. With some other writers, the plot may be clear in advance, but the *dramatis personae* may only gradually emerge and act in terms of their most central thoughts and feelings. This seems to have been true of Shakespeare. Although he selected in advance general plots from history and folklore, it is almost as though the characters emerged with such vividness as to reshape these plots in accordance with their respective natures and the resulting relationships.

Men are continuously struck by the fact that the created or fictitious works of a Shakespeare, a Dickens, a Balzac, or a Tolstoi do not seem to be merely *like* life. Some great works are sometimes said to be *more like life than life itself*. But is this not merely another way of saying that they may illuminate life in a way that our own minds and senses, viewing life directly, fail to do? Perhaps a part of the essential genius of the creators of such works may be some extraordinary sensitivity and receptivity to the realities of life situations, together with unusual ability to transmit through words of their imaginings which draw on this vivid sense of what life is like.

If we recall what has been said about the aims, disciplines, and skills of the case researcher and writer, we may perceive that he too undertakes to render himself into an unusually sensitive receiving instrument to "pick up" real situations. He too must have some skill in transmitting through the medium of words his awareness of these situations. These two attri-

[3] Irving J. Lee, *Customs and Crises in Communication* (New York: Harper and Brothers, 1954).

butes of a "good" case researcher and writer may thereby enable him to illuminate real situations beyond what we ourselves would see if we were to observe the same situations.

The case writer, of course, does not need to have the creative imagination of a literary artist; indeed, to the extent that he has it, he must try to keep it under wraps while he is writing a case. We would see no particular gain and considerable potential loss if the aim of case preparation were changed to permit *fictionalizing* to take the place of trying to reflect real situations as faithfully as possible. The intensive and repeated analyses and discussions to which cases are subject are likely to reveal any basic flaws in them. They must even reflect "naturally" — that is, without excessive self-consciousness on the part of the case writer — the mores, the languages, and the patterns of behavior in the special environment of educational administration. A case that leaves any considerable number of users with the feeling that it is "not like real life" has serious flaws, not the least of which is its failure to interest or challenge persons of administrative bent, who are oriented toward dealing with real-life situations.

The "Human" Nature of Situations

It may appear that we have been talking as though the only important elements in cases in educational administration were human factors. This is not our intent. But the variety of elements in educational administration which involve things thought of as being "other than people" may warrant our stress upon the obvious.

These factors which we think of as different from the "human factors" include the whole range of "substantive" or "technical" or "subject matter" aspects of administrations, such as finance, business management, transportation, budget-making, curriculum, and "practices" of all kinds. The volume of these seemingly impersonal elements is so great that the human factor and the knowledge and skill required to deal with it sometimes seems just one among many. But can we really separate "other" elements from human aspects of administration?

Suppose we make the statement that all elements of administrative situations do, in fact, involve people. This statement is of course a truism. But it would not be surprising if, in repeating it a number of times as an axiomatic statement, it might also suddenly appear as strange. For we are saying that there are no factors in administration consisting wholly of "other than people." We are saying that the data of administration consist of complex combinations of "human and other" elements. Yet much of our approach to administration is made as if this statement were *not* true. Indeed, the degree to which knowledge in the field of administration has been organized as if it could have reality independent of specific human actors in specific situations makes the statement run counter to habits of thinking which have become quite strong in us.

We have tended to forget the "as if." We read about, talk about, and think about "finance," "budget-making," "school plant," or other artifacts (useful ones, as we shall subsequently note) with respect to matters which exist only in combination with human factors.

"Finance," for example, is merely a convenient category which we have invented for organizing certain kinds of data. But some of the most fundamental aspects of finance, as every superintendent confronting a financial problem knows, remain in the original human context; the human data are inextricably interwoven with the "financial" problem — but we do not classify them as finance.

To get at these data, we would have to get at the attitudes, the behavior, and the relationships of people. If in dealing with "financial data" we forget, even for a moment, that there remains in the original situations a great deal more information which has just as much to do with financial problems as that abstracted in a "financial" category, we begin to delude ourselves. We may think of having *knowledge* about "finance." But the only kind of *experience* we have is with many kinds of "fiscal-human" or "social-fiscal" situations.

We shall return later to some distinctions between artifacts represented in specialized organizations of data and experience in administration. At the moment it is pertinent only to underscore the point that whatever may be the utilities of organizing and treating such data as if these had existence independent of social contexts, serious difficulties are likely to arise in our thinking and behavior whenever we lose sight of the qualifying phrase.

In thinking about cases, it is necessary to deal with the fact that administration embraces innumerable combinations of "human and other" data and experience. In the development of administration, the dominant tendency has been to abstract specialized kinds of information from the human settings in which they occur; to analyze and organize these data independently of social contexts; and to generalize principles, or best practices, without reference to any concrete situation involving human factors.

This practice in administration has, of course, been long antedated by somewhat similar processes in the organization and development of knowledge more generally. The formulation of generalizations about special kinds of data abstracted from their original settings has been basic to the rise of "scientific" knowledge. It took firm root in such fields as economics, for example, in the nineteenth century. Virtual social upheavals were subsequently involved in breaking through systems of political power and social sanctions based upon such illusions as "the iron law of wages." In time, workmen organized into unions, and some employers, pursuing different ideas as to what might constitute workable and profitable wage policies, demonstrated that this abstraction of "economic law" was unreal. Numerous other examples could be cited to illustrate a significant tendency for *artifacts of mental abstraction,* originally derived from the attempt to comprehend real experience, to be considered as having existence independent of social situations. We are still bound, perhaps more than we imagine, by belief in generalizations about this or that aspect of reality which had their original roots in particular social conditions at particular points in time.

Many such beliefs, furthermore, tend to create their own evidence that they are true. Presumed "laws" about one or another aspect of society or human behavior may result in behavior which may even strengthen the supporting evidence, as in the case of "the iron law of wages." This phenomenon is referred to as "the self-fulfilling prophecy." Only time may reveal an error in knowledge thus reinforced; the working out of less visible "human and other" forces eventually confronts men with new situations which compel modification or abandonment of the erroneous generalizations. Should we not begin to recognize more clearly that perhaps one of the very few generalizations in terms of which administrators might wisely act is the notion that: (1) all data describing "other than human" elements reflect the operation of arbitrary mental artifacts, and (2) all situations contain elements of the "new" and unexperienced?

Now, we cannot, of course, proceed from such a view to the idea that we should abandon the process of classifying data and attempting to make generalizations about them. We need merely imagine what drastic consequences would follow from such a mode of behavior to see how utterly lost and confused we would become. The problem might be viewed as how to define and abstract various kinds of "other than human" data and generalize about them *and at the same time* provide for the maintenance of the sense of the inseparability of the "human factors" and the "new" of every new situation. It might also be viewed as how to develop more "scientific" knowledge about combinations of "human and other" data as these are experienced in administrative situations. In some way, knowledge in the field of administration must clearly remain far from scientific if it is organized in forms which neglect the essential fusion of "human and other" data.

For the moment, we shall simply touch on the frame of reference we have in mind. Science, as it is usually defined, involves *par excellence* systematic processes of selecting, organizing, and analyzing various kinds of data in the attempt to arrive at generalized statements about these data. The data are always of special types defined according to the interests of the scientists. Since the world around us exhibits innumerable different kinds of data, the systematic task of science involves the phenomenon of the *specialization* of efforts in the development of knowledge.

As we shall subsequently indicate, this can scarcely hold as a sufficient definition of science, if by science we mean a kind of knowledge beyond that given to us by our ordinary experience. For we start with the knowledge, based on ordinary experience, that the data we have separated out were derived from observable phenomena in which many kinds of data are interrelated. Clearly the task of scientific knowledge must ultimately also include putting the specialized knowledges together again into statements applicable to the diverse and interrelated phenomena of our real and direct experience.

Nonetheless, the specialized approach to knowledge tends still to be dominant, as it grows throughout the modern era. It perpetuates itself partly because of the great and continuing prestige associated with the brilliant successes arising out of the physical sciences particularly. From the time of Galilee and Newton until the present, the physical sciences have been extraordinarily successful in pushing forward to discoveries of uniformities of data. However, physical science has been, by definition, that major branch (together with related sub-branches) of science which deals exclusively with data defined not only as nonhuman but also as lacking that essential though elusive quality which is presumed to differentiate between nonliving and living matter. All the data of physical science are thus of a single special class which excludes anything defined as "living."

Since the methods of the physical sciences proved brilliantly successful, it is not surprising that they would be imitated, so far as possible, by efforts with respect to other kinds of phenomena — including the phenomena of living things and of human society itself. Our purpose in citing the "iron law of wages" was to dramatize one kind of possible consequence of this tendency. We made this selection realizing that it might be called an unfair example in that it represented a not very scientific finding in a field which was then very young and which, furthermore, might be viewed as a "borderline" science at best. Yet for a considerable length of time the evidence seemed to support the "iron law of wages" theory quite conclusively.

Is it not possible that the basic error may have been, not in the adequacy and validity of the evidence and what it "proved," but in the use of a model appropriate to physical data but not to "economic" data?

Perhaps there are aspects of administration, including even some human and social factors, which can lend themselves to study that corresponds closely to study in the physical sciences. The values of undertaking to develop scientific social knowledge are not to be belittled; the importance of more rigorously scientific research is probably still too little recognized. *But the essential complement of advancing in the skills of study of each unique situation can easily be neglected if knowledge of specialized aspects of administrative experience is erroneously given a halo of science that needs but to be "applied."*

The tendency both to *think* primarily in terms of specialization and to define "science" chiefly in terms of abstractions of special classes of data, is very powerful in society. The idea that synthesis may be a major, perhaps even the main, task of advancing science is comparatively new and undeveloped. Yet the notion of synthesis, of seeing and acting in relation to diverse kinds of "human and other" phenomena inherent in administrative situations, would seem to be quite basic to the idea of administration itself.

How can administrators use resources of specialized knowledge without just "applying" them? How can administration develop generalizations about special kinds of data, yet remain aware of the nature and limitations of such artifacts of knowledge? How can administrators become adequately aware of concepts arising out of scientific specialization without interposing barriers to awareness of the novel pattern of factors in a given situation?

As we have said, the tendency to think in terms of scientific specialization is powerful in society. It is perhaps particularly powerful in the social and educational environments which have conditioned the habits of thinking of most of those who aspire to the administration of education. This being so, one might even argue that it is safer to approach administrative situations with a minimum of specialized kinds of study but with total concentration on observing new, concrete situations, rather than to make the gross error of assuming that past experience and abstractions describe, explain, and provide the answers to specific situations. In such a view, learning administration would primarily emphasize *unlearning* — that is, reducing the effects of the earlier influence of thinking in terms of scientific specialization.

There are some, indeed, who hold such a theory with respect to learning administration. In this view, the study of concepts and generalizations from past situations and experiences are to be avoided, as blocking the ability to see clearly the immediate, the concrete, the unique, the "human and other" aspects of an administrative situation. It cannot be questioned that such blocking can and does occur when men's minds are so dominated by the formulations of past experience that they cease to approach new situations *as new situations,* or to remember that abstractions of "other than human" data eliminate the one indisputable common ingredient of all administrative situations — people interacting. But it does not seem to us that the extreme of avoiding the study of experience, of specialized resources of knowledge, or of generalizations about administrative experience, as a whole or in any aspects which may be selected, is any happier than the extreme of being so dominated by these mental artifacts that the ability, and perhaps even the willingness, to be open to the realities of each new situation is atrophied.

The problem of advancing in administrative knowledge-and-practice (for there cannot be the one without the other) would seem to lie in bringing together the two aspects of learnings — studying experience and acting in new situations — into a more profitable and continuing synthesis. But how to do it? Whatever may be learned from a field such as medicine, which has had to deal with a somewhat comparable problem, still does not provide some of the keys required for administration. We shall look briefly at some of the experience of medicine in Section Two.

This still largely unsolved problem of synthesis of various kinds of knowledge-in-action has been and is being grappled with in various ways in various fields of administration. The development of the case method has been one of the outcomes of thinking about this kind of problem. In general, the case method has arisen in response to the feeling that the organization of knowledge, of training, and even of function in administration has previously reflected too greatly an emphasis on learning abstractions and generalizations about aspects of administration. These have all too frequently lacked the qualities associated with rigorous development of knowledge. At the same time, consideration of these generalizations has been largely divorced from the specific human contexts in which the data underlying them alone occur. These conditions have resulted in some tendencies to attribute reality to quite tenuous and even amorphous generalizations, yet to induce little familiarity with arenas of social reality. Among those who find the state of knowledge in administration unsatisfactory in these respects, there may also be the contrary tendency to proceed by purely pragmatic handling of situations.

Educational administration appears to have both need and opportunity to make some fresh contributions, through the case method and perhaps in other ways, to the problem of improved knowledge-in-practice. Business administration and public administration have been at the task longer and have much to offer. Educational administration is younger, less highly formulated, and is, furthermore, involved with problems which require some differences in solution.

These historical and special factors may be basically responsible for an approach to cases in educational administration which differs in some important respects from those generally prevailing in the two older fields of administration on the central matters which we have been considering. These differences are reflected in some of the ways in which we define cases. It has been our intent that they be reflected also in some qualities which we have tried increasingly to achieve in the cases we produce and in certain aspects of theory and methods of case instruction.

Cases: Instrument, Content, and Method

In the "Overview" we stated that cases are instruments for use in learning; we have also made frequent reference to "case methods." This kind of language is sometimes associated with a stress on the "process" of learning rather than the "content."

Much of Section One thus far, however, has revolved around the problem of the "content" of administration. Although this question is to be pursued more fully in Sections Two and Five, we have argued that:

1. "Administration" is an abstraction which can be defined only by reference to concrete administrative situations, and to the kinds and relationships of "human and other" data which these contain.

2. Abstractions from numerous administrative situations and any generalizations resulting from their analysis must be considered as statements *about special aspects* of administration. Since these may not necessarily be pertinent to any given situation, they are also indeterminate with respect to their place in a scheme describing administration more generally.

3. Cases constitute abstractions of quite a different order. In our view they more nearly reflect the basic phenomena — situations — which must be examined in order to formulate appropriate descriptions and definitions of "administration" or generalizations about it.

To speak of cases as instruments for learning is therefore not at all to class them merely as aids to learning some content not contained within the cases. The use of a rich variety of "good" cases, by any rigorous and thorough method of study, would, in our view, impart to the student a broad foundation of knowledge *about* "administration." A solitary student reading and studying a wide range of cases could learn a great deal *about* administration. By including in his solitary program the exploration of many kinds of *specialized* knowledge pertinent to administration, he could work at the task of how to relate this knowledge to the case situations and to his emerging concepts of "administration." He might, indeed, through a long period of such solitary study become a quite advanced student of administration, in the sense that he might have a great deal of knowledge about it.

But his achievements would fail to accomplish the task to which our efforts are centrally directed. He would be learning *about* administration; we are concerned with the problem of *learning administration.* There is a vital difference between the two, as we see it.

We are here making, we believe, essentially the same distinction which has been made in a recent report of an important experiment:[4]

> Although related, we assumed that there were two kinds of knowledge that needed to be differentiated. One is the kind of knowledge that is associated with the scientist who is seeking to make verifiable propositions about a certain class of phenomena. The other is the kind of knowledge that is associated with the practitioner of a skill in relation to a certain class of phenomena. This distinction is not original; it has been made over and over again by many different people. To us it still seems important and not too well understood.
>
> The difference between these two kinds of knowledge can be readily seen by contrasting the aim of the scientist with the aim of the practitioner of a skill. The aim of the scientist is to discover and make verifiable propositions about a certain class of phenomena; the aim of the practitioner is the immediate "control" of the phenomena with which he deals. Although

[4] F. J. Roethlisberger and others, *Training for Human Relations — An Interim Report* (Boston: Harvard University, Division of Research, Graduate School of Business Administration, 1954).

the "knowledge of acquaintance" which the practitioner acquires from the practice of a skill often remains intuitive and implicit, it serves his immediate purposes well. . . . He does not have, however, that kind of analytical *knowledge about* phenomena sought by the scientist. . . .

Because of a failure to distinguish between these two different kinds of knowledge, the application of knowledge is often confused with the practice of a skill. The frame in which the scientist's thought is set when applying analytical knowledge, however, is quite different from the frame in which the practitioner's thought is set when practicing a skill. . . . A skill can be practiced with little analytical knowledge about the territory; analytical knowledge, however, cannot be applied to the territory before such knowledge is formulated.

The distinguishing features of the practice of a skill are quite different from the application of analytical knowledge. Skill is the response of a whole organism, acting as a unit, that is adequate to a particular point in a given situation. A skill is always manifested at a particular point as a complex capacity acquired by experience in responding appropriately to particular, concrete, and whole situations.* The applier of analytical knowledge is responding only to those observations which his specialized methods and techniques have said in advance are relevant. In differentiating skill from analytical knowledge, it does not follow that they are unrelated. It does follow that the difference between them needs to be better understood before their relation to each other can be more correctly assessed.

---

* See Elton Mayo, *The Social Problems of an Industrial Civilization* (Boston: Division of Research, Harvard Business School, 1945), p. 15.

Because of connotations which our particular audience may initially attach to "knowledge" and "skill," we use a somewhat different terminology from that used in the above quotation in discussing the same differentiation. When we speak of "learning about administration" as distinguished from "learning administration," however, we are referring to the essential difference between developing a *knowledge* and developing a *skill,* in the language of the report cited.

Despite the largeness and the significance of the difference, few things are more difficult to explain. We are not sure whether the difficulty lies in our inadequacies or whether it is because they cannot be "explained" — that is, communicated through the vehicle of language *alone.* We are certain, however, that the vital difference between *learning about administration* and *learning administration* can be experienced. Furthermore, experience can be *imagined* to some extent, if some of the conditions or framework of the experience are stated.

Suppose we briefly present a quite different way of using cases from the one we have just described. The reader may then be able to imagine to some extent what this second experience might be like and how it would differ from the experience of studying cases as a solitary student. (This will not demonstrate or prove that the second method results in learning administration, as contrasted with merely learning about it. We shall have to say much more about administration and various possible ways of learning it, in the sense of learning a skill, before the notion that case methods result in learning administration, at least to some extent, can be made clear. This we attempt to do in Section Two. But a heightened notion of what experience might be like under the conditions of case study may transmit to the reader's imagination some overtones with respect to learning administration rather than just about it.) Let us note a contrast between the two following conditions of case study:

A. A solitary student studying the cases.
B. A group of students and their instructor *interacting* in the process of *working at* and *working with* these cases in *their efforts* to extract values from them, including, quite centrally, that particular value which we have called "learning administration."

The first of these conditions involves an isolated individual working at a task that centrally involves both *learning* and *administration.* The second involves a number of persons (instructor and students) working together at a task which similarly involves learning and administration. But since administration is itself a function related to persons working together on a task, it is quite clear that (1) the solitary student can learn only about a function related to persons working together in a task, whereas (2) a member of a case study group is working under conditions which contain some of the basic elements involved in the very function he is trying to learn. (We do not say, however, that he is working under conditions *equivalent* to administration.)

Under condition A, what is learned through solitary study will depend upon the relationship of a limited number of variables: (1) who the student is; (2) what cases he uses; (3) what other resources of knowledge he uses; (4) what his methods of study are. Now let us suppose that this same student (1) studies these same cases (2) as a member of a case study class. To the environment of his "individual" experience and learning are now added several new major variables, including (3) who the other persons (students and instructor) are; (4) what kinds of "working at" and "working with" the cases, as a focal task, emerge through the interactions within the group; (5) what other resources of knowledge any others (as well as he) use; (6) what methods of individual study (that is, apart from the class) are used by others (as well as himself).

Of course the relationships among these variables are different in each case study class and situation or series of situations; how any given group will use a case and what values they will derive from it are unpredictable. A class using a case at one time will behave differently and with different results than at another time. For this reason, there is value in using at least one case at two different times in a case course, in order that the students may experience the change in their pattern of going at the task as well as the change in the values derived from their effort. "The Letter" (page 11), for example, might be used at the beginning and also toward the end of a case course.

It may also be pointed out that the two variables (1 and 2) which we carried over from condition A to condition B, as if they remained constant, do not remain constant. Let us see how these two variables change simply as a result of their shift from condition A to condition B.

Shift in Variable # 1. Intensive study of each case by each member of the class prior to class sessions (and by many students subsequently) is not the same thing as isolated study by an "individual" student, such as we described in A. Each member of the class in his perhaps solitary phase of study of a case before (or after) a case session is not a "solitary student" in the sense originally defined. This means, of course, that John Jones learning in isolation is not the same John Jones if he knows that he is to be engaged in a social process of co-learning.

Shift in Variable # 2. The thing that may be much harder to see is that a case does not remain constant when shifted from A to B. A case is not the same case when studied by John as an isolated student as when studied by John as a member of a case study class, even though, from one kind of perspective, the written case consists of exactly the same words in exactly the same arrangements. The words in the case (and the whole structure of the language of the case) have one set of meanings when the student studies the case prior to its discussion; these meanings are bound to change to some extent if he is capable of listening to what any other student tries to say in discussing the case. For every other student has projected into the language of the case certain meanings which reflect his own frames of reference and ways of putting these together. A case, in short, has no reality except as a piece of paper with some marks on it, apart from the different meanings which these marks have for different persons who examine them. There are, of course, many approximations of meaning, arising out of the structure of language as a social tool for communication. Working at a case involves dealing with problems in communication and behavior in the attempt to discover (find correspondences of perceptions and meanings) what the case is all about and what kinds of action might be appropriate to the situation reflected in the case. Interestingly enough, this experience is one of the aspects of case study experience which begins to be sharpened in the awareness of students at a very early stage. It begins to be learned and realized by them.

A group working at the task of case use is doing so with the notion that it may result in learning administration, at least to some extent. This notion must necessarily remain somewhat nebulous; if it could be made definitive by means of oral or written exposition, there would then be no need either for cases or for working with others in the use of them. Presumably the value involves the experience. And the experience will be affected by whatever those involved have in mind in the way of both aims and anticipations. What the various participants in the class mean by "administration," by "learning," and by "learning administration" will affect the experience of each; but not necessarily as anticipated.

A case study sequence for learning administration takes place within an environment composed of adults who have attained the graduate level of study and who have given some conscious thought to the goals of their learning efforts. They will presumably redirect these efforts from time to time in the light of their original goals, of whatever they have learned, and of whatever new goals seem to emerge as worthy of effort. These conscious and self-conscious factors operate as important determinants of case study experience itself.

The kind of awareness *about case methods* which the participants have at the outset may also vary widely. They will have a variety of ideas related to the reports of experience in case methods by others. There will be vagueness in the minds of some and stereotypes in the minds of others. The way in which each person — instructor and student — proceeds to "use" the cases constitutes behavior reflecting many kinds of awareness which are parts of his particular make-up; one awareness, even if it is only a sense of uncertainty, has to do with "behavior" in relation to case methods of learning administration. There is a consciousness about the learning experience about to be undertaken, even if what case methods are all about is unclear. There is consciousness about such things as behavior in a graduate-level classroom, behavior in a group discussion, behavior in relation to others working on a task. There is thus a consciousness of role, however indeterminate.

The case being obviously a paper report of a situation and not the "real situation itself," the initial tendency may be to view it primarily as an instrument. But we have taken the position that cases also more nearly reflect the data and relationships of administration than do compilations of specialized data derived from administration situations.

We might look upon a case as the nearest thing to a first-order abstraction of the "realities" of an administrative situation that can be made available for examination. A case preserves the situation in such a way that it can be studied. Yet the situation itself has meanwhile evolved into a whole new series of situations; it is still alive in the sense of its continuance in persons and relationships affected by it. What the situation was, disappears; it disappears from memory also, or is distorted in recall.

A written case is therefore quite different from a report of a situation made orally, perhaps long afterward by an actor. It is a picture of interactions over a limited period of time taken as close to that time as research and interview conditions permit. It is like the haemulon in Professor Agassiz's laboratory in the sense that it is preserved for examination. But unlike the haemulon, it is not "dead." The real situation is not dead, even though it may have evolved into the context of new situations; these new situations are the result of interactions, including the important factor of decision or action by an administrator and the consequence of this decision. These are unknown to the reader of a case. Any case has to stop at a point in the continuum of interactions involved. This point is a point at which the actual situation was at some time. The user of a case picks up the situation at a point at which, in the original situation, the administrator and the other actors in the case found themselves.

"What is the situation" in any particular case is the initial question. What "is" in the case is partly a function of who is viewing it and what kind of social situation he is in.

To the extent that any participant from time to time asks himself: "What am I learning or what have I learned from my case study experience?", the resulting notions will be highly variable. Indeed, if a student asks himself the question one day and supplies his own answers, he may find that if the group discusses the question shortly thereafter he may emerge with rather different ideas.

In the minds of most students there may first be a tendency, if any ideas tend to crystallize, for them to relate respectively to two "obvious" sides of the question: (1) what has been learned regarding the "content" of the cases; (2) what has been learned regarding one's own and others' behavior in relation to this "content." It may be that no satisfying crystallizations of either kind will emerge soon or easily, or that if they do there may thereafter be a growing sense of dissatisfaction with them. If the aim is "learning administration," it must involve something more than a *duality* of awareness, relating respectively to the content in the cases and the experience in the classroom. The problem of the relationship between the two remains.

It was but a few pages ago that some familiar terms in pedagogy — "content," "instrument," "methods," "learning situation" — seemed to have some more clearly differentiated meanings than they may now seem to have. These terms and their original referents may seem to have disappeared, to have been swallowed up in each other. In their place may be a somewhat nebulous sense of what may be experienced in using cases in administration. May not a lingering sense of these familiar terms or the attempt to hold onto them get in the way of trying to imagine, from what has just been said about case study situations, what the experience may be like?

But the difficulty in imagining may also be due to what may seem to have been an obvious lack in our discussion, so far. We have said very little about administration as a kind of human behavior, in an action role. We have taken it for granted from the outset that our readers are aware that the administrator functions not merely intellectually and verbally. The administrator reflects his knowledge behavioristically in situations of which he is a part. It is not alone what he thinks, says, writes, that affects the situation; his whole being is reflected in the way in which, as an individual and also as an actor in a social role, he interacts with others — influencing and changing their feelings, values, behavior, satisfactions, health, and life careers — — and also their physical environments of school, school district, and community. He cannot but be a judge and a determiner of values significantly affecting the lives of many other human beings — including children who have no voice of their own with regard to their conditions of learning. To learn administration involves learning behavior in the context of situations in which one's own behavior and the behavior of others are interrelated. It is this that necessitates development of new ways of learning administration as contrasted with study about it, or about aspects of it, which has tended to characterize graduate levels of study.

In the nature of the administrative function, many of the kinds of knowledge associated with the humanistic and liberal arts tradition are necessary, but not adequate. The definitions of competences and skills most strongly recognized, inculcated, and rewarded in the purely scholarly field are appropriate up to a point, but they do not cover the need. Furthermore, having an abundance of "knowledge," developing intellectual facility, and achieving competence in oral and written communication are not only not enough: a stress upon such development, at the cost of loss of ability to listen to others, to recognize one's own feelings, to be willing to live with awareness of uncertainty, may shape not merely a poor administrator but a dangerous one.

Similarly, in the nature of the administrative function, many of the kinds of knowledge associated with the sciences are necessary but not adequate. A distinction such as "pure" and "applied," transferred to administration, holds the danger of transforming it into technocracy, with its various levels of hierarchy from "scientist" to "engineer"; the human constituents of the organization become simply a part of the objects to be acted upon and brought into correspondence with "scientific solutions."

Case methods represent a development which has arisen in various fields of *practice* — law, medicine, and several fields of administration — in response to a recognized need for curricula and learning situations more closely corresponding to the conditions of practice. In these fields, for the most part, approaches to learning arising out of the scholarly and the scientific traditions were not abandoned. But emphasis upon them was reduced in the process of making room for case methods. Cases, case methods, and ways of thinking and behaving which are involved in the shaping and use of these, have then increasingly influenced the very idea and direction of the development of knowledge in these fields. The original distinctions between knowledge and skill tend to disappear in a new synthesis.

There have been some tendencies in fields of administration to depend exclusively upon case methods to meet the need, in training programs, for learning the skill. We feel that case methods alone do not adequately meet this need but that they constitute a highly valuable part of a core of experiences which do so more adequately.

We realize that it is possible to use the case method in such a way as to direct primary attention to "the situation in the classroom." Behavior of oneself and of others as revealed in the interactions among the participants can be made the major focus of observation and analysis; under these conditions the case may become somewhat secondary.

A strong emphasis of this kind strikes us as denoting a predominant interest in "human relations" somewhat divorced from the context of administration in which we are centrally interested; it tends to become a study of "human relations in the classroom" by those who are in the classroom, with the case becoming a rather shadowy part of the stage setting. A focus of this kind may well offer important values in both the knowledge and the skill aspects of human relations. And human relations is obviously a basic part of administration. But is it one which is normally separated from other aspects of administration? Or is it an element of administration which simply has to be dealt with as a part of the process of trying to accomplish the tasks toward which the work of the organization is directed? We incline to the latter view, although recognizing that organizations occasionally do set up for their members special programs of education, training, or therapy in human relations which use methods not unlike those involved in studying human relations *in* the class *by* the class. If this is the aim for a class in a graduate program of study, it would seem scarcely necessary to invest heavily in case devices for such programs; the so-called member-centered approach would seem to us to provide a focus.

We therefore have a bias. We view the case approach as a primarily *task-oriented approach* to learning. The task revolves around the idea of using the case for learning administration; the case is the major focus. Awareness regarding behavior and changes in behavior then tends to emerge as part of the problem of the task productivity of the class groups.

This same bias leads us to hold to no particular theory regarding our role as instructors, unless it could be one which has in it such notions as "spontaneity"and "co-learning." Despite the fact that the cases we use have been produced by a case research staff working under our direction, we have usually forgotten, if indeed we ever knew, anything more about the case than is in the written case before us. Nonetheless we have three seeming advantages over our students when it comes to trying to see "what is in the case":

1. We have more familiarity with case methods and case discussion situations than most of our students have at the outset of a course.
2. We may have had longer acquaintance with the particular case being used. If we have used it before, we have the benefit of the analyses and discussions made by previous classes.
3. We presumably have a somewhat larger background in administration, and particularly in the problems of trying to learn it, than most of our students. This is, of course, something quite different from knowing the answers.

(These seeming advantages may be somewhat illusory, since they may induce in us a false sense of security with respect to our insights into the case.)

Assuming that the above are advantages, we recognize that the too early or strong use of them would spoil the game for many of the students, at least temporarily. But as soon, in our work with any new group of students, as we can enter into the process of "working with" and "working at" the case *as a task to which no one knows the answers,* we do so according to our spontaneous inclinations in the case situation. We think that we learn a great deal from case discussions — including what we learn when we jump to premature or oversimplified conclusions as to what to do in the situation, or when we find it hard to decide what we would do.

We are also aware that our status in an academic institution makes our expressed views or other behavior a different influence in a case discussion situation than would similar views and behavior on the part of students in the class. We thus tend to give less expression to our views regarding any particular case at the outset of a new year with a new group of students, but relatively more as the year wears on; as the aura of authority is diminished, we can move more clearly into the role of "co-learners."

As this may imply, we do not hold "nondirective behavior" as an ideal image for an instructor's role in a task-oriented group situation. Nor do we believe that an acute period of frustration which may accompany the maintenance of a persistently nondirective role is either essential or particularly efficient for the achievement of learning. In its own peculiar way, it seems to us, the setting up of a "nondirective" model for the instructor's role can result in behavior that imposes upon others conditions not unlike those associated with authoritarian behavior.

Our sense of our own role includes trying to behave in such a way as to help the case discussion group move on a fairly even keel from the initial novelty of the experience, through a time of increasing uncertainty, to the stage of more conscious learning efforts. These are merely our biases, however. We state them chiefly in order that any stereotypes — probably oversharpened ones — about what the case process "is," and what the instructor's role "is," may be reduced by each instructor's and each student's recognition that there is no prescribed behavior necessarily associated with the case method of learning administration. Nothing that is learned will have been worth the learning, as we see it, if learned at the cost of losing the ability to be "yourself."

We do believe that it is not merely a bias, but an essential part of the definition of endeavoring to learn administration, for students to do more than *analyze* the cases in various ways; these may include attempting to predict what will happen and what the administrator and others in the case are likely to do beyond the point where the case ends. We feel that it is important also, at least in most cases and case discussions, for the student to cast himself in the role of an administrator in the situation and *commit himself to a course of action,* whatever it may be.

Analyses and predictive analyses alone, it seems to us, tend to emphasize knowledge *about* the case and skill in verbalizing this; they do not embrace the doing of something that every administrator must constantly do, namely, commit himself to some decision or course of action under conditions of relative uncertainty, and handle the consequences of his decision.

What has been said may leave the reader little if any clearer on various key problems and questions that have been noted; some of these we have discussed and finally passed without full explanation or definitive statements. We are still groping with the problem earlier raised. Can the things we are talking about be communicated as abstractions by the writers to the readers of a book or must they first be "experienced" at least to some extent?

We indicated that it is sometimes possible, by means of language, to get someone to imagine what some experience might be *like*. We have proceeded accordingly to say some things, but we do not know what the consequences will be in the minds of various readers. What we have said, plus what he has imagined, may affect his notions as to the desirability or potential worth of "having" some of the kinds of experience that are being talked about.

The results may be quite different or contrary to what the writers have intended and sought to communicate by this device. The reader's heightened imagination may result in a quite different sense of "what the experience might be like" from that which the writers have attempted to stimulate. He may decide that the "experience" which we are urging him to "have" is not for him. But we decided to run the risk.

The Situations in the Cases in This Book

We approached case collection with the point of view that administrative problems do not present themselves to the administrator in any neatly ordered array under such labels as "personnel relations," "finance," or "policy," or divorced from the specific human contexts in which they occur. In collecting cases, therefore, we purposely tried to avoid differentiating between "human relations" cases and other kinds of cases by specific substantive categories commonly used in administration. All of our cases, with two exceptions,[5] represent mixtures of both — "human relations" and "other."

From time to time, however, as attempts were made to take stock of the cases, it was natural to think of classification to see what "coverage" was being secured and whether important aspects of administration were being omitted. We played with many elaborate schemes; we finally settled for a simple one. Categories commonly used in educational administration such as "personnel," "finance," "plant," and "educational program" were found useful in assaying our distribution of cases; these categories we have called *Substantive Elements.* We also drew up a check sheet of the various kinds of actors appearing in the cases — school board members, superintendents, principals, teachers, parents, representatives of professional organizations, and the like. But attempts to classify by such categories proved again how

[5] "Salary Schedule" (Case 7) and "Waltham" (Case 12).

arbitrary this sorting out of cases (and administrative situations) could be. None of the cases proved capable of classification in just one *Substantive Element* category, and the specification of key *Actors* was frequently a problem.

In many cases, moreover, a product of some kind of *generality* of actors — such as public opinion or the sentiment of a social segment of a community — may be involved; but we abandoned our attempts to develop schemes that would enable classification of cases in such terms.

A case would be not *finance* alone, for example but finance, law, public policy, and even perhaps in a "minor" way curriculum — an admixture of elements often not clearly separable. In similar fashion, a case always involved a variety of actors. Yet the majority of cases seemed to have at least one "obvious" focus and some reasonably central actors. Other less obvious aspects and actors may eventually emerge as of greater or less importance than the obvious ones, depending on the direction the analysis of the situation takes with different groups of students. This variation in perception and analysis has made us very cautious about presenting tables which list the "coverage" of each case. (In our own classes, we have never made any reference to any kind of category regarding a case to be studied.)

An experience reported by Lindberg illustrates that categorization of a case prior to its use tends to implant a concept as to a particular viewpoint from which it should be examined.

> Since case study thus invites what might be termed a multi-dimensional exploration, it is often somewhat disconcerting to attempt — on a unilateral basis or in a narrow sense — to "classify" each case into a predetermined schematic framework as such. This point, however, may be better illustrated by the account of an actual classroom experience.
>
> The first time I taught the course in personnel administration at the Harvard Business School I classified each case carefully, using the standard functional personnel classifications such as "employment interview," "job evaluation," "testing," and so forth. One of the cases was No. 48 in this book, the "Redmond Manufacturing Company (B)," which describes an altercation between two workers. For some reason, I had classified the case under "recreation," perhaps because it had been my idea at that time that recreational activities sponsored by the company might alleviate tensions induced by latent nationality differences and frictions from the work environment.
>
> At any rate, first one man reviewed the situation, suggesting that a baseball team or a bowling team might be a possible escape valve for these tensions. Another man spoke along similar lines. Later a third man just about repeated the same suggestion. This sudden uniformity of responses so excited my curiosity that I casually inquired from the class where in the case there had been any implication of the need for baseball and bowling teams. Although the men readily admitted that there was no mention of such ideas in the case, one of them said ". . . but this case is classified under recreation . . ." In other words, my carefully structured classification scheme

> had defeated one of the essential features of case study, namely, independent, exploratory, and imaginative thinking.[6]

In spite of these qualifications and reservations, the user of this book will want to know something about the cases — who they are about, what the major problems are, and how the cases are distributed among these problems. Moreover, an instructor may wish to use a case which includes personnel problems, or problems on the level of the principal. He needs information to help him to select quickly special cases to meet his specific need. In order to help give a picture of what these cases are about, we are presenting two distribution tables: one the *Substantive Elements,* and the other the *Actors.* Each case is listed by number in the category of an *obvious* focus and a *major* actor; the obviousness of the categorization will, we think, reduce the tendency to give it too great importance. In addition, each case is given an "x" in each additional category (substantive or actor) which seems to us to be readily apparent in the case. (Thus, the distribution table for substantive elements shows, for example, that in thirteen cases, as listed by number, "personnel administration" is the obvious focus, and that in seven other cases, as indicated by "x's," it is a clearly apparent factor, though not the primary one.) This we hope will suggest the range and distribution of apparent substantive and human factors included in the cases in the volume, yet avoid influencing the analysis of any particular case.

Different categories could of course have been used; they could have been made more detailed or been even further telescoped. But these have been useful to us in our selection of cases for our classes and have provided sufficient identification for the student to see the possible range and coverage of work in a course using these cases. The discovery of the significant problems, actors, and aspects of administration in each case is a part of the task of those using it — as it would be for the administrator in the situation.

[6] Ben Lindberg, *Cases in Personnel Administration* (New York: Prentice-Hall, 1954), pp. 2–3. Reprinted by permission of the publisher.

DISTRIBUTION OF CASES

Substantive Elements

Personnel Administration	2	3	4	6	9	10	11	13	14	17	22
	23	31	x	x	x	x	x	x	x		
Finance	7	x	x	x	x	x	x	x			
Curriculum	8	21	25	34	35	x	x	x			
Plant	12	x	x	x	x						
Law		x	x	x	x	x	x				
Public Policy and Community	1	5	16	18	19	20	24	26	28	x	x
	x	x	x	x	x	x	x	x	x	x	x
	x	x	x								
Organization and Administrative Practice	15	27	29	30	32	33	x	x	x	x	x
	x	x	x	x	x	x	x	x	x	x	x
	x	x	x								

Note: Case A, "The Letter," is omitted.

DISTRIBUTION OF CASES

Actors

Board	9	16	18	19	20	22	32	x	x	x	x
	x	x	x	x	x	x	x	x	x	x	
Individual Board Members	x	x	x	x							
Superintendent	A	1	3	4	6	10	11	13	15	21	
	24	26	27	31	x	x	x	x	x	x	
	x	x	x	x	x	x	x	x	x	x	
	x	x	x	x	x	x	x	x	x	x	
	x	x	x	x	x	x	x	x	x	x	
	x	x	x	x	x	x					
Central Staff	23	33	x	x	x	x	x				
Principal	2	8	14	17	35	x	x	x	x	x	x
Teacher	x	x	x	x	x	x	x	x	x	x	
Pupil	x	x	x	x	x	x	x	x			
Parent	x	x	x								
Professional Organization	28	x									
External Organization	5	30	34	x	x	x	x	x	x	x	
Professional Individual	25	29	x	x	x	x					

Note: "Salary Schedule" (Case 7) and "Waltham" (Case 12) are omitted in this table.

SECTION TWO

THE RELATIONSHIP OF KNOWLEDGE, EXPERIENCE, AND TRAINING IN ADMINISTRATION

The Relationship of Knowledge, Experience, and Training in Administration

PROGRAMS for the training of educational administrators are currently grappling with an increasing abundance of things "necessary to learn." Long lists describing things that superintendents presumably need to know or to do in their jobs have been prepared. From these lists, "competencies" or qualities of thought and behavior have been deduced, and correspondingly long lists have been developed of the "kinds of experience" that individuals need to undergo in the course of preparing for educational administration.

The assortment of items appearing on such lists varies widely. The way they are divided into categories under such headings as knowledge, skills, experiences, competencies, suggests that these terms may not have the same meanings in the various lists; an item designated as a skill in one list may be included as experience in another, and as knowledge in a third.

It is not unusual for these lists and studies to embrace several scores of items. They reflect the problem of defining the content of educational administration, and of relating the variety of activities which it seems to involve, to the problem of defining needs in programs of training. As an illustration of this difficulty, the following items were selected from one such recent study: "pupil accounting; interpreting to the community the philosophy of the school and its implementation; conduct of staff projects for improvement of curriculum and instruction; analysis of school building plans in cooperation with the architect and others; preparation of prediction of financial needs of school system based on economic trends from the community as well as educational trends and predicted needs; accounting and budgetary control; observation and analysis of factual data; adaptation of curriculum to needs of the community; effective written communication, formal and informal; public speaking."

An institution attempting to develop a program of preparation for administration on the basis of such a listing is inevitably faced with some such question as this: "Since no program of any practical duration can possibly impart all the kinds of knowledge, skill, experience, and competence which seem necessary when one defines the things that administrators on the job are called upon to know and to do, what should be included and what should be left out?"

The sheer number and variety of items of quite different orders pose major difficulties of selection and elimination. It becomes almost essential to revise the original question along such lines as the following: "What kinds and combinations of learning are needed for development of the knowledge and skills which would enable the administrator to deal with various *classes* of items which he seems called upon to know about or to handle?"

More concretely, the question as originally posed might be: "What content and methods in an administrative training program would seem to offer promise of developing knowledge and skill with respect to handling specific problems or activities x_1, x_2, x_3, . . . , connected with an administrative job, which may also be defined as including innumerable different kinds of activities of somewhat comparable orders of specificity y_1, y_2, y_3, . . . , z_1, z_2, z_3, . . . , and so on?" On the other hand, the reformulated question would imply finding answers for a more limited set of somewhat more generalized knowledges and skills, *A*, *B*, *C*, . . . *n*, of which all the activities of order *x*, *y*, *z* and so on might be viewed as more particular sub-classes.

But when attention is turned to the reformulated question, the problem of selection remains, and to this is added the problem of systematic organization. What are to be considered as adequate and sufficient more general categories of competence *A*, *B*, *C*, . . . *n*, which may be considered to comprehend particulars x_1, x_2, x_3, . . . , y_1, y_2, y_3, . . . , z_1, z_2, z_3, . . . , and so on? What kinds of study or methods of learning might be most appropriate in providing knowledge and skill for each of the more general categories of competence? Does accepting such an approach imply programs which, so to speak, forget all the particular *x*'s, *y*'s, and *z*'s and transmit learnings which fit only the generalities *A*, *B*, *C*, . . . *n*? Are there kinds of learning or methods of learning which may be capable of improving or developing competencies *A*, *B*, *C*, . . . *n* in such a way that sufficient *x*'s, *y*'s, or *z*'s are embraced in, rather than dropped out of, the scheme of comprehension or behavior?

There are other very central questions which dog us: Assuming that there can be a general kind of competence (knowledge or skill), defined as "*A*," which is important in dealing with various kinds of particular problems, what might be said about the various possible ways of learning "*A*" within the framework of a program under which only a limited amount of time and attention can be devoted to "*A*" as compared with *B*, *C*, *D*, . . . *n*? Any answer given to such a question will reflect (1) certain assumptions regarding the relative importance of "*A*" in the practice of administration; (2) therefore certain assumptions about administration; (3) certain assumptions about the nature of learning; (4) certain assumptions about what is involved in learning administration; (5) certain pedagogical leanings as to effective ways of teaching whatever is involved in (1) through (4) above. (Number 5 is included because, although learning does not necessarily imply teaching in the sense of a conscious role activity by a "teacher," we are here considering programs which imply teaching as well as learning.)

Quite clearly, some particular frame of thought must always lie behind any scheme for relating all the various elements, long before a particular definition of *A*, *B*, *C*, . . . *n* has been arrived at together with the classifications embraced under these various higher categories. This approach, in short, involves the introduction of a conceptual scheme which embraces not only educational administration and all the particular aspects of "doing" assumed to be involved in the practice of educational administration, but also those considerations related to the special problem of *learning administration.*

Perhaps we can start by disregarding the *x*, *y*, *z*'s and also the *A*, *B*, *C*'s which would have to be defined, and consider instead what kind of conceptual scheme we think may be appropriate to administration and to learning administration. This would involve asking ourselves what we mean when we talk about learning anything that involves, not just carrying around some content of knowledge in our heads, but doing something, behaving in a certain way in a certain role in certain situations. We might start with the idea that learning administration relates to the development of patterns of behavior which the person will impress upon the situation as he proceeds to behave as an administrator. Now, this approach could lead us back into a circle of terms — knowledge, skill, and experience. Since these terms apparently have different meanings to different persons, as evidenced by the way they are used in the classifying lists, we might concentrate our attention simply on the idea of a person behaving in a situation. We may then be able to give these terms meanings which are sufficiently close to a universe of discourse, yet sufficiently differentiated from each other, so that they may serve as an elementary set of definitions for use in our subsequent discussion.

Experience as the Basis of Administrative Knowledge and Skill

We have noted a tendency in educational administration to break down the competencies required for it into a variety of classes, in which knowledge and skills are treated as separate sub-categories — for example, "knowledge of finance" and "skills in human relations." Suppose, however, we start with the statement that "Administration is a skill." We are saying that all mental resources and activities (including what we may have heretofore considered as *knowledge* pertaining to administration) must be subsumed as aspects of the skill, that is, the behavior of the administrator in relation to situations. If we accept this definition, there is nothing that we can call knowledge in administration except what inheres, as part of a unity of human action, in the behavior of educational administrators in their respective situations. By this definition, what we have previously referred to as specialized knowledge of various kinds, as well as knowledge based on either study or experience in specific situations, has no meaning except insofar as it is integrated into the behavior of administrators. To define knowledge in this way also means recasting the "frames of thought," to use Professor Roethlisberger's phrase, so that the kinds of mental content that we have previously thought of as "knowledge" simply become aspects of that entirety of administrative behavior which we are calling skill.

Now, whether or not we shall want to hold permanently to this disappearance of knowledge into skill so that nothing previously called knowledge has any meaning unless it has become an integrated element of skill, we shall find the concept useful as a next step. The practice of administration takes place in situations (experience) and involves something different from either knowledge or experience even though these are essential to it. This is not true of all kinds of human activity with which the term "skill" is commonly associated. For example, as a solitary worker you can weave hats of standard design from standard materials. You have experience, skill, and knowledge in relation to weaving hats. If you continue to weave identical hats, your experience increases; your skill may increase; but has your knowledge increased, except as you may consider this as a latent factor in the event of any increase in skill? You can, however, "know how to" weave a hat by observing the process or by having someone tell you about it, without having either the experience or the skill — but you cannot weave a hat. Knowledge does not necessarily imply either experience or skill; it represents mental content not necessarily involving anything but a communication from another mind which may remain in one's own mind unused.

Now, if administrative practice did not involve the novelty of situations, if it were a purely repetitious occupation — such as hand-weaving of hats of standard design and materials — experience alone would be necessary to skill. There would be no need for any knowledge about hat-weaving other than that represented in continuing to weave identical hats. But the novelty of situations means that administrative practice involves *changing* what you do, or dealing with *consequences of not changing.* Administrators have to decide what to do in situations. They must, therefore, have at least some awareness of alternative choices above and beyond those they have experienced.

Let us assume that an administrator has no experience in any situation having fiscal-social aspects and no financial or fiscal-social knowledge from any other source. He is obviously a hypothetical creature, but we can imagine such an administrator if we try. Now let us imagine him in a situation having, to our minds, fiscal-social conditions. With no previous fiscal-social experience or knowledge, he acts in terms of the situation as he sees it. His view of, response to, and behavior in it are simply ways of expressing a dynamic relationship between himself and the situation. How he behaves represents his level of skill at that stage.

The essential first-order relationship is "experience-skill" or "skill-experience" in a situation. (Like the hen-egg question, you can argue the order indefinitely. But the answer is that there is no order; the two are conjoined.)

At this stage, there is nothing separable as knowledge in the sense in which we are using this term. The administrator did what he did; the situation changed as it changed; he has some awareness of relationships in the situation before and after his action. He now has some experience.

Let us suppose he begins to think about the experience. He begins to develop the idea that the situation influenced him to act in such and such a way, or that what he did changed the situation in such and such a way. Reflection on or thinking about "acting in relation to the situation" or "the situation influencing action" (which are the same as skill-experience or experience-skill) marks the beginning of a process of development of a mental resource or abstraction about what has happened. In the process, something new may emerge: the idea that "If I were facing this same situation, *knowing what I now know,* I think that I would act in this way rather than in the way that I did," or "If I were to come up against a situation different in these or these respects from the one I have just experienced, I think that I would act in such and such a way." That is, his thought, acting upon aspects of the experience of which he is aware, results in the formulation of alternative notions about his own possible behavior; these constitute a primitive kind of knowledge, derived from one experience and available for trial in a subsequent experience.

Out of a single experience which alone does not represent any growth of knowledge except in a latent sense, reflection or thought may thus produce a first order of knowledge — an awareness of a choice of possible alternatives of action in either the "same" or a different situation. This knowledge is, however, untested. And in this potential state there is no way for the person to determine which alternative — of the several possible ones he has developed in his mind — is better than others. He can only hypothesize about what would have been better in the former, never-to-be-repeated situation, or what would be better in this or that new situation. His mental preparation, applying imaginative thought to a single situation (including his action in relation thereto), flows back into skill when a new situation arises. He considers: How is this similar to and different from the previous situation? Shall I act this way or that way?

He acts — making a choice and behaving accordingly. (These two facets of action may be so closely conjoined that he is not aware of them as being separate or different.) There are consequences which affect relationships in the ensuing situation. They can remain as undifferentiated experience and latent knowledge. Or reflection and imagination can now range over his awareness of the second situation, construct possible alternatives, and combine these with what has been previously recognized and worked out in the mind. Knowledge thus takes form as a mental resource derived from and flowing back into a series of experience-skill interactions.

Obviously, all we are doing is giving a special definition to knowledge — a definition functionally related to experience and skill *but not equivalent to experience.* One could have a great deal of experience without deriving knowledge or advancing in skill. Knowledge in this special sense can arise only out of reflection on experience of which one becomes aware, and can be tested only as skill. It is never knowledge that is applied to situations; it is the behavior of a person that is applied. What kind of component of behavior any particular knowledge may be is problematical. In this view, any knowledge about administration, no matter how seemingly highly ordered, must be considered simply as a potential mental resource; what the knowledge is, and what its validity may be, can be determined, if at all, only as it flows into skill — by what the effects are when a particular person uses it in practice.

But knowledge has a curious property which sharply differentiates it from skill and gives it a unique value. Administrator A can communicate to Administrator B some of the knowledge which he has derived from awareness of his own experience and which he incorporates into his own skill. Administrator B perhaps does not even attempt to use this communicated knowledge as skill, or if he tries to, is dissatisfied with the results and rejects it; A's knowledge was transferred, but not his skill. Administrator B, however, has already communicated to Administrator C this same knowledge derived from A. Administrator C includes this knowledge as a new variable among his mental resources; he undertakes to use it. Again it is not A's skill that has been transferred, but some knowledge which C has incorporated into his own skill.

Along with this property of communicability of knowledge (as contrasted with experience and skill, which are inseparable from particular persons) goes a difficulty. To Administrators A and C the knowledge was of value; it proved out in test (via them). To Administrator B it was of negative value; it failed in test. To Administrators A and C it becomes "valid knowledge" even if of a very primitive kind. To Administrator B, it is not knowledge but erroneous hypothesis or theory. Thus we have the problem of what constitutes valid knowledge in administration; and this problem cannot be separated from the question of different results by different users.

This problem of knowledge we shall leave for a moment, in order to pursue further the idea of an administrator learning (i.e. developing his skill) merely through reflection on his own experience — or on those aspects of which he is aware.

In the example which we have been using, we have assumed that the situations embrace "fiscal-social" or "fiscal-human" aspects. This is simply our way of describing these situations. In terms of experience-skill, our hypothetical administrator has simply had to deal with certain situations containing factors new to him. For him to think in "fiscal" and "social" terms implies that he has made differentiations between these terms which he now seeks to put together. But in the kind of new experience which we are talking about, it is possible that these elements may not be separated in any such way in his mind. They may be thought of merely as "aspects of the situation" or as categories other than those of "fiscal" and "social." *For how he thinks about his experience and behavior, and the terms and cate-*

gories he uses in his thinking, depend upon their functional utility to HIM *as potential skill.*

We should have to pursue an investigation into his particular structure of thinking, feeling, and behaving in order to find out what ways of organizing knowledge out of his awareness he finds useful. Unless we are able to make statements about ways of organizing experience that can be shown (by administrators in all or most situations) to be superior at the test point of skill, we find ourselves up against a major problem. The difficulty arises when we attempt a comparison between this kind of "knowledge" and the quite different and much more prevalent kind of "knowledge" with which it is confused by the identity of names. This problem we shall consider later in this section.

We may also now ask ourselves what has become of the term "skills in human relations" which we mentioned earlier as reflecting a way of speaking in contrast with the term "knowledge of finance." Clearly something connoted by such a term as "human-relations skill" is involved in the behavior of our hypothetical administrator in his dealing with situations which contain, in our terms, "fiscal-social" aspects. "Fiscal," "social-fiscal," and "human relations" are artifacts resulting from ways of thinking. But are they essential to the development of skill? Do they reflect the frame of thought which is functional to the development of "knowledge about"? The answer is uncertain. They may, of course, be powerful enough in the administrator's environment so that it does become functional to think in these terms even though he may then find it necessary to translate them into terms corresponding to the frame of thought of administrative skill. But this would merely mean that he has to take an extra step in thinking because of the way knowledge has come to be organized and communicated in society. It may be that the peculiar task of administrative thinking is to put together again aspects of undifferentiated experience which have become separated in the social process of organizing and communicating various kinds of knowledge.

We now come to a point where we must recognize that the example we have been using contains an original flaw or impossibility. It is, of course, possible to start as we did with an administrator who, prior to the first situation with which we confronted him, has (1) no fiscal-social experience, (2) no fiscal-social knowledge, (3) no fiscal knowledge. But every administrator has had experience in situations involving other kinds of "human and other" data and relationships. He has responded to situations involving other combinations of people and other things; and the kinds of awareness and behavior he has developed affect his subsequent behavior. Whether his skill has advanced depends on the organization of his awareness of and responses to situations. This development of skill will include certain products of his thought acting upon the content of his recognized experience; but the form which these products take and the kinds of data he assembles in relation to one or another category may well be different if his aim is solely that of improving his own skill rather than that of communicating to someone some knowledge relating to his experience.

A key problem of the administrator is the functional organization of his experience and of any content of knowledge in relation to his role and behavior. And this he must do within the climate of a civilization which has increasingly tended to arrange and order the products of experience in terms of numerous kinds of specialized knowledge whose organization is not necessarily functional to any given behavior in any given situation.

The Problem of Self-Realization in an Administrative Role

Thus far we have attempted to clarify some definitions and relationships which we see as basic in administrative behavior, even under the most elementary conditions such as those in our hypothetical example. To summarize: We have spoken of administrative behavior as involving the entirety of action of a person in an administrative role (his skill may be considered a qualitative description of this behavior). His experience consists of his relationships and interactions in a situation or series of situations. What emerges in his awareness is derived from his experience but is not necessarily equivalent to it. Through the interplay of his thought with the content of his awareness he will imagine alternatives of action under conditions similar or different from those in his experience. These primitive, self-formed resources of knowledge are communicable to others, as in a similar fashion the mental products of others are communicable to him; but this knowledge has no meaning except as its validity is judged through test as skill.

Clearly, there are wide ramifications and complex components underlying each of these terms, "situation," "experience," "awareness," and "behavior." Any attempt at elaboration would lie beyond the scope of this brief discussion. But we do wish to relate them briefly to the framework of administration and patterns of administrative action.

Reference to "an administrative situation" is an arbitrary way of bringing into mental view a particular interaction or series of interactions. Under any real conditions these would constitute merely a brief sequence in longer and larger sequences which comprise the environment and field within which the behavior of any particular administrator takes place. A situation is a snapshot which brings into focus a part of a sequence of interactions; what lies within or outside the frame of the picture is always more or less arbitrarily determined by whoever is referring to the situation. *When* a situation in the life of an organization "begins" or "ends" depends on our notions of causality and the consequences of "visible" acts.

Except in relatively rare cases where an administrator happens also to have been an entrepreneur assisting in the creation of an organization *de novo,* he assumes a role in an organization or institution whose purposes have, at least to some extent, been defined before his accession to the role.

More often than not, the role he assumes has been approximately defined by predecessors in that role.

Yet it is also a part of his responsibility to clarify, reinterpret, and redirect the efforts of the organization, or that sector of it which is embraced in his responsibilities, not necessarily strictly according to his viewpoint, but at least to some extent from his viewpoint. Even if his viewpoint and the viewpoints of others which are effective in giving direction to the organization favor the maintenance of purposes already defined and policies already laid down, the world of change surrounding any organization may mean that the organization must change in order to remain the same.

In one way or another, an administrator must deal with a relative non-correspondence of views as to desirable directions of policy. Those persons who are in any way involved will have formed ideas of what the policies should be — or even of what they have been or are at any given time. These views of others include varying expectancies about the administrator's own role and behavior. And mixed up with these expectancies are varying hopes and fears. The administrator, too, has his own views both as to what have been and what should be the significant directions of effort of the group for whose endeavors he bears a particular responsibility. He has his own ideas about the ways in which his role should be performed. He also has his own deeply built-in patterns of behavior which may or may not always correspond precisely to his image of that behavior — or even to the image of his intended behavior.

In one way or another he must cope with the confusions and cross-purposes which are always potential in a human organization — as may be demonstrated when a vacuum develops at a focal point of administration. How an administrator both conceives of his role and acts in it crucially affects the conditions of activity and the behavior of others. An administrative post carries with it some degree of power, conferred by the traditions of the organization, to make decisions affecting the behavior of others. The administrator's behavior in the role he assumes includes an exercise of power inherited by him. He may inherit either more or less power than he considers desirable for the purposes of the organization. In one way or another, any administrative behavior may have implications for the maintenance or change of the relations of power existing in the organization.

The pitfalls of self-delusion which confront an administrator are myriad, and the key to the kind of perceptions he will have about the relationships in which he is involved lies centrally in his awareness about himself. If, for example, he is unaware of the rise of feelings of irritation in himself when the expectancies of others run counter to his own, he cannot be aware of the numerous forms of reactive behavior with which he may respond, thereby conditioning responses in others, which responses in turn may affect his own. Common tendencies such as imputing invidious motivations to those who resist his will, for example, result in perceptions and responses, in relation to a situation, which will be very different from those he might have and make if he has learned both to become aware of his own feelings and to use them as a warning cue for a fresh appraisal of his own relation to the situation. The dynamics of administrative situations and administrative behavior are such that what he perceives, what he thinks of himself as deciding to do, and what he does, are not neatly separated steps; what seem to lie before or after a visible or conscious act are aspects of an interrelated whole. And what relation his behavior as a whole bears to the conditions unfolding (or obscured) in the continuum of interactions can only be the subject of his continuing study.

It would scarcely seem necessary to labor the point that a large part of the drama of most situations occurs through interactions at levels of feelings and emotion of which the actors themselves may be relatively or wholly unaware. Yet unless an administrator chooses to depend primarily or heavily upon the power of his office to bring about some coordination and control of the activities of those whose effort leans upon the exercise of that administrative function, and unless the institutional conditions permit this choice of means to be effective, the administrator cannot but function primarily as an organizer of consents. But consents may be obtained in numerous ways; the less the desire or possibility of effectuating the ends of joint human action by devices of covert master-minding or manipulation, the more the administrator is confronted with the task of clarifying and harmonizing diverse conditions and motivations.

In order to do this, he must be attuned to the feelings — the desires, the anxieties, the hopes, the resistances — which lie behind the words, acts, tones of voice, gestures, work performances, and social relationships of those with whom he is working. But these feelings and emotions of others will come through to his awareness only in distorted fashion, if at all, if they must first pass through blocks and barriers which stand between himself and his own self-awareness. His ability to differentiate between his own intents and the intents which others will, in some way, try to communicate to him, will play a large part in his ability to distinguish whether a group with whom he is conferring have come to an agreement or have resigned themselves to acceptance of what they perceive as his wishes.

In suggesting that such factors as these are included in what we mean by situation and experience, by awareness and behavior and skill, subtly interlinked with all of them, we do not imply that the administrator must merely respond to the desires and intents of others, or that introspection is the earmark of good administrative behavior. The fact of responsibility carries with it the notion of a voice which is expected to be that of the administrator himself. The fact of power of office is automatically called into play, and does not disappear but merely has unintended consequences when an administrator deludes himself that his behavior does not constitute acts of power above and beyond the "personal" element.

His sensitivity to other persons, in terms of seeking to understand what they are trying to communicate, need be considered merely as a part of his effort to comprehend the situation in which he is involved; it carries no necessary connotation that he conform to their wishes. His need to grow in recognition of his own behavior, and of those forces in him which he perceives to be influencing his action, cannot be met by constantly imagining himself "apart" from the situation, and attempting to analyze himself in isolation. If he learns to perceive himself at all clearly, it can only be because he learns to be aware of and to grow in understanding of his own behavior in relation to his experience in situations.

Whether an administrator thinks about administrative behavior in such terms as these, or whether he tends to think about it in some quite different terms, every administrator has some notion of what he considers good administrative behavior to be. He has some models of administration and of administrative behavior. These models affect his behavior, although they are by no means identical with it. Probably almost everyone has had contact with an administrator whose behavior seems quite at variance with the model he carries around in his head and cites as his. This gap between model and behavior need not signify hypocrisy, as we usually mean this word. Administrators, like many other people, simply behave, in many cases, in ways of which they are apparently unaware and in contradiction to the patterns of behavior which they admire and sincerely wish to make their own.

Now, the fact that many aspects of the role of an administrator are established by the office itself, and by the way that office and similar offices have been conducted by others, means that an administrator becomes a kind of actor, consciously endeavoring to carry out a role as he conceives it, according to some pattern of admired behavior. This role and behavior reflect some selection or new combination of types of behavior which is based on his observation or other knowledge of administrative roles and behavior, on his own experience in relationships with administrators, and on his sense of values with respect to the function to be fulfilled. It is not surprising that the most difficult synthesis for him to make is the readjustment of this model or ideal image so that it more and more closely corresponds to his own behavior. For an administrator cannot become a type (except in the sense that others may class him); he is a person, a unique entity. His behavior has been developing long before he achieved an age and a stage of development which involved him in thinking about being an administrator, or about developing desired models. This behavior may condition his choice of a model to be admired. If the image in terms of which he desires (or thinks he desires) to behave is to be one that he can really call his own, he may have to alter it to fit his self-reality, or he may need to grow to fit it. In fact, both adjustments may be involved, for the comfortable acceptance of the model always requires at least some experience. As so often with analogies, this one has its inadequacies; the image of realizable behavior by an administrator need never be a single one into which, once fitted, he permanently remains; there is always the potential of a better model — or even growth beyond a model that previously seemed well designed.

The problem of shaping a model or image of administrative behavior that is appropriate to a particular person, in terms of both his aspirations as regards behavior in a particular role and his actual behavior as a person, is perhaps the easiest problem to state with respect to administration — and the most difficult to resolve. But is there really any other problem to administration? For here is stated the problem of self-realization in an administrative role — involving the kind of administrator a particular person both desires to be and is capable of becoming, with a minimum of gap or contradiction between the two. No administrator can be a different or a better administrator than he can define in terms of his own values and can realize on the basis of his own awareness of his behavior and capacities. All knowledge he can gain from his own experience and that of others is merely a means to this end: behavior in terms of some consistency with an image of behavior consciously constructed to integrate both personal and social values.

Training for Development of Administrative Skill

If our argument is correct that it is the entirety of behavior of an administrator that affects situations, irrespective of whether or not this behavior conforms to the image about it which he carries in his head, then training for administration must concern itself centrally with the development and test of behavior.

To be sure, the kind of images he has in his head and the kind of mental resources he possesses will affect his behavior. But no mental resources of knowledge and no models of administrative behavior which he has fashioned or acquired are equivalent to that entirety of behavior represented by an administrator interacting in a situation.

If we labor this point a bit heavily, we think that there is justification for it. We do not decry the importance of knowledge — of products of human experience and thought which are communicable from one mind to another in such a way as to extend the mental resources (constituting potentials of skill) of any individual far beyond what he could cumulate from his own experience alone. Before this section has been concluded, we shall discuss, although certainly not presume to answer, the problem of relating to the advance of skill in educational administration those resources of knowledge that arise out of numerous fields of specialized study.

Yet we feel that abundant evidence supports the view that the advance of knowledge, the characteristics of thought which serve the ends of knowledge (though not necessarily of skill), and the prestige acquired by the organization of experience in such forms have resulted in obscuring a prime essential in the training of administrators — learning behavior rather than merely learning knowledge. We hold that knowledge is never enough.

Nor is that kind of thought which has been primarily associated with the development of knowledge in the modern world enough. By this we mean analytical thought — thought which diffracts, separates out elements from a totality of experience, and establishes the bases for construction of various kinds of specialized knowledge. Administrative behavior, in our view, requires also the exercises and development of processes of thought less strongly stressed in the climate of specialization which characterizes the modern intellectual world. We refer to the kind of thought which is concerned with the *synthesis* of experience. Partly because of the tendency toward separation and even fragmentation of various aspects of experience in the modern society and mind, it may require a considerable emphasis on this latter mode of thought to bring the realization that one's attempt to "put together" whole views of situations and one's own behavior in situations is really an illusory task. For those things which seem to be separated, and which the individual must strive to perceive and respond to as wholes, are in truth not separated except through the working of analytical and specialized frames of thought.

But what an administrator must strive to perceive, to respond to, to behave in terms of, are situations which are unique and therefore not previously described. Therefore, for the administrator to perceive them through analytical spectacles and then to try to relate them as a whole through a separate mental act of synthesis is to screen them through thought framed in terms of the symbols of prior experience, even before aspects and relationships of the situation available to him through his new experience have been permitted to arise in his consciousness. Somehow, it would seem, the administrator must develop a mode of behavior in which the process of becoming aware and the respective thought processes of analysis and synthesis can be brought into a new sequence and relationship.

Behavioral learning for administrative roles therefore involves consideration of kinds of mental experience which are not necessarily involved in the development and transmission of knowledge. It cannot be limited to the acquisition of mental content in terms of the various symbols in which all knowledge is organized and communicated. The administrator deals with situations and responds, whether knowingly or not, to cues which are elemental — the feelings of those around him, or perhaps his sense of the suitability of a particular acre of ground for the play of growing children. His non-awareness of these elemental things also conditions his behavior and the influences thereby impressed upon the social institution in which he plays his role. His behavior is a complex force having impact upon the lives of persons both immediate and distant from his sphere of vision. He has learned nothing out of all his knowledge unless he knows what his awareness and behavior are in terms of these elemental relationships; he can learn them only through the practice, the test, and the examination of his behavior in relation to situations.

Unless he grasps this reality sufficiently to come to the realization that he does not *apply* knowledge but merely behaves in such a way that certain resources of knowledge may be a component of his behavior, he will continue to think in terms of knowledge instead of in terms of skill. He will analyze situations as if he were apart from them. He will think in terms of having defined the alternatives of choice in a situation, rather than of recognizing that these are basically his inventions — products of his imagination. He will inadequately recognize that in actual administrative behavior he may often give way to some previously unconsidered choice; he will therefore perhaps not learn to use more skillfully the process of careful reflection plus spontaneous choice which may yield behavior subsequently viewed as superior to the alternatives which he consciously imagined. He will think in terms of finding "the answer," forgetting that it is not some answer in his mind that will enter into the situation but the behavior of himself as a person.

Training in administration must involve exercising behavior (and not just "the mind") if behavior is to be learned. The development of a pedagogical scheme for such training must revolve around the central idea of learning a skill; whatever learning may be acquired symbolically as knowledge is to be considered as an auxiliary and potential resource. For such resources must be translated, by the necessary shift in the frame of thought in which they are cast as knowledge, into skill, if the administrator's behavior is to reflect an integration between "his knowledge" and "himself."

As we have indicated, the acquisition of knowledge apart from one's own administrative experience is not essential to the growth of skill. There have been administrators of outstanding qualities who learned without the benefit of formal programs of training. But to leave the matter at that point would be to argue against the creation of any pedagogical schemes of training. In administration, as in other fields, schemes of learning that involve the use of other than one's own experience, usually develop long before they emerge as concerns of institutions devoted to learning, teaching, and training. Although these pragmatic ways of learning may not be adequate, a recognition of such patterns may suggest the more conscious pedagogical use of them or the invention of better ways.

Administrators-to-be develop models and images of desired administrative behavior through their experience with or observation of the behavior of other administrators. Administrators "teach" administration to others through their practice of it, even though they may not consider themselves as teaching it, and even if their "pupils" accept the opposite of their teachings. Those aspiring to administration begin learning it by having to respond to the behavior of administrators and by acquiring alternative notions through their experience. Experience with a particular administrator or with particular kinds of administrative behavior results in the emergence of "positive" and "negative" models in the awareness of those who aspire to administrative roles. (Parenthetically, the use of a range of cases provides a range of models which may become positive or negative to different students, thereby revealing to them something of their own behavioral tendencies.) Administrators responsible for the advancement of other persons into administrative roles may take these others under conscious tutelage. The training of administrators "on the job" may itself come to be viewed as a function of administration at higher levels of responsibility.

This does not mean that what men learn as knowledge via books or reports written by administrators or about administrators, may not contribute significantly to the models formed in the minds of administrators-to-be. Any communicated knowledge or direct or vicarious experience which alters or affects the system of values a person holds may influence the kind of model which he may conceive of as desirable. But developing a model is not the same as behaving in an administrative role. The crucial aspect of learning lies in the practice itself, whether with the intent of behaving in terms of a model or of discovering one through recognizing a kind of behavior that expresses with some comfort one's own self and values. It is by no means necessary, in short, that an administrator move by the steps of (*a*) constructing a model, (*b*) trying to realize it.

It may be that the oversharpening of a model, without continuous test of its appropriateness either to situations or to one's self, may compound the problem of seeing past the model. It may be well to bear in mind those administrators, and there are many, who develop articulate concepts about administrative behavior largely out of the maturation of their own experience and their direct observation and experience in dealing with other administrators, with little or no attention to recorded knowledge or experience, but whose testimony or behavior is subsequently used by others as a basis for the formulation of models. Perhaps placing too great an emphasis on the construction of mental models and ideal images *in advance* of beginning to develop the elemental skill of learning in relation to behavior in situations, which is crucial, may represent a barrier to rather than an advance of administrative learning.

In this respect, also, it would seem important to submit the student to a development and a test of his behavior in "clinical" activities such as (*a*) learning through case methods and (*b*) serving as a member of a staff responsible for study and recommendations for a school system. The latter, as a developmental and testing program, we shall not discuss here. But we do wish to point out that case methods, in requiring the student to cast himself in the role of an administrator, set crucial tests for the realism of his behavior and responses. For whatever he may indicate would be his action in the situation, he is almost certain to face challenges by others in the case session who tend to see desired action and behavior in terms rather different from his. Any expression of his choice of action may result in his being pressed with such questions as: "What would you say — in what words? Well, if you were to say that, in that way, I (putting myself in the place of so and so in the case) would figure that you were trying to do thus and so, and I would react this way — which I doubt is the way you intended or expected that I would react. Or suppose I were to do this because you did what you have just shown us you would do as the next step in the situation; how would you handle that?" In such a process, when a student assuming the administrative role puts forward images which either students or instructor feel to be inadequate or out of touch with the situation as revealed in the case, those images are likely to be rather forcibly chiseled into different and more subtle forms. And since such images are projections of the orientations of these administrative students as persons, the process of altering the models thus advanced involves the growth of self-awareness. For insofar as the models are themselves, the students change themselves in modifying the images under the impact of the behavior of others toward them.

Administrators whose tutelage in administration has occurred in a largely pragmatic way have also usually had some shocks of experience which have impressed them with the realization of the difference between symbolic models and real behavior. Under the sheer necessity of having had to cope, as underlings, with administrators whose behavior they did not admire, they may have developed patterns of behavior in themselves which subsequently equipped them for more mature administrative behavior. By the necessities of common defense against the arbitrary or incompetent use of administrative power, they may have learned to attune themselves to the feelings of peers and underlings in the structure of their organizations. If the situation has included their having to learn to deal with the boss, while at the same time recognizing behavior on his part injurious to others with whom they sympathize, they may not distinguish in their minds changes in their own behavior which actually represent growth toward becoming administrators of a different model.

But even this behavioral learning is but preparatory to the dilemmas which may arise in the actual conduct of an administrative role, where the conditions of a situation may be perceived as requiring action of a kind quite different from that which may be perceived by those who do not bear the responsibilities of the role. It is the factor of responsibility, as conferred by an organization upon the person who assumes an administrative role, which seems to us to pose what may be the most crucial problems in all administrative behavior. This responsibility is the administrator's by inheritance of whatever values have been contributed by his predecessors; if he is to respect it as a trust, he must be concerned with a future beyond the time when he may be performing in that role. At the same time, he must deal with the living present; his acts and behavior affect the satisfactions and welfare of numerous others in a most immediate sense. These realizations of sense of responsibility involve an awareness not dependent upon any particular situations, however much they may be deepened by particular experiences, and, of course, brought to the only test through the administrator's behavior in relation to situations. But the realization of sense of responsibility is bound up more deeply with the background and the behavior of the administrator as a person.

His weighing and deciding among the frequently conflicting values inherent in the circumstances around him — not the least of which may be a realization of some degree of conflict between his desires as a person and his administrative responsibilities, as he may see them — pose the problem of *integrity,* in the fullest meaning of that term. For integrity connotes an internally consistent whole; in an administrator this wholeness cannot but refer to self, role, and situation. His task of learning is that of developing behavior which represents a continuous advance of integration within himself, in the field for which he is responsible, and between the two.

The Idea of Knowledge in Relation to Administrative Behavior

An administrator impresses upon the situations around him not the model in his mind nor any abstractions of knowledge but the force of himself as a person. Like every other human being, he has tended to develop patterns of behavior throughout his lifetime. These correspond with what he has discovered "works" for him — what kind of behavior results in rewards and satisfactions and what kind is associated with discomforts to be avoided. In early childhood, it is largely these realizations that constitute his knowledge. Whatever other kinds of knowledge subsequently loom large in his mind with the advance of his formal education and training, by adulthood some fairly basic tendencies in behavior have been built into him as a person. The later knowledge superimposed upon his earlier awareness and behavior usually so dominates his mind that he little recognizes the values in terms of which he generally responds. He usually develops some tendencies which are maintained in all the varying experiences and situations of his life. He is, in these respects, a kind of miniature self-fulfilling prophecy.

He may have a tendency to acquiesce in the opinions of others, or, conversely, to assert opinions just a little different from those of everyone else. He may tend to assume a directive role in most situations, or, alternatively, a recessive role, a follower role, a resistor role, a critique role, an "above-the-battle" role. While recognizing the dangers of classifying persons on the basis of narrow tendencies uniformly maintained in all situations, we cannot escape the fact that each person does have some tendencies which are strong determinants of his behavior. Despite the difficulties of establishing operational definitions and empirical tests which fully satisfy scientific criteria with respect to such notions as the authoritarian personality, the dependent personality, the aggressive, the submissive, and the cooperative personality (in the language of some psychological and psychiatric thought), the feeling persists that there is some validity to such notions.

Tendencies in people's behavior are the outcome of what they have learned; their learnings are both conscious and subconscious. In any particular act, each person has certain intents, whether or not he is fully aware of them; he expects certain consequences to follow from his act. Each act whose consequences are seen by him to correspond to the intended consequences reinforces his tendency to act in the same way in what he perceives as similar circumstances. His basic kinds of behavior and response in his interactions with other people are merely the cumulation of these reinforcements, begun in his earliest childhood. These reinforcements finally tend to produce behavior which overrides the conditions of particular situations and relationships.

They become modified, if at all, only as a person may become aware that what is following from his acts is not in keeping with his expectations. But such is the nature of self-reinforcing behavior that when events following his acts cease to accord with his expectations, he will first tend to remain unaware that this is happening. He may, without recognizing it, retreat from the awareness which his experience is trying to force into his recognition; he is, in short, responding to experience in such a way as to maintain his built-in behavioral tendency in the face of circumstances threatening enforced change in it. If, despite this retreat from awareness, he finally cannot escape it, he may then tend to attribute events following his acts to "outside" causes, such as the unreasonable behavior of other people.

It is the responses of others to his acts that provide a person with the experience from which his behavioral tendencies are derived. Since every person's behavior is of this kind, a small group of people coming together for some purpose will interact through their respective behaviors in such a way that their responses become mutually self-reinforcing. They will develop a relationship of acts and responses which results in their behavior as a group — this behavior also being what we have termed a self-fulfilling prophecy, but now on the scale of an organization. And since they have become a group for some purpose, the purpose itself and their direction in terms of it are a part of that prophecy. This tendency and direction of the group will also continue until or unless a correction is forced by conditions of noncorrespondence between the group's intents and expectations and the consequences of their acts.

We need not pursue further the problem of correction of a tendency of behavior which is not in correspondence with the actualities of one's experience. It is our purpose here merely to emphasize that basic behavioral tendencies are essentially self-reinforcing. Each person is, in effect, a self-fulfilling prophecy, which is revised only, if at all, as it becomes increasingly out of correspondence with reality.

The role of an administrator implies the idea of developing some common directions among persons who individually may have quite different and potentially conflicting behavioral tendencies. In so doing, his own behavior is a major conditioning factor; he gives peculiarly significant direction to the institution. Yet there is no way of defining one particular constellation of tendencies in behavior as most consistent with administrative behavior, except perhaps to suggest that they be not too extreme. For we are forced to recognize that persons of rather different basic personal tendencies can function with apparent effectiveness as successors to each other in central administrative roles. Different phases in the life of organizations and institutions may be best served by administrators of different tendencies. It is possible that the birth of an organization, the later stabilizations following a period of great growth, or the reorganization and reinvigoration of an organization somewhat gone to seed may variously be best served by administrators of different temperaments and behavioral tendencies.

Yet we can consider that, whatever the idiosyncrasies of an administrator, some tendencies may be theoretically projected from the circumstances of his role. It is these which we have stressed throughout our discussions. We can furthermore consider that these tendencies are being increasingly buttressed by the pressure of social forces. Perhaps nowhere are these forces now seen operating more clearly than in the administration of public education.

Finally, we do not hesitate to include in our notions of requisite administrative behavior some moral and ethical values beyond those now generally obtaining, since without the idea of advancing values, the idea of training administrators would seem to us to be devoid of meaning.

But the problem of any particular person and any particular administrator relates not only to a generality of trends. How appropriate and how effective in both the short and the long run are his own tendencies of behavior as a person and an administrator? Whither are they leading him and the institution in relation to which he is functioning? When all is going well, does it mean that all is sound and evolving as a sequence of productive correspondences? Or do the smoothly functioning relationships within the institution merely mean that he and those around him (or most of them) are caught up in the operation of a self-fulfilling prophecy which is nonetheless out of tune with social forces? If so, those forces must sooner or later intervene, perhaps abruptly, to compel changes in awareness and in direction of behavior.

Administrators have power to which other members of the organization defer and accommodate to some extent; any direction of behavior may be self-reinforcing within the institution as a whole. Everyone may behave in such a way as to suggest that all is harmonious, thus producing evidence justifying continuance of the prevailing and administratively sanctioned directions and behavior. Yet forces "outside" the organization if not "within" it sometimes have a way of bringing an organization or a unit of an organization to an impasse, an abrupt halt, a sharp conflict, a time of troubles, or an enforced change of directions. These "outside" forces are thought of as the forces of society, of life in general, and even as the conditions and hazards of nature; the forces "within" are of course composed of no different elements, but merely different combinations.

Are there trends which represent a self-fulfilling prophecy for society as a whole? Are there relations between man and nature which are of this order? Do patterns of response and directions of purpose exhibited by an organization have any validity in terms other than those of a purely local and transitory self-fulfilling prophecy? Is there a measure of validity other than the perceptions of the members of the institution itself?

How can we know whether activity of an organization is valid in a more fundamental sense, or whether there is a flaw or error somewhere underlying the self-fulfilling prophecy which only time and the working out of social forces may bring to light? The answer to this problem is bound up with ideas of knowledge — of a mental product derived from the examination of experience which is nonetheless independent of it, and which, furthermore, can predict errors to which experience alone may lead. The idea of knowledge revolves around the possibility of making statements which define and interpret experience in such a way that the description holds good irrespective of how many persons may make different statements on the basis of their private experience.

At the time when this idea of knowledge was taking form, the distinction between human and other than human aspects of experience was much less marked than it was later to become; this distinction was sharpened by the consequences of use of the idea itself. All things were considered animate and as possessing the same kinds of feelings that human beings experienced; furthermore, their behavior was viewed as responsive to the behavior of men. Human beliefs and actions could result in particular kinds of behavior on the part of nature (not then dissociated from men). But in the course of this development, the idea emerged of "things that were so, irrespective of human belief about them." The first strong realization came with respect to the independence of some kinds of behavior in nature from the wishes of men.

Regularities in the motions of heavenly bodies, for example, seemed to occur independently of human behavior. The idea of knowledge "worked" with respect to this kind of other-than-human phenomena. Things could be predicted in the heavens without regard to prevalent human beliefs; indeed, astrology reversed the earlier notions of causality and presumed to predict human events according to earlier conjunctions between the regular patterns of the stars and earlier human events. The idea of knowledge was most successful — indeed, so successful as to revolutionize human awareness — when it most clearly distinguished between nature and man; this permitted a *rational* view of nature, undisturbed by human wishes, or so it seemed. Knowledge became increasingly redefined in these terms; the potentiality of the idea proved itself in isolating and defining aspects of experience apparently unaffected by human behavior, or beliefs inconsistent with them.[1] Knowledge grew enormously in prestige; indeed it appeared

[1] The viewpoint summarized here with respect to the concept of knowledge and its evolution into the concept of science involves a recognition of the extent to which current prevalent concepts of science, how it emerged, and what it is, are mythologies. These myths are only currently yielding to historical and comparative review, and to the critique of the epistemological problem of science — namely, that of the assumptions of the concept itself. Some recent works in these areas may help the reader to an understanding of the thesis which we are able only to summarize in this section, but which underlies our view of the function of the cases-and-concepts approach to the development of administrative behavior. Valuable insights may be obtained through such works as: H. Butterfield, *The Origins of Modern Science* (London: G. Bell and Sons, Ltd., 1951); F. S. C. Northrop, *The Logic of the Sciences and the Humanities* (New York: Macmillan,

magical to men who did not make the separation between human self and nonhuman "nature."

A problem remained, however, with respect to those aspects of experience which are essentially conditioned by the kind of awareness, response, and behavior which men have. The problem of knowledge in the field of human action has been pursued as if "knowledge" in this field were of the same order as in the field of phenomena independent of human action. In all eras since the emergence of knowledge as a major governing concept, there have been men who have voiced views which suggest that they distrusted or opposed the application of the basic concept of knowledge, so defined, to the field of human behavior. But the clarification of the problem to a stage which is enforcing a fundamental re-examination and revision of the concept of knowledge itself is virtually a twentieth-century development.

This problem of the basic definition of knowledge confronts us quite centrally in discussing a field such as administration. For the phenomenon of the self-fulfilling prophecy makes us feel the need for some equivalent of "objective knowledge" as a corrective. In seeking to develop administrative knowledge through experience, we at first cannot escape the problem that this kind of knowledge has no meaning except as skill, hence feeds back into what may merely be self-reinforcing behavior.

Administration and those social sciences which are seeking to discover valid knowledge about human behavior in social settings face the same basic problem. No knowledge of that order (i.e., "objective" or uninfluenced by the act of the human observer) is even theoretically possible in these fields. A fundamental revision of the concept of knowledge is necessary with respect to the phenomena of human behavior (except for those aspects of human behavior which may be observed without awareness of this observation on the part of the human "object").[2]

1947); F. S. C. Northrop, *The Meeting of East and West* (New York: Macmillan, 1946, reprinted 1949); E. Cassirer, *An Essay on Man* (New York: Doubleday and Co., 1951); M. Jammer, *Concepts of Space* (Cambridge: Harvard University Press, 1955); Sir Charles Sherrington, *Man on His Nature* (New York: Doubleday and Co., 1953); A. N. Whitehead, *Essays on Science and Philosophy* (New York: Philosophical Library, 1947).

For more advanced or specialized presentations and treatments of problems involved in the concept of "knowing," the reader may wish to explore such works as: H. Weyl, *Philosophy of Mathematics and Natural Science* (Princeton: Princeton University Press, 1949); J. W. Dunne, *The Serial Universe* (New York: Macmillan, 1938); W. Carington, *Matter, Mind and Meaning* (New Haven: Yale University Press, 1949); E. Froeschels, *The Human Race: A Study in the Nature of Knowledge* (New York: Philosophical Library, 1947); L. Berman, *Behind the Universe* (New York: Harper and Bros., 1943).

For briefer articles suggestive of emerging views and trends of thought concerning the nature of science, see: P. Meadows, "Science as Experience: A Genetic and Comparative Review," *American Sociological Review*, Vol. 14, No. 5 (October, 1949); P. Frank, "The Unity of Science," *Proceedings of the American Academy of Arts and Sciences*, Vol. 130, No. 2 (April, 1950); H. L. Parsons, "The Social Implications of Science," *Main Currents in Modern Thought*, Vol. 8, No. 2 (June, 1951).

See also references particularly relating to definitions of concepts in Section Five.

[2] Some discussion of this problem from the perspective of a social psychologist interested in situational analysis may be found in L. S. Cottrell, Jr., "Some Neglected Prob-

The cumulation of empirical data cannot solve the problem; it will indeed in time merely make the problem more obvious. A belief that the problem is unimportant or can be rendered negligible by the cumulation of empirical data — a belief that is to be found in much of present social science — begs the basic question and reflects what has been called "the fallacy of empiricism." [3] A basic question underlying any system of "objective" knowledge or science relates to the order of validity of the data which the knowledge or science attempts to relate or interpret. The very idea of validity, in the traditional sense, of data about human behavior in social settings is meaningless; human data of this kind are changed indeterminately in response to human observation or examination. The solution, if any, of the problem lies in a new concept of "knowledge" and "science" with respect to human action. Whatever this new concept may be, it will have major implications for administration as well as for those who seek to build a science of men's social acts.

We can, however, imagine that constant increase in administrative skill may be one way out of the dilemma. For if the self-fulfilling prophecy does contain flaws, if there are social forces which will in time render it inoperative, they must earlier exist, if only as traces of data and relationships in various situations. Hence a constant increase in sensitivity to the novelty of situations might theoretically enable the administrator to find new directions, rather than become caught in a self-reinforcing trend. Although this appears to be a theoretical possibility, we cannot be certain that it does not contain flaws even as theory; for the problem of the self-fulfilling prophecy, as a general and fundamental theoretical problem in various fields of study concerned with human and social behavior, is probably not yet definitively solved. Furthermore, even the definitive solution of the theoretical problems would not represent a pragmatically satisfactory solution; for it would involve a kind of perfection of individual administrative behavior which is quite unrealistic.

Let us recognize that all social interactions are self-reinforcing and work out in a direction determined by their own components and dynamics until set off in some new direction by some new force from within or outside the pattern — in short, that all behavior, individual and social, represents the working out of successive self-fulfilling prophecies, however conditioned by new elements of experience. (How any particular person may interpret this statement will depend upon whether he wears deterministic or free-will

---

lems in Social Psychology," *American Sociological Review,* Vol. 15, No. 6 (December, 1950). As indicated in that paper, formulation and understanding of the problem are aided by acquaintance with the experience and thought of H. S. Sullivan, G. H. Mead, Kurt Lewin, J. L. Moreno, T. M. Newcomb, and various others. (Some of these references are noted in Section Five.) For a discussion of a point of view stressing the possibilities of obtaining "hard data" in the field of social sciences, see G. A. Lundberg, "Alleged Obstacles to Social Science," *Scientific Monthly,* 70: 299–305 (May, 1950).

[3] R. Bierstedt, "A Critique of Empiricism in Sociology," *American Sociological Review,* Vol. 14, No. 5 (October, 1949).

spectacles; it can be viewed as supporting either view — or neither.) Let us, on the basis of this recognition, consider a second possibility for discovering flaws in the self-reinforcing behavior of an administrator and/or his institution.

Let us suppose that there is an *observer* of an administrator and of others who are behaving in situations constituting a self-fulfilling prophecy or a complex of changing prophecies. We may readily imagine that an observer may note aspects of the situation and behavior of which the involved persons, or actors, are themselves unaware. He may through his own thought processes become aware of possible relationships between the behavior of the person and the situation which the person himself has not considered. He may not find the relationship between behavior and experience adding up to the same alternative hypotheses or conclusions that the person or persons involved in the interaction have added up in their minds.

His knowledge becomes different from the administrator's knowledge or the knowledge of the other actors. Now, the observer's knowledge *may* be more valid; that is, he may perceive factors or imagine relationships which the self-fulfilling prophecy itself tends to block from the recognition of the actor or actors. But how can this be known? Indeed, how can it be known that the reverse may not be true? What do we mean by the relative validity of these two kinds of knowledge — the knowledge of an actor (or actors) in an interaction and the knowledge of an observer of the interaction?

For it is clear, when we introduce into our discussion, the idea of an observer and *his* kind of knowledge, that we have greatly compounded the problem of what we mean by knowledge with respect to human action. We now have two quite different definitions of knowledge: (1) products of the awareness of persons acting in situations; (2) products of the awareness of persons observing *other* persons acting in situations. The complexities of relationships between these two different kinds of knowledge can only be suggested here. For example, does the observer just stand off and watch the administrator acting in a situation? If so, he can hear and see some things happen in an interaction between the administrator and others in the situation. But each of these persons is behaving in relation to the situation with some kind of intent. These intents are crucial factors in the situation, but they may be unknown to the observer. Or does the observer also have some data in his mind about the awareness and intents in the mind of one of these persons — let us say the administrator? Or of several of the persons in the situation? What are these data? How did he get them? What may happen to such data in being communicated from the actors to the observer?

Many other questions arise. Even the observer who is merely standing off and watching the situation is doing something, behaving, practicing a skill. Can we say more than that he is having some kind of experience related to his behavior in the situation, even though we will assume for the moment that he is not doing anything that affects the situation? What kind of awareness does he have about this experience, and what does his thought do with the content of this awareness, inasmuch as we are assuming that he is *not* using it with an intent to interact in the situation in the sense in which others in the situation are interacting? He is merely trying to develop some knowledge about it and stop at that point, as far as this situation is concerned. What does this frame of thought do to the data of his experience?

But is this product of his experience necessarily in keeping with his intent? Is this not going to be affected by the conditions of his relationship with the situation he is observing? If no one in the situation knows that he is observing, his act of observing may be assumed not to affect the situation. But also, if this is the case, he cannot be aware of the intents in the mind of each person in the situation; these intents crucially condition both the behavior of each person and the pattern of the whole situation. The intents of each person are conditioned by their assumptions about the intents of others.

Suppose, however, that the administrator or one of the other actors knows that there is an observer of the situation. May not this knowledge make that person somewhat more self-conscious and lead him, perhaps consciously or perhaps only partly consciously, to act in a way that he otherwise would not have acted? This would obviously change the situation. Suppose that all persons in the situation are aware that they are being observed. May this not affect their behavior? And if it does, what do we have here?

We have, of course, a situation as affected by the awareness of the actors of the presence of an observer. What would the interactions have been if the situation had not been affected by the presence of the observer? Obviously no one can know. The situation can never be repeated; and the awareness that the persons have after their interaction is not the same as it was before. We have to face the fact that unless no actor in a situation knows that the situation and his behavior in it are being observed, even the experience of the observer consists of "the situation-including-himself." He is a special kind of actor in the situation; he affects it. How he affects it depends upon his behavior (skill). As in the case of the administrator, his awareness, intents, and behavior are a unity; they are bound up together. Yet his intents about his behavior and his sense of what his behavior is may be different from his behavior.

What emerges in his awareness plus how his thought acts upon it determines what knowledge he formulates; but this is an aspect of his tendencies in behavior, which, like those of the administrator, may reach back into his childhood. How he behaves as an observer in a situation is a skill inseparable from him as a particular person, just as it is in the case of the administrator. The situation is not affected by "observation" but by the behavior of a particular observer, just as it is affected not by "administration" but by the behavior of a particular administrator.

A second or *n*th observer watching two different observers, A and B, in similar situations with the same group might note significant differences between the behavior of Observer A and that of Observer B; he might also see different kinds of interactions within the group according to whether Observer A or Observer B was doing the observing. Similarly, watching these two different observers each in a variety of situations, he might note that one tended usually or always to behave in a certain way, and the other in another way; or that one tended to maintain the same kind of behavior in numerous different situations, and the other to change. An observer might also tend to note similar patterns in the behavior of administrators studied in the same way.

By now it must be clear that although an administrator may view his role as that of acting in relation to situations in order to change or maintain the direction in which they seem to him to be moving, an observer seeking "knowledge" may view his role of acting in relation to a situation "as if" he did not effect any change in the direction in which it is moving. Yet, paradoxically, he must be aware that he affects the situation or its direction in some way which he cannot know through his own experience. Nor is there any escape from the paradox through introduction of a second, a third, or an *n*th observer. For each must either remain unaware of crucial factors in the situation by conducting his act of observation unknown to the actors, or have it known and thus affect the situation indeterminately. Furthermore, no situation can be replicated, and every situation contains relationships that are novel.

The idea of knowledge in relation to human situations as comparable to knowledge in relation to phenomena which are presumed to be independent of human action thus constitutes a fundamental semantic error. Without prejudice to the possible validity of this idea of knowledge with respect to *aspects* of human or social behavior not involving the interaction of persons in situations, the idea does run squarely up against the problem of *infinite regress* in any attempt to derive knowledge of a "scientific" order, as now generally defined, about human situations. The communication of observer-knowledge to other persons, like the communication of actor-knowledge, adds nothing to the solution of the problem of *valid* knowledge with respect to human action. Observer-knowledge communicated to other seekers of knowledge cannot be tested by them except as skill. The same observer-knowledge may work out differently for different observers in their attempts to use this knowledge as skill. Or if Observer A's knowledge about skill appears to work in the same way for Observer B but not for Observer C, in terms of their respective testimony about their experience, where are we?

We will not endeavor to elaborate the point that may now suggest itself to any reader — namely, that the behavior of observers, like that of administrators and various others, may constitute a self-fulfilling prophecy. The mere effort to develop skill (behavior in relation to situations in accordance with intents to achieve desired results) makes each observer a miniature self-fulfilling prophecy that can be corrected only by "breaking out of the circle" or by running up against experience that enforces change — that is, experience reflecting forces incompatible with that particular self-fulfilling prophecy.

The above conditions invalidate the idea of knowledge as independent of differentiated private experiences with respect to situations involving human action; each private experience, be it that of "actor" or of "observer," is a function of the situation. But the implications may not be as negative as they may seem. A person involved as an actor in a situation is also a kind of observer in that situation, although not a "neutral" one; a person known to others in a situation as a neutral observer thereby automatically becomes a kind of actor, indeterminately affecting the situation. The actor-observer and the observer-actor have different experiences in the situation and presumably they should differ in their awareness. But there is no way of *demonstrating* that the awareness of one is more nearly "correct" than that of the other. There is therefore no choice but to avoid assuming either absolute or hierarchical superiority to the meanings of these roles or the respective states of knowledge which may result from them; they must be conceived as relative to the situation and therefore to each other. Perhaps sufficient experience and experiment might yield some notions as to patterns of relationship which may exist between such roles.

Since persons involved in such roles in a sequence of situations presumably have some intents in being there and behaving as they do, and can satisfy these intents only if the behavior of others in the situation permits the intended roles to be performed, some degree of mutual understanding and acceptance of the respective roles is involved. This communication and adjustment is but one of the processes which make it more difficult to separate observer-awareness from actor-awareness as the study of a situation becomes more intensive.

The more intensive the study, the more essential for the observer-researcher to try to gain access to the actors' awareness, perceptions, and intents in advance of actions in the situation, as well as explanations and recollections following events; in so doing, he cannot but provide to the actors some cues as to his perception of their behavior. For both the researcher-observer and the actors, this compounds the problem of maintaining awareness separate from the cues and responses involved in this very process of researcher-actor interaction. Inherent in the notion of developing knowledge in any terms that may be defined, with respect to a situation or series of situations in a continuing sense, there must be growth of tolerance that the situation is as multiform as the experience and awareness of the several actors, not finally resolvable, even theoretically, in terms of one objective situation. There is neither person nor point permitting such a perspective. The flow of human interaction itself closes each situation irrevocably, yielding but a transitory condition of relationships which again flow into a new transitory condition, in relation to which any knowledge shifts relatively and indeterminately as a function of the relationships of the respective roles.

But again, this may not be as negative a prospect as it may first appear. Experience in numerous situations involving relationships between actor and observer roles might again yield varieties of testimony within which some patterns might eventually be perceived.

Toward the Integration of Knowledge in Terms of Skill

The experience of every person consists of the impress made on his organism by the environments through which he moves during his lifetime. These environments consist of an undifferentiated complex. By this we mean continuous new combinations of forces resulting from the interlacing of nature and natural forces, other persons in various relationships, and artifacts arising out of the conjunctions of man and nature in terms of particular concepts and products of the mind. But the undifferentiated complex embraces myriad patterns of relationship between person, nature, other persons, and these artifacts; for the concepts of the mind do not constitute frames capable of containing or ordering the relationships actually existing between the human being and its environments.[4]

Between the experience of the person and his awareness of that experience stand those frames of thought that correspond to his concepts. The concept of knowledge, as it has been historically conceived, itself reflects a limiting frame of thought. The historical refinement of the concept of knowledge into the concept of science enlarged the earlier frame of thought in one direction (in terms of permitting constant redefinition of knowledge with changing experience and the action of thought upon it) and narrowed it in another (by sharpening the division between observer and object).

The second of these qualities of the concept of science and its corollary frame of thought has revolutionized man's awareness of numerous *aspects* of his environment and experience — that is, whatever particular aspects he undertakes to examine. But it has done so at the cost of cutting off from recognition, even more sharply than the earlier concept of knowledge had done, basic aspects of this undifferentiated complex, including many of men's psychic relationships. In this respect, the concept of science has intensified the effects on the mental structure earlier emerging as a corollary of the concept of rational and objective knowledge. Historically, the mind has become increasingly separated from the undifferentiated complex of experience. The most powerful consequence is the loss of awareness of the basis of awareness itself.

Behavior ostensibly governed by recognitions emerging through the frames of thought of knowledge and science is, however, actually governed also by the effects of forces and relationships which lie in the shrouded levels of the undifferentiated complex. Consciousness screened through the governing frames of thought can and does seek to *dominate* behavior, force it in various directions, and may appear to govern it, for the reason that one's

[4] E. Cassirer, *op. cit.*

own and others' behavior and relationships are perceived in terms of recognition set by the governing frames of thought. But this limited and skewed awareness does not actually govern behavior. All behavior and relationships respond to conditions and relationships of the entire environment.

These dawning realizations result in part from the first quality of science earlier noted — namely, the redefinability of the concept and frame of thought of science itself. Therefore the problem of redefinition of the idea of valid knowledge, which has confronted us with respect to human behavior and human action, need not be considered incapable of resolution, even if we do not now know how to resolve it.

Even a consideration of possible aids and directions of solution, in the sense of a theoretically satisfying one, is beyond the scope of this discussion. Suffice it that modern physics has also had to face a basic problem which has necessitated a fundamental redefinition of what constitutes valid knowledge. This redefinition pertains to the concept of a science concerned with the sub-atomic field of nature; by the indeterminacy principle of Heisinger, the nature and behavior of this field — even theoretically, let alone pragmatically — are incapable of inspection or examination in terms of the traditional definitions of science. The principle of indeterminacy in physics is not the same as the principle of indeterminacy which must be recognized as inescapable with respect to phenomena of human behavior in the social field; but both have in common the problem of the relationship of mind to aspects of the undifferentiated complex which renders the traditional definition of objective empirical knowledge obsolete.

The problems of administration are pragmatic. They cannot wait upon the discovery of valid knowledge and theoretically satisfying solutions. Indeed, the latter are bound up with the growth of skill developed pragmatically. Training programs must themselves be considered pragmatic inventions.

Yet recognition of conditions and problems which may point to the need for major changes in prevalent theory can positively affect skill, even in the absence of the new theoretical and conceptual developments; indeed, such recognition can actually contribute to such developments. For if there is recognition that the frames of thought under which we are operating are inadequate and stand in the way of the awareness which experience gives to us as a potential, we have started to unlock the mental barriers to new sensitivity to experience and situations. And this *per se* constitutes a development of skill.

By moving behaviorally in this direction, the problem of using knowledge of the various kinds that have been accumulated in any field of knowledge stands in a new light. These kinds of knowledge which we have thought of as "valid and objective" now fall into a perspective based on the realization of their essential relativity. The compulsions which have been operative within administration to use the models of physics, of chemistry, of biology, and of some social sciences, for the examination, analysis, and ordering of data pertinent to administration, become reduced. The errors that result when models appropriate to one field are applied to another in which the order of experience involved makes them inappropriate may be more easily discovered. Administration need not try to compete with the sciences on the terms of traditional definitions. It has its own tasks to perform. The pursuit of skill involves casting aside a narrower frame of thought for a new frame (not yet invented) that is appropriate to the field of its experience. The new frame of thought will in part evolve from the advancing skill; and that which emerges as valid experience, as contrasted with the idea of valid knowledge in the older terms, will represent increasingly organized mental contents of awareness functionally related to skill. In these tasks and opportunities, administration must largely feel its way and invent its models; for there are no models from earlier disciplines which it can copy or easily adapt without danger of reverting to the frames of thought and science still dominant in society.

Yet some food for thought may be gained through recognition of some of the processes of recent evolution which are perceptible in one of the oldest disciplines — the field of medicine. For medicine, as a skill, has likewise had to find a direction for its own development involving use, on the one hand, of numerous findings from the whole range of the ordered sciences, and on the other, of the kind of skill which is associated with the sensitivity of a particular physician to a particular patient in a particular situation. This process of relating the two conditions — accumulated resources of "knowledge" and a unique patient — places the physician in the role of a human interlink between the two. Through a system of mutual feedback, operating via the physician, the direction of the behavior of the patient is influenced but not governed by "knowledge," and the direction in which knowledge develops is influenced by the behavior of patients. Yet it is a personal factor — the skill of the physician — which serves as the key to evolution and development at both extremes of this continuum. Significantly, the use of the case method, involving written reports on the illnesses or deaths of specific persons (including the records of diagnosis and treatment), is one of the basic patterns developed by medicine for the improvement of research, for training, and for continued professional development.

tology, and of some social sciences for the identification, analysis, and solution of data pertinent to administrative [illegible]. The error [illegible] that which [illegible] appropriate to one field are [illegible] in [illegible] the [illegible] may be [illegible] not [illegible] with the [illegible] on the terms of [illegible] has its own tasks to perform. The [illegible] involves [illegible] a particular [illegible] of thought [illegible] in [illegible] of its [illegible] and the [illegible], as [illegible] truly [illegible] for [illegible] to such tasks and [illegible] administration must [illegible] and [illegible] from [illegible] which [illegible] of [illegible] to the [illegible] of [illegible].

[illegible] of some of the processes of [illegible] which are [illegible] of the [illegible]. For [illegible] skill has [illegible] on the one [illegible] the whole range of the [illegible] and on the other [illegible] with the [illegible] in a particular [illegible] — [illegible] in the [illegible] in the [illegible] of the [illegible] and [illegible] of the [illegible] in [illegible] as [illegible] the [illegible] for the improvement of research for training, and for continued professional development.

SECTION THREE

THIRTY-FIVE CASES

1 Shantytown

Woodlawn's elementary school board took the most direct possible means of ending segregation in its school system. As of September, 1951, they closed the Santa Ana School in outlying Shantytown, the largest of the school district's three Mexican settlements, and redistributed the children throughout the rest of the system. Although the decision resulted in an immediate saving of money, board members and the superintendent insisted that their primary interest was in ending segregation. The decision was typical of Woodlawn's school board — it was reached without bothering to consult or to inform anyone in town. The change was effected smoothly and with a minimum of complaints. In fact, when rumors that the Santa Ana School was to be reopened were making the rounds in the spring of 1953, both "white" and "Mexican" elements joined in protest.

Woodlawn is a middle-class suburb in Southern California. Now a thriving residential and small-industry town, it was originally a quiet little business center for a ranching district. Until about 1920 the town presented an almost feudal pattern of wealthy ranch owners and Mexican ranch labor, with very little gradation between these socio-economic extremes. Then the nearby city of San Julian began to make itself felt. Large numbers of white-collar workers from the city moved into Woodlawn, doubling its population in less than ten years and changing its socio-economic picture even more radically. By 1953 the ranches had given way almost entirely to subdivisions, and the once open land between Woodlawn and San Julian had filled in completely with industry and housing. Woodlawn now has a population of over 20,000 and is the business and shopping center for an area, primarily residential, including about another 30,000.

The Woodlawn Elementary School District embraces the town and approximately another 10,000 population in nearby outlying areas. It has under its jurisdiction some 4,000 children from kindergarten through Grade 8, and includes nine elementary schools plus one junior high for all the children in Grades 7 and 8. Board members are elected by popular ballot for three-year terms. The elections seldom bring forth more than 10 per cent of the voters. The elementary and secondary school districts have separate school boards and superintendents.

The Santa Ana School had been built in 1924 for the express purpose of keeping Shantytown's children out of the other schools, and had been condemned because of earthquake damage in 1948. It had been Superintendent Adams' idea to redistribute the children rather than ask for further permission to continue use of the condemned building, undertake the expensive job of repair, or build a new school. The school board had gone along immediately and enthusiastically. Adams was empowered to make the necessary plans, and he had gone about the redistribution of the children of Shantytown in systematic and thoroughgoing fashion. He did not separate brothers and sisters, but he did break up troublemaking cliques and saw to it that each classroom in the Woodlawn elementary system had three to six of the Shantytown children. It turned out that the redistribution would cost $2,000 per year for transportation and would save $20,000 in teachers' salaries. It was not necessary to release any teachers, though, since the normal turnover plus the personnel needs of a system which was expanding at the rate of 15 per cent per year [1] permitted their absorption into the system.

The change was announced to the town through the local newspaper in August, 1951, and it went into effect the following month. All 300 Mexican children (180 from Shantytown and 120 from the two other Mexican districts) were absorbed into the elementary system with only two complaints. One of these came from a Mexican parent who was worried about the amount of time her child had to spend on the bus each day. The other came from a parent who objected to having Mexican children in the classrooms. She had recently moved from a nearby city because of Negro children in her son's class.

The first complaint was handled, at the superintendent's request, by some Shantytown members of the junior high's custodial staff who knew of the reason for the redistribution and were able to explain it to the Mexican parents, many of whom did not speak English. The other complaint was ignored, and the family soon moved on to another town.

About this time the Local Federation of Women's Clubs had studied the redistribution plan in action and had come out in favor of it. The sensitive Shantytown parents had been fearful at first, both because their children might be snubbed and because of the expense of clothing and equipping them well enough to avoid the pity or scorn of children from middle-class homes. But within a year the benefits were so obvious that they had come to be completely in favor of the new order of things. English was replacing Spanish as the accepted tongue among Shantytown's children, although up to this time it had been used only when absolutely necessary. Practice in speaking English was having a good effect on the children's grades. Fights between "white" and "Mexican" youngsters were less and less common, and the Shantytown children no longer kept to themselves when they reached junior high school, but mixed freely with the others in all curricular and extracurricular activities. P.T.A. units were making sincere and increasingly effective efforts to bring the Mexican mothers into their activities. The results were really spectacular, and most heartening to those responsible.

Then, somehow, rumors started to the effect that the Santa Ana School was to be reopened in the fall of 1953 in order to ease crowded conditions in the other schools of the district. Actually, nothing was further from the minds of the board and of the superintendent, although they were concerned with the problem of what to do with the old school. The school's playground had become an impromptu community center for sandlot games.

The area which the school had served included a ranch district across the railroad tracks and quite a distance from Shantytown. This district had recently been subdivided and settled largely by white, lower-middle-class people. These people complained about the rumored reopening because they feared that some of their children, who were already beginning to overflow the school built in the subdivision only two years before, would have to attend a school in which over half of the children would be Mexican. The Mexicans complained because they feared a return of the old segregated conditions.

An informal open meeting for the purpose of drafting a petition of protest was

---

[1] This rate of expansion had been fairly constant since World War II. The best estimate, based on the amount of land still open in Woodlawn for new residential construction, was that the rate of expansion would decline sharply by 1956.

arranged for March 10 by citizens of both groups, including Shantytown's Catholic priest and the P.T.A. officers in the subdivision. The meeting promised to be well attended by both Mexicans and whites. On March 5, Superintendent Adams received a letter from those organizing the meeting inviting him to attend and to speak if he wished.

2 *Applied Science*

In August of 1950, Alden Rice, principal of Sutton High School, interviewed Patrick Thompson, a candidate for the position of science teacher. Thompson was without experience and came to Rice as the third candidate sent by the All-State Teachers' Agency. The two previous candidates had refused the position because of the low starting salary ($2,700 for a teacher with a Bachelor's degree and no experience), the uncertain and indefinite salary schedule (actually the schedule in existence was rarely adhered to), and the isolated location of the Town of Sutton. Sutton, a town of 8,000, was at least thirty miles from the nearest city of any size (North Bank, 30,000). When August came, and the position still had not been filled, Rice had requested that his superintendent wire the All-State Agency to spare no effort in their search for a man. Mr. Thompson was the result of the search.

Superintendent Parkinson interviewed Thompson briefly before sending him to see Mr. Rice at the high school office. While Thompson was en route from the superintendent's office to the high school, Parkinson called Rice. "I just talked to the latest candidate for the science job," Parkinson said. "A Mr. Thompson."

"What do you think of him?" Rice asked.

"Well, I don't know. His scholastic record is good. He's young. . . ."

"I imagined that he would be," Rice said. "What's really the matter with him?"

"Nothing," Parkinson said. "Alden, I'm going to let you make up your mind on this one. After all, he will be teaching at your school."

"We have to get someone," Rice mused. "It's August. I can't go through another year with a parade of substitutes."

"Yes," Parkinson agreed. "Well, see what you think of him. He's got the science background, all right."

Thompson carried his school transcripts and other recommendations in a sealed envelope which the agency had sent along with him. He fumbled the envelope when he passed it to Rice, and they bumped heads in their attempt to retrieve it. Thompson blushed furiously and stammered an apology. While Rice read through the credentials, Thompson drummed nervously on the edge of the desk and tugged at his collar. Rice saw that Parkinson had not exaggerated the quality of the candidate's school record. Thompson had solid banks of "A's" through his high school, college, and university records. He had attended both the State University and a small, first-rate private college where such marks did not come easily.

"I notice that as an undergraduate you majored in geology," Rice said. "Then in the University you seem to have gotten away from geology. These last semester courses are in education."

"Ah, yes, I switched," Thompson said. "I didn't like working with rocks. That is, I thought if I could. . . ." His voice trailed off, and Rice waited for him to get command of his Adam's apple. "What I meant was," Thompson finally managed to say, ". . . was that I wanted to work with people. They are. . . ."

Rice said, "Well, education will bring you into contact with people, all right. Do you think you can get along with high school students?"

"I guess so. I know the work. I've had over ten hours in physics and chemistry.

I know the text you use. I don't think I'll have any trouble." Thompson seemed to have recovered his poise at this point, and he went on to talk to Rice about his hobbies, collecting rock specimens, rebuilding engines, and building model boats and planes. This appealed to Rice, because one of the big problems at Sutton High was the so-called Applied Science class. Rice had no illusions that the class was looked upon by the faculty as anything else but a dumping ground for "the tough and the dumb." The high school, with an enrollment of 325, maintained three curricula: College, Commercial, and a course that was sometimes called "General." The Applied Science class was the senior science course for those in the General curriculum. Rice had no fears about Thompson's ability to teach chemistry and physics to the college group. Thompson could even take one math class from the high school coach, who was not a trained math teacher. Rice did have doubts, however, about putting Thompson into the Applied Science class. Thompson seemed to be strongly oriented to "subject matter." Still, if Thompson could work in his hobbies, Rice felt, something might be salvaged. It was the Applied Science class that had caused the former science teacher to resign in the middle of the preceding year, on the verge of a nervous breakdown. From the Christmas vacation until June, eight different substitute teachers had paraded through the science classes at Sutton, and some of the College Course parents had complained bitterly to the school board.

"I know the material," Thompson said again. "And I think I can teach it. I'd certainly like to try."

"All right," Rice said. "The superintendent and I will go over your record and letters of recommendation in more detail tomorrow. Where can you be reached?" Thompson gave his home address to Rice and left the office.

The following morning Rice and Parkinson met in the office of the superintendent of schools. All the letters of recommendation praised Thompson as a "serious boy" and a "conscientious worker." One of Thompson's professors at the school of education had included the rather cryptic statement, "Mr. Thompson may find close contact with children a trifle upsetting at first, but I have no doubt that a man as determined as he will succeed in the long pull."

"What did you think?" Parkinson asked.

"He appeared to lack poise," Rice replied. "Still, before he left, he was talking."

"We don't have time to psychoanalyze him," Parkinson said. "What do you think?"

"I don't know," Rice confessed.

"We could hire him on a four-month probationary arrangement," Parkinson suggested. "Then if he proved a complete failure, we wouldn't be stuck with him."

"I don't know about probation in his case,'" returned Rice. "It might keep him too much on edge."

"We can't afford to risk a year," Parkinson said. "I've had more trouble from that science teaching spot than all the other teaching positions combined. I'll mail out the contract. I don't like probationary hirings as a policy. And I plan to change it. But since we have it, I think we should use it."

Rice did not see Thompson again until the teachers' meeting on the day before the high school opened. Rice's main purpose in the meeting was to provide orientation for the three new teachers who were coming to the high school faculty that year. After a preliminary speech of welcome, Rice introduced Thompson and the two other newcomers to the older members of the high school staff. After the introductions were over, the three new teachers went to the principal's office for a short talk on the mechanical details of the high school. Rice noticed that

Thompson had seemed flustered and upset during the flurry of introductions in the teachers' room. Rice showed the new teachers where the supplies were kept and explained the report forms and the marking cards. Thompson seemed inordinately concerned about the minor details of school routine and took notes on some of the instructions. He asked to inspect the laboratory and the equipment, which he examined and in some cases tested, while Rice waited anxiously to get out of the building. After examining the equipment, Thompson asked to go over the classrooms again, and it was quite late when they left the building. Rice offered Thompson a ride back into town. Thompson said he was staying at the Y.M.C.A., and he blushed when Rice asked him if he had a girl back in his home town.

Thompson mumbled, "I guess I'll stay here weekends."

"Well, you'll meet lots of people in Sutton," Rice said. "There are church clubs and social groups."

"I'm not much of a joiner," Thompson said. "I guess the work will keep me busy enough."

Rice made it a point to visit Thompson in the Applied Science class on the second day of school. Coming along the corridor toward the room, he heard the rolling sound of a general class disturbance and he hastened toward the door. Inside, the room was in wild disarray. A wastebasket lay on its side, the contents strewn over the floor. All the boys were on their feet milling about and talking. Thompson was standing in the center of the room, flushed and shaking. "I will give you until I count three to pick up that basket," he was saying to a boy student.

"I didn't mean to kick it over," the boy protested sullenly. "And I ain't going to pick it up. I'm not the janitor."

An unpleasant scene ensued in which Thompson stubbornly insisted that the boy pick up the waste paper. The situation was saved by the bell which ended the period. After the students had gone, Rice asked Thompson to forget the incident, assuring him that such things had happened in that class before. "Try not to give an ultimatum to a boy like that in front of the others. Get him aside and he'll eat out of your hand. And keep the rest of them in their seats."

Thompson thanked Rice for the advice, and the principal went on to visit other classes. Fortunately, the other two new teachers, one of whom was inexperienced, were doing outstanding jobs.

There was no further disturbance in Thompson's class that week. Toward the middle of the second week Rice again visited the class, and sat through the entire period. There was no disturbance this time, but the class was as apathetic as any that Rice had ever seen. In fact, he had to wake two boys who were asleep with their heads down on their desks. It appeared that Thompson taught almost wholly from the book. His desk was bare of any demonstration materials, and his voice droned on interminably. After a twenty-minute lecture, Thompson quizzed the class on the lesson assigned the day before. The boys either ignored his questions or made silly guesses at the answers. The three girls in the class made more respectable attempts to answer, but were as hopelessly unprepared as the boys. Rice decided to give the new teacher another week before talking to him.

On the first day of the following week Thompson appeared at Rice's office after school was out. He seemed depressed and a trifle bewildered. "I don't know what's the matter with me," he said. "They aren't learning anything. My other classes do fine. But Applied Science. . . ."

"I think you should relax more up there," Rice told him. "Get them interested first. Maybe slow down the pace. Spend more time on demonstrations. Get them out on field trips if necessary."

Thompson said, "There is no sense in field trips until they get the fundamentals. I'm going to start putting some pressure on them. Keep them after school."

"I wouldn't," Rice advised. "Some of the boys are on the football team, you know."

"With me," Thompson said, "football is secondary. If I can give up my afternoons, they can."

On Monday of the following week, Rice had one call from "Dab" Brennan, the high school football coach. Brennan complained that five of his first team had missed three days of practice the week before because they had been detained by Thompson.

"I offered to straighten them out, but he didn't say anything," the coach said.

"I'll talk to him," Rice promised. After Coach Brennan was gone, Rice sat a long time worrying at his desk. Sutton was a football town, and the coach was a man of considerable influence in the community. Brennan's salary was at least $1,000 more than Rice's own; in fact the coach was the second-highest-paid man in the system. Rice had no wish to get into difficulties with the coach. Rice's predecessor had been reprimanded for interfering with Coach Brennan. The man finally had been hounded from town by the sports writers on the local paper. This had happened two years before under a different superintendent; but Rice felt that Parkinson was too new to give him strong backing. Still, Rice was a man who would not tolerate a threat from anyone. He had let Brennan's implied threat pass because Thompson probably was not in the right. Rice resolved to talk to Thompson and to urge him to relax, rather than to tighten up, in the Applied Science class. In order to present his proposal Rice decided to visit the class that afternoon. He had purposely avoided the class for a week, feeling that Thompson would come around sooner if not placed under the pressure of too frequent visits from his principal. During the noon hour, before Rice could make his visit, he received a call from Miss Archembault who taught French in the classroom next to Thompson's Applied Science class.

"I hate to do this," she apologized. "But I feel something must be done about Mr. Thompson's class. The noise from that room disturbs the entire wing of the building."

"How long has this been so?" Rice asked.

"For the past week. The class sounds as though it is completely out of hand."

"All right, thank you, Miss Archembault. I'll visit the class this afternoon."

That afternoon there were no disturbances in the Applied Science class. Rice sat through the entire period in the back of the room. He noticed that Thompson had improved his teaching. Thompson had brought in some rock specimens collected from the surrounding countryside during the weekend. He gave a short talk on the rock strata and local geology, illustrating it with his rock samples. To Rice's surprise, some of the boys appeared to be genuinely interested. Several of them who were miner's sons tried to guess where Thompson had found his samples. A lively, but relatively orderly, discussion followed and lasted until the bell rang, ending the period.

"Whew!" Thompson said when the class had left the room. "I've been catching it. I guess I tried to bear down too hard. I'd hate to think what they would have used those samples for if you hadn't been here."

"I don't think my being here had a thing to do with it," Rice said. "They were interested in you and in your rock specimens." He put his hand on Thompson's shoulder. "Look, Pat," he said. "I think you're beginning to get the idea here. Do you want me to look in on you tomorrow?"

"I'd like you to," Thompson said. "We will have some work from the book.

I know I'm causing you an awful lot of bother, Mr. Rice. I feel bad about it. God knows I work hard enough at it. I realize I'm on probation here."

"How many hours do you put in on preparation and correction?" Rice asked.

"At least five every night — and all weekend."

"I'll talk to you about this tomorrow," Rice promised. "Meanwhile I'd let up on the detentions a bit."

Late in the afternoon, Principal Rice went to the superintendent's office. Thompson had been teaching in Sutton a little more than a month, and Rice wanted to talk to the superintendent about the matter of probation. It was Rice's feeling that Thompson should either be let out or taken off probation. He judged that Thompson was under considerable pressure because of his uncertain status in the Sutton schools. Thompson was, if any thing, overly conscientious, and not likely to work well in a pressure situation. Rice presented his diagnosis to the superintendent. "The problem is not to spur the boy on to work harder. He's already overworking. I think we ought to try to get him to unwind."

"Is his teaching worth it?" Parkinson asked.

"I think it is. I saw a flash of good teaching today."

"It is a bit unusual," Parkinson agreed. "Incidentally, one of my board asked about the matter of detentions. I asked him whether Brennan had been to see him. The board member denied it. But to get back to Thompson. What will you do — ask him not to work so hard?"

"I've never had that problem with a teacher before," Rice said smiling.

"Well, I wouldn't want to bring the probation matter before the board now," Parkinson said. "Let's give it a week and see what happens."

The following morning Rice was delayed by an office call and did not reach Thompson's class until fifteen minutes after the period began. As he came along the corridor there was the sound of a disturbance coming from Thompson's classroom. As soon as Rice entered the room it became silent. Thompson was at the board drawing a diagram of a plant cell. The floor was strewn with small paper balls; it was obvious to Rice what had been going on before his entrance. Thompson had his back to the class while he sketched his diagram with great care. The students sat quietly, some staring out the window, other staring at the ceiling or doodling on the margins of their notebooks. After many erasures, Thompson had his diagram drawn satisfactorily, and he began to lecture on plant and cell growth, never once looking down at his class. The recitation following the lecture was a complete failure.

"It happened again," Thompson said after the class had gone. "If you hadn't been here, they would have torn the room apart. They were protesting an assignment for next weekend."

"We generally give light assignments during the fall weekends," Rice told him.

"I know, but this class is so far behind schedule." Thompson handed Rice a paper. "This is a list of the boys who skipped detention yesterday."

Rice glanced at the list. Five of the seven boys were on the football team. "I'll talk to the boys," he promised. "I think I had better visit the class for the rest of the week. Incidentally, I wouldn't spend so much time on board diagrams. The same diagram is in their textbook."

Thompson said bitterly, "These boys are bored by everything but football games and automobiles."

"You might try working on something along those lines, then," Rice suggested. "Explain combustion engines to them or something. Look, Pat, neither I nor the taxpayers are expecting you to make silk purses out of sows' ears. This is hard to say, because my job is to see that all pupils get the best education a teacher can give. In this case, though, I wonder if you aren't trying to teach them too much."

"Are you requesting that I shirk on my job?" Thompson asked.

"No," replied Rice, "but your job is more than hammering facts into their heads. Suppose we talk more about it during the week."

Rice sat in on the Applied Science class every day during the week that followed. There was no explosion, but Rice could feel a potential one simmering below the surface. Thompson tried to do what he considered Rice expected of him. He even tried humor, and failed pitifully. After school each day Rice sat down with Thompson and tried to help him with his papers. Thompson's trouble seemed to be that he checked each paper with meticulous care. Rice tried to convince Thompson that some of the routine exercises had only to be spot checked rather than analyzed completely.

Toward the end of the fifth week, Thompson seemed to have the paper situation solved. He submitted a set to Rice who checked them and found them satisfactorily marked. Rice did not order Thompson to stop the detentions, but their afternoon appointments served to cut these down effectively without a direct order. In the same week Rice also scheduled a meeting between Thompson and the football players who had skipped detention. During the course of the meeting an agreement was worked out whereby the boys promised to work off their extra detentions at the end of football season. The boys also promised that there would be no further occasion for them to be detained during the season. Their chief cause of complaint was that often Thompson was unable to pick out "the guilty ones" and kept the whole class except the girls. Thompson listened to the boys' complaint and agreed that group punishment was not a wholly fair procedure. He asked the boys if they had any special preference in the subject matter covered in the class. The boys considered this with obvious sincerity and said that they had no immediate suggestions, but would take the matter up during activity discussion period. Rice felt that the meeting had been completely successful, but after the boys had gone, Thompson seemed to be worrying about something.

Thompson said doubtfully, "I may have weakened my position with them by backing down on the punishment."

"You didn't back down," Rice said. "You worked out a solution with them. Pat, these pupils aren't like some you have been to school with. Most of them are sons of miners or laborers. I don't approve of all the folderol connected with football, but it does keep children in school. Before we had the big team, our percentage of drop-outs was very high."

"Well," Thompson said, "there must be some way we can get some education into them. I feel that I'm failing."

"Relax," Rice said. "Get down to the game tomorrow."

"I'll try to relax," Thompson promised.

That night Principal Rice reviewed the events of the past week. Rice was not certain that he had done the right thing in teaching Thompson how to cut corners in the matter of paper work. Further, he was not certain that it was good policy for a principal to encourage a teacher to relax his classroom standards. There was also the matter of discipline. Rice had recommended that Thompson relax his standards of classroom behavior and let the students talk a bit more freely during discussions. He had also told Thompson to let the boys get off the subject once in a while and "just kick the ball around." As a lifelong resident of Sutton, Rice felt that he knew the town boys and their ways. He had been a classroom teacher for over twenty years, and a principal for two. Rice did not think of himself as a "progressive educator" in any sense of the word. In his day as an English teacher, Rice had been a strict disciplinarian and a stiff marker. His change of view had come not through reading books on education, but rather through experience.

Rice was pleasantly surprised to see Thompson at the football game on Saturday. Rice and Superintendent Parkinson sat together at the game, and Parkinson remarked about Thompson's presence among the students.

"I'd still like to get that probation matter settled," Rice said. " I think if we took him off, it would be a shot in the arm for the boy."

"You seem to have taken quite a liking to him," Parkinson observed.

"I think he'll make it," Rice said. "You have to admire his nerve and the way he is trying."

"I'll get an answer to you this week," Parkinson promised. "I think the next board meeting would be the place to do it. I did get one complaint last week from a parent. Mr. Milch felt that Thompson was working his daughter too hard in College Chemistry."

"Yes," Rice agreed, "and if he wasn't, Mr. Milch would call with the opposite complaint. I know Al Milch from grammar school."

"He's a chronic complainer," Parkinson agreed. "Well, we'll see."

Rice did not get an opportunity to visit Thompson's class on Monday. On Tuesday Thompson asked permission to take the class to a local automobile dealer's showroom where there was a cross section of an engine on display. In the course of this field trip two of the boys skipped away from the class group and went to a local drugstore. Rice felt badly about the incident because he was afraid that it might prevent Thompson from taking the class out again.

The next afternoon Parkinson called to report that he had received a complaint on the drugstore incident. He said, "Some busybody saw the boys there during school hours and reported it."

"That's Sutton for you," Rice said.

"I'm going to take the boy off probation anyway."

"I think you're doing the right thing," Rice agreed.

The following day Rice visited Thompson's class and found him considerably more relaxed with the students. Rice also noticed that Thompson had arranged a display case of rock specimens at the front of the room, and that there were some engine diagrams from a magazine on a new bulletin board. Rice visited the class once more that week and found that things were running much more smoothly. Thompson, freed from his paper correction duties, had his sketches prepared and his assignments ready. All was not completely well. The students still gave pitifully inadequate answers in the question period and wasted time in the discussion, but Rice felt that this was unavoidable. He commended Thompson after the class. Thompson said that he had received word from the superintendent about the end of his probation period. "I think now that I have the discipline problem somewhat settled I can teach them something."

Things ran along fairly smoothly for the next two weeks. Rice managed one class visit during this period. It seemed an orderly class in which the students appeared to be passively interested. During the same period, Thompson took the class out on what they called "a prospecting trip," and everything went smoothly. Rice thought increasingly less about Thompson until the first marking period arrived.

On checking the master grade sheets in his office, Rice was aghast. Thompson had failed two-thirds of the Applied Science class. In his other courses Thompson had been somewhat more liberal, but there were far too many low grades on the reports of the students in the College Course. Rice contacted Thompson after school, and reviewed the marking system with him.

Thompson said, "Well, that's the way they came out."

Rice asked Thompson if he had ever heard of the normal-curve distribution of marking. Thompson said that he had. In the resulting discussion Thompson evidenced considerably more training in mathematics than amenability to suggestion. He pointed out that theoretically the curve had no validity in the Applied Science class. "They're all dumb," he said. "Some are dumber than others. What you are proposing is that I add a constant to each grade to get some of them by."

"I'm not interested in the theory behind this," Rice said. He had been somewhat annoyed by Thompson's lecture on probability distribution and the mutilation of the concept by educators. "What I'm trying to say," he told Thompson, "is that these students should be graded in terms of the general level of the class. You can't flunk this many."

"I can, and I have," Thompson said. "If you want to change them, that is your lookout. But don't try to justify it mathematically."

"Now look, Pat," Rice said. "There's more to this than mathematics. You're new in teaching, and I think you have some promise. But you have to learn that you can't add up people in columns of figures."

Thompson stubbornly shook his head. "I guess I've learned something here today," he said. "You have to change your honest opinion to get along."

"I don't want you to feel that way," Rice said. "But I can't flunk half of the school to please your whim for mathematical precision." Noticing that the argument was getting heated, Rice broke off suddenly and asked Thompson to think it over. Thompson promised to do that, and they scheduled another meeting for the next day.

After Thompson had gone, Rice sat late in the office studying the sheets. The individual reports would be made out and distributed the following day. It had been the first time that Thompson had openly resisted any suggestion. It seemed to Rice that he was being constantly put into a position where he had to counsel Thompson against being honest and conscientious. Rice could change the marks, he supposed, but he had never been forced to do so before. Superintendent of Schools Parkinson was scheduled to stop at the high school office that afternoon. Rice disliked bothering Parkinson with a problem which was internal to the high school, and yet if Thompson's marks went out as they stood, the problem would be more than an intramural one.

"I'm glad you told me," Parkinson said, after he had heard the story. "It seems to indicate a complete lack of judgment in the boy. He thinks everything can be figured out on his slide rule. If these marks went out like this, we would have an explosion."

"What do you suggest?" Rice asked.

"I think it's time that I talked to Mr. Thompson," Parkinson said. "I've kept out of this because you were doing a good job with him."

Rice was not present at the meeting between Thompson and Parkinson. He knew only that one had been scheduled for late that afternoon. The following morning Thompson came into the principal's office. "I'd like to see the grade sheets," he said. Thompson took the sheets and carried them to a small table across the office. He worked at the table without speaking, and finally carried the sheets back and laid them on Rice's desk. Still without a word he left the office. On inspecting the sheets, Rice found that Thompson had raised all marks on a sliding scale. Rice turned the grade sheets over to his secretary.

The following afternoon Rice had an irate football coach in his office. "Three of my boys are ineligible by rule," Brennan stormed. "Thompson flunked them in math and science." Rice didn't say anything. "I want you to talk to that guy," Brennan said. "He just isn't reasonable."

"What would you suggest I say?" Rice asked.

"Tell him that there's more to a kid's education than school work. There's the matter of character and discipline that comes from team play." Brennan went on at great length, and Rice heard him out.

"There isn't much I can do," Rice said. "Thompson is responsible for making judgments in his own class. I'll have him give the boys make-up work and tests. Maybe they can get back up to a passing grade in a week."

"A week!" Brennan snorted. "I want those kids back Saturday."

"That's all I will do," Rice said emphatically.

"Well, I'll see what *I* can do," Brennan said, and stormed from the office.

That night Rice received a phone call from Superintendent Parkinson. "Well," Parkinson said, "they're after us. I've had three calls this afternoon about those ineligible football players. One of them was from Henry Josephs of the *Sutton Times.* Henry is on my board, you know."

"I know all about Henry," Rice said. "He's the leading tub-thumper for a big stadium and a small school building."

"That may be," Parkinson agreed. "But that doesn't help me. I worked all last year to keep Henry and his paper happy. And I suspect that this is only the beginning."

"I don't know as we have any choice in the matter," Rice broke in. "Thompson assigned the marks. He raised them once. I think that's about as far as we can go short of firing him."

"I'm not suggesting it."

"I know that," Rice said. "But quite apart from Thompson, I think it is about time we made a move against the football crowd." Parkinson agreed, but said that this situation was the wrong one on which to make a move. He felt that they did not have a very strong champion to back in the person of Mr. Thompson. Parkinson felt that it would be better to defer the whole football matter, and to take it up in an entirely different context.

"I've got to get a working relationship with my board first," he pointed out. "Once I have that, we can go after these other things." Parkinson said that his first move would be to get a policy committee from within the school system to direct athletics in Sutton. He proposed that he, Rice, and Brennan be on that committee. He also planned to have all game receipts from football and basketball go into the general school fund instead of the athletic fund as had been the case. "We'll just get athletics back under the general school budget. This seems like a bad time for Thompson to create a general fuss."

"My suggestion is that he work with these boys all week," Rice said. "Then he could give them a make-up test, and have them eligible again."

"I guess that's the best we can do," Parkinson agreed.

Thompson was more than willing to tutor the boys during the following week. In a conference with Rice, he indicated that he felt no further animus about the mark incident. Brennan agreed to talk to the boys and get them to study. Rice was somewhat concerned about the outcome in the event that Thompson should fail any of the boys in their make-up tests. But they all passed. Afterwards Thompson said the tutoring experience had been good for him. "I see how to work with individual boys now," he said. "I guess my trouble before was that I saw them as a big blur of faces." Thompson also felt that he had reached a working agreement with the group by helping them after school. As far as Rice was concerned, the incident had been terminated successfully.

In the weeks that followed, Rice spent increasingly less time worrying about Thompson. All his classes seemed to be going well. In the Applied Science class Thompson used more practical laboratory experiments and demonstrations. He also took the class on several field trips to neighboring mines, factories, and farms. Several of the boys came to Rice and told him how much they looked forward to these trips. The Applied Science class, with the exception of a small core of chronic troublemakers, seemed under control. In the marking periods that followed, the group average rose steadily, and in the spring there were no more than the normal number of flunks. Early in the spring Thompson arranged a Science Fair in which his Applied Science class contributed more than their share of exhibits. One of the mine owners was particularly fascinated by the geology exhibits, and called Rice to commend him on "securing a teacher who has some brains in practical matters." The mine owner added, "Some of these kids are going to be working for me some day. What you teach them may make the difference in whether I get foremen or muckers. Latin and French won't help them."

In the College Course Thompson went on as he had from the beginning, doing an outstanding job in the teaching of subject matter. Several parents commented to this effect to Rice. In the spring College Boards Thompson's class did far better than any previous group from Sutton High.

On the social side Thompson was still far from being a "hail fellow," but he had emerged from his shell to some extent. The general attitude of the students and other faculty members was, "Pat is a strange one, but he means well." Others had the feeling that Thompson was "stand-offish" and inclined to be a "longhair." In the school his one active enemy was Coach Brennan.

In the spring Parkinson and Rice conferred about the teaching contracts for the following year. Things went smoothly until Thompson's name came up. "First," Parkinson said, "should we rehire him?"

"I think we definitely should. I can't go through another year with a new man. It would be the same thing all over again with that Applied Science course. No teacher would fit in immediately."

"I am not eager to put a new man into that class either. We haven't a tenure commitment to face. How about salary?" Parkinson asked.

"I propose a $300 raise far all three of my new men," Rice said.

Parkinson hitched his chair closer. "I can't see giving Thompson that big a raise. He hasn't had as successful a year as the others."

"Considering the way he started, he has," Rice argued. "That boy has developed. I see no reason why he won't continue to develop."

"I think there is a little paternal pride here," Parkinson said smiling. "I think this may be influencing your judgment, Al."

"Maybe," Rice admitted. "But that boy needs all the encouragement he can get. Half of his trouble was due to that probation."

"Possibly. I can see your side of it. Let's take mine. I'm going up before the board at the same meeting with my salary schedule. I think this is the root of the matter. If we had had a fixed schedule, we might never have been stuck with Thompson. I need all the board support I can get on this. I need Henry Josephs down at the *Times* with me. Henry has never forgotten Thompson's stand on the football players. Brennan and Henry are like two peas in a pod, and Brennan dislikes Thompson. I'm going after that relationship, but on my own time and when I can win. I'm too old to scrap for exercise."

"I hate to see a boy caught in the middle of a situation," Rice said.

"Let me say this," Parkinson said. "I'm going to put the athletic committee changes on the agenda. The way it stands now, Brennan and two of your teachers are the committee. Brennan gets his way. With us on it, we could get the funds into the general budget, and we could sit on athletics. If I buck him on Thompson, he may take this as an indicator . . .Would you honestly say Thompson is a good teacher?" Parkinson asked abruptly.

"He has improved more than the others."

"That wasn't my question. Is he now as good?"

"No . . . But he started with less."

Rice and Parkinson discussed the matter further without coming to any agreement. As a compromise proposal Parkinson was willing to give Thompson a raise of $200. Both of the other two new teachers at the high school were scheduled for raises of $300. Parkinson said, "It's not a matter of money alone. I'd just as soon give the boy $299.99, as long as it is less than what the others get. Henry Josephs, I might add, is going to move than we don't rehire Thompson. I want to save this as a compromise proposal. After all, Pat would still get $200."

Rice was adamant. "It isn't the money as far as I'm concerned," he argued. "In terms of Pat Thompson's morale, the one-cent differential would be as bad as the one hundred dollars."

"Would you like to see him not hired?" Parkinson asked.

"No. I couldn't stand a new teacher."

"Then this may be your best bet. Let me say this: I don't think we are in danger of losing Thompson, no matter what we offer him. I don't think he would want to face a new situation in his second year. With his shyness, job hunting must be a torture."

"That's taking unfair advantage of a man's weakness," Rice said.

"I guess it is," Parkinson agreed. "But it's a real factor. My interest here is in doing something for the Sutton schools in general. I want a fixed salary schedule. I can get that. I want to get athletics under control. I think I can do it. I want to attract better teachers here, and I want to get certain responsibilities back with the superintendent, where they belong. On the other hand, I'm going to be quite frank with you. I want and need you as a friend. I respect your judgment, and I've never gone over your head on anything."

The following morning Rice arrived at his office early and sat down to mull over the matter of Pat Thompson. He reviewed the entire situation from the first day Thompson, shy and fumbling, had arrived at the office. Rice was proud of what Thompson had made of himself in one year. There was no reason to suppose that Thompson would not go on improving. On the other hand, Rice did not want to set his demands so high that he would lose Thompson and be forced to hire a new teacher. The decision was not in Rice's hands. Rice felt that Thompson would stay on no matter what the salary arrangement — but what kind of teacher would he be, Rice wondered. The whole matter hinged on the lack of a definite salary schedule. Rice was as anxious as Parkinson to settle that matter. Rice also had a stake in the football business. Brennan had been building his athletic empire with increasing boldness of late. Rice had considerable sympathy with Superintendent Parkinson's problems. Parkinson was the first superintendent in Sutton history for whom Rice had the slightest respect. The others had let the present situation develop. Rice had no personal ambitions for the superintendency, and it was to his advantage to have the best man in the job. Parkinson was moving in his own time toward a solution of the problems of Sutton.

Parkinson, in his office, was also pondering the Thompson situation. Parkinson was particularly worried about the effect of his decisions on Rice. In his two years in Sutton, Parkinson had found Rice an invaluable ally. Parkinson also knew Rice could be stubborn and a formidable enemy when aroused. Both men wanted essentially the same thing, but Rice was the type who would go after it more directly. Parkinson had always counseled caution. Parkinson felt that there was a strong personal involvement in the matter of Thompson. Rice had worked hard to make Thompson into a teacher. Any slap at Thompson was an indirect slap at Rice. Parkinson had no illusions about Henry Josephs and his crowd. Eventually there would have to be a showdown, but Parkinson did not think that the time had arrived.

Both Parkinson in the superintendent's office and Rice up at the high school wanted to make certain that they knew what to say when they talked again about Thompson.

3 *Center Hill*—Prologue and Act I*
The Superintendent Recommends

Prologue

CENTER HILL is a pleasant resort town situated in the mountains of New England. The permanent residents total about 6,500, but in the summer an influx of seasonal residents raises the population to 12,000. Part of the charm of the community is its quaintness, which is carefully preserved. The streets are narrow and tree-lined. Old colonial houses face the village green and the pond, and line the winding roads overlooking the mountains.

Mr. Fisher, the superintendent of schools in Center Hill, is a slightly built man of sixty-three, whose white hair and dignified manner seem appropriate to the Center Hill atmosphere. He had come to the town twenty-three years earlier, after varied experiences as teacher of English and high school principal in several New England communities. In his first years in the town he was a great favorite, popular for his gentle, courteous manner, and his friendliness.

The school committee of Center Hill consists of six members. During the years from 1929 to 1944, there had been quite a stable membership composed of prominent businessmen and representatives of the "leading families." In spite of the fact that early in that period the superintendent's private life became a subject of much gossip, there was little evidence of discord between the committee and the superintendent at the time.

Service on the school committee was not regarded as the steppingstone to a political career, as in some communities, but there had generally been candidates interested in filling the vacant positions. Gradually, during the war and postwar years, there had been a shift in membership of the committee. In the records it could be seen that there were many resignations which made temporary replacements necessary. There were lengthy periods in which vacancies existed, because it was not always easy to find candidates.

In the period from 1929 to 1944 the community had not changed much, but the gradual growth of population, slightly accelerated from 1944 on, had finally made it necessary to build a new junior-senior high school. The new building had long been needed by every criterion other than seating capacity. The other school buildings could be rated as meeting minimum standards; most of them were old, but some had been well maintained. There were three elementary schools. The student body numbered about 1,500, and there were 72 faculty members.

Other teaching conditions would probably be termed "fair." The salary range was from $2,300 to $3,800, a scale lower than in many similar communities but comparable to rates in adjoining communities. According to the regulations of the school committee, the automatic pay increments would be given only to those teachers who had earned, within a three-year period, four semester credits for study. The pupil load averaged twenty-six pupils per teacher.

* This is a three-part case (Nos. 3–5). It is urged that each part be studied and discussed before the succeeding part is taken up.

Early in the spring of 1950, annual consideration of faculty appointments for the following year was begun. This had been a problem customarily attended to in April, but a recent state law required all teachers to be notified of appointment decisions before the first of April. This meant that the school committee decisions had to be made in March, and that early March was the deadline for the superintendent to make his recommendations to the committee.

The turnover rate for the faculty was high. The low salary scale had attracted mostly inexperienced teachers who usually moved on to better-paying communities in a few years. There were always some who married and settled in the community, content to live in the pleasant, healthful resort environment. In the winter there was a small-town rural atmosphere; in the summer there was all the excitement and activity of a cosmopolitan center.

There were few prospects of promotion to administrative positions. The rather limited social and financial opportunities of a small town seldom attracted the recent university graduate. During the war the teacher shortage was critical, and in the years since, an increasing number of married women had been employed. The faculty was 77 per cent women, of whom 38 per cent were married. Of the faculty, 12 per cent had training beyond the Bachelor's degree, 57 per cent had Bachelor's degrees, and 43 per cent had only a diploma.

There was a Teachers' Club which held an occasional social meeting or sponsored a lecture on some topic of professional interest. It was not an active or influential group. Most of the teachers were able to find lucrative jobs for the summer season. The community depended almost entirely on tourist trade for economic survival. Quarrying and farming were subsidiary activities, and there were no local industries.

Act I

Mr. Fisher was getting ready to make his recommendations for faculty appointments. It had been his custom each year to give special attention to the teachers who were eligible for tenure appointment. This evaluation of a teacher's ability, based on a three-year record, was a real responsibility. It seemed to Mr. Fisher that it was almost a final judgment, crucial to the teacher and to the whole school system. Of course, tenure contracts could be broken, he realized, but that rarely happened. For the year 1950 there were six teachers eligible for tenure appointment, and there were openings for all of them. As Miss Walker, his secretary, gathered the files of material about each of these teachers, Mr. Fisher leaned back in his chair to consider the over-all school picture.

To an observer, the school program seemed a long-established one. The atmosphere of both the schools and the town was one of calm routine. Mr. Fisher felt that educational experiments were not viewed with enthusiasm by the community, which placed a high value on tradition. The criterion was academic success. The academic standards were firmly set and clearly defined by subject areas. No major change in school policy had occurred since he had taken the position as superintendent. The community had never taken an active interest in the schools, and had provided only a small budget to maintain them. Although its booming summer trade made Center Hill one of the wealthy communities of the state, this fact was not reflected in school facilities.

Mr. Fisher felt that there was no evidence of community dissatisfaction with the state of school affairs, although the school committee in recent years had not been easy to please. He sighed when he thought of his school committee. He wished the town would take enough interest in the schools to elect a more adequate group of committee members. Mr. Kittredge and Mr. Donovan, particularly, seemed to enjoy being rude and pinching pennies. He had never been able to reason with them. In fact, they seemed to want to oppose him. Perhaps they liked the sense of power that an official position, executive meetings, and public recognition sometimes give.

Mr. Fisher sighed again, and mused, "If I were younger, or healthier, I would take them on. . . ." It was really his health which had caused some of this trouble. Some people had gone directly to the school committee with complaints while he was ill, and gradually this had become a habit. Now Mr. Kittredge didn't even feel it necessary to inform the superintendent of complaints made against teachers, or of school committee orders sent directly to the schools. This state of affairs had proved very embarrassing for Mr. Fisher. As he thought of other action taken by the school committee, it seemed to him he had really suffered at their hands. He thought of the removal of his office from the high school to the community office building. The extra walking and the three flights of stairs were an inconvenience, almost a hardship, for a man of his age in poor health.

He felt that men like Kittredge, with only a high school education, could not be expected to know how to assume the responsibility of serving on a school committee. Mr. Fisher often said that there ought to be some educational requirements for school committee members, to get the right type of members. There had been so much turnover in the school committee, anyway, that it was really hard to know just what was going on. But Mr. Kittredge was always there! It was only two years ago that Mr. Kittredge had tried to force the superintendent to resign. Mr. Fisher was proud that he had refused to resign under pressure, and had carried on his work in spite of the many obstacles placed in his path. His health was poor, and he looked forward to the retirement for which he would qualify in two years.

Miss Walker placed on his desk the files of the six teachers to be considered for tenure appointments. Mr. Fisher picked up the familiar rating cards. These contained two lists of qualifications, to be evaluated as *good, satisfactory,* or *poor* by the principal. On one side of the card the check points were:

Preparation
Presentation
Pupil Reaction
Management
Cooperation
Discipline
Progress

There was space for written comment or explanatory notes. On the other side of the card more specific traits were to be similarly rated. These included:

Personal Appearance
Use of English
Initiative
Loyalty
Health
Knowledge of Subject Matter
Industry
Resourcefulness
Training
Reliability
Tact
General Intelligence

As Mr. Fisher considered these categories, they seemed quite sensible and comprehensive. These traits certainly fitted his concept of "the good teacher." As he studied the first card he wondered whether he should not revise his rating method. The form hadn't been changed in ten years, but it had served adequately all that time.

The first rating card was that of Miss Brown, a second-grade teacher in the East Hill Elementary School.

A State Teachers College graduate;
Nine years' experience before Center Hill;
Satisfactory ratings on every trait except two:
  health rated poor once;
  for last two years tact similarly ranked;
Consultations on program, methods, discipline;
Needed help with parent-teacher relations.

The comments were:

"Too hasty when disciplining."
"Talks too much."
"Spends too much time at school."
"Discusses her problems too freely."
"She is a good teacher of subject matter."
"Excellent for slow learners."
"Very conscientious."

Mr. Fisher though of his own impressions of her: Extremely shy, devoted to her work, a careful, precise teacher whose students were thoroughly prepared to meet required standards, health now O.K., no courses taken. She had few friends in the community, and had mentioned the possibility of resigning, as she felt there was criticism of her retiring social habits.

There were really no official records on Mrs. Gordon. Mr. Fisher had first met her three years earlier when she had come to his office to inquire about being placed on the substitute list. She had just moved to Center Hill with her husband to enjoy retirement. She was a lively person of sixty-two, with an unusual background — a degree from Smith College and courses at Columbia University, extensive foreign travel, with study at Oxford. As former owner of a private elementary school, with experience in teacher training and administration, she held modern views on education but was not impractically progressive.

Mr. Fisher enjoyed talking with her, and called her almost immediately as a substitute. Owing to a series of unusual circumstances, she was needed as a permanent substitute. Mrs. Gordon finished out the year on that basis even though she had not wanted to take the full-time teaching job which evolved after two weeks of substituting. Since her husband had died at Christmas time of that first year, it had been a hard year for her at work and at home. Mr. Fisher felt that she had saved an emergency situation for him and done it superbly.

In talking with him, Mrs. Gordon described her difficulties in adjusting to the public schools. She had said, "It is almost impossible for a woman of my age and outlook to change my educational beliefs so completely." It had been very difficult to persuade her to accept a regular teaching contract at the end of her year as permanent substitute. Finally she had agreed to give it another try since some of the most difficult phases of adjustment were behind her. She had been highly valued by her principal, her co-teachers, and her pupils.

At the end of her second year Mrs. Gordon refused to sign her contract for the following year; she felt that the work was too much of a strain on her physically. Her daughter, with whom she lived, thought she should now be enjoying life and taking things easy. Her original intention had been to do only substitute work. After the principal and Mr. Fisher had pleaded with her without success, the parents sent a committee to call on her. The committee discussed with Mrs. Gordon just what phases of the work were especially difficult for her. At first she commented only that the work was too much for her.

Finally she remarked that, "All day long with the children, without even a break to eat alone or to get to the bathroom, is more than I can take." From this discussion a rather unusual plan evolved which proved to be a beneficial experiment for all concerned. The mothers arranged a rotation scheme in which they took turns supervising the noon hour, including the lunch and play period. It relieved Mrs. Gordon of standing out in the play area for a long, hectic stretch, too.

This tentative plan was approved by both the superintendent and the principal. Mrs. Gordon found her new schedule a great help; the mothers found that supervisory experience was interesting and educational. As their interest grew they played a more active part in many phases of the school program. The other teachers, too, benefited, as they were included in the rotation scheme on the playground. Mrs. Gordon, at the end of her third year of teaching, again decided to retire, although she had enjoyed the year under the new arrangement. However, Mr. Fisher felt it would not be difficult to persuade her to stay on since the work was now less of a physical strain.

The next card belonged to Mrs. Marsie, sixth-grade teacher.

Two-year certificate from a small Teachers College in 1920; additional professional courses in various summer schools, totaling 60 semester hours, between 1920 and 1928;
Two hours of credit by taking a psychology course offered in Center Hill the preceding winter;
Applied for position after living in community several years;
Husband owned food locker;
All points checked good or satisfactory by principal.

This principal seldom wrote extensive comments:

"Asks advice, a good sign."
"Shows improvement."
"O.K."
(These were all the remarks for the three-year period.)

Mr. Fisher mentally supplemented the notes on the card from his own observations: her classroom was always calm and busy; she was helpful with students who brought problems to her; her work was always done competently; she was prompt in filling out forms.

He was interrupted by the sudden commotion of samples of school furniture being carried up the three flights of stairs. Five models of movable desks were deposited in his office. He and Miss Walker took a few minutes to examine them and to try them out. "Well," said Mr. Fisher, "You had better tell Mr. Kittredge that there is more furniture here for him to look over."

He turned back to his desk and picked up the next file record. Miss Partington, a pretty young gym teacher, had an excellent set of comments from all the principals.

B.S. State Teachers College;
Two credit hours for taking the course in psychology;
The high school principal rated her as the best gym teacher he had seen;
Her students were devoted to her — previously gym had been a very unpopular subject with the high school girls;
Demanding position, visiting all the schools to do gym work with all the girls;
Program approved by head of department at college she attended;
Seemed to do well with varied ages and interest.

Mr. Fisher felt that Miss Partington was enthusiastic, energetic, and showed responsibility and good judgment. She had talked with him about the possibility of joining the armed services or taking a year to do graduate study. Although she mentioned these possibilities several times it seemed to him that the two ideas were more "food for thought" than "plans for action." She was popular with many people in the community and seemed to have made a happy life for herself.

Miss Rourke was a second-grade teacher.

> B.S. from a State Teachers College;
> She had previously taught one year in New York State — employed by a publishing company — after five years wanted to return to teaching;
> Family had owned summer home in Center Hill and she wrote to Mr. Fisher to inquire about openings;
> All traits checked *good* or *satisfactory* on her card.

There were only two comments:

> "Good pupil-teacher relationship."
> "Would benefit by new methods courses, especially phonics."

Mr. Fisher knew that Miss Rourke enjoyed life in Center Hill. She was cheerful and easy-going. Her work was always completed, although not always on time. She was not particularly ambitious, and could have earned more money by remaining in business. She had taken no courses in her three years of service.

As a matter of fact, the superintendent had never discussed with any of his teachers the possibility of taking courses. Usually one course was offered during the winter, given by some one of the faculty of the university situated one hundred miles away. As for summer study, the pleasant summers at Center Hill and the good job opportunities during the tourist season were a strong inducement *not* to attend summer school. More of the teachers might take the course offered in the winter if special care were taken to select a good subject and a good instructor.

The last teacher to be considered was Mrs. Whittaker, a third-grade teacher in the same school with Miss Brown.

> Four years of training in a Canadian normal school before coming to Center Hill as an inexperienced teacher, in 1935;
> Married after five years of satisfactory teaching to a young businessman in the community;
> All traits and characteristics on her record, for the entire three years, had been checked as good or satisfactory;
> Conferred with principal about phonics work and problems of discipline.

Comments:

> "Too hasty in disciplining children."
> "Would benefit by new methods courses, especially phonics."
> "She is anxious to succeed."
> "Very conscientious."
> "Does a good job teaching subject matter."

In 1949 Mr. Fisher had found it very difficult to find suitable elementary teachers. He had looked back through his files of former personnel, hoping to find a prospect. When he saw Mrs. Whittaker's name he was delighted. Possibly he could persuade her to return to teaching now that her daughter was eight years old, and her family situation demanded less of her time. She had always loved her work, and he felt it would not be difficult to interest her in returning to the profession.

He had immediately called on Mrs. Whittaker to urge her to take on a teaching position. At first she was unwilling to consider the idea. She finally consented to try it after two school committee members called on her to give strong support to Mr. Fisher's idea. She made it clear that she could not do extracurricular activities or attend courses, as well as teach school and take care of her home. She was appointed third-grade teacher, although her earlier experience had been with fifth grade.

Mr. Fisher realized that Mrs. Whittaker was high-strung, dynamic, sensitive, a devoted teacher. It was her custom to spend numerous afternoons after school giving children special help. When he visited her home he saw many evidences of her extremely conscientious preparation, of her diligent efforts to bring herself up to date by reading and talking with other teachers. He had even expressed a worry that she was doing too much, and that her health would suffer.

It was now time for him to make a decision about each one of these teachers. In each case the principal had recommended the teacher for tenure appointment. Any decision given to the school board would be worded as a joint recommendation. The school board had always accepted his recommendation in this problem of tenure appointments. In a sense, his was the final responsibility. He had never had to call any of these teachers to his office for criticism or correction. He wondered how these candidates would be rated in other school systems. At this point Mr. Fisher took out his pen and wrote a neat heading: "Teachers to be recommended for tenure appointment."

4 Center Hill—Act II
The School Committee Acts

At a regular meeting of the school committee on March 21, 1950, the question of teacher appointment for the following year was to be considered. The superintendent had notified the chairman that his recommendations would be ready.

The following five members of the school committee were present:

Name	*Years of Service*	*Business*
Mr. Kittredge, Chairman	7	Bank Cashier
Mr. Donovan	5	Mgr. of Auto Agency
Mrs. Foster	3	Housewife
Mr. Olsen	1	Proprietor
Mr. Fernandez	1	Salesman

The one absent member was Mr. Laird, owner of a cabin rental business, who was a temporary appointment to fill in a vacancy.

The school committee viewed itself as a hard-working group, taking its responsibilities seriously. It had been struggling with the problem of vacancies and turnover during the war years, and had managed, the members felt, to do a good job. During the period following the end of the war they undertook a vigorous campaign for a new high school. This took hard work, and over a period of several years the school committee was one of the busiest groups in the community. Committee members spoke of meeting from four to fifteen times in a month, sometimes even more often. When the building plans were finally accepted, there was a three-year squabble over the site, and then there were the many details of construction to be attended to. At about this time Mr. Fisher had a serious operation, and for six months the school committee carried all his administrative duties as well as their own, including interviewing candidates for teaching positions.

During this same time the committee instituted other changes. There were changes in policies dealing with transportation, student regulations, relationships with principals and teachers, and other matters. The members claimed that the changes merely indicated a more actively interested and independent School Committee. They pointed with pride to their better attendance record, the frequency and long duration of meetings, their decision to join the Association of School Committee Members. Yet several members who resigned were quoted as finding their services too much of a strain, "because of the clash of personalities." Some of the newer committee members were outspoken in their criticism of Mr. Fisher, although no specific charges were made against him publicly.

One of the school committee members described the attitude of the group toward the superintendent as one of "complete lack of confidence." This member went on to say, "Over the period of five years that I served on the committee I found Mr. Fisher very untrustworthy, and I know that other members shared my feeling. Lies and deception do not build confidence. It came to our attention that Mr. Fisher withheld information which we should have been given. We discovered that he had used funds, which we had appropriated for one purpose, for entirely different purposes which would not have been approved by us. In many small instances he acted without authorization. As we took over his responsibilities during his illness we were astonished at the evidence of poor management. Everyone in the organization was doing as he pleased. You can't run a business that way.

"Of course, as we lost confidence in him, an atmosphere of mutual distrust built up. We were very critical of him. It is true that we went into matters which were not our responsibility, but his illness, mismanagement, and unreliability made this necessary. Personally, I feel that a man who has deserted his wife is not a fit person to be school superintendent.

Another committee member commented, "On occasion we asked Mr. Fisher to leave the room when we discussed school matters or his management of them. At one time we had a tie vote on a motion to request his resignation, but one of the members convinced us that we could not force this action because of the difficulty of getting evidence which would satisfy a court.

"In ten years," this member continued, "Mr. Fisher never failed to recommend an eligible teacher for tenure appointment. Many of these teachers were originally appointed in a last-minute rush at the end of the summer because Mr. Fisher was particularly inefficient about scouting for candidates. In September there were usually several vacancies still to be filled. Few of these 'desperation appointments' were eliminated during the nontenure period, and Mr. Fisher then recommended everyone for tenure. We never could get the superintendent to start early in the year to look for teachers, or to visit the normal schools to talk with the prospective graduates. A very large number of his appointments came from one small agency no one has ever heard of. Other members of the committee shared these views, and we had grown steadily more disgusted with the whole situation, especially personnel."

On the night of the meeting to consider appointments for 1950–51, Mr. Fisher was ill and sent his secretary, Miss Walker, to the meeting with the list of recommended candidates. The first teacher Miss Walker put before the school committee was Mrs. Marsie. Her only statement was, "Mr. Fisher recommends Mrs. Marsie, sixth-grade teacher in Woodward Elementary School, for tenure, with the approval of the principal." Mr. Kittredge asked the members of the committee if they had any comments to make about Mrs. Marsie. No member had any remarks, and a motion was then made to give Mrs. Marsie a tenure appointment. This motion was passed.

The second teacher to be considered was Miss Partington, also recommended for tenure by the principal and the superintendent. Mr. Donovan asked to be recognized. "I have heard that Miss Partington left a group of girls who were in her charge alone in a car late at night. I would like to know more about this incident — it sounds pretty irresponsible to me."

Mr. Kittredge commented, "I have heard a vague report about that incident, too. But I don't know the details. Does anyone know about this?"

Mrs. Foster spoke up, "Has the complaint which we referred to the superintendent last year about her wearing gym clothes to the faculty lunchroom been corrected?"

"Well," Mr. Donovan commented, "It looks as if the superintendent should be here to clarify these points."

"In fact," Mr. Kittredge responded, "how can we vote intelligently about these teachers unless the superintendent and the principals are here to give us whatever information we need? We shouldn't be expected to do everything alone!"

The committee nodded in agreement. Mrs. Foster stated emphatically, "Of course Mr. Fisher should be here, and the principals, too. I suggest that we table the problem of teacher appointments until next week, and that we request the superintendent and all of his principals to be present at that time."

The committee quickly agreed to the suggestion. As Miss Walker was leaving, Mr. Kittredge spoke to her, "Thank you for coming, Miss Walker. Would you notify Mr. Fisher and each of the principals that we would like them to be present next week?"

The next week the school committee met again to consider teacher appointments. Mr. Kittredge opened the discussion by saying, "Last week we voted to give Mrs. Marsie a tenure appointment. Now that the superintendent is here does anyone have any questions or comments about her record?"

Mr. Fisher spoke, "Mrs. Marsie is a fine person, a real addition to Center Hill's schools."

After several minutes Mr. Kittredge turned to Mr. Fisher. "There were several questions asked at our last meeting about Miss Partington."

"Questions about Miss Partington?" asked Mr. Fisher with a note of surprise.

Mr. Olsen leaned forward to ask, "Would you explain the circumstances when Miss Partington left some of her students in a car late at night?"

Mr. Fisher looked puzzled. "I'm not sure just what you are referring to. Perhaps Mr. Davis will have a better idea."

They all looked toward the high school principal. He said, "I suppose you are referring to Miss Partington's trip with her students to the square dance. There were some people who complained at the time, but when I explained the situation to them I heard no further criticism. A group of girls went to the dance in two cars. One car was the old and unreliable school department car which Miss Partington had received permission to use. On the way home that night — the affair lasted quite late — the school car had a flat tire. They stopped and put on a spare. Only a few miles later there was another flat tire. There was nothing for Miss Partington to do except leave some of the girls in the school department car while she drove to the nearest telephone to have the parents come to the rescue. She then returned to the group and kept everyone together until help arrived."

Mr. Olsen spoke again, "From what I hear, Miss Partington has used the school department car often enough on weekends for her own transportation. She should have known it would not be reliable for a trip with students."

A variety of responses greeted this. Some of the committee smiled derisively, some frowned. Mr. Fisher looked uncomfortable. Mrs. Foster turned to the high school principal to ask a question. "What is your opinion of Miss Partington's program? I have heard complaints on that score."

The principal responded vigorously. "She has an excellent program which she worked out with the head of her department at college. She is the most popular gym teacher we have ever had."

Mrs. Foster replied, "Some people didn't like those pictures of Center Hill girls posing in bathing suits which were featured in the newspaper. Is that a suitable type of school activity? Of course, I feel popularity is not the way to judge a school program."

Mr. Donovan spoke, "A teacher who wears her gym clothes to the lunchroom could not be expected to show good judgment in publicity poses for students!

Other teachers have complained about Miss Partington. Has she changed her habits?"

"There have been so many comments about Miss Partington during these three years. I wonder," asked Mr. Kittredge, "if the committee feels she is showing improvement?" No one seemed to have an answer to that.

Mr. Fisher spoke, "Miss Partington is a fine young woman who works hard, runs a good gym program, and maintains a good relationship with her students."

Mrs. Foster interrupted, "I have heard a rumor that she is planning to enter the service, or wants a year off to study. What can you tell us about that, Mr. Fisher?"

The superintendent answered, "I believe Miss Partington may be considering both possibilities."

Mr. Kittredge questioned, "Has she actually applied for an appointment in the armed forces?"

To this question Mr. Fisher replied, "Well, I am not sure. She may have done so. Even if she has, it is uncertain that she will be accepted, or, if she is called, the appointment may take a long time to come through." This brought some discussion about the difficulty of replacing a teacher in the middle of the year, the legal responsibility of employers to personnel who serve in the armed forces, and such problems.

At this point the school committee discussed whether or not to vote on each teacher after discussion or to wait for voting until all tenure candidates had been considered. It was decided to consider all the condidates before voting on any. As each teacher's name was given, questions were raised or criticisms offered.

The chief criticism against Mrs. Gordon was her age. Some members of the school committee felt that a sixty-five-year-old woman was not a suitable tenure appointment. Emphasis was given to the fact that she found the physical strain excessive, and that special arrangements had to be made to accommodate her frailty. It was frequently repeated, "She is not able to do a full day's work!" The fact that she had taken no courses for professional improvement during her three years of teaching in Center Hill was cited against her. There were some general comments about some of the unusual proceedings at Willowdale School. Mr. Fisher praised Mrs. Gordon very highly and said that she no longer found the school day too fatiguing. Her principal held her in highest respect and esteem, and stated emphatically, "Here is one teacher it would be impossible to replace.'

Miss Rourke was criticized for not taking any courses. Her principal commented on her steady improvement in the teaching of subject matter, and rated her work satisfactory in all phases. (According to one member of the school committee, the principals all denied having made any critical comments about their teachers until the superintendent"s file with the comment cards was produced as evidence.)

Mrs. Whittaker's name provoked a lengthy discussion. Mr. Kittredge reported that she had struck a child in the classroom. Others reported that parents had stopped them in the street to complain about her. She had a hot temper which led her to pull hair, swear, and thump heads down on desks *hard*, according to an assortment of reports. Mr. Fisher commented that no complaints had ever come to him. He reminded Mr. Kittredge that he was one of two members of the school committee who had personally urged Mrs. Whittaker to return to teaching.

In discussing this case subsequently, members of the school committee stated that for three years the superintendent had been instructed to advise this teacher to take some courses to bring herself up to date on modern educational principles. He had also been asked to warn her about too harsh discipline. The superintendent denied all this, insisted that he had never heard any complaints about the teacher, and had not been instructed by the committee to take any action concerning Mrs. Whittaker.

Miss Brown was criticized for her tactless and peculiar personality, as well as for her failure to take courses. Several of the committee had anecdotes to illustrate how odd and unsociable she was. It was also noted that in her nine years of teaching in another state she had never been given a tenure appointment.

Mrs. Foster made one very emphatic statement. "Center Hill has too many older teachers without four-year academic degrees. It will give us a bad rating if we continue to appoint teachers who barely meet certification requirements, and who make no effort to acquire advanced professional degrees. The State Director of Education commented to me on the proportion of teachers in our community who do not meet the modern requirements. It is my own personal opinion that teaching is a profession, and that people who show no professional interest should be eliminated."

There was some additional discussion, after which the principals were dismissed. When the vote was taken, it was found that the committee had voted unanimously against giving tenure appointments to Mrs. Gordon, Mrs. Whittaker, and Miss Brown. With one dissenting vote they refused to appoint Miss Partington to a permanent position. Mrs. Marsie and Miss Rourke were given tenure contracts. It was after one o'clock in the morning when this meeting broke up. Mr. Kittredge, according to his later statement, then turned to make the following remark to Mr. Fisher, "Will you see that these teachers are notified of this action?" Everyone departed from the meeting in a weary frame of mind.

5 Center Hill—Act III
The Community Reacts

There were various impressions of how the firing of the four teachers was actually made public. Some citizens felt that the action was formally announced in the *Center Hill Herald,* the weekly newspaper which customarily gave only a brief account of the committee meeting. Two of the dismissed teachers felt that "everyone at school knew before I did." Another commented, "No one knew, not even the principal." One of the principals remarked, "I just assumed that the joint recommendation of superintendent and principal would be accepted, as always. There was no reason to think otherwise. When they questioned me I had nothing but a satisfactory report to give. I even told my teacher that she had been given the tenure appointment."

According to Mr. Fisher, the school committee voted on the tenure appointments after the principals and superintendent had made their statements and been dismissed. He described himself as stunned when he received notification in the morning about the committee's vote. Miss Walker said she was alarmed about him, he appeared so shaken and upset. The official notification said, "On March 28 the Center Hill School Committee voted not to grant tenure appointments to the following teachers: Miss Brown, Mrs. Gordon, Miss Partington, and Mrs. Whittaker. Please notify them immediately." Over and over again Mr. Fisher moaned, "What can I say to them? What can I say? They don't deserve this!" He dictated several versions of a letter to the teachers, but none satisfied him. He finally decided to repeat the message sent to him by the school committee.

School Department
Office of the Superintendent
Center Hill, March 29, 1950

Dear Miss Partington,

On March 28 the Center Hill School Committee voted not to grant you a tenure appointment. I was requested to notify you of this action immediately.

Yours truly,

MAF/bw

Morgan A. Fisher

He felt that this communication fulfilled the directive of the school committee. Later the members of the school committee blamed "the unsatisfactory letter" for much of the trouble. At one time Mr. Fisher was called before them to explain why he had not called the teachers in to inform them personally, which was his customary action when a teacher was not to be retained. At this same meeting the school board also questioned him about an expression of loyalty he allegedly made to the teachers. He was reminded that his first loyalty should be to the board. Mr. Fisher denied having made such a comment. For purposes of clarification he asked that the following statement be put on the record. "My loyalty is at all times with the school committee, and my sympathy is with the teachers."

The four teachers were doubly shocked by the letter; they were astonished by the news it contained and by its cold tone. At first they were stunned and totally uncertain what to do. Each one wondered to whom she could turn for help. They appealed to their friends in the community for assistance and advice. The news of the committee action spread quickly.

The other members of the faculty and many people in the community greeted the information with consternation and strong criticism. From parents, from former associates, and from fellow townsmen came words of praise for the teachers. Letters to the editor were written by citizens particularly interested in the schools, and by those concerned with fair treatment for all town employees. The *Center Hill Herald* of April 6 carried on the front page two letters which commented on the action of the School Committee, as reported in the March 31 edition. One letter was written by the president of the Teachers' Club; the other was written by Miss Winslow, an author who had run unsuccessfully for the school committee from the Willowdale district. She was a close friend of one of the dismissed teachers.

Under the direction of Mr. Wendall, president of the Teachers' Club, the action was publicly condemned as unfair, and a demand was made that the matter be reconsidered. The club held a meeting crowded with tense, indignant teachers. A letter was sent from the meeting to the chairman of the school committee, demanding that the dismissal action be reconsidered. The secretary of the club, a fifth-grade teacher who was a close friend of Mrs. Whittaker, delivered the message to Mr. Kittredge, and reported to the teachers that he stood on his front steps and cursed her, threatening to have her fired.

The dismissed teachers requested an opportunity to appear before the school committee for an explanation of the action and for an opportunity to appeal the decision. Individual appointments for the teachers were scheduled with the school committee for approximately fifteen minutes apiece. When the date of the appointments needed to be changed in order that an attorney provided by the state unit of the National Education Association might attend, the school committee denied the request and specifically stated that no one would be permitted to accompany the teachers at the interviews.

Meanwhile irate citizens were informally getting together. The Woodward School P.T.A. denounced the action taken. It demanded that the school committee hold a public hearing, or voluntarily resign. The policy of keeping school committee meetings closed to the public was sharply criticized, especially by the *Center Hill Herald.* In the midst of the community furor the school committee issued a public resolution which stated that the "matter of teacher appointments and reasons for nonrenewal of contracts is not a matter for public debate." The weekly newspaper featured the school committee's difficulties as front-page news. According to Mr. Kittredge, the editor of the local paper had long been angry at the school committee for refusing to withhold information from a daily newspaper which competed for circulation with his weekly. While the dismissed teachers and the critics of the school committee praised the paper highly for its fair coverage, the school committee condemned it for prejudiced and deliberately inaccurate reporting.

A small group of civic leaders informally requested the school committee to meet with a community committee to discuss the matter of the dismissals. According to the town moderator, this request was refused by Mr. Kittredge on the grounds that there would be no time to discuss it with his committee. As the moderator told of this he shook his head and commented, "Such stubbornness!"

At the regular meeting of the school committee on April 18, an informal group appeared in the school office. The town moderator, who was one of those present, described the gathering. "This was a spontaneous group of individuals concerned about the matter. A group of about fifty had gathered by eight o'clock, the hour set for the meeting. The school committee did not appear until nine o'clock, although there was no explanation of this delay. A spokesman for the group of citizens requested that they be admitted to discuss the dismissal problem. His old friend, Mr. Kittredge, replied, 'I'm sorry, but we meet in executive session. No outsider is permitted to attend.' There was further sputtering by some citizens, and a demand for an opportunity to ask questions. This was ignored by the school committee, and the gathering broke up quickly. The citizens had come in calmness, but they left in fury."

Mr. Kittredge felt differently. He stressed that this group of citizens did not attend the meeting spontaneously, although he felt it was possible that some of the individuals came of their own accord without knowing what was afoot. "Actually, several days before the meeting took place one person called me to request a meeting. I told him I would take it up with my committee and try to arrange a date. On the day of the meeting I had several people call me to warn me, 'there would be trouble' that night. People were being rounded up to attend. We didn't meet until nine o'clock because one member was involved in a church supper, although people seem to think there were other reasons. As we climbed the stairs we could hear people talking. It sounded like the angry buzzing of bees. You could feel the hostility. When we were asked to discuss the teacher dismissals, I asked my committee what they wanted to do. We decided to hold a regular executive meeting with the business we had planned. I announced the decision to the people there. There were glaring faces, the shaking of fists, shouting, threats hurled at me. I will never forget it as long as I live. It was a disgusting exhibition — people who had the advantage of excellent education and environment doing what you would expect a mob to do. It was a difficult thing to control. Nothing could have been accomplished. They had come to spank, not to listen. I would still refuse to yield to mob pressure and divulge private information."

Community feeling climbed higher. The teachers who were fired came from different schools, under the supervision of different principals. As a result, all sections of the community were involved. The suggestion that the entire committee resign voluntarily seemed to grow in community favor. To this request the committee paid no heed, although one member informally expressed his willingness to resign if the other members would join him. Gradually there developed a demand that the group be ousted. This would require action by the state legislature. The idea of involving outsiders in an unpleasant community episode did not appeal to many people, but there were abundant signatures for a petition demanding the removal from office of all concerned.

The group which felt rebuffed by the school committee when they attempted to attend a regular committee meeting had taken immediate action. They had crossed the street to the home of one of the group and established themselves formally as the Citizens' Committee. Miss Winslow was chosen as chairman. The tentative plan of the Citizens' Committee was to attempt to sound out community feeling and to make a thorough investigation of the whole situation. Miss Winslow said that they wanted to work cautiously in the hope of developing a constructive plan of action. Legal counsel was retained.

The school committee took no official cognizance of the existence of this group, and repeated its statement that this was "not a matter for public discussion." Some in the community interpreted this remark as meaning that "something about morals must be involved." The Citizens' Committee did not want to publicize any behavior which the school committee might be keeping quiet to protect the reputation of some individual. But at the same time, they felt that the unexplained action was itself having a damaging effect on the reputations of the teachers.

At first the school committee had flatly turned down a suggestion that an "impartial" committee be allowed to consider its action in not appointing the four teachers. However, after some persuasion by businessmen and other community leaders, who feared the school scandal would have a bad effect on the summer tourist trade, the school committee did consent to the formation of an Arbitration Committee composed of nine members: three members from the school committee, three members from the Citizens' Committee, and three members-at-large to be chosen with the approval of the six partisan members. The nine-man committee met for two long sessions to consider the evidence presented by the school committee to explain and justify their action. The final report of this group was never made public.

Mr. Kittredge quoted the report as stating, "The school committee was clearly acting in good faith. . . . In view of the community uproar it might be wise to reconsider the action and rehire Miss Partington." A member of the Citizens' Committee commented, "There was no evidence presented which could not have been made public. I still feel that the action was arbitrary and unjust."

The school committee rejected the recommendation of the Arbitration Committee, although the Citizens' Committee, which had wanted to rehire all of the teachers, was willing to accept the compromise suggestion. The school committee apparently felt that to make any change under public pressure would weaken its own position, and be unfair to all of the teachers who had not been rehired. Actually the arbitration procedure did not seem to satisfy either group. The citizen group had expected to find "the real reasons" for the action. The school group had expected to find "support" for its action. The fact that none of the report was made public caused some community dissatisfaction.

As they probed the problem of the tenure appointments, the Citizens' Committee felt that there were many problems related to the total educational program of Center Hill which needed scrutiny. The Puerto Rican population of the town (about 28 per cent of the total population) claimed that their children were discriminated against. The schools in their section were less well-maintained, and there had been a long struggle to have even adequate lunchroom facilities provided. The lunchroom quarrel had been brought to the floor of the town meeting, against the wishes of the school committee. The town had granted funds to equip the cafeteria over the objection of the school committee. An attempt to form a P.T.A. group at one of the primarily Puerto Rican schools had been resisted by the principal and the school committee for years. This long struggle had reached "riot" proportions at one meeting where a school committee member referred to the pupils as "brats." All the elementary schools now had P.T.A. groups, but there was nothing to indicate that they ever met together or worked on common projects.

There were many specific criticisms of the school system. Retardation in the Center Hill schools was about 30 per cent, and Puerto Rican parents particularly complained about this. Evidence was produced to show that the chief activity in the Special Class was wood handicraft and that there was little effort to teach these children to read or write. In spite of the apparent unity of community opinion about the firing of the teachers, there seemed to be wide racial and economic splits, and many other divisions of opinion, when it came to judging the local school situation. The Citizens' Committee realized that deep-seated community fissures were growing ever wider under the pressure of these school arguments.

In spite of all the inquiry no further statements were forthcoming to explain the reasons for the four dismissals. The only reason which was officially disclosed was the failure of the teachers to take courses for purposes of professional improvement during their three years of service. Actually, one teacher had been given an appointment who had not met this requirement either. Other members of the faculty declared that they had interpreted the clause about taking courses as necessary for salary increments, but not as required in order to receive a contract. This was the way Mr. Fisher had interpreted the statement. None of the teachers felt they had any warnings or complaints which would have led them to expect dismissal. Mrs. Whittaker, particularly, stressed her shock at being dropped as a teacher when she had never been criticized or warned, and therefore had no opportunity to improve or resign. Miss Winslow, a good friend, commented that everyone was worried that Mrs. Whittaker would have a complete nervous breakdown as a result, because she showed little improvement as time went by, and definitely felt her whole life had been ruined.

Each of the teachers finally had her individual interview with the school committee. The superintendent of schools was also invited to attend the sessions. Each teacher faced her interview as a great ordeal. Mrs. Whittaker had to be given sedatives by her physician before she could attend. Each teacher returned from the meeting to report to representatives of the Citizens' Committee, including its medical and legal counsel. All felt humiliated by the school committee procedure. They reported that no further charges were made against them, that no additional explanation was given, and that no apologies were offered. Each felt that the committee sat merely to go through the motions of providing an opportunity for an appeal. Each described the atmosphere as hostile. Mr. Fisher had sat with his head bowed through most of the session. The school committee said that each teacher was given the reason for the action, and an apology for the rude letter of notification.

On April 26 an open meeting was sponsored by the Citizens' Committee. The meeting was publicized in the press as an opportunity for citizens to get together to exchange opinions on what could be done, and to find out more about what had been going on. The school committee was invited, but none of the members appeared. About 350 people attended the meeting, which was held in the Town Hall. The town moderator complied with a request to attend the meeting in the capacity of chairman, and a popular minister of the community gave the invocation. The Citizens' Committee explained to the moderator that they wanted a dignified meeting, with no name-calling, and that they felt he could "set the tone" on that level by assuming his customary presiding duties, although the meeting was not an official town meeting. The school committee interpreted the use of the "moderator" and the "invocation" as an attempt to create an official town meeting atmosphere.

Miss Winslow gave an explanation of the Citizens' Committee, how it was formed, its purpose, and the details of becoming a member. Any who were interested were invited to join. The first business was a report by two teachers concerning their private interviews with the school committee. One described her feelings as "disgust and humiliation." It was clear that the assembled group were predominantly in sympathy with the dismissed teachers. The account in the *Herald* stated: "The men and women who gathered last night had made up their minds on the school controversy. They came together to vote a protest and not to talk about it. There was restraint in the management of the proceedings, and restraint in the remarks. There were no fireworks. Applause was frequent. Even the observation that a 'million-dollar school and a ten-cent school committee don't go together' was put mildly."

The meeting passed several resolutions. The group charged the school committee with failing a public trust. They demanded that the entire committee resign, "not later than 4:00 p.m. EDT, May 7, 1950." The failure of the committee to attend this meeting was heartily condemned. It was resolved that in the event the school committee refused to resign, a petition to have a special town meeting to recall the school committee be circulated, and people were asked to sign such a petition as they left the hall so that it would be ready when and if needed. (Actually such action by a town meeting would have no legal basis.)

As the Citizens' Committee met night after night to consider the situation, they began to feel that there was more behind the community furor than the four dismissals. The consternation arising out of this action was not, in their opinion, merely the result of this immediate situation. Many felt that it was not suitable for a school superintendent to be boarding at the home of an unattached woman. His personal charm and friendliness had caused many others to overlook some aspects of his private life. He also had powerful friends in the newspaper editor and in the popular high school principal. Others emphasized that the situation between Fisher and his school committee had long been strained. There had been a long struggle for power, and the school administrator had lost much of the authority of the position. The relationship between Fisher and Kittredge was particularly poor; they had been at swords' points for a number of years. Another member of the school committee was reported to have long held a grudge against the superintendent for the firing of a relative from the school system.

Yet no one felt well enough acquainted with the schools to make specific suggestions, and while the committee wanted to give full consideration to all segments of feeling in the community in accomplishing their stated objective, "to undertake constructive action to improve the Center Hill school system," they wondered how widely to spread their activity.

6 Insubordination

Ralph Nash, Assistant Superintendent of Instruction in Southern City, found a note on the desk when he returned to his office in the administration building. It said only, "Call from Miss Ella Morss, 12:15, November 16. Please call back." Mr. Nash reached for the phone. Ella Morss had recently been appointed principal of Booker T. Washington School, a Negro seven-grade elementary building on the western edge of Southern City. Mr. Nash was a bit anxious as he waited for the call to go through. Miss Morss was a Negro woman who was not given to making unexpected calls to headquarters. Above all things, she had considerable stability. Nash had heard rumors at the time of her appointment that some of her own race had made the comment, "Why, Ella is just plain slow stuff! But maybe that's what they want uptown." Nash sighed. He held the wire while someone went to search for Miss Ella Morss, who was out of her office.

Mr. Beauregard, Assistant Superintendent in Charge of Personnel, and Mr. Nason, Superintendent, had spent considerable time in consultation with the Negro principals before making the Morss appointment. All of the staff had then felt that the Negro principals were wholeheartedly in favor of her. Still, as Mr. Nash knew, it was never possible to be absolutely certain what they wanted. A session of that sort was generally a push-and-pull affair where the Negroes attempted to guess what the white administrators wanted in order that they might want the same thing. It was hard to get a frank opinion from them when the "people from downtown" came around for a consultation. Nash guessed it was just lack of practice in decision-making, or perhaps it was "loyalty to the administration" which had done more for them than had any previous one. Finding the right kind of leadership among the Negroes was a problem, the complexity of which never failed to amaze Mr. Nash, a lifelong resident of the South.

At last Miss Morss was on the phone. "Hello, Mr. Nash, I'm sorry that I was out of the office when you called."

"Perfectly all right, Miss Morss," Nash said. "We'd be worried if you weren't. I had a message on my desk saying you called."

There was a long silence at the other end of the wire. "Mr. Nash . . . I wonder if we could talk frankly about a certain matter . . . not on the phone. I'd rather . . . I mean, it is pretty important."

"Certainly. Would you like me to come out there?"

"I'll come downtown if you'd like."

There was another lengthy pause. "Would you like me to come out?" Nash asked again. He debated the matter with himself, and decided that Miss Morss wanted him to come out but was too polite to say so. "I'll come out," he told her. "I have something to do out in Thomas School anyway."

"Well, I don't want to trouble you."

"No trouble at all. I'll be out there around 1:30."

Driving out through the crowded Negro district on the western edge of town, Nash wondered what had occasioned the call from Miss Morss. If he could have gotten a hint on the phone, he would have had a bit more time to think about it, but Miss Morss had said, "talk frankly," and that meant that it would have embarrassed her to talk on the phone. He couldn't think what the reason for the call might be.

Washington School was overcrowded. All the schools in the western district were. A new elementary building was through the planning stage, and although things were moving slowly, they were moving, and Nash rather doubted that Miss Morss would concern herself with matters outside her building. She was the solid kind who knew her job; as she said, "I mind my business, which is teaching children." She had been in the system over twenty years and she was well liked by Negroes and Whites. More than half of her staff were older teachers, like herself, without as much formal training as many of the younger Negro teachers in other schools, but to Nash's way of thinking just as good. They did their job and stayed away from headquarters. There was also a sizable group of new teachers. One teacher in the fifth grade there, a Miss Davis, did have considerably more formal training than the others. She had a year of course work beyond her Master's degree at Columbia, and she had almost six years of teaching experience in both Northern and Southern schools. Mr. Nash wondered a little about Miss Davis. She had asked for a transfer to Washington School from her former position in an elementary school across the city. The reason for the transfer had been "to be nearer my home." Nash had heard rumors that there was more behind it. About two years before, Miss Davis had gained national recognition for a student project in Democracy and a series of papers written by her seventh-grade children giving their interpretation of Democracy. She was bright, Nash knew, but he had heard rumors that Miss Davis could be hard to handle.

Miss Morss was in her office, and it was obvious to Nash that she had been waiting there since his call. The office clerk went out and closed the door.

"I don't want to complain about anybody," she began. "Don't think I'm that kind, Mr. Nash. I'm not."

"Suppose we hear about it," Nash suggested.

More agitated than Mr. Nash had ever seen her, Miss Morss launched into a lengthy and rapid recitation. It appeared that Miss Davis had been a constant source of friction since her appearance at Washington School in September. Washington School furnished all new teachers with a Course of Study Guide and a booklet entitled *A Summary Statement of Philosophy at Washington School.* At the first teachers' meeting of the year, upon receiving her copy of these documents along with the class schedules and other mimeographed material, Miss Davis had given a loud groan, and had then begun to laugh. " 'We believe that a democratic political system is the most desirable way of life,' " Miss Davis read from the first paragraph of the *Statement of Philosophy.* "Why, that's fine — just fine." She continued to read. " 'He — I guess they mean the student — must be cognizant of the supreme value of personality, freedom, equality of opportunity, and social change.' Freedom and equality," she said. "Fancy that!" The rest of the staff of Washington School were silent. Miss Morss had been explaining a matter of routine to one of the new teachers. She turned toward Miss Davis. "Don't you believe in our philosophy?" she asked.

"Believe in it," Miss Davis said. "Why, Miss Ella, there isn't anything to believe in here. This is just words. How are some of these fine phrases going to be translated into something real?"

"I guess that's our job," Miss Morss said simply.

"Well, I'd sure rewrite this book," Miss Davis said. "I'd make it real and meaningful. Not just words."

Miss Morss turned back to the new teacher. Miss Davis, seeing that the other teachers were staring at her, became silent.

From that day on Miss Davis had done nothing but carp and criticize. She referred to Miss Morss openly as "Miss Ella," a title Miss Morss found embarrassing. She openly ridiculed the rather conservative views Miss Morss expressed at teachers' meetings. "I know I'm not as smart as she is," Miss Morss admitted to Mr. Nash. "But I've been around long enough to know how to get along with people — Negro or White."

During the fall Miss Davis continually caused trouble in the school. She had criticized the study guide and this had provoked a quarrel with Miss Morss. "I guess I handled that wrong," Miss Morss admitted. "I blew up and told her to teach the way it said in the book. This was wrong. When I thought it over, I went to her and told her to make any revisions she wanted to. She did a good job, but then she went around telling all the other teachers that I had to back down and depend on her for ideas."

It also appeared that Miss Davis was not happy with the fifth grade. She had been with seventh-grade children before and with children from more prosperous Negro families. These children had been able to "think," according to Miss Davis. She complained that the children in Washington School were nothing more than "citified field hands." Miss Morss had explained that three of her oldest teachers were in the seventh grade, to which Miss Davis had replied: "That's what I mean. Everything around here is moldy. We need new ideas." Miss Morss had tried to pacify her by promising that she would get the first seventh-grade opening, but Miss Davis was not easily put down.

"The thing is bringing about a split among us," Miss Morss said. "A lot of the new teachers are following Miss Davis. They are impatient and want things done faster. The older ones are like I am. They go slower."

As he listened to Miss Morss, Mr. Nash began to remember some things about Miss Davis. Two weeks before he had heard a rumor about Negro teachers who had quarreled among themselves over the matter of inviting a Negro college professor to address a P.T.A. meeting. The professor had a reputation for making explosive and embarrassing statements on the question of segregation. According to the story, the older members of the staff of one Negro school had held out for not inviting the professor. The younger members, led by a teacher who had transferred to the school, had resisted the advice of the older teachers and the principal. Nash and the supervisory staff had made no effort to check the accuracy of the story. It was the sort of thing that was best handled by the principal. Furthermore, cooler heads had prevailed, and the professor had not been invited. Nash now felt certain that the story had originated at the Washington School. In all probability this had occasioned Miss Morss' call. She felt that the situation was getting outside the school and beyond her control. And yet she would never specifically tell Nash of that incident. Women of Miss Davis' talent were all too few, and no other member of her race would jeopardize Miss Davis' career by reporting her to the people uptown as an "agitator." Nash felt that the Negro principals trusted the administration and were extremely loyal to it, but that they had their own problems and worked them out in their own way.

"Well," Mr. Nash said, when Miss Morss had finished, "do you want me to talk to Miss Davis?"

"Oh, no. I don't think that would be good. She isn't easy to talk to. And I don't want her reported uptown. She's a good teacher." Miss Morss thereupon launched into fulsome praise of Miss Davis. Miss Davis had started a committee to re-evaluate the whole curriculum of Washington. Miss Davis had interested the students in historical trips, and in projects in state history. Miss Davis was functioning as a critic teacher with the new staff members. Miss Davis had rejuvenated the P.T.A. Miss Davis had organized a rhythm band and reorganized the school paper and the debating club. She had interested the P.T.A. in a drive to collect the money for basketball uniforms. "If she were punished," Miss Morss said, "people would say I was jealous of her." She smiled and added: "Maybe I am at that. But for the good of the school I think something should be done."

Miss Morss thereupon proposed that Miss Davis be transferred to another elementary school in the western district. She suggested Franklin School and advanced two reasons for requesting that school: Mr. Powers, the principal, was a man universally respected by other Negro educators. Because Powers was a man with considerable status, Miss Morss felt that Miss Davis would be less of a problem there. Miss Morss pointed out that she herself was a new principal and had not yet won the respect of her associates. "I order people too much," she said. "I know it, but I can't help myself. Miss Davis can't be ordered."

Mr. Nash nodded. It was a problem common to many of the Negro principals in their first years in office. It was difficult to find leadership that would be both firm and democratic. Often the chain of communication stopped at the principal level. He noted with approval Miss Morss' analysis of her problem, and decided that they had made the right selection in her case. It would be a matter of time. He agreed that Mr. Powers was a man who could handle Miss Davis, get the most out of her driving energy, and still not lose the respect of his staff.

"You said there were two reasons," he prompted Miss Morss. Miss Morss pointed out that there was presently a vacancy in the seventh grade at Franklin School. This job was being held by a substitute teacher until the end of the present half-year. Miss Morss had obviously been in contact with Mr. Powers. She said, "I'm only suggesting now. Miss Davis would be happier in the seventh grade. Those two years between the fifth and seventh are important. She is used to getting more mature children to work with. And the children from Franklin are from better homes. Understand I'm not sticking my nose into other people's business. I'm only suggesting."

"Of course," Mr. Nash agreed. "I won't make the decision anyway. Mr. Beauregard is in charge of personnel. He and Mr. Nason, the superintendent, have the say in the matter."

"Well," Miss Morss said, "I'm only suggesting. I don't want Mr. Beauregard or Mr. Nason to think I'm presuming."

"That's all right," Mr. Nash said. "I'll talk to them about it." He walked with Miss Morss to the door, and they said goodbye. Nash was fairly certain that he had understood Miss Morss. She had called him because she knew he had no official power in the matter of a transfer. She knew, however, that he would contact Mr. Nason and Mr. Beauregard who had the decision. It was an informal procedure, but it was one which was favored by many Negro educators.

Mr. Nash informed Mr. Beauregard and Mr. Nason of the matter at a staff meeting the following morning. Both Mr. Beauregard and Mr. Nason had heard rumors that Miss Davis was "troublesome" to her principals. Both had had the feeling that her last principal had been relieved to get rid of her.

After being informed by Mr. Nash of the situation in Washington School, Mr. Nason and Mr. Beauregard consulted briefly. Mr. Beauregard proposed that the transfer be made as suggested by Miss Morss. He and Mr. Nason agreed that there was no definite proof of censurable conduct on the part of Miss Davis. However, it was probable that Miss Morss' complaints were justified. Neither man wished to stir up racial controversy in the schools. They did not want to "martyr" Miss Davis, a woman of talent and energy. Nason had met her briefly when the national award was presented to her. He remembered her as a clever, intense woman.

Beauregard and Nason didn't want to jeopardize the leadership of Miss Morss, a woman whom both men respected. Southern City schools operated on a half-year basis, with promotions in January and June, and it was not unusual to make teacher transfers at the end of the first half-year. Mr. Beauregard agreed that if anyone could handle Miss Davis, Mr. Powers was the man for the job.

Mr. Powers was a man of considerable ability in human relations. A big, forceful man, in his mid-fifties, he had a sense of humor and considerable shrewdness in the diagnosis of human motivation. He was born in the deep South, but he had spent most of his early years in the North where he had come by his formal education after being a professional baseball player, a Pullman porter, a construction worker, and an employee in the U.S. Government service. Mr. Beauregard promised to contact Mr. Powers about the impending transfer.

Mr. Powers was in favor of the transfer. He knew Miss Davis by reputation as an able woman, not overly favored with tact but with genuine talent and energy. He suggested that he should call Miss Davis and explain that he had a vacancy in the seventh grade. He proposed to ask her permission to request the transfer. In mid-December he called Miss Davis. She was in favor of the transfer. The superintendent's staff heard no further comment on Miss Davis from Miss Morss. They felt that perhaps the impending transfer had served to quiet both teacher and principal. At any rate, there was no open trouble, and at the end of the half-year the transfer was effected.

In the early spring, Mr. Nash, through one of the supervisors, heard rumors that all was not well at Franklin. Mr. Nash had no direct factual information, but he gathered from the conversation with the supervisor that there was a certain amount of difference of opinion among the teaching staff and Mr. Powers, the principal. Mr. Nash was surprised by this news, for he knew Mr. Powers as a man who got along well with his teachers. While Powers was not a man who yielded easily on an issue, he was no dictator either. Remembering the transfer, Mr. Nash asked, "Does this have anything to do with Miss Davis?"

"I wouldn't want to say," replied the supervisor. "I'm only a visitor to the school. I don't think I should presume to talk about something I don't know about."

A week later at a general meeting of principals and administrative staff, Mr. Beauregard happened to be discussing a matter of personnel policy with Principal Powers. During the course of the conversation, Mr. Beauregard sensed that Mr. Powers had some matter which he hesitated to mention. Beauregard hesitated to press for information, but having worked for many years with Powers he felt that he knew him well enough to do so. "How is Miss Davis working out?" Beauregard asked.

"Well," Mr. Powers said, "since you have asked me officially, and I didn't bring the matter to you, I'll tell you. Not so good." Mr. Powers then went into detail.

The pattern was much the same as it had been at Washington School, only slightly more intense. Because Franklin School already had "things going," as Mr. Powers put it, Miss Davis found considerably fewer outlets for her energy than she had had at Washington. To compensate for this, she had become involved in matters of school policy which Powers felt were no concern of hers. She was constantly opposing him in staff conferences. He had at first ignored her opposition or attempted to joke her out of it, but this seemed only to provoke Miss Davis. Her attempts to set herself up as the unofficial critic teacher on the Franklin staff were welcomed neither by Mr. Powers nor by his teachers, who had had considerably more experience than this new member of the staff at Franklin.

Miss Davis had had less than six years' classroom teaching experience. Some of the teachers she was attempting to advise had more than twenty. "And two or three of her years were spent teaching in the North," Powers said, "where things are different. I think she has too many years talking and reading about teaching and not enough doing it." Powers, as Beauregard knew, was not an opponent of graduate training for teachers. Powers held an advance degree from Columbia as did Miss Davis. Powers said: "I think the difference is that I've put ten years of experience on top of that training. She hasn't. It's still shiny for her."

Powers also alleged, and this seemed more serious to Beauregard, that Miss Davis persisted in getting between him and the parents in the P.T.A. Powers had organized a strong P.T.A. in his school. He had built it around recognized leaders of the district. Miss Davis was already coming into conflict with these people, who advocated a much slower program than she. At one meeting she had openly criticized people who "dragged their feet while big things were in the wind."

Powers, then, was in an unusual spot. Miss Davis was an able teacher, admired by other Negro educators. Powers could only gain unpopularity for himself if he brought her before the administration with a charge of insubordination. Beauregard felt that this was what was involved. If Miss Davis had provoked Powers into going as far as he had, there was much more to it that the administration had not heard.

"I'm not saying this to get you to take action," Powers said. "That is exactly what we don't want. I just want you and Mr. Nason to know what's going on here." Mr. Powers then recited the same litany of praise for Miss Davis which Miss Morss had given. Miss Davis was a good teacher. Her students were devoted to her and worked up to capacity. A citizenship exhibit by her class had occasioned much favorable comment among Negro educators in the area. Her Social Studies program was a model for other Negro teachers. She enjoyed the support and admiration of many of the parents, and she had done some notable guidance work with some of Franklin School's severest problem cases. "I'd like to give it another month," Mr. Powers said. "Perhaps in that time I can catch it. If I can't . . ." He lifted his shoulders. Mr. Beauregard made no specific recommendation to Mr. Powers. He knew that Powers would talk to Miss Davis, and that Mr. Powers would do anything possible to prevent an unpleasant situation.

When Mr. Beauregard reported the matter to Mr. Nason, the superintendent expressed some concern. "What we need least of all," Nason said, "is an agitator. But I don't guess we can take any action now."

Two weeks had scarcely passed when the administration began to notice portents of a coming storm at Franklin School. Articles in one of the extreme Negro papers criticized the present "go-slow policy" of the Negro educators.

The articles bore the unmistakable sign of having been written by a Negro teacher in the schools of Southern City. One of the office staff had a copy of some of the material which Miss Davis had prepared at the time of her national award exhibit. Some of the phrasing matched the articles word-for-word. News also traveled in from some leading Negroes that Miss Davis was making "a big stir" in the town.

In the first week of May, the administration received an unsigned letter which alleged that Miss Davis had delivered several "inflammatory speeches." Mr. Nason ordered the letter destroyed and requested that its contents be forgotten by members of the staff. At the end of the same week a second letter came to Superintendent Nason from Mr. Powers. Mr. Powers described a situation at a staff conference where Miss Davis had refused to obey orders. The occasion for the dispute involved a procedural matter — the forming of lines to enter the building after recess. The doorways at Franklin School were narrow, and Mr. Powers had decided that, to insure the safety of the younger children, straight and orderly lines had to be formed by the teachers on recess duty. The recess ran into two shifts, one group going out to the play-yard while the other entered. Miss Davis said: "I agree on the safety angle. But I'm not making *my* kids do a lock step into school."

"It's either an orderly line or no line at all," Mr. Powers argued.

"Well, I won't pull kids into line like they were soldiers or prisoners," Miss Davis insisted. "Its not good for them."

Mr. Powers confessed that at this point he had lost his temper. "You'll do it," he told her. "And I'll be out there tomorrow to see you."

"We'll see," Miss Davis muttered.

The next morning, according to Mr. Powers' letter, Miss Davis had deliberately turned her back on him and the line of children. Mr. Powers had gone to her room immediately after school and informed her that he was going to bring the matter to the attention of the superintendent. Miss Davis had laughed.

Powers, in his letter, did not request that a charge of insubordination be formally lodged against Miss Davis. He suggested only that the superintendent write Miss Davis a letter censuring her for "unprofessional conduct." A copy of the letter could then be put into her record folder. Mr. Powers pointedly added that he felt any further punishment would be unwise. Behind this Mr. Nason sensed a warning not to make a martyr of Miss Davis.

Nason followed the suggestion and sent Miss Davis a letter of official censure. He received in reply a letter from Miss Davis which said that she did not clearly understand the charges against her. Mr. Nason wrote her that he did not propose to go into the formal aspects of the charge at that time because she was not formally charged with anything. There was no further communication from Miss Davis.

During the last part of May and early June there was no open activity on the part of Miss Davis. Rumors and hints of trouble, however, still drifted in from time to time. The administration guessed that Miss Davis was still active but that she was more guarded in her operations.

In late June the administration staff had sent out most of the contracts and assignments for the following year. Mr. Powers appeared at Mr. Beauregard's office with the request that Miss Davis be transferred from his school. Mr. Nason was called into the conference. Mr. Powers detailed a long list of instances which involved insubordination in the school and agitation in the community.

"Would you like to file formal charges against her?" Mr. Nason asked.

"No, Mr. Nason, I wouldn't. I'd just like to see her out of my school."

"Well," Mr. Nason said, "we've been pretty patient with her. This is the third request for transfer in a year. We can't go on passing her around the system forever."

"Lord knows I tried to work with her," Mr. Powers said. "I tried and I tried."

"Maybe we should get rid of her," Beauregard suggested. "Some of these things have happened since the letter of censure."

Mr. Powers did not favor this suggestion. He said, "I know it's not up to me to suggest what to do. Let's put it this way. I don't want to charge her formally with insubordination."

Mr. Nason agreed that they should think the matter through more carefully. After Mr. Powers had gone, Mr. Beauregard and Mr. Nason went over the case. The administrative staff had good reasons not to want Miss Davis speaking as the official representative of the schools of Southern City. If she alienated enough people, the program for new buildings and general improvement of facilities would be jeopardized. Some of the more active Whites had already approached Mr. Nason in the matter of Miss Davis. Nason had pending before the City Council requests for two million dollars in capital expenditure for new buildings. The City Realtor's office had several requests for land-taking to expand playyards and to build additions to existing plants. Behind it all, the question of integration was causing both Whites and Negroes to be restive and tense. Mr. Nason feared that some radical elements among the Whites might make proposals to sell the schools to private interests for one dollar, a move which would jeopardize the general structure of public education in the South. The Plan of South Carolina was enough to give Mr. Nason great concern. He was professionally committed to public education, and he felt considerable loyalty to his profession. For this reason it was a most inopportune time to have Miss Davis making rash statements in the community.

On the other hand, he had no wish to antagonize the Negroes or to provide the more radical among them with a "martyr." He was unable to assess exactly the degree to which Miss Davis had the backing of her people. He knew that some of them were opposed to her tactics. Also to be considered was Mr. Powers' recommendation not to take the matter any further. It was upon men like Powers that the administration would have to lean in the difficult times ahead. Powers, with his immense popularity, was the sort of man who could be depended on to see that a sane program of change could be implemented.

Within the school there was no question that Miss Davis was a handicap rather than a help. Franklin had been a good school before her arrival. Whatever good she had accomplished was more than offset by her fractious behavior.

There was no real sources of guidance in the matter of Miss Davis. Most Whites would have recommended her immediate dismissal. Most Negroes would have favored patience. Mr. Nason sat down to consider her contract for the following year. Mr. Beauregard favored not giving her a contract. He felt that the administration had a clear-cut case of insubordination against Miss Davis. After considerable debate Mr. Nason and Mr. Beauregard agreed that the best course of action was to put Miss Davis on probation for one semester, to transfer her, and to offer her a one-semester contract.

Miss Davis was brought down to the office the next morning, and Mr. Nason and Mr. Beauregard informed her of their decision. Without going into full details they told her some of the charges made against her by her last two principals.

Miss Davis said, "Well, I'm a little startled by the suddenness of this. I mean I had no idea this was going on."

"We exchanged letters back in May," Nason said. "You must have had some idea at that time."

Miss Davis requested that some of the charges be repeated, and Mr. Beauregard read them to her.

"I guess I had better go home and think about this," Miss Davis finally said. "I'm too unsettled to give an answer at this point."

Two days later Mr. Nason received a letter from Miss Davis. She said that the charges against her were unclear, and that she could not understand them. Nason sent her a letter giving the charges in detail.

A week later Nason received a letter from Miss Davis saying again that his letter was unclear. At this point he decided that she was "baiting" him, and he sent back a short note in which he informed Miss Davis that she was not being dismissed, and that she had an option of signing or not signing the contract. Miss Davis then sent a letter saying that the contract was not clear. She said that she wouldn't sign. Mr. Nason did not answer this letter. Miss Davis waited a week and then sent a letter saying that she was being forced to withdraw and that she would like a formal hearing in the superintendent's office.

Mr. Nason was somewhat agitated by the whole matter at this point. It meant that he had to bring Mr. Powers into the case and proceed with formal charges of insubordination. When informed of what had happened, Mr. Powers said that he would appear and back up his charges. He said that he felt that Miss Davis had been given her chance and had "lawyered her way out of it."

Mr. Nason had the hearing before a three-man subcommittee of the nine-man school board. He had specifically requested that one Negro member of the school board be assigned to the subcommittee to hear Miss Davis. He also hired a court stenographer to record testimony. Mr. Nason anticipated that Miss Davis, who was obviously negotiating with a lawyer, would appear before the committee with counsel.

Nason had called Powers before the meeting started and told him that his appearance was not necessary. He felt that it would seem that Mr. Powers was "on trial." Therefore, the superintendent's office had to take full responsibility for Miss Davis' probation.

Miss Davis appeared before the committee alone. She said briefly that she was not there to contest the charges, that she did not want reinstatement, and that she only wanted a recommendation from Mr. Nason. Mr. Nason answered Miss Davis' request for a recommendation by saying that he would write a letter in which he would give the facts, "good and bad," on her. This was not satisfactory to Miss Davis. After protesting this briefly she left the meeting. After she had gone the committee unanimously upheld Mr. Nason's recommendation. The Negro member came to Mr. Nason and said he considered that Miss Davis had received very fair treatment from the administration. Mr. Nason assumed that the matter was closed.

A week later Miss Davis called Mr. Nason and asked for a "blanket recommendation" which she could use for a teachers' agency form. Mr. Nason said, "I will give you a statement which will say that you have taught three years here and that we offered you a contract which you refused." Miss Davis said that she would think this over.

In a few days Miss Davis appeared at the office and requested the letter. Mr. Nason offered her the letter. At the same time he gave her a letter which contained the complete details of the charges against her and the action taken to date. Miss Davis did not want to accept the second letter, but she finally took it.

Mr. Nason again felt the case was closed. He had refused to give her a blanket recommendation for many reasons. One was the plain matter of professional ethics. He felt that in such serious matters the facts should be on record and not glossed over. Furthermore, a woman like Miss Davis might have used a satisfactory reference against him at a later date. Now he heaved a sigh of relief. The case of Miss Davis was finally closed.

Two days later the secretary on the switchboard sent a call in to Mr. Nason's secretary. Mr. Nason's secretary asked the caller to hold the line while she went to talk to the superintendent. "Mr. Nason," she said, "there is a call for you."

"Who is it?" Mr. Nason asked.

"Miss Davis."

7 *Salary Schedule*

In July, 1950, three "union free" school districts and nine "common school" districts in New York State initiated preliminary talks on the possibility of centralization. Pushed by the lack of adequate elementary school facilities in the predominantly one-room schoolhouses of the common districts and the lack of one first-rate high school unit in the area, the district representatives reached agreement rapidly and petitioned the Commissioner of Education to lay out the area. The Commissioner laid out the area and ordered a vote in which the centralization was passed 856 to 560. The Commissioner thereupon ordered Central School District Valparaiso-1 to be formed; the district was to be joined on July 1, 1951. The total population of the combined area was 6,458.

In July, 1951, a five-member board was elected for the new central district, Valparaiso-1. This board appointed John Racine superintendent of schools, and ordered him to engage teachers for the following year. The estimated enrollment of the new district was 1,345; 952 children were enrolled in Grades 1–8; 394 children were in Grades 9–12. Racine faced a considerable number of problems in the matter of plant consolidation — for example, there was no building wholly adequate to serve as the district high school. Hence he wished to finish the matter of personnel appointment as quickly as possible.

As he understood his mandate from the board in the matter of personnel, three things were involved: (1) retain all teachers presently teaching in the former district schools (common and union free) who wished to continue in the new central district; (2) place all teachers on the Valparaiso-1 schedule according to the minimum salary schedule established by state law; (3) make no salary commitment — at least during the first year when so many other matters were pressing — which was not absolutely necessary.

With these considerations in mind, Racine called for the personnel records of all teachers who wished to teach in the new central district, Valparaiso-1. Forty-six full-time teachers had been employed in the districts. Of this number, two were retiring and hence were not considered. One teacher had married and moved out of the district to a new job. One teacher, who was obviously unfitted by reasons of mental health for her job, had been persuaded not to continue. Racine then was left with a group of forty-two teachers from the former districts, and the necessity of appointing two and perhaps three new teachers for the coming school year.

For his own purposes Racine had constructed forty-two cards, with a summary of pertinent information taken from the personnel records. He grouped the fourteen teachers from the nine common school districts into one class. He had entered the following information on his cards:

TEACHERS FROM NINE COMMON SCHOOL DISTRICTS

Name	*Experience in Years*		Degree	Present Salary	Comment
	Continuous	*Noncontinuous*			
1. Arthurs	2		B	$2,200	
2. Calan		2–1	M	2,300	
3. Davison	18		cert.	2,600	
4. Easley	8		B	2,400	First-rate teacher
5. Johnson	7		B	2,300	
6. Josephs		10–4	B	2,500	
7. Kelley	1		B	2,100	
8. Kuhn	1		M	2,200	
9. Lathrop	17		cert.	2,600	Supervisory experience
10. Lodge	4		B	2,300	
11. Mason	1		B	2,100	
12. Moore	1		B	2,100	
13. Parker	5		B	2,400	
14. Yeats	12		B	2,500	

Racine then took the teachers from Coghill-1, the smallest of the three union free districts. All seven Coghill teachers were to be placed on the schedule. The following salary schedule was in effect in Coghill-1 prior to the consolidation:

SALARY SCHEDULE FOR COGHILL–1

Salary Steps or Years of Service		
1	$2,550	$100 more for Master's degree, or 30 graduate hours beyond the baccalaureate degree.
2	2,650	
3	2,750	
4	2,850	
5	2,950	
6	3,050	
7	3,150	Merit Level One
8	3,250	
9	3,350	
10	3,450	
11	3,550	Merit Level Two
12	3,650	
13	3,750	
14	3,850	

The cards from Coghill-1 showed that all seven teachers from the Coghill District wished to be considered for positions in Valparaiso-1.

TEACHERS FROM COGHILL–1

Name	*Experience in Years*		*Degree*	*For 1951–52: salary step on old schedule*	*Comment*
	Continuous	*Noncontinuous*			
Bodert	26		cert.	14	
Gordon	20		B	14	
Harriss		8–6	M	Step 10 with Master's $3,550	
Kiely	14		B	14	
Love	6		M	Step 6 with Master's $3,150 (first-rate teacher)	
Narricci	5		B	5 (first-rate teacher)	
Welsh	2		B	2	

Racine noticed that while the Coghill-1 schedule had two merit levels [1] beyond the sixth (the usual custom was to have three levels in districts of more than eight teachers), there was no stated per cent of teachers that had to be at the various levels. There was no state requirement for schools with seven teachers or less to do so. All the teachers were placed at the level determined by years of teaching experience with the exception of Miss Flora Harris, who had interrupted her teaching career for five years while serving with her husband in overseas mission work. Apparently the Coghill-1 merit levels had not meant anything, and had never been operative in determining a teacher's position on the salary schedule. Among the Coghill-1 group were two teachers known personally to Mr. Racine as extremely capable people — Miss Love and Miss Narricci. Mr. Racine was very anxious to retain these teachers in the new Valparaiso-1 district.

Racine knew that in order to determine the salaries of the teachers he must consult Article 63, Sections 3101–3104, of the Education Laws of New York. He found the appropriate sections in McKinney's Consolidated Laws of New York, Book 16. Racine also knew that Article 63, Section 3101, of the Education Laws of New York had been changed effective July 1, 1951, and that the articles as set down in the Law of 1947 had been modified and reworded. He knew that both the salary schedules and the manner in which teachers were to be entered on the new schedule were prescribed in the new law. He determined to consult the law and make his calculations exactly in conformance with its provisions.

He decided to finish computing the new salary schedules for all the teachers, including those from the two union free districts, and to fix each teacher from the old districts on the appropriate place on a new schedule, as determined by the Law of 1951. He procured the two schedules from the union free districts and constructed a complete roster of teachers from the cards.

---

[1] The New York State Law of 1947 required the establishment of merit levels to advance fixed percentages of the total teaching staff to each level for all but the smallest districts.

SALARY SCHEDULE FOR LAMBETH-2

Salary Steps or Years of Service	*Bachelor's*	*Master's*	
1	$2,000	2,200	
2	2,150	2,350	
3	2,300	2,500	
4	2,450	2,650	
5	2,600	2,800	
6	2,750	2,950	
7	2,900	3,100	Merit Level One
8	3,050	3,250	(after 6th year 50% of
9	3,200	3,400	teachers)
10	3,500	3,700	Merit Level Two
11	3,500	3,700	(30% at this level or
12	3,500	3,700	above)
13	$3,800	4,000	Merit Level Three
14	3,800	4,000	(not less than 20% of
15	3,800	4,000	teachers)
16	4,100	4,300	Maximum (not less than 10%)

TEACHERS FROM LAMBETH-2

Name	*Experience in years*		*Degree*	*Present Step on Old Schedule for 1951–52*
	Continuous	*Noncontinuous*		
1. P. Astroth	12		M	9
2. Cone		4–3	B	4
3. Dunning	3		B	3
4. Ebring	8		B	8
5. Hubbard		18–4	cert.	16
6. McCarthy	7		B	7
7. Moon	14		B	12
8. Norton	1		B	1
9. Zara	17	9–8 1 yr. leave for Master's	M	15

TEACHERS FROM LAMBETH-1

Name	*Experience in Years*		*Degree*	*Present Step on Old Schedule for 1951–52*
	Continuous	*Noncontinuous*		
1. M. Astroth	15		B	12
2. Booth	12	6–6	B	12 (1 yr. leave)
3. Comptom	7		B	6
4. R. Kelley	3		M	3
5. Levering	13		B	13
6. Newcombe	4		B	4
7. Olsen	10		B	10
8. O'Ryan	13		B	12
9. Perrone	6		B	6
10. Rogers		8–10	M	10
11. Williamson	21		cert.	16
12. Yablonski	2		M	2

SALARY SCHEDULE FOR LAMBETH-1

Salary Steps or Years of Service	*Bachelor's*	*Master's*	
1	$2,150	$2,250	
2	2,300	2,400	
3	2,450	2,550	
4	2,600	2,700	
5	2,750	2,850	
6	2,900	3,000	
7	3,050	3,150	Merit Level One
8	3,200	3,300	(50% of teachers)
9	3,350	3,450	
10	3,600	3,750	Merit Level Two
11	3,600	3,750	(30% of teachers)
12	3,600	3,750	
13	3,900	4,100	Merit Level Three
14	3,900	4,100	(20% of teachers)
15	3,900	4,100	
16	4,200	4,400	Merit Level Four (10% of teachers)

After completing his roster of teachers to be transferred to the Valparaiso-1 schedule, and after studying the schedules from the former districts, Mr. Racine contacted the State Department of Education. He received a copy of the new law, effective July 1, 1951, and with this in hand he began the arduous task of computation and transfer to the new schedule, which was Schedule A of the law effective July 1, 1951. He hoped to have the transfer completed within a week and have a complete estimate of his total teaching salary for the year 1951–52, so he decided to select every third card from his deck of forty-two to see how the transfer would work out.

New York State Law

ARTICLE 63 — SALARIES OF TEACHERS AND SUPERVISORS

Sec.
3101. Definitions.
3102. Powers and duties of school authorities as to salaries.
3103. Minimum salary schedules.
3104. Method of transfer to new schedules.
3105. Minimum salaries for substitute teachers.
3106. Minimum salaries for administrative and other employees.
Schedule of sections added by L.1951, c.756, §5, eff. July 1, 1951

L.1949, c.687, §39, eff. April 18, 1949, repealed former Article 33; section 40 of such chapter renumbered former Article 33–b as added by L.1947, c. 778, to be Article 63.

L. 1949, c. 687, §41, eff. April 18, 1949, renumbered former sections 882–885 as added by L.1947, c.778, to be sections 3101–3104 of this Article.

§*3101. Definitions*

1. "Teachers" shall mean all full-time members of the teaching and supervisory staff of each school district of the state, including, if employed in such district, the superintendent of schools, associate, district or other superintendents, members of the board of examiners, directors, inspectors, supervisors, principals, administrative assistants, first assistants, teachers, lecturers and special instructors, except employees holding the positions enumerated in section thirty-one hundred six of this article.

2. "Year of service" shall mean the number of years which a teacher has served in the school district in which he is employed including the year for which a determination for salary purposes is made. Added L.1951, c. 756, §6, eff. July 1, 1951.

Former section 3101 as amended by L.1949, c. 687, §§41, 42, was repealed by L.1941, c. 756, §2, eff. July 1, 1951.

§*3102. Powers and duties of school authorities as to salaries*

1. The school authorities of each school district of the state employing three or more teachers shall adopt by-laws fixing the salary schedules for all full-time teachers, which schedules shall not be less than the minimum schedules set forth in section thirty-one hundred three of this article.

2. In school districts employing eight or more teachers, such schedules shall provide for regular annual increments for each year of service, except that such by-laws shall incorporate standards and conditions under which each teacher who qualified therefor shall be granted an increment following his twelfth and fifteenth year of service. Such standards and conditions shall be adopted and placed in effect prior to July first, nineteen hundred fifty-two. The school authorities shall provide for the participation of classroom teachers in the formulation and subsequent revision of such standards and conditions.

3. The school authorities shall also adopt by-laws fixing the salaries of administrative and other employees.

4. The school authorities may adopt schedules providing for higher rates of pay than are required by the provisions of this article, through higher salaries and more frequent, larger or additional increments, provided, however, that no salary differential among members of the teaching and supervising staff shall be established on the basis of sex.

5. Nothing contained in this article shall be construed to alter the practice, in certain school districts, of granting salary increments on the anniversary date of appointment.

6. A certified copy of the by-laws containing the salary schedule and the standards and conditions adopted pursuant to subdivision two of this section shall be filed by the school authorities with the state commissioner of education within thirty days after the adoption thereof and not later than July first, nineteen hundred fifty-two. Amendments shall be filed within thirty days after their adoption. Added L.1951, c. 756, §6, eff. July 1, 1951.

Former section 3102, except subd. 11, as amended by L.1948, c. 860; L.1949, c. 775; L.1950, c. 821, §2, was repealed by L.1951, c. 756, §2, eff. July 1, 1951. Said subd. 11 is now subd. 3 of section 3106.

§3103. Minimum salary schedules

1. In school districts employing less than three teachers, the annual salary for teachers shall be not less than two thousand five hundred dollars.

2. In school districts employing at least three teachers, but not more than seven teachers, the minimum salary schedule for teachers which may be fixed in the by-laws adopted pursuant to section thirty-one hundred two of this article shall be as follows:

Step or Year of Service	*Salary*	*Increment*
1	$2,500	
2	2,600	$100
3	2,700	100
4	2,800	100
5	2,900	100
6	3,000	100

3. In school districts employing eight or more teachers, the minimum salary schedules for teachers which may be fixed in the by-laws adopted pursuant to section thirty-one hundred two of this article shall be as follows:

Salary Steps or Years of Service	SCHEDULE A (1)	SCHEDULE A (2)	*Increment*	SCHEDULE B (1)	SCHEDULE B (2)	*Increment*	SCHEDULE C (*refers to New York City*)
1	$2,500	$2,700	....	$2,700	$2,900	....	
2	2,600	2,800	$100	2,815	3,015	$115	
3	2,700	2,900	100	2,930	3,130	115	
4	2,950	3,150	250	3,195	3,395	265	
5	3,100	3,300	150	3,360	3,560	165	
6	3,250	3,450	150	3,525	3,725	165	
7	3,400	3,600	150	3,690	3,890	165	
8	3,550	3,750	150	3,855	4,055	165	
9	3,700	3,900	150	4,020	4,220	165	
10	3,850	4,050	150	4,200	4,400	180	
11	4,000	4,200	150	4,350	4,550	150	
12	4,000	4,200	0	4,350	4,550	0	
13	4,300	4,500	300	4,680	4,880	330	
14	4,300	4,500	0	4,680	4,880	0	
15	4,300	4,500	0	4,680	4,880	0	
16	4,600	4,800	300	5,010	5,210	330	

a. Schedule A shall apply to school districts having a population of less than 100,000 except in the counties of Nassau and Westchester.

b. Schedule B shall apply to school districts having a population of one hundred thousand or more and less than one million, and to school districts in the counties of Nassau and Westchester.

c. Schedule C shall apply to the city of New York.

d. Schedules A (1), B (1) and C (1) shall apply to teachers who hold valid certificates pursuant to the provisions of this chapter.

e. The differential of two hundred dollars provided in schedules A (2), B (2), and C (2) shall be paid to such teachers who have completed a fifth year of preparation; that is, thirty semester hours of approved study beyond the baccalaureate degree, immediately upon their qualifying for such differential. Added L.1951, c. 756, §6, eff. July 1, 1951.

Former section 3103 was repealed by L.1951, c. 756, §2, eff. July 1, 1951.

Public Policy. Laws 1951, c. 756, §1, eff. July 1, 1951, provide: "It has been the declared public policy of the state of New York to require all school districts to pay to each teacher in the public schools a salary not less than a minimum amount at which he can maintain himself, with an appropriate allowance for years of service, educational qualifications, and quality of teaching ability. The establishment of such minimum standards has served to encourage the school districts to employ teachers at a high level of competence and to offer sufficient inducements to retain qualified teachers in the educational systems of the state. Many school districts should and do pay salaries in excess of such state minimums. Others must be directed toward such levels of pay as will maintain and raise standards of teaching. It is a matter of state concern that greater recognition be given to ability, outstanding service and teaching excellence by local initiative in developing workable measures of teaching performance."

§3104. Method of transfer to new schedules, except for substitute teachers.

1. In school districts employing at least three but not more than seven teachers, the school authorities shall not be required to credit any years of service prior to July first, nineteen hundred fifty-one, in placing teachers upon the appropriate schedule contained in section thirty-one hundred three of this article.

2. In school districts employing eight or more teachers, the school authorities shall transfer each teacher to the appropriate schedule contained in section thirty-one hundred three of this article in the following manner: Each teacher whose salary on July first, nineteen hundred fifty, plus any increment regularly granted since that date, was at least as high as a given step in the state minimum schedule in effect on that date, but not as high as the next higher step on such schedule, shall be placed as of July first, nineteen hundred fifty-one, on a step not lower than such given step in the appropriate schedule contained in section thirty-one hundred three of this article. In addition, each teacher shall be entitled to receive an annual increment not lower than that specified in such schedule on July first, nineteen hundred fifty-one, or on such other date during the ensuing school year as may be fixed by the school authorities for payment of increments as provided in subdivision five of section thirty-one hundred two, provided, however:

a. the school authorities shall not be required to place any teacher on a salary step higher than that corresponding to his year of service,

b. each teacher, whose step on the appropriate salary schedule on July first, nineteen hundred fifty-one, is less than his year of service, and whose salary as determined under this subdivision would be increased by less than five hundred dollars as a result of such transfer, shall be entitled to receive an increase in his annual rate of salary not less than five hundred dollars in excess of his annual salary on July first, nineteen hundred fifty, plus any increment regularly granted since that date. This five hundred dollars shall be exclusive of the increment he would be entitled to receive during the school year beginning July first, nineteen hundred fifty-one, according to such schedule. The school authorities in computing such five hundred dollars may include any increase applying to all steps on local schedules granted since June thirtieth, nineteen hundred fifty.

c. No school district shall be required to pay to any teacher the salary provided, beyond the twelfth step on the appropriate schedule prior to July first, nineteen hundred fifty-two.

3. The step upon which a teacher is placed in accordance with paragraphs one and two of this section shall be the base from which advancement on and after July first, nineteen hundred fifty-two, shall be computed, according to the appropriate schedule of section thirty-one hundred three of this article, and no increment shall be paid thereafter less than the increment provided in such schedule except that the increment following the tenth step is not required to raise a salary beyond that prescribed for the eleventh step.

4. Nothing contained in this article shall require a school district to pay to any teacher a salary in excess of the highest step provided in the appropriate schedule contained in section thirty-one hundred three.

5. Any teacher receiving an annual rate of salary, exclusive of any increase provided under a chapter of the laws of nineteen hundred fifty-one entitled "An act to provide for increased compensation for teachers during the period April first to June thirtieth, nineteen hundred fifty-one," higher than that corresponding to his year of service may be retained at such salary until his year of service requires the granting of a whole or partial increment.

6. The compensation to which any teacher would otherwise be entitled on July first, nineteen hundred fifty-one, exclusive of any increase provided under a chapter of the laws of nineteen hundred fifty-one entitled "An act to provide for increased compensation for teachers during the period April first to June thirtieth, nineteen hundred fifty-one" may not be reduced by reason of any provision contained in this article.

7. Notwithstanding any other provision of this article, in the city of New York the compensation to which a high school teacher shall be entitled under the laws in effect prior to July first, nineteen hundred fifty-one, shall not be reduced, irrespective of whether such compensation is greater than that of the highest salary step contained in the schedule appropriate to him contained in section thirty-one hundred three of this article. Added L.1951, c. 756, §6, eff. July 1, 1951.

8 Three Credits in Music

"You know those two boys you asked me to talk to? Well, I did, and I think this is more of an administrative problem than a guidance one. You got a minute?"

"I think so," replied Dan Bennett, the assistant principal at Lincoln Technical High. "Those boys can wait another minute or two, I guess. They've been truant for five days now; another ten minutes won't hurt them. What's the story?"

Malcolm ("Mac") Woodbury, math teacher half-time and guidance counselor for the general-curriculum boys in the other half, lowered his big frame into a chair by Bennett's desk. "You remember those kids wanted to be transferred from Boys' Chorus into some other class. Well, they had a reason for it.

"Apparently that's a hell-raising class they've got there, and these kids don't want any part of it. They're afraid that the teacher's going to flunk the whole class — said she threatened to, or some such thing — and since they're seniors and don't have any extra credits, that would mean they wouldn't graduate.

"I told them they didn't have to worry about it — that they must have misunderstood her, or else she was just mad and spoke before she thought. But they're still worried, and I think I would be too if I were in their shoes.

"They want to switch classes, but there's not a heck of a lot they can take. The only electives open for them are music, astronomy, and art. One of them wants to take art and the other wants the general music appreciation class, but neither of them really cares anything about those courses except as the least of the possible evils. For that matter, they aren't exactly wild about Boys' Chorus, but it seemed like the safest way to get the credits they need to graduate, so why not?

"Now, I've known these boys since they came here three years ago, and they're both O.K. Neither of them's going to set the world on fire, but they mind their own business and keep their noses clean. I don't think they have anything to do with the ruckus that seems to be going on in that class. After all, it's about all you could expect there, anyhow. The class is sort of a dumping ground for loose generals, so half of the kids who are in there don't give a darn about what they're doing, and some of them go a lot further than that. There are troublemakers in that crowd. That Sanborn kid is in there, for instance, and he's got some of his buddies with him."

"I'll tell you what," Bennett broke in. "I could go in that class and yank out three or four right now, and that would end the trouble. And just let me look at the bunch there once and I'd know which three or four to yank, too. When you've been in charge of discipline around here for a few years, you learn fast who the troublemakers are."

"Yeah, that's true," said Mac. "I think I could put my finger on the kids who are causing trouble, too. The only thing is, if you yanked them where would you put them? They've got to go somewhere, don't they?"

"Throw them out," replied Bennett. "If they won't behave themselves, suspend them a while and make their parents come with them before letting them back in. Make them know that they've got to behave themselves, that they've got to respect the rights of the others around here if they're going to stay. After all, the kids in this school are here because they chose Tech. We don't require them to be here. They can go on to the classical or the vocational high if they don't like it here."

"Yeah, I suppose so," said Mac. "Still, we've tried that before, and we've still got the problem on our hands. Another way to get at it might be to transfer the kids who were squawking about the class. That's what they're asking for, anyhow. Or something might be done about the class as a whole. Sooner or later that will probably have to be done anyhow. You know, that's the class with a new teacher. It's kind of tough on her to give a new teacher a class like that. And she's not really the one for such a class anyhow, aside from her lack of experience. Since something's going to have to be done with that class sooner or later in any event, I think it's really more of an administrative problem than a guidance one. I can transfer those two kids O.K., but that won't take care of the problem of the class itself. *You're* going to have to do something about that."

"Before you do anything about switching classes for those boys," said Bennett, "let me talk to the teacher. You and I can get together later and decide what to do about it."

Woodbury heaved himself out of the chair and headed for his classroom to catch up on his paper work. Bennett summoned the two waiting truant boys from the outer office, and the day resumed its normal routine.

Later in the day, Bennett took advantage of a lull to visit Mrs. Bondsen, the teacher of the boys' chorus class. On the way to her room he reviewed what little he knew about her. He remembered that after working as an elementary music supervisor in a nearby system she had come to Lincoln Tech this year to teach part-time. Before that, he remembered, she had taught in a small college somewhere in the Midwest. He wondered whether her husband was living and whether she needed the job or was just interested in keeping occupied. One thing was sure; the school surely needed her. They had one full-time music teacher, and they didn't quite need another such. And part-time music teachers were hard to find — at least those with any experience in the public schools. It would be different if there were a symphony orchestra around; symphony musicians very often would take a part-time job like this — but there just weren't any in this town. They couldn't afford to lose Mrs. Bondsen.

He found her in her room, correcting papers, and introduced himself.

"I'm sure we've met before, and I'm ashamed that I don't remember it. My work keeps me in the office so much that I just don't get around to visiting the teachers as I should. I'm the assistant principal, Dan Bennett. Just stopped in to ask how you're doing. I'm afraid we've given you quite a row to hoe in Boys' Chorus."

"Oh, I have no complaints, really." The reply came in a quiet, well-modulated voice. "I do find that trying to fill Mr. Logan's shoes is a bit difficult at times, but I'm sure it's just a matter of not relaxing my efforts to reach the children. It will work out, with time and effort."

"You have the boys' chorus and the recreational music classes, don't you?" asked Bennett.

"Yes," she replied. "I'm here only on a part-time basis to take some of the load from Mr. Logan. I teach only those two classes. They're something of a problem, too. I think the title 'recreational music' is a bit of a mistake and helps to account for it. The children come in expecting to be entertained, you see, not to learn anything. The connotation there is all wrong. I can see why they changed it from 'music appreciation,' since that normally means all manner of dullness, but there must be some other more suitable title.

"I think I have the problem solved in that class. At first I was way over their heads, so naturally they were bored. Since then I have come down to their level, and it's incredibly low. I have to remember, too, that I must reach listeners, not performers. I'm teaching children with no talent, drive, or training, and that makes it a much harder job. I'm trying to start where they are. They ask to hear popular music, so I play some records, and let them bring some to be played — all the while trying to keep them from the more dreadful things, of course. They ask to study popular music, but I tell them there's no need for that, that there's nothing there that can't be understood on the first hearing — that it doesn't need and won't even repay studying.

"In the chorus I have some boys — about ten or twelve out of thirty-five — who simply don't want to be there. They're boys who needed three more credits in order to graduate and just looked around for a course with no homework. That's music. You'd think, then, that they'd be grateful for music, but they're not. They won't sing at all, and they just wait for the bell to ring so they can get out. I tried appealing to school loyalty, but without success. I told them that the chorus puts on a concert every year, and a good one, and that this group won't let down the tradition. But it just doesn't reach them. They don't care.

"I've hit on a plan which might help. The next time they meet I'm going to have them elect a president, vice president, secretary-treasurer, librarian, and assistant librarian. The president will then have the job of calling the group to order and keeping discipline, the vice president will act in his absence, and the secretary-treasurer will take the roll. The librarian and the assistant librarian will see to getting out the music and getting it back. It may help to give them some responsibility.

"Mr. Logan had the same problem when he got here three or four years ago. He simply kept at it, though, and won them over by sheer force of personality. He's talented himself, and children come to recognize and respect talent after a while. As I say, he did it by sheer personality. Then the children come into the class and expect the wonderful Mr. Logan, of whom they've heard so much, and he's not there. Worse yet, it's a woman who is there. I have a sizable handicap to overcome right from the start, you see.

"Now, I suppose the administration might reasonably be concerned, but I don't want to start right off by going to you people. I don't think a new teacher should presume to question until she's had time to look around and gain some perspective. And I hope I will be able to handle my problem myself. At least, I'm going to try.

"I've never encountered such a situation before. I've taught in a teachers' college in Illinois, and I was music supervisor in one of the neighboring towns before coming here. But I've never run into anything remotely like this! I'm afraid I'm something of a failure, although I can't give up trying. I must confess, though, I'm really disturbed about the situation."

"Well," said Bennett, "I wouldn't get disturbed about this if I were you. Having trouble with that class is not being a failure, by any means. You just keep your head above water and keep trying. I'm sure you'll make out fine. And if you do have any more trouble, don't hesitate to ask for help. If any kid gets out of hand, send him to me — I'll straighten him out. Meanwhile, keep up the good work. I'm sure you're doing a good job and will be doing an even better one before long."

"As a matter of fact," Bennett was telling Mac Woodbury later, "I think she probably is doing a good job. At least she talks a good fight, and she seems to know pretty well what she's up against. It really was kind of a dirty trick unloading those two classes on her right off the bat. I can understand Logan's wanting to get rid of them, but it doesn't seem right to fire them both to her, especially when they're the only classes she's got. Those are the two classes that boys who need three more units will take, and sometimes counselors will shove them in for that reason alone. Naturally, some of the boys resent that.

"But these two boys I sent on to you are a problem too. They see trouble brewing and so they want to get out. I don't know but that the thing to do is to yank the troublemakers out and give her a chance. At the same time we'll give these other two boys a chance to finish the year without any trouble. It's really a little late [the time was mid-October] to transfer them to other courses now."

"That would be the one way to do it, all right," said Mac. "I was looking over the schedules of these two kids to see what they could transfer to without trouble. It doesn't look hopeful. One of them elected music, which I hadn't remembered, and he has a pretty good voice too, so he could be switched over to the choral group that Logan teaches [an advanced chorus class which attracts those who have been through the beginning classes who elect to go on with chorus singing]. One trouble with that is you might have trouble between Logan and Mrs. Bondsen over all of the good voices being taken away from her class. That's your problem though, not mine. The other one could probably go to an art class that meets at that time. I see on his record that he wanted typing, but — and again I was wrong — he's a technical curriculum student and so can't take the typing. While we're on the subject, when are you going to do something about that foolishness? You and Hal [Harold McManus, the principal] can tackle it, can't you?"

"Not quite," said Dan. "We'd have to get together with the assistant superintendent in charge of the secondary schools and with the superintendent, but it's not a board matter. I don't know why we should, though. I know it would be handy for technical curriculum kids to be able to take typing. But we have only a few machines, and one teacher. There just wouldn't be enough room if we opened the gates like that."

"Well," Mac answered, "you ought to be able to do something about it if there were enough kids who wanted it. After all, we're supposed to help them, not to hinder them. Think about it, will you?

"But to get back to these kids and their problem. I suggested that they could stay in the class and do their bit to help the teacher straighten out the class. But I'm not dumb enough to expect them to. And as far as bouncing the troublemakers, that's all well and good, but where would they go? Some of them need credits to graduate, you know. You just can't stick them in a study hall somewhere. And if they were transferred to any class of mine at this late date, I'd want to know why. I think most of the teachers feel as I do, that if it's a case with a legitimate excuse — been in the hospital or something like that — good enough. They'll do their best to help bring them up with the rest of the class. But the others — I dunno! I'd resent it myself. Nobody likes to have his classes made into a wastebasket, a dumping ground for anything that can't be taken care of anywhere else."

"I guess I better see Hal about this one," sighed Dan. "It's such a little thing, just two kids out of 1,600. But if teachers come into it, I guess it's his baby really. I'm pretty much discipline, safety patrol, and attendance man myself, so this is a little out of my bailiwick. I'll see what he thinks. He's the principal, not I."

"So you see, Hal," he told the principal the next morning, "that's how it stands. We could let it ride, but if we do we might lose our part-time music teacher, and you remember as well as I what a tough time we had finding her. It wasn't till after school started that we did find her. If we just transfer the two out of the class, we might still lose Mrs. Bondsen, since that wouldn't help her problem at all — gets rid of two of her better pupils, in fact. If we boot the troublemakers, then we've got to figure out what to do with them, assuming we have to do anything more for them. They're all old enough to quit school if they want to. I know it's a little matter, but if we start losing teachers it stops being such a little matter. What do you think we should do?"

9 *Mrs. McNutt's Demotion*

George Thompson was the new superintendent of schools in Westover, a community of high socio-economic level; the per pupil expenditures for public education were the highest in the state. The school system, staffed by about 200 teachers, was generally regarded as outstanding. Many people in the community took great pride in their schools.

Superintendent Thompson was particularly pleased with the Board of Education. Seven members, all well-educated and respected citizens, composed the group. The chairman, Foster Harris, was a brilliant, decisive, and highly successful business executive, an individual with such a strength of personality that few people ever crossed him. Among the other members, Albert Lockhart was an older man who was impulsive and also set in his opinions. In general, Superintendent Thompson's first impression of the remaining board members was that they were thoughtful, fair-minded, and solidly behind the chairman.

At the second meeting of the board after Mr. Thompson assumed his position as superintendent, Mr. Lockhart appeared excited as he commented that there had been a P.T.A. controversy at the Lincoln Elementary School. One P.T.A. mother had opposed a plan to raise money for purchasing a gift for the school. The objection was based on the premise that the objective of the P.T.A. was to further understanding and cooperation between parents and teachers and not to raise money. After much discussion by the mothers, according to Mr. Lockhart, Mrs. Dorothea McNutt, the school principal, made an impassioned speech to the group, stating that the members should be glad to work for physical improvements in the school. Mr. Lockhart criticized Mrs. McNutt for antagonizing the mother who opposed the fund raising. Chairman Harris then recalled that Mrs. McNutt had personally called on him the previous summer, before the new superintendent had arrived, to express dissatisfaction with the amount of her salary increase.

As the situation developed, Superintendent Thompson gradually came to see that the board had an unwritten but understood policy which opposed any fund-raising by pupils or individual schools. It appeared to be the sincere opinion of the board that an honorable school system solicited financial support through taxation only. When Superintendent Thompson asked if the board had any jurisdiction over P.T.A. policies, the chairman stated that in his opinion the P.T.A. should itself decide such things but that no school employee should ever *ask* the P.T.A. for school gifts. There was no further discussion of the incident, and attention turned to the business listed on the agenda.

In the next few months, though quite busy with details and the problem of getting oriented in a new position, the superintendent did pay particular attention to the situation involving Mrs. McNutt. After listening to comments from the elementary supervisor, and doing some classroom visiting, he came to the conclusion that Mrs. McNutt was sincerely interested in her school. In her early forties, she appeared to be rather serious, persistent, and even tense at times. She drove herself and her staff in providing experiences in art, music, and folk-dancing for the Lincoln pupils. She had an M.A. — one of the two elementary principals holding a Master's degree. He also learned that she had originally been a very successful teacher in Westover, later in a larger city nearby. After marriage and return to Westover, she had been asked to be principal at the Lincoln School, and had served in this capacity for three years.

As time for the annual re-election of teachers drew near, Thompson surveyed his staff generally. Two probationary teachers were not doing well after two years of experience. Feeling assured that they had had professional help from their principals and from the elementary supervisor, Thompson persuaded them to plan on looking elsewhere for another year and not to seek re-election. He felt that the rest of the staff should be re-elected, though many complaints from parents had been made about Miss Carey and Miss Sanders. Both were eligible for retirement income, though neither had quite reached compulsory retirement age.

At the February meeting of the board, the superintendent's nomination list was presented. Mr. Lockhart exploded. He said he was "sick and tired" of continuing to re-elect Miss Carey and Miss Sanders in the face of their obvious incompetence and the long-standing complaints of parents.[1] He also deplored Mrs. McNutt's poor public relations and felt that she should be replaced. Three other members joined in. Chairman Harris asked Superintendent Thompson if he wished to change his nomination, but before the superintendent could reply, Mr. Lockhart commented that Superintendent Thompson was new and should not be expected to settle that question. His motion was that the teachers be elected as nominated except for Miss Carey and Miss Sanders. He also made the provision that Mrs. McNutt be assigned as teacher rather than as principal. His motion was passed by a vote of 3 to 2, after general agreement that the board should take responsibility for the action and not embarrass the new superintendent.

Mrs. McNutt was informed that she was to become a teacher instead of continuing as principal, because the board was dissatisfied with her public relations. A wave of protest ensued. Board members, as well as the superintendent, were deluged by telephone calls from members of the P.T.A. Letters praising Mrs. McNutt were received from the teachers of the Lincoln School. A committee from the Westover Teachers' Association was appointed to seek from the superintendent the reasons for Mrs. McNutt's demotion and to act in her behalf. It was also clear that Mrs. McNutt was deeply hurt and emotionally upset.

The following month at the annual school board election in March Mr. Lockhart and one other board member were not re-elected. The daily paper's front-page headline read, "Teachers Ired Over School Board's Action." The accompanying article stated that teachers and their friends or relatives were active in the board election and really responsible for the defeat of the unsuccessful candidates. Board members, except for those newly elected, were indignant and disappointed over the election results. Mr. Harris made it quite plain to Superintendent Thompson that he thought Mrs. McNutt was not a first-class principal and that the Lincoln School would improve under different leadership.

At the organization meeting of the board, the two new members inquired

---

[1] New Hampshire State Law: "Dismissal of Teacher. The school board may dismiss any teacher found by them to be immoral or incompetent, or one who shall not conform to regulations prescribed; provided, that no teacher shall be so dismissed before the expiration of the period for which said teacher was engaged without having previously been notified of the cause of such dismissal, nor without having previously been granted a full and fair hearing."

about the demotion. The chairman answered summarily that the action was in the past; that, even though many people objected, Mrs. McNutt had not appealed the decision by asking the board for a hearing.

Superintendent Thompson was disturbed over the whole situation. After thinking the matter over very carefully, he had a long talk with Mrs. McNutt, urging her to request a hearing before the board. Even though she dreaded such a difficult ordeal, she later decided to make the request.

The hearing consisted mainly of statements by the demoted principal, who throughout the hearing was straightforward, though obviously under great strain. Asked by Mr. Harris if the previous superintendent had not warned her orally that her work as principal should be improved, she expressed real surprise and stated that she had never understood that this was so, although the former superintendent had seemed impatient once or twice. After a few general questions were asked, Mrs. McNutt left.

The board chairman then proposed taking up the regular agenda, whereupon Mrs. Penney, one of the new members, spoke up. "Before doing anything else, I'd like to hear the superintendent's opinion on the McNutt case."

10 The Advisory Council

NONE would deny that Superintendent Carlyle E. Wellington had the best of intentions in setting up an Advisory Council of teachers elected by representatives of every public school faculty in this large industrial city. Widely acknowledged to be an educator of the highest professional standing, Dr. Wellington was a man of unassailable integrity. Many a time had he assured large groups of his teachers that he wanted them to regard him as their "colleague with special responsibility." His office was open to teachers who had grievances. Proposed policies and rules changes were frequently submitted to teacher organizations for study and suggestions before being submitted to the Board of Education for adoption. It is true that teacher recommendations were not always favorably considered, but enough were accepted to give teachers both individually and in organizations, the feeling that their superintendent meant what he said in the matter of wanting a democratic school system.

At some time in 1949, after about five years of service in Shane City, Superintendent Wellington announced a plan for setting up the Advisory Council. The purpose of the council, he said, would be to give the superintendent the opportunity to meet with representatives of *all* teachers to get their reactions to certain policies and conditions in the schools. The teachers' union (A.F. of L.), having a membership of 4,000 and being the majority organization of teachers, wrote to the superintendent, after due consideration and vote by the union's House of Representatives, that the council would merely duplicate functions now performed by the union and other organizations. Dr. Wellington replied that it was not his plan to have the council vote or advise him on matters pertaining to teachers' welfare. He said he had no intention whatever of having the group usurp the functions of teacher organizations. "All I want to do," he wrote, "is to meet with teachers to interpret certain policies and programs of the administration and to have the group advise me informally of its feelings on certain questions relating to the educational program of our schools." Despite a mild protest from the union, Dr. Wellington proceeded to set up the council.

Since its membership included roughly two-thirds of the teachers, the union decided to deal with the council threat in another way. It decided to elect, through the machinery set up by Dr. Wellington and his aides, a majority of union members to the council to ensure that it would not become a "company union." The union, working quietly through its delegates and representatives in the schools, caused teachers to elect union members to three-fourths of the council membership.[1] Elected during the school year 1949–50, this group composed the council through the year 1950–51.

Reports of council deliberations in its monthly meetings with the superintendent gave the union executive board increasing concern. The superintendent's bulletin carried rather detailed accounts of these meetings, at which some questions of teacher welfare were raised.[2]

The executive board, with the approval of the House of Representatives,

[1] It is not known to what extent the superintendent was aware of this.

[2] For example: questions of sick leave benefits, salary schedules, and length of working day.

ordered John Greeley, union president, to write Superintendent Wellington to the effect that the union still regarded the Advisory Council as a threat to legitimate teacher organizations. Greeley was also directed to call Dr. Wellington's attention to the fact that the council was discussing questions of teacher and pupil welfare on which the union, a voluntary association of a majority of the teachers, had already made known its position. Dr. Wellington replied that the council's discussions were most informal and that no vote was taken to indicate the thinking of the council in these areas. He said, however, that in view of the union's opposition he would submit to the council the proposal that it be dissolved. He did so. The council promptly voted to continue its existence. Union leaders were nonplussed to see that their members were ignoring the known official position of their organization.

The union was a voluntary association of 4,000 teachers affiliated with the City Federation of Labor, the American Federation of Teachers, the State Federation of Labor, and the American Federation of Labor. It had come into prominence at the time when Shane City teachers were not being paid and teacher demonstrations against payless paydays were being led by John Greeley, and again when a battle was being waged to break the tyrannical hold of the former superintendent and board of education on the school system and its employees. Many citizens and teachers felt that through its efforts to obtain a school system free of politics, in which teachers would be elected on the basis of merit rather than political influence, the union had given its finest demonstration of educational statesmanship. Too well did its members remember the former administration's system of espionage and repression. The scars of long educational misrule were still too recent to be forgotten.

It is clear, then, how memories of this experience colored the union's reaction as an organized group to Dr. Wellington's proposal to work toward the democratization of the school system through the establishment of the Advisory Council.

Shane City is a large industrial city that has a strong labor movement. Most nonprofessional employees are unionized. The school system could be paralyzed completely by a strike of these workers. For example, school engineers could close the schools and through picketing prevent unionized truck drivers from making deliveries.

Union teachers' association with these groups — however remote — hardly gives the union full respectability in the eyes of teachers who feel that professional people should not affiliate with labor. Nevertheless, Dr. Wellington had several times pointed out to John Greeley that he would gladly join the union if its constitution permitted his membership to be accepted. The State Educational Association, affiliated with the N.E.A., accepted everyone — administrators and teachers alike. Moreover, Dr. Wellington pointed out, the union represented only *some* of the teachers. Through his Advisory Council he could meet with representatives of *all*.

The union, although it felt kindly toward Dr. Wellington and respected his good intentions, pointed to the threat that lay in the coming of an administration that might use the council to destroy the union. It also contended that since it represented a majority of the teachers, it could not understand the extent of his concern for the minority which it did not represent. Dr. Wellington was asked whether he felt that he should permit his concern for this minority to cause him to disregard the wishes of a voluntary association of the majority.

The superintendent of a school system, large or small, has many pressures acting upon him to move in this or that direction. No doubt pressures were operating to get Dr. Wellington to reduce the strength of the union. It is to be expected that representatives of large industrial and business establishments, as well as groups interested in tax reduction, should not want labor-oriented groups to become dominant among teachers. However, union leaders did not suspect that Dr. Wellington would attempt to placate this source of pressure by seeking to destroy the union; its relations with him had been too good. He was by disposition too worthy a man to succumb to such pressure. Besides, he had said on several occasions that the Shane City Teachers' Union was one of the most highly professional organizations that he had ever dealt with. He had addressed general sessions of its annual education conferences. Too, he knew of the union's considerable financial support of the Citizens' Schools Alliance, a kind of federation of public-spirited organizations working for good schools. He knew of the union's work in the legislature to increase state support of Shane City schools. Indeed, he had expressed gratitude for the genuine efforts of union committees to improve the quality of instruction in the schools. However, he would not give in to the union on the council issue.

In his last conference with the superintendent regarding the council, John Greeley had said, "This most recent audit of our finances shows that out of a total of 6,500 teachers and principals, we have 4,000 paid memberships."

Dr. Wellington countered, "But you don't represent all the teachers. Other organizations, although they don't have a majority of the teachers, do have a considerable number. I cannot regard the positions taken by your group on certain issues as representative of the entire staff. Other organized and unorganized teachers have to be considered."

Greeley paused a moment; then he said, "We have never sought to get all teachers into the union. As you know, membership is purely voluntary. If you were to submit the question whether the Advisory Council should be continued to a vote of all teachers, I have no doubt that a majority would vote 'No.' "

"But that is not the way the council voted — and no doubt many of your people are council members," said Dr. Wellington.

When John Greeley reported the result of this conference to his associates, the union executive board voted to carry the matter to the Grievance Committee of the Shane City Federation of Labor. It hoped that the committee would help to show Dr. Wellington the threat to teacher organizations that lay in the "company-union" type of Advisory Council.

The chairman of the Federation's Grievance Committee [3] (a committee used by all A.F. of L. unions of the city) was also a member of the Board of Education. In addition, there was a prominent C.I.O. labor man on the board. The remaining nine members were three businessmen, two Women's City Club members, one physician, and three lawyers.

The Executive Board's decision to seek the aid of the Federation of Labor revealed its feeling that this issue, which had had its inception in Superintendent Wellington's desire to democratize the school system, was of critical importance to the union's future both as guardian of the interests of Shane City teachers and, in one sense at least, as guardian of the integrity of the Shane City schools.

Finally Dr. Wellington received a letter on Shane City Federation of Labor stationery, over the signature of the Grievance Committee chairman, requesting an appointment for the committee and John Greeley to discuss the advisability of continuing the Advisory Council.

---

[3] The Federation's Grievance Committee is used by all A.F. of L. unions to settle union–management disagreements. The disputants talk informally in the presence of the Grievance Committee until they are able to reach an agreeable compromise. If they fail to reach an agreement, the Grievance Committee will make a recommendation, which will be supported by all A.F. of L. unions.

11 Squeeze Play

DURING the month of November, 1949, School Superintendent William Rice received three calls of complaint from parents. All three charged that Philip Camlin, a mathematics instructor at Brandton High, had neglected his job. Specifically, the parents alleged that:

1. Camlin had conducted his classes indifferently and had failed to cover essential work in trigonometry and solid geometry.
2. Camlin had refused to give extra help to students.
3. Camlin had not set up the usual extra-work classes to prepare students for the College Board Examinations.

The calls surprised Superintendent Rice. Brandton (population 53,000) was not so large that he needed to consult a file card on Camlin. Camlin had been at Brandton High School for ten years, the last five on tenure. He was a driving, nervous teacher, not always popular with the slower students but highly regarded by parents and by other teachers. His students had a fine record in college mathematics. Allied Electric, Brandton's main industry, ranked Camlin's former students high in their apprentice training courses.

Superintendent Rice referred the complaints to Frank Riley, principal of Brandton High School. He was even more surprised when Principal Riley substantiated the parents' charges. Riley described Camlin's teaching as "listless" and "indifferent." Camlin had neglected extra-help sessions. He had not set up any class for the students who planned to take the College Board Exams. Although it was only late November, Camlin had already used his entire ten days' sick leave.

Riley knew of the reasons for Camlin's slump. In the fall of the previous year his wife had been crippled by an attack of polio; Camlin had had to hire a woman to take care of her and their two small children. Both children had been hospitalized during the past year. The resultant crushing expenses were the real reason for Camlin's school troubles. Riley explained that Camlin had driven himself mercilessly to get out of debt. He had started a tutoring school in his home, sometimes teaching as many as eight hours in addition to his regular sessions. Riley felt that it was not surprising that Camlin had become unable to perform his school duties.

While he was on the subject, Riley mentioned two other high school teachers who were also involved in outside jobs. Robert Wilson and Joseph Mejick were as much overburdened as Camlin with outside employment. The only difference, according to Riley, was that Mejick and Wilson were younger than Camlin and the strain of overwork showed less on them. Riley felt that nothing could be settled in the Camlin case until a general policy could be formulated to deal with the problem of outside work. He said that Mejick, who taught history and coached baseball, often cut afternoon sessions to coach basketball at one of the private schools near Brandton. Sometimes Mejick traveled to distant college towns to officiate at night basketball games.

Riley was even more concerned about Wilson, who taught French and Latin in the high school. Wilson worked five nights a week as a bartender in Brandton's largest hotel. Although a member of Wilson's family owned the hotel, and it was a well-run place, Principal Riley did not think the job an appropriate one for a high school teacher. Rice agreed; he asked Riley if there had been any open comment on Wilson's job. Riley said that he had heard of none.

Superintendent Rice scheduled a meeting to discuss the outside-work problem more thoroughly. It was not news to Rice that some of his teachers were working at extra jobs. He supposed that it was inevitable that a family man would be driven to supplementing his salary in the midst of an inflation, but he had not realized the extent of the problem.

In December, Rice and Principal Riley decided to take action. The Superintendent of Brandton Schools sent a circular to all the teachers in the system. The circular did not single out any teacher for individual censure, nor did it forbid outside employment. But it did remind all teachers that their primary duties were within the schools. It said that no teacher would be permitted to leave the school during the afternoon when he was scheduled for extra-help sessions. Further, it warned teachers against swapping sessions in order to meet other obligations outside the school. It also stated that teachers should be prudent about their ouside activities.

The circular caused widespread resentment among the teachers. It was so ambiguous that each teacher interpreted it in a different way. Some felt that it was an attempt to keep them from taking jobs during the Christmas vacation. Others interpreted it, not as applying to outside work, but as an attempt to regulate their private lives. Most of the teachers felt that the superintendent should have had "whoever was guilty" into his office for a talk. The meaning of the superintendent's message was uncertain in the minds of many, partly because the school regulations made no mention of the question of extra work for teachers. Rice soon realized that his circular had been a mistake. He had hoped to avoid an open fracas because of another matter that was being agitated in the city. Brandton needed two new junior high school buildings. Some of the leading taxpayers were opposed to Rice and to all who advocated the new buildings.

Rice's position in the community was not quite so strong as it had been. He had been superintendent at Brandton for fifteen years and had early gained the respect of many townspeople as a "practical" rather than a "visionary" educator. Recently, however, he had been taking courses in educational psychology and curriculum theory, one result being a considerable shift in his educational philosophy. Some of his old friends among the businessmen had become alienated thereby, although he suspected that he had gained some compensatory support among the younger townspeople.

By January the "outside-work" situation had not improved, and Rice decided that he would call Camlin, Mejick, and Wilson to his office.

Camlin was the first to appear. He said that the call was not unexpected. He offered no defense and added little to what Riley had already said. The tutoring was necessary if Camlin's family were to live decently. The only alternative, as Camlin saw it, was to resign and take care of his family himself. He was six years and $600 away from the maximum salary he could expect with a Bachelor's degree. His present salary of $3,100 was inadequate to maintain his family. He could not afford to continue to work for his Master's, and he had only four of the required thirty-two credits. He could not afford a summer in school. Camlin finally became so overwrought that Rice had to excuse him.

Wilson came to the superintendent's office four days later. He said that with his M.A. and five years' experience he earned $3,100. He was ten years away from his maximum of $4,100. "I have five kids, Mr. Rice. Ten years is a long time to keep the grocer and the milkman waiting." Rice pointed out that a bartender's job was not suitable outside employment for a teacher. Wilson countered with, "Maybe you should take that up with my uncle, Arthur Fuller. He owns the hotel." Wilson's retort angered Rice. Arthur Fuller, one of Brandton's largest property owners, was chairman of the City Council. He had not opposed the new school building program, but he had not backed it either. Rice hoped to have Fuller on his side when the school buildings came up for final consideration in March. However, he felt that Wilson had intended his remarks as a threat. Superintendent Rice reminded Wilson that he would come up for tenure at the March meeting of the school board.

Mejick was the last one to appear before Superintendent Rice. He had three years of teaching and earned $2,900, plus $300 for coaching the baseball team. He was married and childless; his wife worked at Allied Electric. Mejick said that he needed the money to meet payments on the new house they had bought that year. He needed every outside job he could get. He did not feel that his outside work would prejudice his chances of being made a permanent member of the school staff. His team had gone to the state finals the year before, and the local papers and the townspeople were for him even if Rice were not. Superintendent Rice made no answer to that.

Before he left Rice's office Mejick added one significant statement. Labor Department statistics showed that the median salary of Brandton workers exceeded the national average for cities of the same size, and that the average total "take-home" pay exceeded that of the average teacher. Allied Electric, which employed more than 5,000 Brandton residents, paid well above the national average wage. Mejick reminded Superintendent Rice that the Brandton schools, with more than 7,500 enrolled, paid its teachers well below the average for a system of comparable size. "We are caught in the middle," Mejick said. "If I'm willing to work, why shouldn't I live as well as a mill hand at Allied Electric?" Rice told Mejick that no further permission would be granted to be absent from afternoon sessions. Mejick conceded that he had abused that privilege and promised to make up any sessions that he had neglected.

After Mejick had gone, Rice took out the 1948 school budget. Comparing it with the 1945 budget, he saw that the operational budget for 1948 was $1.5 million, almost double that of 1945. Of the $1.5 million operating budget for 1948, over a million would be tagged for the salaries of 312 teachers, administrative personnel, and staff in Brandton's twenty schools. There were about 286 classroom teachers.

In 1949–50 the pupil-teacher ratio varied from 38:1 in some elementary classes to less than 25:1 in the high school. Rice was alarmed not so much by the ratio figures per se as by the fact that there was so much difference between them. The distribution was out of line; there were too many teachers in the high school and too few in the elementary schools. Teachers from the high school were resistant to what they considered a "demotion" to the elementary schools. Several years previously, Brandton had changed from an 8–4 to a 6–3–3 system. The change was largely one of name, however, as the two buildings being used as junior high schools were really converted elementary schools. Brandton had adopted a single preparational-type salary schedule in 1948, but there was still a lingering aura of discrimination against elementary teachers, a feeling that they were somehow of lower rank. It was common knowledge that the high school teachers grouped junior high teachers with elementary teachers.

In 1949 there was talk of another raise for teachers. The issue was scheduled to come before the Brandton School Board in March, 1950. Rice had favored the raises previously given to the teachers. He had sat with the committee of the Brandton teachers' association when the raises had been proposed. He had advised the teachers to ask for a series of small raises rather than request a large raise in any one year. As a result, the teachers had been granted every raise which had been requested, but none of the raises had been large. Rice felt that in 1950 the teachers should not try for another raise. He had therefore counseled them to "skip this year" and try next year. He had pointed out that they had been granted four raises since the war. The teachers pointed out, in turn, that all four raises had been small, and that Brandton teachers' salaries were still below the national average. They said that this was a particularly acute problem for married teachers supporting families, because the general level of wages in Brandton, owing to the high rates paid to Allied Electric workers, was far above the national average for cities of similar size. Rice had answered, "Up to now you have never lost a wage request. If you go before the board and lose one this year, it might establish a bad precedent."

After the meeting, one of the teachers' representatives had characterized this as "a lot of nonsense." Fully aware that the superintendent could hear him, the teacher had continued, "If there's any logic to the superintendent's argument, I'm darned if I can see it."

Rice had said to this teacher, "We had an open meeting, at which you could have expressed your opinions."

The teacher's answer was, "I'm not so sure that it meant that much to me, sir. I'm leaving education at the end of this year."

"Well," Rice had said, "I'm sorry to hear that young men like you feel that way."

Rice felt that another teachers' raise would inflate the Brandton operational budget dangerously. Although there was no direct connection between this operational budget and the capital expenditure for schools, which would be arranged through bonding, there was a definite connection in the minds of the members of the school board and of the city council — and particularly in the mind of Councilman Arthur Fuller. At a preliminary joint meeting of the board and council, Mr. Fuller had stated, "Money outlay is money outlay. It doesn't matter how long you put it off; somebody has to pay for it." For this reason Rice felt that there would be an inevitable connection between the teachers' raises and the capital outlay for buildings. He felt that the building problem was the more urgent of the two items, but that was before he had become fully aware of the effect of inflation on his staff.

The teachers' raise was scheduled to come up at the March meeting of the school board. Wilson and Mejick, among others, would be up for tenure at the same meeting. There was also the question of Camlin, who had been absent five days during January. Camlin was on tenure — and during Rice's fifteen years as superintendent of the Brandton schools he had never been forced to take action against a teacher on tenure. Rice had over a month before the meeting. He had planned to spend the month in proving his case for the new schools by taking board and council members on a tour of the present junior high schools and in preparing statistical tables. One of the backers he hoped to gain was Wilson's uncle, Councilman Arthur Fuller. Rice had not many more years in education before him. He had always felt that he enjoyed the backing and respect of his teachers. He had never openly opposed them in anything. Still, he felt that 1950 was not the year for them to seek a raise. He felt badly about the young teacher who was leaving the schools. Probably still others were leaving whom Rice did not know about. In the closing years of his career in public education, Rice did not enjoy having this on his conscience.

12 *Waltham**

Introduction

UNTIL recently the City of Waltham (1950 pop., 47,187) could have been described as a manufacturing center that revolved in its own orbit not greatly affected by developments in the Greater Boston metropolitan area. Now, however, highway expansion and a gradual filling up of nearby municipalities are placing new pressures on the city. The city government has not been unaware of this, and of an urgent need for intelligent planning to meet this latest development. The planning board is now in the process of producing a master plan with which to face the problem of proper use of all available land. Careful consideration is being given to topography, road networks, and other related factors in order to anticipate and prepare for the most desirable industrial, business, and residential sections.

The urgency of the present building situation is due largely to the development of new sections within the city boundaries. The population has been very largely concentrated in the southern section of the city, except for a small post-World War I development in the Hardy Pond area. The northern section until recently had been largely undeveloped. The holding of land by the federal government, state and county agencies, and charitable organizations has contributed to the virtual isolation of this section, by partially cutting it off from the rest of the city. As will be pointed out later, this northern geographic area is now evidencing tremendous school housing needs; yet the lack of roads, of public services, and particularly of a master plan, makes school planning for this section extremely difficult.

The following report includes a comprehensive treatment of the problem of school population prediction, both for the city as a whole and for the several geographic subsections. An analysis of the capacities and relative educational usefulness of the elementary, junior high, and senior high buildings now in the school plant follows the section of the report on population. By merging this analysis with an estimate of the future needs, there naturally develops a differential which must be taken care of through a planned program. . . .

Chapter I

Present and Future School Enrollments

Part I: A Discussion of the Method of Estimation

In order to plan for future school housing needs in any community, the estimator must know the total number of pupils who will be enrolled in public schools at specified times in the future, the age-distribution of these totals, and where

* Adapted from a report, "Meeting Present and Future School Building Needs," made by the Center for Field Studies, Graduate School of Education, 1951. This case consists of material excerpted from the full report so as to provide the rationale of the analysis and findings. Chapter II has been most sharply edited, but for the purposes of case analysis, the information is retained to give the student some "feel" of the present school plant.

these children will be living within the city. To arrive at this information, the estimator must first study, as contributing factors, the sources of school-age children; births to residents of the school district; and movement in and out of the school district. He must also study those factors which act as deterrents to public school enrollments, such as membership in nonpublic schools, the policy and public acceptability of kindergartens, and the proportion of children who do not continue through to high school graduation. In addition, he must study the possible changes which these contributing and deterring factors may undergo in future years.

With all of this information, he is then in a position to estimate the total numbers of expected public school enrollments. Then by subdividing the total city area into smaller, possibly neighborhood sections, and studying the conditions affecting enrollments in these subdivisions, he can predict the numbers of children expected to attend public schools from each area and thus provide more exact information about future school plant needs.

This method of estimating has not previously been used, however, because little has been known about contributing and deterring factors and how they might be quantified. In the past, the method has been to project school enrollments on the assumption that the average of the conditions of the immediately preceding period will reasonably accurately represent future conditions. This method of estimating, however, is subject to severe limitations: (1) future conditions are almost certain not to be like past conditions, and (2) when a condition does change, it is almost impossible to revise estimates because the many contributing and deterring factors have not been dealt with separately and therefore cannot be isolated. These limitations make such estimates very uncertain, particularly at this time when the nation and its cities and towns are undergoing so many rapid changes.

Although the estimates made here are dependent upon many carefully considered assumptions about future conditions, what is important is that the factors affecting school enrollments are defined and the assumptions concerning these factors stated, so that changing conditions can be followed carefully and analyzed for their possible impact on enrollment figures as presented.

A final word before turning to the analysis: the high enrollments expected for Waltham *for the very near future* are not the result of *speculation,* but result from the large number of preschool-age children *now living in Waltham.*

Part II: Total Enrollment Estimates

Today many new homes are being built in Waltham (Map I). Table I is a record of new dwelling units planned each year from 1920–51 as measured by building permits. (There appears to be in Waltham practically a one-to-one relationship between permits issued and actual construction during the following year. Hereafter numbers of permits will be used to estimate numbers of dwelling units available one year after the issuing of the permits.) The extensive building during the last five years is equaled only by the building during the period 1925–30 when the region south of Hardy Pond was developed.

Over the State of Massachusetts, there has been a drop of nearly 25 per cent in the number of homes built in the first eight months of 1951 compared to the number built during the same period in 1950. *There has been no drop at all in Waltham.* This may be due to the fact that Waltham has considerable open land available for new homes near the metropolitan area. Also, the new circumferential highway gives increased access to a larger metropolitan area

MAP I

EACH SYMBOL EQUALS ONE BUILDING PERMIT

- ISSUED IN 1947
- ISSUED IN 1948
- ISSUED IN 1949
- ISSUED IN 1950
- ISSUED IN 1951

and thus increases the desirability of home ownership in Waltham. Industry seems oriented toward Waltham rather than away from it as evidenced by recent petitions for industrial sites before the City Planning Board. . . .

Table I

NUMBERS OF NEW DWELLING UNITS AUTHORIZED BY BUILDING PERMITS*

Year	*Number*	*Year*	*Number*
1920	45	1937	47
1921	65	1938	87
1922	120	1939	126
1923	170		
1924	183	1940	219
		1941	283
1925	350	1942	164
1926	322	1943	0
1927	332	1944	0
1928	318		
1929	196	1945	29
		1946	272
1930	131	1947	132
1931	78	1948	423
1932	31	1949	315
1933	30		
1934	20	1950	277
		1951**	215
1935	43		
1936	71		

* Data from city documents.
** To September 1.

In the Warrendale section and the housing north of the Beaver Brook reservation, there are (including streets, schools, etc.) about three houses per acre. Thus, should the present building rate of 300 houses per year continue, about 100 acres per year or 1,000 acres per decade will be required for the new housing, *assuming the housing to be of the general type of Warrendale.* Housing of the Chesterbrook Garden Development type would require less land for the same dwelling unit density. But the current construction as well as the presently planned new construction resembles the Warrendale type housing.

There are about 2,500 acres of open land in Waltham, of which nearly 1,400 are available for new housing at any time. Thus, if building lots of a size consistent with City Planning Board policy are assumed, 4,200 houses of the single-family type could be built on immediately available land and as many as 7,500 houses if all the open land were made available.

Whatever building estimates are made, yearly checks will have to be made with the facts of development as they become known. But considering the growth factors impinging on Waltham and the current experience, it will be assumed in this study that new building will continue for the next twenty years at the rate of the last few years. This amounts to the addition of 6,000 new dwelling units during the next twenty years.

What effect will all this building have on the public school enrollments? It is evident that the location of children is affected by families moving into these new homes, but how is the total number of children also related to this building activitiy? . . .

The results are interesting. For preschool-age children, Waltham appears to have had migration outward from 1935, gradually decreasing to zero net migration [1] in the five-year period ending in 1950. Examining the school census data, and noting the fact that families from outside of Waltham are settling in the new housing in Trapelo Road, it is possible that a slight outmigration stopped about 1948 and a slight inmigration began in 1949, thus resulting in zero net migration in the 1945–50 period. Without yearly census data, however, it seems unwise to attempt quantifying yearly changes. . . .

The next consideration is births to Waltham residents. The most recent year for which the age distribution of Waltham residents is available is 1940. (1950 census data will not be available until 1952–53.) Using these 1940 data and making corrections for survival and migration, estimates of the age distribution of women of child-bearing age can be obtained for each year to 1965, a span which includes all the years required for estimates of public school enrollments to 1970. . . .

Having estimates of the age distribution of women of child-bearing age living in Waltham, a measure of *birth rate* is still required in order to get estimates of future numbers of births. . . .

One of the most difficult estimates to make is what the birth rates will be in future years. Experts on this subject themselves disagree. There are few empirical data or theories on birth rates in local areas. Some experts feel the rate will return to the 1940 level by 1955 and continue at this rate. Others feel the birth rate will continue much as it is at present. For purposes of this study, the average of the 1940 and 1950 birth rates will be used for estimating births in 1955, 1960, and 1965. This average will be called the *projection birth rate.* Births during intermediate years will be estimated on the basis of a regular decline in birth rate from the present high level to the projection rate by 1955 and a constant birth rate at the projection rate from 1956 to 1965. This projection birth rate is applied for each year to the previous estimate as to women of child-bearing age in the Waltham population for that year, thus giving an estimate of births.

The estimation of birth rate and the consequent estimates of births are likely to cause the greatest error in estimates of future public school enrollments. Each year the actual numbers of births should be checked with the estimated numbers of births. . . .

With the migration, births, and survival estimates accumulated, it becomes possible to determine the potential *public school enrollments* for any year to 1970. (By potential public school enrollments, we mean the total number of school-age children living in Waltham for any particular year.)

Assuming that all the *potential* enrollees would distribute themselves in grades, if they went to public school, in the same way that children distribute themselves who are in public school, it is possible to convert the age potential to a grade group potential (Table II). Thus, we obtain estimated enrollments in terms of grades rather than ages.

---

[1] Reports sometimes state that a certain number of families moved to Waltham but do not state how many moved out. Net migration here means the difference between the number moving in and the number moving out.

But all the children who are potential enrollees do not enroll in public schools. We now come to an examination of possible deterrents to public school enrollment. Each deterrent is discussed individually. Each year the effect of each deterrent should be re-evaluated so that estimates of public school enrollments can be kept as accurate as possible.

1. Only four-year old children, who will be five on January 1 of the school year in which they intend to enroll, are admitted to kindergarten. (A child must be four years and eight months old to be admitted.) Thus, about three-fourths of the four-year-old children are not allowed to enroll in kindergarten in September.

2. The greatest deterrent to public school enrollment in Waltham is nonpublic school enrollment. Virtually all the Waltham children going to nonpublic schools are enrolled in parochial schools. Over the last ten years, the parochial schools have been filled to capacity and drawing an almost constant number of Waltham children. In the past, the number enrolled in nonpublic schools has been very nearly 27 per cent of the total number of children. But now that Waltham is entering a period of high enrollment due to the postwar births, it is unlikely that nonpublic schools will continue to draw this high a percentage without a change in facilities or a change in class size. As a result, it seems most wise to subtract from each grade group the number of children served by nonpublic schools. These numbers are obtained from parochial school enrollments of the last ten years and agree almost exactly with the 1951 school census data of *all* nonpublic school children. This census reveals that very few children, less than fifty, are enrolled in nonpublic schools other than parochial.

Table II

POTENTIAL PUBLIC SCHOOL ENROLLMENTS BY GRADE GROUPS, 1950

Age	*Births*	*Expect to Survive to 1950*	*Migration*	*Potential*	*K*	*1–3*	*4–6*	*7–9*	*10–12*
4	950	893	0	893	893				
5	790	743	0	743	609	134			
6	829	779	−20	759		759			
7	853	802	−20	782		782			
8	775	729	−20	709		525	184		
9	733	689	−20	669		100	569		
10	664	624	−20	604			604		
11	628	590	−65	525			389	136	
12	613	576	−65	511			123	388	
13	631	593	−65	508			20	488	
14	647	608	−65	543				451	92
15	635	597	−65	532				170	362
16	635	597	−65	532				64	468
17	635	597	−65	532					532
18+									

Table III

ESTIMATES OF WALTHAM PUBLIC SCHOOL ENROLLMENTS, 1950

Age	*Potential*	*K*	*1–3*	*4–6*	*7–9*	*10–12*	*Total*
4	893	893					
5	743	609	134				
6	759		759				
7	782		782				
8	709		525	184			
9	669		100	569			
10	604			604			
11	525			389	136		
12	511			123	388		
13	508			20	488		
14	543				451	92	
15	532				170	362	
16	532				64	468	
17	532					532	
18+	---					100*	
Total Grade Potential		1,502	2,300	1,889	1,697	1,554	8,942
Deterrents:							
(1) Not of legal age		−670	0	0	0	0	
(2) Nonpublic enrollment		−140	−650	−525	−450	−310	
(3) Special classes**		0	0	− 50	− 50	− 20	
(4) Nonacceptance		−165	0	0	0	−208	
Total Deterrents		−975	−650	−575	−500	−538	32,38
Estimate		527	1,650	1,314	1,197	1,016	5,704
Actual		524	1,699	1,241	1,176	1,025***	5,665
% Error of Estimate		+1%	−3%	+6%	+2%	−1%	+1%

N.B. An error of 10 per cent would correspond to three children per classroom, assuming an average of 30 children per classroom.

* In recent years about 100 students 18 or older have been enrolled in the High School.

** 1950 estimate only.

*** High School enrollment, 1950, plus 100 Waltham residents in the Trade School.

A change in the amount of parochial school facilities or class size policy would have a direct bearing on public school enrollments, so that it becomes very important to keep informed of parochial school plans and to revise estimates of public school enrollments accordingly.

Consistently, the nonpublic school enrollment of Waltham during the last ten years has been very nearly:

Grade	*Children*
Kindergarten	140
1–3	650
4–6	525
7–9	450
10–12	310
	2,075

Our estimates of future nonpublic enrollments will be those of the above table.

3. Kindergarten enrollment and enrollment over sixteen years of age are optional. Not all children or their parents decide in favor of enrollment.

Recent experience in Waltham public schools shows that 86 per cent of the number who enrolled in first grade had been enrolled in kindergarten one year earlier. Thus, it seems reasonable to estimate for the future a kindergarten attendance based on 86 per cent of the children who, according to our estimate, will subsequently attend public school. Also, about 71 per cent of the children who enroll in the tenth grade enter twelfth grade three years later. If we assume an average drop-off in the eleventh grade, then of 100 children entering tenth grade each year for three years, we would estimate that at the end of the three-year period there would be 100 in the tenth grade, 86 in the eleventh grade and 71 in the twelfth grade, making a total of 257 enrolled as compared with 300 originally entering. We assume that 85.7 per cent (257 divided by 300 times 100) is the percentage of attendance of the high school. This percentage will be used for estimation of future high school enrollments.

4. One hundred and twenty children are presently enrolled in special classes. As the numbers enrolled in special classes are very much determined by local practice, no correction will be made for special classes. These children will be included in their regular grade group.

5. The Trade School draws some of the students who would ordinarily go to Waltham High School. In making enrollment estimates, however, these students will be regarded as tenth- to twelfth-grade students.

By determining the potential enrollment for any year in the future and by adjusting for the deterrents, it is possible to obtain estimates for future years as long as the deterrents are constant. It is possible to check our procedure by making an estimate of 1950 enrollments for which actual enrollment data are available. This is done in Table III.

The close agreement of the *1950 estimates with actual 1950 enrollment figures* suggests that the contributing and deterring factors considered in making the estimates adequately account for the numbers of public school enrollments.

With present-day knowledge, it is unrealistic to try to predict how the deterring factors may change in future years. But estimates of future public school enrollments must be made. Thus, estimates of future enrollments are made on the basis that the deterring factors will operate in the future as they have in the past. Should any changes occur in any of the factors, the estimates can be very simply brought up to date by making suitable adjustments. . . .

Table IV summarizes the estimates of future public school enrollments.

Table IV

SUMMARY OF ESTIMATES OF TOTAL PUBLIC SCHOOL ENROLLMENT

Year	*K*	*1–3*	*4–6*	*7–9*	*10–12*	*Total*
1950	530	1,650	1,310	1,200	1,020	5,710
1954	770	2,380	1,870	1,660	1,000	7,680
1958	630	2,320	2,660	2,180	1,460	9,250
1962	540	1,840	2,390	2,850	1,880	9,500
1966	540	1,740	1,970	2,470	2,170	8,890
1970	560	1,800	1,920	2,110	1,830	8,220

The large increase expected in enrollments can be attributed to three major factors:

1. The coming of school age of children born during years of high birth rate and the simultaneous leaving of school age of children born during the years of low birth rate. Thus, birth rate changes have a double effect.

2. The fact that nonpublic schools will not draw a *constant proportion* of the total number of children but rather a *constant number* of children. Thus the impact of large numbers of children born during years of many births is felt almost entirely by the public schools.

3. The estimate that new construction in Waltham will make possible the housing of Waltham's expected natural increase, thus reversing a trend of outmigration in the past.

Put another way, the 1962 estimate is greater than present enrollments by approximately 3,500 children. Of these, about 3,000 result from increased births, and the fact that under present conditions the nonpublic schools cannot increase their enrollments, and the other 500 result from the estimate that outmigration will stop in Waltham.

Even though new construction is expected to continue unabated through the 1960's, enrollments are expected to drop off after 1962 because children born during the immediate postwar years, the period when the number of births is greatest, will be completing school.

Part III: Distribution of Present and Estimated Enrollments

For school-building purposes it is not enough to know the total numbers of children alone; it is also necessary to have information about their location in the city.

Using the school census data, "dot" maps were made showing the location of all preschool children by ages and all public and nonpublic school children up to eighteen years of age by grades.

To study distribution of preschool- and school-age children in Waltham, the city has been divided into sixty-five study areas, which are shown on Map II.

The basis of division has been to make each area a natural neighborhood in the sense that the areas are not cut by railroads, bodies of water, large parks, and most important major traffic arteries. Where possible, the areas have been kept of reasonably uniform size. In some cases, the divisions are along back ends of lots or through the center blocks in order to preserve the neighborhood idea and still keep reasonably uniform size. The numbers of children in each study area were then counted, giving numerical data about the distribution of children by areas. For the initial examination, the data for each study area are grouped into preschool, public school, and nonpublic school totals. These data are recorded in Table V along with the grand total of children in each area, the approximate acreage of each area and the density in each area measured in terms of public school children living in each area per acre. . . .

An over-all feeling for the present enrollment situation in Waltham is provided by Map III, which shows the density of public school children by study area.

Although Map III gives some idea of the distribution of school children, it is necessary to work with the actual numbers. Table VI lists the present numbers of school children grouped K–3, 4–6, 7–9, 10–12, according to sections corresponding approximately to *elementary school attendance* areas.

Our question now becomes: Can we provide for future years a table of estimates similar to Table VI?

MAP II

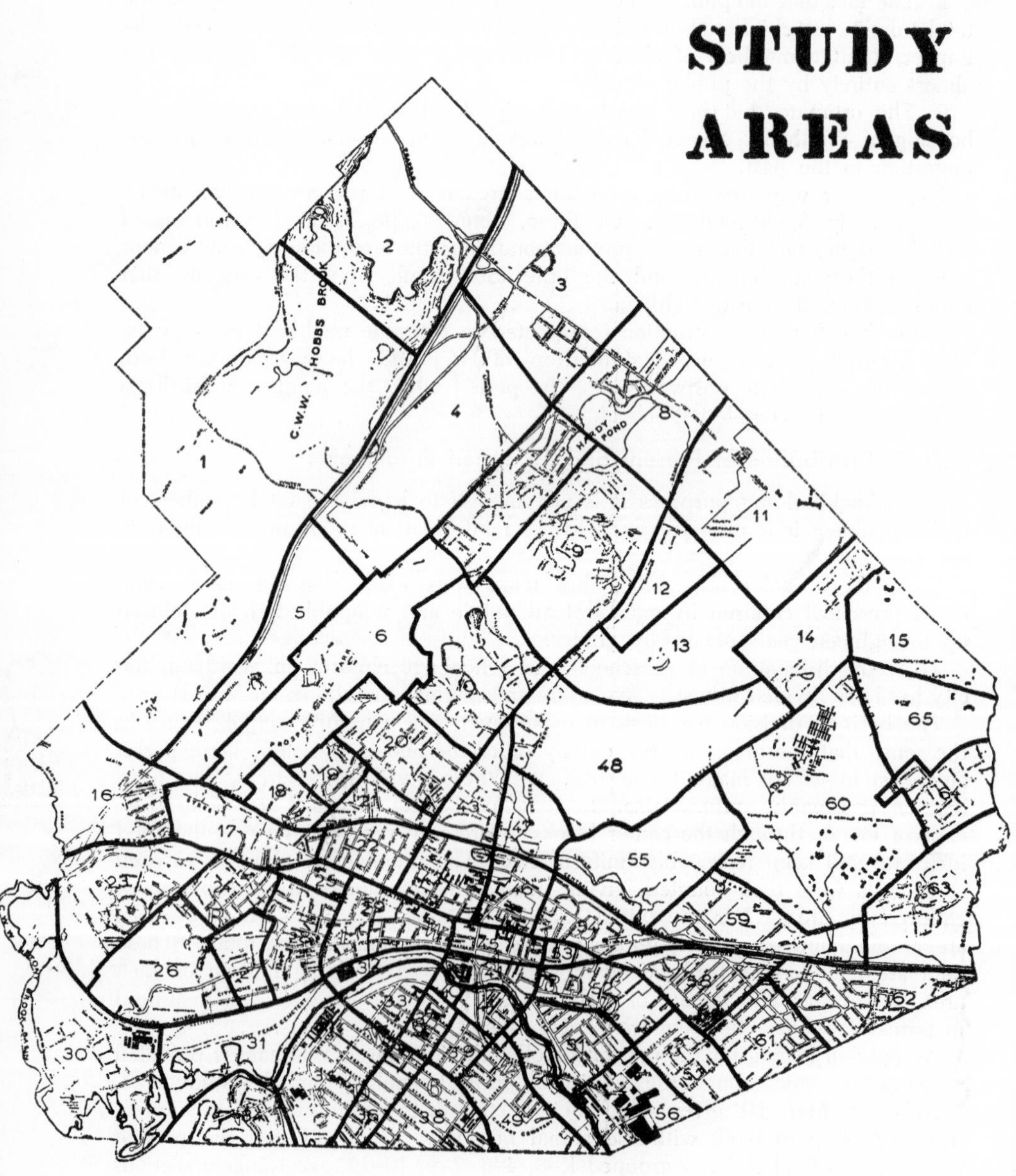
STUDY
AREAS
HOBBS BROOK
C.W.W.
HARDY POND
1
2
3
4
5
6
8
9
10
11
12
13
14
15
16
17
18
19
20
21
22
24
25
26
27
30
31
36
38
48
49
55
56
59
60
61
62
63
65

MAP III

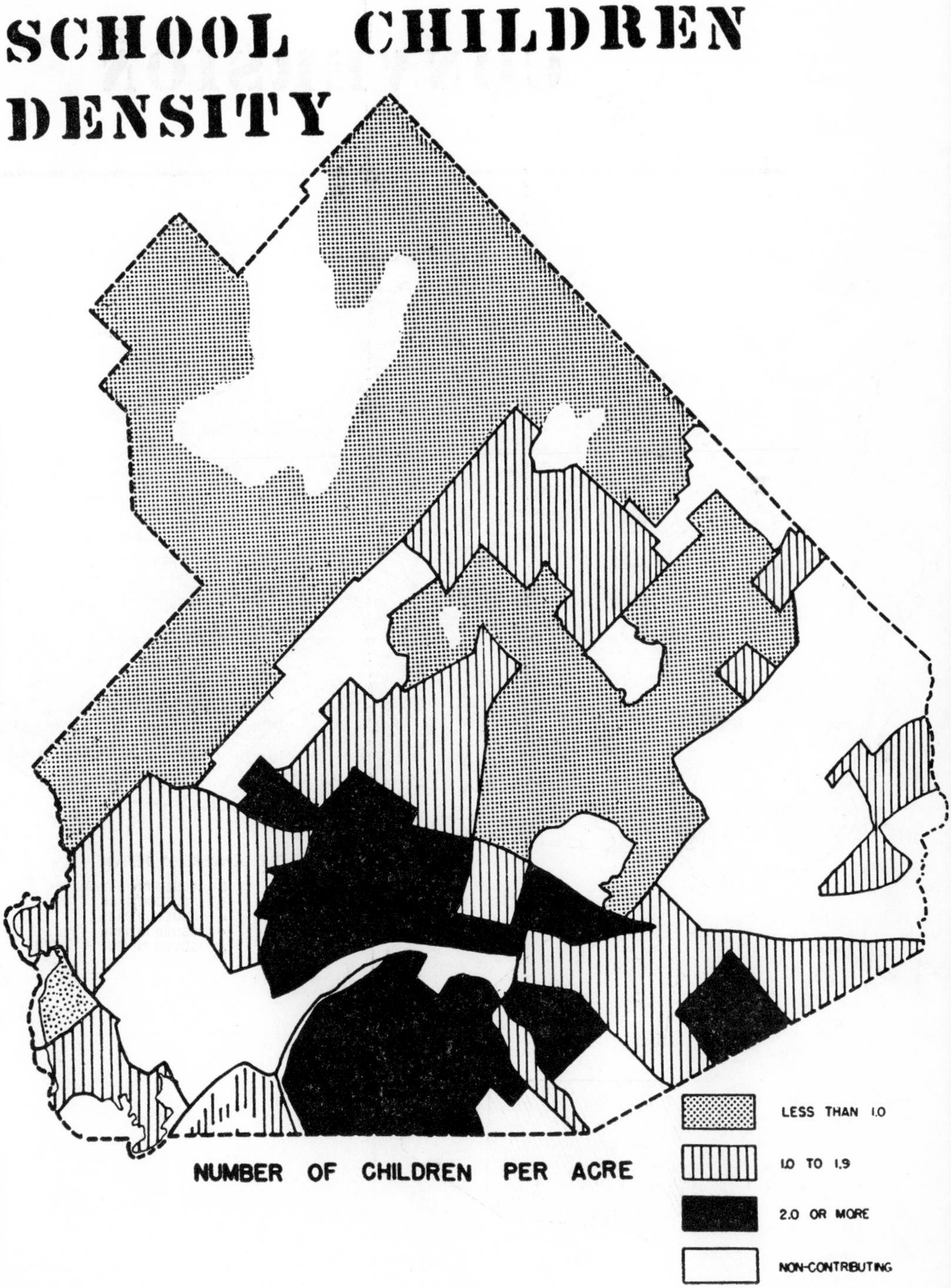

SCHOOL CHILDREN DENSITY

NUMBER OF CHILDREN PER ACRE

LESS THAN 1.0

1.0 TO 1.9

2.0 OR MORE

NON-CONTRIBUTING

MAP IV

CONVERSION

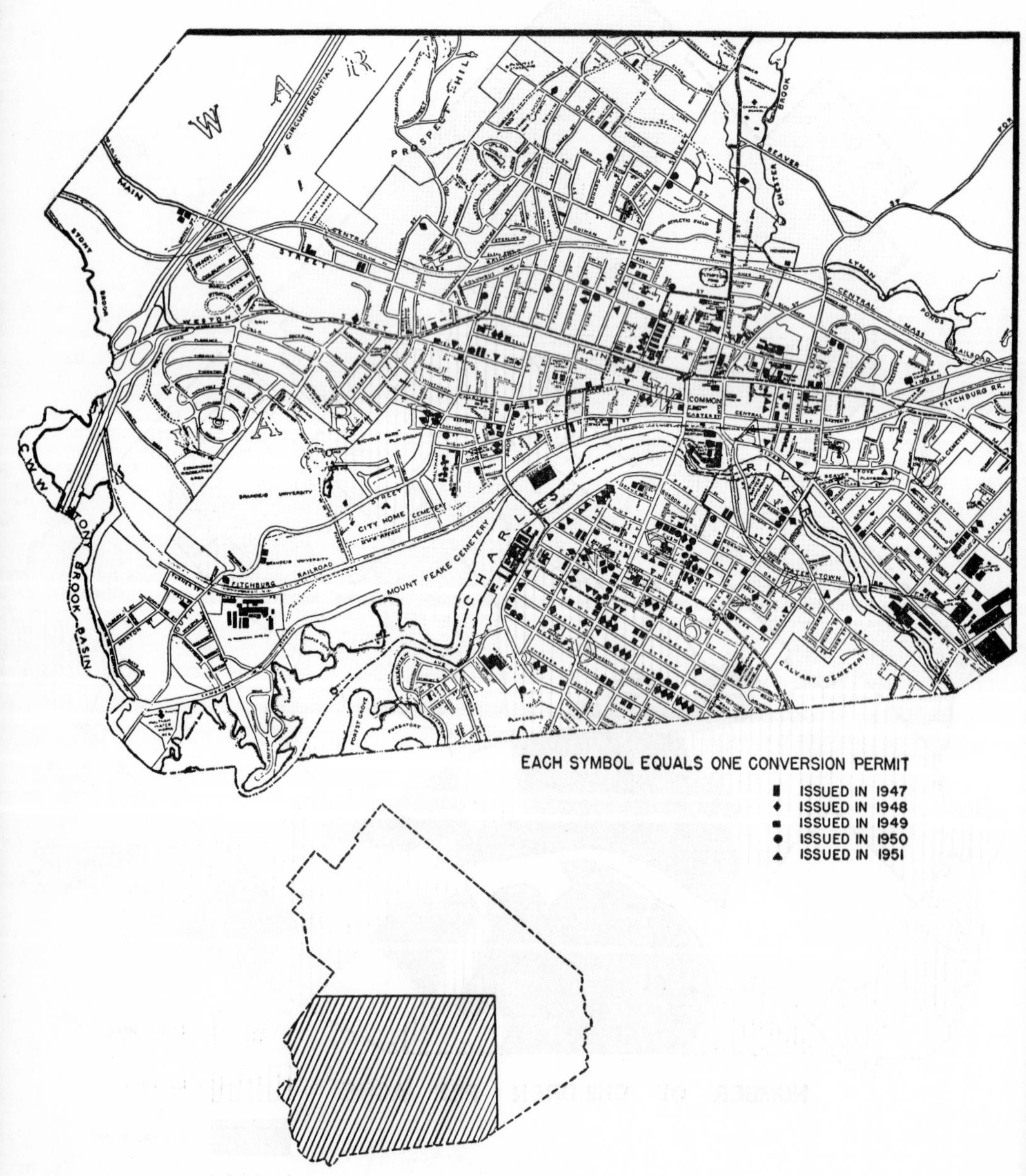

Table V

STUDY AREA BASIC DATA: APRIL, 1951

Area No.	*Approx. Area (Acres)*	*No. of Preschool Children*	*No. of Nonpublic School Children*	*No. of Public School Children*	*Total No. of Children Birth to 18*	*Density of Public School Children S.C./acre*
1	1,080	0	5	11	16	0.01
2	420	12	1	9	22	0.02
3	240	24	2	40	66	0.17
4	380	30	3	16	49	0.04
5	180	4	0	0	4	0.00
6	240	9	0	8	17	0.03
7	140	178	17	162	357	1.16
8	200	48	6	69	123	0.35
9	250	149	17	182	348	0.73
10	180	65	7	35	107	0.19
11	240	9	0	27	36	0.11
12	90	3	0	13	16	0.14
13	180	0	0	0	0	0.00
14	130	42	1	30	73	0.23
15	110	0	0	6	6	0.05
16	150	42	5	40	87	0.26
17	100	176	61	166	403	1.66
18	40	244	27	96	367	2.40
19	40	25	19	34	78	0.85
20	120	110	66	137	313	1.14
21	40	97	94	139	330	3.48
22	60	188	140	213	541	3.55
23	150	88	38	119	245	0.79
24	50	49	12	83	144	1.66
25	20	46	18	56	120	2.80
26	20	9	3	3	15	0.15
27	50	25	4	23	52	0.46
28	80	185	69	199	453	2.49
29	90	273	156	324	753	3.60
30	270	75	16	93	184	0.34
31	120	0	0	3	3	0.02
32	25	0	0	7	7	0.28
33	50	80	43	86	209	1.72
34	60	44	6	62	112	1.03
35	130	255	50	292	597	2.25
36	50	183	80	250	513	5.00
37	30	67	95	83	245	2.76
38	80	253	59	257	569	3.21
39	30	128	56	87	271	2.90
40	8	0	1	3	4	0.38
41	35	45	16	42	103	1.20
42	70	230	199	147	576	2.10
43	60	30	14	36	80	0.60
44	25	35	34	30	99	1.20
45	40	86	41	67	194	1.67
46	60	83	88	62	233	1.03
47	60	11	5	16	32	0.27
48	320	26	4	22	52	0.07
49	90	141	101	156	398	1.72
50	40	42	24	71	137	1.77

Table V (continued)

Area No.	Approx. Area (Acres)	No. of Preschool Children	No. of Nonpublic School Children	No. of Public School Children	Total No. of Children Birth to 18	Density of Public School Children S.C./acre
51	70	154	88	185	427	2.64
52	70	63	23	62	148	0.90
53	15	16	11	6	33	0.40
54	70	370	57	132	559	1.90
55	200	2	2	5	9	0.03
56	80	28	9	31	68	0.39
57	60	77	25	98	200	1.63
58	90	115	27	152	294	1.70
59	100	33	3	32	68	0.32
60	400	3	0	6	9	0.02
61	80	146	32	200	378	2.50
62	120	154	13	123	290	1.02
63	150	27	0	40	67	0.27
64	80	71	5	104	180	1.30
65	110	0	0	9	9	0.08
Totals	8,418	5,203	2,000	5,297	12,500	

From the building that is under way and certain building petitions existing for the near future, we can reasonably estimate building to 1954 and thus proceed to estimate the distribution of children. Also we can easily identify the general area in which building will occur from 1954 to 1958. But as the master plan for Waltham has not yet been worked out, to go beyond 1958 would imply more knowledge than it is possible to have at present.

However, an estimate of distribution in 1954 will provide the pertinent information for building needed immediately, and an estimate of 1958 distribution (which should be reasonably accurate at the level of attendance area analysis) will provide rough information for long-range planning and immediate selection of school sites.

Before discussing possible locations of future homes, it is interesting to see the location of the postwar housing planned by August, 1951. Map I shows the location of new houses authorized by building permits, and Map IV shows the location of conversions. Conversions are houses divided in such a way as to create a new dwelling unit.

Now let us turn our attention to new dwelling units expected by 1954 and by 1958. For each four-year period, 1,200 new units are expected.

Considering conversions first, we find that the rate is steadily declining from the approximately 60 conversions per year which occurred during the immediate postwar period. At the present time, the rate is about 30 per year. The area south of Main Street is becoming saturated and will soon contribute practically no conversions. On the other hand, the section north of Main Street and west of Lexington Street (with the encouragement of city planning authorities) will probably continue to add conversion units. We estimate that, on an average for the next eight years, 30 conversions per year will go into the north region.

The Cedarwood and Warrendale areas are reaching saturation. Assuming a steady decline of new building in these areas as available lots are used up,

Table VI

NUMBER OF CHILDREN * BY ELEMENTARY ATTENDANCE AREAS: 1950

Area	Sections	K–4	4–6	7–9	10–12	Totals
Banks	16, 17, 23, 24, 25, 26, 27, 30, 31	171	100	83	74	428
Bright	51, 52, 56, 57	126	81	88	75	370
Fitch	32, 33, 34, 35	316	175	195	98	784
Hardy	1, 2, 3, 4, 7, 8, 9	224	111	100	36	471
Hill	41, 45, 46, 47, 53, 54, 55	159	68	63	41	331
Lawrence	11, 12, 13, 14, 15, 48, 60, 63, 64, 65	116	78	58	39	291
Newhall	28, 29	183	92	52	35	362
Plympton	5, 6, 10, 18, 19, 20, 21, 22, 42, 43	371	185	173	155	884
Warrendale	58, 59, 61, 62	249	86	77	81	493
Whittemore	36, 37, 38, 39, 40, 44, 49, 50	308	215	240	120	883
Totals:		2,223	1,191	1,129	754	5,297

* Does not include special students, trade school students, or students over 18.

we estimate that by 1954 there will be 80 new houses in the Cedarwood and 40 new houses in the Warrendale area. After 1954 the contribution of new houses in both of these sections is expected to be negligible.

Considering new housing east of Lexington Street near Beaver Street, there is acreage for about 140 new houses at three houses per acre. It is assumed that by 1954 there will be 60 new homes in this area, and 80 more by 1958.

Moving to the north part of Waltham along Trapelo Road, we estimate that by 1954, 300 houses will be built in study area 2 of the general type already there. (A petition is now before the City Planning Board for this amount of construction.) By 1958, 200 more will be built in this area. In study area 3 the same estimate is made as for area 2; Realty Construction Company has plans to place 300 homes in this area with construction beginning in March, 1952. In areas 11 and 14 it is believed that 200 houses will be added by 1954 and 100 more by 1958. One hundred fifty-four houses are already under construction in area 11.

In areas 9 and 10, building seems steady. Although the building rate is less spectacular than along Trapelo Road, it is reasonable to believe that 25 homes will be built in this area each year for the next eight years.

Finally, to meet the estimate of 1,200 new dwelling units every four-year period, it is believed that as many as 300 new units will go into study area 4 near either Trapelo Road or Prospect Park. As yet the Planning Board is uncertain whether to allocate land for residential or industrial purposes in the region near Prospect Park.

With preceding estimates, a table of anticipated building can be made up. Table VII shows the anticipated new dwelling units by study areas. Table VIII shows the anticipated new units by school attendance areas, which will be the data used in continuing the analysis of distribution of children.

Once the location of new dwelling units is estimated, the problem becomes one of determining the distribution of children in the study areas.

We must be specific about the kind of dwelling unit most likely to be constructed in Waltham. Immediately after the war, single-family homes, conversions, and multi-apartment units were built in Waltham. At present the building

Table VII

NEW DWELLING UNITS PER SECTION

Section	*1954*	*1958*
17, 18, 19, 20, 21, 22	120	120
23	80	---
58, 61, 62	40	---
47, 48	60	80
2	300	200
3	300	200
11, 14	200	100
9, 10	100	100
8	---	100
4	---	300
	1200	1200

under way consists entirely of single-family dwellings and a few conversions. Future developments already in the planning stage are for single-family dwellings. We are assuming, therefore, that save for a few conversions, the single-family dwelling will be the predominant kind to go up in Waltham during the next eight years.

Table VIII

NEW DWELLING UNITS PER ATTENDANCE AREAS

School Area	*1954*	*1958*
Banks	100	20
Bright	0	0
Fitch	0	0
Hardy	650	900
Hill	30	40
Lawrence	230	140
Newhall	0	0
Plympton	150	100
Warrendale	40	0
Whittemore	0	0
	1,200	1,200

We feel it reasonable to expect that in 1954 the distribution of children in the new dwellings will compare to the city as a whole just as in 1950 the distribution of children in sections 23, 62, and 64 (containing mostly housing built in 1947–50) compares to the city as a whole. The comparison of distribution of children in sections 23, 62, and 64 with the distribution of all Waltham children is given in Table IX.

From the data of Table IX, one would argue that the distribution of children in the new housing areas is no different from that in the whole town. Thus, in estimating distribution of children in the new areas in future years, we will assume that the new areas will have the same distribution as the city as a whole is expected to have in the year under consideration.

An important anomaly appears at this point. It is possible (although not

Table IX

DISTRIBUTION OF CHILDREN FROM NEW DWELLINGS COMPARED TO WALTHAM AS A WHOLE

Section	*Preschool*	*K–3*	*4–6*	*7–9*	*10–12*	*Total*
23	88	61	37	24	35	245
62	154	60	27	24	25	290
64	71	29	29	27	24	180
Total	313	150	93	75	84	715
Per cent	43%	21%	13%	11%	12%	
Per cent distribution whole city of Waltham	42%	22%	13%	11%	12%	

likely) that Waltham will experience new construction of multi-unit dwellings of the sort at Prospect Hill, Garden Circle, etc. Sections 18 and 54 consist almost entirely of housing of this type. Examining sections 18 and 54 in the same way as the previous sections, we note the distribution of children is not at all the same as that for the whole town. (Table X.) (The new Chesterbrook Garden development is also of this type.)

Table X

DISTRIBUTION OF CHILDREN FROM MULTI-UNIT DWELLINGS

Section	*Preschool*	*School Age*	*Total*
18	244	123	367
54	370	189	576
Total	614	313	926
Per cent	66%	34%	100%
All Waltham	42%	58%	100%

Should new construction follow the pattern of multi-unit dwellings, this anomaly would have to be considered. In fact, in the absence of these multi-unit dwellings, the distribution of children in other sections might be altered. But in terms of the accuracy involved in distribution estimates, this possibility does not seem serious enough to warrant special corrections.

In sections 62, 63, and 64, we also note that nonpublic school enrollments are relatively small from the new housing areas as compared to Waltham as a whole: 6.7 per cent compared to 27 per cent. This is probably partly related to the inability of existing nonpublic schools to service more than 2,075 children, so that children in new housing areas are not able to enroll in the nonpublic schools. Since this problem appears to be getting more intense, we will assume *all* children of school age in the new units will seek enrollment in the public schools.

One further factor is needed before projecting the distribution of children in 1954 and 1958. In the past, the size of families occupying new homes has run about 3.4 persons per unit. Although there are probably a few children over high school age and some adults besides parents, we will use as a basis of computation 1.4 children from birth to age eighteen per dwelling unit.

It is assumed in making the estimates that the part of the town existing in 1950 will contribute *public school students* in 1954 and 1958 in the same *proportion* as in 1950; the numbers change because the age distribution changes, but the proportion remains the same.

The estimates of public school enrollment distribution appear in Table XI for 1954 and Table XII for 1958. . . .

Table XI

1954 ESTIMATE OF DISTRIBUTION OF PUBLIC SCHOOL ENROLLMENTS

School Area	*New Dwellings*	*	*K–3*	*	*4–6*	*	*7–9*	*	*10–12*	*Total*
Banks	100	(43)	243	(21)	156	(18)	125	(14)	96	620
Bright	0	(0)	148	(0)	107	(0)	114	(0)	83	452
Fitch	0	(0)	374	(0)	237	(0)	250	(0)	109	970
Hardy	650	(282)	545	(137)	289	(118)	247	(91)	131	1,212
Hill	30	(13)	205	(6)	97	(5)	86	(4)	49	437
Lawrence	230	(99)	238	(48)	155	(42)	117	(32)	75	585
Newhall	0	(0)	219	(0)	125	(0)	68	(0)	38	450
Plympton	150	(65)	505	(31)	291	(27)	247	(21)	193	1,236
Warrendale & Warren	40	(17)	312	(8)	125	(7)	105	(6)	95	637
Whittemore	0	(0)	365	(0)	292	(0)	305	(0)	133	1,095
	1,200		3,154		1,874		1,664		1,002	7,694

* Numbers in parentheses tell how many of the total result from estimated new homes.

Table XII

1958 ESTIMATE OF DISTRIBUTION OF PUBLIC SCHOOL ENROLLMENTS

School Area	*New Dwellings*	*	*K–3*	*	*4–6*	*	*7–9*	*	*10–12*	*Total*
Banks	120	(45)	192	(31)	198	(27)	148	(22)	122	660
Bright	0	(0)	109	(0)	135	(0)	130	(0)	102	476
Fitch	0	(0)	278	(0)	295	(0)	284	(0)	134	991
Hardy	1,550	(558)	779	(414)	604	(348)	494	(283)	332	2,209
Hill	70	(26)	166	(19)	132	(16)	108	(13)	68	474
Lawrence	370	(140)	239	(98)	231	(83)	168	(67)	120	758
Newhall	0	(0)	156	(0)	155	(0)	75	(0)	47	433
Plympton	250	(95)	414	(66)	389	(56)	305	(46)	257	1,365
Warrendale & Warren	440	(151)	354	(11)	157	(9)	122	(7)	116	749
Whittemore	0	(0)	263	(0)	364	(0)	346	(0)	162	1,135
	2,400		2,950		2,660		2,180		1,460	9,250

* Numbers in parentheses tell how many children of the total result from new homes.

Chapter II

Waltham's School Plant Today

In Waltham, as elsewhere, school buildings are much more than the inanimate heaps of masonry that they appear. Belying the inert quality their exteriors sometimes present, school buildings have a definite function to perform — a function beyond that of mere shelter. This function is to provide the means, through proper facilities of design, of aiding and stimulating the educational program itself. Rather than as an element of passivity, therefore, the school building should be thought of as an active force. . . .

The age of the school building often is related to the positive or negative influence which the school exerts. Most well-planned and soundly constructed school buildings maintain their educational usefulness, or positive action, for a period of about thirty-five to forty years. After that, they frequently descend the road to obsolescence at an accelerated rate, so that a half century of use usually means that the building is acting negatively by limiting and interfering with the educational activities of the occupants.

Age is but one factor that affects educational utility, however. Of great importance also are the basic design of the building, the manner in which it has been maintained, and how much it has been improved to approach modern standards of safety, comfort, and efficiency. Some school buildings become obsolete before they have stood twenty years; others, through intelligent initial design and good maintenance and rehabilitation practices, extend their period of usefulness beyond the usual span.

Waltham's School Buildings

The Waltham School Department at present operates eleven elementary school buildings, one special school (Robbins), two junior high school buildings, one senior high school plant, and one trade school. The location of these buildings, together with the major traffic arteries, are given on Maps V and VI. Trade school classes are also held in quarters on Main Street, at School and Exchange Streets, and at the Waltham Watch Company. These latter will not be considered in this section except indirectly, since they are not properly a part of the Waltham school plant under the complete control of the School Committee.

The median age of the remaining sixteen school buildings is forty years, based upon the age of the original building in those areas where an addition has been erected. The original portions of four of Waltham's schools are sixty-four or more years old.

General Characteristics of the Present School Plant

Certain common characteristics are observable in the Waltham school plant. These involve not only the buildings themselves, but also the sites upon which the schools are located.

School sites in Waltham are generally inadequate in area and are sometimes poorly placed to serve best their potential enrollments. Only two schools, Lawrence and Warrendale, even approach present standards for size of school sites. A few, such as Hill and Plympton, have no outdoor play area on the site. While standards call for sites of fiteen to seventeen acres for a junior high school, North and South Junior Highs have only about one and a half acres each. The Whittemore School is an example of where *not* to place a school building.

MAP V

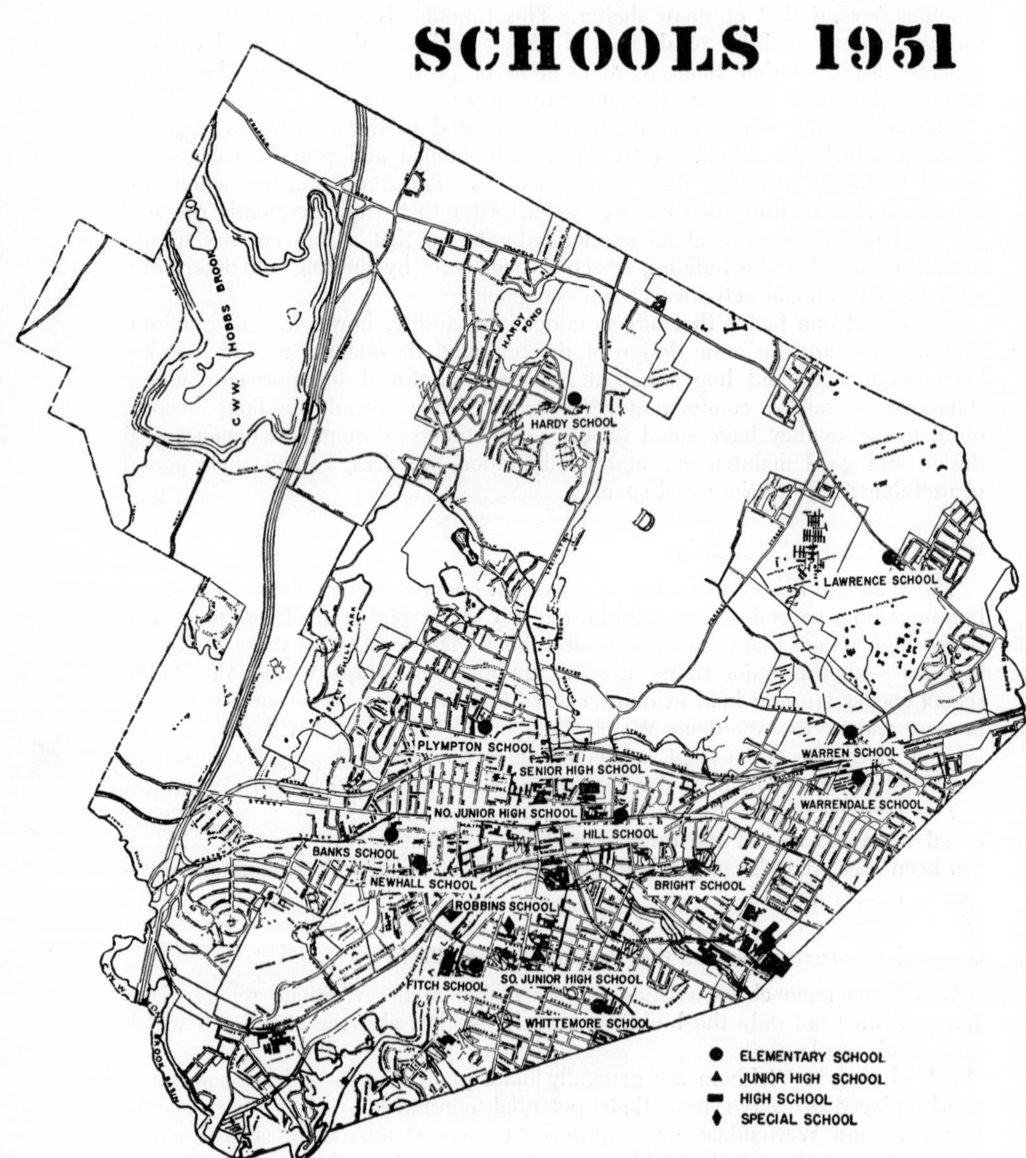
SCHOOLS 1951
HOBBS BROOK
C.W.W.
HARDY POND
HARDY SCHOOL
LAWRENCE SCHOOL
PLYMPTON SCHOOL
WARREN SCHOOL
SENIOR HIGH SCHOOL
WARRENDALE SCHOOL
NO. JUNIOR HIGH SCHOOL
HILL SCHOOL
BANKS SCHOOL
NEWHALL SCHOOL
BRIGHT SCHOOL
ROBBINS SCHOOL
FITCH SCHOOL
SO. JUNIOR HIGH SCHOOL
WHITTEMORE SCHOOL
ELEMENTARY SCHOOL
JUNIOR HIGH SCHOOL
HIGH SCHOOL
SPECIAL SCHOOL

MAP VI

TRAFFIC
HOBBS BROOK
C.W.W.
HARDY POND
10,000
5,000
1,000
VEHICLES PER DAY

The city line and an adjacent cemetery effectively cut off two directions from which the school should draw its pupils. Clearly, study of placement and attainment of adequate area must attend future site selections in Waltham. . . .

As regards the buildings themselves, art, music, audio-visual, and guidance rooms are missing from nearly all schools. Only a few schools have any kind of health clinic, and where such facilities do exist, they are of minimum area and quality. Administration space, including that designed for storage of supplies, also tends to be minimal. Fireproof storage of pupils' records is almost totally unavailable.

Classrooms in the elementary schools are generally small, even in the recently constructed Warrendale School where rooms are about 23′ × 28′.

A commendable effort to supplant the fixed, screwed-down furniture with movable desks and chairs is noted in many school buildings. This move is in keeping with modern trends in education, and all possible support should be given to this replacement program.

Other school building details that deserve favorable comment include the steel staircases and the upstairs toilet rooms in many schools. In addition, most Waltham schools have had good maintenance over the years, and there has been continued attention to the elements that affect pupil safety. Exterior masonry, paint, and roofs are also apparently well maintained.

Method of Evaluation

Each of Waltham's school buildings has been carefully studied to determine its acceptability as an educational tool and its destiny in the planning of an ultimate school plant for the city. Each has been evaluated by using a measuring instrument through which a numerical score is earned by each building, comparable to that of an ideal school building rated at 1000 points.

Into this evaluation have entered hundreds of criteria ranging from such items as size of classrooms to adequacy of the school site. In Table XIII these criteria have been summarized under five principal headings, and each school has been scored in terms of the ideal scores shown in the column headings.

Table XIII

SUMMARY OF RATING OF PRESENT ELEMENTARY SCHOOL PLANT

School	*Site (120)*	*Building Design Structure (170)*	*Service Systems (225)*	*Classrooms (315)*	*Special Rooms (170)*	*Total (1000)*
Banks	15	120	170	185	85	575
Bright	32	96	133	176	53	490
Fitch	67	128	164	186	112	657
Hardy	35	102	146	179	95	517
Hill	10	92	135	164	63	464
Lawrence	90	108	158	170	79	605
Newhall	18	95	134	170	48	465
Plympton	12	97	140	150	72	471
Robbins	16	84	132	150	50	432
Warren	35	42	138	142	62	419
Warrendale	110	152	197	200	116	777
Whittemore	50	132	163	182	120	647

School buildings attaining a total score of less than 500 points are classified as generally poor, while those scoring less than 400 may be said to be basically inadequate. Schools in these categories would naturally be the ones selected for abandonment, all other things being equal, when that step is indicated. In the case of Waltham, however, there can be no program of abandonments until the peak enrollments are past, thereby pointing to another decade of use for all these buildings.

[We are omitting the detailed descriptions of individual school buildings, contained in the survey report, except for abbreviated comments on the secondary school buildings.]

THE NORTH JUNIOR HIGH SCHOOL

Outside of the two wood shops and the homemaking room in the basement, this 1920 building has sixteen classroms, a fair basement gymnasium, and a flat-floored auditorium. There is an inadequate cafeteria in the basement consisting of a modest kitchen and little dining space.

Most of the regular classrooms are about 23′ × 30′, and contain forty seats. No special rooms for art, music, guidance, or pupil activities are provided. The only shops are woodworking rooms. There is no library, although one small room, equipped with about fifteen seats, does have a few books in bookcases.

The science rooms are poorly equipped, and the homemaking rooms are in a dark section of the basement. The office, the teachers' room, and the health room are quite modest in size and appointments. . . .

Instead of the fifteen or more acres of school site necessary for this plant, the building is placed on a two-acre plot at a busy intersection. At the rear of the school is a small unpaved area which is the only outdoor recreational space available. . . .

THE SOUTH JUNIOR HIGH SCHOOL

Counting the so-called library, there are seventeen classrooms, two shops, and two home-making rooms in this school. There is a long narrow gymnasium (about 46′ × 100′) and, across the corridor, a kitchen and serving counter so that pupils can eat in the gymnasium, although there are no tables. There are also two small shower rooms at each end of the gymnasium.

In the basement, under the auditorium, are the two shops for printing and woodworking. Nearby in the basement are a foods room and a sewing room. Also in the basement are the only toilet rooms in the building.

The classrooms (about 23′ × 32′) have forty seats per room. . . .

There are fairly good science and biology rooms on the second floor, and the teachers' room and health room on that level are also acceptable. However, there is no provision for special rooms for art, music, crafts, or exploratory experiences in such program areas as typing or home economics. . . .

This school was built in 1923 on a site of about two acres, when it should have been about seventeen or eighteen. Consequently, there can be little outdoor activity on the limited site which is located at the busy intersection of Moody and High Streets.

THE SENIOR HIGH SCHOOL

The central section of the High School was erected in 1902, and both the east and west wings were added in 1935. The older portion is three stories and a basement in height, while the wings are two stories and a basement high.

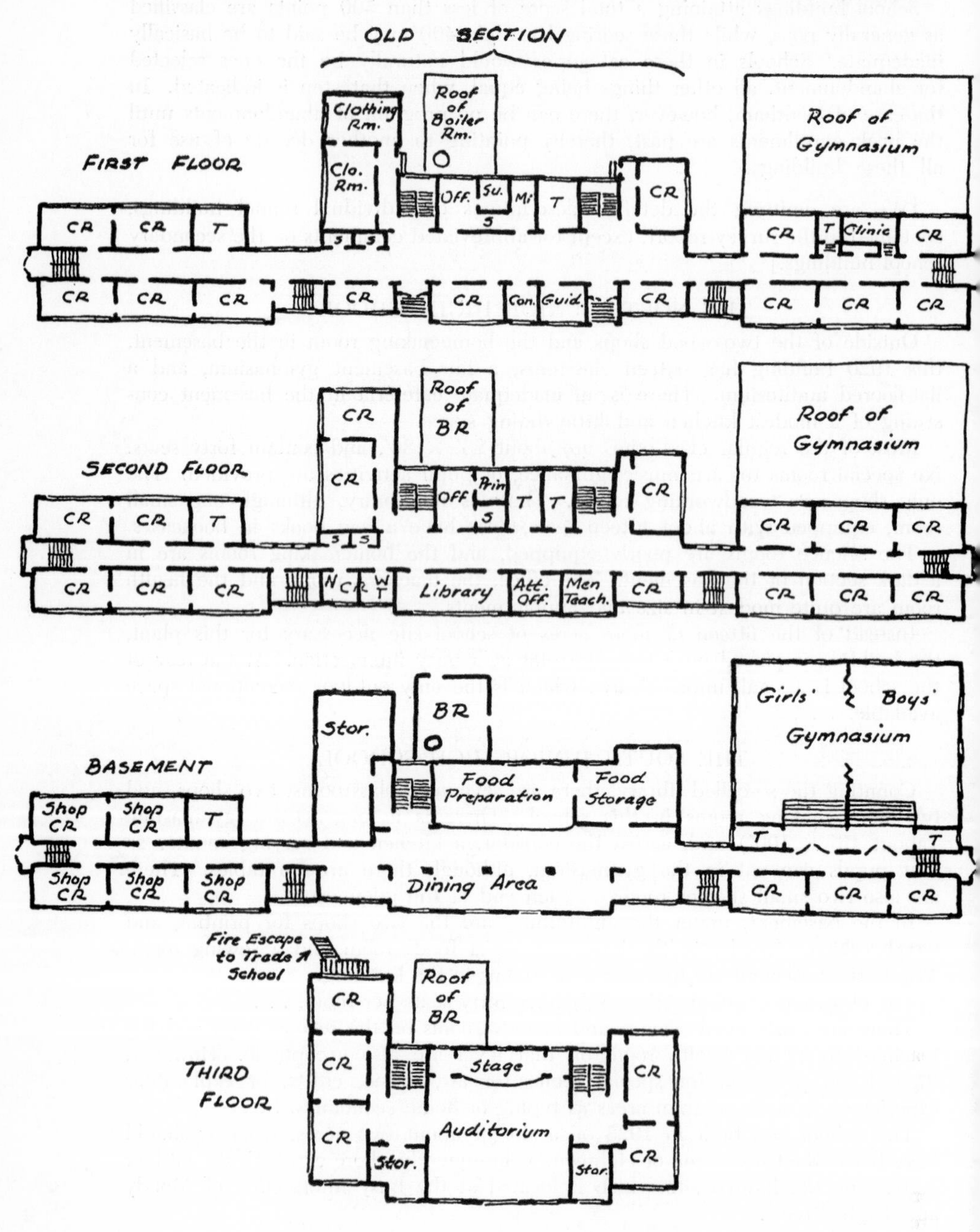

SENIOR HIGH SCHOOL

These wings, which are worthy of retention as part of Waltham's ultimate school plant, are of fire-resistant construction and have a number of good features. Recessed corridor lockers, partially recessed bubblers in corridors, asphalt tile floors, cream colored face brick lower walls, a telephone intercommunication system, good window-sill height, and excellent toilets have been put into these buildings. . . . In the basements are the gymnasiums and some shop rooms which are used as adjuncts of the grade school. With the exception of a clinic, the remainder of the rooms are classrooms.

The half-century-old center section has outlived its educational usefulness. Its antiquated assembly hall is three and a half stories above the street, its staircases and corridors are wasteful, and its rooms are ill-suited to their purposes. Its basement cafeteria is what would be expected of a cellar space of fifty years ago — cut up, poorly lighted and ventilated, restricted; in short, anything but a contribution to the socialization process which is a vital part of today's education. The library, which should be the resource and research center of the school, is a dull, uninteresting, uninspiring, totally inadequate room. . . .

There are no specially equipped rooms for music, art, consumer education, or the modern phases of homemaking. All in all, this building tightly restricts the educational experiences of the senior high pupils in Waltham.

Table XIV summarizes the scores for the junior and senior high schools.

Table XIV

RATINGS OF JUNIOR AND SENIOR HIGH SCHOOLS

Items	*Maximum Score*	*North Junior*	*South Junior*	*Senior**
Site	120	15	15	20
Building Design, Structure	170	115	140	118
Service System	225	142	165	129
Classrooms				
Regular	245	148	174	132
Special	70	18	30	23
Special Rooms				
Pupil Activities	70	34	46	18
Service	50	32	36	15
Administration	50	30	32	20
Total	1000	534	638	475

* This is a composite score, including both the old and the new sections.

THE TRADE SCHOOL

This two-and-a-half story building was constructed in 1905 at the rear of the senior high school on a site that is inadequate for either school separately. A fire escape connects the roof level of this building with the upper floors of the Senior High School, bridging an intervening driveway.

The Trade School is badly overcrowded and needs about twice the floor space for its present activities.

The auto shop, with related activities, is in the basement, the machine shop on the floor above, and the printing room, some carpentry, and a stock room on the top floor.

Planning activity, physical education, and other special functions are not provided for, except on an expediency basis in the Senior High building. This focuses attention upon its dependence on the Senior High School, of which it might well be a part. The high quality of some of its equipment deserves a better, less crowded physical plant. . . .

THE SCHOOL ATHLETIC FIELD

Although this field is in fairly good condition, well located from a community standpoint, and has fairly adequate seating capacity, the concept of placing recreational facilities in a spot remote from the related school plant is open to question. Most authorities today agree that the school site itself should include enough usable land to have the recreational activities right there. In this way the convenient use of the shower and locker rooms, as well as equipment, is possible, without the expensive duplication of these items. In this particular instance, transportation from a remote school building to the athletic field should be regarded as only an expedient. . . .

Chapter III

Conclusions and Recommendations

I. The Use of the Present School Plant

From the foregoing analysis, it is obvious that Waltham is faced with a large discrepancy between present school building capacity and what will be needed to meet future enrollments at all grade levels. There are many ways of computing the capacity of a school building. One acceptable method for estimating elementary school capacity is based on the average number of pupils per classroom.

In Table XV the planned capacity for each of the elementary buildings now in use is computed on the basis of an average of 30, 28, and 25 pupils per room.

Table XV

SUMMARY OF PLANNED ELEMENTARY CLASSROOM CAPACITY FOR WALTHAM

Attendance Area	*No. of Rooms*	*Building Capacity*		
		30 pupils per room	*28 pupils per room*	*25 pupils per room*
Banks	15	450	420	375
Bright	9	270	252	225
Fitch	7	210	196	175
Hardy	8	240	224	200
Hill	9	270	252	225
Lawrence	7	210	196	175
Newhall	8	240	224	200
Plympton	18	540	504	450
Warrendale	7	210	196	175
Whittemore	26	780	728	650
	114	3,420	3,192	2,850

The school committee believes that 30 pupils should be the maximum average class size. It recognizes that some classes operating within the city may contain

34 or 35 pupils, and others less than 30, in order to achieve this average. The committee would also like, as soon as possible, to lower this average to approximately 25, thereby maintaining a range of from 23 to 27 or 28. This is a desirable stand for the committee to take, since it is generally held that a class of more than 30 pupils reduces the possibility of individual attention.

As enrollments have steadily increased during the past two years, it has become necessary to take over emergency facilities. Extremely small basement areas have been converted, and teachers' rooms and other special activity areas have been utilized to handle the mounting demand for classroom space. Everyone concerned with school administration has realized that the educational experiences of the children have been significantly impaired by the cutting down of building facilities. (It stands to reason, for instance, that the educational program at the Warrendale School has been hampered by the subdivision of the basement all-purpose activity room.)

These statements are not meant to be critical. They are included merely to emphasize the fact that the number of children presently housed in Waltham school buildings does not indicate a true capacity based on an unfettered educational program. *The survey staff recommends that all emergency classrooms be abandoned as soon as possible so that these areas may revert to their original functions of assisting in diversifying the children's education.* The staff realizes, of course, that the magnitude of the present over-all need for space is such that these emergency rooms may have to be utilized while new construction is made available, but in spite of the extensiveness of the problem, the abandonment of these substandard facilities is recommended . . .

Table XVI shows the distribution of school building capacity when these emergency facilities are included in estimating available classroom space.

Table XVI

EMERGENCY CAPACITY

Attendance Area	*Planned Capacity, 30 pupils per room*	*Emergency Capacity (incl. unplanned areas) at 30 pupils each*	*Expected Enrollment 1958*	*Plus or Minus*
Banks	450	480	390	+ 90
Bright	270	270	244	+ 26
Fitch	210	300	573	− 273
Hardy	240	270	1,383	−1,113
Hill	270	270	298	− 28
Lawrence	210	210	470	− 260
Newhall	240	300	311	− 11
Plympton	540	540	803	− 263
Warrendale	210	360*	511	− 151
Whittemore	780	960	627	+ 333
	3,420	3,960	5,610	−1,650

* Including 60 at the Warren School.

The need for additional school facilities is not distributed evenly throughout the city. However, no school attendance area has what can be considered surplus school facilities, except possibly one — the Whittemore School in the southernmost section of the city. Due to the tremendous need for school facilities, therefore, it is self-evident that *all available capacity must be utilized to the full.* The survey staff, fortunately, can conscientiously recommend the adequacy of all the present elementary and junior high buildings from the point of view of safety, although in any long-range program certain of the buildings should be slated for abandonment.

II. Recommended Rehabilitation Practices

It should be remembered that the bulk of Waltham's school children will continue to be housed in the present school buildings. It is important, therefore, that these buildings be made attractive and comfortable as part of the program for developing desirable classroom environment. . . .

III. Needed New Schoolhouse Facilities

Waltham is facing an almost simultaneous need for additional school housing at the elementary, junior high, and senior high school levels. This need is felt unequally in the several sections of the city and at varied school levels within these sections. Moreover, additions to the present school buildings cannot be considered as contributing significantly to the solution of the problem. Indeed, in only one case is the site large enough to permit an addition. The recommendations for the solution of the complex building problem are perhaps most clearly seen if they are presented in four parts by dividing the city as a whole into the following general areas:

A. The section south of the Charles River extending to the Newton line,
B. The section north and east of the Charles River running from the Waltham Railroad station south and east of the railroad track to the Watertown-Belmont line,
C. The section north of the Charles River, west of the Common, south of Main and Weston Streets, and
D. The remainder of the city north of these three sections.

13 *Blackboard Hodson*

THE Ludington school district is located in a residential town (population 28,000) about twenty-five miles from a large commercial city. Last year the gross cost of the schools was just under one million dollars. Over two-thirds of this cost went into salaries for the superintendent, the teachers, the principals, and the supervisors. Edison Pines School will be completed in 1952; it is a fine example of modern elementary school building. Last year 4,390 were enrolled in the eight elementary schools, two junior high schools and one high school.

In the Ludington School Report for 1951, just following the School Calendar and the Financial Statement, there appears "The Report of the School Board." It says in part:

> Your Board convened at 32 meetings this past year and many perplexing problems confronted them. As we pointed out in the school report last year, the problems for the most part were in five categories:
>
> 1. Proper maintenance of present school physical plant.
> 2. Future expansion of school physical plant.
> 3. Salary adjustment for all employees.
> 4. Transportation of children.
> 5. Standardized educational opportunities.
>
> A sixth problem may be appropriately added at this time:
>
> 6. Revamping of the administrative organization.
>
> We report on these problems as follows:
>
> 1. A maintenance group which supplements regular custodial repairs is accomplishing much towards keeping our plant in proper condition. They are working on a schedule which takes them methodically from school to school. Results have been most effective.
>
> 2. The new elementary school in the Edison Pines area should be completed in the spring or early summer of 1952. This excellent example of a modern school, housing the latest and best educational features, will, to a great degree, ease the elementary problem on the north side of town.
>
> 3. The School Board over the last five-year period has endeavored to adjust the salaries and wages of its employees with a twofold view in mind: (1) To pay salaries and wages which befit the particular position and its concomitant duties. (2) To bear firmly in mind the expansions of the town's obligations in all fields of government and the ability of the taxpayer to absorb the ever-increasing financial burden that is the inevitable part now of expansion growth. We feel that our employees, as of this date, are being compensated fairly in respect to points 1 and 2 above.
>
> 4. The full impact of the transportation problem has not yet been felt by the Board. This problem is growing steadily, however, and as a present solution we are strongly recommending the purchase by Ludington of another school bus in 1952.

5. Through the leadership of the superintendent and his cooperative fellow administrators, the principals, we are arriving at a more standardized educational system. We can definitely report progress at this time.

6. Study is now being given to the revamping of the administrative organization of the school system. While it can be safely said that no sweeping changes are contemplated, it is fair to say that consistent with progress in the other fields of our system, some changes will be effected by the Board during the year 1952. A proper distribution of administrative assignments will make for a better and more progressive school organization.

The school committee report concluded: "Some (administrative) changes will be effected by the Board during the year 1952."

"Blackboard" Hodson, the superintendent, came to Ludington five years ago from a smaller superintendency in the western part of the state. He had his A.B. from Colgate and his Ed.M. from the University of Michigan in 1928. He had taught in elementary and in high school, and had been high school principal and coach. Forceful, colorful in speech, "Blackboard" Hodson spent his first six months in the Ludington System as an "associate without specific duties." He moved among the teachers and principals of the eight schools talking to everyone — students, teachers, janitors, and principals.

This is what he told an interviewer: "I spent my time investigating every nook and cranny of the school system. I wanted to see and not to criticize. I wanted to get a knowledge of the system, to hear all the gripes, and to discuss problems with the personnel without making any promises to anyone. The Ludington system seemed to revolve around the personalities of two people — the outgoing superintendent and the high school principal. Do you want to hear about it, fella?"

Mr. Hodson went from his desk in his dingy office across the room to his blackboard. He had to speak loudly, as the school band was practicing "The Black Watch March" in the music room directly under the superintendent's office. He wrote "Superintendent" and "Principal" on the board and continued to speak.

"When I came here five years ago, the outgoing superintendent had been here thirty-three years. He was a gentleman of the old school. During the last ten years he appeared to be waiting out retirement. Probably he had had his battles and rebuffs earlier, but when I got here, things appeared to be rosy. He had urged my election to the job, and he gave me a free hand to look into anything in the system. A nice old guy!

"Actually, the real superintendent seemed to be the principal of the high school. He was 54, married, had three grown children and had fair to good health." Hodson wrote on the blackboard:

Education: High School, Western Reserve Academy, Oberlin College, B.S. 1918. Two summer sessions at Columbia. Extension courses, Michigan State College.

Teaching Experience: High School, Elementary, Science, Biology; Assistant Principal and teacher, two years; Assistant Principal and Director Trade Division, two years; Principal of High School from 1927 to this date.

References: Very best recommendations possible from the Superintendent, the former Principal of the High School, and others.

Personal Qualities: Sincere, honest, hard worker even to a point where he sometimes takes it out on his own health and time for social contacts.

"He had applied for the job of superintendent, too. He had some support around town, even among some school board members. They said he knew the system better than anyone and that he had deserved the superintendency. I remember the day I got my letter from the school board. Right after it, I got a letter from my professor at the University congratulating me and along with it a letter from Principal Marshall also congratulating me. The first time I met him, I found him in the supply room of the gym trying on new football uniforms like a kid. He said he was getting them ready to issue that afternoon.

"He had no assistants — though there was a Dean of Girls. He handled everything himself. Every time I suggested that he let others do some of the things, he took it as a criticism. He worked from dawn to midnight. Checking the buses, checking attendance, distributing visual aids and checking the equipment, supervising the cafeteria, supervising the athletic program, checking tickets for the games, collecting the money, taking it to the bank himself, and so on. Finally I asked him to write down what he thought the duties of the principal were and ought to be. I like to get things reduced to paper. These are the things he submitted. Look them over."

Memo From: Principal
To: Superintendent and School Board Members
Subject: Duties of the Principal

The duties which I believe I should cover, subject to revision and with the understanding that all cannot be reduced to writing, are:

1. In complete charge of all phases of attendance, including tardiness cases, absence excuses, daily checking of absentees, receiving weekly attendance reports and compiling school summaries.
2. Disciplinary problems not requiring final action by the superintendent, continuing or not continuing the present assistance of floor masters.
3. Supervision of problem situations such as corridor, basement, and cafeteria passing and in charge of cafeteria while high school pupils are in attendance. For another year this might also include supervision and direction of the pupil marshal system.
4. Supervision of physical arrangements of the building, reporting needs to the Director of School Buildings.
5. In charge of pupil transportation to and from school, in keeping with schedules to be established by the School Department; also arranging plans and executing same, for transportation of pupils to games and special events.
6. Student council adviser in charge of the student participation in government organization and activities, including class elections, social activities, and service projects of the school, as well as the other many ramifications of student council work.
7. Screening reports of teacher advisers and teachers, relative to guidance problems, and assistance in solving the perplexing difficulties which retard pupil progress.
8. Organize and administer the part-time job placement of boys, and assist in the vocational plans of boys, especially those not continuing their education in college.
9. To assist the dean of girls in matters pertaining to admission of pupils to schools and colleges.
10. In charge of visual aid equipment and use.

11. Major assistance to be given in the making of the annual school program which extends over many weeks in spring and some weeks in summer.
12. Checking supplies received and assisting in preparation of supply orders.
13. Responsibility for much of the detailed work of graduation exercises and plans.
14. Full responsibility as acting superintendent in the absence of the superintendent.
15. Assisting the superintendent in many activities which arise from day to day, impossible to list as a part of any schedule.

Hodson said: "I made up a list of duties I thought he ought to be responsible for and told him to study them. Then two things happened which looked as though I was forcing him into something."

Hodson erased the blackboard and wrote:

1. Appointment of a new administrator for the Athletic Program, heretofore under the direction of the principal.
2. Appointment of a new administrator for the School Lunch Program, heretofore confined solely to the high school and under the direction of the high school principal.

"You know, when Marshall heard about this he burst into my office about ready to cry, all shaking and wanting to know if I had thought that he was incompetent in these areas. Well, fella, I tell you, he was in bad shape. So I went to my blackboard and showed him how it had come about. These are the reasons I gave him."

> (1) Article 151, Section 92, of the Acts 1951, in terms of appropriations, gate receipts, purchasing of supplies, etc., established a separate division for this field of activities. (2) At the same time the Town was appointing a new full time Athletic Director. (3) There had been a feeling that the local school board had abdicated its position of direct control or assigned control of athletics and that they should take such steps as they deemed best to accept the responsibility of such a program. Thus, by reason of the law, the separate appropriation for athletics and the election of an Athletic Director and Head Coach, the change was made. (4) Article 148, Section 202, of the Acts 1951 established the Lunch Program as a separate item and isolated the program from the school budget proper. This, coupled with the thought that there was need for an expansion of school lunch facilities in the junior high and elementary schools made for a desire on the part of the board to have one person be responsible for all school lunch programs throughout the system.

"His reaction was one of resentment. With the part-time assistance of two or three men school teachers, he had totally supervised the Athletic Program. When the board established the new 'chain of command' he interpreted it as a personal criticism, which was not intended. It has taken considerable time and interpretation to remove the feelings but it has been accomplished and I feel certain that the principal would now be the first to approve the plan in operation. As far as the lunchroom situation went, unfortunately, when that step was taken the only lunchroom in operation was the one located in the high school so . . . . Notwithstanding the fact that it had been thoroughly discussed that there was additional need on a district-wide basis for cafeteria facilities, he felt that this was another move on the part of the school board to usurp some of his duties and obligations. He took it as a personal rebuke. But again, by reason of time and interpretation, he now agrees that it was the thing to do.

"I kept working with him. We looked at his list of duties and we looked at mine. The dawn came slowly. He argued that he couldn't do all the things on both lists, but that everything was important. I kept hitting both lists, spelling the duties out in time and so forth. Finally one day he suggested that he would need an assistant if he was to carry out all the duties under discussion. 'What will the assistant do?' he wondered. I told him to figure that out and let me know. He said he would. Later he came back with the whole thing reduced to paper. It was a good job. I'll have to give him credit. He's a fine old-timer, despite everything. Here is the page that he worked out. I presented it to the school board and they voted through his recommendation for an assistant principal." (See Exhibit 1)

Hodson took his time to unsnarl and clarify the lines of administrative responsibility in the Ludington system. For the first time in the history of the schools he began weekly Wednesday morning meetings with all the principals. This was accomplished only after teaching and administrative schedules were straightened out so that they could meet together. The principals drew up their lists of responsibilities. So did Hodson himself, and so did the supervisors. (See Exhibits 2 and 3 and "Additional Notes.")

Running continuously with this revamping of the administrative organization from within the system, the superintendent said he was faced with a school board that didn't know just what it was doing.

The six-member board had three persons who had been on it for over ten years. None knew what the law stated pertaining to the responsibilities of school boards. Mr. Hodson took upon himself the task of enlightening the board whenever he got the chance. He spent ten or fifteen minutes at each meeting going over the laws of the state with them. He said he and three secretaries spent a great deal of time going over the rules followed by the school board of the previous decade, and reducing them to paper. Glaring disparities appeared. Contradictory rulings stood side by side. "In short," Mr. Hodson wrote on the blackboard, "things were in one hell of a mess."

Meeting by meeting, members of the board willingly and gradually learned more about their specific responsibilities. "When I got a chance to read from Article 21 to them, I did so, and interpreted it to them. They are beginning to see themselves as a state function and not a local function. They are beginning to work with the law." He and his board developed a list of eighteen duties of the school board to serve as a common denominator in discussions and deliberations concerning present and future organizational structure. These are the duties of the school committee as Mr. Hodson and the board worked them out over a period of four years.

ADMINISTRATIVE AND SUPERVISORY DUTIES OF SCHOOL BOARD

1. Set salaries, increments, and schedules for all personnel.
2. Determine school districts and provide adequate school housing.
3. Establish school bus routes by such means as the board thinks is in the best interest of all concerned.
4. Establish courses and approve the use of all types of instructional aids.
5. Sanction purchases and approve bills for payment.
6. Enforce laws of attendance.
7. Determine school programs, school year, and vacation periods.
8. Set regulations for all school personnel.
9. Engage, demote, and discharge, and pass on resignations of members of school staff.
10. Provide for education of physically and mentally handicapped.
11. Provide for physical education and health examinations.

12. Provide "released time" for religious education.
13. Provide for Supervisor of School Attendance and work conditions for minors.
14. Make annual report to town.
15. Permit sale or exchange of school property other than school buildings.
16. Set tuition rates for out-of-town students.
17. Determine proper supervision of athletics and School Lunch Program.
18. Make and cause to be enforced any regulations which the body determines is in the best interest of the student body.

Just recently the master administrative plan for the Ludington system had been mimeographed and sent to everyone in the system. "It was drawn in the form of a chair, with the various parts all flowing back and forth and interlocking," Hodson continued. "Of course, not everything is on the chair yet. I have no Assistant Superintendent. I need one, but the school board has not seen the light yet. I just keep presenting them with the situation, and all the things I do which I would not have to do. An assistant would free me to do other more important things. Don't worry; some meeting, someone will say, 'I think Old Blackboard needs some help. The job is too much as he cuts it out.' When they say that, I'll tell them I have someone in mind, and that'll be that. What do you think of the chair? I dreamed it up in two nights." (See Exhibit 4)

EXHIBIT 1 The Administration and Supervision of the High School

The total high school program is under the direction of the principal. But in a school of this size as it is now and as it will be in the near future, he needs capable assistants who will and can accept certain duties and responsibilities. In the first instance it is most desirable that the several people concerned take an active part in the planning process. Once this has been accomplished, the principal's administrative and supervisory program becomes twofold: (1) He is directly responsible, i.e., it is mainly by reason of his personal attention and guidance that the item needing attention is successfully concluded. (Such an item is identified by the letter "R" in the accompanying chart.) (2) He serves in an advisory capacity. Although he does not abdicate his responsibility to expedite matters, he delegates the responsibility to others who take an active part, to the end that the item is successfully concluded. (Such an item is identified as "A" in the following chart.)

Duties, Responsibilities	*Principal of High School*		*Vice-Principal of High School*	
	Responsible for	*Advisory*	*Responsible for*	*Advisory*
1. Establishing building policies in harmony with State Regulations Chap. 53, *et al*, and school committee regulations	R			A
2. Organizing and supervising extra-curricular activities		A	R	
3. Organizing teaching schedules and room assignments	R			A
4. Homeroom activities		A	R	
5. School discipline		A	R	
6. Supervision of teachers	R			A
7. School records, adm. clerical duties		A	R	
8. Recommendations for selection, rating, assignment of teachers	R			A
9. Public relations	R			A
10. Guidance		A	R	
11. Department heads and assistants	R			A

EXHIBIT 2 The Administration and Supervision of the Junior High School

Duties, Responsibilities	*Principal*		*Vice-Principal*		*Dean of Girls*	
	Responsible for	*Advisory*	*Responsible for*	*Advisory*	*Responsible for*	*Advisory*
General care–oversight of building	R			A		
Set policy for staff and students	R			A		
Interview teachers	R			A		
Determine periods and classes for school year	R		R			
Supervise instruction	R			A		
Hold teacher meetings	R			A		
Plan social functions for teachers and students		A	R			
Provide adequate cumulative and anecdotal records for pupils	R		R			
Determine health					R	
Conditions of girls		A			R	
Provide for discipline cases		A	R			
Establish program-school	R		R			
Check attendance of student body		A	R			

This chart suggests that the vice-principal cooperates with and accepts training for a principalship. He should be free of homeroom duties and have two free periods a day for the above duties. In case of absence of principal, the junior high vice-principal classroom duties should be filled by a proper substitute. He should be selected for the position because he has those potentialities which make for a good principal.

EXHIBIT 3 The Administrative–Supervisory Structure of Our System *(as we recommend it to you)*

The superintendent shall serve as the administrative agent of the school committee and as their educational adviser. He is immediately responsible, as an administrator, for all school personnel. The scope of his duties is as broad as the entire school program and as specific as the policies adopted by the school committee. Many of his duties are and should be delegated to other responsible, experienced administrators. This chart indicates some of the necessary items of responsibilities which need to be performed by the administrative staff; (R) indicates the individual immediately responsible for a given item; (A) indicates the assisting or advisory agent; two (R's) indicate joint responsibilities.

TO WHOM EACH ADMINISTRATOR IS DIRECTLY RESPONSIBLE

A. The School Committee
B. Supt. of Schools
C. Supt., thence Committee
D. Supt., thence Committee
E. Supt., thence Committee
F. Supt., thence Committee
G. Supt., thence Committee
H. Supt., thence Committee
I. Supt., and/or Principals
J. Supt., thence Committee

Duties and Responsibilities	*A* Supt. of Schools	*B* Ass't. Supt.	*C* Supervisors	*D* Directors	*E* Maint. Sup.	*F* Attend. Off.	*G* Lunch Supr.	*H* Clinic Staff.	*I* Clerical Staff	*J* Principals
1. Adult education	A	R	--	--	--	--	--	--	A	--
2. Administrative meetings	R	A	A	A	A	A	A	A	A	R
3. Attendance — work permits	A	--	--	--	--	R	--	--	R	R
4. Art education	A	A	R	--	--	--	--	--	--	--
5. Budget preparation	R	A	A	A	A	--	A	A	R	A
6. Business administration	R	A	--	A	A	--	A	--	A	--
7. Building program	R	--	--	--	A	--	--	--	A	--
8. Curriculum — development	A	R	A	A	--	--	--	--	A	A
9. Evening schools	A	R	--	--	--	--	--	--	A	A
10. Finance — accounting, purchasing	A	A	--	--	--	--	--	--	R	A
11. Health — safety	A	A	--	R	--	--	--	--	--	A
12. Improvement of teaching staff	R	R	A	A	--	--	--	--	A	R
13. Lunch programs	A	A	--	R	--	--	--	--	--	--
14. Maintenance of property	A	--	--	--	R	--	--	--	A	--
15. Selection and nomination of teachers	R	R	R	R	--	--	--	--	A	R
16. No-school schedule	R	A	--	--	--	--	--	--	A	A
17. Office personnel	R	--	--	--	--	--	--	--	--	R
18. Preschool clinic	A	A	--	--	--	--	--	R	--	A
19. Public relations	R	R	R	R	--	R	R	R	R	R
20. Physical ed. — recreation	A	--	--	R	--	--	--	--	--	--
21. Salary schedule preparation	R	A	--	--	--	--	--	--	A	--
22. School calendar	R	A	--	--	--	--	--	--	A	--
23. Sports program	A	--	--	R	--	--	--	--	--	A
24. School report	R	A	A	A	A	--	--	A	R	A
25. School committee Work	R	A	--	--	--	--	--	--	R	--
26. Testing — measurements	--	R	--	--	--	--	--	R	A	R
27. Transportation — routes	R	--	--	--	A	--	--	--	A	A
28. Vocational education	A	--	--	R	--	--	--	--	--	--

COMMENTS ON EXHIBIT 3

1. Either in district or out of district schools; i.e., tray painting, possible opening of H.S. for language classes.
2. Meaning local meetings with staff members.
3. Issuing work permits — truancy — court cases.
4. Referring to fine arts.
5. The collective result for school board.
6. The method and procedure, as well as ways and means.
7. New building and renovations.
8. Curriculum revision pointing to a 12-year program.
9. Americanization and Adult Evening School.
10. For board use — ordering, delivering supplies.
11. As indicated.

(continued on next page)

(*comments on Exhibit 3 continued*)

12. In-service-training meetings, class visits, teacher courses, reports.
13. Townwide in scope, including personnel — records.
14. Supervisors and staff, clerical work.
15. After visits in other systems or colleges, applications processed, candidate interviews.
16. Temporary closing of school due to weather.
17. Clerical staff.
18. Before opening of first grade.
19. Radio — newspaper — public meetings — P.T.A.
20. As indicated.
21. In keeping with local and state practices.
22. Meaning opening and closing of school.
23. Meaning all organized sports under Athletic Director.
24. Yearly publication for district.
25. Carrying out of board action.
26. Meaning preschool, individual, yearly testing programs.
27. Meaning contract process, school owned, bus ticket.
28. Meaning local Trade School: ed. in or out of district.

ADDITIONAL NOTES ON EXHIBIT 3

1. The Supervisors' functions in the total program: Since they are specialists, their main concern is with their respective subject areas. It is the supervisor's duty to plan and prepare his 12-year program and to cooperate with the building principal for its successful conclusion. He is likewise responsible for the selection and direction of his staff but not without consultation with the respective principals. He is directly responsible to the superintendent of schools.
2. The Department Head in the High School is responsible to the Senior High School Principal for his staff, the course of study, the instructional aids, and the general improvement of his department. He should have adequate time for classroom visits.
3. An Elementary School Building Assistant is one who takes charge of the elementary school in the absence of the principal. Such a person holds a teaching position but is relieved of such duties when there is a long period of absence.

EXHIBIT 4

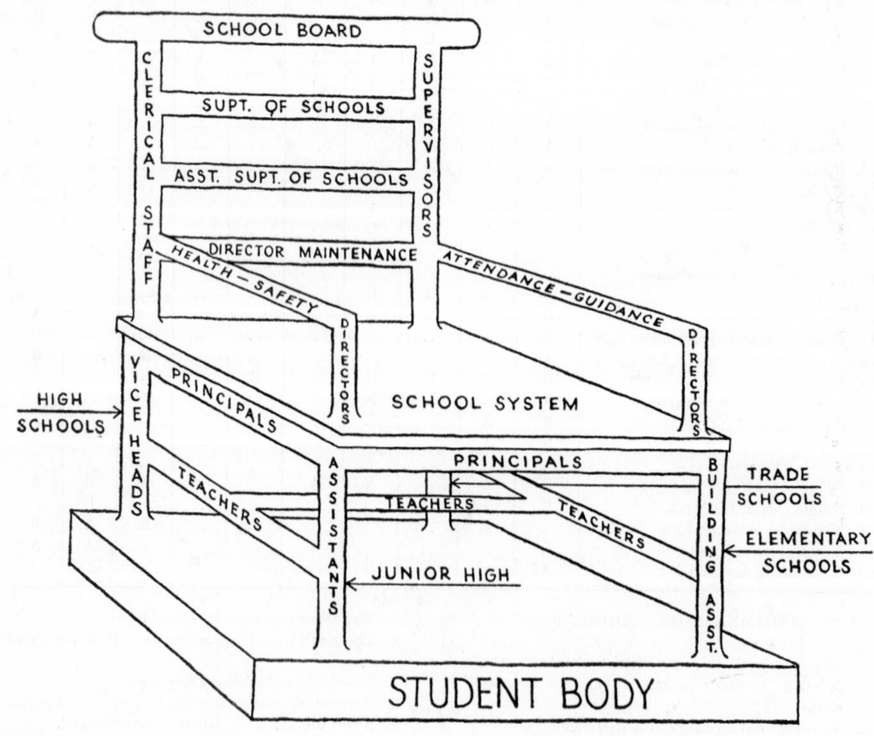

14 *The Conference*

Mr. O'Shea . . . Principal of Central High School, Middle City

On December 14, 1952, I instructed my secretary to write a memo to Miss Marie Leduc, one of my French teachers in Central High School, and to Miss Dora Fine, Head of the Modern Language Department. The note instructed Miss Leduc and Miss Fine to appear in my office at 3:30 for a conference. The occasion for the note was a situation which had been brewing for some time in Central High School. In fact, the thing had started during the first week of the fall term in 1952. Miss Leduc and Miss Fine, her department head, didn't hit it off from the first. There is probably something to be said on both sides. There always is. Naturally I've had to be cautious in the matter. A principal always has to back his department heads. Yet he has to keep a happy teaching staff. I've always felt that if I can get both sides to sit down and talk over their troubles with me, the thing can be settled in short order. I've been upset by this situation. It's not the usual one in my school.

I guess the trouble began when I hired Miss Leduc. There was no question as to her competence in the language. She spoke it like a native. In fact, her father was French, the family had lived in France, and Miss Leduc and her mother still used French at home. Maybe that was one reason for the trouble. Dora Fine, the department head, does not speak French as well as Miss Leduc. Not that Dora isn't good in her field. She spends almost every summer traveling in France. She published a textbook for teaching French in high school. We used the book in all four high schools in Middle City, up until a year or two ago. Dora Fine is also well recognized by other language teachers. Still, she may have had some feeling against Miss Leduc. After interviewing Miss Leduc, Dora recommended that I shouldn't hire her. Dora had one of her former pupils, a bright girl, slated for the job, but at the last minute Dora's candidate backed out, and I had to hire Miss Leduc.

Miss Leduc had her experience and training in elementary education. I'm not so sure that I approve of women like Miss Leduc teaching anyway. Her mother spends more on servants than I earn in a year. It's hard to deal with a woman like Miss Leduc. Any time she wants to, she can walk out of the school and never come back. Her mother is a power in the town. She comes from a family that doesn't have much to say, but when they do people sit up and take notice. I suppose this may account for a certain amount of jealousy among the staff. Miss Leduc's mother invites the Superintendent out to tea once a year, and he goes.

I wasn't completely sold on Miss Leduc either. She had swallowed the elementary school approach pretty thoroughly. Still, she knew a lot about her subject and she had the courses in French teaching. Even Dora Fine had to admit that Leduc had the course work and spoke the language well. I felt maybe we needed a new approach in our classes. Our faculty is "old."

The "old" staff may have had something to do with Miss Leduc's trouble. It isn't easy to break into the group, and some of the old teachers are cliquey. Naturally they would favor Dora who is one of their own. I guess Miss Leduc must have sensed this at the start, or maybe she is just naturally strange and standoffish. At any rate, she went too far in the opposite direction. She seemed to try to avoid all of the teachers. When you met her in the corridor it was like pulling teeth to get a "hello." I don't like that. People should be friendly when they work together.

I suppose Dora Fine paid a visit to Miss Leduc's class the first week. Dora always does. I didn't ask her to submit any report, but I happened to meet her in the cafeteria and I said, "How is your new teacher doing?" I could tell by the look on her face that all was not well.

"I don't like to comment so soon," Dora said, "but . . . I think she may need help. The noise level in the room is terrible. She seems to let every child talk at will. Her accent is good, however. She does have some problems with her teaching. She doesn't seem to catch mistakes in time."

"Did you talk to her about it?" I asked.

"Yes, and that's what is bothering me most. She is on the defensive. Instead of taking my advice as well meant, she argues. I'm afraid her viewpoint doesn't fit her too well for being a high school teacher. She was probably excellent in elementary school. But I don't know about that either."

"Well," I said. "I would worry if I didn't know she was in your department, Dora. I know you'll bring her around." But after that first talk with Dora I suspected that we might be in for trouble.

My first real chat with Miss Leduc, except when I interviewed her, came after a staff meeting one day. I didn't want to come right out and say that I had heard complaints about the noise. I said, "One trouble new teachers have in this building is noise. I guess the walls are pretty thin."

She said, "Yes. Some of the classes are noisy. But then, coming from an elementary school I'm used to it. It doesn't bother me too much."

I said, "Well. How are you getting along?"

"Very well." The rest of the interview went pretty much like that. Miss Leduc is one of those people who can't realize that a problem exists.

In late October before I could actually visit Miss Leduc's class, Miss Fine came to me with the results of some standardized language exams given to the students of Miss Leduc's second-year class. The results were alarming. They showed that after two months in Miss Leduc's class, her group had actually lost ground since the previous June. This was serious. Central has always done better than the other three high schools in Middle City. We get the good students. I had both Miss Leduc and Miss Fine into the office and I went over the test results. Miss Leduc's answer was open criticism of the exam, and an implied criticism of Miss Fine. I made a mental note to visit her class at the earliest possible date.

I made a series of three visits; each visit was followed by a conference. All the complaints I had heard about the class proved to be accurate. She allowed the children almost unlimited freedom to talk out, to move around. The one good feature of her class was that the students seemed to be interested. Without commenting on her knowledge of the language or of language-teaching techniques, I tried to point out that there were many general teaching procedures which she was neglecting. She either argued needlessly, or ignored what I said.

During this same period of time her attendance slips were invariably late or did not arrive at my office at all. I found students from her class wandering about the corridors without "travel slips." I think I held my temper remarkably well until the conference after my last visit. I entered the class after it had been running for fifteen minutes. The floor was littered with bits of crushed chalk.

Miss Leduc was at her desk with her head in a book. I waited until the end of class, and then I approached her desk. She was not even aware of the chalk on the floor until I pointed it out to her. She denied that the chalk had been thrown during her class. She said, "It was on the floor when I came into the room." I knew this was not true, but I pointed out to her that if that were so, then it must have been the fault of the teacher who had had the class before her. She said, "That must be true. It didn't happen during my class." She even grew nasty about it and said, "Mr. O'Shea, I am not the janitor. This is not my responsibility. I resent your even questioning my word about the chalk." I got out of there without losing my temper. Just as I had suspected, the other teacher denied that the chalk was thrown on the floor during her class. Well, this story got around the faculty in some way and the other teachers resented Miss Leduc's version of the incident.

After that I requested Miss Fine to visit Miss Leduc's classes more frequently, but to try to handle her carefully. At the same time I took every opportunity to talk to Miss Leduc informally. She showed the same indifference to Miss Fine's efforts to help her as to mine. The woman was unapproachable. Miss Fine found that Miss Leduc corrected papers very badly. She took several sets of assignments and quiz papers, corrected them, and handed them back to Miss Leduc, but apparently this had had no effect.

During this period, Miss Leduc's relationships with the rest of the faculty deteriorated rapidly. She lunched alone, and spent the rest of her free time doing "busy work" in her room. I think that fact revealed more than anything else that Miss Leduc did have a personality problem. I tried to talk to her about cooperation and friendship among teachers being essential for a happy school, but I feel that I made no impression. I had to keep from being too pointed.

Toward the end of November, I again asked Miss Fine to check on Miss Leduc's papers. After a week passed, Miss Fine reported that Miss Leduc had refused to submit the papers. I asked Miss Fine to have another conference with Miss Leduc. Miss Fine came back from this conference white-faced and shaken. According to Miss Fine, Miss Leduc had accused her of being "mentally ill." I knew then that the matter had to be brought into the open.

In early December I called the superintendent and informed him of everything which had transpired to date. Mr. Patterson, the superintendent, encourages us to make decisions in our own schools. Sometimes I think he encourages too much independence. But that is his concern, not mine. While I think he is sincere about it, I still feel that he should know about what goes on in the schools. In that way I'm protected in case the matter gets out of hand. I asked Mr. Patterson point-blank whether Miss Leduc had a history of trouble in our schools. He said: "Not that I recall. At least it was nothing big that I remember. There was some unpleasantness due to that language experiment at Baker. I think, however, that it was a difference of opinion among language teachers."

"How much of a difference?" I asked.

"It was pretty much on the technical level," he said. "I didn't get too involved in it."

I said, "Well, I just want you to know how it is here."

I didn't hear any more from downtown on the matter. Around the middle of December, Miss Fine came to my office. She reported that she had absolutely no success with Miss Leduc. She said that her job as a department head was being impaired. She said, and I could fully believe the woman, that she had tried as best she could to work things out with Miss Leduc. That was when I called

Miss Fine and Miss Leduc to the meeting. I tried to sketch a few notes beforehand. I knew it would be a tense session. I wanted to be prepared. At the same time I notified the superintendent that I was calling the conference. I felt that in dealing with a woman like Miss Leduc, it was wise to be covered in such a matter.

Miss Fine . . . Head of the Modern Language Department, Central High, Middle City

The memo from Mr. O'Shea which had been placed on my desk during the morning recess period read: "Miss Dora Fine, Head of the Department of Modern Languages, Central High School: Dear Miss Fine . . . Could you attend a meeting in the Principal's office this afternoon, December 14, 1952, 3:30–4:30 P.M.? Miss Marie Leduc, a teacher in the Modern Language Department of this high school, will be present. The matter is quite urgent."

I suppose my first reaction to the note was relief. I hadn't wanted to get Mr. O'Shea into the situation, but apparently he had been aware of the impending crisis. In my thirty-two years of teaching, I had never met a more difficult teacher to deal with than Miss Leduc. I pride myself on my ability to get along with my fellow teachers. I cannot remember having exchanged more than a few cross words with any of them during my long years of teaching French and heading the Modern Language Department in Central High School. I think I can safely say that most of the faculty support me in my assessment of Miss Leduc. The woman is remote and unfriendly. She does not openly antagonize people, but she makes her feelings abundantly clear by sullen silences and glances which evidence complete weariness. She can say cruel things, and she has said them to me, but her usual defense is a sullen, brooding silence which is unnerving.

I interviewed Miss Leduc when she requested her transfer to the high school. The woman was not suited for the job, and I so informed both Mr. O'Shea and Mr. Jordan, the assistant superintendent in charge of personnel. It was not that she lacked preparation in her subject. She speaks beautiful French, although I would not say that this fact would automatically fit her to teach the subject. Miss Leduc's lack of suitability for high school teaching stems more from her training, experience, and personality.

Her attitude toward students has reflected this background. She feels that students should be allowed to run the class. I have found that high school students in an academic course need and expect much more guidance than do younger students. Discipline in a class of forty language learners must be strict. She keeps her head down most of the time while the class is in progress. In general she has the habit of never meeting a person's eye. I suppose she is shy and this affects her fitness for teaching.

As a teacher she has many faults, and this has not been my observation alone. We have always had a close faculty group at Central High. Most of us have been teaching here since the building opened. In fact, the teachers here have had more experience than Principal O'Shea.

I made the usual routine visit to Miss Leduc the first week, and after thirty years of teaching I am in a position to know when things are wrong in the classroom. She had no control over her group — a second-year French class. The noise level in the class was high, the attention level low. Some of the children were speaking French, some were just talking. After they had finished, she attempted to point out their errors, but then of course it was too late.

I made these observations the subject of our first conference, and I chose the subject deliberately because it was a minor matter which could be easily remedied. She was not amenable to correction. She hardly listened to my comments, and when I had finished she said, "Are you finished, Miss Fine?" When I said that I was she launched into five minutes of utter gibberish which seemed to have compounded all the worst features of modern progressive education, along with the most esoteric points made by the lunatic fringe of the linguistic scientists. I am not opposed to either modern pedagogy or scientific linguistics, but all things must be leavened with a grain of common sense. I think I can say that I have pioneered many of the new things in language teaching. Until recently my textbook was used exclusively in the four high schools of Middle City. It needs some revision now, but it has generally been hailed as a standard work in the teaching of high school French.

Before Miss Leduc came to the high school her sole experience in the teaching of French was a series of experimental classes which she and another elementary teacher had conducted in the third and fourth grades at Baker School. It has generally been agreed that controversy over these classes prevented her from becoming principal at Baker School, and when she lost this opportunity she put in for a teaching position in the high school.

Some of the teachers felt Miss Leduc was a snob. Her mother is a very wealthy woman and a "social power" in Middle City. She and her mother live in one of the largest houses in the city, and she often arrives at school in a chauffeur-driven Cadillac. The woman has no real reason to teach. She missed several days of class in the early fall, and the usual excuse was a "sick headache."

I had urged her through most of the first weeks in October to administer the department language exams. She promised to do this but she did not actually keep her promises. Instead, she gave a constant series of pretexts and excuses. In late October, when it became apparent that she was not going to test her groups, I tested them on a day when she was absent. A glance at the results in her three second-year French classes showed me that the time had come to bring the matter before the principal.

The resulting interview served to alert Mr. O'Shea to the problem, and from that time on he asked me to visit her class regularly. There was no apparent result. He also visited her class and talked to her. On one of these occasions, Mr. O'Shea found the floor littered with bits of chalk. She said that the chalk had been on the floor when she entered the class. Mr O'Shea checked with the other teacher, who denied it. The principal wanted to bring the matter to a head then, but I managed to dissuade him. The result was that Miss Leduc lost the sympathy of her fellow teachers as well as Mr. O'Shea's support.

During the fall I had attempted to help her with her correction work, and I had reviewed her marking of tests and home assignments. I found that she did very poorly with her paper work. She gave all manner of partial credit for vocabulary words which were misspelled. I tried to point out that this was contrary to department policy. At the end of November, I again asked her to submit a set of papers for rechecking. This she never did, pleading that she was too busy getting ready for the Christmas Program. After a week of this, I went to her. I did not accuse her of refusing to obey orders, but she seemed to have the feeling that I had. No doubt it was on her mind, for she said, "I feel you are accusing me of failure to follow directions." At this point I admitted the situation was getting out of hand. I pointed out to her that this was not alone my view, but it was the opinion of Mr. O'Shea and the other teachers.

I had no other choice but to take the matter to Mr. O'Shea. I told Miss Leduc that I had been patient and kind with her but that the situation required the entrance of the principal. Her accusation that I was mentally ill was one which I could not tolerate. She also accused me of turning the other teachers against her. It was quite apparent who was ill.

I went to Mr. O'Shea and detailed the problem to him. He was extremely upset and wished to send for Miss Leduc immediately. After discussing the case further, we decided that it would be better to give her one more week. During that week I tried extremely hard to work with Miss Leduc. She paid absolutely no attention to me. She seemed to have adopted a new tactic. She crept into a shell and refused to answer me. In the middle of December I reported this to Mr. O'Shea. He said, "Lord knows we've been patient with that woman. I think the time has come to take action."

Miss Leduc . . . French Teacher, Central High School, Middle City

This is the note Mr. O'Shea sent me: "Miss Leduc, could you attend a meeting in the Principal's office this afternoon, December 14, 1952, 3:30–4:40. Miss Dora Fine, Head of the Modern Language Department of this high school, will be present. The matter is quite urgent." The note marked the first time that Principal O'Shea had taken official recognition of the trouble between my department head and me. In a way I was glad that the matter had finally come out into the open. There had been far too much talking behind hands in the cafeteria and in the teachers' lounge.

I suppose it was inevitable that most teachers supported Miss Fine. She is after all, one of the senior members of the faculty that is generally "old." I think I should be charitable and refrain from saying "ancient." Not that Dora Fine has a warm personality . . . far from it. However, she saves most of her asperity for her students or for teachers in her own department. She can be quite charming to her "equals" — the other older teachers on the faculty. And there is no denying that she is well thought of professionally. She has even written a textbook which, significantly enough, is no longer in use in any of the four high schools in Middle City. Miss Fine knows everything about French, except how to speak it. I really feel that this was the root of our trouble.

My parents both spoke French, and I passed the first eleven years of my life in schools in France and Switzerland. I speak the language fluently. Miss Fine likes to inform her fellow teachers and students — she teaches the two classes in French conversation, unfortunately — that she has missed only six summers "abroad" in all of her thirty-two years of teaching. "And this, of course," she always adds, "was due to the war." As one might guess, she speaks a better than average brand of tourist French, and I'll give her credit, her knowledge of French drama and literature is excellent.

I've been teaching in Middle City Schools for ten years, and, oddly enough, in the beginning I had no intention of teaching French in high school. My Master's Degree is in elementary education, and I have been certified to serve as a principal in the public schools of our state. When I did not get the principalship at Baker last year, I decided to go up to the high school. I had the training in French, of course, and Mr. O'Shea favored my candidacy, but Miss Fine did not. She attempted to conduct our first interview in French, and it was actually embarrassing. I had never lost contact with the language, and in fact I might say that I was one of the first to introduce experimental classes in conversational French into the elementary schools. In one way this was the reason for my being passed over for the principalship at Baker. There was a squabble among the language teachers and I was drawn into it. Our Director of Curriculum, Mr. McGraine, after first supporting the project, withdrew his support, and I was forced to go to Superintendent Patterson to get permission to finish it. There is no question that I and Miss Folson, the sponsors of the program, suffered. Miss Folson left the system at the end of the year, and I requested a transfer to the high school.

I don't know why I stayed on in Middle City schools. Mother wanted me to resign and travel with her. Mother has always been opposed to my holding a job. She often points out that it costs more to keep the house in Middle City open and staffed in the winter than I earn in a year of teaching. When she is at the Palm Beach house she calls Middle City constantly to make certain that I am well.

I learned one valuable lesson from the Baker experience. One must be careful when talking to fellow teachers. I tried to use this lesson after coming to the high school, and I suppose this hasn't made me too popular among my fellow teachers. I suppose some of them think I am odd and "standoffish," but I'm not actually. I learned my lesson after missing the principalship at Baker due to a whispering campaign by the other teachers. I had been a very close friend of Jane Folson, and after she left the system I had no interest in being friendly with other teachers.

There have been a lot of changes in the teaching of modern foreign languages in recent years, and I fear that Miss Fine has not followed them as closely as she should have. My special interest is in the teaching of foreign languages by direct methods and by using the principles of scientific linguistics. I tried to discuss the problem with Miss Fine, but I gave that up after one meeting.

I suppose where we differ most is in the matter of handling the children. I have found, after nine years of experience, that a teacher simply has to let the children be free from needless restraint. I am not a "progressive educator" in any sense of the word, although Miss Fine did make that charge in a department staff meeting. I know that my classes are a bit noisy. There is no way to teach children to speak without letting them make some noise. One has to encourage spontaneity in language classes. And I do just that. I guess this is the one thing that Mr. O'Shea objects to. He reads the books on democratic processes of education, but his ideas as to how the theory should be put into practice are strange indeed. "Understanding leadership" and "loyalty" are the keynotes of most of his staff conferences. To this Miss Fine will inevitably nod agreement, although to her way of thinking the "understanding" could best be left off.

Miss Fine began coming into my classes before I had been in the school a week. She stalked in and sat in the back of the room with disapproval plainly written on her face. She never actually interrupted me, but I could see that she restrained herself with an effort. We had the usual conferences following her visits. In the first conference she was quite indirect, but I sensed that she was criticizing my teaching techniques, which put emphasis on the oral presentation of the language. I suppose she wanted me to have the children recite in cadence and on command. I refuse to muzzle healthy, young children. I tried to give a reasoned technical defense of my methods. She sat through it, but I could tell that she paid absolutely no attention to my explanation. In her second conference she was more open and she criticized my classroom discipline. I tried to point out that I did not view discipline as an isolated problem but rather as something which was tied into a general technique of teaching.

The first open sign I had of her attitude was when she gave the departmental tests to my second-year group on a day in late October when I was home with a sick headache. I was not surprised when my three second-year classes scored low on items of vocabulary and formal grammar. The vocabulary selection in the test was outlandish. The grammar items actually contained certain constructions which are no longer in use among intelligent and educated French people. Nevertheless, I would not have pointed this out if she hadn't called me into the Principal's office. She had no real argument after I pointed out the poor items in the test. In fact, shortly after that, she stormed out of the office. I think Mr. O'Shea was actually embarrassed by the whole affair. At any rate, he mumbled some vague thing which I did not even hear and then waited for me to leave the office.

Then in early November he appeared in my class to visit. He did not criticize my competence in French, but after his visit he made a few criticisms of minor matters in classroom routine. His approach is always fatherly. He places his hand on your arm or shoulder — which makes me uncomfortable — and talks in a low, friendly tone and complete platitudes. After a conference with Mr. O'Shea it is very difficult to remember what has actually been said. Perhaps this is just as well. The only trouble I have had with the man came after his final visit to my class. After I had dismissed the group he approached my desk and pointed to the floor of the room. "Miss Leduc," he said, "have you by chance looked at the floor of this room?" I confessed that I hadn't, it being essential that a teacher look everywhere else but the floor.

"It is littered with chalk bits," Mr. O'Shea pointed out. I looked, and it certainly was covered with chalk. Furthermore the children had walked on the chalk and ground it into the floor. He had entered the room halfway through the class, and he assumed that the children had thrown the chalk during the first half of my class. This was not so, because I had noticed some chalk on the floor when I entered the room at the beginning of class. I told Mr. O'Shea this.

"All of it?" he asked.

I told him quite patiently: "Mr. O'Shea, I am a teacher, not a custodian. I have had very little experience in estimating the quantity of chalk on a classroom floor. There was chalk there. I see no reason to doubt my word."

"All right," he said, "I'll talk to the other teacher."

Apparently Mr. O'Shea discovered that I had spoken the truth because I heard no more about chalk. However, from that day on I was more or less an outcast among the other teachers. Not that I had been close to them before. The atmosphere around the high school was that of an exclusive club, closed to any teacher who had been there less than twenty years. The older ones sat at particular tables in the cafeteria and had their special seats in the teachers' lounge, and it was dangerous to take these self-appointed places. I found it easier to spend most of my free time in my own room.

In November Miss Fine increased the frequency of her visits. She also changed her tactics to some extent. She never aimed a criticism at my work directly, but always her criticism was implied. Her usual approach was to beam at me and say, "The class is progressing beautifully in pronunciation. Don't you think that you should spend more time with the sentence workbooks?" It did no good to tell her that I did not approve of workbooks. I nodded agreement and did try to spend more time with the workbooks.

Miss Fine also asked me to submit my test and homework papers to her, so that she could check on my paper work. I turned in one examination and a week of written exercises. At the end of the week she returned them to me without a word. Almost every mark which I had put on the papers had been penciled through by Miss Fine. Her general comment was that I had been much too lenient with spelling errors in French. I could have pointed out that, using a more direct method and emphasizing the sound rather than the sight of the language, spelling errors in the early stages were to be expected.

Toward the end of November Miss Fine again requested that I turn papers over to her to be checked. I was busy that week getting the class play in French ready for the annual Christmas Program. I did not refuse to bring her the papers, but when a week passed, she came to my room at the close of school and accused me of refusing to obey the order of a department head. I pointed out to her that this was absurd.

She said: "Miss Leduc, frankly I don't know what to do in your case. I really think it is getting beyond me. I've noticed and the other teachers have noticed your behavior. I feel that Mr. O'Shea is beginning to notice. You just will not cooperate."

I was simply amazed. I said: "Miss Fine, you must be ill. I'm sorry we had to have this meeting today when you aren't yourself."

At this point she flew into a rage. "I will not tolerate that sort of accusation," she screamed. "I've tried to be kind and patient with you. I've attempted to work with you. I've made suggestions. Miss Leduc, I haven't been the only one to notice this. All the teachers have." Her constant references to the other teachers made it quite clear to me what she was doing. Once when I had come into the teachers' room I had actually overheard her talking about me to three of the other teachers.

"Are you stirring up the other teachers?" I asked her. I shouldn't have said that. It provoked her into a further display of temper. The woman had absolutely lost control of herself, and I felt sorry for her. I said nothing further during our talk, and she continued to upbraid me for another fifteen minutes. At the end of that time she left the room. I resolved then that the only way to get along with Miss Fine was to be absolutely submissive.

The first week in December she came to my room at least once a day. At the same time I noticed that the general attitude of many of the teachers grew increasingly hostile. Miss Fine was obviously ranging them against me for the purpose of providing support for her position when the break came. I didn't see Mr. O'Shea at all during this time. I had made a resolution to be patient with Miss Fine and I followed that resolution to the letter. I made absolutely no comments to her when she came to the room. When she pointed out something which I was doing wrong, or merely hinted at it, I agreed with her silently. I did not encourage her but I did nothing to offend her. I spent even less time in the company of other teachers. Instead of pacifying Miss Fine, my silence seemed to irritate her all the more. On Monday of the second week in December she stormed out of my room. Two days later the summons to meet with her and Mr. O'Shea was on my desk. I have no idea what to say in the coming meeting. There is nothing to say, really. I have tried to get along with Miss Fine, and failed.

The Conference

(Present at the conference were: Mr. O'Shea; Mr. O'Shea's secretary; Miss Leduc; Miss Fine. Time, 3:35; place, office of the Principal of Central High School, Middle City)

O'SHEA: I've called you to this office this afternoon to have a frank and open discussion of a matter which concerns all of us. I've always felt that only a happy staff can run a good school. I guess we all know that things aren't completely happy here. It's always been my belief that if people can let their hair down and really speak their minds, the situation can be straightened out. I know there is something to be said on both sides of every situation. It takes two to make a quarrel.

FINE: I beg your pardon.

O'SHEA: I said, Miss Fine, it takes two to make a fight.

FINE: Mr. O'Shea, are you implying that I am *equally* guilty of fighting?

O'SHEA: My dear lady, I'm not implying that anyone is *guilty*.

LEDUC: I'd like to bring this matter into the open now. It appears that you both have pretty well decided that I am at fault.

O'SHEA: I don't think that's true at all, Miss Leduc.

FINE: Well, I think we should be honest about it. If there *is* blame, it should be laid at the proper doorstep. I know Miss Leduc has her side of the story.

LEDUC: I'd prefer to hear the charges first.

O'SHEA: There are no charges. The reason for this meeting is to avoid that sort of thing . . . to nip the matter in the bud while it is still among friends.

LEDUC: *Friends!*

O'SHEA: I know Miss Fine has tried to work with you. I think she has made every effort. . . .

FINE: I certainly have. I have tried to point out Miss Leduc's problems. . . .

LEDUC: I have no problems that. . . .

O'SHEA: Every new teacher has problems, Miss Leduc.

LEDUC: I'm hardly a new teacher, sir. I've had ten years' service in Middle City schools.

O'SHEA: I think what I intended to say was that you're new to us here.

FINE: The teaching of modern languages in secondary schools has many problems. I don't think that Miss Leduc should feel *alarmed* that she has her share during her first year. They can be worked out. But we *must* have patience. We must first of all face the fact that we *have* these problems. It shouldn't be a source of embarrassment for anyone to do this.

LEDUC: Well I'm ready at any time. But I think we should be honest and direct. I gather that you feel I spend too much time on oral practice.

FINE: I don't think it is exactly that. We all realize that the student must practice speaking the language. I would say that you spend too *little time* on other things.

LEDUC: Well, Miss Fine, there are only so many class hours in a week. If we spend the time on one thing we will not have it for another.

O'SHEA: That's very true. But I think what Miss Fine is attempting to point out is . . . there are certain things that all teachers should do . . . certain formal requirements. These are part of the routine in any school . . . absence slips, corridor permissions, a reasonable spread in the mark range.

LEDUC: I have no faith whatsoever in marks, Mr. O'Shea. I feel that *entirely* too much weight is given to them.

FINE: And it requires *effort* to make them out accurately.

LEDUC: I'm quite able to make out marks.

FINE: I'm sorry, I didn't mean that you weren't. I merely meant that you must pay more attention to formal requirements. I didn't mean to imply that you were careless with your paper work.

LEDUC: I'm sorry too, then. I felt that was what you meant.

O'SHEA: I think we're beginning to get somewhere now. I think both of you are able teachers. With her training and experience Miss Leduc is *bound* to do things differently. I guess what we have to do is find out what those differences are.

LEDUC: That would be helpful. If I could get specific examples of what I'm doing wrong. . . .

FINE: This has been done, you must admit, Miss Leduc. I think I have been quite clear in our conferences.

O'SHEA: I don't think Miss Leduc meant that you *weren't*. I think what she wants is a list of suggestions put down in black and white. Am I right, Miss Leduc?

LEDUC: I guess so. Frankly, I'm getting confused. I've tried to avoid unpleasantness. I know that the staff feels that I am remote. I don't suppose that is easy to change, but I could try.

FINE: I think it would help if you did. You *do* have a personality problem.

LEDUC: (*angrily*) And I think it would help if you stopped trying to get the other teachers over to your side of the issue.

FINE: That is *not true*. . . .

LEDUC: Are you implying that I don't tell the truth?

FINE: I think that you are sometimes careless with the truth . . . the matter of the chalk on the floor, for instance.

LEDUC: I explained that.

FINE: Yes, but Miss Danvers denied that her group was responsible. She was quite upset about it.

O'SHEA: I think we're getting off the point again, ladies. Miss Danvers has forgotten the incident.

LEDUC: Why wasn't I allowed to know about that? Why wasn't I permitted to defend myself against Miss Danvers' accusation?

O'SHEA: Miss Danvers made none. The incident is closed.

LEDUC: And I am made to seem a liar.

FINE: I think we should go back to the list. We've talked about marking and reporting. I think the paper correction is improving. It could be better . . . but it has improved.

LEDUC: How could it be better? Could you give me some specific examples? Why should this constant talk in generalities go on? How does it help?

FINE: I think we should be careful of our spelling. A vocabulary word is either right or wrong. There is not partial credit for a misspelled form.

LEDUC: There is a wide latitude given in the matter of pronunciation even in the *advanced* classes. Why not spelling?

FINE: Are you saying that my classes do not pronounce accurately?

LEDUC: I'd rather not say what I mean. I think I'd like to go home now. I'm afraid I feel ill.

O'SHEA: Now, Miss Leduc. I think we owe it to ourselves to see this through.

FINE: I think that poor health may be one of the problems here. Miss Leduc has used most of her sick leave already.

LEDUC: That is no concern of yours, Miss Fine. Remember that there are other forms of sickness besides physical.

FINE: Are you saying . . . ?

O'SHEA: Miss Leduc is not saying anything. I feel. . . .

LEDUC: I'm trying to . . . I'm willing to go along with any reasonable request.

FINE: I think the choice of the term *request* is unfortunate. It is simply not department policy to mark partial credit on misspelled words. I am not *requesting* this.

LEDUC: Very well. I will agree to give no partial credit.

O'SHEA: Now we are getting somewhere. Let's get to the matter of discipline. I know it's not Miss Leduc's *fault.* I'm sorry, *fault* is not the word I meant to use. I mean, just because Miss Leduc's classes are noisy and disturb other teachers.

LEDUC: I have heard no complaints.

FINE: I have.

O'SHEA: The south wing of the building is old. The walls are thin. Sometimes disturbance is unavoidable. We have to be patient with this. While Miss Leduc's technique may be fine in an elementary school, with older students the teacher has to be a bit more formal. All teachers have difficulties. Keeping children in their seats and quiet during classes is difficult.

FINE: I don't think I would say that *all* teachers have this trouble. I think Miss Leduc does.

LEDUC: I am trying to teach my class to speak. To speak they must talk.

O'SHEA: Well, I'll get to the point. Your classes are not as orderly as they might be. This I feel is a difference in approach, rather than a lack of ability.

LEDUC: Well, if you feel that I should put the children into a straitjacket, I shall do so. You are the principal.

O'SHEA: Well, I think we are moving toward something here now. Don't you, Miss Fine?

FINE: I don't know. I don't feel there is much conviction.

LEDUC: Is there anything else? I'd really like to go. I'll try to follow your wishes. I'll be inflexible in my marking and teaching.

O'SHEA: I think you've missed the point. There are certain formal matters which *all* teachers do.

LEDUC: I don't think *all* teachers. Let's say most of the teachers in this school.

O'SHEA: Now, I think we ought to talk about attendance and excuse slips. Miss Geron, the assistant principal, is in sole charge of discipline and attendance. She has had problems . . . your failure to be prompt with office reports. I have a list here of things I wanted to talk about.

LEDUC: A list of my failings?

O'SHEA: No. I have some good points here, Miss Leduc. I think your class is pronouncing beautifully. Don't you, Miss Fine?

FINE: Yes, I do. I listened to your group rehearse for the Christmas play. I think they were splendid.

LEDUC: Well, Miss Fine, I do speak the language myself.

FINE: And *so* do I.

LEDUC: I didn't mean that you *didn't.* It is just that I come from a bilingual home. I think accent is important.

FINE: And I do too.

O'SHEA: I think . . . to go back to the slips . . . the usual procedure is to send attendance slips to Miss Geron before the beginning of the third period. Tardiness should be reported on this slip.

LEDUC: I didn't know that. At Baker we sent in our daily report at noon.

FINE: It was on the mimeographed instruction sheet which Mr. O'Shea distributed to all new teachers.

LEDUC: (*faintly*) I'm afraid I didn't read it thoroughly.

O'SHEA: After all, Miss Leduc, I have over one hundred teachers in this school. I can't see that each one reads the instructions.

LEDUC: You might have reminded me before this.

O'SHEA: I *did* remind you . . . once in the corridor.

LEDUC: I can't remember that.

O'SHEA: Are you implying that I'm not telling the truth?

LEDUC: I'm not saying that at all, sir. I'm saying only that I can't remember. If you say it happened then I *believe* you.

O'SHEA: I hope so, Miss Leduc. I certainly hope so.

FINE: I think we should get back to classroom matters. I feel that Miss Leduc needs the most help in this area. I think her assignments are often too easy. Or too vague. In the reading book for the second year, the usual procedure is to assign one complete story a night. That was the intention of the author. The stories are not more than three pages in length.

LEDUC: You are *quite* positive about the intentions of the author?

FINE: I happen to know the author. And furthermore, it is not necessary to have them read the complete story through in French. Translation is the challenge.

LEDUC: I am trying to develop students who speak French, not translators.

FINE: I'm telling you what the usual routine in the department is.

LEDUC: All right, Miss Fine. Rain or shine, one story a night. Read aloud one half the story in French. Then translate.

O'SHEA: I think we are reaching agreement in classroom matters. I propose that we go back to school-wide matters. I think if Miss Leduc would look in her manual, she would find it says on page three: "Any student excused from class for any reason will be provided with a 'travel' slip, made out by the teacher in charge."

LEDUC: I know that, Mr. O'Shea. And I have complied with it.

O'SHEA: During the fall term I found children wandering around the corridors. In all cases. . . .

LEDUC: How many cases?

O'SHEA: Perhaps three, perhaps more. I didn't count. At any rate, in *all* cases these children were from your class. They had no travel slips.

LEDUC: It has never happened to my knowledge.

O'SHEA: This makes it even more serious. I thought perhaps you sent the student on an errand and had forgotten the slip. I know this was true in one case.

FINE: This is another indication that Miss Leduc is sometimes careless with the truth. Or forgetful.

LEDUC: I refuse to be subjected to that sort of thing. (*Rises noisily*)

O'SHEA: Now, Miss Leduc, sit down and be calm. I think we're making real progress here. Miss Fine did not mean that. I think she meant to say . . . there was some inconsistency in your statement. If you knew about the student then you excused her without the slip. This is a minor matter.

LEDUC: I have the same feeling.

O'SHEA: Well, I don't view it as a minor matter. I think school regulations must be maintained. Mr. Pine, the custodian, says that you often forget to send him the room-temperature report.

LEDUC: That is *not* true.

O'SHEA: Now wait a minute, Miss Leduc. I think you owe it to professional ethics to be patient and listen to us.

FINE: I agree.

LEDUC: I am as sensitive to professional ethics as any teacher. Are you charging me with unprofessional conduct?

O'SHEA: Miss Leduc, I have explained that we are not charging you with anything. This is not a session of that sort. At least it wasn't intended to be. It was intended for us to talk frankly about an unpleasant situation. I've always felt that if people could sit down and talk things out, the world would be better. I don't know how you can expect nations to be at peace, when we — members of the same family, as it were — are squabbling. I think we should all just sit quietly for a moment and meditate. At least let's think this whole thing through before we speak again. The damage that has been done by hasty speech.

FINE: Well, I'm not certain that we should just *sit* here. I think there are still things that have to be settled. I don't feel that Miss Leduc *really* wants to cooperate. I will say now, Miss Leduc, Mr. O'Shea has been very patient . . . far more so than I would be. I would. . . .

O'SHEA: Miss Fine! *I* am principal here.

FINE: I know that, Mr. O'Shea. But I think there is a limit to everything. If you won't charge Miss Leduc with unprofessional conduct, I shall. Here and now. There is *something* wrong here. Either Miss Leduc is to blame or I am. *That's logical.* It *has* to be one or the other.

O'SHEA: I don't think it does.

LEDUC: Well, I would prefer that you be frank about things. If you feel that way, say it. If you want to bring the matter before Superintendent Patterson, I am quite ready to go there. I think I've listened to quite enough innuendo for today. (*Again rises*) I think I need the advice of someone. Make your charges.

O'SHEA: Sit down, Miss Leduc. I mean that. I've had my secretary taking all of this down. I sense in your last statement a threat . . . and I will not be threatened in my own school.

LEDUC: I didn't intend to threaten you. I can sense that you are arrayed against me. I feel it.

O'SHEA: We aren't. But you clearly implied that you are going to the superintendent. You further hinted that you are going to seek legal aid. I didn't want the matter to come to this, but since you choose to. . . .

LEDUC: I hinted at no such thing.

O'SHEA: Miss Leduc, your unprofessional conduct has been apparent throughout this whole meeting. You have consistently refused to adhere to the spirit of regulations governing this school. Your attention has been perfunctory.

LEDUC: I'm going to leave this minute!

O'SHEA: I want to tell you this, Miss Leduc. If you do, I will carry the matter to Superintendent Patterson. I will send him a complete report of this meeting, and a history of the case. I will send you a copy of the letter. And you, Miss Fine.

FINE: I'd like to say, Mr. O'Shea, that I agree with you completely. You have made every effort. I have made every effort. We all have made every effort.

LEDUC: I'm sorry, but I feel ill. I really think that I will have to go. (*Exit Miss Leduc*)

O'SHEA: *Well!*

FINE: Well indeed, Mr. O'Shea! Mr. O'Shea, I think you handled it very well. It's so tragic.

O'SHEA: Yes, tragic, Miss Fine. This has been the most difficult case I've ever had to deal with. I'm sorry about this. It's the first time it has ever happened to me. Miss Templeton, would you make up a transcript of these notes for Mr. Patterson. I'll write a letter covering the entire matter. I'm upset about this.

15 Next in Line

Bob Donovan graduated from a state college in Ohio in June, 1948. Bob was the youngest of the six children of "Big Jack" Donovan, a sometime railroad laborer, and Martha (Grey) Donovan, daughter of a small merchant in Maybank, Ohio. With two and a half years of credit under the G.I. Bill, and the aid of his brothers and sisters, Bob had managed to get through college without suffering any undue hardship. He had majored in history and minored in education, and his aim all through college was to teach social studies in the public schools. He had not been an exceptional student, but he had been a fair athlete and popular with his classmates. In the summer of 1948 Bob considered going on for his Master's degree in Education, but decided that he owed it to his family to work for a few years before going on to graduate school. In June he applied for a teaching job in his home town of Maybank.

After his first interview with J. Gordon Phelps, Superintendent of Schools of Maybank, Bob concluded that he had little chance of getting the job. Superintendent Phelps said: "Social Studies teachers are a dime a dozen around here. Particularly ones with no experience and no advanced study like you."

"Well, I plan to do advanced study," Bob said. "I guess I'll enroll next summer at Ohio State."

"What are your plans for this summer?" Phelps asked.

"I'm working as a lifeguard for the Park Department."

"Humph. Pretty easy job for a strong young fellow like you. Well, we always welcome applications. We'll see what comes up." Throughout the interview Phelps had shuffled papers on his desk, and Bob had had the impression that the superintendent was anxious to see him leave.

After the interview Bob told his mother that he had small hope of teaching in Maybank. Still, he was quite certain that there would be vacancies in the Maybank schools in the fall of 1948. The town, a suburb on the eastern edge of Carter, a large Ohio city, had, since 1940, increased in population from 10,000 to over 20,000. New industry was moving into Maybank; there was a building boom in all classes of housing. The boom was due partly to the influx of industrial workers and partly to the numbers of city families who were building one-family houses in the North Farms district of Maybank. The result had been a large rise in the Maybank tax rate, to support a school-building program that was somewhat out of joint and to hire new teachers for the schools. Phelps, who had been superintendent of schools since 1941, was in 1948 a man with problems. Hence Bob was not upset by the brusqueness of his reception at the school office. Superintendent Phelps had a reputation for being direct and gruff. He was, in fact, a controversial figure in the town. His knowledge of the technical aspects of his job was admitted by all. On the other hand, his strong-mindedness, his dictatorial tactics, and his attempts to dominate the school board had made him many enemies within the community. Two of his opponents had joined the school board in the last election, and the rumors were that they were "playing hell with old J. Gordon." Bob supposed that this accounted for his own rather gruff reception. The two new members had announced their intention of "ridding this town of J. Gordon." One of these men worked with Bob's older brother, who was a foreman in a local factory.

Early in July Bob received a call from the superintendent. Phelps requested that Bob come to his office for a second interview. The second interview was quite different from the first. "Bob," Phelps began, "I think we can hire you. I've sounded out your candidacy with some of the board members, and they are all for it. I think I can safely promise that you will be a candidate for a junior high school job in the fall."

"Well that's very good, Mr. Phelps," Bob said. "I'd about given up hope. You see, I want a job in this town for many reasons. I came from here. What I've gotten came through education. I'd like to pay something back to the other kids like me. I guess I'm not making myself clear."

"I understand perfectly," Phelps assured him. "You're the kind of boy we need in public education."

During August it was announced in the local paper that Superintendent of Schools J. Gordon Phelps had been given a new five-year contract and an $1,800 raise in pay. Some people in the town exchanged knowing smiles and the usual comment was: "Well, old J. Gordon has done it again. You've got to hand it to him. What he sets out to get he gets. He can be pleasant when he has to be."

At the general faculty meeting, held before school opened in September of 1948, Bob learned that he was not going to teach social studies but instead was scheduled to teach seventh- and eighth-grade math and science in Maybank Junior High. Bob had had no specialized work in this field, and had not had a course in science since his high school days. When he approached Mr. Phelps after the meeting Phelps smiled and pumped his hand. "Yes," Phelps said, "I know you asked for social studies. But some things have happened. I was forced to do some shifting. It's in line with the certification law in Ohio, though; I checked that. Donovan, I know you'll get in there and do a bang-up job no matter what you are teaching." Phelps stepped in close to Bob and shook his hand, adding: "Good luck to you, son."

So Bob Donovan went into Maybank Junior High and taught math and general science. According to parents, other teachers, and Principal Ned Burton, Bob was "a born teacher." In 1951, when Ned Burton was made principal of the Maybank High School he strongly recommended that Bob be chosen to succeed him. "I know he hasn't had too much experience," Burton told Phelps, "but that kid . . . I'd like a dozen like him. He really produced for me down there. He coached, he served committees, he souped up the P.T.A. He has a way with parents." Phelps listened to Burton's recommendation and made no comment. A week later it was announced that Hi Cole, a principal from an elementary school in a nearby town, had been chosen principal of Maybank Junior High.

"I didn't expect it," Bob told his older brother, Pete. "After all, I don't have the years of teaching experience. Mr. Cole has more than ten."

"He's an old fuddy-duddy," Pete said. "I've heard about him. I think that's what Phelps wants. He's scared of young, smart lads like you. I'll get Art Shibley to land on him at the next school board meeting."

"I wish you wouldn't do anything," Bob said. "My turn will come. I'm not even sure I want to get out of the classroom yet."

"Look, Bob," Pete said. "Let's get with it and learn how things run in this town. You wouldn't have even gotten into this system if Art hadn't gone to bat for you."

"I didn't know about that," Bob said. "And I'm sorry to hear it. I don't want you to do anything."

"O.K. boy," Pete told him. "It's your life."

Bob Donovan produced the same results for Hi Cole that he had produced under Ned Burton. Cole cited Bob in his school report and referred to him as "an outstanding classroom teacher." In the same report Mr. Cole outlined the out-of-class contributions which Donovan had made to Maybank Junior High. There was no guidance officer, as such, at Maybank Junior High, and at the request of Principal Cole, Bob was freed from six teaching periods a week to handle guidance at the school. Bob also handled the club and activity program, and in addition to coaching the school basketball and baseball teams he had persuaded another teacher to start an intramural softball league. Bob found Hi Cole far from an "old fuddy-duddy." Cole enthusiastically backed Bob's projects and took every opportunity to bring them to the attention of Superintendent Phelps. Hi Cole told Bob on numerous occasions: "I'm just waiting to catch J. Gordon in a good mood. I'm going to request that you be given an assistant principalship here."

This request was never made, because before the first year was over Phelps and Cole had quarreled violently, and Cole accepted a principalship in a small high school in the southern part of the state. That same year two more of Maybank's most able school men left the community. It was rumored, but never confirmed, that these men had left the community because they saw no hope of advancement under Phelps. The general complaint was that Phelps was inclined "to sit on the young men with ability within the system." When appointments were made they went either to men brought in from the outside or to older men in the system. This accusation was directly put to Phelps by a member of his board in June, 1951. Phelps denied the charge. He offered as proof of its falsity the fact that he was considering two young men for the principalship of Maybank Junior High. He named the men as Bob Donovan and Jim Barnet. "I want young men with ability in our schools," he told the board. "I think my choice of these two young men, both from our town, demonstrates this."

In the following week Superintendent Phelps called Bob Donovan to his office and informed him that he and Jim Barnet were being considered for the Maybank Junior High School principalship. Jim Barnet was a teacher in a local elementary school. He had been a lifelong friend of Bob Donovan's and had preceded him through college by one year. He called Bob that night after the meeting with Phelps and said that he had been called into the office and told of his candidacy for the job. "I'm surprised about it," Jim said. "To be honest with you, Bob, that job should be yours with no questions asked. You know the place and all. I'm in for a principalship here next year when Foss retires." During the course of the conversation Jim offered to withdraw his name from consideration. Bob spoke strongly against this, pointing out that it might cause trouble for both of them with Phelps.

A week later Bob received notification, in the form of a letter from Superintendent Phelps, that Jim Barnet had been appointed principal. Phelps stated, as the reason for the selection, that Jim Barnet had had one more year of teaching experience than Bob Donovan had. Barnet also had his Master's degree, and Bob was still six credits short of his. He had been forced to miss one summer of study when his mother was ill. Phelps went on to praise Bob extravagantly. He said that the president of the local P.T.A. had written letters to him and to the board members urging the selection of Bob Donovan. Phelps said that Principal Ned Burton at the high school had recommended Bob highly. He also said that he had had letters and phone calls from parents and other "interested parties" who had unanimously recommended Bob for the position. He said that in view of this he felt that Bob was the logical choice for the principalship of the new junior high school when it was opened. Meanwhile he promised that he would make Bob the assistant principal at Maybank after mid-term. Phelps further stated that if Bob wished he could go "up to the high school" and teach social studies. Phelps pointed out that there would be an assistant principalship vacant there at the end of the year. He said that Ned Burton had requested that Bob Donovan be assigned there. Bob said that he would consider both positions and let Phelps know before the week was out. Before the end of the week Jim Barnet called at Bob's house. He urged Bob to stay on at the junior high school with him. Jim said, "I need you there. It's a new situation for me." He also argued that Bob would be getting his assistant principalship by mid-term and that Bob would find the experience valuable on his record should he wish to move on later. Phelps had made no definite commitment on the high school assistant principalship. He had only stated that it would be open. Bob, influenced by his loyalty to Jim and to the school, decided that it would be best to stay on at Maybank Junior High School. When he informed the superintendent of his decision, Phelps said: "I think you've made the wisest choice. I wish we had more loyal young men like you in our schools."

The mid-year arrived, and there was only silence from the superintendent on the matter of Bob's assistant principalship. The mid-year passed, and still there was not word. Bob's older brother called in early March to say that Bob had not even been mentioned in the personnel plans which Phelps had submitted to the school board. Again Bob requested that his brother not interfere. Late in March Bob received a call from Ned Burton. Burton said that he had just been appointed principal of schools in Arthursville for the coming year. He said: "They've given me carte blanche on building up a team of smart young school men there. You know how slow and stodgy the Arthursville schools have been." Arthursville was a wealthy old suburb on the western edge of the city of Carter. It was thirty miles from Maybank. Although the town was wealthy, it had never been noted for the quality of its schools. It had provided the bare minimum support, favoring a traditional system, with a high school which emphasized the college preparatory course. Many of the children of the wealthy citizens of Arthursville went East to preparatory schools, and this was sometimes reflected in the attitude of the taxpayers. "They want a new look over here," Ned Burton said. "And I want you as part of the team. We can make you assistant principal of the high school right away. I'll have you in my office before two years are over."

"I'd like to have my name submitted for the job," Bob said.

"O.K.," said Burton. "That's all I wanted to know."

Early in April the contracts for the Maybank schools came out. The usual note was attached — that the contracts were to be signed before the end of the month. Bob's contract called for $4,400, an eight-hundred-dollar raise. He was to be assistant principal of Maybank Junior High. Phelps enclosed a note saying that he had upgraded by $200 the original salary estimate for an assistant principal at Maybank, because of Bob's unusual ability. The same week Bob was notified that he had been selected for the job in Arthursville at a salary of $4,600. Ned Burton had enclosed a note saying that he had strongly urged Bob's appointment and that he was looking forward to having Bob with him next year.

Two days later Phelps called Bob to the office. He said that he had been approached by "people from Arthursville" in the matter of a recommendation for Bob, and that he had recommended him highly for the job. He wanted to know if Bob had been made a definite offer by Arthursville. Bob gave the superintendent the details, and explained that he thought the Arthursville job offered the better opportunity. He said that he thought that he would take the position.

Phelps agreed that Arthursville had made the better offer. Then he said: "It's one of those rich towns. The kids there aren't our kind, Bob. I guess I'm old. I just can't see running off to these towns to teach rich kids. Everybody can't teach in gold-plated towns like Arthursville. Some of us have to stay here and provide an education for the poorer kids. Well, good luck to you, son. You're going places in education."

Bob had no answer to that. He said, "Well, I'm sorry you feel that way, Mr. Phelps. I'm certainly influenced by more than the money involved." As he drove home, Bob pondered Phelps' remark. It was quite true that it looked as though he were running out of his town to chase the first good offer that came along. He thought back to his first reason for entering public education, and his reason for wanting to teach in Maybank. He remembered that he had done some apprentice teaching in Arthursville when he had been back in college. It was quite true that he had found the children different; he had often been ill at ease with them. Still, this could have been caused by his own feelings of inadequacy rather than by any true difference in the children. He had had no problems with the wealthy families who were moving into the North Farms district of Maybank; in fact, many of them were his prize pupils.

Two hours after he reached home Bob received a call from Phelps. Phelps said: "I'm just not going to let you leave us here, Bob. What would it take to keep you in Maybank?"

"I don't know," Bob said.

"Well, let me work on it," Phelps said. "I think you would be making a mistake to leave us. And I'm not going to let you make that mistake for a few hundred dollars." Bob promised to think the whole matter over and Phelps said that he would contact him within the week.

The next day at the close of school Bob received a visit from Dr. Kermit Shipton, president of the Maybank School Board. Dr. Shipton said: "Mr. Donovan, I've called about a matter that is causing us increasing concern on the school board. Our town is growing. We are attracting industry and householders. Yet our young school men are leaving. We of the board wonder why."

"Well, I don't have the answer to that, Dr. Shipton," Bob said. "I guess the opportunities are better elsewhere."

"We have been very much interested in your particular case," Shipton said. "You seem to be typical of the kind of men we are losing. Frankly, the board was shocked when it heard about your impending move to Arthursville. Let me say this: We will meet to the dollar any offer they make. Furthermore, we will appoint you to the high school in September of next year as Dean of Boys. You will be in line for the next suitable administrative post in the system. And I might add that at the rate Maybank is growing we will very soon need a new assistant superintendent. I can't promise you anything there, but you will receive consideration if and when this vacancy occurs. Now . . . what do you think of that?"

"Well," Bob admitted, "it certainly influences my decision. I don't know what to say. I'll think it over."

"I'd like to ask you a few more questions, if I might, Mr. Donovan. What exactly have been your relationships with Mr. Phelps? What is your considered professional opinion of him? If you did leave Maybank, would you consider coming back later, if there were certain changes?"

"Well," Bob said. "I'd rather not answer those questions off the top of my head. I'd like to submit my answers in writing if I could, sir. It's not the sort of question which should be answered in conversation."

Dr. Shipton nodded. "Very good. You'll write me a letter, then."

On the following day Bob composed his letter to Dr. Shipton. In it he stated that the reason why many of the men were leaving Maybank was that they were being offered jobs with higher pay and professional status in other towns. He wrote: "My relationship with Mr. Phelps has always been satisfactory. He has dealt with me in an open and honest way. My professional opinion of Mr. Phelps is that he is a capable and intelligent man. He has had many difficult problems in a town which is growing so rapidly. His decisions have been, to the best of my knowledge, the wisest possible under the circumstances. In closing, I would say that I would consider coming back to Maybank, depending on the job offered me here. I received my education in the Maybank schools, and naturally I feel that I have some debt to them." Bob signed the letter and mailed it.

That night Bob sat down to think over his answer to the Maybank and Arthursville school authorities. He had no wish to let Ned Burton down, and he realized that Ned Burton had pushed his candidacy to the limit in Arthursville. He had also kept Arthursville waiting longer than was customary. The opportunity at Arthursville was there, and it depended on the promises of Ned Burton, who had never broken his word. In Maybank it depended on a temporary situation in which the school board was putting pressure on Phelps. Bob had seen Phelps come out on top with past school boards. Dr. Shipton had no permanency on the board; if he were replaced, Bob could not be certain that his future was secure. Maybank was a growing community, and Arthursville was a stable one. As long as Ned Burton was supported by the new group at Arthursville there was hope of a challenging job, but if control should pass back to the old group, Arthursville could go back to its former school slump. Maybank was bound to grow and increase because the area was there. Arthursville was built up as much as the space and zoning laws would permit. He had just built a new house which he and his mother occupied, and he hoped to be married within the year. Arthursville was directly across the city of Carter, an impossible daily drive, and housing in the town was scarce and expensive. Bob could not afford to run two homes after his marriage. Furthermore, he felt some obligation to the Maybank schools. He had taught there only four years; he had made his mistakes and now was in a position to make a contribution. When he reviewed the past four years he saw that he had come along much faster than most young teachers. Still, in the past year he had come to understand the sort of man Phelps was. Although he had no particular grudge against the man, Bob was no longer as naïve as he had been. Bob realized that Phelps was an "operator" and an opportunist. Viewing him as such, Bob neither blamed him nor admired him, but he was certain of one thing: At the start of his own career in education, he had no intention of patterning himself after J. Gordon Phelps.

16 Request for the Name

In mid-April, 1953, the Superintendent of the Public Schools of Boston, Dennis Haley, and five members of the Boston School Committee, Patrick J. Foley, Alice M. Lyons, Isadore H. Y. Muchnick, Mary K. Fitzgerald, and William F. Carr, attended a meeting sponsored by the League of Women Voters in Boston, Massachusetts. In the course of the meeting, as a reporter subsequently remembered it, Superintendent Haley spoke of the first-rate job the Boston School Department was doing in meeting its problems squarely.

Dr. Haley described the way he had handled the case of a Boston public school teacher suspended in late March for conduct unbecoming a teacher and insubordination. He went on to say, in language recollected by the reporter approximately as follows, "and there may be another similar problem that we will have to handle. There is another teacher scheduled to appear before the subversive investigating committee in Washington."

A few days later on April 17, at a school committee hearing originally called on the matter of custodial assignments, the following interchange took place between the committee members and Dr. Haley.

(*Transcript taken from the Proceedings of the School Committee of the City of Boston, 1953.*)

Mrs. Lyons: I think we are all here. Would you. . . .

Mr. Muchnick: Madam Chairman, before we start in this, I have one short motion I would like to present. A couple of nights ago there was a meeting of a certain group of people at which all members of the school committee — at which the superintendent and some assistant superintendents and various others from the administrative end of the School Department were also present.

At that meeting, the superintendent stated substantially the following at one stage of the discussions. . . .

Miss Fitzgerald: Madam Chairman, may I ask if this is to be a meeting or a hearing to the custodians? I don't wish to interrupt the proceedings, but I wonder if this motion is particularly relevant at this time.

Mrs. Lyons: I think if one of the members wants to make a motion. . . .

Miss Fitzgerald: I didn't understand that this was to be a meeting, and there was no public notice given. I understand in the near future we will have a school committee meeting and this motion can be taken up at that time.

Mr. Muchnick: Madam Chairman, just a few minutes ago we met in the superintendent's office on something that wasn't scheduled for this meeting. This is even more unusual, frankly, if I may be permitted. . . .

Miss Fitzgerald: I just wish to offer for the record. . . .

Mr. Muchnick: There was stated at the time substantially the following: That the superintendent, as he put it, had knowledge of the fact that there was a member of the School Department personnel — I assume a member of the teaching force — who was suspected or engaged in — I don't know the exact details of it — in Communism or subversive activity and that that information would become public within a short time.

Now, if it is a fact that the superintendent or any other person has knowledge or reason to believe that any member of our teaching force or custodial force or any other division of the School Department is in that category, then it seems to me we should not wait until any federal government agency or state government agency brings that to our attention or to the public's attention.

It is our duty under those circumstances to move and to move as quickly as possible to eliminate from our school system that type of person. Therefore, I move, that the superintendent be instructed to furnish the name and address of that person to the chairman of the school committee forthwith, and that the school committee communicate with that person this evening and direct that person to appear before us here tomorrow morning at 9:30 to answer such questions as may be put to that person, and to show cause why that person should not be immediately suspended by the school committee for engaging in that kind of activity; for conduct unbecoming a teacher and for any further reasons that may appear as a result of that meeting and hearing.

MISS FITZGERALD: I just want to say that this is a very serious motion; that it is not a full board, and I certainly can't be here in the morning at 9:30; and if there is anyone — and I certainly feel I, as an individual member, am as concerned as any of the other members over the presence of any Communist or other subversive personality who is in our teaching force. I didn't happen to have heard that remark made, although I was there but had to leave early.

DR. FOLEY: It might be instead a good suggestion that the superintendent get in touch with you, as chairman of the school committee, and you, if you felt the problem was severe enough or of interest enough to the school committee, could be delegated, I am quite sure, to inform the members of the school committee whether or not it is of urgent character or what the particulars are.

SUPERINTENDENT: Madam Chairman?

MR. MUCHNICK: Madam Chairman?

MRS. LYONS: Mr. Muchnick.

MISS FITZGERALD: Madam Chairman, I think the superintendent. . . .

MRS. LYONS: Miss Fitzgerald, I will conduct this meeting. You are dictating to me altogether too much and I will decide who is to have the floor, and I will run this meeting. The person who is entitled to the floor will be recognized and they don't need you to tell them. I don't need you to tell me either.

Mr. Superintendent, if you wish the floor you may have it now; but Miss Fitzgerald, I don't need your suggestions. The Chair will handle the meeting very, very capably.

SUPERINTENDENT: Madam Chairman and members, at the present time I do not wish to reveal the name of the individual concerned. I have certain information at my disposal which was given to me through the proper channels. I have conferred with the Corporation Counsel in regard to the information which I have at my disposal, and following the advice of the Corporation Counsel, there is nothing for me to present to the school committee or to present to anyone at this particular time.

MR. MUCHNICK: I don't know what conferences the superintendent or anybody else has had with the Corporation Counsel. I not only don't know, but I don't care. Under the law, under the Constitution of the Commonwealth of Massachusetts — as a matter of fact, in compliance with the oath we severally took the other night — it is our duty not only as citizens but it is our duty as public officials — members of a school committee — to run a School Department. It is our duty as well as the duty of the other people to see to it that the kind of person described in the motion, the kind of person referred to by the superintendent at the meeting Wednesday night, doesn't stay in our school system for five minutes, if the facts are as indicated just now by the superintendent, and the other night by the superintendent.

The Corporation Counsel isn't running the School Department. The superintendent isn't running the School Department. The school committee is obliged by law to run the School Department, and I press you, Madam Chairman, this motion that the superintendent be directed as indicated in the motion first stated, as an employee of the School Department, the same as anybody else in the employ of the School Department, to furnish you with that name forthwith so that the necessary arrangements can be made to bring that person here tomorrow.

This isn't the kind of thing that waits on any situation. I, too, am busy tomorrow morning. This is far more important than anything I personally have to do tomorrow; or, in my opinion, than anything that anybody has to do tomorrow.

Just because the Corporation Counsel has told the superintendent not to do it now is in no way binding on the school committee.

The superintendent is not working for the Corporation Counsel. He is working for the City of Boston. He is working for the City of Boston under the direction, supervision, and control of the school committee; and, as he himself stated last Wednesday night in response to a question having nothing to do with this particular item — he said he didn't wish to get involved in a discussion with the members of the school committee who were his superiors without it being for the record, as I remember the phrase. He knows that he is an employee of the school committee and therefore, I ask that the school committee pass that motion and direct one of its employees to furnish vital, necessary information to it as called for by the motion.

MISS FITZGERALD: May I ask the superintendent this question through you, Madam Chairman?

Is there some reason why the Corporation Counsel stated that information should not be presented to the school committee at the present time?

SUPERINTENDENT: Madam Chairman and Miss Fitzgerald, the information which I have at the present time does not, I would say, incriminate the individual to the extent that I should make any accusation in any way, shape, or manner toward him.

When the facts in the case were before me, I followed the advice of the Corporation Counsel and I acted in the best interest of the service as the executive head of the school system.

Now, there is another problem before me, and I am certainly not going to reveal any name to anybody at the present time that in any way might affect the case or affect the proper dealing with this particular case.

Now, when the matter is of a nature that I feel it should be presented to the school committee, I shall do so officially. I am not going to make any statement to any individual member of the school committee until I am in a position to know more about the individual case.

MR. MUCHNICK: Madam Chairman, it is not the province of the superintendent or any single individual, whether it be a member of the Law Department or any other department in the city or state or anywhere else, to decide for himself or themselves what must be decided by the school committee. The fact that the superintendent says that there isn't enough evidence to incriminate Mr. or Miss or Mrs. X in his opinion is of absolutely no importance.

The matter is one for the school committee and it is the opinion of the school committee as to whether the person presently unnamed, of whom we are speaking, is guilty of communistic or subversive activity or conduct unbecoming a teacher, or insubordination. The superintendent has no right legally or morally to refuse to give this information or any information, Madam Chairman, to this school committee who are his employers. Refusal, as a matter of fact, seems to me would be tantamount to insubordination on his part. I am not going to go into the question of the superintendent's duty as a citizen, or this or that. That is something between him and his conscience.

He has absolutely no right under the law, under our rules or under any conceivable or imaginable document or interpretation to keep confidential from the school committee any information so vital affecting the schools. It is not up to him to decide as to whether there is or isn't sufficient information that will incriminate a person.

Again, I repeat, I must press for a vote.

DR. FOLEY: I would say, at the meeting the other night, I think it was, an inference was made by the superintendent that he had such a question now before him with regard to undoubtedly a subversive nature that was related somewhat to the —— case or was just the same as the —— case. I would say, Madam Chairman and Superintendent, that inasmuch as that was a public utterance to a public group, I think it behooves you to impart that knowledge to the recognized head of the school system.

SUPERINTENDENT: Madam Chairman and members, I have discussed the matter with the Corporation Counsel from the standpoint of affairs both in regard to myself and in regard to the individual concerned. I can say this: The individual concerned is being summoned to Washington before an investigating committee.

MRS. LYONS: I think that was in the newspapers at the time of the —— case.

DR. FOLEY: Why is it we are left in the dark and we don't — we don't come into your confidence, sit down in man-fashion and discuss these things? Why run to the Corporation Counsel when you have five members of a school committee who are interested in the welfare of the schools?

I knew nothing about it until you made the statement at the League of Women Voters the other night, and as the sponsor of this oath now going through the City of Boston, I felt I would have liked to have known what that information was.

I would like to feel as though I know what is going on in the system, and I get a little put out if I don't.

MRS. LYONS: It was in the papers.

SUPERINTENDENT: It was in the papers. Now, the information came to me and I in turn discussed the matter with the Corporation Counsel.

Madam Chairman, I certainly am very willing to reveal everything to the school committee that I should. On the other hand, I don't want to make any accusations or have any names involved officially before the school committee until the time comes where I feel it really belongs there. In other words, right at the moment the Corporation Counsel has said to me, "Well, now, in the meantime, there is no report that you will have to make at the moment."

MRS. LYONS: May I say something first? I think the last time there was considerable resentment, Mr. Superintendent, on the part of the committee members. Everybody seems to know a great deal about it but the school committee; they were never taken into confidence. Until we were sitting at the public meeting, is the first time anyone of us knew what the story was about Mr. ——.

I think they felt — I know what their feelings were because people said to me, "You don't know anything about it?" I would say, "No, never discussed by the superintendent."

Even the newspaper reporters I really don't feel believed me that night when I said that I didn't know anything about it.

Mr. Muchnick: I can't get this business, frankly, of an employee of the School Department, regardless of title, taking things up with the Corporation Counsel and following the advice of the Corporation Counsel as to whether he should tell the people who are his superiors about anything that has to do in the school system which these people are obligated under the law to run. I don't know of any person in the City of Boston who voted for William Baxter [Corporation Counsel] as the man to run the School Department.

I do not ask further that the superintendent make any accusations. I merely ask that the superintendent tell us or you, so that you can notify this person to be present, and the superintendent can or cannot be present — as far as I am concerned — as he wishes. If the discussion that takes place with this school employee warrants the making of an accusation, I will be very glad to assume the responsibility of making the motion which involves making the accusation.

I for one, don't need any Congressional committee to make the accusations for me. I think I know something about the ascertaining of facts from people. I think I know something about the applicable law in relation to the obtaining of facts and to the evaluating of facts. I do not ask that anybody make any accusation and thus put themselves on a spot.

The mere fact that this person is currently being summoned to Washington — and this is the first I have heard of that, was the discussion a couple of minutes ago — is added proof to the argument which I have been advocating during the last few moments.

Now, under our regulations it is the duty of the superintendent to report to the school committee everything that is of an unusual nature in connection with the school system as soon as that happens. It is not his duty to report it to the Corporation Counsel.

Now, we, under the law and under the rules, must have this information if this person is of the type who shouldn't be connected with our schools. We must act immediately, just as the superintendent took action in the —— case in a matter of hours. This case should be handled the same way if it is to be handled at all.

It does not have to wait and mustn't wait on anything that happens in Washington, New York, or Chicago, or any place else.

Nobody in this city, members of the committee, or the governor, or the superintendent, or anybody else, has any right to keep that information from us, much less that person who is an employee of the Department, the School Department, and who is charged with the responsibility and duty of giving us information of any unusual incident.

I am sure that the superintendent or nobody else will claim that the existence of a person in our employ who is of the type that I am afraid this unnamed person is, is the usual thing in our system. This is the kind of thing that we are trying to fight and trying to get rid of — not next week, not next year, and not forty years from now — but today is when it should be done and must be done.

SUPERINTENDENT: I am sorry, Madam Chairman and members, if the committee resented anything I did, for this reason.

DR. FOLEY: I would like, Madam Chairman, to get all this information possible before suspension orders are declared by the superintendent. In the process of suspension, I believe that the process up to the time of suspension should be made known to us so that we would have the information before suspension.

I really believe that the chairman of the school board should be then informed. And then let us determine what the action should be.

MRS. LYONS: I think that has been what has been done in other communities. I think in New York there have been several cases and it has come to the attention of the board, and the board didn't wait for the Jenner people to tell them or anybody else.

They brought these individuals before them and they said, "You can't ask those questions." The board said, "We are sorry. We are going to ask those questions."

DR. FOLEY: I do believe local boards should assume responsibility to track down those that are not fit as Americans and dispose, if it so sees fit, to take care of them. I don't feel we should wait for the Jenner Committee or any federal group to so inform us as to who is in this group.

I believe local boards, local school boards, or any educational board that is set up, that is elected for the primary purpose of running local schools, should receive all this information as quickly as possible.

MR. MUCHNICK: That is correct, Madam Chairman. The superintendent said once it became an official matter, he told the school committee about it. Well, it becomes an official matter as soon as the superintendent learns about it. That is the time it is to be told to the school committee without any question.

It is official as soon as anybody learns about it. It doesn't become official sometime in the future by action on the part of the superintendent or headmaster or anybody else. It is something not only to which we are entitled to have information; it is something which the law compels us to know about and to act about, and properly so.

The superintendent said something about the Law Department saying that we didn't know what the superintendent was going to recommend. Well, suspension and dismissal are not in the sole province of the superintendent. It is as much the province and the duty of the school committee to suspend and dismiss improper people as it is the province of the superintendent or anybody else.

Regardless of what the federal government does about these things; regardless of what the state government does about these things; regardless of what the municipal government in Boston — outside of the School Department — does in these things, it is clearly the established policy — and again properly — of the school committee that we don't want improper people teaching; whether that improper trait is based on Communism or subversive activity or morals or anything else.

Once we have information or an inkling of information, we must act; if it is a question of Communism or subversiveness, what we do here tomorrow — if we do it — may help whatever Congressional committee has summoned this person. Because the question of desire not to incriminate under the Fifth Amendment while I believe it is a matter of constitutional law, the privilege could be exercised.

It seems to me the proper kind of questioning might adduce certain facts that could be helpful in the overall attempt of the federal government to see if there is a pattern of subversiveness and Communism fostered among school personnel. But that being aside, I think it is even our province, as a school committee, to do that if we can. There is no question but what it is our duty to act immediately in the situation that we have under discussion at the moment.

MISS FITZGERALD: I have been here since four o'clock. We were scheduled to have a hearing at five. It is now ten minutes past seven, and these good gentlemen have been kept waiting all this time. I have been subjected to discourtesy and I don't intend to remain for the rest of it. I hope you will excuse me.

MR. MUCHNICK: I would like a vote on the motion.

MRS. LYONS: Would you call the roll?

(*Rollcall:*)

MR. CARR: [Absent.]
MISS FITZGERALD: [Absent.]
DR. FOLEY: Yes.
MR. MUCHNICK: Yes.
MRS. LYONS: Yes.

17 *Popular Bandmaster*

Mr. Phipps' Request

In late July, 1953, Cyrus Phipps, music supervisor of the secondary schools in Fern City, appeared at the home of Francis Carroll, principal of Carter Junior High School.

Mr. Phipps had been on the staff of the Fern City schools as a part-time supervisor since 1927, and a full-time supervisor since 1929. Now he requested that during the next school year he be relieved either of duties as director of the school sing, an activity which was held every Tuesday from 11:40 to 1:00 at the Carter Junior High School, or of the regularly scheduled music class which immediately preceded the noon activity. He said that before going to Carter in the morning, he had to teach two periods at the high school — choral singing and glee club from 8:30 to 9:21 and band from 9:21 to 10:21. He then came "down to the junior high school" to begin his teaching day.

Mr. Phipps, who worked between the Fern City High School and the Carter School, the one junior high school in the city, requested the relief on the grounds that his schedule was already overly long. He felt that the school sing was not primarily a music department activity, but rather an extracurricular recreational program which could be handled by the regular staff at Carter. Mr. Carroll pointed out that Phipps actually did not begin to teach until 10:50, which allowed him thirty minutes between the high school and his first class at Carter. That class ran from 10:50 to 11:40, and from this class Mr. Phipps went to the auditorium to conduct the Tuesday sing, usually making his entrance between 11:45 and 11:50.

Phipps felt that there was more than a matter of time involved. He said: "I object to the load coming like that. I have to run from a teaching class directly into the songfest. The only way a person can realize how hard I work is to follow me around all day. Sometimes I can't eat. I have charge also of the discipline in the auditorium. I would like more time for a change of mental environment."

Mr. Carroll did not see it the same way. He pointed out to Phipps that the activity program was very important, and besides it would be difficult to replace a man of Phipps' ability.

Cyrus Phipps agreed that the activity periods served an essential purpose. He also agreed that the songfest was one of the most important and popular of the noon programs. "The kids like it," he said. "Mainly it's recreational singing. We flash the words on the screen, I play the piano, and the kids sing. But sometimes I get a chance to slip in a real worth-while record for them to hear."

Phipps also agreed that it would be difficult to find a replacement for him. He said that the job required a man with a good heavy touch on the keys. He also found it easy to get along with the children and felt that some substitutes wouldn't find it so easy. He said that ten years previously he had volunteered to take the noon sing on a temporary basis. Before this a woman who had "a strong touch on the piano" had been hired to play for the sing. Phipps had directed the singing from the floor. One of the piano players had sent a bill to the superintendent, and according to Phipps, the superintendent complained about the expense. Phipps had agreed to take over temporarily; ten years later he was still "stuck with it."

Mr. Carroll and Mr. Phipps discussed the problem for some time, and finally Phipps indicated that he would see the superintendent.

He thought he had a good case, and reviewed the points in his favor.

Cyrus Phipps, as director of the school band and the school glee club, played an important role in the community and was before the public on many occasions. He had, for example, aided in a Christmas musical program put on by the Woman's Club, a memorial program put on by the Elks, and a breakfast sponsored by the Knights of Columbus. Recently the city had celebrated its founding, and he had supervised an enormous musical program. A fifty-piece band and a chorus of over two hundred had performed under his direction during the celebration.

When a citizens' committee had organized a program for a state music festival, Phipps had directed a seventy-piece band; and the concert had raised over $1,300. On another occasion, a program directed by him had raised over $1,700. There was in the city considerable interest in the high school football team, and he and his seventy-piece high school band were an important part of the ritual surrounding the games. Phipps knew he had played no small part in the community programs which were put on to raise money for the elegant band uniforms.

None of the other supervisors had duties which were directly comparable to his. The one similarity was that they were required to travel between schools and consequently were subject to the same time and scheduling problems. It was customary to allow half an hour from the end of one class to the beginning of another in a different building. Traveling from the high school to the junior high, approximately a quarter of a mile distant, he had half an hour between his second class at the high school and his first class at the junior high. But all the supervisors agreed that it was better to devote a full morning to one school and a full afternoon to another. This cut down needless running between schools. Most of them, he knew, experienced no problem of "mental adjustment" and were able to go directly to their classes to teach.

He found it difficult to work in time for lunch at Carter Junior High School. In addition to the ten class hours a week he taught at the high school, he carried a teaching load of about twelve forty-minute class periods a week at the junior high school. In addition to this, he had a full activity session throughout the year during the Tuesday sings, and an activity period on Wednesday when he handled the band and the music club. These club activities began in October and finished some time before the end of the school year in June. On Friday, he was usually involved in an activity period when he brought the band before the school assembly. He was free of class and activity duty on Monday from 11:40 to 1:00; Tuesday 1:00 to 1:40; Wednesday 11:40 to 1:00, except when he had orchestra and club; Thursday 11:40 to 1:40. On Friday, he spent twenty minutes of the time from 1:40 to 2:00 with his orchestra in the assembly, and then was free from 2:00 to 2:30. He had no afternoon sessions for make-up work and extra help as did the other teachers. He was also exempt from recess duty.

As compared with the regular teaching staff at the junior high school, Phipps granted, he perhaps had a trifle lighter schedule. But as compared with music supervisors in two nearby towns, Phipps felt, he had a full teaching load.

Mr. Carroll's Response

Mr. Carroll felt that Mr. Phipps was not being reasonable in his request to be relieved of the sing or the class before it, in view of the total picture.

The activity schedule kept the staff busy at Carter. Carroll had said repeatedly, "The activity program is extremely important because space is tight at Carter."

Carroll reflected that the school sing was divided into two sections, with one half of the school assigned to the first session, while the other was at lunch. The sections then changed places. The first section ran from 11:50 to 12:20; the second from 12:20 to 1:00. Approximately fourteen homeroom teachers were in the auditorium with the children at each session. Furthermore, both Mr. Carroll and Mr. Duchaine, the assistant principal, were in attendance when their duties permitted.

Mr. Carroll felt that Mr. Phipps had sufficient time for lunch from 1:00 to 1:40. The songfest came only once a week, on Tuesday, and the other teachers on his regular staff were far more burdened than Phipps, who was free on Monday from 11:40 to 1:00 when the activity period consisted of the assignment of topics and orientation on class club procedure. In the Wednesday activity hour, Phipps met with his band club, but the clubs did not get under way until early October. On Thursday, he was again free from 11:40 to 1:00 when the activity consisted of a movie shown to both halves of the school. On Friday there was a general school assembly during activity period.

Carroll had often said, "Our noon programs are an absolute necessity. You should see the place on a rainy day." After the ten or fifteen minutes required for lunch the students were confined to two raised cement walks which ran on either side of the lunch room in the basement.

Carroll knew that it would be very difficult to get a replacement for Phipps. Phipps knew how to handle students and get the most out of them. The whole system was experiencing a shortage of qualified substitute teachers. Moreover, the state teacher licensing requirement was strict in the matter of certifying teachers who did not have the exact course preparation. For this reason, there was little hope of getting anyone qualified to fill in for Phipps if he were excused from a class instead of from sing activity.

Carroll surmised that there were several things behind Phipps' request. In the first place, Carroll judged that Phipps was nearly sixty-five and was close to the retirement age. "You can't blame a man for wanting to cut corners at that age. He's getting along, and I have tried to free him from some of the load," he thought. Phipps no longer had to run the two operettas staged each year. Miss Carpenter, the auditorium teacher, coached the dramatic part of the program, and either the music was put on tape, or they hired a girl to help with the music. "I had to pay the girl," Carroll recalled, "and maybe Cyrus feels that I should have paid him."

Carroll offered Mr. Phipps very little encouragement or sympathy in the matter of dropping the sing from his schedule. It was the principal's impression that Phipps had already consulted Superintendent of Schools Phillip Utley about the matter before coming to Carroll with his request.

Mr. Utley's Problem

Some time in late July or early August, Cyrus Phipps went to Superintendent Utley with his request. Utley said later, "I was surprised. It was the first I'd heard of it." When questioned about the sequence of Phipps' visits, Utley said, "I think he went to see Carroll before he came to me."

Mr. Utley pictured himself as a superintendent who was "community-oriented." He was concerned with the internal problems of the school, but he had considerable faith in the ability of his staff to handle the day-to-day details of their jobs. This was acknowledged by members of his staff who stated, "If you do your job, he lets you alone."

Utley had an assistant superintendent, Martha Holmes, who had been in the system for over twenty years. He had considerable confidence in Miss Holmes, with her thirty-odd years of experience and training in elementary schools. She supervised the elementary schools, consulting Mr. Utley only in "unusual cases." Utley encouraged the same initiative in his high school and junior high school principals, stating, "I make the decisions. I mean I have to say 'yes' or 'no' thirty or forty times a day. But the staff handles most of the day-to-day problems."

Mr. Utley's concern with community problems meant that the school system had made it a policy to cooperate in all sorts of community-wide projects. School auditoriums and facilities were made available to programs sponsored in the community. And Cyrus Phipps was important to the success of many of these activities, Utley knew. He knew also that Phipps was very popular with many community groups.

In the school-wide picture there were a number of factors which, in the judgment of Utley, had weight in the case of Mr. Phipps. There were six supervisors in the Fern City Schools, including Phipps, supervisor of music in the secondary schools, and Miss Thompson, supervisor of music in the eight elementary schools.

Miss Thompson had come into the Fern City Schools in 1927, the same year that Mr. Phipps had been hired. The previous supervisor, who had handled the entire system, had suffered a collapse from overwork; hence the job was cut in half. Both of the present supervisors operated entirely independently, and there was no case when their duties overlapped or when they consulted on a general program of music. Miss Thompson had worked with Mr. Phipps on some of the community projects; she had trained half of the chorus (one hundred boy sopranos) for the celebration of the city's founding. Except on these occasions Miss Thompson and Mr. Phipps had infrequent contacts.

The matter of equipment storage seemed to have a certain bearing on the problem. Cyrus Phipps' second class in the morning at the high school (9:21–10:21) was with the band, and involved instruments and music which had to be stored in some semblance of order in the high school music room at the end of rehearsal. The principal of the high school, John Flynn, told Mr. Utley that there were occasions when Mr. Phipps had to leave for the junior high school class without supervising the storage of the equipment. The principal pointed out that this, in his estimation, was not the fault of Mr. Phipps, but rather of the schedule. Mr. Phipps had stated that he felt he should have an assistant for this work.

Flynn was not sure that this would be a completely fitting solution to the problem. He did say, however, that for his own purposes he would have welcomed a chance to get more of Mr. Phipps' time. He pointed out that two-thirds of Phipps' teaching day went to the junior high school rather than to the senior high school. In contrast, the time of the practical arts teachers, also shared by both schools, was apportioned in reverse ratio so that two-thirds of their day went to the high school. Flynn pointed out that having a music man for only two periods a day necessitated certain administrative shifts in the high school program. The inflexibility of the music supervisor's time schedule made it necessary to jam all students interested in music into the first two periods of the day. As a result, the students were either forced to shift their scholastic programs or to skip the music elective.

As for equipment, he pointed out that the high school band uniforms were stored in the junior high school basement. It was the custom for the high school football team to play its games either on Sunday afternoon or on Friday night. "Cyrus has to be with the band at all these games," Flynn said. "That's a chore. Then he has to go down after the game and see that the uniforms are put away. He supervises this, and I'll bet there are nights when he doesn't finish until ten-thirty, eleven, or even later. He puts the uniforms away, but you can't expect him to sweep the floor afterwards. This means that they have to keep an extra janitor on hand at the junior high. Maybe this has caused him trouble. I don't know."

The junior high school picture was somewhat different in the matter of equipment. The principal did feel that the music supervisor was occasionally lax. Two of the regular staff of classroom teachers at the junior high school supported the principal's statement. At Carter it was the custom to have student committees assigned to take care of instruments and music. In general the school was organized to run with almost military precision; and both the principal and the assistant principal, with extensive backgrounds in military service, operated on the basis that "a busy ship is a happy ship."

Superintendent Utley felt that the differences in orientation and procedure between Carroll and Phipps could be one cause of possible friction. A principal and a music man might well be inclined to look at things differently.

Furthermore, Phipps did not appear to some of his more intimate friends to be as set on retirement as Carroll had judged. Phipps said that, although he was near the retirement age, it was still possible for the school board to vote him back into office for one-year terms. He seemed to feel that this might be the situation in his case, although it appears from other sources that the usual policy was to retire candidates when they reached the age limit.

It was not apparent that Phipps had slowed down to any extent because of age. He was an alert, active man with a mane of white hair and a healthy look. The guidance teacher in the junior high school stated that Phipps was quite capable of keeping up with the most active children. "He's wonderful with them," she said. "I've seen him pick the problem children out and get them working. He kept one of our most difficult cases in school through the twelve grades, because he had him carrying the bass drum in the band. And that boy had been badly truant in the seventh grade and ready to drop out of school." The principal of the Fern City High School, where Phipps worked two periods a day, substantiated this. "He'll get right out there and march the band around the block," the principal stated. The principal did agree, however, that Phipps may have preferred high school work to work in the junior high.

Before Mr. Utley decided on the request of Cyrus Phipps, certain personal considerations had to be thought about. Utley and Phipps were and had long been on friendly terms. Utley knew that Phipps was capable in his special field and a person of considerable importance in the community. As Phipps himself said of his community status, "You don't see the English teacher marching down the street with seventy men behind him reciting Shakespeare."

Looked at from the school-wide view, Phipps did have a full schedule.

To hire a substitute for Phipps, Utley would have to go before his school board to get the extra money. Even were Utley to get the money, there was no reason to suppose that substitutes would be readily available who could handle the school sings as Phipps did, or meet state licensing requirements so as to fill in for him at regular music classes. On the personal side, Utley felt reasonably secure with Phipps. Utley had always backed Phipps to the hilt on the procurement of equipment, a thing dear to the music director's heart. Phipps admitted this quite readily. Utley had been considerate of Phipps when he was requested by other school departments to take the band out of town for concerts or programs. Utley ruled this extra work and always found a way to get Phipps reimbursed for the duty. In the summer Utley had obtained extra money so that Phipps could run a band training school in the town. On the other hand, Utley knew that Phipps had been working extremely hard on the town celebration during the previous three months. Phipps was perhaps justifiably tired and overwrought.

18 *Laketon* — Prologue and Act I District Reorganization*

Prologue

Laketon, with a population of 60,000 in 1950, occupies ten square miles on the shore of Lake Tawana. The community serves as a residential area for commuting business and professional men and women; furthermore, because of its location astride major rail and highway facilities, it is also a center of light industry and shopping. Within the community are the estates of millionaires and the slums of the poor; its citizens represent diverse religious, racial, and national groups. The city is less economically and sociologically homogeneous than many of the other suburbs of the so-called "South Shore." Additional demographic and community data are given in Exhibit 1 and Map I (pages 247–254).

Asked about the community and its schools, five citizens commented as follows:

Anthony Cenci

[Anthony Cenci, 33, who worked for a taxi company owned by his uncle, was born of Italian parentage in Laketon and educated in the local schools. After returning from military service he married a girl from his neighborhood near the Garibaldi Elementary School in the fourth ward. He and his wife and their three children, the oldest in the first grade, lived in a six-family wooden apartment house, owned by his uncle, in the same neighborhood where he had grown up.]

"Laketon is a swell place to live. It's lots better than New Dresden or Rock Haven [two nearby suburbs similar to Laketon]. It isn't a millionaire's town like Lake Shore or Valley Forest; an Italian can't even live in those places. After all, we are all Americans. That's one of the bad things about Laketon. When you drive a cab, people seem to think you're deaf. My blood just boils when I hear somebody talk about us as 'wops' just because our folks came from the old country. I have a pretty good way of handling that: when they get out, I just say, 'No tips today, thank you ma'am,' and they know what I mean.

"I went to school here and it was pretty good. I learned to be a mechanic; but most of all, I guess, I played basketball. Horace Mann [Junior High] was a high school then. [Before 1939, Laketon's school system had seven-year elementary schools and two five-year high schools; but in 1939 the school system was changed so that there was one three-year high school and two three-year junior high schools. The Horace Mann School became a junior high school for the south end of town, and all high school students were sent to the Laketon High School.] When they changed the system over, that really ruined things. The guys who'd played on the Horace Mann teams didn't have a chance on the high school teams. My brother Joe really got rooked. He spent his senior year warming the bench instead of playing regular quarterback.

"Things are a lot different, I hear, now that all the kids go to the same high

* This is a three-part case (Nos. 18–20). It is urged that each part be studied and discussed before the succeeding part is taken up.

school. The kids from the north end are really snotty. They've got too much money. They don't mix with kids from my neighborhood or date 'em or anything. It's the kids whose families are goin' to send them to college that cause the trouble. It's undemocratic. The school ought to do something.

"To tell you the truth — I mean I don't know whether you're a Jew or a Catholic or anything; but it's really the Jews that cause all the trouble. They've got too darn much money. And did you know, those Jews are tryin' to keep their children from bein' sent to the Garibaldi School even though they live closer to the Garibaldi School than they do to the Marshall School. That is so undemocratic it makes my blood boil.

"I want my kids to go to public schools. I went to St. Joseph's [Parochial School] for a couple of years, and I didn't like it. I think maybe its O.K. for Mary; I mean it's good for girls; but I want the boys to be doctors or lawyers. A kid who grew up in our neighborhood is a doctor. He has two Cadillacs, which you can see is pretty good. All the rich people in our part of town are doctors or lawyers.

"Things are different from when I was a kid. Most of the people in my neighborhood came over from the old country, but we are just like everybody else; but people who have a lot of dough always think they are better than you are. That's not democratic. I think that is because so many Jews have moved to Laketon."

Mercer Babcock

[Mr. Mercer Babcock, 38, an executive of a large corporation with headquarters in a nearby city, had previously lived in a suburb of another large metropolitan city. When he received a promotion and transfer in 1950, he had moved his wife and family, a daughter in the sixth grade and a son in the eighth grade, to Laketon. The Babcocks owned a house in a fashionable section of the third ward.]

"When we moved here, I came out first and looked for houses. I liked Laketon and I saw this house which is my idea of a perfect home. I wired Peg. She flew out, and we bought the place, just like that. Of course, we knew that the schools were good.

"Things haven't worked out quite as we expected. In most suburbs — the kind of places where I've always lived — everybody is pretty much the same. What I mean is that nobody had any reason for being suspicious of anyone else. For the first two years that we lived here Peg and I were very much interested in the P.T.A., but this year I have sort of dropped out of sight, if you know what I mean. Everybody seems to have an axe to grind. They grind it according to whether they are Catholics or Jews. This prayer business and the fight over the football coach were the kinds of things that made me sick.

"We didn't know anybody in Laketon when we moved here. We didn't exactly move in with our eyes open. One of the boys at the office said to me the day before we bought the house, 'You won't like Laketon; there are a lot of Jews there.' Well, I didn't think that should matter.

"Peg and I have tried to be friendly with our Jewish neighbors. Everything is very polite and all; but frankly, we haven't been accepted. Peg arranged a cocktail party last September. We invited everybody we knew in Laketon. It was awful. We'll never do that again. It wasn't that anything happened. The people whom we had met through the church [Laketon Community Church] didn't mix with our Jewish friends, and vice versa. We don't belong to the Country Club. Haven't been invited.

"We think we'll move up to Auburn or Valley Forest when we can find a house to our liking. We can get our money out of this one anytime. Those communities are more homogeneous. There aren't the tensions that Laketon has. It would be nicer for the kids because they are beginning to pick up prejudices, I hope not from us. Maybe if we lived here a couple more years we would be accepted by the nice people, but I'm not sure."

Morton Glasser

[Mr. Morton Glasser, 47, an executive of a cosmetics firm, had moved to Laketon in 1944 with his wife and four children. The oldest Glasser child was a senior at Laketon High School, another was also in the high school, and the two youngest were junior-high-school age.]

"Laketon is one of the finest suburbs in the United States. Our schools are looked upon as being among the best in the country, especially in the sciences. That is a fact.

"You cannot imagine how much more we have enjoyed living out here. My family is of the Jewish faith, you know, and we have some special problems. We would not have wanted to move into a neighborhood where there were no other Jewish families. I don't think we would have wanted to live in an all-Jewish neighborhood, either.

"A lot can be done to improve Laketon. Most people seem to be apathetic to this need. There doesn't seem to be any unwillingness to join sides in a scrap, but very little constructive effort seems to come out of these fracases. Nobody seems to look at the problems of Laketon as a community. It's always a matter of doing battle for or against prayer in the schools or something like that.

"I don't know what is going to happen to the town. We have a terrific problem of discrimination against the Negro minority. We have our own 'Black Belt.' If these problems aren't licked, Laketon will get to be like Sunnytown [a residential area which had deteriorated very rapidly in the 1930's and 1940's].

"My wife and I are most concerned about the schools. Our schools are just as good as the private school everybody sends their children to in town. For the last couple of years there have been a couple of really bloody fights over the schools. I don't care how much I pay in taxes. I want the children to get the best education they can. I would like to have the boys go into the professions; that's where the best opportunities are. They need really good schools. Most of our friends feel that way, but I don't think people in the other parts of town really care."

Mrs. Mary Martin

[Mrs. Mary Martin, a housewife in her thirties, lived in an apartment development built after the war by the Laketon Housing Authority. Mr Martin worked for a storage warehousing firm. Their two children were in the John Brown Elementary school.]

"My husband and I were born and brought up in Laketon. Not many of us [Negro citizens of Laketon] can say that. We like it fine. We are very lucky; we have this swell apartment which is sure better than the place my family lived in.

"A Negro boy was elected president of the high school student council a couple of years ago. That couldn't have happened when I was going to school here. That is very good, but we are still much discriminated against. When I went to the John Brown School there wasn't a single white child in the school, and it hasn't changed so much since.

"That is not good, and the city should do something about it. Reverend Simpson is on the school board. He represents us but he hasn't been able to change things. Somebody ought to do something.

"It was the same way with this apartment. We moved in in the beginning. There were some white families and some colored families. Nearly all the white people have moved out. Everything would be better if we could associate with white people instead of all living here together. They would know us better and then things would be different.

"We go to school at the high school with white children, and it works out fine. It ought to start that way in kindergarten. Everybody feels that way, and we can't do anything about it.

"You know how everybody loves their children and wants them to have it better than they did. Well, that's the way it is. We are treated pretty second-class. They are all the time saying that the John Brown School is just as good as the other schools, but I know it just isn't. How can you have a segregated school and have it just as good?"

Cobb Burnham, M.D.

[Dr. Cobb Burnham, 57, had lived all his life in Laketon, where his father had been a physician also. His two married daughters lived in other parts of the country. He and his wife were prominent in the social activities of the Country Club and Yacht Club.]

"I've seen Laketon change considerably in the last fifty years. My father, who started my practice, was a combination of country doctor and court physician. The farms have given way to apartment houses and the estates have become housing developments.

"Many of the old families still live here, but most have moved on up to Valley Forest or Auburn. We have a mixed population now. When I was young, the poorer residents of Laketon were all Germans and Swedes. Today many of these people live in the white-collar area around the Joliet and Daniel Boone [Elementary] Schools. The Italians and Portuguese took over the western part of the South End, the 'fourth ward' to us. We developed a Negro slum during the First World War, and it has remained ever since. During the last war it started to spread. It was originally limited to the John Brown School area, but now it is overflowing toward the Adams and Pilgrim schools. Those big old houses behind the Dewey Junior High School, close to the commercial district, are being sold to Negroes now. Mark my word: there won't be a white family in the neighborhood in five years.

"Jews from the city have moved out here in droves during the last twenty years. They make up most of the population of the better residential areas. There are no poor Jews in Laketon. I must say that they have been good citizens. They are, as a group, very much concerned about the welfare of others. I have a great deal of respect for them. They are not particularly active in politics like the Catholics; that may be because the City Council is elected on a city-wide rather than a district basis. They have been the backbone of most of the civic organizations and, I guess, the P.T.A.

"Another group of people which I haven't mentioned are the young commuters. I mean they are Protestants who live here and work in the city. There is quite a turnover in that group. They live here a couple of years and then move up the shore some place to a community where they can get into the social swim a little more. You see, the old families have a sort of closed society in Laketon. You don't get into the Country Club or Yacht Club until you have been around long enough for people to know you fairly well. Frankly, I don't see how the Country Club can hang on financially much longer with that policy.

"I don't know what is going to happen to Laketon. Except for the people who own homes, I personally don't think that many people care. We have a lot of teapot tempests: the *Observer* [the local daily newspaper] thrives on the fights about the schools. Not many people pay any attention to local politics because we have a city manager. I'm afraid that the population pressure from the city will gradually overwhelm us; but not until after my time."

Act I

Twice during recent years controversies over the redistricting of schools had arisen. The first dispute developed during the summer of 1950; the second in January, 1953.

During the spring of 1950 Mr. Reynolds, the superintendent of schools, informed the board of education that on the basis of the first school census report certain schools would be crowded beyond capacity during the 1950–51 school year. The board concluded that school district lines (Map I, pages 248–251) should be altered in order to adjust school facilities to meet school population. (A description of the school districts is given in Exhibit 2, pages 254–258.)

The board of education consequently appointed a Citizens' Advisory Committee to investigate the redistricting problem. This committee received instructions that the school districts should be arranged so that no elementary school classes would contain more than twenty-nine pupils (except kindergarten classes which had a maximum of fifty). The board also informed the Advisory Committee that it would be desirable to equalize the utilization of physical facilities without increasing the number of teachers.

The Citizens' Advisory Committee submitted its report on June 20, 1950. The report was published in the *Observer* on June 22. A new north-end school district was to be created. The children in this school district would no longer attend the Taft School, but would instead be transported by bus to the Jackson School in the south end. Although the specific areas to be affected by the redistricting were not announced, the numbers of school children to be transferred were reported as follows:

1. In September, 1950, eighty-four children would be transferred from the Taft School district to the north-end school district.
2. Thirty-eight children would be redistricted from the Pershing School to the Pilgrim School, and forty-one would be transferred from the Pershing School to the Joliet School.
3. Sixty-five children were to be redistricted from the Joliet School to the Adams School.
4. Forty-one children in the Daniel Boone School would be transferred tc the Jackson School and seventy-eight more to the Adams School.
5. Twenty-three children in the Jackson School district would be placed in the Adams School district.
6. Fifty-nine children in the Adams School district would be trasnferred to the Garibaldi School district.
7. Twenty-one children in the Marshall School district would be transferred to the Garibaldi School district.
8. Twenty-seven children in the Lincoln School district would be transferred to the Adams School district.

On the day following the publication of the Advisory Committee report the board of education made two announcements. The board scheduled a public hearing on the redistricting plan to be held on July 7. The board also announced its own amendment to the redistricting program of the Advisory Committee: namely, the transfer of half of the fifth- and sixth-grade students of the John Brown School to the Marshall School. The reasons given for the amendment were, first, that transfer would be the beginning of a program to integrate the Negro students of the Brown School into the predominantly white schools and thus eliminate a segregated school; and, second, that the transfer would allow the Brown School to function with two less teachers without adding to the teaching staff of the Marshall School.

On the evening of June 23, residents of the northern end of the Taft School District, who believed they would be in the new north-end school district, held a mass protest meeting at the Taft School. About 150 persons attended. One parent, who had organized the "Paul Revere Committee" to inform north-end parents of the meeting, acted as moderator. He opened the discussion by denouncing the plan to transport children to the Jackson School as "physically dangerous" and "psychologically harmful." A series of speakers from the floor stated that they agreed with the moderator's stand. The moderator's suggestion that a permanent committee be established to "represent the north-end parents and school children" was approved by acclaim. A man who had spoken in favor of a new north-end school as "the only equitable solution of this problem" was named chairman of the committee.

P.T.A. meetings were held at the Boone, Joliet, and Marshall schools on June 26. The Daniel Boone School P.T.A. announced to the *Observer* after the meeting that it "opposed in principle an inadequate solution to the school population problem such as that proposed by the board of education." The grounds of objection were not stated in the public announcement. The Joliet P.T.A. announced through its publicity chairman that it objected to the proposed redistricting "because the small children involved in transfer to the Adams School district would be at the mercy of commercial district traffic." The P.T.A. of the Marshall School passed a resolution objecting to the transfer of students to the Adams School on the grounds that the abandoned roadbed of a defunct railroad running through the upper edge of the Adams School district constituted "a natural obstacle." The Marshall P.T.A. also passed a resolution condemning the "integration policy" of redistricting as proposed by the board of education.

On June 28 the officers of the Joliet P.T.A. sent an open letter to the board of education asking that the Pioneer School (which had been converted from a school to the school administration building during the 1930's) be reopened to receive children from the new north-end district and the Pershing School.

On June 29 the Colored Women's Club of Laketon held a meeting to protest the transfer of fifth- and sixth-grade students to the Marshall School. A spokesman for this group explained to a reporter of the *Observer* that the transfer had been made "in order to prepare for the reopening of the Garibaldi Junior High School for Negroes and poor people." The Colored Women's Club requested that the board of education change the school district lines so that children of all grades could attend either the Marshall or the Pilgrim School. On the same day the residents of Woodhill Park, the part of the Marshall School district nearest the Garibaldi School, organized a neighborhood association to fight against "changes in school district lines which will ruin property values in Woodhill Park."

The Laketon Corporation Counsel advised the board of education, on July 6, that under an antidiscrimination statute passed by the state legislature it would be illegal to transfer children from one school district to another because of their race. Mr. Blanc,[1] a member of the board, announced that the board would drop its plan to move fifth- and sixth-grade students from the John Brown School to the Marshall School because of "the unfortunate and unintended effect of the state antidiscrimination laws."

The public hearing on school redistricting held on July 7, took place in the 600-seat auditorium of the school administration building. The auditorium seats were filled at 7:45 P.M., although the meeting was not to begin until 8:00 P.M.; and the room was still filled to capacity when the meeting ended at 12:15 A.M. Large delegations identifying themselves as "north-end parents," "Joliet School parents," and various neighborhood groups from the Marshall School district presented prepared statements opposing redistricting. A number of individuals identifying themselves with other interests also opposed the redistricting. The president of the P.T.A. Council and a spokesman of the Garibaldi School P.T.A. were the only speakers who were wholeheartedly in favor of the redistricting plan. The former praised the Advisory Committee's proposal as "a temporary solution until new buildings are erected." No members of the Citizens' Advisory Committee spoke at the meeting. Representatives of the Council of Unity, the National Association for the Advancement of Colored People, the John Brown School P.T.A., and the county lodge of B'nai B'rith criticized the board of education for maintaining the Brown School as a "segregated school."

During the remainder of the month of July the redistricting controversy was carried on in the "Letters-to-the-Editor" column of the *Observer*. On July 31, the board of education announced that plans for the creation of a "north-end school district" had been dropped and that all north-end children would remain in the Taft School. The board also declared that the other changes in district lines would be implemented at once.

On August 1, after a closed meeting, the board announced that all plans for redistricting had been cancelled, except those pertaining to the Boone and Adams school districts and the transfer of students between the Brown and Adams schools.

On August 7, the Garibaldi School P.T.A. sent an open letter to Mr. Reynolds deploring "snobbish and disparaging remarks about Americans of Italian descent which have appeared in letters to the editor and in public hearings." The letter suggested that the school administration should not try to please people expressing "such un-American attitudes." The *Observer* published a letter from the Brown School P.T.A. several days later condemning the redistricting of children from the Brown School to the Adams School because "the effect of the redistricting is to transfer a substantial number of white children attending this segregated school to another school which is predominantly white."

Redistricting: 1952–1953

The redistricting question did not attract public attention again until November 1952. At the November open meeting of the board of education, Mr. Blanc stated that preliminary school census figures for 1953 indicated overcrowding in several schools and that the board would need to re-examine its stand on redistricting. There were no further public statements on this matter; but on January 13, 1953, twenty-six representatives of "service, social, and political organizations" were invited to join the board of education for a special meeting to discuss "school utilization."

[1] See Exhibit 3 (pages 259–263) — "The Board of Education, (*c*) Composition."

The meeting was reported in a front-page article of the *Observer* under the headline "Redistricting Backed at School Conference." The article is quoted below:

> Redistricting — which would affect approximately 400 public school students — was supported as the solution to the problem of full school utilization by a large majority of the 26 civic leaders invited to meet with the board of education last night.
>
> The guests, representatives of various service, political, and social organizations, were asked to express individual opinions which were not construed as the views of their organizations.
>
> Crux of the situation is that Taft, Pilgrim, and Marshall schools are overcrowded and Garibaldi and Adams Schools are under-utilized.
>
> The consensus was that the main difficulty in redistricting would be "selling" the idea to the people affected by any changes, and allaying the "emotional upset" evoked by such a move.
>
> If the board adopts a redistricting policy, the technicalities of exact changes in districts would be handled by the administration. It is apparent, however, that the districts would be revised southward and would probably mainly affect parts of the Taft, Pilgrim, John Brown, Adams, Marshall, and Garibaldi districts. The 400 students involved represent approximately 5 per cent of the total student population in the city.
>
> According to opinions expressed last night, redistricting is the "best possible solution" because it would eliminate capital expenditures for additions to Taft and Marshall, and would enable all schools to carry full programs. At the present time some of the facilities for special services have been curtailed in the overcrowded schools.
>
> Except for minor district changes in the past few years, the school districts have remained static for more than 20 years.
>
> "It is quite evident that you people think redistricting is the answer," board president Melvin Blanc declared, requesting that the representatives continue support of the idea if the board adopts it. He pledged that any changes in district lines would be "equitable and with the least possible disturbance," and said the board would meet with the P.T.A.'s to explain the situation. Before any change is made there would also be a public hearing, he said. Mr. Blanc also offered to have board members address any organization on the subject.
>
> Consolidation of Garibaldi and Adams schools, which had been suggested as a solution, received only minor consideration last night on the grounds that, while this would effect economies in certain salaries and in maintenance and repair of one school building (as well as returning one school site to tax rolls), this step would not relieve the overcrowded conditions in the Taft, Pilgrim, and Marshall schools. (Superintendent of Schools Rodney Reynolds said that additional space at Pilgrim will be needed, whatever the solution.)
>
> Several of the speakers, residents of the Fourth Ward, spoke firmly against the closing of Garibaldi or Adams.
>
> "If the Garibaldi district line were logically drawn, the school would be filled," Luigi Bugatti of the Fourth Ward declared. "Now students from Woodhill Park, Blaine Avenue, Courtney Manor, and that general area are not going to the proper school — they live nearer Garibaldi but are in the Marshall district."

Mrs. S. L. Stone, P.T.A. Council, pointed out that it is a misapprehension that redistricting concerns only those people physically affected. She said that a broad program of education should be undertaken so people would realize that under the present circumstances redistricting would be in the best interests of the entire city.

"The eventual solution is getting around the feelings of the affected residents and then redistrict," said Joseph Florentino of the Garibaldi Society. "Why do people feel so strongly about individual schools? Is there a difference? You have to find the objections people have in sending their children to certain schools."

Mr. Blanc assured the group that educational standards in teaching and equipment are alike in all schools and that differences arise only when there is insufficient space to carry out the full program.

Mr. Harold Abernathy, of the City Affairs Committee, commented, "Maybe the multiplicity of schools has made the selectivity." He also stated that the increasing enrollment will probably taper off and that adaption "of what we have" to meet the problem was the only answer.

"Whatever is done, there are going to be emotional upsets," Samuel Rose of the League of Neighborhood Associations, declared. "But if instruction and management of all schools are the same, that should defeat most of the arguments. I agree that the only solution is redistricting and making it stick.

"It is true that people select neighborhoods with regard to schools, but it is physically impossible to accommodate everyone in the school he'd like. If the reasons for redistricting are properly presented, there will be some hullabaloo but stress on education equality, etc., should offset this," he continued.

Charles MacDougal, of Rotary Club, commented, "It comes down to selling the idea and showing that all schools are the same and that realty values are not affected."

Thomas Lombardi, of the Retailers' Association, said he would consider it "wasteful to leave some classrooms empty and build in other places" and said that city economics must be considered. He also urged redistricting.

Mr. Blanc explained that the group had been invited to express their opinions so the board could get a cross-section of feeling before acting.

"This group is not a true cross-section," Fred P. Farmer, general manager and editor of the *Observer,* commented. "That's the nub of this thing — how people are going to react. Most of the people here tonight are looking at the subject objectively. The families who will be affected are not represented."

Paul Davidson, of the Council for Unity, suggested that the full facts be presented to the public so all citizens can learn what is involved, and what the alternatives are.

Mrs. Mary-Lou Lee, of the N.A.A.C.P., inquired whether district changes would increase the Negro population at John Brown School.

The emotional aspects of redistricting were also cited by board member John J. Rhodes, who noted that it was not only a matter of dollars and cents, but feelings of people.

In summing up, Mr. Blanc asked support from individuals and any organizations which might take action on the matter, should the board decide on redistricting.

> Mrs. Charles Ernst, of the Woman's Club of Laketon, observed: "Public hearings are usually attended only by those who think they are adversely affected. The 'voices on the other side' should get out so the board would not appear to be taking a stand opposite to public clamor. Other parents must realize they are just as much affected by this matter and offer support."

One week after the special meeting of civic leaders, Mr. Blanc announced to the *Observer* that the problems of school crowding would be "presented to the public in meetings of the elementary school P.T.A.'s." Mr. Blanc stated the problem as follows: "The shift in our school population has created overcrowding in some of our schools, while in some districts there are empty classrooms. A simple way of meeting this problem is to increase the number of classrooms in the congested district. This, however, involves a heavy capital expenditure, and still leaves other school buildings under-utilized, with the consequent high cost of operation. A consolidation of school districts and the elimination of a school building would meet this latter point, but would not relieve crowded conditions in other areas. These dilemmas complicate matters, and what the board of education is seeking is a solution which will make maximum use of existing facilities without incurring more expense. This aim leads to a third approach — to readjust school district lines, thereby keeping our existing buildings but redistributing the children. Economy of operation should result. But here we run into more difficulty. A change in school districts usually provokes deep feeling among the residents concerned, besides having its bearing upon other community values, thus affecting the city at large. For this reason the board wishes to proceed with caution, and get the best thinking of the citizens of Laketon."

Mr. Reynolds issued a statement "in order to supply a factual background to Mr. Blanc's remarks." Mr. Reynolds pointed out that the Taft and Marshall schools were overcrowded and that "the quality of the educational program at Taft and Marshall has been suffering because of the overcrowded condition of those buildings." He said that the John Brown, Pilgrim, Joliet, and Daniel Boone schools were full currently and that the Pershing, Hemingway, and Jackson schools would be full by September 1, 1954. He explained that both the Garibaldi and Adams schools had unused rooms.

Mr. Reynolds suggested two possible solutions. The first was to consolidate the Adams and Garibaldi schools "since the pupil population of both schools can be held in either building" and since "consolidation would save $10,000 in teachers' salaries and $32,000 in administrative operational expense." Mr. Reynolds said that the consolidation would allow "a capital return from the sale of the Garibaldi School and income from the return of this property to tax rolls. The second solution was to redraw district lines in order to reduce the Marshall and Taft school districts. In this way, Mr. Reynolds explained, the salaries of six teachers could be saved, a sum amounting to approximately $20,000 a year. The alternative to redistricting, according to the superintendent, would be to build additions to the Marshall and Taft schools at a cost of about $28,000 per classroom. Mr. Reynolds concluded his statement by saying, "Public school business is everybody's business."

The statements of Mr. Blanc and Mr. Reynolds were printed in the *Observer* with an announcement that public meetings would be held at each elementary school to discuss the school-crowding problems. The meetings were scheduled to take place between January 26 and February 10. Each meeting, the announcement said, would have one member of the board of education and

Mr. Reynolds present to explain the overcrowding problem and to answer the questions of citizens.

The first public meeting was held at the Pilgrim School. The *Observer* reported that with a few exceptions those in attendance were wholeheartedly opposed to the redistricting plan. The chief objections voiced were the following: Many residents in the Pilgrim School district had bought their homes in order that their children might attend the Pilgrim School; these residents would move out and their large homes would become multiple dwellings, causing both a decline of realty values and further overcrowding of the school. Children would suffer by having their education interrupted in moving from one school to another. Redistricting would be only a stopgap since the northern section of the city is growing so rapidly. Pilgrim School children would suffer the most under the redistricting plan because the school would be overcrowded by Taft School children transferred to the Pilgrim School to replace the Pilgrim School children transferred to the John Brown School.

Mr. Reynolds explained to the audience that the board of education had hoped that the people attending the meeting would discuss the possible solutions suggested in the statement of the board to the *Observer*. Several speakers received considerable applause after accusing the board of education of "trying to force down our throats a solution they have already decided on." Mr. Reynolds and Mrs. O'Brien (the board member present) denied that the board had made any decision to redistrict the schools. Mr. Reynolds explained that there was no need to be concerned about the extent of the changes because no final district lines had been drawn, and that if the board decided on this solution a "public hearing will be held, probably in March."

A former president of the Laketon Republican Club asked for a show of hands as to the willingness of those present to pay for new schools as an alternative to redistricting. Most of those present raised their hands. Mr. Reynolds attempted to say something about the expenses of building and operating new schools, but his efforts were met with boos and catcalls. The president of the Pilgrim P.T.A. adjourned the meeting after several more speakers had bitterly attacked the redistricting plan on behalf of several neighborhood associations.

Two days after the meeting at the Pilgrim School two letters appeared in the "Letters-to the Editor" column of the *Observer*. A Mr. Becker, who identified himself as a resident of the Pilgrim School district, wrote that new construction alone could meet the needs of the school system. He said that the plan to shift 200 pupils from the Taft School to the Pilgrim School, while shifting 200 others from the Pilgrim School to the John Brown School (neither Mrs. O'Brien nor Mr. Reynolds had hinted how many children might be affected by the changes in district lines) was "only a temporary expedient." Mr. Becker pointed out that the growth of the north end would continue and 500 or 600 more families would be moving into the south end shortly "so that the dominoes won't topple." Mr. Becker also wrote, "I realize no one likes to face unpleasant facts, or indeed to voice them publicly, but the plain and unvarnished fact is that placing the southerly portion of the Pilgrim district in the John Brown School district would result in serious depreciation of property values. . . ."

Angelo Cipriano wrote to the editor saying, "Every speaker [at the Pilgrim School meeting] had some lame excuse. . . . None had the temerity actually to state that they did not want their children to attend certain schools in certain sections. . . . Let us practice the American way as well as preach it." Several days later a letter replying to Mr. Cipriano's charges was printed. A Mr. Campbell, the author of the letter, declared that the Pilgrim School parents were justified in their attitude because "the practice of investing life savings in purchasing a home partially, if not totally, predicated on school locations is universal." Mr. Campbell accused the board of being "insincere," in that "they invite us to discuss the alternatives to redistricting and then they have a million reasons why there are no alternatives."

During the last week in January meetings were held at the Daniel Boone, Jackson, Pershing, and Joliet schools. Between twenty and forty persons were present at the meetings. Various groups in the Pilgrim School district sent representatives. In each case the group expressed an informal approval of redistricting plans, on the grounds that the city's voters would be unlikely to approve further funds for capital outlay until all available school space was utilized.

The Taft School meeting on February 1 attracted an audience of approximately 300 men and women. No speaker from the floor favored redistricting. Most of the speakers asked that a referendum be called to secure the voters' permission to expend public funds for a new school building and additions to existing buildings. One speaker received an ovation when she proposed that classrooms could be freed for elementary school use if the kindergarten classes were moved to new buildings which might be constructed in the school neighborhoods.

The meeting at the Marshall School on February 6 followed a pattern similar to that of the Pilgrim School meeting. An audience which filled the school auditorium to capacity criticized with considerable bitterness the plans for redistricting. A number of alternative proposals were offered from the floor. Among these were: the construction of additions despite the effect on costs; the operation of overcrowded schools on two shifts; the study of the entire matter by an impartial professional consultant; the transportation of the excess school population of the whole city to either the Adams or the Garibaldi School.

The Hemingway, Garibaldi, and Adams schools held a joint meeting in the Adams School auditorium on February 10. Most of the 250 people present were from the Adams and Garibaldi school districts. Ten speakers from the floor were enthusiastically applauded after each had stated that he favored the redistricting plan and opposed the closing of any school. Two speakers from the Marshall School district presented their arguments against redistricting, after which Mr. Florentino of the Garibaldi Society said in rebuttal, "When the logical decision is made, namely, to send the children in the crowded school districts to the uncrowded ones, the voices of the people so affected rise in protest. What do they say? . . . redistricting will lower property values. . . . children will be upset emotionally. With respect to these foolish opinions, the Garibaldi Society goes on record as claiming, (1) by redistricting we shall not lower property values, and (2) if anyone is going to upset children emotionally, it is the individual who hysterically shouts that a change of school would do so. (3) We further think that all schools are on an educational par, and we feel that those persons unaware of this should be pitied, and those who are aware of it and still oppose redistricting are guilty of hypocrisy born of a dangerous form of undemocratic snobbery." After Mr. Florentino's speech the moderator adjourned the meeting because he was unable to restore order.

The board of education held its final public meeting at the John Brown School. The president of the John Brown P.T.A. opened the meeting with a short speech attacking racial discrimination as an "undemocratic practice which harms our children, whom we love more than anything else in the world." The Reverend

Edward Simpson delivered a statement on the overcrowding problem of the Laketon schools. Mr. Reynolds, who had attended and spoken at all the meetings, then spoke briefly about the "solutions that seem to meet our needs" — redistricting and consolidation of the Garibaldi and Adams schools.

When Mr. Reynolds had finished, a man in the audience directed the following question to him: "If you are going to redistrict schools why don't you abolish this segregated school?" Mr. Reynolds explained that as a school superintendent he did not make policy on such matters, and therefore, the question should be addressed to the board of education. A number of hands went up at this point. A series of speakers from the floor stated that the board of education should not allow any one school to have a student body drawn largely from one race or one religion. Mr. Simpson was laughed at when he said that the board of education accepted this principle but that practical difficulties made it nearly impossible to put it into practice. Finally, one speaker stated that the Brown School was "educationally inferior" to the other schools. Mr. Reynolds vehemently protested that all the schools of Laketon were "on a par" and called on the Brown School principal to testify on this matter.

Mrs. Mary-Lou Lee of the N.A.A.C.P. asked how the redistricting would affect the proportion of Negro and white students in the Brown School. Mr. Reynolds pointed out that the new lines had not been drawn. On further questioning, he said that redistricting between the Adams and Brown schools "might" leave fewer white students in the school, but that a change in the Pilgrim School district would "probably" bring more white children into the school. Mrs. Lee said that Mr. Reynolds was mistaken because the ultimate effect of the adjustments would be "to take all the white children out of the south side of the district and send them to the Adams School while taking all the colored children out of the southern end of the Pilgrim district and sending them to the Brown School." Mr. Reynolds said that he was under the impression that the areas just north of the Brown School were white residential areas. Mrs. Lee replied, "They may have been a couple of years ago, but they aren't now."

The theme of the discussion was changed only once when a man representing a Marshall School neighborhood group attempted to explain the disadvantages of redistricting. He was booed by the audience when he finished. Immediately afterwards, Mr. Simpson asked for a voice vote in favor of redistricting. The request for those in favor to say "aye" provoked only a few voices; but the request for "nays" led to a prolonged uproar. The meeting was then adjourned.

The board of education announced in the February 12 issue of the *Observer* that an open meeting would be held on February 18 to announce the board's "decision on the problem of overcrowding in the Laketon schools." On February 16 the board announced that the open meeting had been cancelled because "the overcrowding problem at the Taft and Marshall schools has been solved for the coming year." The announcement explained that the congregations of the Laketon Reformed Synagogue, adjacent to the Marshall School, and of the First Baptist Church, next to the Taft School, had offered the use of church property for school use during the coming year. The board declared that it planned to construct an additional classroom at the Pilgrim School at an expense of $25,000 and that certain remodeling at the Marshall School, costing $40,000, would make one more classroom available in that building.

The *Observer* subsequently published a series of open letters from individuals and neighborhood groups complimenting the board of education on the wisdom of its decision. One strongly worded protest signed by a group of prominent political party and civic organization officers in the Garibaldi and Adams school districts was also printed. This group charged the board of education with "a surrender to snobbery and undemocratic attitudes" and pledged itself to fight for redistricting and against "those who have insulted our children in their opposition to a common-sense solution of the school problem."

19 *Laketon—Act II*
School Elections

Two school district elections had taken place in 1951. The first of these, in May, 1951, was a referendum on an increase in school taxation power of one-quarter of one per cent. The second referendum took place in December, 1951, on the approval of bond issues for school construction. The election aroused in a number of groups an interest in the issues presented at the polls as well as in the system of election.

The Tax Increase Referendum

The possibility of a referendum to increase the school tax was first discussed at an open meeting of the board of education on October 31, 1950. At that time the board announced that no suggestions requiring additional expenditures for the school year 1951 could be accepted because the budgeted appropriations were within $960 of the constitutional taxation limit. On February 15, 1951, the board announced that it would hold a referendum on the question of a quarter of one per cent increase in the tax limitation on May 1, 1951.

If the referendum passed, the net increase in the school tax allowed would be $2.50 per $1,000 assessed valuation. The rate could not be raised again until the school year beginning October 16, 1956. Under the legislation governing school district fiscal affairs, the tax for any given year could not exceed the budgeted expenses for that year; thus, any tax funds collected and not expended, as appropriated, were to be credited against taxes for the ensuing year. Under these conditions the actual tax might be less than the allowed rate.

The election laws pertaining to school district elections established franchise requirements that were superimposed upon the requirements of general suffrage. These requirements restricted the franchise in school elections to (1) the holders of title to taxpaying real estate in the school district, (2) owners of leaseholds, and (3) the parents (or guardians) of children attending the public schools.

The P.T.A. Council established a Referendum Committee to investigate the need for an increase in taxation authority. This committee reported to a P.T.A. meeting held April 2, 1951, and announced that it emphatically favored the proposal of the board of education.

The report of the P.T.A. Council Referendum Committee pointed out that because of rising costs an increase in taxes would be necessary if the present educational standards were to be maintained. The elements of these educational standards were enumerated as follows: "(1) fine instructional facilities, (2) neighborhood schools, (3) limited class size, (4) enriched curriculum, (5) special services such as health and guidance programs, remedial reading, and speech correction." The committee reported that without increases in educational funds the program would be cut. They commented that teaching salaries in Laketon were $100 to $400 less than those of any nearby suburban community and that 68 out of 360 classroom teachers received less than the lowest paid janitors.

The two methods of economizing which the committee saw were, first, to close several neighborhood schools and eliminate special services, and second, to increase the maximum class size to some level above the present maximum of twenty-nine pupils. The former economies, the committee stated, would not free enough revenue to meet the pressing needs, and a change in class size would produce "reading disabilities, emotional disabilities, and . . . superficial understanding of individual cases." In conclusion, the committee presented a comparative exhibit showing that the educational tax was lower in Laketon than in any nearby community.

The P.T.A. Council accepted the report of the Referendum Committee and resolved to campaign for passage of the referendum.

The superintendent of schools, Mr. Reynolds, was invited to address the Kiwanis Club and the Realty Board on the subject of the tax-increase referendum. On both occasions Mr. Reynolds was asked a number of questions about the possibilities for economy in the school system. He answered that economies would require reduction of the teaching staff and of the maintenance expenditures on school property. He pointed out that $160,000 of the anticipated increases in the school budget for the next year were accounted for by mandatory automatic increases in salaries ($46,000) and pension fund payments for teachers ($15,000), costs of tax collection ($14,000), and reserves for uncollected taxes ($85,000).

On April 4, 1951, Messrs. Harold Abernathy and Morton Gore of the Civic Affairs Committee publicly called upon the board to allow the opponents of the tax increase to distribute pamphlets to school children to counteract "propaganda for extravagance fostered by school teachers." At an open board meeting on the same day, the request was refused. Mr. Abernathy accused the board of education of "interfering with the democratic process." The Laketon *Observer* reported a heated debate which followed. Mr. Gore commented that most of the adults of Laketon had attended schools with far less "frills" than the ones provided today and that the results of the "reading, writing, 'rithmetic" education were apparently quite satisfactory.

Several days later the League of Women Voters resolved to support the proposed tax increase, announcing that "the present limitation simply does not provide sufficient revenue to maintain our schools under today's conditions." The resolution was based on the findings of a committee, several of the members of which had previously been active in the affairs of the P.T.A. Council.

On April 11 a group of teachers' organizations active in the Laketon schools announced to the Laketon *Observer* that they were raising $1,500 by salary assessments to aid the P.T.A.'s campaign for the tax increase.

The board of education held a public meeting on April 15 in order that interested groups could air their views on the referendum. The meeting opened with an announcement that voters who met the franchise requirements and who had registered for the elections of November, 1950, would not have to register again. Messrs. Abernathy and Gore, representing the Civic Affairs Committee, presented a proposal for meeting the anticipated needs in excess of the tax limitation (a sum of $170,000). They proposed that one school be closed and sold, thus creating economies of $50,000 and proceeds of $100,000 from the sale. They stated that yearly increases in the assessed valuation would yield $23,000, and that $16,000 in the contingency fund could be used for regular expenditures. They also criticized the expenditure of $50,000 for maintenance. The spokesmen for the P.T.A. and the League of Women Voters pleaded for the passage of the referendum to maintain educational standards and preserve real estate values.

On the day after the public meeting held by the board of education, the Laketon *Observer* pointed out that the referendum measure required approval by 60 per cent of the voters. The editorial pointed out that a small turnout at the polls would assure passage of the tax increase. It further stated that the true feeling of the community could be made clear only by a large vote. For the next eleven days the "Letters-to-the-Editor" column of the *Observer* was devoted entirely to correspondence by P.T.A. members, teachers, and writers identifying themselves as "taxpayers" or "parents of school children."

On April 26 the *Observer* announced, "In the name of what is best for the community, and in the belief that Laketon voters generally are fair-minded, we strongly urge all to go to the polls next Tuesday and vote 'yes.'"

During the final week before the election the P.T.A. canvassed all parents of school children and arranged for transportation to the polls for those who wished it. The P.T.A. Council sponsored a full-page advertisement in the *Observer* on the day before the election. The opponents of the tax increase conducted no organized electioneering.

The total vote cast on May 1, 1951, was 5,495. The 60 per cent majority required to carry the referendum was 3,297. The measure passed on the following vote:

	Yes	*No*
Ward 1	494	439
Ward 2	533	436
Ward 3	1,941	908
Ward 4	386	358
	3,354	2,141

Several people who had been active in the electioneering activities in favor of the tax increase subsequently stated that they were surprised by the narrow margin of victory for the proposal. They commented that the measure probably would have been defeated if there had not been a general abstinence on the part of those interested in the parochial schools.

The board of education subsequently passed a budget for 1952 requiring the use of $.16 of the $.25/$100 taxing authority.

The Bond Issue Referendum

At the monthly open meeting of the board of education in September, 1951, Mr. Blanc announced that the board would submit a bond issue to the voters on December 11, 1951. Mr. Blanc said that the board would ask for a $1,900,000 bond issue "to replace the antiquated Daniel Boone Elementary School which was built in 1884, which cannot be remodeled to contemporary safety and educational standards." Another bond issue of $360,000 would be requested to build an addition to the Pershing Elementary School because "an increase in the school attendance in this district has overwhelmed the facilities of the Pershing School." Architect's drawings of the proposed project were made available to the *Observer*. The board announced that registration for the special school elections would take place October 22–26 in the evenings at the several elementary school buildings.

The board of education held a special meeting to discuss the details of the proposed building program. The *Observer* appearing on that day carried an editorial criticizing the inconvenience of special school elections held at times other than the regular municipal-state-national elections. The editorial also attacked the special qualifications for voters as "iniquitous and undemocratic." The proceedings of the meeting of the board of education were not made public; Mr. Blanc announced, however, that the board had passed resolutions in favor of holding school elections at the time of regular elections, and in favor of discontinuing the special franchise requirements.

When the registration period began, the P.T.A.'s of the Daniel Boone and Pershing schools canvassed the parents in their school districts. Other P.T.A.'s sent out leaflets to members asking that they register and vote for the bond issue. The board of education provided school children with printed brochures to take home to their parents. The board also prepared special statements of qualification to be filled out by registrants. These statements could be taken home by a husband or wife to be signed by his or her spouse, so that only one needed to go to the registration place to register two votes.

On October 30, the *Observer* printed in its "Letters-to-the-Editor" column a communication received from an opponent of the bond issue stating that the P.T.A. canvassers were bringing registration statements to the homes of parents of school children, obtaining signatures, and turning in the registrations. The writer stated that the result of this practice was "the packing of the voting list by the P.T.A." In the next week a number of letters condemning the P.T.A.'s actions were printed in the *Observer*.

At an open board meeting on November 8, the canvassing procedures of the P.T.A. were attacked by Mr. Gore of the Civic Affairs Committee. He commented that of the estimated 12,000 to 15,000 eligible voters, only 3,000 were now registered for the election, and that a large proportion of this number had been "fraudulently registered by a special interest group." He suggested that the only way of redressing the wrong and assuring a democratic election would be to send registration forms to the home of every eligible voter.

Messrs. Parish and Reynolds both stated that they doubted whether direct mail registration would be desirable because of the cost and because it would result in inaccuracies on the voting list. Messrs. Harrison and Ferris disputed the prediction of the superintendent and their fellow board member. They claimed that direct mail registration would assure a "really democratic referendum." Mr. Abernathy criticized Mr. Parish's objection to the expense of direct mail registration, saying that the board did not show such consideration of the taxpayer when it spent public funds "for propaganda brochures favoring the bond issue." A woman in the audience accused Messrs. Abernathy and Gore of bad faith in that "their zeal to pinch pennies blinded them to the real needs of our children."

Mr. Parish commented that the initiative on the matter of registration lay with the citizens, not with the board of education; he then suggested that the board request an opinion from the Laketon Corporation Counsel as to whether direct-mail registration was legal or not. Such a resolution was voted.

A closed meeting of the board was held during the next week. The *Observer* reported that the Corporation Counsel had advised the board that its legal responsibility was discharged by the maintenance of registration places. The City Clerk reported that direct-mail registration would cost between $1,000 and $3,000 and that many inaccuracies would result from such a practice. The board voted not to adopt direct-mail registration. It announced that any citizen could register at the school superintendent's office at any time before the election day. Mr. Ferris told the *Observer* reporter that he and "several other board members still favored direct-mail registration."

A series of pre-election forums were held by the various P.T.A. groups at each Laketon school. At these meetings a spokesman of the board of education explained why the bond issue had been proposed. The spokesman described the overcrowding at the Pershing School and the expected increase in enrollment. The Daniel Boone facilities were described. The plumbing, heating, and lighting were termed inadequate in terms of contemporary health and safety requirements. The classroom and play areas were described as unsuited to modern teaching and organized recreation. The architect's estimate of the cost of renovating the Daniel Boone School was set at $1,500,000, of which the net result would be undersized school facilities, even though surrounding property assessed at $450,000 would have to be condemned to make room for the required changes. The anticipated increase in taxes required for servicing the bonds was set at $6.78 per $10,000 assessed valuation for the Daniel Boone project and $1.50 per $10,000 for the Pershing project. The bonded indebtedness of the Laketon school district would be increased from $3,450,750 to $5,710,750 by the proposed issues. The constitutional limitation on the bonded indebtedness of the school district stood at $8,503,917.20 as of September, 1951.

At each of the meetings a discussion followed the statement by the spokesman of the board of education. Except for the large audiences at the Daniel Boone and Pershing schools, it was unusual for more than eighty persons to attend the forums. Mr. Abernathy and Mr. Gore usually were present to lay their views before the audience. They announced that the Civic Affairs Committee favored the addition to the Pershing School, but opposed the building of a new Daniel Boone School on the grounds that the "inadequacies" pointed out by the board of education were "extravagant frills" that the school had done without for nearly sixty years. They also indicated that the cost-free solution of changing school district lines so that Daniel Boone pupils could go to the Adams Elementary School had not been considered. They stated that it would be wiser to renovate the Daniel Boone School and use the savings to improve the other schools, such as the one where the meeting was being held. A heated debate usually followed these remarks.

On December 5, the League of Women Voters announced that it favored the two bond issues. The Real Estate Board simultaneously announced that it did not favor the new Daniel Boone School because the population in the area surrounding the school was more likely to decline than to increase.

By election day, 4,766 people had registered. Of these, 3,756 voted and both measures passed. The election results are shown in the tally below.

BOND ISSUE REFERENDUM

District	Registration	Votes Cast	New Daniel Boone		Pershing Addition	
			Yes	No	Yes	No
Adams	107	82	32	46	49	29
Daniel Boone	1,180	920	628	261	690	163
Garibaldi	133	100	38	58	52	42
Jackson	341	282	111	162	192	78
John Brown	156	112	45	59	64	39
Joliet	403	295	103	185	208	79
Marshall	408	356	171	179	271	75
Pershing	808	634	395	190	584	28
Pilgrim	533	446	216	222	343	95
Taft	697	529	325	186	450	62
	4,766	3,756	2,064	1,548	2,903	690

When the election returns became known, Mr. Gore made a statement to the *Observer* that the election result was "not a triumph for the democratic process."

School Elections: An Addendum

On January 22, 1952, Mr. Gore, representing the Civic Affairs Committee, appeared before the Laketon City Council to ask for that body's support in reforming the school election laws. Mr. Gore described the special franchise requirements as "flagrant discrimination." The special elections, held at times other than those of general elections, were described as an "opportunity for fraud, irregularity, and illegality . . . by which well-organized minorities are enabled to exercise unwarranted control over the majority." The City Council passed a resolution asking the Laketon Corporation Counsel to draw up two reform bills, one on franchise requirements and the other on times of election, to be introduced by a local legislator at the state capitol, during February.

The proposed bill was introduced as the Hittinger-Moseley Act during the third week in February. When the bill went to the committee, a "home rule" provision was attached to the election date act. This provision allowed the board of education the option of setting election dates on the same days as those on which general elections were held.

Several days later a city newspaper reported that the P.T.A. lobby and the boards of education of a number of the state's cities were opposing the Hittinger-Moseley Act. The reported basis of the opposition was the belief that education matters would become involved in political partisanship. The Laketon *Observer* responded to the opposition in an editorial, stating: "This is not a political question at all. Seemingly, it is this: if you are in favor of everyone who is qualified to vote at a general election also being qualified to vote on school propositions, then you are in favor of these bills. We believe all fair-minded voters are for such a change."

Both the franchise and election-date measures had been voted through the legislature by March 14, 1952. The organized opposition to the bills was, according to a political commentator, taken by surprise when the measure passed the state senate. According to reports, the P.T.A. lobby, the counsel for the State Education Department, members of boards of education, and superintendents of schools from many localities sought to dissuade the governor from signing the bills, particularly the bill allowing changes of election dates.

On March 24, 1952, however, the governor signed the franchise bill, but not the election-date bill. The Laketon *Observer* reported that "it was learned over last weekend that opponents, including some state officials as well as a Laketon group of citizens, attempted to influence the governor to disapprove the bills." The paper then commented editorially as follows:

> Why there is sufficient opposition to this measure to make the governor hesitate is difficult to understand. It would not change the system of school elections where such elections are now held, unless the board of education wanted to change it. But it would make unnecessary special elections such as Laketon was forced to hold last December 11. . . .

Two days later the governor vetoed the bill which allowed the combination of general and school elections.

In January, 1953, the City Council, at the behest of the Civic Affairs Committee, passed a resolution suggesting that the vetoed part of the Hittinger-Moseley Act be reintroduced in the legislature. The *Observer* complimented the council editorially for its stand. The P.T.A. Council, which had taken no public stand on the election law during 1952, now announced that it opposed further alteration of the school election system because "school issues would be subject to misinterpretation and misuse by political factors, school issues would be snowed under in the shuffle and excitement of political campaigns, and another safeguard to public education would be irrevocably lost."

The new Hittinger-Moseley Act was still in committee at the end of February, 1953.

20 Laketon—Act III
The "Prayer Issue" and the "O'Riley Affair"

The "Prayer Issue"

The "prayer issue," as it was called in Laketon, developed rapidly. On December 3, 1951, the Laketon *Observer* carried on its front page a statement by Mr. Ferris that he would introduce that evening at the meeting of the board of education a resolution that each day's classes in the public schools should begin with a prayer. The State Education Committee had recently announced that boards of education might, at their option, take such measures.

When the resolution was presented to the members of the board, Mr. Ferris explained that the inclusion of prayer in the public education program would help inculcate reverence in the minds of children. He asked for a vote on the resolution.

Some of the board members were surprised by the resolution, as they had apparently not seen the statement that had appeared in the *Observer*. Mr. Parish said that he did not believe that the board was prepared to act on the measure without time to consider the legal implications of a question involving religion in public schools. Mr. Rhodes seemed incensed by Mr. Parish's comment; he asked, "Why would anyone but an atheist be opposed to prayer?" Mr. Blanc pointed out that there might be some religious groups who would be offended by the prayer or the manner in which it was offered.

Mrs. O'Brien read the prayer that Mr. Ferris had included in his proposal and asked Mr. Blanc whether he could see any grounds for objection. Mr. Blanc stated that he saw no specific objections, but he added that before a vote was taken the people in the community ought to be given the time to state any objections they might have. Dr. Simpson said that he thought Mr. Blanc's suggestion was wise, and that as a minister he believed there might be grounds for objection by some groups.

Mr. Blanc proposed the appointment of a committee, headed by Mr. Rhodes, to investigate the problem and report to the board at the next meeting. Mr. Rhodes stated bluntly that he saw no need for such a committee and would not serve on it. Mrs. O'Brien and Mr. Ferris supported him in this stand. Mr. Parish moved that the resolution be tabled until the next board meeting when the board would meet as a committee of the whole. A heated discussion followed, but the tabling motion was finally voted. It was agreed to ask each P.T.A. group for its opinion on the resolution.

The *Observer* reported the board meeting the following day. A day later the *Observer* printed a letter from Rabbi Nathan of the Laketon Reformed Synagogue. Rabbi Nathan asked the board of education not to institute prayer in the schools because the state would then be teaching matters which only the family has the privilege and duty to teach. Rabbi Nathan also pointed out that there were sectarian differences in prayers that mystified and embarrassed children, such as the practice of Roman Catholics of crossing themselves or the practice of Orthodox Jews of covering their heads when praying.

Rabbi Nathan's letter prompted a flood of letters in the "Letters-to-the Editor" column of the *Observer*. A number of writers, identifying themselves as Roman Catholics, advocated that prayer be instituted in order to improve the spiritual quality of public education. Some pointed out that religious education was a defense against Communism.

Meetings were held by the various school P.T.A. groups. It became apparent that each P.T.A. group was split. The discussion of the resolution in the meetings led to bitter debates with the sides drawn on religious lines. A number of Roman Catholic organizations sent representatives to the meetings to speak in favor of the resolution. Several Jewish groups issued statements attacking the resolution, and many individuals who identified themselves as Jews spoke against the measure at the P.T.A. meetings. The various Protestant organizations took no stand. The Protestant ministers' association held a meeting, after which it announced that the members unanimously favored inclusion of prayer in the school program. A week later the same group announced that on reconsideration it was opposed to the inclusion of prayer.

A Roman Catholic explained as follows the viewpoint of those who favored the inclusion of prayer, according to her understanding: "All religious groups agree that the encouragement of reverence for the Almighty is in itself good. The community recognizes this in nearly every form of social activity. Why should this attitude not be encouraged in the schools?" A Jew expressed his understanding of the Jewish viewpoint as follows: "My family's religion is somewhat different from the other religions of the community. It has been passed on from father to son for 4,000 years and more. I want my children to learn our faith at home and in the Synagogue. I don't want my sons to be subjected to social pressure from the community at large on religious matters, and I don't want them stigmatized by other children because they put their hats on during prayer."

The two viewpoints offered above are less extreme than the accusations that became more frequent as the controversy continued. Some proponents of the inclusion of prayer claimed that the only opposition to the resolution came from "atheists and Communist sympathizers." On the other hand, some of the more violent members of the opposition called the prayer resolution "the first step in a Catholic conspiracy to take over the public schools," pointing out that Messrs. Ferris and Rhodes and Mrs. O'Brien were all members of the Roman Catholic Church.

At the next meeting of the board of education an open discussion of the prayer issue was held. The board heard some sixteen speakers present different views. The general opinion of those who had watched the controversy develop was that the Roman Catholics favored the proposal and that the Protestants and Jews opposed it. The view seemed to be borne out by the statements made by various speakers at the meeting. It was believed that only the Roman Catholic members of the board of education, Messrs. Ferris, Palermo, and Rhodes and Mrs. O'Brien, would vote in favor of the proposal, and that the five other members of the board would oppose it. Mr. Blanc did not allow the issue to come to vote; instead he proposed a compromise. He suggested that the question of whether or not prayer should be included be left to each individual principal to decide for his school. This measure passed unanimously. The more impassioned partisans of both sides were disappointed by the compromise, but the opponents of the resolution later stated that the compromise satisfied them, while the proponents of the resolution considered the compromise better than defeat.

The "O'Riley Affair"

In February, 1952, the director of health and physical education for the Laketon schools died suddenly. The Laketon High School football coach, Mr. Francis O'Riley, submitted to the superintendent of schools an application for the vacated post. During March Mr. Reynolds, the superintendent, wrote Mr. O'Riley that the latter's application would not be forwarded to the board of education.

Mr. O'Riley consequently told some of the high school boys whom he had coached that he would not be the new director of health and physical education. Thereupon a group of the high school football players organized a petition among the students at the high school requesting that Mr. O'Riley be appointed to the vacant position.

The petition had been circulating for several days when, on April 3, 1952, the board of education announced the appointment of Mr. Gordon Piper to the post of director of health and physical education. Mr. Piper had formerly held the same post at a high school in the suburbs of San Francisco. According to the announcement of the board of education, Mr. Piper held a graduate degree in physical education; he had been a high school coach for several sports; and he had had considerable experience in teaching and administration.

Within two days after the announcement of Mr. Piper's appointment, an informal group of former Laketon High School athletes organized in order to exert pressure on the board of education to appoint Mr. O'Riley in place of Mr. Piper. Mr. O'Riley had coached the football teams of Laketon High School for twenty years. Many of the boys whom he had befriended during this period, as one expressed it, "saw their opportunity to show their loyalty to old Frank." Under this impetus the petition, which was first circulated in the high school, soon accumulated the names of adults in the community. By the time the board of education met on the first Tuesday in May, the petition listed more than 8,000 names.

During April the controversy over the appointment of the director of health and physical education became progressively more bitter. The Knights of Columbus passed a resolution, reported in the Laketon *Observer*, condemning the failure of the board of education to appoint Mr. O'Riley as "religious discrimination against a member of the Roman Catholic Church." This charge was echoed in letters appearing in the "Letters-to-the-Editor" column of the *Observer* during the following month. Letters from former high school athletes also appeared in this column. The athletes' letters pointed to Mr. O'Riley's popularity and success as a football coach and then commented in effect that "after twenty years of loyal service we see our old friend passed over and snubbed by the board of education for an outsider."

The chairman of the board of education, Mr. Blanc, issued a statement to the *Observer* explaining why Mr. Piper had been appointed. Mr. Blanc explained that the board was required by law to request nominations from the superintendent of schools for any post requiring a teacher's certificate. The post of director of health and physical education required a teacher's certificate; and although Mr. O'Riley had such a certificate (it was required for all teaching posts in the Laketon schools), the superintendent had not nominated Mr. O'Riley. Mr. Blanc also stated that Mr. Piper seemed to be eminently qualified for the job.

Mr. Reynolds, who was also interviewed by the *Observer*, declared that the post of director of health and physical education involved the teaching of several courses in hygiene and psychology in the high school as well as the administration of the school health and physical education programs. He explained that Mr. Piper had had considerable training and experience in these fields.

The *Observer* took an editorial stand in opposition to the appointment of Mr. Piper and in favor of the appointment of Mr. O'Riley. In an editorial the *Observer* stated, "The circumstances, we believe, place the whole question in the lap of the board [of education], and void, in effect, any 'nomination' the superintendent has made. . . . " In a subsequent editorial the newspaper accused the board of "abdicating" and "flaunting its indifference to the will of the citizens." The editorial finally suggested that "if the board is going to let the superintendent run the schools in this manner, the Mayor should not reappoint the two members of the board whose term expires in June." (These members were Messrs. Blanc and Harrison.)

The P.T.A. Council announced that it planned to poll the teachers of the Laketon school system to find out whether they approved of the appointment. The Reform League, a civic organization which had spearheaded the movement for the city manager form of local government, announced that it planned to investigate the whole matter of appointments. Prominent members of the P.T.A. Council and the Reform League had written letters to the *Observer* favoring Mr. Piper's appointment.

Before either the P.T.A. Council or the Reform League had announced the results of their investigations, the *Observer* published a lead story concerning a letter which the newspaper had received from Dr. Raymond Burke, Mr. Reynolds' predecessor as superintendent of schools. Dr. Burke, who had left Laketon to become the superintendent of schools in a large neighboring city, stated that the news of the controversy over the appointment of the director of health and physical education had reached him in Michigan. He explained that the question of appointing Mr. O'Riley to this post had arisen six years earlier when he had been superintendent of schools. On that occasion Mr. O'Riley had applied for the position but he, Dr. Burke, had not nominated Mr. O'Riley because the football coach "was not qualified for the administrative or teaching duties that are required for this position." Dr. Burke declared that he had informed Mr. O'Riley of the reasons which prevented his nomination; and Dr. Burke also stated that he had told Mr. O'Riley that the post was open to him if he would take the summer school courses at the University of Metrosa which provided the necessary training for the job. Mr. O'Riley, according to Dr. Burke, had not made any effort to prepare himself for the job. Dr. Burke said that the teaching of hygiene and psychology and the administration of the health program for the school system required a special type of training which Mr. O'Riley did not possess. Dr. Burke concluded his letter by saying that he was sorry to see the community divided over the appointment because he did not believe Frank O'Riley's "ability and loyalty" were impugned by the appointment of Mr. Piper, and further, as a Roman Catholic himself, he could not believe that the Laketon board of education would allow religious discrimination to influence any appointment.

After the publication of Dr. Burke's letter the P.T.A. Council and the Reform League made no public announcements concerning their investigations. The *Observer* continued to receive and publish letters pertaining to the controversy. Most of the letters criticized the board of education for disregarding the public sentiment expressed by the O'Riley petition.

During the first two weeks of June the mayor made no announcement concerning the expiring appointments of Messrs. Blanc and Harrison to the board of education. During the third week of June the P.T.A. Council, the League of Women Voters, and the Council for Unity announced their endorsement of Messrs. Blanc and Harrison for reappointment to the board of education. The *Observer* did not take an editorial stand on the matter. The newspaper's "Letters-to-the-Editor" column contained a number of letters from citizens demanding that new members be appointed to the board. On the last day of June, however, the mayor announced that he had reappointed both Mr. Blanc and Mr. Harrison for the new five-year term. The mayor made no comment on his appointments.

EXHIBIT 1 The Development of Laketon

In the northern and southern ends of the city had once been the large country estates of wealthy families. The belt along the railroad track, covering the First and Fourth Wards, included the main shopping district and the older residential area. (Map I) During the period between 1900 and 1910 a large number of Italian immigrant railroad workers settled in the area of the Fourth Ward. During World War I a number of Negro families from the South moved into Laketon in the northeast corner of the Fourth Ward. After World War I a tremendous expansion of the city's population took place. Between 1920 and 1940 the population doubled.

In the 1930's, however, the growth of the community was considerably reduced. A change in ownership in the residential areas took place. A number of Jewish families moved into the most expensive residential neighborhoods, and by 1950 those areas, which had been predominantly Protestant in the 1920's, became predominantly Jewish.

By 1940, there were about 5,500 single-family houses and about 8,200 apartments of various sizes in the city. The land near the railroad station and on the fringes of the shopping area was dominated by apartment districts. The upper end of the Second Ward and the lower end of the Third Ward had become residential localities for well-to-do-commuters.

Since the end of World War II, a new era of development had been in progress. New residential and industrial expansion had taken place. By the end of 1952, about 1,100 one-family dwelling units and approximately 1,400 apartments had been built. Most of the apartments were located on the eastern edge of Ward Two. The new one-family houses were constructed principally in the southern end of Ward Two and the northern end of Ward Three, the greater number in the latter area. New industries and shopping areas were brought to Laketon during this period. More than 14,000 people were employed in Laketon businesses.

Accurate information about the population of the several wards of Laketon was not available in the spring of 1953. The city clerk, however, made the following estimates:

Ward 1	10,000 persons
Ward 2	14,000 "
Ward 3	22,000 "
Ward 4	14,000 "

MAP I Laketon

3rd WARD
Taft

MAP I Laketon (continued)

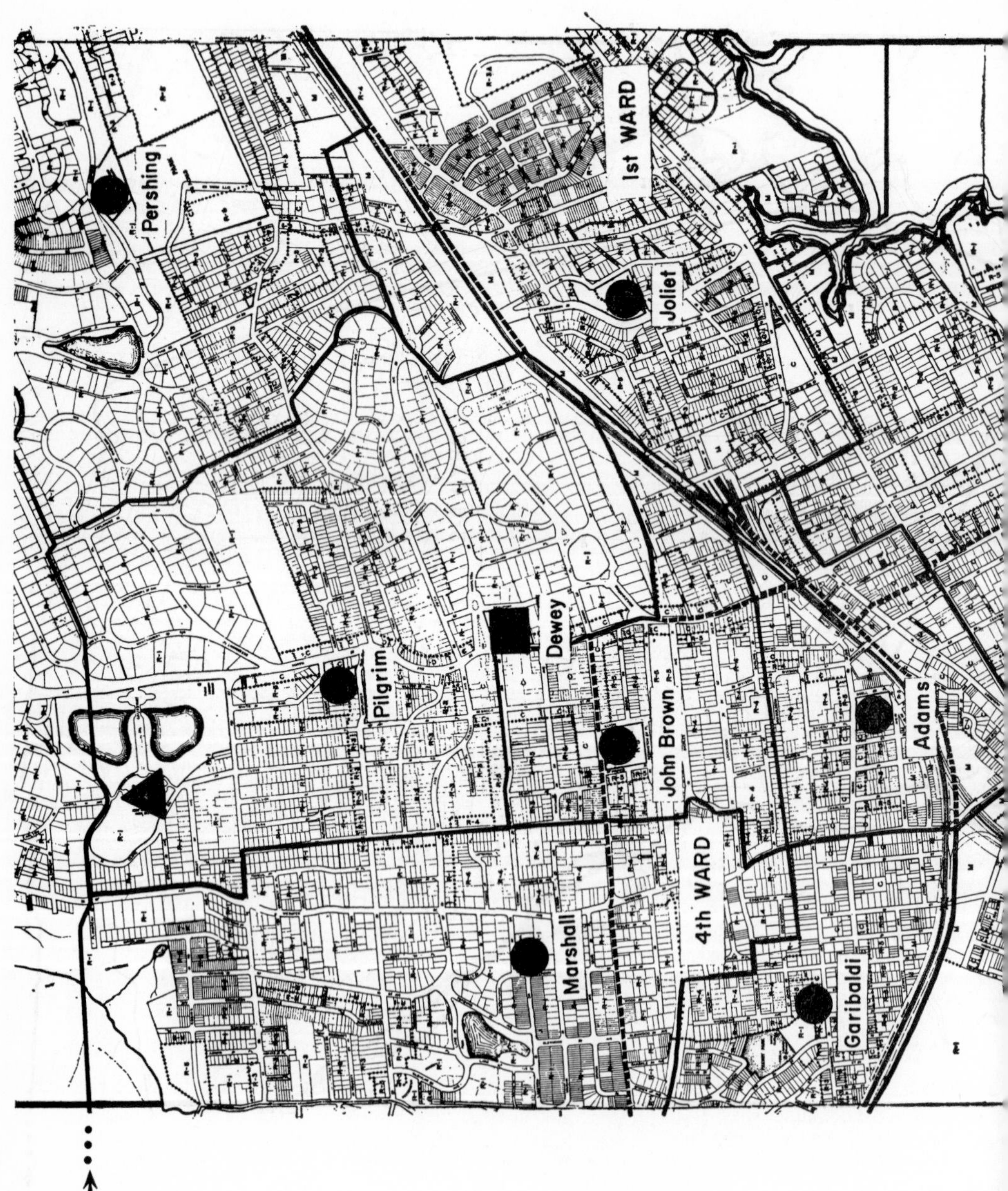

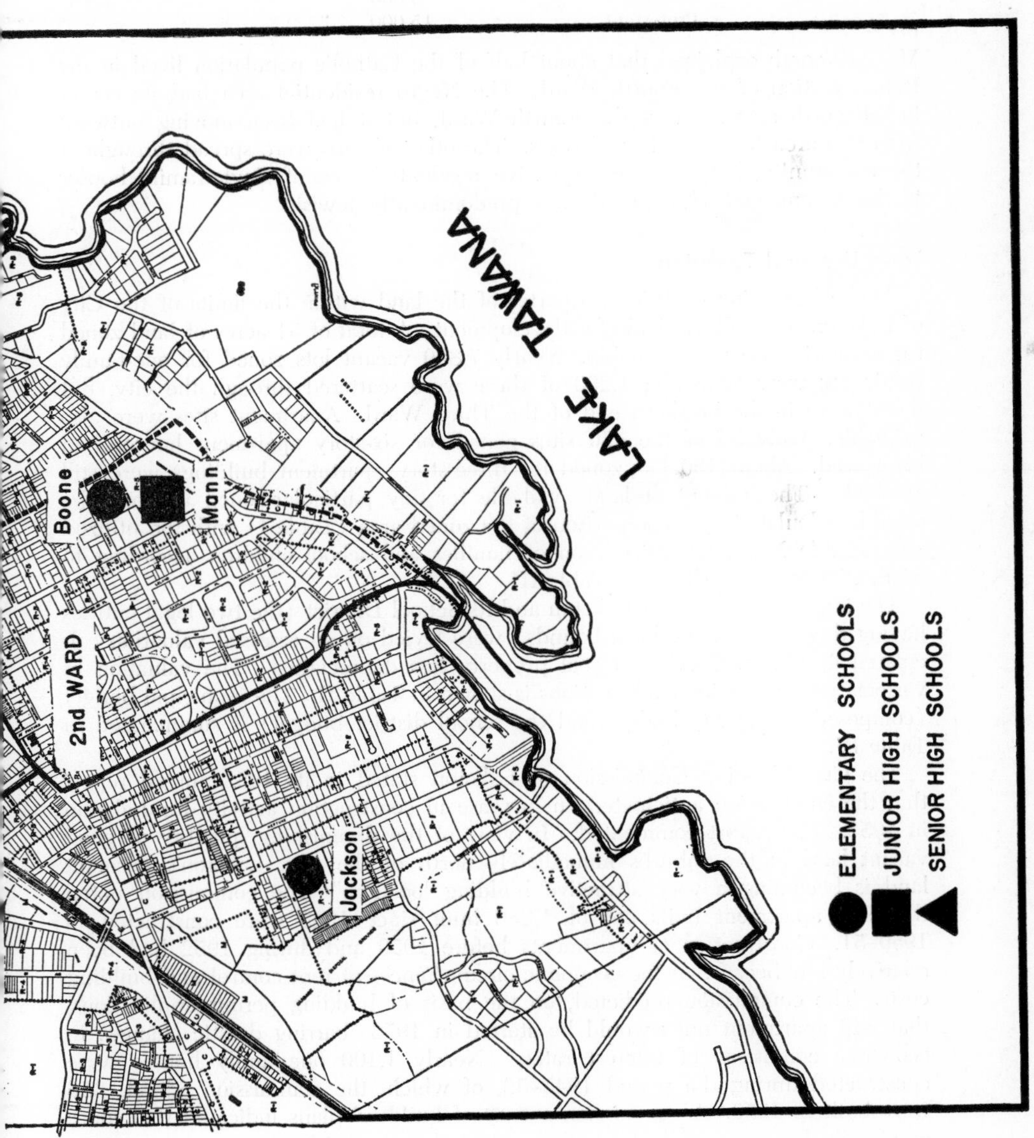
LAKE TAWANA
Boone
Mann
2nd WARD
Jackson
ELEMENTARY SCHOOLS
JUNIOR HIGH SCHOOLS
SENIOR HIGH SCHOOLS

Mr. Harvey Newcomb, a member of the Laketon Real Estate Board, provided an estimate of the sociological division of the population:

Catholic	16,000 persons
Jewish	20,000 "
Negro	9,000 "
Protestant	15,000 "

Mr. Newcomb explained that about half of the Catholic population lived in the Italian section of the Fourth Ward. The Negro residential area had its center in the northeast corner of the Fourth Ward, but it had been moving outward from this area for a number of years. The other groups were spread throughout the community, although the expensive residential area of single-family houses in the Second and Third wards was predominantly Jewish.

Land Use and Taxation

At the beginning of 1953, a quarter of the land within the limits of the City of Laketon was still available for development. A total of 51 acres of land zoned for industrial use was available. Nearly 7,800 vacant lots zoned for one-family residences were available; 1,200 of these were scattered through the city, but 6,600 were in the northern end of the Third Ward. Apartment sites were also available. Only 56 of the 430 sites zoned for six-story apartment houses had been used. About 150 lots zoned for three-story apartment buildings were still available. The amount of land available for any particular-zoned use may be roughly calculated by a comparison of the zoned area (Table I) with the utilized area (Table II). The distribution of families and school children according to residential zoning is shown in Table III.

The taxes for the City of Laketon and its School District (the two legal entities having the same geographical bounds) were levied on an assessed valuation calculated as the 1940 value of real property less depreciation. The valuation of various types of zoning classifications is shown in Table II. The municipal budget (composed of the city budget and the school district budget) is summarized in Table IV.

The City Planning Commission of Laketon stated in its 1952 annual report that the commission anticipated an increase in construction activity for Laketon in 1953. The report commented, "In view of the diminishing quantity of good vacant land in the suburbs immediately north of the city, Laketon's dormant land is becoming a very attractive building location." The commission noted that 980 apartment units out of 1,286 built since 1945 were constructed in 1950–51. Construction of apartments before 1950 and during 1952 had been relatively low because of the economic circumstances of rent control and building costs. The commission predicted, on the basis of building permit applications, that 840 apartment units would be started in 1953 "barring drastic changes in economic conditions of interest rates." Nearly 1,100 one-family houses were constructed during the period 1945–52, of which, the commission added, 356 were built in 1952. A commission survey of builders' plans indicated that more one-family houses were to be built in 1953 than in 1952. The apartment construction for 1953 was apparently to be concentrated in the southern end of the city whereas nearly all the one-family houses were to be built near the northern tip of the city.

Table I

BUILDING ZONE AREAS

*Type of Use**	*Total Acreage*	*Per Cent of City Area*
Single-family	4,285	64.38
Large two-family	108	1.62
Small two-family	246	3.70
Garden apartments	12	0.21
Three-story apartments	183	2.75
Six-story apartments	430	6.46
Temporary housing	6	0.09
Neighborhood shopping center	5	0.08
Business	301	4.52
Industry	186	2.80
Streets	894	13.43
	6,656	100.00

* Tax-exempt property classified by adjacent use.

Table II

LAND USE: AREA AND VALUATIONS, 1950

Land Use	*Areas in Acres*	*Per Cent of Total Area*	*Assessed Valuation*	*Per Cent of Total Valuation*	*Number of Units*
Estates	277.79	4.17	$ 1,583,600	1.01	17
Single-family	1,670.58	25.10	75,144,685	47.72	6,019
Two-family	244.48	3.67	13,025,450	7.99	2,931
Three-family	66.18	0.99	3,818,950	2.42	1,215
Four- to six-family	41.79	0.63	2,911,235	1.85	822
Multi-family	56.14	0.84	11,246,150	7.14	2,844
Store and Apt.	33.89	0.51	7,997,550	5.08	1,627
Business	132.48	1.99	22,276,280	14.15	
Industry	36.68	0.55	2,957,450	1.88	
Public utilities	89.29	1.34	4,414,500	2.80	
Quasi-public (clubs, etc.)	340.36	5.11	2,485,650	1.58	
Vacant	1,728.39	25.97	10,042,145	6.38	
Vacant (city-owned)	159.98	2.39	(963,485)	0.57	
Total Valuation Excluding City-owned Property			$157,970,245		
Exempt	889.16	13.28	$ 31,431,650		
Streets	893.83	13.43			
Total Area	6,656.	100%	Total Number Residential Units 15,475		

Table III

ZONING CLASSIFICATION OF RESIDENCE: FAMILIES AND SCHOOL CHILDREN

Zoning Classification	*Percentage Families*	*Percentage School Children*
Estates	Less than 1%	Less than 1%
One-family	39	50
Two-family	18.49	16
Three-family	7.83	9
Four- to six-family	5.3	5
Multi-family	18.39	15
Stores and apartments	10.48	5

Table IV

MUNICIPAL BUDGET: 1953

General government	$ 907,068.14
Protection of persons and property	1,347,106.06
Conservation of health	120,864.57
Sanitation and promotion of cleanliness	500,962.57
Highways, bridges, and parks	541,085.41
Welfare	68,993.75
Public library	130,842.54
Recreation	93,897.25
Down payments for capital improvements	150,000.00
Municipal indebtedness	1,156,036.98
State and county payments	1,341,500.00
County sanitary sewers	28,840.00
Provision for uncollectible taxes	35,000.00
Municipal garage	96,140.99
Gross city budget without education	6,518,338.26
Less income from franchises	1,529,306.00
Net city budget	$4,989,032.26
School district budget	2,972,218.50
Net cost to real properties	$7,961,250.76

EXHIBIT 2 Laketon Schools and School Attendance Districts

The Laketon public school system consisted of eleven elementary schools, one of which was under construction in the spring of 1953, two junior high schools, and one senior high school. The elementary schools had Grades 1 through 6 and kindergarten as well. The junior high schools contained the seventh, eighth, and ninth grades. The three-year senior high school offered either college preparatory or vocational courses. The school district lines are shown in Map I, and the 1953 enrollment of the various schools, totaling 8,007 pupils, is shown in Table I, together with a summary of their capacities.

Table I

SCHOOL ENROLLMENT AND CAPACITIES

School	*Enrollment*	*Constructed**	*Class-Rooms*	*Normal K ***	*Capacity Grades ****
Laketon Senior High	1,506	1931	60	--	1,500
John Dewey Junior High	950	1906–18–22	36	--	900
Horace Mann Junior High	753	1928	40	--	1,000
John Adams Elementary	262	1921	18	50	450
Daniel Boone Elementary	526	1884–1909	19	50	475
Garibaldi Elementary	300	1909–26	34	100	850
John Brown Elementary	429	1898–1910	12	50	300
Ernest Hemingway Elementary	153	1953	12	50	300
Andrew Jackson Elementary	492	1932	22	50	550
Joliet Elementary	472	1913	18	50	450
John Marshall Elementary	482	1930	14	50	350
Gen. John J. Pershing Elementary	584	1931–52	18	50	450
Pilgrim Elementary	431	1910	17	50	425
William Howard Taft Elementary	659	1920–31	20	50	500

* The first date given is that of the original construction. The subsequent dates are the years in which additions were made.

** Kindergarten capacity is calculated on a base of 50 pupils to a classroom.

*** Normal capacity for Grades 1 through 12 is calculated on the basis of 25 students to a class.

Each elementary school was surrounded by a school district. The children of residents of a school district were not permitted to go to any public school other than the one serving their district. The junior high school districts were composed of several elementary school districts. The John Dewey Junior High School included the Hemingway, Taft, Pershing, Pilgrim, Marshall, and Brown Elementary School Districts. The other elementary school districts made up the Horace Mann Junior High School District.

Although the board of education and the superintendent of schools frequently declared that there were no qualitative differences in the instruction offered at the several elementary and junior high schools, the citizens of Laketon appeared to agree that the schools could be placed on a scale of educational value. With minor differences of opinion, there seemed to be substantial agreement that the schools could be ranked according to "quality" as follows:

Junior High Schools:
1. John Dewey Junior High
2. Horace Mann Junior High

Elementary:
1. Taft Elementary School
2. Pershing Elementary School
3. Marshall Elementary School
4. Pilgrim Elementary School
5. Jackson Elementary School
6. Daniel Boone Elementary School
7. Joliet Elementary School
8. Garibaldi Elementary School
9. Adams Elementary School
10. John Brown Elementary School

The Hemingway School, which was still under construction, had not yet achieved a "rating" in the minds of the persons who had formed opinions about the "quality" of the various schools. The Hemingway School was operating a kindergarten and first and second grades in temporary facilities.

The characteristics of the various elementary school districts were generally acknowledged by citizens of Laketon as an influence on the "quality" of the schools. For this reason a brief description of each elementary school district is given below:

(1) *The Andrew Jackson Elementary School District.* The Jackson School District contained the largest estate in Laketon, and a residential area where some of the old families of Laketon lived, but most of the population in the district lived in two-family frame dwellings or apartment houses built in the early 1920's. Most of the population of the area were in the $3,500–$6,500 income group. The greater part of Laketon's undeveloped land zoned for manufacturing was located in this area. There remained enough undeveloped land zoned for one-family residences to build at least 250 homes. Very little building of this type had taken place within this school district since the 1930's, and a prominent local realtor did not believe that new houses priced over $12,000 could be sold in the Jackson School District. A number of apartment sites overlooking Lake Tawana were available, several of which were held by owners planning to build 400 units in 1953. The Jackson School District had more vacant land for multi-family building than any other school district.

(2) *The Daniel Boone Elementary School District.* The Boone School District contained a part of the Laketon commercial district, a large number of older apartments, most of the apartments built since World War II, a residential area zoned for single-family dwellings on small plots, and an expensive residential area on a neck of land jutting out into the lake. The only undeveloped land in the district was the land zoned for apartments near the Horace Mann Junior High School and the land zoned for single-family units on the neck. Building plans for 1953 called for 450 apartment units in this district. The City Planning Commission estimated that the neck contained land for at least 200 new single-family homes on large lots. Most of the residents of the district were in the $4,000–$6,000 income groups, except those living on the neck (an area of estates, old family homes, and luxurious postwar houses that included some of the wealthiest residents of Laketon).

(3) *The John Adams Elementary School District.* The Adams School District had been a semi-slum residential area when the school district was established. Subsequently about 75 per cent of the area of the district had been zoned as "commercial" property. By 1953, more than half of the district was used for business purposes. The remaining dwellings comprised Laketon's poorest housing. The income of the residents was believed to be below $4,000 a year. The population was predominantly Italian-American with a growing proportion of Negro families on the northern fringes of the area. It was believed that the presence of a parochial school in the area had contributed to the reduction of the public school population.

(4) *The Garibaldi Elementary School District.* The population of school children in the Garibaldi School District had been the most dense in Laketon at the time the original school had been erected. In 1926 the board of education ordered the erection of an addition to the building in order to provide a second

junior high school for Laketon. The junior high school had been closed in the early 1930's when a series of readjustments had been made in the Laketon school system. A general reduction of the school population in the area and the opening of a parochial school adjacent to the Garibaldi School had reduced the enrollment of children in the school. The Garibaldi School District covered a residential area which was almost exclusively Italian-American. The range of incomes in the school district was believed to be very broad, from under $4,000 to over $12,000.

(5) *The Joliet Elementary School District.* The Joliet School had at one time served a school district consisting entirely of one-family houses, a white-collar residential district. When the Pioneer Elementary School had been closed during the depression, most of the Pioneer School District had been added to the Joliet School District. The new area added by the change in district lines had contained commercial property and two-family apartments. Although the district had remained predominantly a white-collar residential area, beginning in the 1940's numbers of laborers began to move into the region. The Joliet School District was Laketon's principal residential area for its German, Irish, and Swedish population. The range of income was believed to be between $4,000 and $6,500. The undeveloped land was zoned for manufacturing, garden apartments, and single-family dwellings. There was enough land of the last type for only about sixty homes, but the land available for garden apartments could accommodate about 350 units. Laketon realtors did not believe that the residential land would be developed in the foreseeable future.

(6) *The John Brown Elementary School District.* The John Brown School had been given its name to honor an early citizen of Laketon. By 1953 most of the citizens of Laketon assumed that the school, whose students were almost all Negroes, had been named in honor of the famous abolitionist. The district in which the school was located was not so predominantly Negro as the school population would seem to indicate, but the white children in the area, Protestant and Catholic alike, usually attended non-public schools. The housing in the area was superior, in general, to that in the Adams and Garibaldi school districts. The income level of most of the residents was believed to be below $4,000.

(7) *The John Marshall Elementary School District.* The John Marshall Elementary School had been built to serve a residential area that had grown rapidly during the 1920's. Previously the children in this district had attended the Pilgrim School. At the time the Marshall School District lines had been drawn, the board of education had established lines which excluded every Italian and Negro family from the school district. As a result of this practice, some children living within two blocks of the Garibaldi and John Brown schools attended the Marshall School. After the lines were drawn some of the real estate bordering the Brown and Garibaldi school districts had changed hands so that some Italian and Negro families lived in the John Marshall district. The remainder of the population was mixed, although the largest single group was Jewish. The district contained neighborhoods of four-story brick apartments, $17,000 to $24,000 homes, and an area of $35,000 to $45,000 homes. All Laketon's social, ethnic and economic groups were represented in this school district, although most of the residents were of the upper middle class.

(8) *The Pilgrim Elementary School District.* The Pilgrim School District covered an area of $15,000 to $35,000 homes and two-family apartments. The

areas adjacent to the John Brown School District and behind the John Dewey Junior High School had become Negro residential areas after World War II. About 10 per cent of the pupils came from these areas. The greater part of the population of the area was Jewish and Catholic. The presence of a parochial school within the district had reduced the number of Catholic children in the Pilgrim School. It appeared that the school's capacity would be seriously strained in September, 1953, because of the opening of a 150-family cooperative apartment building near the school. There remained practically no undeveloped land within the bounds of the school district.

(9) *The General John J. Pershing Elementary School District.* The Pershing School had been constructed in an area containing the most expensive residences in Laketon. At the time the building was erected, the area north of the school contained large homes selling for over $50,000 in 1953. The area south of the school consisted of two-family apartments. An area of park and vacant land stood between the two districts. Immediately after World War II about 180 homes costing $9,000 to $12,000 had been built in the northern part of the district. Undeveloped land for several hundred more single-family dwellings remained in this area. The residents of the Pershing School District represented all the economic and social groups in Laketon, but most of the residents belonged to the upper income groups and were Protestants.

(10) *The William Howard Taft Elementary School District.* Until the new Hemingway School District was established, the district of the Taft School had covered an area almost as large as all the other school districts combined. With the exception of two large apartment buildings, the entire developed area of the district contained houses which sold for over $35,000 in 1953. Most of the residents of the area were Jewish families who had moved to Laketon within the past twenty-five years. Sufficient land remained, after the Hemingway School District was established, to build about 250 more large homes, and if the property of the Laketon Country Club should become available, 750 additional building lots would be created. The Taft School had been crowded beyond its normal capacity for several years, but the 1953 enrollment was reduced by approximately 100 pupils as a result of the creation of a temporary Hemingway School for the first- and second-grade children living in the new school district.

(11) *The Hemingway Elementary School District.* The areas to be served by the Hemingway School had until very recently been large estates and vacant land. Although most of the estates were still intact, the vacant land had been bought up by real estate developers. Building in this area had started in 1951, and it appeared that a substantial number of new homes would be built there in the future. More than 300 homes would be constructed in that district during 1953. For practical purposes, the whole district was available for construction. Several of the realtors developing property there said that they planned to construct $16,000 to $24,000 homes, and they supposed that most of these would be purchased by Jewish families. The new school had given considerable impetus to residential development in the area. The school, to be opened in September, 1953, was planned for a normal capacity of 300 children; one developer, however, commented that if the number of children per new house remained a constant proportion, there would be 450 children in the district by the time the school opened.

EXHIBIT 3 The Board of Education

(a) Powers and Functions

The Laketon board of education derived its powers from enactments of the state legislature. The powers of the board of education are set forth below as stated in the enabling statute:

> The right, subject to the general regulations of the Commissioner of Education, to prescribe necessary regulations for the conduct of its business; to establish free elementary schools, high schools, and training and vocational schools; authorize the general courses of study which shall be given in schools, authorize and determine the text books to be used, regulate the admission and transfer of pupils, create and fill positions such as those of superintendent, principal, teacher, secretary, and clerks; take care of and maintain all school property; purchase necessary apparatus, books, furniture and other equipment; operate and maintain cafeterias or restaurant service for pupils and teachers; purchase real and personal property; designate sites for new school buildings; reconstruct, improve or enlarge existing buildings; adopt an annual budget; levy and raise taxes and disburse the funds raised.

Before January 1, 1950, there had been no statutory limitations on expenditures for school purposes. The annual school budget had been prepared by the board of education for approval by the city council. In November, 1949, several amendments to the state constitution had been passed: one amendment established fiscal autonomy for school districts, establishing a limited taxing power for school districts; another amendment established limitations upon the bonded indebtedness of school districts.

The taxation power of the Laketon board of education was established in terms of rigid limitations. The base tax rate was established on the annual school district budget for the year 1948. In the case of Laketon the tax rate was 1¼ per cent because the 1948 school budget was a trifle under 1¼ per cent of the five-year (running) average of assessed valuation. The constitutional amendment stipulated that the tax rate could be increased in increments of ¼ of 1 per cent with the approval of 60 per cent of the voters participating in a special school election. If such an increase were granted by the voters, no further raises could be approved for a five-year period. The ceiling tax rate set by the state constitutional provision limited the amount of school taxes to 2 per cent of the five-year average assessed valuation.

The constitutional limitation on bonded indebtedness set by the amendments effective January 1, 1950, was 5 per cent of the five-year (running) average of full assessed valuation. Each bond issue within this debt limitation had to be approved by a majority of the voters participating in a special school election for this purpose. The 5 per cent bonded indebtedness limitation could be extended within the provisions of the new constitutional amendment "for specific objects or purposes (*a*) if approved at a referendum by at least 50 per cent of the qualified voters participating in the election; (*b*) if the consent of the State Commissioners of Education is obtained and (*c*) if the consent of the state comptroller is obtained."

Working within the legal framework mentioned above, the board of education acted as a policy-making body over the Laketon schools. The administrative functions for the school system were managed by the superintendent of schools,

Mr. Rodney Reynolds, and his staff. The board of education held monthly evening meetings, although special committees made up of part of the membership met more frequently.

(b) Organization

The members of the board of education were appointed by the mayor of Laketon. The appointive system had been required for Laketon by an enactment by the state legislature until the constitutional amendments, ratified in 1949, came into effect. The amendments required that the members of the board of education should be elected unless the majority of the voters in the school district should vote in favor of the appointive system in a referendum during the regular elections held in November, 1950.

The appointive system for selecting board of education members had been an issue of community concern several times in recent years.

In 1944, a local attorney, described in the Laketon *Observer* as "long active in the Republican Party," proposed that legislation be initiated in the state legislature to make the Laketon board of education elective. The mayor, the only Democratic officeholder in traditionally Republican Laketon, protested that an elective system "would throw the board into politics." At that time a committee was appointed by the P.T.A. Council to investigate the question of whether the board of education should be appointive or elective.

The chairman of the P.T.A. Investigating Committee, Mr. Ralph Parish, announced its finding that there seemed to be no evidence that any board member had allowed the favor of appointment to influence his behavior. The report, however, did criticize the board of education for delegating authority to the superintendent of schools "without establishing machinery for obtaining information other than that provided by the superintendent, without a check on execution of its policies, and without contact with parents." The committee recommended that an elective system be established for the board of education, stating that "election is the traditional democratic way of selecting policy-making bodies" and "the popular arguments against elective school boards are refuted by the experiences of towns which use the elective system." The several P.T.A.'s in the various schools accepted the report and passed resolutions requesting the state legislature to repeal the statute requiring appointive boards of education in cities of less than 125,000 population. No action was taken by the legislature on this resolution because, according to the Laketon *Observer*, other communities which would have been affected by the change lobbied against the proposal.

On May 19, 1950, the governor of the state signed a bill making boards of education elective unless communities now using the appointive system voted in a referendum during the November, 1950, elections to retain the appointive system.

In August, 1950, the board of education announced that it favored the appointive system and therefore would request that a referendum proposition be included on the November 7 ballot. Subsequently, the mayor announced that he also favored the appointive system. In both cases the reason given for favoring the appointive system was that the board of education had operated satisfactorily under the present system. The P.T.A. did not announce a stand on the issue, but it did hold a forum. At the forum a number of speakers mentioned the 1944 Investigating Committee report. The Civic Affairs Committee, a taxpayers' group, announced that it favored the appointive system "because under the conditions of discriminating franchise in school elections all community interests would not be represented in an elective system." The *Observer* commented that the attitudes expressed at the close of the forum seemed to indicate that the audience favored the appointive system.

The resolution establishing the appointive system passed in the November 7, 1950, election. The vote ran as follows:

	Yes	*No*
Ward 1	1,262	913
Ward 1	1,715	1,076
Ward 3	4,045	2,573
Ward 4	1,132	781

In 1953 most of the citizens of Laketon regarded as a dead issue the question of whether the board of education should be elective or appointive; some of the advocates of an elective system, however, thought that the issue might be re-examined. A local politician stated that changes in the school election laws might change people's perspective on the board of education. He said that he regarded membership on the board of education as an important determinant in community fiscal policy and as a "wonderful opportunity to develop vote-getting power in candidates for other offices."

(c) Composition

The board of election of Laketon is composed of nine members. All the incumbent members of the board have been appointed or reappointed by the present mayor. Among the people who had followed school affairs closely there was a widespread belief that the mayor adopted certain unstated principles in appointing board members. There was a difference of opinion about some of the "unwritten laws." One member of the board had always been a prominent member of the Italian-American community in the Fourth Ward. Another appointment seemed always to go to some prominent Roman Catholic layman. Similar representation seemed to be given to the Jewish faith. On a suggestion of several civic groups that "the Negro community of Laketon should be represented on the board of education," the mayor had appointed in 1946 a Negro member, who had subsequently been reappointed. For many years one appointment had gone to a woman; since 1944, however, two women had been on the board. One appointment had been filled by a succession of appointees whom the mayor had described to the press as "representative of the south-side parents and taxpayers"; those to whom this description applied had been members of the Laketon Community Church, the Protestant church to which many of the members of the Yacht Club and Country Club belonged.

The mayor's appointments were for five-year terms. Two appointments expired on the last day of June each year, although every fifth year only one appointment had to be made because of the odd number of members on the board. During the two months before the new appointments were announced, several civic groups usually reported through statements published in the local newspaper their recommendations for new appointments. The P.T.A. Council made a practice of endorsing candidates each year. Two former presidents of the P.T.A. Council had stated, however, that an endorsement by the P.T.A. Council was "the kiss of death" for any candidate. On two occasions when the P.T.A. Council, the League of Women Voters, and the Council for Unity (formerly the Mayor's Interracial Committee) had joined in endorsing a candidate, the candidate had been appointed. The recommendations of civic groups did not always follow the unwritten law of board appointments, but in the case of the first Negro appointee the leaders of these civic groups claimed that they had created a new rule of representation. The mayor apparently made a practice of reappointing board members whose terms expired until the appointee resigned voluntarily, except under special circumstances such as the appointment of the first Negro member to the board.

The membership of the board of education was as follows:

Terms expiring in 1957: Melvin W. Blanc
Frank T. Harrison

Mr. Blanc, the chairman of the board of education, was an attorney practicing with a law firm in the nearby metropolis. He was a resident of the Third Ward and a member of the Laketon Reformed Synagogue. His children were attending the Laketon public schools.

Mr. Harrison, who owned a small manufacturing firm, lived on an estate on the neck in the Daniel Boone school district. He belonged to one of the socially prominent old families of Laketon. His children had attended the Laketon schools at one time, but were now grown. Mr. Harrison had been described by the mayor as "a representative of the south-side parents and taxpayers." Messrs. Blanc and Harrison were serving their second terms.

Term expiring in 1956: Reverend Edward A. Simpson

The Reverend Edward Simpson was the pastor of the Calvary Baptist Church, a Negro congregation. He lived across the street from the John Brown School.

Terms expiring in 1955: Mrs. Sean O'Brien
Ralph Parish

Mrs. O'Brien had been a widow with three school-age children when she was first appointed to the board of education in 1935. She had been a probation officer for the County Juvenile Court for many years. She had served in an official capacity on the boards of a number of charitable organizations, and she was active in several Catholic women's organizations. Her home was near the Jefferson School.

Mr. Parish was a senior partner of the local law firm of Parish & Coe. He had been president of the Council for Unity, chairman of the Mayor's Interracial Committee, and an officer of the P.T.A. He had two children in the public schools. His family lived in the Third Ward. At the time of his appointment the mayor made no other comment than that Mr. Parish had been endorsed by more organizations and individuals than any other appointee in the mayor's memory. Mr. Parish was serving his first term.

Terms expiring in 1954: Mrs. Hobart H. Clifton
Salvatore Palermo, M.D.

Mrs. Clifton was the wife of a former city councilor and a close personal friend of the mayor. Mrs. Clifton had three children in the Laketon schools. She had previously served on the Municipal Housing Authority. She was active in the Laketon Humane Society, the Garden Club, Nurses Aid, the Better Homes Council, and the Women's Council of the Y.M.C.A. Her husband was an attorney practicing in Laketon. They lived near the Pilgrim School.

Dr. Palermo was a general practitioner from the Italian-American part of

Laketon. He had formerly been elected a county supervisor for that district. His children were grown. He was active in the Garibaldi Society, an Italian-American social club. He had been appointed to the board in 1944.

Terms expiring in 1953: Francis A. Ferris
John J. Rhodes

Mr. Ferris, the president of a local soft-drink bottling company, resigned from the board of education in January, 1953, because of a state statute pertaining to board members associated with firms doing business with the public schools. Mr. Ferris was a director of the Laketon National Bank, which had purchased tax anticipation notes from the board of education. No successor had been named to his post. Mr. Ferris' children attended parochial schools, and he himself had been prominent in the activities of several groups and charities of Catholic men.

Mr. Rhodes was a local undertaker. He had been appointed to the board of education in 1928; thus he was the only member who had not been originally appointed by Laketon's incumbent mayor. Mr. Rhodes had announced that he would retire from the board at the expiration of his appointment. He belonged to the Roman Catholic Church. His home and funeral parlor were located in the Daniel Boone school district.

21 Elementary French

IN March of 1951 Dr. Lane, head of the French Department at Westwood, one of Wisconsin's oldest private schools for boys, approached the superintendent of schools in the town of Cameron about the possibility of teaching conversational French in the elementary schools. Dr. Lane and three of his colleagues at Westwood wanted to experiment in the third grade of the LaFollette School, one of the four elementary schools in Cameron.

Mr. Carlson, superintendent of schools in Cameron, expressed interest in the proposal of Dr. Lane and his three associates to give short periods of conversational French each day to the four third-grade classes in LaFollette. To initiate the experiment they wished to offer their services free for one year. It was decided that the experiment could be tried only in the elementary school nearest Westwood, since the schedules at Westwood would not allow the teachers time enough to include the three other schools. "As a matter of fact," Dr. Lane said, "this whole idea can be carried out only if our headmaster can schedule our classes so that we may be released for forty-five minutes a day."

"I certainly hope he can," said Superintendent Carlson. "Meanwhile, I'll mention the proposition to my school board."

As he went about his work for several days, Mr. Carlson frequently thought of his conversation with Dr. Lane and wondered what, if anything, would come of it. On several previous occasions teachers from private schools and even from colleges had approached him with proposals which involved experiments in one or another of the Cameron schools. Since most of them had been abandoned for such valid reasons as lack of time or funds or the disapproval of the school board, Carlson didn't dare become too hopeful or enthusiastic about the latest proposal. After a week or so he scarcely thought about it.

At the April meeting of the school board there were many important things to be discussed. The board was holding its meeting that night in an elementary school in one of the outlying sections of the town to decide on future repairs to the building, enlargement of the playground area, and the possible addition of a cafeteria.

The recent election had given the board a new member, Allison Kent, a city bank official who had followed school problems closely before running for office. Since Mr. Kent had just discovered that arrangements had been made for him to spend the next two months in Europe, he was eager to know about any long-range plans which would require discussion and decision before his return to Cameron.

In answer to Mr. Kent's question about long-range plans, Superintendent Carlson mentioned several things: an additional teacher in the Music Department to instruct in violin and cello; planning for two additional rooms in the basement of a crowded elementary school; and removing an antiquated cupola from the roof of the same building. Finally he said, "I don't know what it will amount to, but there are four men at Westwood who would like to experiment with teaching French to our third-graders in the LaFollette School next year. They propose to start in October sometime."

"Sounds interesting," said one board member. "Going to cost us anything?"

"Nothing," replied Carlson. "It's all a sort of project with them."

"Great opportunity — we'll want to hear more about it later," said Miss Nelson.

"Long as it won't add anything to the budget, I'm all for it," said the chairman. "Any motion necessary, Mr. Superintendent?"

"Not at this time," said Carlson. "I'll handle it until there's more definite information."

"Good enough," remarked Mr. King. The meeting was adjourned.

It was a busy spring for the School Department in Cameron. Since two new elementary schools were near completion, there were many details that required the Superintendent's attention. Teachers helped to choose the pastel tones they wanted in their classrooms and transferred books and supplies to the cupboards and shelves in the new schools. With one of its members in Europe, the school board comprised only four members.

In May and June several special meetings were held to consider items that couldn't be covered at the regular monthly sessions. However, on the night of the senior-high graduation exercises in June, the chairman said, "I guess the job is done until September. Everything seems to be under control. I, for one, am going on a good long vacation — a camping trip with my wife and kids. Here's hoping we won't need to have a meeting in July or August."

"I don't see why we should," said Superintendent Carlson. "Anyway, I've got to go on a trip to the West coast the first two weeks in July. I'll be around during the rest of the summer, though, if any of you want to see me."

Late in June, Mrs. Atwood, a member of Cameron's school board, saw Dr. Lane at a party. When he went over to speak to her, his first words were: "It's wonderful that the board is going to back our project! My colleagues and I are really enthusiastic about teaching French to young children. We can hardly wait for October to try it out!"

"Yes, indeed," replied Mrs. Atwood, "and you men are most generous to give us your time and the benefit of your experience. We all hope to hear more about it at our September meeting. In fact, I'd like to hear more about it right now — especially since my daughter will be in one of the classes. Incidentally, I taught French in high school years ago. I'm more than interested in your project."

"That's wonderful!" said Dr. Lane. "You can be very helpful in interpreting what we're doing to the rest of the school board." He went on enthusiastically to outline his aims and hopes. "You see, the University is behind the idea one hundred per cent. They've got a foundation grant to use to train teachers and to get the project rolling in various school systems all over the country. I'm going down to the University for six weeks this summer to study. We're going to teach a group of third-grade boys and girls in a demonstration class down there."

"Are you planning to keep on with these third-graders of ours when they become fourth-graders," Mrs. Atwood asked, "or does the experiment end with a year's instruction?"

"No, indeed," Lane answered. "We hope the teaching will be continuous from the third grade through the sixth grade. This means that in the fall of '52 another third-grade group will start. Eventually we'll have a bilingual group of children entering junior high school. Of course, even next year there'll be more divisions than my colleagues and I can hope to handle, so you'll have to find yourselves a good full-time French teacher. He must be a very good one. Someone who speaks French fluently and is especially good with small children."

Somewhat puzzled, Mrs. Atwood said, "It's really an extensive, long-range project then. I'm not at all sure that our school board members understand how involved it may be. Do you think Superintendent Carlson fully understands the responsibility we are assuming?"

"Why, yes, I think he does. Otherwise I wouldn't undertake it for this coming year. It's going to be quite a task for us to plan the course and put in the necessary time. If you weren't going to carry on for several years, it wouldn't be worth while to start, and the University wouldn't be interested in our sponsoring the project in Cameron. I think I made that clear to Mr. Carlson."

Later, Mrs. Atwood mentally reviewed what had gone on at the school board meeting when the Superintendent had mentioned the French project. She felt certain that no commitment or obligation had been mentioned in connection with it. To verify this she phoned the two board members who were still in town. The first response — from Miss Nelson — was: "No, I feel no sense of obligation for us to carry on such a project for several years. We don't know how it's going to work out or what the elementary-school teachers and parents will think about it."

The chairman's reaction was quick and definite: "We can't promise a thing. There's not much chance that we'll put money in next year's budget for French with all the other expenses we have to meet. Let's wait and see how the idea catches on. We didn't sign a contract or even make a motion on it."

At the opening board meeting in September, Mrs. Atwood asked the Superintendent if he would again talk with Dr. Lane about what, if any, responsibility the school board was assuming in regard to the French project. Carlson's response was: "I'll be glad to. But I'm sure we understand each other. After all, it is only an experiment. It sounds wonderful, but it is almost a revolutionary idea. We'll want to see how it works for a while before we decide anything definite, don't you think?"

One week before actual instruction in French was to begin, Dr. Lane and his wife invited Miss Williams, the elementary-school principal, and the third-grade teachers in the project to tea. They discussed such details as the division of the third-grade class and whether it would be wiser to have ability or alphabetical grouping, such as they had in their homerooms. It was decided to leave the groups as they were, since each room had a fairly representative range of mental abilities. Dr. Lane remarked, "Language ability sometimes crops out in strange places. It's not always in the otherwise strong or gifted pupil." Together the teachers decided on four twenty-minute classes a week, with no classes on Wednesday, since all the elementary schools closed at noon that day.

The first French classes started on October 10. Thereafter, at approximately 10:30 each morning the three instructors greeted their young charges with "*Bonjour, mes enfants!*" Within a few weeks most of the children could converse in a limited way with their instructor and with each other. Every Friday there was an oral quiz and someone was declared "*Le Champion.*" Teachers were loud in their praise and agreed that the French period was a stimulus to good work in general. One little girl who had never seemed to "click" in the school was suddenly a responsive pupil who waited eagerly for the French teacher to come.

Many parents, too, were amazed at the reactions of the children. Instead of being reticent, they were eager to tell their parents the new words they had learned. Many mothers and fathers "hunted up" their old French grammars or bought French-English dictionaries so that they might keep up with their children's progress. Older children in some families learned along with their younger brothers and sisters and often asked if they could have lessons in French. Occasionally some parent would remark, "My only objection is that it must take valuable time away from the important subjects like reading and arithmetic. It seems to me that eventually the children will suffer from this added course."

But both Dr. Lane and the third-grade teachers insisted that nothing was skimped to allow time for the French. It usually meant that there was less time for creative activities such as finger painting or modeling in clay but still ample time for regular art work.

In the short time between October and November a great deal of interest was aroused. The newspapers in the nearby city of Milton gave ample coverage to the project as did the local press. There were pictures of classes in session and of children singing French songs. There were reports of interviews with the instructors and with Dr. Lane, who discussed with reporters the reasons for starting instruction at the third-grade level. Lane stated that some of the nation's leading universities were behind the idea. He discussed how the children seemed to react. School board members found themselves answering questions and listening to opinions. People were generally enthusiastic. Only a few asked, "Where is it leading?" or "Who in the world needs to speak French nowadays? Do the French learn to speak English? We're the leading nation of the world today!"

In November Dr. Lane spoke to the elementary school P.T.A. groups, using as his subject "Why Teach French at the Third-Grade Level?" A convincing and scholarly speaker, he captivated his audience. He told them that young children were naturally bilingual and ready to absorb another language with the least possible effort. He pointed out that this experiment had proved completely successful in several communities in various parts of the country. Furthermore, he said, World War II had shown that it was a great advantage to the armed forces to have men trained to speak more than one language. He claimed that those who learned in childhood had a decided advantage. He explained that as countries united in efforts for world peace and the betterment of mankind, the need for understanding each other's language increased. "There is also," said Dr. Lane, " a great cultural gain in the mastery of a language other than our own. It opens up new fields in literature, music, and art."

The response to this speech was striking. Several people said to Dr. Lane afterwards, "If the school board doesn't see its way clear to financing this project for next year, the P.T.A. will. We'll pass the hat. It wouldn't take long to get enough for the French teacher we'll need when you have to give it up."

Two members of the five-man school board were present, and they observed the strong reaction of the P.T.A. group. At the present time the board was working on the budget and soon would have to decide whether or not to include the salary for a teacher of French.

At a meeting in mid-November a preliminary draft of the budget was carefully studied. It included salaries for six new teachers. The chairman said, "Will you please explain how you plan to use these additional teachers, Mr. Carlson?"

Carlson said, "We need three new elementary school teachers: one physical-education instructor to help Miss Snow with the girls' program, and two teachers to be assigned to the junior and senior high schools. These people are all quite necessary because of increased enrollment. For example, next year's first grade in the LaFollette School will have five sections instead of four. The bulge in school population is also hitting the junior high.

Mrs. Atwood observed, "You are not planning on a French teacher to take over next fall?"

"Yes, I'm keeping that in mind. If you people vote to continue the experiment, there are several ways we can handle it. For example, one of the elementary school teachers might be able to take the French classes. At the State Teachers College the other day I heard of a sixth-grade teacher (and we need one), a native-born French girl, who would be available in September. She could be released from her own room each day to go to the fourth-grade rooms for perhaps half an hour for each room, if that would be enough."

Miss Nelson spoke up: "That would be possible only if we limited the French to the present third grade and let them continue it next year. Do we want to do that when everyone seems so much in favor of it? What do you think, Mr. Kent?"

"I question whether we have the right to spend the taxpayers' money for something which benefits only a small portion of the school population. Just what would be gained by it? I admit it may be fun in the beginning, but how many of them will ever use it? I've just been to France, as you know, and I didn't have any difficulty getting people to understand my English!"

The chairman joined in emphatically. "I never got anything out of French in either prep school or college, and I've never had any need for it in my business. It seems to me to be only an educational frill. I hate to think what those old boys at the bank will have to say about it."

The fifth member of the board, Mr. Dabney, whose chief interest was usually buildings and repairs and not curriculum, said: "But doesn't it seem a shame to have to tell those people who are giving us their time that we don't consider the project worth while? It seems ungrateful, to say the least."

"I'll grant that," said the chairman, "But this board made no promise. One of our chief duties is to the taxpayers. You can't dodge that. French is decidedly an extra, and you'll have plenty of criticism if you move to continue it. We could lose the whole budget, which is plenty big, just because of that one item. It's happened before."

"Well," Mrs. Atwood said, "it seems to me that we should either adopt the program for the whole system or tell Dr. Lane that we are not prepared to. If we put it into operation in the LaFollette Elementary School, as a matter of policy we should add it next year to the curriculum for the third grade in the other elementary schools in town. That is the only way we can gain acceptance and support from people in all sections of town. This would mean a full-time teacher next fall who would travel from school to school each day. She would teach, as I see it, about twelve sections a day. Quite a program in itself. Why don't we invite Dr. Lane to come to a special meeting and discuss it with us?"

"I like that idea," said Mr. Dabney. "After all, we want to be fair about it."

The time for the special meeting was set for the following Tuesday, subject to Dr. Lane's convenience and approval.

On Saturday evening Miss Nelson met Dr. Lane at a concert. "I think it's wonderful that you people are going to put through the whole program, Miss Nelson. I shall be happy to help you find a teacher. The University will have some excellent ones to suggest, I'm sure. I know of one especially able young lady, French-born and college-trained here in the United States, who has just taken her master's degree in the teaching of French. Mr. Carlson tells me that you may decide on someone like that."

"Well, I wish the whole board felt the way I do about it," replied Miss Nelson. "There seems to be some doubt of the real value of such a program."

"Really?" said Dr. Lane, surprised. "Do you think, then, that perhaps we had better not continue the course after the Christmas holidays? We are all too busy at Westwood to pursue it if your school board isn't going to assume the responsibility for next year. There is no point in doing it for only one year. The University staff, which is watching the experiment very closely, will be most disappointed."

"That's why I'm glad you're going to meet with the board soon, Dr. Lane. It's what we should have done before the whole thing got under way in October."

During the next few days, board members held informal discussions with each other and with Superintendent Carlson. The Superintendent felt that several courses of action were open; the board was still divided in its opinion.

Finally the night of the special meeting arrived. Dr. Lane was pleasantly greeted by everyone. For half an hour he spoke convincingly of the responses of the pupils, of the splendid cooperation of the principal and the room teachers, and of the aims of the project and the means of achieving them. He said in part, "It has taken a good deal of time to organize this project. But my colleagues and I believe in it so wholeheartedly that we won't give it up unless you tell us you're no longer interested in it."

As he finished, Mr. Kent smiled at him. "You're a persuasive speaker, Bill!"

Mr. Dabney said, "Well, Dr. Lane, I hope you don't change your mind when you get my daughter Sally in the course. She's eight and she can scarcely speak English!"

"Thank you very much for coming, Dr. Lane," said the chairman. "We won't take any more of your valuable time now, but I'll call you later and tell you what we've decided."

As the goodbyes died away, Mrs. Atwood turned to the Superintendent and said, "Since this is our last opportunity to appropriate money for a French teacher before going over the budget, I feel we ought to reach some decision now. Mr. Carlson, what is your recommendation?"

22 *The Motion Is Seconded*

The Board Meeting

"I MOVE," said Mr. Joseph Kelly, "that we place all names in nomination and proceed to the election of principals for the Spring Street and Wenton schools. Do you have any ballots, Dr. Mitchell?"

"I second the motion," said Mr. John O'Neal.

"I second the motion," said Mrs. Ellen Reilley.

"I'm new here," said Mr. Stein, "but do you customarily vote by closed ballot for appointments?"

"I thought we did," replied Mr. Kelly.

Superintendent Mitchell was surprised. "We never have in the six years I've been here," he said, "but if you want to. . . ."

Everyone sat silent for a moment after his voice trailed off.

Then Mr. Stein asked, "Isn't anyone going to talk about the qualifications of the candidates?"

There was a little shifting in the chairs, but no one said anything. Then Mrs. Reilley blurted, "Who do you think is the best candidate?"

"Mr. Shane," said Mr. Stein. "Mr. Shane stands head and shoulders above any of them." Mr. Stein mentioned Shane's four years of teaching the Special Class in the Bellwood schools and his previous experience in special schools in New York; his professional training; his reputation for solid accomplishment with the difficult children in his classes. Mr. Stein pointed out that Superintendent Mitchell ranked Shane first among the fourteen candidates. There seemed to be little response from the others as he talked, and finally he stopped.

They sat there a moment, and then Joseph Kelly said, "Let's vote."

They voted for the Spring Street principalship first. No one spoke as the pens scratched and the ballots were laid on the table. Mr. Stein flung his sheet of paper face up with the word "Shane" plainly visible.

The Reverend Richard Fulton glanced at the ballots and announced, "Miss Greenwald is elected by a vote of three to two."

"I move," said Joseph Kelly, "that we vote for the Wenton School."

"Second the motion," said Mrs. Ellen Reilley.

Mr. Stein and Mr. Fulton said nothing at all, and in a moment the pens scratched again.

Mr. Fulton announced, "Miss Flanagan is elected, three to two."

Mr. Stein

Leaving the meeting, Mr. Stein was boiling. He had three children in the schools, and concern for their well-being had prompted him to run for the school board — a job he had never wanted in the first place. For two years before he announced his candidacy for office, he had attended practically all meetings. Time after time he had seen Superintendent Mitchell's recommendations for appointments disregarded as the board "literally pulled candidates out of their pockets." Now it had happened again, just three months after he had joined the board.

Inwardly he called the roll of fellow members:

"Richard Fulton: Protestant minister, on the board for five years. Nice fellow and willing to talk principles, but he'd never fight for them.

"Joe Kelly: Auditor with Houghton Machine Company, on the board for ten years; definitely qualified as 'Dean of the School Board.' Makes deals on school appointments right and left. Active politically, and politically oriented in everything he does.

"John O'Neal: Young lawyer who has just joined the board. Wants to be Mayor some day. He'll play ball with anyone who can help him along.

"Mrs. Reilley: Pleasant and well-meaning, but stupid. Wife of fireman 'Slats' Reilley, one of the most likable fellows around. Ran for the board on the basis that she has six children. Her concept of her relation to the school system seems to be: 'I will be a mother to all the school children in the city. I have six children and "Mother knows best."' She seldom understands what is going on — especially if figures are involved."

Mr. Stein was almost amused as he thought of a recent report of a school board meeting published by the *Bellwood Citizen:*

> Mrs. Reilley interrupted the discussion of the Meade Elementary school teacher appointment with "What about my nephew?" Dr. Mitchell told her that he stood ninth in a list of sixteen according to qualifications as evaluated by the principals and the superintendent.
>
> "Well, I understand that both Jim Turner and Joe Shehane want him for the job and think he's swell," she replied. She was informed that the position in question was for a second-grade teacher whereas her nephew had applied for a position teaching grade eight.
>
> A discussion of the appointments ensued when Mrs. Reilley asked why the positions weren't filled by men instead of women candidates. "It seems funny that no local men get appointed," she said. "They all must be pretty stupid around here." Dr. Mitchell told her that he considered teachers' qualifications, not their sex and place of residence, the main factors to be considered.

Mr. Stein reflected that Mrs. Reilley had just announced her candidacy for the Legislature.

Kelly, O'Neal, and Mrs. Reilley, reflected Mr. Stein, are becoming bold. As three Catholics they'll stick together against the Protestant and the Jew, and they can control the board; so why bother with formalities?

Clearly, something had to be done. There was always the possibility that a letter to the local papers might stir things up. Well, he'd see.

Dr. Mitchell

Dr. Mitchell didn't like it, but there wasn't much he could do about it. Joseph Kelly had done it again.

Dr. Mitchell had come to Bellwood in 1948, when Superintendent Sullivan had finally retired. Sullivan had been there for many years and should have retired earlier, but World War II had made the task of finding a replacement especially difficult. When he did retire, Dr. Mitchell and a man from Pennsylvania had emerged as the leading possibilities among fifteen candidates for the job. Dr. Mitchell had come up from his New Jersey school job to talk to the board and tell them his ideas on education. Among other things, he told them that if he took the job he would want to have full authority in the nomination of teachers. No promises were made, but an informal understanding seemed to have been reached.

The position had first been offered to the man from Pennsylvania on a vote of 3 to 2 by the board. He had refused the position on the grounds that he would not care to accept such responsibility unless the vote was unanimous. However, when the position had been offered to Dr. Mitchell on the same basis, he had accepted. At that time the five-man school board had been composed of two Catholics, two Protesants, and a Jew. Mr. Kelly and the Jewish member had supported the candidacy of a local principal for the superintendency.

Salaries in Bellwood had been very low. As a matter of fact, Superintendent Sullivan had, during his last year, secured Mr. Kelly's support for a salary increase, but the full board had refused to take such a step. At his first meeting with the Bellwood teachers, Dr. Mitchell admitted that salaries were much too low and promised to work for increases. He had little difficulty. As soon as his recommendation was placed before the school board, the increase was approved.

During Mr. Sullivan's term of office, candidates for teaching positions and principalships had regularly contacted school board members to discuss their candidacy. Dr. Mitchell immediately requested that this practice cease. Instead, the candidates were to be interviewed by him, their professional qualifications tabulated, and both the tabulated qualifications and the superintendent's recommendations given to the school board for official action. The new superintendent felt very strongly that candidates should be chosen on the basis of their professional qualifications and not of "personalities." He also felt that his own professional training gave him special competence in judging candidates.

At school board meetings Dr. Mitchell customarily presented the list of candidates with their qualifications and his recommendations. He would then give his reasons for recommending the particular candidates, and if the board members wished, they could then ask about other candidates. If the candidate preferred by some member of the board was about as well qualified as his own choice, Dr. Mitchell would not quibble over the matter.

Ordinarily, all such discussion of candidates took place in executive session, since this gave the members more freedom to discuss the candidates with frankness.

Mr. Kelly seemed to dislike the new system; he said that he liked to see and talk with prospective candidates, and that he felt the superintendent might not stress points that the candidate might like to have emphasized. Dr. Mitchell recalled how, about six months after he had become superintendent, Mr. Kelly had said to him, in effect, "I am on this school board to see that Catholics get into teaching positions." The superintendent had been shocked.

For the first two years of Dr. Mitchell's superintendency the board had followed the procedures which he insisted upon concerning the selection of personnel. However, when the Catholics gained a 3 to 2 majority on the board, they began to fight, and slowly the old method returned to use. Time and again, the majority disagreed with his recommendations, and once more candidates were contacting the board members. Some members accused others of interfering with the established procedure of the board, and the situation began to receive some notice in the local press.

By 1950 the majority of the board finally recommended and passed a vote to have applicants for *teaching* positions interviewed by a "board of examiners," consisting of the superintendent and the principals of the elementary and junior high schools. At such interviews the candidates were questioned, and they were later discussed and rated by this board. Under this arrangement, candidates did not contact the members of the school board, and on the whole the school board followed the recommendations of the board of examiners very closely. However, no similar routine was established for the selection of *administrative* personnel. Candidates for principalships continued to be interviewed by the superintendent, and their qualifications were presented to the school board in tabular form. A number of the candidates also continued to get in direct touch with the board members.

In 1949 Mr. Stein, a Jewish lawyer, had begun attending school board meetings regularly. Rumors were rife in the city that appointments being made by the board were highly questionable. Mr. Stein had made no secret of the fact that he wanted to see what was going on.

In the fall of 1951 Mr. Stein ran for the school board. During his campaign he did not hesitate to name names and debate issues. His campaign stirred up unusual interest in the election, and he polled the highest number of votes ever given to a candidate in a school board election.

In that same election Mr. John O'Neal, a young Catholic lawyer, was elected to the board. These two new members joined Mr. Kelly, Mr. Fulton (the chairman), and Mrs. Reilley on the board as the school year 1951–52 began.

During the following spring the principal of the twelve-room Spring Street School (Grades 1–6) and the principal of the six-room Wenton School (Grades 1–3) announced their impending retirement. On February 4 Dr. Mitchell sent out a bulletin (Exhibit 1) inviting applications for the positions. Fourteen applicants responded, two applied specifically for the Wenton School only, and the remaining twelve presumably sought either position.

As usual, the superintendent tabulated the qualifications of the candidates and presented copies of the tabulation (Exhibit 2) to members of the school board at a meeting held on March 31. At the same time he recommended the appointment of Mr. Shane for the Spring Street principalship and of Miss Steinlieb for the Wenton position.

After his recommendations were made, there was no discussion. Rather surprisingly, John O'Neal asked the superintendent to rank all the candidates in the order of acceptability to him. Dr. Mitchell took a little time to think, but he finally ranked ten of them, with Mr. Shane first and Miss Steinlieb second. He lumped the remaining four in a group at the bottom of the list. (See Exhibit 3.) When Dr. Mitchell had finished his ranking, Mr. O'Neal suggested that the election be put over another month and that the superintendent be instructed to contact all applicants and tell them that members of the board wanted an opportunity to talk with each of them and to examine any material that they might care to submit in connection with their applications.

The board adopted Mr. O'Neal's suggestion, and the meeting broke up. The next day Dr. Mitchell sent word to the applicants that members of the board wanted to interview them.

He presumed that the board members had been busy interviewing, but nothing noteworthy happened until the final meeting, when Miss Greenwald and Miss Flanagan were chosen as the new principals.

The worst thing about Miss Greenwald was that for a month she had been boasting to other teachers that she was to be the new principal — even before any discussion of her qualifications had taken place, and before the board had been given the names of the candidates. Joseph Kelly was a good friend of her brother and thought he owed the brother patronage.

Kelly had probably been the prime mover in Miss Flanagan's election, too.

The trouble there had very likely begun four or five years ago, when the superintendent had to send Miss Flanagan a disciplinary letter and give her a lecture for professional misconduct. There had been considerable controversy over the question of equal pay versus a single salary schedule. The single salary schedule was better for most Bellwood teachers, but Miss Flanagan wouldn't advance as quickly or as far as some of the younger teachers if it were adopted. The school board and the Teachers' Association had printed and circulated an explanation of why they recommended voting for the single salary schedule. Miss Flanagan received the material in her classroom and tore it into tiny pieces in front of the children, saying, "That's what I think of that kind of rubbish!"

The material was an official communication, and Dr. Mitchell had decided to reprimand Miss Flanagan. Kelly had later tried to get him to destroy the file copy of the written reprimand. Mitchell thought Kelly probably didn't like to have him reprimand a Catholic.

It was too bad about Shane and Miss Steinlieb, he reflected. This was the third time Shane had been turned down for a principalship. He's a Catholic, too. He has been teaching a class of backward children, mostly big boys who are close to delinquent. They respect him and think of him almost as a father. He has taught them manners and how to take care of themselves. He helps them get jobs and follows them up — really a professional educator. It's hard to see why he was turned down. Miss Steinlieb is good, too. She has the experience and the background to do the job, and she has been assistant principal at Lee Junior High.

Nothing much could be done, though. There was no legal redress. The vote had been taken and the choice made. If he tried to do anything about it, the three who voted for the successful candidates would block it. He decided to see what would happen at the next board meeting.

The *Bellwood Citizen* of June 12 reported:

STEIN CLAIMS SCHOOL JOBS SET BEFORE MEETING

School Board Member Says Secret Caucus Held; Hits Failure of Board to Consider Qualifications before Filling Vacancies

"A move on the part of school board member Melvin Stein to have included in the official minutes of the last school committee a statement that the election of two elementary school principals took place without any discussion of the qualifications of the candidates failed to pass at the meeting of the school board Tuesday evening.

"Stein asked to be recorded as having voted against both appointees. He claimed that a caucus had been held prior to the meeting, and that the elections had been agreed upon outside the board chambers — a procedure which is contrary to law, he said.

"Board Member Stein pointed out that Joseph Kelly, Mrs. Ellen Reilley, and John O'Neal had all voted for the two candidates, although no discussion had taken place.

"When Board Member John O'Neal claimed that he must receive proof that Chairman Fulton had not voted for the two selected, Stein declared that he had such proof and Chairman Fulton backed him up, stating that he hadn't voted for the two appointed.

"Stein's motion was defeated by a vote of 3 to 1, with Chairman Fulton abstaining.

"Stein later told the *Citizen* that his claim that a caucus had been held was based on the results of the secret balloting.

" 'According to all the information I have been able to gather from 20 years back, this is the first time in the history of the board that an election has been held by secret ballot. It seems to me more than mere coincidence that without any discussion of the qualifications of the candidates, three of the school committee members voted for identical candidates for each position,' he asserted.

" 'We had 14 candidates for these positions,' he continued. 'Some of them were very fine people, well qualified for the vacancies, yet we dismissed them with no consideration whatever.' "

Editorially, the *Citizen* went on to comment:

> "School Board Member Melvin Stein brought out in the open Tuesday evening at the school board meeting and substantiated what many persons have been hinting at the past few weeks. He made a vain attempt to have inserted into the school board record the statement that the two principals selected two weeks ago for the Wenton and Spring Street schools were chosen without a comparison or even inspection of any of the records of the applicants for the position.
>
> "At that meeting two weeks ago, the school board excluded everyone, as it often does, went into executive session, and then selected the two principals by secret ballot, for the first time in history, so far as we know.
>
> "Now, Board Member Stein has in fact substantiated what many teachers and other persons interested in the schools have only hinted at — that the selection of the two new principals was made without open consideration and discussion of the merits and weaknesses of the entire list of candidates. The votes in both instances were 3–2, and disregarded the professional opinion of Dr. Mitchell, the superintendent of schools.
>
> "Without involving the personalities of the two new principals, we hold the opinion that such actions by the school board are not in the best interests of the city's school system, or of the children in the schools. Without an open and frank discussion of the relative merits of the candidates, how can the members of the school board arrive at the best-qualified persons? And if the best-qualified persons are not to be selected for the vacancies, what hopes of advancement can teachers in the system have? We are, in effect, telling the teachers in our school system to improve themselves by devoting extracurricular time to working with the children and taking additional courses, but that when it comes to promotions, the yardstick will not be, 'Who is the best-qualified candidate,' but rather 'Which candidate can secure the most school board votes?'
>
> "We are deeply disturbed by the implications of the school board's principal elections of two weeks ago, and we are sure others are as intense in their feeling. We cannot believe that the school board, in future appointments, will continue to dismiss the qualifications of many fine teachers, simply by not discussing them. The taxpayers who foot the bills, and the parents whose children are in the schools are entitled to at least that much consideration by school board members."

After the news broke, Mr. Stein's telephone rang continuously as people thanked him for bringing the situation out in the open. The other of Bellwood's two papers was, as usual, silent.

Publicly, there was not a word from any of the three offenders denying the situation or mentioning it in any way. Privately, though, Mr. O'Neal and Mr. Kelly had something to say:

John O'Neal

Mr. John O'Neal explained that he felt justified in the choices the board had made. His own choices had won, and he felt certain that they were good choices.

When the positions were first posted, Mr. O'Neal had been contacted by eight or nine of the candidates. Probably the others had not done so because they thought that doing so might be ethically questionable. He was glad, therefore, to have the opportunity to interview the other candidates when the election was postponed.

Mr. O'Neal felt that the personality of the individual candidates should carry considerable weight in the matter of whether or not they should be selected. While in school himself he had come in contact with a principal whose academic background might easily have been considered not as good as that of some others but who had been able to get along with people. And this, to O'Neal was very important.

In thinking about these present candidates, he had tried to give each question in his own mind the proper weight. First, he felt, the candidate would have to have the proper educational background. That was almost automatic, though, because they couldn't be teachers without sufficient education to qualify for a principalship.

Next, he felt, he should consider the superintendent's recommendation and give it weight — *if deserved.*

Finally, he gave weight to his own impression of personality and ability to get along with children and adults.

After looking over and talking to the fourteen candidates, O'Neal felt that all were qualified. Then it became a question of which two were best qualified, plus suitability and adaptability to the job.

Martha Greenwald had made a tremendous impression on him. She was the only one who had been a Phi Beta Kappa in college. He did some racial thinking in connection with the Spring Street School, which is in a Jewish neighborhood. His personal feeling was that there might be some problems that a person of the same racial background could understand and solve more easily — with both pupil and principal Jewish. In that way he had narrowed his consideration to Miss Greenwald and Miss Steinlieb. Miss Steinlieb had a better background on paper and had served as an assistant principal for a number of years as well. One thing, however, disturbed him about her: her attitude in approaching this thing. She came with a chip on her shoulder; she had been a candidate twice before and had not been selected either time and felt that this should be it. She impressed him as a very strong-minded and even headstrong person. He had the feeling that on her own she might not fit too well into the position. As an assistant she could be guided and influenced by the principal, and undoubtedly she was good in the capacity of assistant — her principal had recommended her. Temperamentally, however, Miss Greenwald was the better person to handle people and get along with them.

For the second position, Miss Flanagan seemed to have the necessary qualifications. She had been a teacher for thirty-three years and had spent her entire teaching life in Bellwood. She had started out in elementary school and had made her way up into junior high, even though she wasn't trained for that work. She had had a fine career in teaching, and her application was partly endorsed by her principal.

Mr. O'Neal had been much impressed by the complaints of John King, one of the older candidates, who had been a candidate before and who said that the board paid very little attention to practical experience.

The Wenton School covers only the first three grades. At that level only women are fitted to teach; hence he had considered only women candidates.

Mr. Shane was apparently disqualified, because they needed a Jewish person and a woman, and Shane was neither.

Then there was a Miss Reed, who was Dr. Mitchell's third choice. Her background was in remedial reading, and at his interview with her Mr. O'Neal had asked if she wasn't more interested in a position as Director of Remedial Reading. She frankly told him that she had applied for the principalship because she was too old to travel around among the schools as much as she had in the past and was anxious to settle down in one spot.

Dr. Mitchell had apparently recommended people on the basis of educational background alone, and Mr. O'Neal could not subscribe to that. Personality was an important factor and should be given considerable weight.

Not all of Dr. Mitchell's recommendations had been wise. He had recommended Miss Roark for the position of assistant principal some time back, as had her principal. Now the superintendent admits that she hasn't worked out.

Then, too, in two previous elections the board did not follow the superintendent's recommendations, and the two men selected have done excellent jobs.

Because Dr. Mitchell is an educator — he has spent his whole life in education and has advanced far in the field — he has a tendency to assign a disproportionate amount of importance to the educational background of the candidates.

Anyway, the selection of Miss Greenwald and Miss Flanagan seemed pretty reasonable.

Joseph Kelly

As Joseph Kelly told it later, the meeting had been just another one of a great many that he had attended since he was elected to the school board in 1942. That was long before Mr. Sullivan retired, although Sullivan had already been there for thirty-odd years.

Sullivan should have retired during the war, but it was hard to replace him. Mr. Kelly was sorry to see him go when the time finally came. He had his feet on the ground and knew how to handle employees and get along with the public. Improvements in the schools couldn't be made under his superintendency — guidance work, testing, visual education, and the like — but financial affairs were always handled in a very sound way.

When they had finally had to replace Sullivan, they had offered the job to a fellow from Pennsylvania — a Mr. Robson. He had turned it down, and they had elected Mitchell. Mr. Kelly had voted against Mitchell in favor of a local man. Mr. Kelly felt that it was a good idea to recognize local people who had bettered themselves and handled their jobs well. A man from within the system might have bright ideas and be well informed about new educational methods just as much as an outsider. A man who had started from the bottom and worked up and learned the fundamentals and had good personal characteristics, could do a better job. Still, Mitchell had seemed like a good prospect.

Originally, Mitchell had insisted pretty strongly that candidates not come to see board members, but they do come to see some board members now. It's better that way. It's better for a board member to see the people he votes for. Then, with Dr. Mitchell's recommendations and the list of qualifications, members have a pretty well rounded picture.

On the night they voted for the principals of the Wenton and Spring Street schools, they had followed normal procedure in using written ballots. The superintendent gave his recommendations, and Mr. Kelly had then asked that all names be placed in nomination so that each member could vote for anyone. Then they had voted.

Mr. Stein had later accused the board of electing candidates whom they had not discussed. Actually, to Mr. Kelly's way of thinking, each member had all the information he needed, between the tabulations and the knowledge of candidates acquired through interviews and occasional contacts at the schools. There wasn't too much to discuss; he wasn't interested in discussing — that was just wasting time. If anyone wanted to give a speech for his candidate, O.K. Mr. Stein did make a lot of comments on his two candidates. Later on, he said that the election had been fixed all the time. Usually people do talk things over among themselves, and they know which way the votes are going before the actual day of election; this can be pretty well said about any organization. At the polls people make up their minds by themselves.

For years Mr. Kelly had found himself voted down 3 to 2 or 4 to 1. He knew that other members had made up their minds and talked it over and decided what stand to take. He had warned them in the past that they had made mistakes on votes. One time the majority of the board had to reverse their vote because of a court ruling.

When they had come to the salary program Mr. Kelly had objected, but the majority voted to put it in, and all of them had agreed ahead of time to vote as they did. Salary is Mr. Kelly's field, but they wouldn't listen to him. There have been several court suits about that vote, too.

For these two principalships Mr. Kelly had interviewed about three fourths of the candidates. He has been a board member for a long time and knows the teachers better than anyone else — especially better than Dr. Mitchell.

Mr. Shane, the superintendent's first choice, spent all his time on work with a Special Class. It didn't seem that he could do any better job as a principal than some of the other candidates. The others had been in the elementary and junior high schools all along. Shane is a very smooth talker, and he's not a local man. Both of those who were finally appointed are local people and have been in the system longer than Shane.

As for the Spring Street School, a majority of the children are of Jewish extraction, and the neighborhood will soon be mostly Jewish. It seemed that one of their own race would better understand the parents and children than anyone else would. Miss Greenwald was chosen, and she is of Jewish extraction. She is a Phi Beta Kappa and very brilliant. She kept on studying and took many courses after she graduated from college. She never got her master's degree, because others were going after it for the financial reward and she would not lower herself to that.

Mr. Kelly had had some experience with this Miss Steinlieb whom Dr. Mitchell recommended. Last year he had talked with her, and in the course of the conversation found she wasn't as sharp as he had thought she was. Things had come up during the year that indicated that her judgment wasn't good. A good part of the work of a principal is to meet the public and be in close contact with the children. It was too risky to take a chance on this particular girl. Others were better suited and more reliable in judgment and in meeting the public.

The superintendent's judgment hasn't always been too good. Recently a group was formed of persons purportedly interested in bettering the conditions in the Bellwood schools. The group wanted the superintendent to place his problems before them; they would make recommendations as to how to meet them. Dr. Mitchell was extremely enthusiastic about the whole idea. Mr. Kelly wasn't quite so sure, so he joined the group by paying his dollar and attended a meeting. He asked the purpose of the group, and when they told him they wanted the superintendent to bring his problems to the group for solutions, he told them that the city paid Dr. Mitchell to solve those problems. He did not go to another meeting. Later it was revealed that the group was partially a front for a Communist group; two members were questioned about Communist leanings. Dr. Mitchell made a bad mistake on that one.

All in all, there doesn't seem to be much to all the noise Mr. Stein is making about that meeting.

EXHIBIT 1

OFFICE OF THE SUPERINTENDENT OF SCHOOLS
Bellwood

Bulletin #16
February 5, 1952

PLEASE POST

TO ALL EDUCATIONAL PERSONNEL:

Because the principals of the Wenton and Spring Street schools are retiring at the close of the current school year, the Superintendent of Schools invites applications from school personnel who feel themselves qualified to fill those vacancies. Appointments to the positions will be effective September 1, 1952.

The last date for filing the applications for the positions will be March 20, 1952, at 3:00 p.m. in the Superintendent's Office.

Those applying should have had a *minimum* of five years successful teaching experience; have demonstrated marked ability to get along well with pupils, parents, colleagues, and the public; should have a real interest in and capacity for the organization, administration, and supervision of elementary schools; and should not only subscribe wholeheartedly to our accepted Philosophy of Education but also stand ready to make it function *effectively* when we begin our work in the fall in the two schools above-mentioned.

Applicants should furnish information on the following points:

1. Name, address, and phone number
2. Name of the college(s) attended
   a. Number of years in attendance
   b. Degree(s) earned and date(s) granted
3. Experience in teaching
   a. Position held or grades taught and where
   b. Number of years of teaching experience
   c. Administrative or supervisory positions held and where
   d. Number of years in such positions
4. Other experience in fields allied to teaching, if any
5. Specific courses taken in recognized colleges or universities dealing with
   a. School administration or supervision
   b. Tests and measurements
   c. Guidance techniques and practices
   d. Curriculum construction
   e. Specialized teaching procedures in
      i. Reading
      ii. Arithmetic
      iii. Any other fields
6. References from persons who are in positions from which they can judge competently the ability of the applicants to meet the qualifications listed in the *third unnumbered* paragraph above.

JAMES T. MITCHELL
Superintendent of Schools

EXHIBIT 2 Survey of Qualifications of Candidates for the Spring Street and Wenton Schools Principalships

March 30, 1952

Name	Education	Courses in Education	Teaching Experience	Professional Memberships
1. Martha Greenwald, teacher of French in the Lee Junior High School	a. B.A. from N.Y.U. in 1931	a. Educational psychology b. Principles of primary and secondary education c. Teaching methods in Latin and mathematics d. Practice teaching e. Principles and practices of guidance	a. Industrial School for Girls b. Substitute teacher for several years in Bellwood c. Permanent substitute in Bellwood elementary schools d. Evening school in Bellwood e. Teacher of French since 1941 in the Lee Junior High School in Bellwood	a. Phi Beta Kappa
2. Susan T. Landon, teacher of social studies in the Barton Junior High School	a. Graduate of 3-year normal course of State Teachers College in 1930 b. B.S. in Education from same college in 1944 c. Candidate for Ed.M. from C.C.N.Y. in August, 1952	a. Supervision in elementary education b. Problems of the elementary principal c. Tests and measurements d. A study of failures in the Bellwood Schools e. Practices and technics in guidance f. Studying the modern school curriculum g. Cooperative laboratory in secondary-school curricula, toward a 12-year program	a. Kindergarten in Bellwood, one year b. Fifth grade in the Tarn School, Bellwood, 1931–44 c. Mathematics, 1944–50, in Barton Junior High School d. Social studies, from 1950 to present, in Barton Junior High School	

(continued on next page)

Name	Education	Courses in Education	Teaching Experiences	Professional Memberships
Susan T. Landon (cont.)		h. A study of the curriculum guide for the primary grades i. Social studies in the elementary school j. Psychology of the adolescent		
3. Francis X. Farrell, teaching principal of the Prince School	a. B.A. from Fordham University in 1937 b. Ed. M. from Syracuse University in 1951, with a major in elementary administration	a. Administration of an elementary school b. Public-school administration c. Tests and measurements in the elementary school d. Bases of behavior e. Curriculum construction in: science, social studies, arithmetic f. Improvement of reading g. Teaching of arithmetic in the elementary school h. Teaching in the primary grades	a. Mathematics teacher in Swett High School, 1945–46 b. Grade 7 teacher in Newark, 1946–47 c. Teaching principal of Grade 5 of Allbritton, Connecticut, Elementary School, 1947–48 d. Grade 6 teacher in Lee Elementary School, Bellwood, 1948–50 e. Grade 5 teacher in Bellwood Summer School—1948 f. Teaching principal of Grade 5 of the Prince Elementary School, Bellwood, 1950 to date	a. Bellwood Teachers' Association b. Bellwood Men Teachers' Club c. Prince P.T.A.
4. Mary T. Roark, assistant principal and teacher of Grade 5 in the Spring Street School	a. Graduate of 2-year normal course of State Teachers College in 1928 b. Graduate of 4-year normal course (same College) in 1931 c. B.S. from Teachers College in 1950	a. Tests and measurements b. Guidance technics c. Measurement and evaluation d. Studying the modern school curriculum e. Analysis of pupil failures f. Improvement of arithmetic in the intermediate grades	a. Teacher of Grades 1–7 in Certes, Va., 1928–29 b. Teacher of Grades 1–6 in Sheffield, Vt., 1929–30 c. Departmental teacher in Grades 6–8 in Painted Post, N.Y., 1938–40 d. Teacher of Grades 5–6 in same town, 1940–46	

Name	*Education*	*Courses in Education*	*Teaching Experience*	*Professional Memberships*
Mary T. Roark (cont.)			e. Teacher of Grade 5 in Spring Street School, Bellwood, 1946 to date.	
5. Edward R. Shane, teacher of the Special Class at the Barton School	a. Ph.B. from Holy Cross in 1936 b. State Teachers College teaching certificate in 1939 c. Ed.M. from Fordham University in 1950 d. University Extension Work e. i. Adult Education at Yale; ii. Aeronautics: Navigation, Meteorology, Dynamics, at State Dept. of Education iii. Special Education of Exceptional Children, at same place	a. Organization and administration of guidance b. Psychology of the subnormal c. Methods in educational research d. Seminar in education e. Educational measurements f. Methods of teaching the mentally retarded g. Principles of guidance h. Teaching the slow-learning child in the regular classroom i. Methods of teaching aeronautics j. Workshop in adult education k. The improvement of reading l. Teaching the retarded child in the special class m. Seminar in education for exceptional children n. Industrial arts in secondary schools	a. Teacher in Phillips School in New York, 1939–41 b. Teacher in Southerly High School, N.Y., 1941–42 c. Teacher in Williams School in New York, 1942–46 (junior high school) d. Teacher in Burley High School, N.Y., 1946–47 e. Teacher of a Special Class in the Bellwood Schools, 1947–51 f. Teacher of Special Class in the Barton Junior High School, 1951 to the present	a. Bellwood Teachers' Association b. State Teachers' Federation c. State Special Education Association d. Association for Help for Exceptional Children e. National Education Association f. Men Teachers' Club of Bellwood
6. Rose T. Steinlieb, assistant principal at the Lee Junior High School	a. Graduate of 4-year course at State Teacher's College in 1929	a. Supervision of classroom instruction b. Supervision of the elementary school	a. Teacher and principal's assistant in the Chandler School, 1929–1931	a. Bellwood Teachers' Association b. Lee P.T.A.

(*continued on next page*)

Name	Education	Courses in Education	Teaching Experience	Professional Memberships
Rose T. Steinlieb (cont.)	b. Graduate of Evening Secretarial School in 1931 c. Ed.M. from Univ. of Wisconsin in 1949, with a major in elementary-school administration and supervision	c. Problems of the elementary school d. Causes of failures in the elementary school e. Measurement and evaluation in education f. Methods in educational research g. Principles of guidance h. Practices and technics of guidance i. Analysis of school failures j. Elementary-school curriculum k. Improvement of reading l. Improvement of instruction in English m. Teaching the slow-learning child n. Literature and voice choir in the elementary school o. Social studies in the elementary school p. Modern methods of teaching arithmetic q. Methods of teaching prevocational subjects r. Teaching arts and crafts in the elementary schools s. Teaching the language arts in the elementary school t. Audio-visual education in the elementary school u. Problems and procedures in working with adults	b. Teacher in various grades in the Birch School, Bellwood, 1931–40 c. Teacher in the Lee Junior High School, Bellwood, 1940–49 d. Assistant principal of the Lee Junior and Elementary Schools, Bellwood, 1949 to date e. Chandler and Lee Schools: teacher of Adult Civic Education in beginners' and intermediate classes	c. Bellwood Women's Civic League

Name	*Education*	*Courses in Education*	*Teaching Experience*	*Professional Memberships*
7. John S. Kyser, teacher of mathematics and science at the Lee Junior High School	a. B.A. from Hiram College in 1931	a. Statistics and measurements in the learning procedure b. School administration c. Methods and technics in testing d. The teaching of junior high mathematics e. The unit in secondary education f. Audio-visual aids in education g. Supervision of elementary education in the field of arithmetic	a. Evening-school teacher of algebra and geometry in Bellwood Evening School, 1931–37 and 1941–43 b. Teacher in the Lee Junior High School, Bellwood, 1937 to date	
8. John King, teacher of industrial arts in the High School	a. Graduate of Sedley Institute in 1925 b. Training School for Teachers of Mechanic Arts in 1928 c. B.S. in Education from N.Y.U. in 1938 d. Ed.M. from N.Y.U. in 1949 e. Has completed 25 hours of credit towards the Ed.D. degree at N.Y.U. f. Has also studied at Columbia University and C.C.N.Y.	a. Supervision in the secondary schools b. The superintendent administers the schools c. Teachers and school administration d. Elements of statistics e. Measurements in secondary-school subjects f. Seminar in measurements g. Measurement of intelligence h. Measurement in educational and vocational guidance i. Classroom-teacher problems in the junior high school	a. Substitute in the elementary grades, Providence Public Schools, 1927–29 b. Teacher of pattern-making, cabinetmaking, wood-turning, and foundry work in the junior and senior high schools in Bellwood, 1929 to date c. Evening-school teacher in Bellwood in architectural and machine drawing and cabinetmaking, 1938–42	a. Bellwood Teachers' Association b. Bellwood Men Teachers' Club c. State Teachers' Federation d. State Vocational and Industrial Association

(*continued on next page*)

Name	Education	Courses in Education	Teaching Experience	Professional Memberships
John King (cont.)		j. Problems of adjustment in the home and family k. Problems in teaching high school economics l. Problems in teaching high school sociology m. Elementary school problems n. Individual health guidance o. Character education p. Problems in personal adjustment q. Seminar in current educational problems r. Practice and teaching of guidance s. Technics of the interviewer t. Guidance in the elementary school u. Cooperative laboratory in the secondary-school curriculum v. Specialized teaching procedures in i. Industrial arts ii. Shop mathematics iii. The unit method		
9. Elizabeth Reed (for Wenton only) teacher of Remedial Reading	a. Graduate of 2-year course of State Teachers College in 1928 b. B.S. in Education from Boston University in 1940 c. Has attended summer schools at the Univ. of	a. Curriculum building b. Tests and measurements c. Remedial reading d. Reading in the first six grades e. Language in the primary schools	a. Teacher of Grades 1–3 in Nowell, N.H., 1921–28 b. Teacher in Grade 1 in Parson, Mass., 1928–46 c. Teacher in Grade 1 in the Oak Park School, Bellwood, 1946–51	a. President of Parson Teachers' Association (two years) b. Bellwood Teachers' Association

Name	*Education*	*Courses in Education*	*Teaching Experience*	*Professional Memberships*
Elizabeth Reed (cont.)	Tennessee and Colo. State College d. Has 16 semester hours of credit toward master's degree	f. Visual education	d. Remedial Reading teacher in Bellwood public schools, 1951 to date	
10. Jane C. Caldwell (for Wenton only) teacher in Grade 2, Lee Elementary School	a. Graduate of 3-year course at Collins Kindergarten and Normal School in 1935 b. Will receive the degree of B.S. in Education from N.Y.U. in June, 1952	a. Home and school relations b. Measurement and evaluation in Education c. School and society d. Child psychology e. Adolescent psychology f. Teaching reading in the elementary schools g. The improvement of primary-grade arithmetic h. Teaching the mentally handicapped i. Social studies in the elementary schools: Methods and materials j. Workshop in elementary music k. Arts and crafts in the elementary school l. Folk dancing m. Choral speech	a. Teacher of Grade 3 and assistant to the principal in the Wenton School, 1935–36 b. Teacher of Grade 1 in the Wenton School, 1936–45 c. Teacher of Grade 1 in the Lee Elementary School, Bellwood, 1945–50 d. Teacher of Grade 2 in the Lee School, 1950 to date	a. Lee P.T.A. b. Bellwood Council of P.T.A's (legislative chairman) c. Past president of the Bellwood Teachers' Association d. Director of the State Teachers' Federation e. Troop leader of Girl Scouts
11. Timothy J. Duffy, teacher of academic subjects in the Vocational High	a. Graduate of 3-year course in Practical Arts at State Teachers College b. B.S. in Education from the same college in 1951	(No special courses listed. Here follows a list of additional teaching experience to supplement the list in the next column to the right.) a. Industrial-arts instructor in Baltimore recreation center	a. Teacher of industrial arts in elementary school, in Fall River, 1928–31 b. Teacher of industrial arts in two Baltimore elementary schools, 1931–41 c. Vocational instructor on	a. Member of the Board of Directors of the Baltimore Teachers' Association b. One of the founders of the Baltimore Teachers' Federal Credit Union and its first treasurer

(*continued on next page*)

Name	Education	Courses in Education	Teaching Experience	Professional Membership
Timothy J. Duffy (cont.)		b. Shop instructor, evenings, for the National Youth Administration c. Shop instructor in the Evening School, Bellwood d. Home-repair instructor in Bellwood Vocational High, evenings e. Instructor of apprenticeship class in Bellwood Vocational High, evenings f. Has given demonstration lessons while teaching in Baltimore schools and also was engaged in teacher-training work there	junior- and senior-high levels in Nantucket, 1941–42 d. Industrial-arts instructor in two Bellwood junior high schools and academic teacher in Vocational High, 1943–51 e. Assistant supervisor in education for the State Department of Education from January 15, 1951 to January 2, 1952 (on leave of absence from the Bellwood Schools) f. Academic teacher in the Bellwood Vocational High School from January 2, 1952, to date g. Taught a college course in the summer of 1949 at State Teachers College	
12. Eileen N. Flanagan, teacher of mathematics in the Meade Junior High School	a. Graduate of two-year course at State Teachers College b. B.S. in Education from N.Y.U.	(None listed)	a. Primary teacher in Meade Elementary School b. Teacher in Meade Junior High School (Total years of teaching in Bellwood — 33)	
13. John R. Swanson, teacher of biology and chemistry in the High School	a. Graduated from the $2\frac{1}{2}$-year course for grade-school teaching at State Teachers College, Utah, in 1940	a. Administration and supervision of home and school relations b. Educational measurement c. Analysis of school failures	a. Grades 1–8 in Township School in Nanton, Wyo., 1940–41 b. All subjects in Grades 7–8 of the Consolidated School	a. President of the Bellwood Men Teachers' Club

Name	Education	Courses in Education	Teaching Experience	Professional Memberships
John R. Swanson (cont.)	b. B.S. in Education from N.Y.U. in 1947 c. Ten semester hours' study in mathematics and science in the Bates College Summer Session in 1949	d. Technics of the interview e. Cooperative laboratory in secondary-school curricula f. Studying the modern curriculum g. Audio-visual aids in education h. Introduction to child and educational psychology i. The unit method j. Observation of grade-school teaching methods in: i. Public-school music ii. Public-school art iii. Upper-grade methods	of Carlson, S.D., 1941–42 c. Teacher of biology, chemistry, and general science in the High School, 1947 to date	
14. Joseph J. Kelly, teacher of geography in the Junior High School	a. Graduated from State Teachers College with B.S. in Education in 1942 b. Attendance at the Preflight School of the U.S. Navy, held at the University of N. Car. during World War II c. Completed 43 semester-hours of graduate work and lacks only the completion of his thesis to receive M.A. from N.Y.U.	a. Supervision in the secondary school b. Cooperative laboratory in secondary-school curricula c. Tests and measurements d. Group guidance e. Technics of the interview f. Status and trends in secondary-school curricula g. Teaching the language arts h. Methods in the social studies in the elementary schools i. Methods of teaching arithmetic j. Science in the elementary schools	a. 22 weeks of teacher-training in the 6th grade of the Baker School in Haughton, 1941–43 b. Teacher of the Social Studies in Junior High School, in Bellwood, 1946 to date c. Staff officer in charge of recruit-training program of the U.S. Navy for the summers of 1949 and 1950	a. Bellwood Teachers' Association

(*continued on next page*)

Joseph J. Kelly (cont.)		k. Music in the elementary schools l. Arts and crafts in the elementary schools m. Physical-education methods in the elementary schools n. Methods in health education o. Psychology of learning p. World community — sociology q. Teaching the social studies in the secondary schools r. Geography of North America s. Geography of New England t. History of American civilization u. History of the United States (1865–97) v. Frontier in American history w. Seminars		

EXHIBIT 3 Rating of Candidates by Supt. Mitchell

1. Shane
2. Steinlieb
3. Reed
4. Landon
5. Farrell
6. Duffy
7. Greenwald
8. Kyser
9. Caldwell
10. Kelly

Roark
King
Swanson
Flanagan

23 *Hamilton Clerks*

SUPERINTENDENT Arthur Allen buzzed for his administrative assistant, Bert Wilson.

"Mr. Wilson," Allen said, "I have here a request from a newly formed clerical staff salary committee, which is headed by Miss Sharpe."

"I guess she'd be my choice to represent me if I were a clerk looking for a raise," Wilson answered. "She's not bashful about speaking her mind. She has a good head on her, from what I've seen."

"That's right," Allen replied. "She's asking for a boost for herself, too. The clerks were disappointed that the clerk personnel classification program initiated by City Hall recently did not provide grade readjustments for civil service positions or salary increases for School Department clerks.

"As I figure it out, our clerks are asking for an increase in the salary maximums. Principal Clerks want a raise from $3,465 to $4,200; the Senior Clerks want to raise their maximums from $3,150 to $3,700; the Junior Clerks want their maximums increased from $2,750 to $3,000 for the lower grade 'B' and to $3,200 for the higher grade 'A.' They want these adjustments of maximums to be retroactive to January 1, and in addition to have certain increments leading to the new maximums paid immediately.

"Of course, salaries here are set by the School Committee but the clerks want their jobs re-evaluated on the same basis as was done for personnel at City Hall. I'd like you to look into the situation and get all the information you can so that we can make some decision about the petition," Allen said.

He handed over the petition and other papers to Wilson (Exhibits 1, 2, and 3) and remarked that all the Principal Clerks were already at maximum as were four of the Junior Clerks and three of the Senior Clerks. Eleven out of eighteen employees were at maximum. The Secretary to the Superintendent, a Principal Clerk, had a $200 supplement over her $3,465 maximum for taking the minutes at school committee meetings. Allen had made a quick rough estimate, and it appeared to him that the suggested new salary schedule would cost about $6,000 more a year, if granted as requested.

Bert decided that the first thing to do was to see Miss Marshall, Director of Personnel for the city, to get details on the methods she used for job classification of city personnel.

At City Hall, Miss Marshall greeted Wilson with a wry grin.

"I thought somebody from the School Department would be here one of these days," she said. "Millicent Sharpe has been calling for information on job grades and salaries of city clerks for weeks. What's she up to now?"

Wilson showed her the petition.

"Well, Mr. Wilson, we don't like to get too much involved in school personnel affairs if we can help it. We've got plenty of our own headaches. I suppose we should have included all your people in our job study and made suggestions to the school committee, but the forms we sent over to be filled out were not returned to our office, and we felt we didn't know enough about the fine points of the positions without this information. On the other hand, since school clerks are civil service employees like ours, we don't feel that your classifications or salaries should be out of line with the other city employees. We're all working for the city you know."

Wilson tensed a little on hearing this old phrase. Hamilton's officialdom liked to think that the schools were just another city department. Sometimes, it seemed to educators in this city, the school committee had a hard time maintaining its independent prerogatives under the state law. Fixing the salaries and making appointments of school clerks was a responsibility of the school committee that the City Council had not challenged. Yet, city employees and nonprofessional school employees constantly compared notes on each other's salaries and conditions of employment.

Miss Marshall anticipated Bert's next question. "I'd like to show you how we handled job evaluation, Mr. Wilson. The principle we follow is that the *position* is evaluated rather than the person. This is up-to-date procedure in the personnel practices of many business houses all over the country."

Miss Marshall handed Wilson a copy of the Job Evaluation Guide (see pages 294–295).

Attached to the Job Evaluation Guide was a multi-page schedule of all municipal jobs. Based on the number of points required by each job, a grade number running from I through XI was assigned to each position. Starting rates and a series of increments leading to a maximum for each grade were also listed. Clerical jobs went from Grade I to Grade VIII. Above that, jobs were no longer considered clerical, but professional.

ALLOCATION OF POINTS TO GRADE

Point Spread	*Grade*
100–110	I
111–122	II
123–137	III
138–155	IV
156–177	V
178–205	VI
206–239	VII
240–280	VIII
281–330	IX
331–390	X
391–462	XI

"Well, Miss Marshall," Bert exclaimed after scanning the Guide, "this must have been a hard job at times when you had to make borderline decisions in assigning grades."

"Yes, the survey took us a number of months, but we think we have our positions properly graded. I will admit, though, that it is sometimes difficult to weigh each job as if we were weighing potatoes. There are intangibles in personality and job demands. That's why we worked out a system where each position, after being evaluated, results in a point total. We fit the point total into the proper grade.

"For example, a Principal Clerk was scored at 174 points placing her in Grade V. However, the Principal Clerk in the Department of Welfare, a very responsible position there, is Grade VII. The Secretary to the City Manager is Grade VI; the Secretary to the Mayor is Grade V."

JOB EVALUATION GUIDE, CITY OF HAMILTON

Job Factors	Definition of Factors and Degrees				
	1st Degree	*2nd Degree*	*3rd Degree*	*4th Degree*	*5th Degree*
1. *Education*	*15 Points*	*30 Points*	*45 Points*	*60 Points*	*75 Points*
Formal preparation required to perform the job. Need not be obtained in school, but assume school standards in this rating.	Grammar school education; not applicable to office jobs.	High school education; — ordinary clerical, typing jobs, etc.	2 yrs. college or high school plus vocational school.	College graduate; advanced office, engineering, major supervisory jobs, etc.	Graduate study leading to a master's degree.
2. *Prior Experience*	*4 Points*	*8 Points*	*16 Points*	*48 Points*	*75 Points*
Consider the actual experience on this type of job which is essential to proper performance.	Requires up to 3 months prior experience.	Requires more than 3, but not more than 6 months prior experience.	Requires more than 6 months, but not more than one year prior experience	Requires over one but not over 3 years prior experience.	Requires over 3 and up to 5 years prior experience.
3. *Training Time*	*3 Points*	*6 Points*	*12 Points*	*36 Points*	*60 Points*
Time required to learn the job well enough to perform it in a satisfactory manner. Assume necessary education and prior experience.	Training period of not more than 3 months.	Training period of 3 to 6 months.	Requires 7 to 12 months training.	Requires one year up to 3 years training.	Requires training over a period of more than 3 years.
4. *Initiative Ingenuity*	*12 Points*	*24 Points*	*36 Points*	*48 Points*	*60 Points*
Necessity for self-reliance, adaptability, and resourcefulness in meeting new and changing conditions; ability to develop new methods of procedure.	Requires ability to handle details with occasional minor decisions. Supervision available at all times.	Standard procedures available; decisions may be required to determine order of operations. Small amount of planning.	General procedures available. Decisions involving judgment and the planning and performance of somewhat difficult work. General supervision. Independent action and thinking almost daily.	Works within latitude of specific department policies. Decisions involve use of considerable judgment and planning and performance of unusual and very difficult work. May initiate new procedures. Supervision only as to results.	Outstanding ability to plan and devise new methods and meet new conditions with high degree of initiative, ingenuity and judgment. Plan complicated jobs involving own and others' work.
5. *Damage to Employer's Propert y*	*6 Points*	*12 Points*	*18 Points*	*24 Points*	*30 Points*
Responsibility for preventing monetary loss to property such as equipment or materials. ("Average probability," rather than the "maximum possibility.")	Probable loss would not exceed $10.	Probable loss would not exceed $100.	Probable loss would not exceed $250.	Probable loss would not exceed $500.	Probable loss might run into thousands of dollars.
6. *Employer's Funds*	*2 Points*	*5 Points*	*10 Points*	*16 Points*	*25 Points*
Extent to which job may require the handling of employer's funds, such as petty cash, employer's collections.	Requires only occasional handling of money. Up to $25.	Seldom requires handling of money. Up to $100.	Requires collections, etc. Up to $500.	Requires handling large sums; does not include disbursement of funds. Up to $1,000.	Requires handling large sums, control of bank account, disbursement of funds.
7. *Employer's Operations*	*6 Points*	*15 Points*	*28 Points*	*47 Points*	*75 Points*
Consider necessity for, and extent of, decision affecting money, economy of operations, service to other departments and associates, or to public. ("Average probability," rather than the "maximum possibility.")	Makes practically no decisions which have any effect on operations. Decisions concern only routine tasks in employee's own job.	Makes some minor decisions affecting routine procedures. Improper action would retard work of others.	Makes routine decisions which may be subject to review before being put into effect. Improper decisions would be of some consequence but not serious.	Interprets results of work of others and translates into course of action or policy in a specialized field of operation.	Makes major decisions at second level of management. Decisions would be of considerable magnitude affecting over-all operations.

8. *Public and Other Contacts*	*4 Points*	*9 Points*	*15 Points*	*22 Points*	*30 Points*
Consider extent and degree of importance of contacts with general public, organizations, and within organization. Consider both personal and telephone contacts.	Direct contact is negligible. Routine contacts with other employees.	Some contact with public through telephone or personal calls. Contacts within organization.	Contact with public through medium of letters, personal interviews, or telephone. Ability to deal effectively with all levels of people.	Considerable contact with other businesses and/or general public. Responsibility for creating and maintaining morale.	Has responsibility for building and maintaining good will for employer. Responsible for public relations.
9. *Safety and Welfare*	*4 Points*	*8 Points*	*12 Points*	*16 Points*	*20 Points*
Consider extent of responsibility for safety or welfare of other employees.	Little responsibility for safety or welfare of others.	Responsibility for 10 or fewer people where no physical hazards are present, but small degree of responsibility for welfare must be assumed.	Responsibility for safety and welfare of 15 to 25 persons employed on tasks of average hazardousness.	Must assume responsibility for safety and welfare of group of 50 or more people. Hazards present.	Responsibility for safety and welfare of large group of more than 150 people.
10. *Supervision of Others*	*15 Points*	*32 Points*	*53 Points*	*74 Points*	*100 Points*
Responsibility for effective use of men, materials, and equipment. Do not give credit unless job requires actual supervisory responsibilities. Training helpers or replacements or substitutes is not to be considered.	Very little responsibility except for own work. May exercise some minor supervisory functions, such as assignment of work, directing without authority.	Some delegated supervision. Controls flow of considerable work.	Supervises number of workers or department. Organizes and coordinates work of employees within the department. Requisitions new personnel, requests transfers and termination.	Responsible for supervision and coordination of a group of departments involving comparatively large groups of people. Accountable for cost control results and personnel.	Responsible for supervision of policies. May have control of training and coordinating work of large number of people. Devises and establishes methods and procedures.
11. *Mental or Visual Effort*	*12 Points*	*24 Points*	*36 Points*	*48 Points*	*60 Points*
Consider necessity for mental or visual effort such as concentration on difficult problems involving mental process or coordination of senses; or protracted visual attention to unusually complicated problems.	Occasional mental or visual attention required; but not exacting or concentrating in nature.	Requires close visual but limited mental attention.	Requires close mental and visual attention throughout major portion of work period.	Requires very close visual and/or mental attention for performance of exacting tasks. Requires either concentration to a very high degree or lesser degree continuously.	Requires very high degree of concentration. Close and continuous mental application is imperative. Strain is quite severe at times.
12. *Physical Demands*	*8 Points*	*16 Points*	*24 Points*	*32 Points*	*40 Points*
Physical requirements including work position, amount and degree of energy required, and continuity of effort should be considered.	Comfortable work position. Minimum of lifting and other physical exertion. Work varied: frequent steps are possible.	Some physical exertion, resulting in fatigue. Work somewhat varied and some steps are possible.	Frequent repetitive movements of mechanical nature. Small amount of lifting and/or carrying may be required.	Considerable work of a strenuous nature; or sustained effort due to physical position. Considerable walking, standing or stooping.	Work results in strain caused by continuous pressure of work. Work is constant and very tiring, or complicated because of constant interruption.
13. *Surroundings—Environment—Hazards*	*6 Points*	*12 Points*	*18 Points*	*24 Points*	*30 Points*
Consider surrounding physical conditions, such as presence of dust, dirt, noise, heat, cold and other detracting conditions. Also consider hazards such as possibility of bodily injury, or damage to health caused by work or surroundings.	Tasks pleasant, little noise and confusion; small chance of injury; very little clothes spoilage; air and light good.	Slight noise of office or other equipment. Tasks as a whole pleasant and agreeable. Slight chance of injury or damage to health. Little clothes spoilage.	Some dirt or discomfort caused by noise or vibration of office or other equipment. Slight chance of injury or damage to health. Average clothes spoilage.	Considerable dirt or discomfort and noise. Some chance of injury or damage to health. Relatively high clothes spoilage.	Noisy, monotonous, repetitive work. Chance of bodily injury or damage to health relatively great. High clothes spoilage.

Miss Marshall explained further that after evaluating all city jobs and setting maximum salaries, there was the problem of where to place the individuals on the salary scale for the given grade. When people were placed in the appropriate grade classification, it turned out that for most of them their old salary was somewhere in the middle of the proposed salary scale for that grade. Then, to provide raises for everyone, employees were generally moved up one step in the scale. In some instances, to provide incentive to long-time employees, people were moved up two and even three steps toward their maximums. For example, most senior clerk-typists had been earning a maximum salary of $2,600. When their jobs were evaluated they were placed in Grade IV with a maximum salary set at $2,950. Those who had been earning $2,600 were immediately moved up one step to $2,700; those who had been earning the maximum $2,600 for five years moved up two steps to $2,800; for ten years they were moved up three steps to $2,950.

Miss Marshall gave Wilson a number of City Hall forms he could use in the job study, and as they looked them over they discussed some of the positions in the school department. Miss Marshall said that she did not have an intimate knowledge of the clerical jobs in the school department. However, from what she did know about them, the salaries as then constituted for school clerks were not out of line with comparable salaries for equivalent positions on the city list. She mentioned again that all city employees and all school department employees were under state and city civil service regulations, and she thought it would not be wise to have any great discrepancies between City Hall clerical workers and those in the School Department.

Miss Marshall also indicated that she thought Miss Sharpe was too aggressive. She admitted that Miss Sharpe was extremely capable and had many years of service as chief payroll clerk of the School Department, but she also considered her too much of an agitator and so painfully blunt in interpersonal relationships that people actually dreaded to disagree with her. And Miss Marshall thought that $4,200 for a Principal Clerk in the School Department was too high.

As Wilson left City Hall, he started musing about the two "old-timers" on the School Department's clerical staff. He'd picked up enough information among the staff to give him some background on Miss Sharpe as well as Miss Fuller, the superintendent's secretary.

Miss Sharpe was in her fifties, vital, full of nervous energy, and thoroughly acquainted with her job as chief payroll clerk. She had served twenty-eight years in the School Department and remembered everybody and everything involved in operations at the central offices. Although she had a reputation for a sharp tongue and an insatiable curiosity, her efficiency went unchallenged. The girls in the office seemed to look to her for leadership, and thus she was selected as their salary committee chairman. She was respected for her sincerity and efficiency by the Administration, even though she was highly vocal — to the point of being annoying at times. Miss Sharpe had often stated that if she were in charge of the other girls in the central office and the principal's office, things would run much more smoothly.

But it was Miss Fuller, the superintendent's secretary who was the clerk-in-charge. She had been with the School Department for thirty-eight years and had been a friendly (and sometimes an unfriendly) rival of Miss Sharpe's for twenty-eight years. It was known that Miss Fuller considered Millicent Sharpe to be "too bossy." And it was not hard to observe that Millicent's bossiness and her loud voice were getting more and more on Miss Fuller's nerves. Miss Fuller was beginning to have difficulty in asserting herself and in gaining the complete and ungrudging cooperation of the lesser clerks. Perhaps she was feeling the weight of increased responsibility; perhaps she was apprehensive about her status as the senior clerk in the office. At any rate, Wilson noticed that she did not appear to fraternize with the other clerks. She had the reputation of being a mild sort of person, but of late she had become increasingly nervous and even her memory was not so clear as in the past. Nevertheless, her years of experience made her hard to replace, especially as stenographer for the school committee.

She, like Miss Sharpe, felt strongly that she was entitled to a salary increase, for she had long since reached her maximum. The school committee meetings, held twice a month, netted Miss Fuller $200 over her regular annual salary. And she was determined to stay $200 ahead of Millicent Sharpe, too.

Wilson returned to his office and prepared to dig into the problem. For about a week he pored over data from the State Department of Education, the Teachers Association, the National Education Association and other materials pertaining to salaries of noninstructional personnel. He compared the Hamilton scale with those of nearby school systems, with the state medians and the national medians. He secured figures from a local Chamber of Commerce survey which reflected the salaries paid stenographers, typists, bookkeepers, and other clerical help employed by business groups and industrial firms in the area.

Superintendent Allen had requested all clerks to write a job description of their respective positions so that when a job analysis was attempted the clerks' listings of duties could be used as a guide (provided that the job descriptions seemed realistic to the Superintendent).

All the charts, graphs, and other material on Bert's desk drew glances from the clerks as they passed. One day Miss Sharpe leaned over his shoulder and said, for all to hear, "Mr. Wilson, I don't know why you are fooling around with all those comparisons. All we want is to be compared with the other clerks who work for the city. I hope Dr. Allen isn't going to make this thing a big production. What are you trying to prove, anyway?"

Bert gave her a friendly but vague answer.

Finally, Bert Wilson felt that he had enough information to present to Superintendent Allen and Assistant Superintendents Hanson and Renson, and a meeting was arranged to work out a classification of each job in the School Department.

They met in one of the classrooms of the old annex building next to the high school. Wilson, Hanson, and Renson watched Allen draw on the blackboard a chart with each School Department position in the left-hand column and thirteen columns across representing the thirteen job factors used in the City Hall evaluation. Wilson had before him the City Hall outline of job factors and the degrees for each, and as the administrators discussed each position, agreement was reached on the number of points which should be assigned for each position.

It developed during the discussions that each administrator tended to rate highly the employee who worked for him personally. Wilson made his own ratings for purposes of comparison.

After the chart was completed, it appeared that there was agreement on the switchboard operator's job (which compared with Grade III on the city list with a total of 128 points for the job). But on the other positions there was quite a discrepancy between Wilson's ratings and the ratings made by the others. For example, Mr. Hanson graded his secretary (a junior clerk) on a par with Grade V on the city payroll, the grade which included the secretary to the Mayor. Wilson had graded her III as a clerk-typist-stenographer. Again, Superintendent Allen rated Miss Semple (the head stenographer) the equivalent of

Grade VIII on the city list, whereas Wilson made her Grade VII. Her current salary level would have put her in Grade VI. The administrators placed Miss Sharpe in Grade IX, the top clerical grade on the city list, whereas Wilson pegged her at Grade VIII. Miss Fuller was also evaluated in Grade IX, by both Wilson and the administrators. Bert wondered at the time if he was not being partial to her because he liked her personally. It seemed to him that the element of subjectivity was continually creeping in.

The final results of the evaluations showed that eleven out of fifteen positions evaluated would be placed in a higher job classification, if they were to be compared with City Hall grades, and thus the clerks would be entitled to an increase in salary maximums. When this fact became obvious, the administrators were somewhat surprised and a bit apprehensive.

At the next school committee meeting, Superintendent Allen told the members about the Clerical Committee's petition, but did not give details on the evaluation study just completed. The school committee appointed two of its members, Mr. Danvers and Mr. Arletta, as a temporary committee to discuss the petition, and arranged a luncheon meeting for the following week.

At the luncheon, Committeeman Danvers opened immediately by saying that he was concerned about the agitation for increased salaries for clerical personnel who would like to receive the same salaries as teachers. He didn't think that clerks who held no degrees should expect to compare in salaries with teachers. This tendency would increase, if the clerks' maximums were increased.

Danvers, looking directly at the superintendent, said, "I suppose that Miss Sharpe and Miss Fuller, being old-time employees, might get something of a raise. But I don't think these other people are in line for any kind of increase now. After all, they don't hold degrees, and they are only high school graduates. As far as I can see from what they are getting now, they are getting enough for the kinds of jobs they hold. We have been trying to increase salaries for the teachers. We owe a lot of money for school buildings. The custodians have been on our necks and will continue to be. God knows who we will hear from next. The custodians have an association, and that makes it tough."

Committeeman Arletta nodded in agreement.

It was then that Superintendent Allen mentioned that an analysis of duties had been made and meant the upgrading of many of the clerks. He thought that Miss Semple, in particular, should receive more recognition, as well as Miss Fuller and Miss Sharpe. He named a few other senior clerks in the same situation.

Arletta said it might seem to add up that way, but as a practical matter the School Department couldn't pay ordinary stenographer clerks more than the secretary to the City Manager was getting. The job evaluation did not impress him. A general raise for the clerks might start a chain reaction to change the schedules for teachers, supervisors, custodians, and cafeteria workers. Where would this sort of thing end?

There were a few moments of silence and then Committeeman Danvers said that he agreed that Miss Fuller and Miss Sharpe should probably receive $150 to $300 a year more and that Miss Fuller should continue to receive her $200 supplement for keeping up the school committee minutes.

Allen suspected that Danvers wanted to oil the "squeaky wheels," and thus pacify the leadership behind the salary requests. If Sharpe got her raise, the drive would "peter out."

The Superintendent told the committeemen that Miss Fuller was finding it very difficult to maintain her job as secretary in his office, keep up the school committee duties, and in addition act as chief clerk in the office. The recent friction between Miss Fuller and Miss Sharpe was not doing the general efficiency of the office much good. On the other hand, Miss Sharpe, in spite of her somewhat aggressive personality, would be able to run the central office better. The clerks seemed to like her regardless of her manner, because they felt she knew what she was doing all the time.

As the result of the luncheon meeting it was agreed that Miss Fuller would be relieved of the supervisory phase of her job. She was to be told that, in view of the increasing amount of school committee work, it was felt that the supervisory duties placed too much of a burden on her. And the hope was that this diplomatic phrasing would not offend Miss Fuller's feelings and would make her feel that she was being relieved rather than down-graded in favor of Miss Sharpe.

It was also agreed that Miss Sharpe and Miss Fuller should have their maximum salaries increased by $275. This would place them in the equivalent city grade of VII; but Miss Fuller would keep her $200 school committee supplement. The only other increase agreed on was for Miss Gorman, who had taken over the work of the chief bookkeeper in the latter's absence. She was voted $100 for assuming extra duties. Nothing more was said about new salary schedules for the other clerks.

Superintendent Allen gave considerable thought to the situation that evening. He had tried to be scientific and just in evaluating positions. According to the evaluations, higher maximums were in order for some of the other clerks. But the temporary committee obviously did not see the practicality of this procedure. In fact, they did not even want to talk much about it.

Of course, Wilson had given Allen other data which had to be taken into account. For instance, compared to all other systems of comparable size in the area, the Hamilton School Department clerical salary average would rank in the top 20 per cent. And median salaries for clerks in Hamilton were generally higher than median salaries for clerks in cities of like size in the whole nation. Also, school clerks in Hamilton received more money, on the average, than clerks employed by private enterprise in the city. And finally, without job evaluation procedures, the school clerks at junior and senior levels compared favorably with positions of similar nature on the city payroll. The more he thought about the problem, the more complicated it seemed to him.

Three days later, when the school committee met and the chairman introduced the topic of school clerks' salaries, Committeeman Danvers made the following statement:

"Gentlemen, Mr. Arletta and I met in temporary committee session the other day with Mr. Allen, Mr. Wilson, and Mr. Hanson and decided that on the basis of the information available Miss Fuller and Miss Sharpe should each receive increases of $275 in their maximums in $100 steps. Miss Gorman should also receive $100 for taking on extra duties while the chief bookkeeper has been away. No other clerical salary should be changed. Our clerks compare very favorably with clerks in other parts of the state and also with City Hall clerks."

Fred Chalmers, vice-chairman of the school committee, and a loyal supporter of Allen's, looked at the superintendent and said, "Well, Dr. Allen, do you have anything to add?"

Allen knew that the five members of the clerks' salary committee, headed by Miss Sharpe, were waiting outside to hear the results of the executive session. He knew that the salary problem would be with them for a long time, and that they could expect to hear soon from the custodians' association and the cafeteria workers as well. If these groups asked for and received more money, perhaps the clerks would get in on a general increase later. But how would the clerks react to being turned down while Miss Sharpe and Miss Fuller were "pacified." And would Miss Sharpe let it rest there, or would she think her increase was a bribe? Would Miss Fuller feel that giving up her supervisory duties was a reflection on her efficiency? Even though the clerks did not know of it as yet, the evaluation of positions had justified their petition. If they found out, what about morale?

There was enough money left in the salary account for the year to absorb the increased costs if granted. But there were also political factors to be weighed — and City Hall was critical of School Department "extravagance."

EXHIBIT 1

April 28, 1953

Dr. Arthur Allen
Secretary of School Committee

Dear Dr. Allen:

The clerical staff of the School Department would like to present a request for an increase in their salary schedule.

As you recall, it was first understood that our clerical staff would be considered in the salary schedule set up for other City employees, but inasmuch as we have not been listed along with them we have been obliged to submit our own request and have tried to obtain as much information as possible from City Hall and have attempted to set up a new salary schedule more or less in keeping with the new salary schedule adopted by the City Council.

Attached is a schedule showing the various grades and salary schedules of all the City clerical staff (exclusive of the School Department) and below, on the same page, the present salary schedule for the School Department clerical staff. You will note that the City has graded their clerks in seven different grades depending on the importance of the position which they hold.

We have also attached a proposed schedule for a new salary schedule for the School Department clerical staff and have based our figures on the following: Principal Clerks (in the Administrative Office) we have considered in the same category as City Hall clerks Grade VII, VIII, and IX and found that the average for the three groups gave us a figure close to $4,200. We have suggested a differential of $500 between the Principal and Senior Clerk maximums and a differential of $500 between the Senior and Junior Clerk "A" maximums, and a differential of $200 between Junior Clerk "A" and "B."

We would like to suggest further that there be a breakdown in the Junior Clerk title of "A" and "B" clerks. The "A" clerks would be the three persons in charge of the junior high school offices and the other Junior Clerks would be classified as "B."

We realize that this will require study by the School Committee and will be glad to assist in any way possible.

Very truly yours,

Clerical Staff Salary
Committee

EXHIBIT 2 Information Regarding Clerical Salaries in City of Hamilton

SALARY SCHEDULE OF CITY HALL CLERKS ACCORDING TO THE NEW SALARY PLAN ADOPTED FOR 1953

Grade		*Starting Rate 1st 6 mo.*	*Base Pay Beginning 2nd 6 mo.*	*1*	*2*	*3*	*4*	*5*
III	Clerk Clerk-Steno Clerk-Typist Telephone Operator	$2,100	$2,200	$2,300	$2,400	$2,500	$2,600	$2,750
IV	Acct. Machine Operator Senior Clerk Senior Clerk-Steno Senior Clerk-Typist	2,300	2,400	2,500	2,600	2,700	2,800	2,950
V	Principal Clerk Sec. to Mayor Sr.-Clerk-Steno } Welfare Sr.-Clerk Typist } Tel. Operator (Head)	2,500	2,600	2,700	2,800	2,900	3,050	3,200
VI	Prin. Admitting Clerk Sec. City Manager Sr.-Clerk Typist (Welfare)	2,700	2,800	2,900	3,000	3,150	3,300	3,450
VII	Asst. Treasurer Head Clerk Principal Clerk (Welfare)	3,000	3,100	3,200	3,300	3,450	3,600	3,750
VIII	Accountant Head Clerk (Pub. Works) Statistician	3,300	3,400	3,500	3,650	3,800	3,950	4,100
IX	Senior Accountant	3,750	3,900	4,050	4,200	4,350	4,500	4,650

PRESENT SALARY SCHEDULE OF SCHOOL DEPT. CLERKS

Jr. Clerk-Typist } Jr. Clerk-Steno }	$2,250	--	$2,350	$2,450	$2,550	$2,650	$2,750 Max.
Sr. Clerk-Steno	No established schedule						3,150 Max.
Principal Clerk-Steno							3,465 Max.
Principal Clerk-Steno and Sec. to Supt. of Schools							3,675 Max.

EXHIBIT 3 Suggested Salary Schedule for School Department Clerical Staff Effective January 1, 1953

	Present Rate or Minimum	*Steps*					
		1	*2*	*3*	*4*	*5*	*6*
Junior Clerk "B"	$2,250	$2,400	$2,550	$2,700	$2,850	$3,000	
" " "A"	2,450	2,600	2,750	2,900	3,050	3,200	
Senior Clerk	2,850	2,950	3,100	3,250	3,400	3,550	$3,700
Senior Clerks (special)	3,150	3,250	3,400	3,550	3,700		
Principal Clerks	3,465	3,600	3,750	3,900	4,050	4,200 *	

* With the proviso that Caroline Fuller retain the differential she has been allowed as Secretary to the Superintendent.

Step-ups as follows: Two step-ups for persons who have received no annual increment for a year or more. One step-up for others.

24 *Beaver Bowen*

GERALD BOWEN was appointed Superintendent of Schools in Oxford, New Jersey, in July, 1950. Bowen came to the Oxford schools from West Ashby, Pennsylvania, where he had been principal of the high school for fifteen years. At the time of his appointment to the Oxford Superintendency, Bowen was forty-nine years old. He had spent twenty-seven years in public education: three years as a junior high school English teacher; six years as an English teacher in the high school; three years as the head of the English department in the high school; and fifteen as principal of the high school.

All twenty-seven of his years were spent in Ashby, and for this reason the move to Oxford was a difficult decision. The Oxford salary however, was $8,500 — $2,000 more than Bowen was earning at West Ashby — and Bowen frankly confessed to a colleague: "This move isn't easy to make. But Gerry junior will be out of high school next year. Then Ann and Jimmy will be coming along. I guess I should be ashamed of myself as an educator. I mean making a choice on the money alone. But that's the way it is. I need the money."

Bowen also confided to Jack Whiting, the teacher who was to replace him as principal: "It's a funny thing, Jack. We're no more than thirty miles from Oxford. It's right outside of Trenton. Yet I know practically nothing about their set-up. I went through the plant in July, but it's hard to judge the nut by the shell. I'd have liked to see the place when the children and teachers were there, but of course I didn't interview for the job until late June. Their last man left rather suddenly, I guess."

"Well, I wouldn't worry about it," Whiting said. "Knowing the way you work, I'd say give you the plant and you'll do the rest."

Bowen said, "I'll give it the big try all right. I had to sweat my way through Penn State, and I don't want the children to do the same. I don't agree that working your way through school is best. I did it and I don't want my children to do it."

In mid-August Bowen moved his family to Oxford. Bowen busied himself settling his family in their new home in the "upper town," and he worked to clear his desk of the administrative routine which had piled up since the departure of his predecessor. He had little time to explore the community, but he did discover that Oxford, population 8,000, was a community of strong social and economic contrasts.

In the "upper town" the streets were wide and shaded by towering elms; the homes were tall and heavy and looked like battleships, each anchored in its private sea of grass. The "lower town" was a district of mean streets. In the center of the town were textile mills, lofts, bars, and tenements. A line of shacks, in which the migrant truck-garden "pickers" lived, straggled out of the center of the town to die out along the highway.

Bowen had one unnerving experience when he went to the local golf course as the guest of the Chairman of the School Committee, banker Frank Lynch. After coming into the clubhouse, Lynch introduced Bowen to some of the local men, saying only, "Gerry is new here," but not mentioning in the introduction that

Bowen was the new Superintendent of Schools. Bowen exchanged the usual pleasantries, after commenting on the wisdom of the rule that all shop and business talk was banned in the club bar. Mr. West, who ran a local market, asked Bowen if he had any children.

"Three," Bowen said, "all school age."

"Well, you better start hopping if you want them taken into Mount Pleasant." Mr. West explained: "Mount Pleasant is the only local private school worth a damn. That means they get jammed with applicants. But I know Storrs, the headmaster. You'll meet Fred Storrs at Rotary. If you want, we can see him about your youngsters."

Mr. Bowen thanked Mr. West, but said, "I plan to send them to public school, since I always have." Mr. West shrugged.

On the way home, Bowen mentioned the conversation to Lynch who apologized and said, "It's the custom not to mention a man's business up there, or that wouldn't have happened. But that school situation is something you might as well know about. Jeff West is no snob. He sends his children to Mount Pleasant, same as I do, because the public schools are just no good. That's why we brought you in at that salary. Maybe in a few years you can do something about it."

"I'd hope to do it sooner than that," Bowen said.

"Look," Lynch explained, "One-third of the pupils in the public schools are colored. Not that color alone means everything. But these people came up right out of the deep South in the days when a dollar a day was big money. They get more money now, but some of them haven't changed much. They live ten to a shack out on the highway and are bussed in to our schools. You'll see what I mean the first time you walk into a class."

Bowen made his first class visit on the third day of school, walking in on a high school class unannounced, and without formality, as he had done back in Ashby. There were two eight grade elementary schools and one four-year high school in Oxford, and Bowen decided to visit the high school first. He was appalled by his first class visit to the high school. He sat in on a fourth-year English class where the group was struggling with relative clauses — rather, two or three students and the teacher were struggling, the rest of the class had surrendered.

In the Modern Language class he discovered the students and the teacher speaking "parley voo" French, and making a joke out of it. Most of the group spoke no French at all. The advanced algebra class was doing first-year work in the multiplication of polynomials; the social studies teacher was having a quiz session — "Name the first four presidents of the United States, and one thing that they were famous for." The Latin class, supposedly a third-year group, was floundering through Gaul and having heavier going than the legions of Caesar had.

After the first class, Bowen checked the attendance and personnel records again. He knew that the high school enrollment was lower than in other towns of like size, and that the attendance of the children at Mount Pleasant school accounted for some of the difference. However, there also seemed to be a heavy drop-out among children of the poorer parents. Teacher personnel records were not so bad as he had estimated from the classroom performance. At least on paper, the teachers looked good, and many of them had advanced degrees. Bowen decided that before he did anything about the high school he would check the two elementary schools.

After spending a day at Rand, the elementary school he chose for his first visit, Bowen went home and went to bed and asked not to be called for dinner. He lay sleepless on his bed, listening to his family tiptoe past his door. By the time his wife joined him Bowen felt more like talking, but all he managed to say was: "Never in twenty-seven years have I seen anything like that. I'll tell you, Emma, in twenty-seven years I never saw anything so awful. Awful! Awful! Awful!"

The next day Bowen visited Bayliss, the other elementary school. The school was on double session; the first session was to begin at 9:00 A.M. Twenty minutes after the nine o'clock bell rang, the third-grade teacher was still caroling at the children: "All right now, boys and girls, let's settle down, please. Quiet, boys and girls. We have a visitor today. . . . Ralph, will you please get into your seat. Our Superintendent. . . . Norman! All right, boys and girls. Our Superintendent, Mr . . ."

The ruckus went on, but the teacher finally managed to introduce Mr. Bowen above the din. Mr. Bowen said, "How do you do, boys and girls," and while the teacher continued smiling sweetly, Bowen made for the door with the noise of the mob already swelling in volume behind him.

The other classes were little better. Teachers were "sassed" and interrupted, and one fifth-grader who was ordered to the office swore at the teacher before leaving the classroom. The sixth-grade teacher confessed frankly that she could do little with recitation periods. She said she assigned seat-work — checking fractions and division problems, copying names from the geography atlas, and looking up definitions in the dictionary. It seemed to Bowen that no more than one-third of the students did the seat-work. The desks were carved with all manner of initials and messages. Mr. Bowen ordered the building janitor to efface three obscene jingles from the walls of the boys' room.

Playgrounds and corridors seemed dangerous places to Bowen. The older pupils bulled their way through lines of younger children. On the playground all the soccer balls and footballs were captured by the largest boys. It was dog-eat-dog in that school. Bowen decided that his first necessity was a good strong man to supervise the corridors and playground. The entire staff at the school were women, most of them married women who lived in the town. Again on the record they seemed well educated, and socially they seemed personable.

Scholastic standards were low, and in every grade up through the sixth there was a group of children struggling through the primer and first-grade readers. The principal told Bowen that she estimated that one-third or more of the pupils were either discipline problems or mentally retarded.

Bowen's next step was to interview all three school principals. He discovered that the high school principal, Mr. Wilkerson, had been on his present job two years. He had a total of six years' teaching experience. Miss Watson, the principal of the second elementary school — Bayliss, was fifty-eight, and a lifelong resident of Oxford. She lived with her bachelor brother, Brewster Watson, who was owner of several farm properties and a farm equipment agency, and a director of the largest bank in the community. Mrs. Hilferty, the principal of Rand, sent word that she could not attend the meeting due to "illness in her family." Later Bowen discovered that this would be a constant excuse, since Mrs. Hilferty's son was blind. She hurried home from school each day to relieve the woman who stayed with the child in the morning. "That's her whole life," Miss Watson said. "It's marvelous the job of training she's done with that boy. He's smart as a whip."

Bowen also learned that Miss Watson and Mrs. Hilferty were lifelong friends, and that Miss Watson's brother had interceded strongly in favor of Mrs. Hilferty when the appointment had been under consideration by the school board. His argument had been, "Here's a chance to do a real work of charity. God knows the gallant little lady needs it." Mr. Lynch reported this to Mr. Bowen, and said that the school board had been deeply impressed by Watson's plea. "The Watsons are great people," Mr. Lynch explained. "Brewster Watson, Junior, is just like his father. Old Brewster was president of the school board for years. He gave the money for the high school gym and auditorium, and the town library. Great people!"

Bowen tried to be mindful of all these things as he talked to Mr. Wilkerson and Miss Watson. He said, "I know some of those children are beyond the point where we can help them. We may be able to get some of them into institutions specially equipped to handle them. But the general level has to be brought up." When asked how he proposed to separate the children, Bowen suggested an I.Q. test. Miss Watson winced. Bowen also said that discipline would have to be tightened up. "I almost favor corporal punishment in some of those cases," he said. "If they still don't respond — expel them! If they are out a certain number of days we can have the parents fined. These parents have to take responsibility for their children. I'm not having the whole school dragged down by a few."

"If it only were a few," Miss Watson said softly.

Bowen also said, "In some cases this automatic promotion seems dead wrong. I observed a sixth-grade teacher who had to teach reading from every level book, from primer to seventh-grade readers. No wonder things are confused. Also look at it from the point of view of the pupils. They know they can just sit there and get promoted, whether they work or not, behave or cause trouble."

"Well," returned Miss Watson, "if we don't have social promotions we'll have an awful jam in the first grade."

Mr. Bowen looked at her to see if she were joking, but she seemed to be serious. He said, "Perhaps you have some suggestions or comments. I don't want to take all the time here."

Miss Watson said: "I think elementary school children need sympathy and kindness from their teachers. This is something I require of all my teachers. I feel certain that children improve with teachers who are gentle."

"Well, I don't know," Mr. Bowen responded. "I couldn't see any particular improvement in those children I observed. I'm telling you honestly that I never saw schools which were lower academically."

"Well, perhaps so," Miss Watson agreed. She seemed never to lose her temper or raise her voice. "But we must remember, mustn't we, that there are extenuating circumstances. Our high school doesn't get the students with the best potential. *Their* parents have sent them to Mount Pleasant. We get only the residue. These children who do stay will never go on to college, nor is it even likely that they will do highly skilled work. I do feel that it's better to have those unfortunate children stay in school as long as possible. I know you'll agree with me," she smiled at Mr. Bowen, "that they will learn a little."

Mr. Wilkerson said nothing, but nodded agreement to Miss Watson.

"And we must remember, mustn't we," Miss Watson continued, "that a failure at this point would be serious for them. Some of them would have difficulty getting any sort of work. They would simply roam the streets . . ."

Mr. Bowen said nothing.

"There is also the fact," Miss Watson continued softly, "that more than a quarter of our elementary children will never attend high school at all. As for corporal punishment, I'm sure you didn't mean that, Mr. Bowen, for it is forbidden by state law. Why, a teacher could be arrested for even slapping a pupil! And I for one would have no sympathy with that teacher." Miss Watson flushed. "Why, if one of my teachers should even think of touching a pupil . . ."

Miss Watson also commented on the "special school" problem. She said that almost all of the "slow children" would be colored children from migrant families. "If these children were sent to special, segregated schools, you could not convince their parents that it was because of low ability. Especially not with a score from an I.Q. test. The parents would feel that it was their color and their poverty which brought the transfer. Mr. Bowen, that would set off a racial bombshell in this community!"

"Well, could they be given extra work?" Mr. Bowen asked.

"Usually no. Usually they are bus pupils from out on the flats. They can't be kept after."

There seemed very little else for Bowen to say. He chatted pleasantly with Mr. Wilkerson and Miss Watson for a while, and then they left the office.

During the following weeks Mr. Bowen worked long hours at his job. He tried to be at the elementary schools, where he often entered noisy classes and brought them to order. He interviewed behavior cases in the principal's office and was firm but nonviolent with the children. He took a special class of big boys and met with them twice a week for extra reading sessions. He requested that the board hire a male teacher for each elementary school for the following year, but he was told that a vacancy was not likely. Apparently the staff, made up mostly of married women native to the town, had very little turnover.

Bowen tried to bring his case before the substantial citizens of the town, but he got little encouragement. Most of them shrugged and said, "Well that's the way it is. No sense stirring up trouble for the town. Race riots, that sort of thing." Nobody came right out with it, but Bowen could sense the attitude that "*our* children are taken care of at Mount Pleasant."

Bowen also tried to meet some of the Negro parents. He talked several times in the Negro church to a parents' group. He found his audience friendly, but listless. He never brought up the matter of a "special school" until his final private talk with the pastor. The pastor, an extremely gentle man, reacted rather violently when Bowen pressed him privately on the matter.

The pastor said, "I'd like you to know that that was what happened to your predecessor. He tried to stir up racial trouble. Wanted to segregate our kids from the others. No, sir. I don't favor that at all. No, sir." Bowen was not invited back to the church.

Bowen continued to work at his job, but around Christmas time he was startled when he was not invited to speak at the annual town Christmas-tree-lighting. He had heard that it was traditional for the superintendent to speak. At the same time he began to get hints from Lynch and West that, "Perhaps you ought to slow down a bit, Gerry. Don't try everything at once."

In January, while working in his study, Bowen heard the piping voice of his son Jim calling from the kitchen, "Mama, why do they call daddy 'Beaver'?"

"I didn't know anyone did," Mrs. Bowen answered.

"Oh, they all do," Jimmie said. "The kids, their mothers and fathers, and the teachers. 'Beaver' Bowen! That's what they call him."

Mr. Bowen put down his pencil and stared at the wall.

25 Test Evidence

One August afternoon Mrs. Arnot entered the office which she occupied as a part-time psychologist for a small pediatric hospital in a large Northern city. Children were referred to the hospital's Psychiatric Service and Child Guidance Clinic for evaluation, and a complete "team" of psychiatrist, two social workers, two psychologists, two nursery school teachers, and secretary, constituted the staff.

The age-range served was from infancy through fifteen years of age, and the cases were of both in-patient and ambulatory variety. Many of the cases were screened before reaching the social worker and the psychiatrist; these were handled by the psychologists and the teachers. The special task of the psychologist was to observe the child, to do psychometric testing as indicated, and to talk briefly with the parents. Sometimes further visits were needed and play therapy was instituted for diagnostic purposes. The clinic was set up principally for diagnosis and short-term therapy.

The teachers were in charge of the playroom, which provided recreation space for the recuperating in-patients, and also a setting for the observation of special psychiatric patients. An observation (one-way vision) mirror was available for this latter purpose. The clinic worked actively with doctors, hospitals, schools, and welfare agencies.

On her desk this August afternoon Mrs. Arnot found some newly typed reports of tests she had administered during the past week. Sitting down to proofread them, she saw that the first in the pile was the report of the ambulatory visit of Teddy Snow, a boy of five years and three months. Teddy had been referred by a resident in the Medical Clinic who had felt that the child needed a psychological examination. Mrs. Arnot read her own words:

> Teddy is very tall and muscular for his age — a blond, wide-eyed, good-looking boy who appears at least seven years old, yet hangs onto his mother and shakes his head "no" at the examiner's request that he come into her office. The mother remains present, therefore, throughout the test. Teddy sits limply on the edge of the chair, gazes out the window, shakes "no" to each demand, but does comply when asked again more affirmatively. He accidentally knocks test objects off the desk and laughs when his mother and the examiner pick them up. Smiles broadly, but as though embarrassed, when examiner tries to make the test "fun." When not smiling, his expression is vague and seemingly preoccupied. He does drawings and puzzles quite willingly, but refuses most verbal tasks, including vocabulary. He often appears to be teasing as he refuses to obey and the mothers begs him "not to be stubborn." She sits behind him, appearing anxious, unhappy, and childlike herself. She states her main worry to be his language, which is notably babyish and sparse. He attends a weekly speech clinic but never went to nursery school. He is healthy and eats and sleeps well, but sometimes he "hurts people" — slapping or pinching or running into them with his bike (his favorite toy.) He always says he is sorry afterwards. The mother is very eager for a definite "diagnosis" but agrees to

wait until her doctor has the report. She says sadly and in a whisper that the neighbors do not know that he is adopted; that Teddy does know but doesn't seem to understand the fact at all. He plays only with girls on his block, one aged six and one aged three — the boys are all older. She is very eager for him to begin kindergarten in the fall, as it is such a "nice, new, modern school building," but she states that he is too much tied to her. He will never leave her at all: "It's as though he's afraid we'll leave him altogether." He's just school age (entering age is 4–9) but she wonders how he will get on there. Examiner asks how old he was at the time of adoption, and tears come to the mother's eyes as she answers ten weeks.

All test scores on Teddy are indefinite and inconclusive, and there is a wide range, due to his negativism and many refusals. On the Stanford-Binet (L) his minimal I.Q. is at a Dull Normal level — 81; Mental Age 4–3; possible M.A. up to 4–7 if certain marginal failures were passed. His base is 3 years and highest successes at 6 years. On the Merrill-Palmer Performance Scale (all verbal tests omitted) he achieves a minimal level of I.Q. 90 with a potential range up to above average (110) if only the completed items are counted. He draws a house, a tree, and a man on request — pale, feeble, infantile, almost unrecognizable, on the top of each page given him. He refuses to talk about his drawings. He uses his left hand, but mother says he can use both. "Will you like to go to school, Teddy?" asks the examiner. He shakes "no," smiles momentarily, and then looks frightened.

This is certainly a puzzling enough picture to warrant further observation. We suggest another visit in early September when the psychiatrist can observe him in the playroom and interview the mother more completely. Teddy enjoyed painting at the easel in the playroom today, paying little attention to the other children, and seemed to acquiesce to return for another visit without his mother present. The clinic will notify Mrs. Snow as to when his appointment will be, should she wish to come.

E. B. Arnot
Clinical Psychologist

One copy of this report was to be sent to the referring resident. He in turn would contact the Snows' private physician, who sent the child to the clinic originally. Mrs. Arnot brought the report to the resident and suggested that he incorporate its main points into his medical report. He said that he intended to send the report attached to the completely negative report of his physical examination. He had no reason to see the boy again, and felt that this was "purely a case of adoptive parents who have to recognize the fact that their boy is dull." The reports were sent.

About ten days later, Mrs. Arnot received a phone call from Dr. Dawson, the Snows' pediatrician. He thanked her for her report, and told her he had showed it to Mrs. Snow, who, however, had refused the suggested visit to the psychiatrist. She said that there was nothing "crazy" about Teddy, that all she needed to know was whether he could begin school that fall. She said she would gladly return to the clinic for more observation and testing if they would give her some definite statement about the child. She said she was reluctant to go to the school herself because she feared that the adoption story would "get out." She had made it a point, as stated earlier, not to "let it get around the neighborhood." Mrs. Arnot made the appointment for a morning in the second week of September and thanked Dr. Dawson for his interest.

As she hung up the phone, Mrs. Arnot thought back to the times when the clinic staff had debated the advisability of sending I.Q. reports to outside doctors. She had proposed then that only very limited reports be sent. The psychiatrist, on the other hand, felt that it was the duty of the clinic to send all findings to the doctor. As she continued her work, she found herself glad that there was almost a month before the Snows would be in again, and she made a note in her appointment book for that week to remind herself to check on all the educational facilities in the town where they lived. She wondered how useful her report would be to a schoolman who had to decide whether Teddy Snow should be sent to a class for special help, or admitted directly to regular classes. She wondered further what the school department psychologist, Dr. Rand, would suggest, and what would be the reaction of an elementary school principal to the report on Teddy Snow.

26 Long Beach

Mr. Douglas Newcomb, Superintendent of Schools in Long Beach, California, wrote as follows to an educational consultant for a publishing firm, on August 24, 1952.

"It seemed quite timely for us to have the Board of Education give consideration to an instructional policy that would guide our teachers. I submitted to the Board a bulletin entitled *An Instructional Policy on Controversial Issues.*[1]

"As soon as this statement hit the reporters, it apparently made newspaper copy — in fact, there was some editorial comment. The *Long Beach Press-Telegram,* which is the evening paper, suggested some need for clarification, but this need was expressed in a very fine spirit, I thought. Mr. George Weeks, a member of the editorial staff, wrote the editorial; and as he mentioned that the statement needed clarification, I suggested that he clarify it for us. His letter to me is as follows:

> In regard to the statement of instructional policy on controversial issues, I would suggest only minor changes in the first paragraph. It might be more acceptable if changed to read something like the following:
>
> Controversial issues arise from conflicts in the interests, beliefs, or affiliations of large groups, either in this country or in the world at large. Controversial issues are important proposals or policies concerning which our citizens hold different points of view, or on which the prevailing American view differs from those of some other nations. Controversial issues may be fostered by political parties, by management and labor, by city and country, and by other large groups inside or outside the United States.
>
> This particular wording can be improved upon, but I think it reaches the point mentioned in our conversation and in the editorial.

"As a whole, the statement seems to me to be a fine one. As you probably know, there has been a great controversy in the Los Angeles School District about United Nations and particularly UNESCO. This apparently has spilled over into this district because of television and newspaper copy. The result is that we had about a dozen people at our board meeting last Monday who would eliminate any studying whatever of United Nations and UNESCO — in fact, when they were asked where a youngster would learn about the United Nations, one person mentioned they should learn it in the home the same as they learn about religion. A pretty high plane, don't you think?

"We have regarded the United Nations and UNESCO as in a controversial area and will continue to do so until instructed otherwise. As to what will come of the entire matter, no one at this time can foretell. However, we don't anticipate that the Board of Education will want to give up much ground, because they believe as you and I do that democracy is built on understanding."

---

[1] See Appendix, page 315.

EXHIBIT 1 From the *Long Beach Independent Press-Telegram*, August 20, 1952

Should Our Schools Study UN?

Here's the Question?

Should principles of the United Nations be studied in our schools?

Last week a group of citizens shouted NO at a Long Beach Board of Education meeting.

The attack followed School Superintendent Douglas A. Newcomb's statement of school policy providing for study of controversial interests.

Because crucial issues are at stake, The Sunday Independent Press-Telegram on this page presents a written debate on the question.

Taking the affirmative is Edwin Castagna, city librarian, who emphasizes that he is writing as a citizen rather than an official.

Taking the negative is Miss Fanchon Battelle of 330 W. Willow, who told the board of education meeting she represented the Friday Discussion Club, the Southern California Republican Women and the Liberty Belles.

In a third statement, Superintendent Newcomb gives his position.

Foe Attacks UNESCO as

A bill is before Congress to withdraw from the U. N.

The Senate Subcommittee on Internal Security held hearings on this subject. Their finding was that UNESCO is subversive. Sen. William Benton, a UNESCO representative,

"Why Not Teach Facts?"

By EDWIN CASTAGNA

"To correct the evils, great and small, which spring from want of sympathy and from positive enmity among strangers, as nations or as individuals, is one of the highest functions of civilization." With many other Americans I subscribe to these words of Abraham Lincoln and I believe they relate directly to the controversy raised by the policy in teaching adopted by the Long Beach Board of Education.

As a citizen I ask why anyone should object to having facts about the United Nations taught in our schools. With bipartisan agreement, the United States was one of the leaders in the founding of the U. N. Our country is an official U. N. member and active in U. N. specialized agencies. With 60 members the U. N. is certainly the biggest organization working for international peace and understanding. To ignore its existence in courses in current

leaving out the facts about gravitation.

How can it possibly hurt any of us for students to learn that there is a world-wide program to teach hundreds of millions of people to read and write?

What danger is likely to result if students hear about a global plan to help many peoples toward the independence and freedom we are so proud of?

These are a few of the programs in which the U. N. is cooperating.

No one pretends the U. N. is perfect. What human institution is? The organization established for peace has heard international insults hurled across its conference tables. There is a war in Korea that the U. N. didn't prevent. The world's problems are many, overwhelming and often disheartening. No one knows how many of them the U. N. will be able to solve.

Subversive

By FANCHON BATTELLE

My objections to UNESCO in the public schools are the same as those of the American Legion, Veterans of Foreign Wars, Knights of Columbus, Sons of the American Revolution, Daughters of the American Revolution, Native Sons of the Golden West, Southern California Republican Women, Liberty Belles, the Junior League of Los Angeles, and members of Congress and citizens who have investigated the aims of UNESCO propagandists.

UNESCO is a typically totalitarian effort to control students' thinking by presenting its propaganda for world government in a favorable light and withholding information about its true aims to eliminate American sovereignty, freedom of speech, press and private property; take an American citizen to a foreign land for trial, and inter-marry the faces — a familiar pattern of communism.

To answer the claim of school board spokesmen that the Long Beach schools are studying U. N. rather than UNESCO, my contention is that the two cannot be separated, as UN ESCO is a specialized agency of the U. N. ning of a long process of breaking down the walls of national sovereignty. In this process UNESCO can be—and indeed must be — the pioneer."

Congress recognized the diabolical nature of UNESCO by enacting the following law: "None of the funds appropriated into law shall be used for the promotion, direct or indirect, of the principle or doctrine of One World government or One World citizenship."

"The United Nations, a Teacher's Handbook" published by the Long Beach Public Schools for the use of our teachers in the classroom, says: "The world-minded American knows that unlimited national sovereignty is a threat to world peace." There is not one word in this book to counteract this corrupt propaganda.

The appendix of this Long Beach "Teacher's Handbook" lists numerous un-American UNESCO books and moving pictures in our local schools, among which are "How the United Nations Works" by Tom Galt and "In Henry's Backyard; the Races of Mankind" by Ruth Benedict and Gene Wetfish, and the moving pictures "Brotherhood of Man" and "Quest for Tomorrow."

"The Races of Mankind" was considered so communistic and disruptive of harmonious race relations that the War Department barred it from the use of soldiers taking orientation

would be like trying to teach the physical sciences while

---

courses in training for World War II. But the Board of Education has permitted it in our junior high school libraries, call No. 572, according to the "Teacher's Handbook." It is also in the Children's Department of the Public Library.

The moving picture "Brotherhood of Man," in our schools, is based on this vile book "The Races of Mankind."

The State Education Code provides: "No bulletin, circular, or other publication of any character whose purpose is to spread propaganda . . . shall be distributed or suffered to be distributed or shown to the pupils of any public school, on the school premises during school hours or within one hour before the time of opening or within one hour after the time of closing of the school."

This un-American propaganda is being distributed to the school children of Long Beach by the Board of Education in violation of the law.

The hysterical scream of Communist-minded UNESCO-World Government advocates that freedom of education is under attack is easily answered: Good people who love their children, home and country demand freedom of the minds of children from subversive indoctrination.

UNESCO is founded in infamy and must be stopped now.

founded so our country would always have an oncoming generation of well-informed young people, able to carry on the best traditions of our American heritage. This American heritage includes a persistent interest in ideas from all over the world, and a continuing belief in the brotherhood of man.

The Declaration of Independence and the Constitution are the pride of our people. They are goals toward which less fortunate people strive. The ideas in these great documents of freedom came from many "foreign" places. Suppose our founding fathers had not had access to information on what was going on in the world in their time?

The UNESCO charter states: "Since wars begin in the minds of men, it is in the minds of men that the defense of peace must be constructed." I believe this statement. Where better to begin constructing the defense of peace than in the minds of the boys and girls who would suffer the agonies of another war? How can we do more to assure freedom from war than by organizing for peace?

I have great confidence in Long Beach teachers, administrators and members of the Board of Education. This confidence is based on knowledge of their ability, skill and devotion to the public interest.

EXHIBIT 2 From the *Long Beach Independent Press-Telegram*, August 20, 1952

"Youth Must Understand Menace of Communism"

By DOUGLAS NEWCOMB

Democracy is not a controversial subject in America. There is only one side to democracy in the Long Beach public schools.

The public schools of this country must teach and teach well the basic principles of democracy. They must teach our youth to understand our rich heritage and must pass on to them our cherished freedoms. The public schools must do all within their power to develop in our youth a loyalty and a passion for democracy. Now, more than ever before, we must guard against any spoken or written word which will undermine our American democracy.

In America there is only one side to communism. We don't believe in it. It is not a controversial subject.

We believe, however, that our youth must understand the menace and the evils of communism. They must know, for example, that freedom of the press, religion, and speech can exist in a democracy—but never in a communistic society. We further believe that consideration of communism should be limited to mature students.

Communism, however, is not controversial in America any more than arithmetic, reading, spelling, and English. In fact, almost all of the school curriculum is not controversial.

There is a small part of the curriculum, probably less than 5 per cent, which is controversial. This part includes subjects about which large groups of our citizens disagree. There is, for example, a difference of opinion in America about such subjects as the Marshall Plan, Taft-Hartley law, labor, management, and the United Nations.

The policy currently being considered by the Board of Education states, in substance, that controversial subjects like the United Nations shall be "studied" but not "taught." We teach our rich heritage of democracy; we teach the evils of communism. These subjects are not controversial.

On the other hand, we "study" controversial subjects. By "study" we mean simply that the facts and arguments for and against a controversial subject must both be presented.

Under the proposed policy the teacher would continue to be required to approach controversial issues in the classroom in an unprejudiced manner. Further, he would refrain from using his classroom privileges and prestige to promote his own points of view. Good teaching of subjects in which there are controversial issues requires great skill. Therefore, teachers of superior ability should be assigned to these classes.

The proposed policy recognizes the United Nations as a controversial subject. Because it is controversial, facts and points of view on both sides must be presented.

APPENDIX Controversial Issues of the Educational Platform*

Controversial issues arise from the conflicts in the cherished interest, beliefs, or affiliation of large groups of our citizens. Controversial issues are important proposals or policies concerning which our citizens hold different points of view. Controversial issues are those on which conflicting views are held by political parties, by management and labor, by city and country, and by large groups of our people who disagree on the proposed solutions to important problems.

The American heritage and our established traditions are not controversial. Most of the school curriculum is composed of established truths and accepted values, but it also includes many controversial issues. Gradual social change is inevitable, and the public schools include the study of some important unsolved problems which involve controversial issues. These are appropriately studied insofar as the maturity of pupils and the means available permit. Only through the study of such issues (political, economic, social) does youth develop certain abilities needed for citizenship in our democracy.

The schools do not *teach* controversial issues, but rather provide opportunities for their *study*. The schools *teach* the American heritage (our established truths and accepted values) and, in doing this, provide opportunities for pupils to *study* controversial issues under competent guidance. For example, the schools provide opportunities for pupils to *study* other forms of government, such as communism and fascism, in order to *teach* pupils the values of American democracy. On all grade levels, the schools provide opportunities for pupils, according to their maturity, to analyze current problems, gather and organize pertinent facts, discriminate between fact and opinion, detect propaganda, identify prejudice, draw intelligent conclusions, respect the opinions of others, and accept the principles of majority rule and the rights of minorities.

Free discussion of controversial issues is the heart of the democratic process. Freedom of speech and free access to information are among our most cherished traditions. Most pupils in the senior high school are mature enough to study the significant controversial issues facing our citizens. It is the responsibility of the schools to make provision for this study.

For the public schools, policy on controversial issues is defined in terms of the rights of pupils rather than in terms of the rights of teachers. In the study of controversial issues in the public schools, the pupil has four rights to be recognized:

(a) The right to study any controversial issue which has political, economic, or social significance and concerning which (at this level) he should begin to have an opinion.
(b) The right to have free access to all relevant information, including the materials that circulate freely in the community.
(c) The right to study under competent instruction in an atmosphere free from bias and prejudice.
(d) The right to form and express his own opinion on controversial issues without thereby jeopardizing his relations with his teacher or the school.

* An Educational Platform for the Public Schools, 1952. (Developed and endorsed by school superintendents of cities in the United States and Canada with population over 200,000.) Used with permission.

The study of controversial issues is objective and scholarly, with a minimum emphasis on opinion. The teacher approaches controversial issues in the classroom in an impartial and unprejudiced manner, and must refrain from using his classroom privileges and prestige to promote a partisan point of view. Good teaching of subjects containing controversial issues requires more skill than most other kinds of teaching and, so far as possible, only teachers of superior ability are assigned subjects in which a large body of the material involves controversy.

Instructional policy on controversial issues should be defined by constituted authority in order to protect teachers and school administrators from unwarranted attack by pressure groups, and to insure youth a well-balanced preparation for American citizenship.

27 Dr. Allen Kratt

HARVARD UNIVERSITY

GRADUATE SCHOOL OF EDUCATION

CENTER FOR FIELD STUDIES

SPAULDING HOUSE, 20 OXFORD STREET
CAMBRIDGE 38, MASSACHUSETTS

October 8, 1952

RECEIVED
School of Education
OCT. 14, 1952

Dr. Allen Kratt
Superintendent of Schools
Sprucefield

Dear Dr. Kratt:

Since our recent telephone conversation regarding an interview with respect to administrative problems as you perceive them in your school system, I find that it will be possible to schedule the interview for either of the days you suggested. Thomas Andrews, one of our field workers, will be pleased to meet with you either Thursday or Friday, October 16 or 17 at whatever time is most convenient for you.

Most sincerely,

Doris Valentine

Doris Valentine

DV/lt

Andrews
I can see
Friday
2 p.m.
Kratt

The interviewer met Dr. Allen Kratt in his office in the new wing of the Sprucefield High School. He told Dr. Kratt who he was and said that he was interested in hearing what problems and experience Dr. Kratt was finding as head of the Sprucefield-Lyonville Union School District.

His reply, which took sixty-five minutes, was uninterrupted by the interviewer. This is what Dr. Kratt said:

"I don't know of anything going on around here of special interest to you. Sprucefield is a town that wants better schools, and as you can see, we are now building an eight-room wing onto the high school. It's just about finished and we're holding classes in it already — some elementary school grades. We had to move in early, about five months early. You see we have the usual problem. Four hundred seventy-seven in the first four grades; in fact, more kids in any one elementary grade than in any two grades in high school. We used $1,500 getting these rooms ready for occupancy early, and there was nothing in the budget for this. So I went to the Finance Committee of the town and got them to give me the money, rather than necessitating a special school town meeting. I just tell you this by way of showing that the town is behind us.

"Sprucefield's people are young, forward-looking, most of whom have come to town since 1940. The schools were in terrible shape. Interested citizens ran for the School Committee in order to get at the situation, but they found out that you can't do much until you control the money of the town, so they worked their way up on other committees until they got to the Finance Committee which controls the school budget. They wanted control and went out and got it.

"But the other town in this union school district, Lyonville, is backward, ingrown, and unshakeable. Nobody wants progress there. The schools are fine in their minds. There are a few new families in the town — about fifty new houses a year — but their interests are not in the town. The old guard still runs the town. Any committee in that town goes along fine until they come up against the Finance Committee. It stops them dead in their tracks. They have their own schools, of course, and I am the superintendent of both towns. Sprucefield is a fine town to deal with, but Lyonville is different. I need to be two different kinds of people in this job, one kind here and another type over there. This is very hard to do. I think one town is enough — I don't care — there are other school systems very near here, Mount George, for example, which are smaller even than Sprucefield; and they have only one superintendent, but these union districts are here for a while, so there you are. I don't really care, it's just a job — the schools don't belong to me. I think there is too much ownership of schools by superintendents these days. I'm here to spend the money the best we can, get the most out of it.

"I came here a year ago this last fall from Braddock, which is a larger system. I was assistant superintendent there. I think one of the toughest problems here is communication, whether you should set up some system for it, or whether you should just let it go, or what. There are eighty teachers in this union district. Let me tell you a story in this connection.

"This fall a teacher came to my office. School had been going a week or two. She said she had a son in the seventh grade last year who had failed two subjects and was therefore repeating the seventh grade. He had passed arithmetic with a very high grade, and she was wondering if the boy could take eighth-grade arithmetic while in the seventh grade, that is, if scheduling permitted it. The teacher confided that she would not have said anything to me a year ago had this come up, but now she feels she can talk to me. This I think is an indication of some progress in communications around here. One-third of our faculty is new every year and it's hard to get teachers interested in anything except their own department; they don't want to see the whole school picture.

"The middle of last year I did something in a very arbitrary fashion. I created a vacuum in the curriculum. I didn't consult a soul, just sent out word that there would be no more special handwriting classes with the specialists coming in once a week to give lessons and check on progress. I just fired the guy. This company he works for has some deal, I tell you. They go around with handwriting booklets and specialists and instruct in school systems around here. I didn't see that it amounted to a thing. There was better use for that money for specialists in other lines than in handwriting. Nobody said a word about the situation one way or another. Very mysterious.

"Later that year the teachers asked for a raise in salary. I didn't want to carry it to the School Committee without some justification for the increase, so I proposed to the School Committee that the teachers get their $300 increase and that the school year include five extra days for professional meetings of the teachers of the system. Everybody thought it was a good plan. I remember one worker in town telling me he was in favor of it since he had to work year round and he didn't see why teachers couldn't work a little more of the year. The teachers got their raise and we also got five additional days of school for professional meetings. These meetings could be called any time during the year either by the Superintendent or the School Committee. I told the teachers of this. I understand one teacher said she would have to pay another week's rent now and another replied to her she would still be making money as rooms don't cost $300 a week.

"Later last year teachers met to plan the first fall professional meeting. Throughout all the planning the elementary teachers were very good to work with; not so with the high school teachers. They met to discuss agenda for the fall meeting and to determine what they might need in the way of help in carrying on the session. They decided to keep the meeting among themselves — no outsiders at all — so they could work out their own problems. At the last school meeting of the faculty in June, we made final preparations and set the meeting for the first week in September, that is, the last four days of that week. Attendance was not compulsory; they were paid for coming and were not paid if they didn't come.

"This Teachers' Institute was held for four days. The first day the new teachers met and I discussed with them the town, the kids, and so forth. In the afternoon they met the others in a general meeting. Then people split up to their own school building groups and met. The final day reports were made and an evaluation of the series of meetings. I haven't had a chance to go over that stuff yet, but on the whole I don't think it was world-shaking — some profited I think. The new teachers got acquainted, which was a good thing. The elementary teachers did some work in Social Studies, combining geography and history in more meaningful ways, reorganizing the units — they're really chapters — and so forth. And at least there was some organization for communication of the whole group. One mistake in it all was that the teachers should have been issued their supplies first, and their room assignments — so as to feel that things were really starting. Also, unfortunately, there was no crayon in the supply room; the order had not come through, so things were pretty tough the first few days of school. If we had given out supplies earlier, we might have been able to take care of this before the kids got here. I think teachers, some of them anyway, thought that the Institute was too long — at least some of the high school people thought so. They didn't know just what to do. Instead of staying with their departmental sections they split up into eight areas of interest, like guidance, library work, homework, and so forth. But there were not enough specific problems to work on. I let it go just as they wanted it; it was their organization and agenda. I just hoped they wouldn't submit recommendations I knew couldn't be put through. You must always respect the findings of a committee, but if you don't put into practice what they recommend, they say it was all a waste of time. You try to honor as many of their proposals as you can. Everyone showed up except four, three sick and one 'bastard' down in Kentucky — he had quit without letting me know it, some family trouble — and he had taken his kids and gone down there. I called him after tracking him down the first afternoon of the Institute. Can you imagine! These teachers and their ethics — I could tell you about them.

"I try to hire a teacher by giving him an hour myself, having him visit the school, talking around with different ones. I want someone who wants to work on committees and who wants to improve the school and the whole system.

"Teachers in one elementary school are working on a problem now. They want to change the home report card to a progress profile type. So they asked the other elementary school faculty to come in on it too. One thing, they found that to have a progress profile they had to have a lot more information about the kids and their homes and so forth in order not to sound stupid on the reports. I am pleased with their progress; those elementary teachers are good to work with on committees.

"I don't know whether or not we will have another professional meeting this year. We can have one more day if we want it. But when to hold it? What to do at it? It's hard to know how far to go. But it's up to the teachers."

28 Corning*—I

"A Valley and a Decision"

At the Annual Meeting of the Erwin School District No. 1 (Painted Post) in July, 1950, a committee was appointed to gather and assemble facts with respect to "centralization" for Painted Post and some adjacent areas and report prior to considering a building program.

In May, 1951, this committee submitted a report which included the following findings:

1. Promote formation of committee of representatives of the three major districts in the area — Corning 9, the city district; Corning 13, the village district of Corning; and Erwin 1 which is Painted Post.
2. Painted Post cannot solve its problems without consideration of other larger districts as well as the rural districts.
3. Need for action is pressing.
4. Curriculum in the local schools should be expanded.
5. Believe entire area should be centralized.
6. Some data have not been obtained.
7. Services of experts in the field of the high school curriculum may be necessary.

[While this committee had been thus engaged, Corning 9 School District had engaged the services of professional building consultants to prepare a study of building needs for their district. Their report was submitted in February, 1951, recommending the construction of two elementary schools.]

A committee of thirty-six persons representing the three major districts was formed, and with some assistance from members of the State Department of Education prepared a report between June, 1951, and April, 1952, which was presented to an Advisory Committee of thirty-six consisting of representatives of the larger districts with some representation from the rural districts.

The report recommended "consolidation" of the entire area and was approved by the Advisory Committee. It was then taken to Albany by the committee on May 12, 1952. The group remained in Albany for two days to discuss the finding with the State Department personnel.

The department agreed to take the report under advisement and prepare recommendations as well as estimate costs of a program which they would recommend for the area.

On November 10, 1952, the report of the State Department was received by the Advisory Committee. The program suggested was similar to that prepared by the Study Committee and approved by the Advisory Committee, except that it recommended one senior high school and three junior high schools where the original report had recommended three six-year high schools, the same as they then had.

* This is a three-part case (Nos. 28–30). It is urged that each part be studied and discussed before the succeeding part is taken up.

In March, 1953, the Advisory Committee of Thirty-Six was enlarged by vote of the committee to an Advisory Committee of Ninety so as to include representatives from all the districts in the area. The new committee signed a contract for the conduct of a study of the area with the Center for Field Studies, Harvard Graduate School of Education, on June 15, 1953.

The Act of 1812 created the system of common schools in New York State. The structure of the districts followed the same pattern as that which existed in the New England states until the middle of the nineteenth century. Each district embraced an area with a radius of approximately two miles, with a school in the center.

In 1915 there were 10,383 school districts in the state. Of these, 57 were cities, 38 were villages, about 700 were union free and about 9,500 were common districts. Many remained as they had been originally organized, though the Act of 1812 permitted adjoining districts to realign as one district if they so desired. By 1946 the total number of school districts had been reduced to 5,112, with 4,215 common districts remaining. Subsequent years have seen this number further reduced.

This reduction in school districts has been largely the result of an act passed in 1925 setting up centralized school districts and making favorable provisions for state aid to encourage the small districts to form a larger unit.

The Rapp Committee [1] in 1946 and 1947 studied the rural districts as they existed at that time for the purpose of discovering effective territorial organization for the formation of additional central districts. This Committee found that around many of the cities of the state there were districts which could not be organized into logical centralization. Rather, their socio-economic, geographic, and educational relationships to the city made it advisable that these districts should consolidate with the city district. In the Master Plan the committee listed these districts adjacent to cities as being "left for future determination." This did not mean that the organizational changes were in doubt, but that the legal procedure for effecting these changes had to be left for future solution. The Corning Area was one of those "left for future determination."

In December, 1947, the State Comptroller appointed a committee to review tax limitations and to study city-school fiscal relations. The second report of this committee stated: "Satisfactory solution of the problem of city-school fiscal relations in some cities depends in no small measure upon a better adjustment of the boundaries of the school districts within and around cities.[2]

With this in mind, the State Comptroller requested the State Education Department to study city-school district boundaries with a view to "a better arrangement of school district boundaries in the urban areas and consequently to a fuller solution of city-school fiscal relationships." A study was made of thirteen of a total of thirty-six such territories in New York State (including the Corning area — Map I). This study recommended new legislation which would permit con-

[1] Joint Legislative Committee on The State Education System, *Master Plan for School District Reorganization New York State,* Legislative Document No. 25 (1947) (The Rapp Report).

[2] Frank A. Moore, Chairman, New York State Department of Audit and Control, *Second Report of the State Comptrollers Committee on Constitutional Tax and Debt Limitations and City-School Fiscal Relations,* 1949.

solidation of city-school districts and neighboring districts, and suggested that some form of "incentive aid" be set up to encourage such consolidations.

Subsequently legislation was passed to facilitate reorganization of the city-rural type of areas. This became known as the "Enlarged City School District Act."

❧

The City of Corning (population 17,684) provided education under the legal structure of two school districts, Corning 9 (the city district) and Corning 13, a union free school district. These districts were divided by the river which ran through the city, and together they exceeded at points the corporate city boundaries. Corning is the home office and major production plant of Corning and Steuben Glass Works, the largest employer in the area, drawing both from the area generally and from as far as fifteen miles into Pennsylvania.

Painted Post (population 2,405) a village abutting Corning and not distinguishable as a separate community to the casual traveler passing through the urban center of the Greater Corning Area, is the location of the Ingersoll-Rand Co., makers of air compressors and second largest employer in the area. Painted Post was the initial settlement in the region, and there is strong local sentiment attached to its entity.

❧

The Harvard Study was conducted in an area which had seen three earlier studies made, for a committee which had as members major executives of the two largest industries of the area, four school superintendents, lawyers, farmers, factory workers, clergymen, research physicists and chemists, and housewives, in a climate of labor-management difficulty and recent political reverses for the Corning 9 Board.

The fact that the boundaries of the sixty-three school districts, the superintendency areas, the city, the towns, the counties, and other administrative areas constitute noncoterminous historical overlays made for numerous technical difficulties. (Map I) These emerged in the procurement, estimation, and organization of the data with respect to demographic, economic, social, and fiscal aspects of the problem for the area as a whole and for the several alternative proposals for new combinations of school districts.

The relationship of the study and any subsequent action to the policies and procedures of the State Department of Education in New York State was an important consideration. The legislation concerning consolidations places wide administrative powers in the hands of the Department. The Department had made one of the earlier studies in the area. The Harvard study pursued a method of analysis not followed by the Department, and concluded that prediction of future operating costs was of doubtful validity because of the numerous arbitrary assumptions involved, thus taking a position contrary to that of the Department study. Finally, recommendations were made which differed in certain major respects from those made by the Department.

To plot and maintain a course for the study in such a way as to work through the technical problems, and at the same time cope with the social factors involved, demanded constant attention and thought. In a community where the accustomed procedure had been to "give orders and get results," there was the problem of protecting the integrity of the study by not being swayed by a controlling group of the "Steering Committee." The work involved satisfying the "slide-rule group" of scientists, engineers, and technicians comprising the majority

MAP I Greater Corning Area

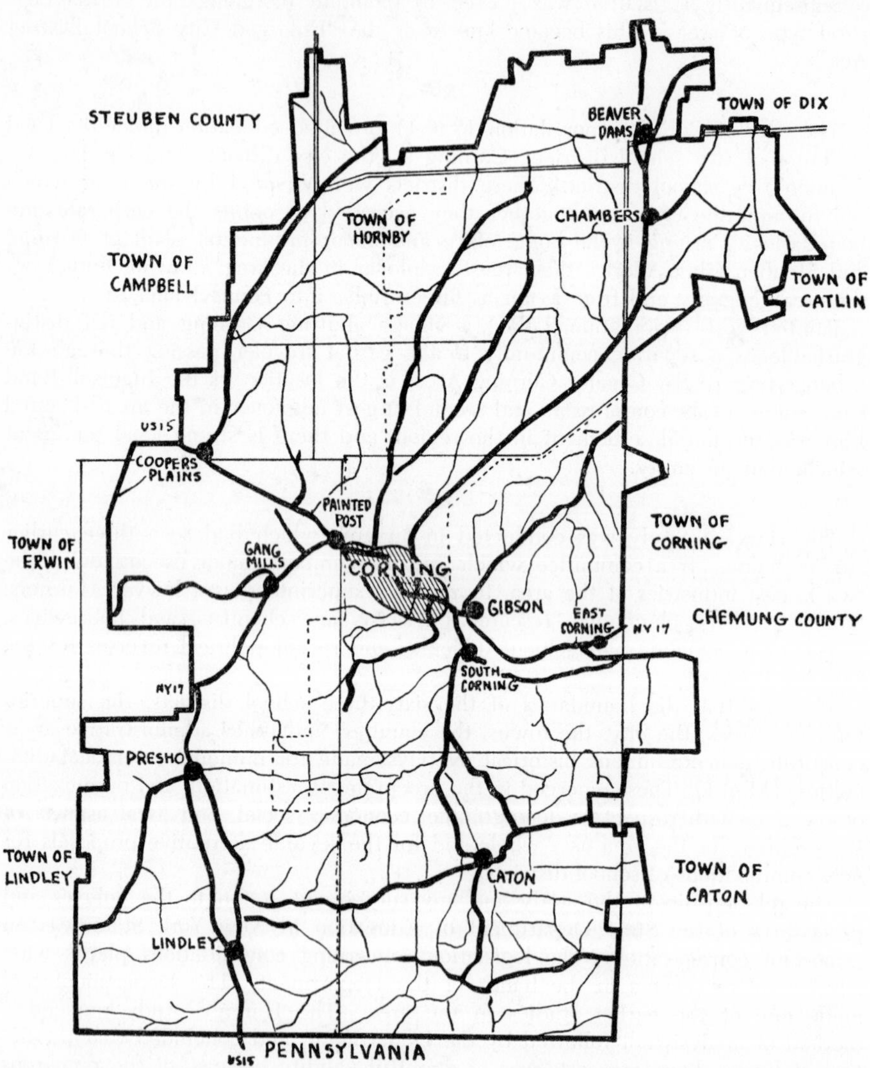

of an estimated three hundred Ph.D.'s in this 30,000 population area, yet communicating with the relatively inarticulate rural people. It was necessary to risk the impatience of some by discussing problems on which they already had "the" answers because of previous study, in order to enable those new to the problem to catch up. A problem from the outset was to allay suspicion that the study would "rubber stamp" a conclusion representing the viewpoint of the industrial interests of the area. The task of establishing a receptive climate for any recommendations that might be made remained a major one almost to the end of the study; achievement of rapport with some segments of public opinion in the area represented in the Committee of Ninety became evident only in the closing weeks. In all a total of 41 public meetings were held in nine different parts of the area with an attendance of 1,920. Ten of the meetings (attendance 730) were with the Committee of Ninety itself.

The Harvard Report

Nine months after the agreement was signed, the Center for Field Studies presented their final recommendations on the problem of school district reorganization in the Greater Corning Area. The final chapter of the report, "A Valley and a Decision," is as follows:

Recommendation for a Decision

The preceding sections of the report have presented basic facts and a detailed analysis on a number of the major aspects of study pertinent to the question of district reorganization in the Greater Corning area.

What factors should now be taken into account in viewing, as a whole, the structure of information that has been developed? The choice of a solution, when more than one possible solution exists, reflects the application of some value judgments to facts and conditions. A recommendation is one part of an attempt to change things as they are, or as we see them, into a new reality — at once grounded in fact, possible of attainment and fundamentally worthy of first choice and effort.

We set down some factors which we wished to keep in mind in arriving at our final recommendation. We do not consider all of these factors to be of equal weight. In our view, a conclusion on a question of this kind involves more than adding up the ratings of alternative plans. But, here, in brief, are some major criteria we had in mind for a preferred plan, in reviewing the study and reaching our conclusion:

Enlarging and equalizing educational opportunity for all the children.
Relating school district organization to geography and community.
Providing equity to all the taxpayers.
Providing for economical and efficient school buildings and educational programs.
Recognizing the desire for adequate representation in shaping decisions on school problems.
Recognizing community sentiment and traditions.
Safeguarding the interest of the state as the responsible agency of education.
Providing a sound framework for future growth and change.

Those who may not agree with the above standards, or who would not give significant weight to one or more of them, may well arrive at a different conclusion than we have done. But if a different set of factors is to be applied by anyone, as each person surely has a right to do, or if a particular standard is to be selected out above all others as the one which should largely govern the choice, we feel that it is only fair to say so.

We do not give any one of these criteria a position of supremacy, relegating the others to unimportance. But we must frankly acknowledge that there is one concept, running through several of these standards, to which we avowedly grant particular importance. This concept is, we believe, so much a part of the basic substance out of which the whole life and structure and values of American society have been created, that few will quarrel when we single it out as of particular importance.

Legally, this concept might be expressed as equity. Politically, it is often expressed as equality or as equal rights and equal privileges. In business, it is frequently called fair trade or fair dealing. And adolescents phrase it "give him a break." All these, as we see it, are ways of expressing some balance between our most immediate, narrow, selfish interests and the necessary fairness and cooperation with others. Without some largeness of viewpoint as to what is fair, ours would be not a society, but a jungle.

In the various and multitudinous ways in which this ideal is expressed, we have a major goal of the American people. We are continually seeking, as a people, to raise the level of our vision and accomplishment in order to transform this concept more into reality.

Working toward this goal, in its better sense, does not mean moving toward dull uniformity. It means moving toward excellence — together. To paraphrase the Harvard report on General Education in a Free Society, the problem is to raise the level while speeding the able — of any bent.

In examining the alternatives for district reorganization in the Greater Corning area, therefore, the staff is acutely conscious of existing inequities. We find these inequities in school facilities, programs, location of resources, tax rates, and even judgments as to what good education is. Although many of these inequities are due to historical circumstances, one of the strong aims of America, in its struggle toward equal opportunity for all, is to overcome the accidents of history and conditions of birth, in order that all children may increasingly have a more nearly equal chance. We know that we cannot overcome history overnight. But we can move forward with it. And, as a people, we can move vigorously when we know that it is time to overcome lag.

In the judgment of the staff, the plan that promises to yield the most equitable education programs and physical facilities for children, with justice to the individual taxpayer regardless of where he may live, is the most worthy plan.

We believe that on these counts, as well as on other counts, the organization of a single school district for the entire study area stands as the preferred choice. Legally, this would mean proceeding in accordance with Plan II [see page 342] to constitute an enlarged city district for the area.

Yet, while we feel that of all the plans considered, this yields most promise in terms of improving educational opportunities, of spreading tax resources behind each child, and of organizing all aspects of the school system efficiently and economically, we do not mean to imply that one such district in and of itself will produce all of the desirable and possible equalities. We feel that there is need for advance in adequacy of citizen representation for the governing of an enlarged city district.

We believe that if the people of the area should see fit to accept both the one enlarged city district structure and at the same time move to achieve the proposed School District Assembly, there would be both larger opportunity for participation and a greater potential for the development of better education for the people of the valley.

It is our belief that in the complex totality which constitutes the social, political, and economic life of the valley, there is no single more important common institution than public education. We feel that establishment of a single school district will strengthen the ties of association and identification which increasingly unite the people of the area as members of the same community. We have envisioned extending this public education through the proposed community college, thus making it possible to offer education — cultural, technical, social — at an advanced level for the entire area.

From time to time during discussions in the area, sentiment has been expressed that the present legal and fiscal framework was not in every way favorable to a reorganization of this type. We would rather say that the present is both a necessary and a propitious time for the Greater Corning area to consider moving in this direction. The proposed single enlarged city district would be able to proceed immediately to operate and construct the needed schools under existing state fiscal provisions and controls.

The time for a decision is now. We are confident that the citizens and voters of this area will face their problem squarely, see it clearly and choose wisely — for today's and tomorrow's children in this valley.

Excerpts from "A Valley and a Decision"

Social and Economic Factors

Population. In 1950, the population of the Greater Corning study area consisted of about 30,719 persons. This total was divided approximately as shown in Table I.

Table I

DISTRIBUTION BY GEOGRAPHICAL AREA

Area	*1950 Total Population*	*Per Cent of Total*
Caton Town	1,199	3.9%
Lindley Town	1,043	3.4
Erwin Town	1,988	6.5
Painted Post	2,405	7.8
Corning City	17,684	57.5
Other Corning	4,275	13.9
Hornby Town	1,014	3.3
* Campbell Town	320	1.1
* Orange Town	299	1.0
* Dix Town	216	.7
* Catlin Town	276	.9
	30,719	100.0%

* Part of total town included in study area.

The study area population constituted about 30 per cent of the population of Steuben County, which showed a total of 91,439 in the 1950 census. Corning constitutes about 19 per cent of the county population.

Steuben County is classed as about 44.6 per cent urban, 35.0 per cent rural nonfarm, and 19.9 per cent rural farm. The study area probably consists of relatively more urban and relatively fewer farm families. Density in Steuben County is about 64 per square mile, as compared with about 112 per square mile in the study area.

During a period of fifty years prior to the 1940–50 decade, Steuben County showed relatively little growth. For the early decades of the same period, Corning experienced very rapid or relatively rapid growth; but during the period from 1920 to 1940, the city also showed virtually no growth. Behind these comparative changes in population, decade by decade, lies a series of changes in the livelihood bases of the county, the city, and the area.

Economic Background. Between 1830 and 1860, lumber, grain, coal, and canal shipping had made Corning the fifth largest port in New York State. The canal was abandoned with the rise of the railroad and the disappearance of its major cargoes. Virtual disappearance, by 1870, of the vast lumber and grain production which had stimulated county growth to 66,000 by 1850, left a labor force which was rapidly drawn into manufacture in Corning.

Although the majority of residents in the area work in Corning, the factories of Elmira and Bath draw also on the local market, and Corning similarly provides jobs to workers from outside the area. Some growth in industry from Elmira to Bath appeared during World War II, and more industries have located in these three industrial centers since 1950. Of some significance to school planning is the increased industrial employment of women in the industrial region embracing Elmira, Corning, and Bath. Of the 7,618 civilian labor force in Corning in 1950, some 5,344 were men and 2,274 were women; in Steuben County as a whole, the proportion of women employed was smaller.

Manufacturing Significance. Steuben County is one of the approximately 6 per cent of the 3,000 counties in the United States which account for 75 per cent of "value added by manufacture." Value added by manufacture provides the best census measure of the relative economic importance of manufacturing in different industries and areas. It measures the approximate value created in the process of manufacturing. High value added by manufacture is ordinarily associated with highly skilled industries and a relatively large capital investment per worker. . . .

Future Trends. In the past, about 85 per cent of the population of New York State has been concentrated along a belt extending only about thirty miles each side of the water-level route from New York City to Albany to Buffalo. Future industrial and population growth will develop along the main secondary routes.

The dieselization, road-bed improvements, and industrial development, since World War II, by the railroads serving this area are related to the clear future prospects for new industries in the Southern Tier region. Establishment of new industries from Elmira to Hornell during the same period and particularly since 1950 are straws in the wind. The long-range plan for highway development in New York State has pointed to a new east-west super highway across the state via Corning and a new north-south route from Pennsylvania to the New York Thru-Way, also via Corning, as two major projects for next consideration. (Map II)

New housing developments in the Greater Corning area are indicative of a long-term rise in the labor force needs and opportunities in the Elmira to Bath industrial zone. After nearly fifty years of little growth in Steuben County and nearly thirty years of very slow growth in Corning, the next two decades are likely to show major growth. The timing and rate of this growth cannot be estimated, nor can the degree and timing of its impact on schools. But it is more likely than not that by 1960, if not earlier, the rise in school enrollments in this area will be sharper than can now be forecast on the basis of computations which are presented elsewhere in the report.

Industrialization, moving ever more strongly along the secondary routes, of which those crossing at Corning are among the most important in the whole New York State area, will bring many new people, homes, and children and many other major changes to the valley, certainly before 1970.

MAP II Corning in Relation to Highway Planning

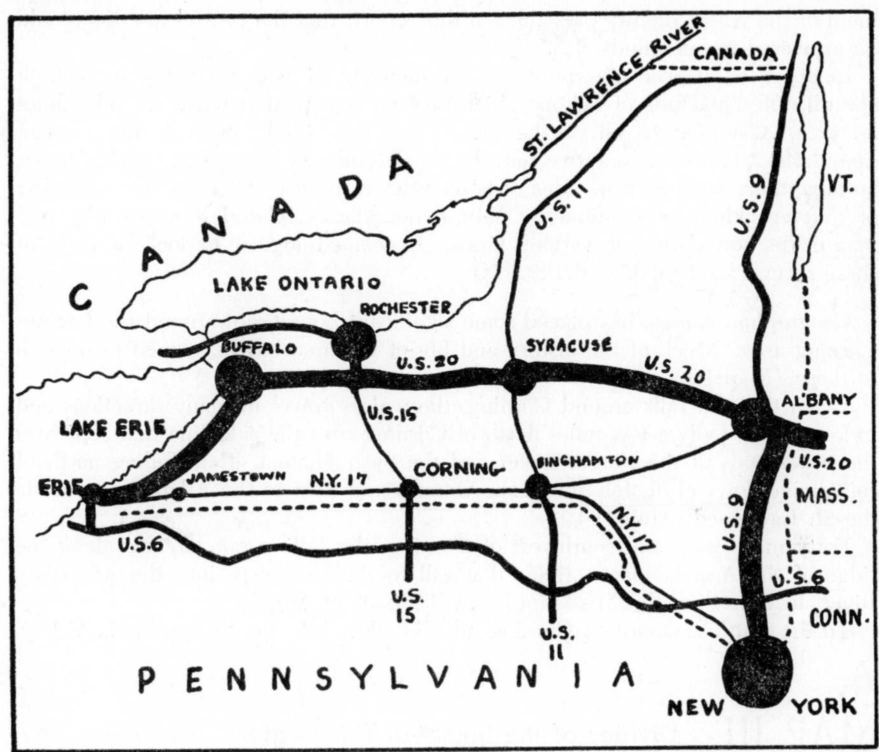

A Valley

Thus far this report has not dealt with a central question involved in the study: Is the "study area" truly one area?

Fairly early in the course of the study, the staff began to search for certain facts and answer certain questions about the so-called "study area" itself in order to deal with this central question. Some of the initial questions were:

1. Should all of the school districts represented on the Advisory Committee continue to be considered as logical members of an "area," even for purposes of study? Or were there any districts perhaps along the outermost boundaries of the area as defined, which might be advised to consolidate with one of the several central districts or other large districts lying outside the "study area" boundaries?
2. Assuming that all of the districts should continue to be included, were there any basic reasons for looking at the totality not as one area, but as two or more distinct areas? Are there fundamental divisions and boundaries within the area which would make it more suitable to treat each of two or more parts quite separately?

Early answers to some of these questions were obviously needed, both in fairness to all districts concerned and in order to plan the organization of efforts in obtaining, organizing, and analyzing facts and information in all the various aspects of the study. But it was only through the slow, piece-by-piece development of the whole picture presented in this report, that the central question could be answered in our minds. . . .

In order to answer the questions satisfactorily, it was necessary to look at several different kinds of factors which may be represented when we talk about an area. Common to all of the factors we may think about is the idea of boundaries. However tentative may be the boundaries in mind in talking about an area, there must be some idea of boundaries or limits. But there are a number of different kinds of boundaries: natural boundaries related to geography and man-made boundaries of various kinds. It seemed logical to look at each of these several kinds of boundaries.

Geography. Nature has placed some significant boundaries around the Greater Corning area. Much of the history and life of the area has developed in relation to these (Map III).

When the rain falls around Corning, the waters travel in many directions and to far places. Only a few miles north of Corning runs the ridgeline that separates the watersheds of the Finger Lakes and the Susquehanna. Rain falling north of this divide flows ultimately into Lake Ontario and then to the Atlantic Ocean via the St. Lawrence (Map IV).

Forty miles west and southwest of Corning, the falling rain divides along the ridge of the Appalachians. Rains that fall to the west flow into the Allegheny River, to the Ohio, the Mississippi and the Gulf of Mexico.

To the south and east of Corning all rains flow into the Susquehanna Valley,

MAP III **Divides of the Southern Tier Region**

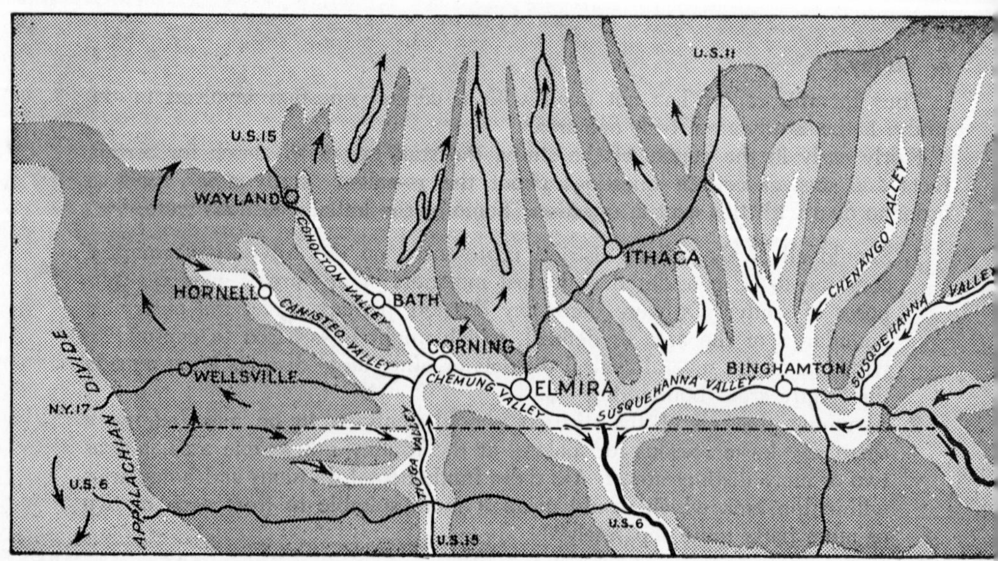

MAP IV Greater Corning Study Area

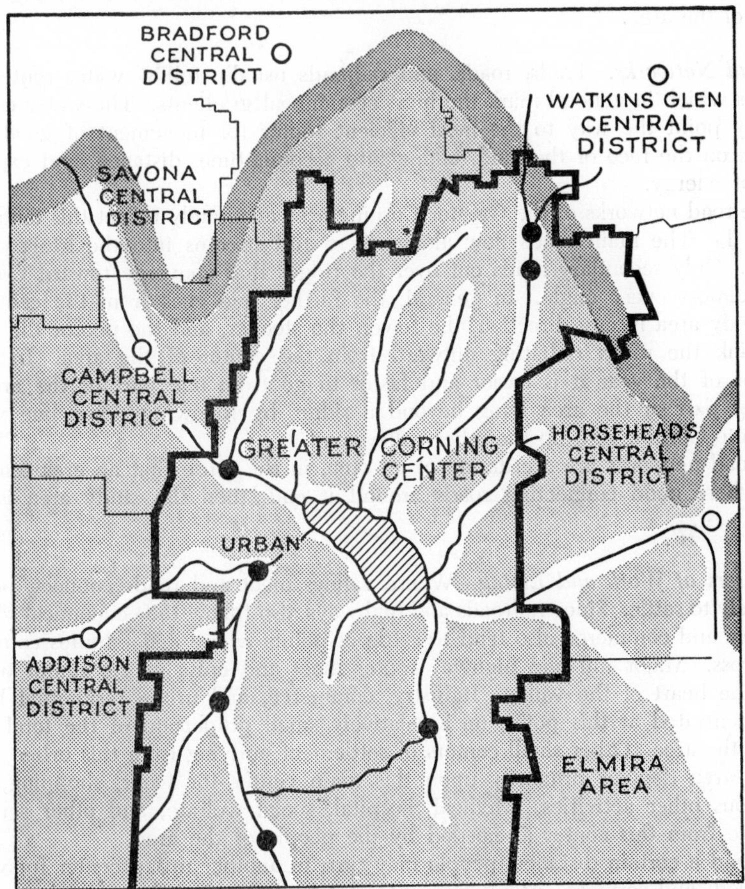

until, a few miles east of Binghamton, runs the sharp divide separating the watershed of the Susquehanna to the west and the Delaware to the east.

Thus, the valley of the Chemung is surrounded by some of the great divides of North America. It is a valley within the much larger valley system of the Susquehanna. The smaller valley systems of the Cohocton, the Canisteo and the Tioga to the northwest, west, and south join to make a valley of which Corning is the heart. The southward plunge of the ridgeline of the Southern Tier to Horseheads and Elmira Heights just beyond Big Flats almost encloses the Greater Corning valley to the east.

All of the Greater Corning study area lies within the Chemung valley area above described. Even the streams to the east of Corning, almost to the eastern boundary of the study area, flow in westward directions from their hillsides north and south of the Chemung and turn eastward only after joining it. Corning is almost like the hub of a wheel whose spokes are the smaller rivers and streams joining the Chemung within the study area.

If the divides and boundaries fixed by natural geography are any criterion, the Greater Corning study area is one valley and one area. And Corning is the heart of the area.

Road Networks. Trails, roads, and railroads usually follow water routes and valleys which in general mark the most economical gradients. The water courses usually point the way to the most efficient routes for movement of goods and people on the face of the land, taking into account time, distance, and expenditure of energy.

The road networks of the Greater Corning area accurately reflect this tendency. (Map I) The main roads flow along rivers and streams into the heart of the valley. Only secondary roads cut over the ridges that converge toward Corning from almost every angle. In general, the farther one goes from the center of the study area in any direction, the fewer, the steeper, and the poorer the roads that link the roads radiating outward from the center of the area. In some seasons of the year it is easier and faster to go from one part of the area to another part of the area lying beyond a ridge, by following down one valley road into Corning and up the other valley road.

If road networks are a criterion of an area, in the sense that an area tends to end where good connecting roads around it end, then the study area is one area.

Centers of Work and Living. Where valleys meet and roads connect, people are likely to settle. Since railroads and highways also follow the economical routes, industry and commerce also tend to settle at points where major routes converge and cross. Major rail and highway routes meet and cross in the center of the area, the heart of the valley. Industry, commerce, and urban residential living is concentrated at this point, on a relatively small proportion of the total land within the area. Other small centers of settlement outlying from this urban heart of the area depend primarily upon this main center for work, shopping, and numerous other activities. Medical, hospital, social welfare, and other services emanate from this center as needed by the people of the area.

Beyond a certain distance, people may turn to another urban center for work, livelihood, and services. Along some not clearly definable line to the northwestward, people go toward Bath rather than to Corning. At some similarly indefinable line to the east, they gravitate toward Elmira. But both of these somewhat indefinable lines appear to lie outside the study area. Within the study area, the great preponderance of movement toward work, shopping, and other services related to the urban core is toward Corning.

Responses to the questionnaire and some other information obtained suggests that at least 70 per cent of the persons residing in the area also work in the area. The major concentration of these work activities lies in the industries, stores, offices, and other business activities located in the urban core of the area. Similarly, the preponderance of other activities related to an urban center — church, recreation in various forms, medical care — brings most of the area residents to this urban center.

Even those villages and rural neighborhoods closest to the boundaries and farthest from the center are more closely linked with Corning than with cities or towns outside the area.

If the existence of somewhat indefinable lines around a major center of work, commerce, and services which constitute a kind of divide or boundary, beyond which the preponderance of movement by people is toward other centers, is a criterion for bounding an area, the study area lies within such boundaries.

Formal Boundaries. If we disregard the highly artificial, but certainly not unimportant, boundary line drawn by man, the answers to the original questions are clear in all but one respect — namely, whether the people of the area identify themselves as belonging to an area.

We suspect that the children increasingly do. They go on to school in the center of the area, relinquishing the exclusiveness of their tie to the small sub-area served by the primary school.

And although their identification is expanded to include primarily that part of the area served by the high school they attend, this shift of identification from the smaller to the larger represents the process of growth — of broadening of identification — which makes an area of land an area also of people.

The formal boundaries of the existing individual school district tend to dissolve in actuality and meaning under conditions which result in children from many districts coming together for learning as they move toward adulthood. The realities of new associations and social relationships diminish the smaller district boundary lines in all but the formal legal sense. The present study constitutes merely a step in carrying forward this process, by seeking to find a pattern and a way in which to dissolve out the now obsolete legal boundaries and build more surely on the broader social realities.

The outermost boundaries of the districts that border the study area are not inconsistent with the boundaries drawn by nature.

Sentiment. Perhaps the most difficult kind of boundary line that must be considered is one that is highly intangible. It relates to the way in which people identify themselves with particular areas of land and particular groups of other people. These sentiments are related to both past traditions and current associations.

Being a resident and a voter of a particular city or town, with its sometimes wholly artificial, man-made legal boundaries, creates a tie. Working in a particular location may create a tie. The sense of belonging to a particular group of neighbors creates a tie. Thinking of oneself as a member of a community with a long history and strong local traditions creates a tie.

The feeling of identification, the feeling of a particular local tie, is thus bound up with human associations, and not alone or even primarily with land and natural geography in the local sense. It is intertwined with the structure of social relationships as they exist among people distributed over the land. Numerous traditions, sentiments, past and present associations result in undoubtedly strong local ties within the area. These local identifications divide the area into numerous small groupings. But because of the centering of so many of the life activities of the great majority of people within the area rather than outside of it, the division of identifications within the area is secondary to the fact that these are *within.*

Do the people of the study area think of themselves as belonging to an area, and not just to one or another sub-locality of the area? Do they feel themselves to be a part of a closely interrelated human community, with its sub-clusters of smaller communities and neighborhoods, partly urban, partly suburban, partly rural? Do they think of themselves as inhabiting together a natural area, a cup in the land surrounded by great divides? Is the valley just a valley of land? Or is it a valley of people?

The answers to these questions are beyond the knowledge of the study staff. Yet the answer to them would determine clearly whether this is an area, in the most significant sense of the term.

Citizens and Schools

. . . A study endeavoring to propose a solution of a problem which depends, in the last analysis, upon the way in which large numbers of voters exercise their franchise must take into account the views of citizens. Not all decisions regarding schools can be made on the basis of proved standards resulting from scientific and professional study.

Certain values and ways of life which are represented in the views and activities of the people of the area must be given weight in arriving at standards or facts or both which are pertinent to the study or conclusions.

Questionnaire Survey. Early in the process of the study, therefore, a questionnaire survey was undertaken through the cooperation of the Advisory Committee with the assistance of a large number of volunteer citizens. The survey sought to obtain information as to some of the opinions and values held by the adults of the area regarding their schools, as well as information as to where those responding to the questionnaire live, work, shop, attend church, and engage in other activities. The latter information assisted the study staff in perceiving to what extent the outlying areas and the urban center are linked together in the daily life and activities of the people. . . .

Some Responses to Questionnaire. . . . Clear signs of a widening interest and growing understanding on the part of citizens both as to conditions as they are and as to standards against which these conditions might be viewed gives promise of educational progress. But a large task in informing greater numbers of people regarding the problems and conditions with which they must come to grips as voters undoubtedly remains to be done.

Solving the problem of education for children and youth in the area clearly involves a considerable problem in adult education. Twenty-two per cent of the respondents, for example, expressed the view that the present district boundaries are either "entirely acceptable" or need "only minor adjustments" relative to a desirable educational system.

More than 35 per cent believed that "most of the buildings are adequate, a few need improvement." Granted that views as to the educational adequacy of buildings are relative, the condition of numerous buildings with regard to health and safety factors alone would seem inconsistent with such a view. . . .

Desire for Representation. In considering various plans for reorganization of the existing sixty-two districts into one or more larger districts, the question of citizen responsibility and representation in the determination of school policy has come strongly to the fore in other ways. It is recognized that some voters in existing smaller districts who take an active interest in their schools are concerned lest their votes and voices be lost in joining with other districts. Such fears of lessening representation are an indication that they value their rights and responsibilities.

Absence of Representation. Actually these small districts have no representation or rights now in one of the most important areas of educational policy — the high school. Under the laws of the state, no one of the fifty-nine common school districts in the area can maintain a high school, even if it could afford to do so. As contracting districts they have no legal voice in either the educational or the financial policies of the system to which they send their high school students; yet they can be charged tuition and a proportionate share of the insurable value of the high school building which their students attend.

They have no legal recourse if their students are denied admission to a high school already overcrowded with students from its own district.

Two Meanings of "Representation." Neither the present set-up of school districts nor the formation of larger districts seems therefore to satisfy entirely the two different kinds of "representation" which are important to citizens and voters in connection with school policy. One of these is a legal status as voters who can cast votes for a school board which has legal power to govern the schools which the children from the district attend. With regard to this kind of representation, nearly one-third of the voters in the Greater Corning area are in effect disenfranchised, in whole or in part, under the present situation — until they vote for a school district reorganization.

The other kind of representation people want is a feeling that their votes will really "count." In any type of reorganized district, merging school districts in this area, the school board is limited by state law to not more than nine members whether the voters electing them be many or few. The voters from small districts in different parts of the area wonder whether any one of these members elected by many voters throughout a wide area will really "represent" them in the sense to which they are accustomed. These concerns are perhaps most acute when a proposed merger of districts would include a district or districts within a city, with many voters concentrated into a small area. . . .

Informal "Representation." It was recognized that apart from the formal structure of qualified voters, regular elections, and official boards, citizen representation in relation to schools is possible in many unofficial forms. Parent-teacher or home-and-school or similar associations flourish in school districts in many parts of the country, working closely but informally with the official school board, the superintendent, the principals and the teachers. In some communities, there are citizens' commissions dedicated to better understanding, constructive criticism, and public support of schools.

In some communities school boards or administrators have appointed or encouraged the formation of citizens' advisory committees to work with them on specific or continuing problems. In one way or another — and sometimes through pressure groups who are ill-informed or even hostile to the schools — interest and participation by citizens in school problems is increasingly manifest. But these alone do not solve the problem which has been voiced by citizens and voters in the area.

Proposed School District Assembly

We have concluded that a possible answer lies in a new kind of governing body for any school district reorganization involving the recent "enlarged city district" legislation.

In brief, the idea would be a representative School District Assembly. If all the districts in the Greater Corning area were to merge, the Assembly elected to represent the new school district would consist of about sixty members. The district would be divided into about eight "voting areas" simply for purposes of representation. The voters in each voting area would elect their own representatives.

The number of representatives from each voting area would be in proportion to the number of voters in the area they represent. No area would have more than perhaps 15 per cent of the voters or of the members of the Assembly, and none would have less than perhaps 6 per cent.

Powers of the Assembly. This Assembly would meet at least three times a year. It would elect the school board for the district from its membership. Its approval would be required for the annual budget. The school board would, of course, attend the meetings of the Assembly to report on activities and decisions and to join in discussion of educational policies. Apart from the powers specified, the Assembly's functions would be advisory. The power to authorize bond issues or tax rate increases, within the limitations which already govern such districts, would remain as now in the hands of the voters.

The Assembly plan would not be used unless a majority of the voters in the district chose to adopt it by referendum vote. The plan represents an effort to devise a system of representation which may be suited to an area like Greater Corning where many people are understandably fearful of losing "representation" if their district merges with a much more heavily populated city district. Whether the people of the area want to be represented under a plan of this kind is for them to decide. We think that it might be an important step forward, fair to all.

New legislation would be required to make the Assembly plan possible. . . . We urge, however, that decision and action on the immediate, urgent question of district reorganization not be delayed in order to await possible legislative approval of the proposed legislation permitting voters to govern their schools through a representative School District Assembly.

School Buildings – Existing and Needed

[The Harvard staff found that the Greater Corning Area would have a pupil increase of nearly 50 per cent in the next ten years. Coupled with this factor was the fact that there had been, in the area, almost no building in the previous twenty-five years. Thus the staff found themselves in the position of making building recommendations in the light of both a predicted increase in enrollments and over two decades of almost no building. The report makes the following recommendations.]

Elementary Schools (Map V.) Stage I consists in starting immediately with plans for making available by September, 1955, the following new facilities:

1. A 250-pupil elementary school in Chambers.
2. A 420-pupil elementary school in Painted Post.
3. A 420-pupil elementary school in Corning Northside.
4. Continue the already committed plan of East Corning for a six-room building for 180 children.
5. Continue the plans of Corning Southside for two eighteen-room buildings for 1,080 pupils.

Stage II provides for:

1. A 250-pupil elementary school in Caton Center.
2. A 350-pupil elementary school in Gang Mills.
3. A 250-pupil elementary school in Lindley in the Presho area.

MAP V Existing Elementary and Secondary Schools by Study Area, 1953

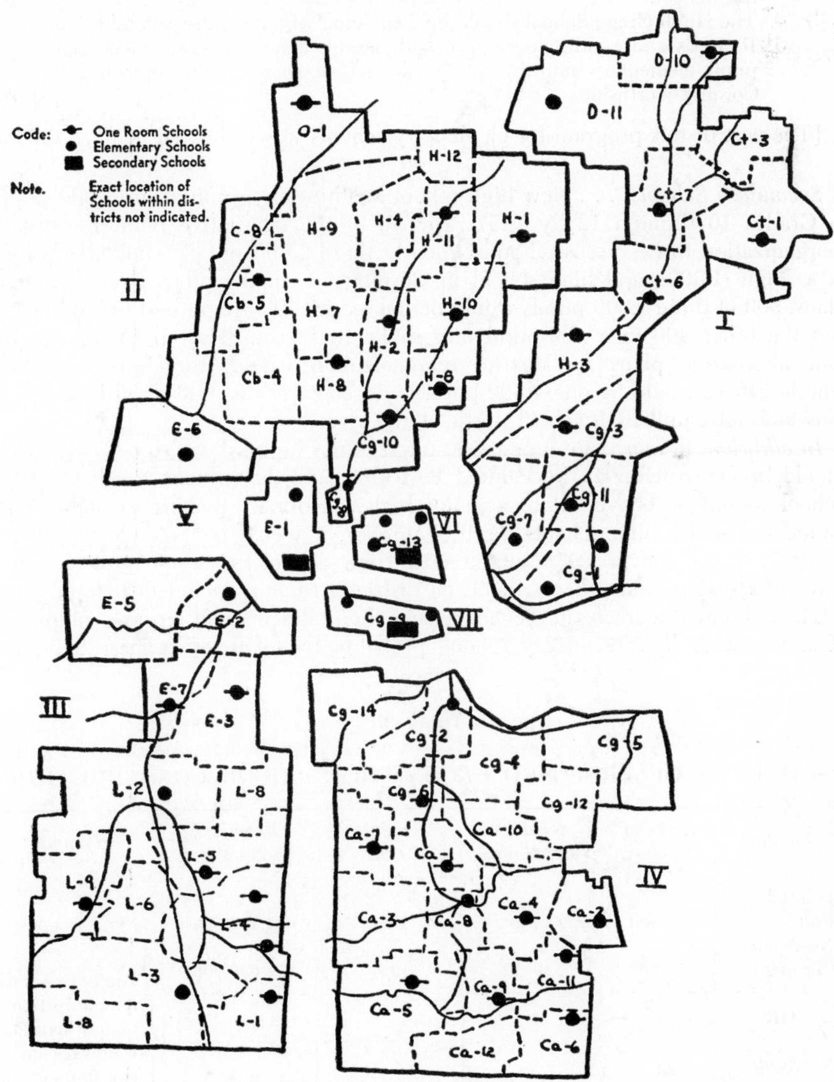

Stage III would provide either four or five additional units, depending on the reassessment of need for 1957.

1. A 250-pupil elementary school in Coopers.
2. A 420-pupil elementary school in Painted Post.
3. A 180-pupil unit in South Corning adjacent to the present South Corning School.
4. The Hugh Gregg School should be completed with a seven-room addition.
5. If needs and conditions require and permit, a new fourteen-room 420-pupil elementary unit by 1957; this school should be constructed in Corning Northside.

[The cost of this program for elementary schools was estimated at $7,170,000.]

Secondary Schools. . . . New high school facilities are required for 1,300 pupils in Grades 10 through 12 by 1957. In two of the alternative plans for district reorganization to be discussed subsequently these 1,300 pupils would be housed in a single 1,300-pupil high school in Corning 13; in the other two alternative plans, 900 of these 1,300 pupils would be housed in a 900-pupil unit in Corning 13 and the other 400 in a 400-pupil unit in Painted Post. The choice among the four alternative plans for district reorganization would, therefore, determine whether there would be one 1,300-pupil high school *or* one 900-pupil high school plus one 400-pupil high school north of the river.

In addition, in *any* plan, a new 550-pupil junior high school (for Grades 7–9) should be constructed in the Painted Post area, and the present Northside High School should be converted to a junior high school. By making available both junior and senior high schools for this number, it would be possible, beginning in 1957, to use the present Painted Post High School for administrative offices and other public offices for whichever district structure included Painted Post.

The continued increase in secondary school enrollments will require completion of still another new secondary school, probably by 1959, of at least 820-pupil

Table II

SCHEDULE OF PROPOSED SECONDARY SCHOOL CONSTRUCTION

Location	*Size of School*	*Grades to Be Housed*	*Available Date*	*Estimated Cost*	*Comment*
Painted Post	500	7–9	1957	$1,100,000	
Northside Corning	1300	10–12	1957	2,600,006	Under two of the reorganization plans, this school would become two units as indicated here
OR					
Northside Corning	900	10–12	1957	1,800,000	
Painted Post	400 *	10–12	1957	800,000 *	
South Corning	800	10–12	1959 or 1961	1,600,000	
Total	2,650			$5,300,000	

* As a smaller unit this school might be expected to cost more than is estimated here.

capacity, but certainly no later than 1961. This second three-year senior high school might logically be located in South Corning. As soon as this school is available, the Corning Free Academy would become an area junior high school. The precise capacity and timing of this construction should be reviewed in 1956. . . . (Table II)

The Harvard Study staff thoughtfully considered the possible advantages which might accrue with one senior high school for the valley. Estimates of enrollment make it clear that a conservative figure would bring the size of such a school to between 2,500 and 3,000 by the 1970's. The disadvantages that arise from the administration of such large schools, the frequent loss of identification of the individual student, the necessity for duplicating the majority of shops, cafeterias, gymnasiums, and other special facilities, all tend to outweight the possible merits of a single high school plant.

Proposed Community College

The answers to the questionnaire concerning public education in the Greater Corning area indicated a strong interest in education for youth and adults beyond the high school level. It so happens that an unusual opportunity exists for this area to acquire, at a lower than normal cost, a major new educational asset which would meet the needs expressed by many citizens.

Recently enacted legislation in New York State gives substantial financial aids toward both construction and operation of two-year "community colleges." Inasmuch as new high school facilities must be constructed in the area anyway, in order to meet the sheer pressure of increasing enrollments, a community college unit could be planned and built in such a way as to fit in with the new high school facilities and teaching staffs. The cost to the area for the community college would thus be much less than would otherwise be necessary.

The community college itself would be, at one and the same time:

1. *A two-year general college* along the lines of the community junior colleges that have been established so widely in California and other states — their growth being evidence of a real need and demand for this kind of educational opportunity.

2. *A terminal technical institute* to enable young men and women past the traditional high school level to grow in their knowledge and appreciation of culture, while advancing those skills which are in demand as a result of industrial diversification and growth in the Chemung River valley area.

Programs of study in technical, industrial, skilled crafts, commercial and other fields would be mapped in keeping with emerging opportunity and demand. Possible programs involving alternating periods of a few weeks of work in industry and of study on the campus could be explored in cooperation with industries in the general region.

3. *A center for continued education at the adult level.* These adult educational programs could be of whatever type people in the area find would contribute to their knowledge, satisfaction, and well-being. Adult education programs in other communities often include small informal classes, ranging widely as to subject. Current events discussions, woodworking, music, painting, and world affairs may be offered alongside the vocational, technical, and academic courses which people with jobs may want to pursue on the basis of evening school attendance.

In brief, the provisions of the state law enabling community colleges call for the state to pay one half the costs of construction with the other half paid by the local sponsoring agency — which may be a city school system, an enlarged city school system, a county, or other area of enough population to warrant it.

Thus, use by the community college of certain facilities required anyway by the high school could be credited toward the share of local expense. In addition, many or all of the same teaching staff could be used jointly. Administration, financial control, and at least some building would be separate, however.

A Note on School Districts

Common School Districts. In the Greater Corning area there are fifty-eight common school districts, of which thirty-two operate schools. By law no single common school district can establish a high school. By various combinations, these fifty-eight common school districts are under four different superintendents. These four supervisory districts also include common school districts located outside the Greater Corning study area.

Union Free School Districts. There are two "Union Free School Districts" Erwin 1 (Painted Post) and Corning 13 (Northside). Erwin 1 is a part of the Steuben I supervisory district; by law, it cannot have a superintendent of its own because its population (2,400) is under the legal requirement for such a district (5,000). It maintains both elementary and secondary education within the district. In addition, Erwin 1 receives more secondary school students (Grades 7–12) from nearby common districts on a contracting basis than it has of its own resident students.

Corning 13 is a Union Free District with its own superintendent of schools serving an area which lies largely within the boundaries of the City of Corning. Corning 13 is able to have its own superintendent of schools because the number of inhabitants of the district is over 5,000. This district numbers among its secondary school students (Grades 7–12) almost as many from contracting districts as from within the district itself.

City School Districts. "City School Districts" are divided into those in cities of over 125,000 and those in cities of 125,000 or less. In the Corning area, specifically, there is one city district in the legal sense. This is Corning 9 which is located largely within the city boundaries. This district itself is constituted by a part of the city and a small part of the area outside of the city. The combination of the areas encompassed by Corning 9 and Corning 13 includes all of the City of Corning and some small adjacent areas.

As in the case of the union free districts in the area (Corning 13 and Erwin 1), outlying common districts send children to Corning 9 on a contracting basis. Slightly less than two hundred students are presently attending Corning Free Academy under this arrangement. Corning 9 has its own superintendent of schools.

An act of the legislature in 1950 designated existing city districts within cities as the city district in perpetuity. In the Greater Corning study area, therefore, the term "city school district" always means Corning 9.

Combinations of Existing Districts. Groupings have been possible in the past which provide separate elementary and separate secondary districts through legislation known as "central" elementary and "central" high school districts. Post-World War II legislation now makes it possible for districts to combine only if they offer all educational functions and services. Further organization of "central" elementary and "central" high school districts is now specifically prohibited and cannot enter into consideration with respect to the present problem.

Since the 1920's, state policy has moved increasingly, through legal, fiscal, and administrative acts, to promote enlargement of districts to a size which will provide for all the educational offerings of an area from kindergarten through high school education under one structure.

Reorganization Laws Available to This Area. There are two methods of reorganization available to the Greater Corning area. They have important variations.

The first is by "centralization." This method is available to union free districts, common districts, and city districts *in cities under 10,000 population.* Districts so combining receive incentive aid in the form of increased annual general aid, a transportation quota, and a building aid.

In 1951 a second method was made possible which provided for "consolidation" with a city school district *in cities of less than 125,000 population.* No incentive aid was provided. In the absence of such incentives, it was a question as to whether the new law would be used. The New York legislature recognized this and so passed legislation, effective in 1953, providing incentive aid over and above the regular state aid for districts combining with city districts in cities greater than 10,000 population, under the act entitled "Enlarged City District."

Four Redistricting Patterns

In seeking ways by which school districts may be grouped together, the starting point is, of course, the legal options that are available. Since Corning 9 is a city school district in a city of over 10,000 population, it must reorganize under the provisions of the enlarged city district statute.

All other districts in the area qualify for either a centralized district or an enlarged city district. This applies even to Corning 13 (a union free school district), although it is located within the city.

An opinion from the Division of Law of the New York State Education Department states that, "Inasmuch as Section 1801 of the Education Law states that the Commissioner of Education may lay out territory 'not contained within a city school district in a city having a population of more than 10,000 inhabitants,' it would appear that the law envisioned that only the territory contained within a city school district in such a city could not be laid out in a central school district. Consequently, all territory in a city having a population of 10,000 inhabitants which was not within the limits of the city school district of such city could be included and laid out by the Commissioner in a central school district."

The four alternative plans which have resulted from this analysis represent, in the judgment of the staff, the only reasonably defensible ones for final consideration, although some slight changes in the boundary lines proposed under one or another of the alternative patterns may be in order, to avoid injustice to a few families.

Plan I, as shown in Map VI would divide the sixty-two districts of the area as follows:

1. An *enlarged city district,* which would include Corning 9, the Catons, South Corning, East Corning, and in addition, Corning 3, 4, 5, 6, 7, 11, 12, and 14. In general, this area follows the road network to the east and south of the city. In this district the pupil population would be 2,333, using the 1953 enrollment figures; the assessed valuation per pupil would be approximately $10,280.

MAP VI The Four Redistricting Plans

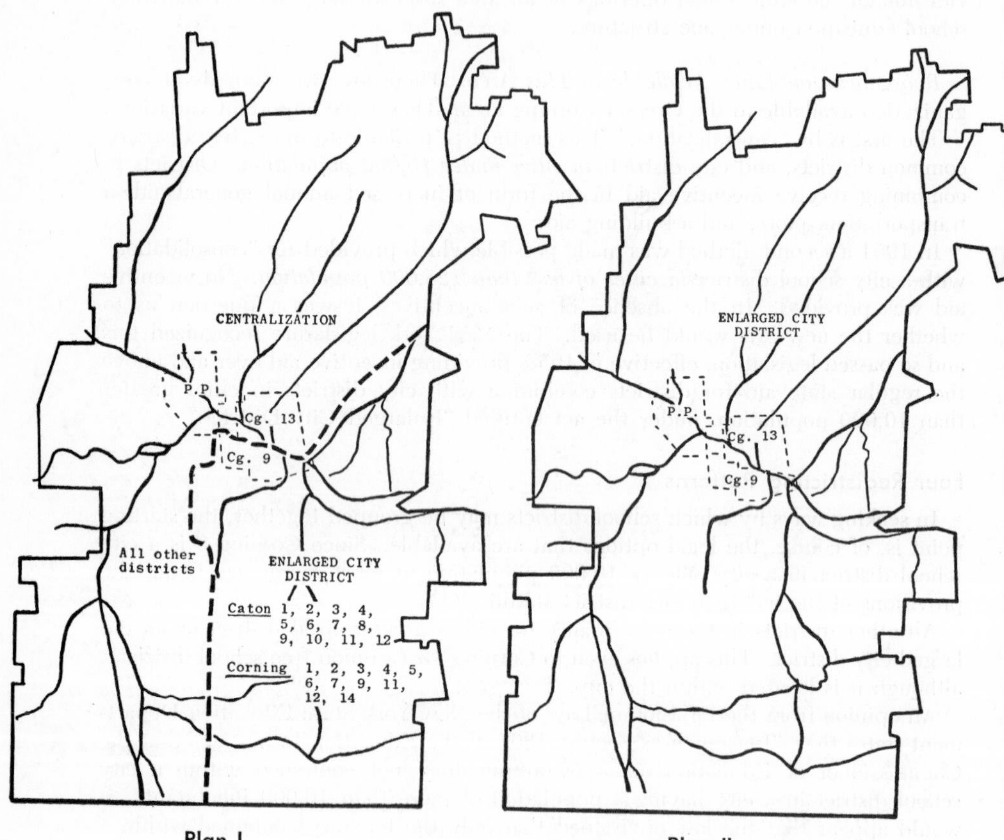

Plan I

Plan II

2. A *centralized district* embracing the entire remaining part of the area, which consists of Corning 13, Painted Post, the Lindleys, the Erwins, the Campbells, Orange 1, the Hornbys, Dix 11, the Catlins, and Corning 8. In these districts, the assessed valuation would be $5,180 and the pupil enrollment in 1953 would be 3,937.

Plan II considers the entire Greater Corning area as one enlarged city school district. This plan spreads the tax base of the area equally behind each of the 6,270 children enrolled in the entire area in 1953, and the assessed valuation per pupil is $7,060.

Plan III is similar to Plan I in that the enlarged city school district would have exactly the same boundaries, but the centralized district of Plan I would be divided into two parts: one to the north and east including Corning 13, the Hornbys, except for Hornby 7, 8, and 9, Dix 11, and the Catlins; the other to the west would include Painted Post and all the other Erwins, the Campbells, Hornby 7, 8, and 9, and Corning 8. The assessed valuation per pupil would be $10,280 in the enlarged

MAP VI (continued)

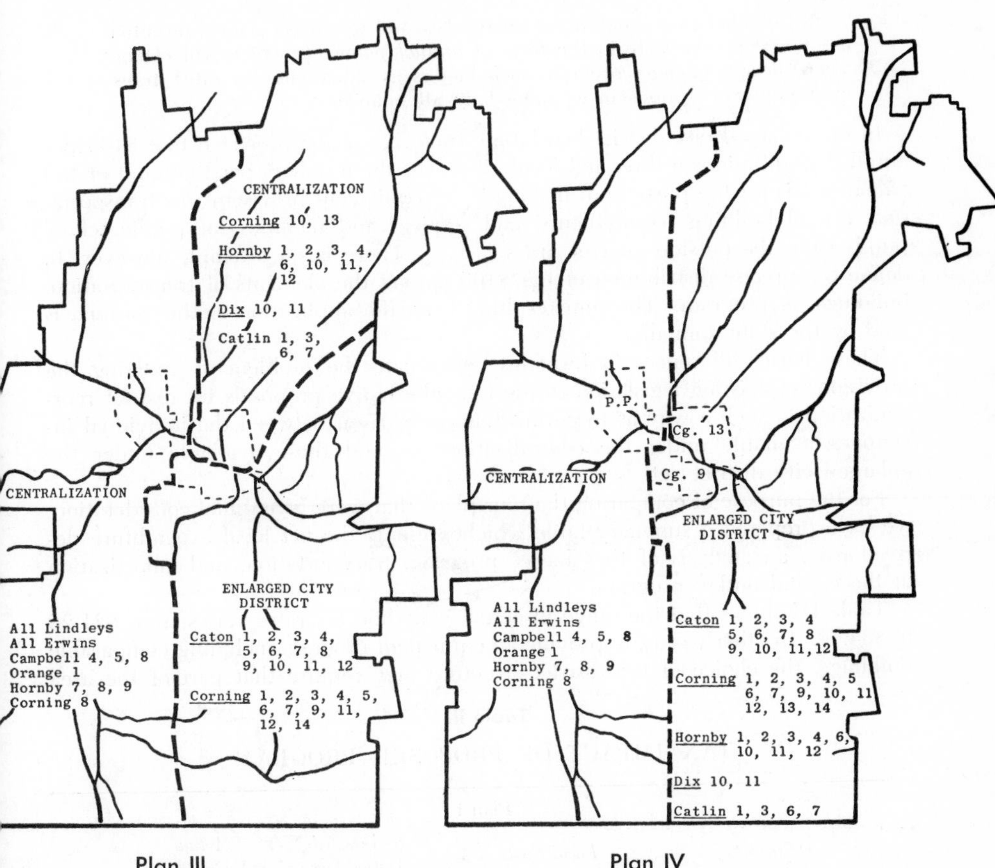

Plan III Plan IV

city district, $5,440 in the centralization which includes Corning 13, and $4,840 in the western centralization which includes Painted Post. Children would be distributed as follows: enlarged city district, 2,333; northeast centralization, 2,239; and the west centralization, 1,698.

Plan IV combines the enlarged city district and the east centralization as outlined in Plan III into one enlarged city district; the west centralization of Plan III remains the same. The enlarged city district in Plan IV would now have an assessed valuation per pupil of approximately $7,886; the centralization would have $4,840 per pupil. There would be 4,532 children in the enlarged city district of Plan IV, and 1,698 pupils in the centralized district.

Fiscal Implications of Four Redistricting Patterns

The basic formulas with respect to state financial aid, the relationships among the variables represented in these formulas and the methods of computations are all different. To oversimplify, for purposes of initial explanation:

In one case (the enlarged city district law and formulas) a fiscal incentive toward reorganization is offered by the state in the form of a *single lump-sum payment* to the newly reorganized district based on "things as they are" as of the date of reorganization — valuations, tax rates, numbers of pupils enrolled.

In the other case (centralized district law and formulas) a fiscal incentive is offered by the state in the form of *annual payments* which will *change every year* if changes occur in such factors as valuations, tax rates, transportation costs, pupils in average daily attendance.

In the enlarged city district legislation, there is specific provision that $100 per enrolled pupil minus a three mil local effort (or three dollars per thousand of full valuation) is for the purpose of making ". . . equivalent provisions for transportation, school building requirements, and services and facilities for public school pupils from the outside area or areas. . . . " There is no attempt, however, to define the precise distribution of the $100 among the elements of transportation, buildings, or program. The sum resulting from the application of this formula is paid by the state annually.

These basic differences in formulas complicate the problem of applying the provisions of existing legislation to the four alternative proposals for district reorganization in such a way as to permit fair comparison between the individual incentives available under the centralization act and those available under the enlarged city district act.

For the purpose of comparing the four plans that were given final consideration, we have prepared a summary table which presents the *net* local expenditure derived from an analysis of the "basic" program, transportation, and amortization of the capital outlay program.

Table III shows that the range in actual valuation tax rates varies from $21.23 to $34.16. In other words, to provide an equivalent program including comparable buildings, the choice of the district structure may require that part of the area

Table III

TAX IMPACT OF PROPOSED PROGRAM

District	*Local Costs*	*Assessed Value Tax*	*Actual Value Tax*
	Plan I		
Central	$ 697,234.37	$46.50	$33.31
Enl. City	506,995.31	30.39	21.23
Total Local	$1,186,229.68		
	Plan II		
Enl. City	$1,200,835.41	38.38	27.13
	Plan III		
Enl. City	$ 506,995.31	30.39	21.23
Cent.-West	280,552.84	45.29	34.16
Cent.-East	361,476.91	42.96	29.68
Total Local	$1,204,113.97		
	Plan IV		
Enl. City	$ 930,654.24	37.09	25.81
Central	280,552.84	45.29	34.16
Total Local	$1,276,295.99		

spend over 50 per cent more than another part of the area to achieve this equal situation. The net local expenditure varies among the plans to the amount of $90,000 per year.

We described at the beginning of this section what we termed a "no plan" attitude and mentioned that sizable inequities would result if this attitude prevailed. What these inequities would be can be shown by contrasting the fiscal situation which will obtain under an enlarged city district pattern for the entire area with the fiscal situation which would result if the "no plan" attitude were to prevail.

The proposed plan for a single enlarged city district would make available special state aid in the amount of $265,764.71 for the total area. This amount when divided by the assessed valuation of the total area ($31,289,491) shows that the state would be contributing additional tax relief to the local real estate taxpayer in the amount of $8.50 per thousand of assessed valuation. This is an annual aid, and the legislation states that the area will receive this benefit every year in the future under the enlarged city district plan.

The cost of the "no plan" will, however, vary considerably in its impact from district to district. The capital program of $12,470,000 which is recommended irrespective of district reorganization would have a total annual cost of $622,377-.70. This figure represents a computed average of $19.89 on the assessed valuation tax rate. Further, the computed level of annual expenditure of $323 per pupil represents a weighted average increase of $61 per pupil over that presently offered in Painted Post, Corning 9, and Corning 13. To offer an equivalent program under the "no plan" approach, we must multiply the average daily attendance of 5,643 by $61 and divide by the assessed valuation. This results in an average assessed tax rate cost of $11.

The sum of these two, or $30.89 *over and above the present average tax rate* will be the actual cost of the "no plan" attitude. The "no plan" attitude would unquestionably result in the highest cost to the average taxpayer in the area.

The official responsibility of the Harvard Staff was completed upon the submission, at a series of public meetings, of the report briefed above. Among generally favorable first reactions to the recommendations, some contrary sentiments by the residents of Painted Post were among the first to be heard, such, for example, as the views expressed in the following "letter to the editor" published in the *Corning Leader:*

Painted Post, N. Y.

Editor:
Corning Leader
Dear Sir:
RE: Enlarged City District.

There are many things about the Enlarged City District which I fail to understand. First and foremost, I am told now is the time to make a choice — but I'm not given any choice to make. . . . Many citizens of Painted Post have repeatedly asked the State Education Department for a comparable study of Centralization and in every instance have been refused.

I'm being fed with all sorts of propaganda FOR the acceptance of the Harvard survey; being told all the advantages, etc. Now isn't it true there are two sides to every story. What about the disadvantages — such as, our

Painted Post children (at the critical age of 13 thru 18) being away from home all day; the extremely large classes in senior high school with a graduating class of three or four hundred pupils. One of the hilights of commencement is the personal opportunity for each graduate to accept their diploma. This could not be a reality with a class of this size. There would be this same lack of opportunity to develop leadership in many other instances. How many of our boys and girls would have a chance in Varsity extra-curricular activities — Sports, Music, Student Council, Senior plays, etc? What about students who did have a chance to participate in these activities and could not leave the high school until long after the bus had left. Would our Painted Post parents know whether they were detained at school or on the streets of Corning?

Why should we have to abide by decisions made by a School Board on which we would have no representation and not much chance of ever electing a member due to the difference in voting power?

We have four fine churches in our own Painted Post community. What would the decision be if we were asked to discontinue these churches and combine them with the Corning churches. How would we react to combining our Village and Town Government with the Corning City Government, with no representation on that body?

Painted Post has had one of the finest school systems in New York State since 1848. The decision we are asked to make has already been delayed eight years. Let's not be fooled now. Let's wait and have what will be OUR OWN school, supervised by citizens of our own community. . . .

Sincerely,
Vuran B. Allen

29 Corning—II

Choice of Directions

Prior to March 15, 1954, the date on which the final report of the Center for Field Studies was to be presented to the Advisory Committee, the Director of the Harvard Center received a letter from Mr. E. E. Teach of Painted Post. The author of the letter had been a member of the original Painted Post Committee of Six (July, 1950) and of the subsequent Committee of Thirty-six, but he had not been a member of the Committee of Ninety, nor had he participated actively in any of the area study of the problem between June, 1953, and March, 1954. As Chief Engineer of the Ingersoll-Rand plant in Painted Post, he was, however, closely associated with Mr. F. W. Parsons, comptroller of the company and a member of the Steering Committee of the Committee of Ninety. Mr. Teach had been kept informed of the progress of the Harvard Study by Mr. Parsons, who had consulted him from time to time.

EXHIBIT 1 Letter to C. G. Sargent from E. E. Teach

March 1, 1954

Dr. Cyril G. Sargent, Director
Center for Field Studies
Harvard University Graduate School of Education
Spaulding House, 20 Oxford Street
Cambridge 38, Massachusetts

Dear Dr. Sargent:

Mr. F. W. Parsons has asked me to write to you concerning future plans for school district reorganization in the Corning area. On Saturday he discussed this situation with me at length and asked my opinion as to the best procedure to follow from now on. Mr. Parsons wanted me to tell you that he is in full accord with these opinions and he urged me to write them down and send them directly to you. It is not my intention to inject myself into this situation now, having withdrawn from public participation. However, at Mr. Parsons' request I am pleased to submit the following ideas for what they may be worth.

Shown below is a date in the left-hand margin indicating the suggested timing for the item listed. Below each item is a discussion pertaining to that item.

Date	*Item*
March 15	1. Present the Harvard Report. Harvard statement that one plan is to be recommended with no alternatives. Reasons for selecting this plan, carefully outlining the advantages, are to be presented.

March 15 to May 1

2. Prepare a brochure covering the plan.
   This brochure should be a first-class job on quality paper, in color, with maps, descriptions, and statistics presented so that it can be understood by people at the eighth-grade level.

March 15 to May 1

3. Reorganize over-all committee with new work objectives.
   To explain this, we should consider a few distinct needs:
   a. The Steering Committee is unwieldy. Freedom of action is needed with about three people empowered to represent the over-all committee.
   b. The over-all committee should be held together for work to come on publicity, obtaining signatures on petitions, and for representation throughout the area.
   c. The over-all committee should think of itself as a work team to complete the necessary steps so that it and the public together can vote on the plan.
   d. The over-all committee must not think of itself as a congress or representative of the area to sit in judgment on any or all plans. It should not vote on the Harvard plan until the public votes.

   You, therefore, have a delicate situation. You will need the over-all committee to do much work in the coming months yet, in my opinion, a vote by the committee on the plan you recommend should be avoided. I believe this for the following reasons:

   a. Much depends on the atmosphere of the meeting. If the meeting gets off to a wrong start, four years of work might be scrapped in 30 minutes.
   b. Before any vote is taken by any group, several months should go by. The brochure should be in the people's hands and there should be ample opportunity to study the plan.
   c. There is doubt in my mind that all of the members of the over-all committee will know enough to vote intelligently until the brochure and simple facts are in their hands.
   d. A negative vote will result in ultimate disorganization of the committee.

   The Steering Committee should be reorganized with an Executive Committee of three people selected to implement plans to bring the Harvard plan to public vote. The Executive Committee would call upon chairmen of seven sub-groups (which you developed during your studies) to carry out the various work load ahead which will involve obtaining signatures on petitions and conducting an area-wide publicity program to explain your plan to the public.

May 1

4. (A) Distribute the brochure covering the Harvard Plan to the public.
   (B) Organize teams for obtaining signatures on petitions.
   Distribution of the brochure could be handled in the same manner as distribution of the Harvard Question-

naire of October 1, 1953. The seven sub-groups would be organized during May and possibly expanded for the purpose of obtaining signatures on petitions. The responsibility of obtaining signatures may be divided according to these areas and the job assigned to the chairman of each area.

June 1 to June 15 — 5. (A) Obtain signatures on petitions.

(B) District 9 adopt a resolution with respect to this plan. Petitions must be signed by voters equal to 10% or more of the number of children in the area.

In my opinion, District 9 should adopt a resolution endorsing the Harvard plan (assuming, for the moment, that the plan involves one enlarged city district). This resolution should be submitted to Albany as early as possible but certainly not later than the time the petitions are submitted to the Commissioner. It would be desirable for District 9 to adopt this resolution as soon as practical after March 15 because their adoption would strengthen the Harvard plan and assure people that they would not be wasting time in preparing for the vote.

July 1 — 6. (A) District 9 submits resolution to the Commissioner (unless submitted earlier).

(B) Advisory Committee submits petitions to the Commissioner.

It would be desirable to have the resolution and the petitions submitted, personally, by representatives from the District 9 School Board and by the new Executive Committee of the Advisory Group to the Commissioner. These representatives should suggest to the Commissioner that a three-month period is desired for the purpose of informing the public about the Harvard plan. A great deal of time and money has been spent in studies of the past four years, and while there are some people well acquainted on area school problems, it is my candid opinion that this period is necessary, particularly since two of the three months occur during the summer. I believe the best chances for a successful vote will come if the Commissioner selects a date sometime around the first of October.

July 1 to October 1 — 7. Inform and educate the public on the proposed Harvard plan.

During this period, the concentrated selling plan will take place. Graphic media, radio and television, together with local discussion groups and lectures, should be arranged by the Advisory Committee. The Executive Committee will be responsible for implementing this campaign.

October 1 — 8. Vote on the Harvard plan

General Comments

It is assumed, in the foregoing, that the Commissioner will be willing to officially lay out the district to correspond to the Harvard plan. Petitions are not usually filed until the Commissioner has laid out the district. I think that it is reasonable to assume that the district in this case has already been defined by the Rapp Commission Report, together with such subsequent changes to the fringe areas as have occurred since this report. Perhaps this should be discussed with the Commissioner immediately after the Harvard Report is presented to make sure that an additional step to lay out the district is not necessary prior to filing of petitions.

Mr. F. W. Parsons asked me just who is eligible to sign a petition. As I have been out of touch with the latest school law, I hesitate to answer positively on this matter, but according to my notes, the petitions are signed by voters equal to 10% or more of the number of children in the area, as mentioned under Item 5 above. I am guided entirely by my notes of March 3, 1952, at the time this bill was introduced in the legislature but before it became law.

Early in 1951, I became convinced that a solution for the entire area was mandatory but at that time, legislation was inadequate and there was nothing to encourage the city districts to absorb the other areas except as the intelligent thinking people would recognize the grave future of the rural districts. I have followed your progress in the newspapers and through frequent conversations with Mr. Parsons. I am still convinced that one enlarged city district is the best solution for this area. I have felt this way as a result of our studies made from August, 1950, to May, 1952, and your investigation confirms my opinion.

The 1952 law helps but is still inadequate. I feel, with the present District 9 administration, that there is an excellent opportunity to accomplish this project in spite of the legislation. I have faith that Albany, although slow moving, will eventually correct the shortcomings in the law so that, in the long run, District 9 will not be penalized for absorbing their neighbors and becoming involved in this large program. There are, of course, some spotty objections to this course of action both in and out of District 9. In my opinion, the sore spots are not of major consequence and, generally speaking, the situation is quite healthy. I believe the chances for a successful resolution of this school area problem are better than at any time in the past.

Yours very truly,
/s/ Edwin E. Teach

A few days later Mr. Sargent wrote the following reply to Mr. Teach:

EXHIBIT 2 Letter to E. E. Teach from C. G. Sargent

March 8, 1954

Mr. E. E. Teach
123 Grace Boulevard
Painted Post, New York

Dear Mr. Teach:

Thank you very much for your letter and the suggestions outlining the procedure to be followed after March 15. I am heartily in accord with them, although I had personally hoped that a decision might be reached by the middle of June. But you would certainly know the local political climate much better than I and would be able to judge whether this might be thought of as thrusting a decision on the area too rapidly.

As you may know, we talked in a general way about the procedure after March 15 at the Steering Committee meeting on Sunday evening, February 22. I need not tell you that some members of the Steering Committee held at that time, and still hold as best I can tell, the opinion that they should study our report for a two-week period and then vote to either accept or reject it, and if they accept it and approve of the plan, to then proceed with an information and public relations program. We did our best that evening to persuade them otherwise with very little success until we made an analogy between this procedure and the earlier one followed by District 9 with respect to its school building site selection. Although it seemed to me that subsequently several members of the Committee saw the similarity of procedures and were inclined to agree that a vote by the Advisory Committee was not only not mandatory, but possibly politically unwise, subsequent discussions with members of the Committee during the week led me to believe that they had not changed their position but were still contemplating securing a formal vote by the Advisory Committee.

I sincerely hope that you, Mr. Parsons, and others can be effective in persuading a change of point of view on the part of the Steering Committee before the March 15 meeting; for I do not feel that we can advance this position much more ourselves without presuming both on our relationship and our responsibility.

Another issue in the public relations problem is a decision to be considered by the Board of District 9 as to whether or not they wish to have the voters of their district express themselves, either formally or informally, by some referendum method on the question of District 9's participation in any proposed plan. I sensed that this was already in their thinking, and if this is so, I would suppose that it would significantly affect any organizational or informational plans that might be developed.

As to the political aspects of the situation, our somewhat restricted observations would lead us to feel that Corning 13 holds the key to the voting in the area. I would be bold enough to hazard a guess that the sentiment has been swung in the surrounding areas so that it is now at least 60–40 favorable to some form of reorganization. But we have been unable to sense any real concern, interest, or spread of information within District 13. Here we have had our consistently smallest attendance, and for the most part it has been limited to members of the Advisory Committee and the school personnel. We have, therefore, thought that one of the major problems ahead lies in developing favorable sentiment in this district and that the series of activities between March 15 and any date on which a vote on a plan is taken would involve some very astute political strategy and timing in this district.

You mention the question of the number of votes required. You are correct in stating that it is ten per cent or more of the number of children in the area, where by area is meant the area exclusive of the city school district itself. The question of the eligibility of a voter has not previously been raised, but my understanding from the statements made in Albany is that anyone who was eligible to vote in the school district meeting (and as you know, there are some restricting factors here) is eligible to sign a petition.

I share your general optimism with respect to the successful outcome of the study, although realizing there are major problems ahead. We certainly hope that a successful resolution of the issue can be forthcoming, because so many people in the area have committed so much time and study to the problem, and the needs are so demanding that it would I feel be a tragedy for the future well-being of the community should further impasses develop.

Sincerely yours,
/s/ Cyril G. Sargent

On March 19, 1954, Mr. Teach wrote Mr. George Farrington, staff member of the legal division of the New York State Department of Education. The purpose of the letter was to seek an understanding of the legal steps which would be required to bring the question of school district reorganization to a decisive vote. Mr. Farrington sent back the following letter to Mr. Teach. (See Exhibit 3.) Two days later Mr. Teach contacted by phone another member of the State Department, Mr. Francis E. Griffen, Chief of the Bureau of Rural and Administrative Services. Mr. Teach's record of the telephone conversation is given in Exhibit 4.

EXHIBIT 3 Letter to E. E. Teach from George B. Farrington

March 23, 1954

Mr. Edwin E. Teach
Ingersoll-Rand Company
Painted Post, New York

Dear Mr. Teach:

This is in reply to your letter of March 19, 1954.

It is my understanding that the various districts listed in your letter anticipate that they would wish to request the Commissioner of Education to lay out such districts in an area constituent to the school district of the City of Corning, with the intent of creating an enlarged city school district, pursuant to the specification of Section 1526 of the Education Law.

Basically, the procedure to effect a consolidation as an enlarged city school district is as follows:

1. Informative petition from each school district other than the city school district should be filed with the Commissioner of Education through the Superintendent of Schools. I am enclosing herewith a few sample forms of such informative petitions to the Commissioner which you may desire to duplicate and utilize. I regret that I am unable to furnish you with a complete supply. There is no requirement of law which specifies the number of signers to the informative petition, but I would suggest that it would be well to obtain as many signatures as possible in order that the Commissioner may be assured that the people from each district desire to be consolidated as an enlarged city school district. Every attempt should be made to get as many qualified voters to sign the petition as possible, because the stronger the majority that is obtained from each school district, the stronger position you are in to request the Commissioner to lay out the area for consolidation and an enlarged city school district.
2. Since the consolidation can not take place until the Board of Education of

the city school district by resolution consents to the proposed consolidation, it might be well at this time to forward a certified copy of such resolution.

3. Once the Commissioner of Education receives the material mentioned in one and two, he, understandingly, will send his representative into the area to analyze and study the feasibility of the proposal.
4. The next step would be to lay out the area for consolidation as an enlarged city school district. Assuming the Commissioner so acts, an order will be made, entered and posted as set forth in Sub-Division III of Section 1526 of the Education Law, and thereafter it will be necessary that petitions be again presented to the Commissioner requesting him to call a meeting of the qualified voters within the area outside of the city school district to vote upon the proposed consolidation. This procedure is set forth in Sub-Division V of said Section 1526. As you know, this provision of law requires that these petitions must be signed by a number of qualified voters to at least ten percentum of the children in the area of Corning to the latest school census in such area.

As you will note, both the enclosed forms and the laws speak of qualified voters. These voters are qualified voters under the provision of Section 2012 of the Education Laws, which fact governs the qualifications of voters in school districts other than city school districts. It is important to bear in mind that the qualifications of voters will be governed by said Section 2012 until after the meeting to vote upon the proposed consolidation and the enlarged city school district is created.

I am enclosing herewith three copies of Law Pamphlet Two entitled "School Meetings," which sets forth the aforementioned Section 2012 as well as a discussion of the qualification of the voters pursuant of such Section. I should again point out the distinction between the first informative petition and the petition called for by Sub-Division V of said Section 1526. The number of signers of informative petition, as has heretofore been stated, is not governed by the provisions of the Education Laws whereas the number of signers of the petition seeking to call the meeting of the area is set at ten precentum of number of children of the latest school census. The number of signers on the informative petition only goes to the favorability and desirability of the Commissioner to proceed to issue an order laying out the enlarged district.

Mr. Griffin of the Bureau of Rural Administrative Service has checked the district mentioned in your letter, and at this time there appears to be no reason why such district could not be included in the proposed consolidation.

Very truly yours,
George B. Farrington

cc — District Superintendent, Calvin U. Smith
Superintendent, William E. Severn
Superintendent, Hugh W. Gregg
Mr. Francis E. Griffin

[Note: Enclosures not included with the case.]

EXHIBIT 4 Memorandum of Conversations with the State Education Department Tuesday, March 23, 1954 and Wednesday, March 24, 1954

At the Monday, March 22, meeting of the Steering Committee, the Acting Secretary was authorized to contact Albany to determine the proper procedure with respect to petitions and, particularly, to seek an answer to a letter written March 19 to Mr. George B. Farrington, Division of Law, at the request of the Harvard Group.

On Tuesday, March 23, Mr. Farrington advised that a reply would be put in the mail that night and should be received the next day. The letter was not in the Albany mail received at our Post Office at 12:30 P.M., March 24; hence we called Mr. Farrington, asking him to read the letter to us and it was taken down in shorthand and later transcribed. This was considered necessary because we needed this information for a Wednesday night discussion to determine if we should start out immediately with petitions.

Mr. Farrington was very obliging and cooperative and the letter, together with the petition, was available for discussion by 4:30 P.M.

Soon after this, Mr. Francis E. Griffen, Chief Bureau of Rural and Administrative Service, called me, asking if I had seen a copy of Mr. Farrington's letter, and I explained to him that while the letter had not yet been received, we had its contents as outlined below:

1. He stated that the reply we had received from Farrington gives the correct legal procedure but he felt that he should amplify somewhat on Mr. Farrington's letter and outline the relative importance of these steps. He particularly cautioned against excessive haste and wanted to emphasize that they consider the presentation of the informative petition as the most important step.
2. He stated that experience in successfully reorganizing other districts had indicated that all of the selling campaign should come prior to the time that the petitions are circulated. (Although this does not follow the Harvard representatives' suggestion, it is more in line with the procedure I had outlined in my letter of March 1 to Dr. Sargent, Item 5. We should not judge Harvard's suggestion too severely, however, because it must be remembered that they made this suggestion before they had either had the procedure outlined by Farrington or before the comments from Mr. Griffen, as recorded in this memorandum.)
3. He, therefore, considers Item 1 of Mr. Farrington's letter of March 23 as the most important step. I asked him what percentage of signatures they would require before laying out the district. He said they would not lay out the district until they had substantially more than 50% of the entire area. This does not mean more than 50% of every single district, but it does mean more than 50% of the over-all area (excluding District 9) and they would want at least some signatures from all the districts. Griffen stated that the Commissioner was not going to lay out the district until he was reasonably assured that there would be a favorable vote; that the petitions were the most important part, and that allowance must be made for people who sign petitions simply to get rid of the solicitor, and who would vote negatively.
4. I said that we had thought that the second petition, as required by law, was

the important one, and that the first petition was to get an indication of how the people felt. He said that this was quite the reverse and said that the second petition was merely a formality and that once the Commissioner has laid out the district, all that is necessary is for us to send in the 10% quantity of signatures as required by law. The Commissioner must then act to call a vote whether he likes it or not. My impression from this conversation was that the Commissioner must make up his mind at the time the district is laid out, not at the time he calls the vote. It would appear that this point was missed in the past.

5. Griffen has not seen the Harvard Report. He understands Dr. Schmidt (the Assistant Commissioner of Finance) has seen it. He seemed to think that Harvard had proposed alternate plans. I told him this was not true; they had published alternate plans prior to their March 15th Report, but they had recommended one enlarged city district as the only plan, and in answer to questions raised in public meetings during the week of March 15, had definitely stated that they were not recommending any alternates or any plan as "next best." Mr. Griffen seemed exceedingly pleased at this situation and said that this was proper.
6. Mr. Griffen said that he had been tied up with the Commissioner on March 23 when Mr. Farrington's office had contacted his staff with respect to the legal procedure we had asked for. He said that he did not realize the letter had gone out until he received his copy. I note this for whatever significance it may have.
7. I asked him about a recent letter that Cal Smith (Superintendent of Steuben County, Supervisory District #1) had written, suggesting another meeting to discuss this matter, and how he felt about going ahead with such a meeting. He did not answer this question directly but said that he called me because of Cal Smith's letter and that he would simply caution us not to move too fast for fear of setting this plan back three or four years through getting petitions signed before the people are ready.

The above summarizes the conversations with the State Education Department and I would like to make the following observations as I now see the picture.

Conclusions

Up until now, the proper procedure for bringing this study to a vote has not been clear. We have been handicapped by not knowing the relative importance of the steps through which we must go.

Bringing pressure upon the Legal Department to give us Farrington's letter of March 23 has resulted in a clear-cut situation:

1. Farrington's letter of March 23 definitely spells out the step-by-step procedure from the legal view, and he has given us the proper form for the informative petition, which is the first step.
2. Mr. Griffen's phone call of March 24 indicates how the State will act on the steps in Farrington's letter. This phone call indicates their position which has not been reduced to writing in any definite commitment. I believe Mr. Griffen is sincere, is not trying to stall this plan, and is hopeful that we will weigh carefully how we carry out the procedure as outlined in Farrington's letter.

/s/ E. E. Teach

On the evening of March 25 the Advisory Committee of Ninety held their first meeting since the meeting at which the final report had been presented by the Harvard group. Exhibit 5 is the newspaper account of the meeting and its decisions as reported in the *Corning Leader* on March 26, 1954. A brief description of the people referred to but not already identified in the newspaper article is as follows:

Theodore Daddow: Engineer at Ingersoll-Rand; aged 39; father of two school-age daughters.

Dr. Kent Phillips: Dentist and real estate owner; aged 70; has been a member of the Board of Education of Corning 13 for twenty-six years; had been selected chairman of Advisory Committee, as citizens of the area said, "because he was neither Ingersoll-Rand nor Corning Glass Works" (the two major industries in the area).

Norman Markle: Head of Computational Division of Corning Glass Works; considered by citizens as "our expert on community drives"; aged 41; no children.

Mrs. Charles King: Wife of research physicist at Corning Glass Works; mother of four school-age children.

Orville Reed: Chief engineer in blueprint department of Ingersoll-Rand, lifelong resident of Painted Post; aged 53; father of three school-age children.

John B. Ward: Director of Design for Corning Glass Works; member of the city district school board (as is Mr. Parsons); aged 45; three school-age children.

EXHIBIT 5 Account of Meeting of Advisory Committee of Ninety, March 25, 1954, as reported in the *Corning Leader*, March 26

AREA VOTE ON SCHOOL PLAN

Group Accepts Responsibilities Resulting from Findings; Plan Setup to Provide Facts to Public

A resolution "to take whatever steps are necessary to bring the question of one enlarged city school to a vote by the citizens" was adopted Thursday night by the Advisory Committee at a meeting in the Northside Grammar School. The committee also heard an outline of the procedure required to effectuate the Harvard-recommended plan through petitions to the State Department of Education and eventual vote of the taxpayers.

The resolution was suggested by Theodore Daddow of Painted Post who said the committee has a responsibility to the public to go on record, indicating where the committee "plans to go from here." The following resolution was adopted unanimously:

"Having caused the Harvard Graduate School of Education to make a study of the school problems in our area and having influenced the various school districts to underwrite the cost of this study, we, the Citizens Advisory Committee, resolve to accept our responsibility to study the recommendations of the Harvard Study

Group, to explain them to the other citizens of the area; to make known our opinion of their merits; and, in any case, to take whatever steps are necessary to bring the question of one enlarged city school district to a vote by the School Board of District Nine and by the citizens of the surrounding area."

The Advisory Committee unanimously approved reports and recommendations of its Steering Committee and adopted a resolution accepting the evident responsibilities resulting from the findings of the Harvard Field Studies.

About 56 persons attended the meeting in the Northside Grammar School auditorium. It was conducted by Dr. Kent W. Phillips, chairman of the steering and advisory committees.

The committee members Thursday night were generally agreed on the need for a wide distribution of copies of the Harvard final report and an intensive program to reach as many people as possible with a full explanation of the recommendations for one enlarged city school district. The committee expects 500 copies of the report to be delivered soon but voted at Thursday's meeting to ascertain the cost of obtaining additional copies to assure wider distribution.

Need Sound Presentation

Norman Markle said the presentation of the recommendations requires a "sound and broad educational base" with representative groups prepared to make presentations at small group meetings throughout the area.

Mrs. Charles King of District Nine suggested that members of the advisory committee could be trained and be made available to address civic, service and social groups and other gatherings to outline the recommendations and steps required to bring about one enlarged city school district.

On the suggestion of Orville Reed, a former member of the Painted Post Board of Education members agreed to submit written questions as received by them, to the steering committee for publication in a bulletin to be widely distributed later.

Hugh W. Gregg, superintendent of School District 13, agreed on the need for an educational program throughout the seven areas involved in the proposed consolidation. He said, "It is not wise to start throwing out petitions now, although some could be accumulated through those already familiar and in favor of the program." He said the circulation of petitions should be coordinated with an expression from all the districts involved.

Calvin U. Smith, superintendent of Supervisory District One, said that "thousands of persons" have got to become interested in the program and it "can't be rushed." He added:

"We've got to go at a rate the people will follow us. We can't get ahead of the people. We must also work with the Department of Education and I understand they haven't seen the report yet."

He added that definite dates for advisory meetings would be desirable, pointing out that four members he knew of were unable to attend the session because of conflicts in dates. He mentioned two at South Corning, who planned a meeting with their Village Board on the program, and others at Hornby and Lindley.

On March 26, 1954, a member of the Advisory Committee sent a letter to Mr. Sargent of Harvard. Enclosed with the letter were copies of Exhibits 3, 4, and 5. The sender cited a group of questions he called "key" and asked for Sargent's reactions and suggestions. The letter, in part, (Exhibit 6) follows:

EXHIBIT 6 Letter to C. G. Sargent from a member of the Advisory Committee

March 26, 1954

Dr. Cyril G. Sargent
Director of Center for Field Studies
Harvard University
20 Oxford Street
Cambridge 38, Mass.

Dear Dr. Sargent:

You can see by the three enclosures the Advisory Committee has decided to take some steps, whatever they will be, to bring the question of your recommendation for our area to a decisive vote. When should we vote, in October, next June, or this June? What do you make of Farrington's letter and Griffen's conversation with our Ed Teach?

We are in considerable confusion as to next steps and would greatly appreciate a letter from you outlining your ideas as to where do we go from here? What do you see as the major decisions we will have to make?

I confess I am perhaps talking about the planning for a program of public information on the recommendations of the report. Realizing your job has been one of analysis and not of selling your recommendations, it has occurred to me that you might be willing, time permitting, to give us some ideas as to how to sell the idea of the single over-all school district. What kind of program of public relations should we develop and how should we organize it? Some of my colleagues here would also appreciate it if you would have some of your staff work out a list of possible questions we may get. In other words, what kinds of questions can we be expected to get; what form do you think the opposition to your recommendation will take? Do we need a brochure; and if so, what would its focus be? What do you suggest we do about the State Department of Education?

I realize I have expressed a number of questions of lesser and greater importance to us, and it may be your present and future commitments will prevent you from taking a greater part now that the report is in our hands. However, it might be that some member or members of your staff will be willing to delve into these questions and assist us. We would be happy to pay the expenses of anyone coming out here in the next week or two to assist us.

Once again, you know how delighted we are with the fine work you have done for us. I hope now we can take the ball and run for a touchdown, educationally speaking. It will be a tremendous job.

Cordially yours,
/s/ F.W.P.

30 Corning—III

The Campaign and the Outcome

After the presentation of the Harvard Study's final report, "A Valley and a Decision" (March 15, 1954), and the subsequent expression of intent (March 25, 1954) on the part of the Advisory Committee of Ninety to disseminate the recommendations and to work to bring the question of district reorganization to a decisive vote, the Advisory Committee engaged the services of two advisers in public information and community organization who were familiar with the Corning school situation. It was the specific assignment of these advisers to take an active part in the development of a planned course of action leading to a vote.

Two memoranda — one by the advisers (Exhibit 1) and one by Mr. Eugene L. Belisle of the Harvard staff (Exhibit 2) — were prepared and presented to the Steering Committee. They recommended that the first phase of the program be geared to presenting a nonpartisan view of all sides of the central issues in the district reorganization question. This was to continue while discussions and agreements were being sought between the state and the locality as to timing of subsequent steps leading to a vote. Following this, Phase II would seek to develop support for the Enlarged City District plan.

The Advisory Committee accepted the recommended organization (Exhibit 1) as proposed by the Steering Committee. However, members of the Steering Committee wished to study further the second memorandum (Exhibit 2) and decided not to make this memorandum available to the Advisory Committee. The Steering Committee also decided not to present to the Advisory Committee as a whole the recommendation for separating the responsibility of Phase I (nonpartisan educational activity under Advisory Committee sponsorship) from Phase II (campaign organization and publicity under a committee composed entirely of supporters of the enlarged city district plan).

The Educational Campaign

During the April 15th meeting of the Advisory Committee it became clear that there existed differing perceptions as to how the program of public relations should be organized, how it should be staffed, and what the tentative target date for a vote should be. Rural members of the committee, represented by Walter Freeman, trustee of Caton 5, tended to feel that the target date should be in June. Members of the management segment of the Advisory Committee felt the same way. Two members of the professional educator group, Superintendent Calvin U. Smith, Supervisory District No. 1, and Hugh Gregg, Superintendent of Corning 13, tended to feel that a June date would be rushing the necessary educational process. Superintendent Smith and the public relations consultant clashed openly at the Advisory Committee meeting, but the motion to try for a June date, as proposed by Walter Freedman, carried 23 to 14.

The consultants were asked to suggest personnel for the program as approved by the committee. (See Exhibit 3.) They also were made responsible for recommending a nucleus for each of the main committees, who in turn would select their own committee members.

The actual pattern of activities, as planned and as carried out, from April 12 to the week of May 24 is summarized as follows:

SUMMARY OF ACTIVITIES

1. Speakers bureau	About 55 speaking engagements were met.
2. Home meetings	About 40 coffee hours were held, attended by over 450 people.
3. Brochures	Seven brochures were developed and circulated, between April 12 and the voting date, June 22, in a distribution pattern which did not include direct mail. Elementary school children, stores, kits of speaking aids for speakers and home meetings, and other methods of distribution were used.
4. Posters	Three posters were made and distributed in quantities of 250 each. The first poster urged people to read "A Valley and a Decision" and listed places where copies could be borrowed. The second poster announced the petition campaign; the third poster announced the date and time and place for the vote.
5. Resolutions, Endorsements	A leaflet was issued containing endorsements of the enlarged city district plan by the Commissioner of Education, all of the chief public school administrators in the area, the school boards of the four largest districts in the area, heads of the principal labor unions, and chief executives of the major corporations.
6. Radio	Both Corning stations were used in presenting panel discussions, spot endorsements, news.
7. Television	The local channel offered time for four half-hour panel discussions in which twenty different people participated.
8. Press	The local daily paper, the *Corning Leader,* cooperated fully, and gave extensive coverage to the whole phase of the study. The local weekly paper, the *Corning News,* was antagonistic to the Harvard Report and to the program of educational interpretation. The nearby *Elmira Advertiser,* although less comprehensive in its coverage, did report various activities.
9. School Conferences	Student and faculty conferences were held in each of the three main school districts (Corning 9, Corning 13, and Painted Post.)

The total involvement of volunteer personnel varied during the whole program from as few as five persons to as many as six hundred.

The Informative Petition

Under the final decision of the State Department, the "informative petition" effort was defined as that of obtaining *as many signatures as possible* (with the understanding that these would have to total *well over 50 per cent* of the voters in the area) on petitions so worded that the signers would know that their signatures meant that they were asking the Commissioner of Education to lay out the area as an Enlarged City District and that they wished their school district to be included. The text of the petition read:

> We, the undersigned, legally qualified voters of school district .... town of ...., county of .... New York do hereby request that the Commissioner of Education lay out an enlarged city school district in and about .... and that said school district number .... town of ...., be included therein.

Since the aim, with the tentative agreement of the State Department, was to bring the matter to vote before the end of June if sufficient signers were obtained, the program of *education* by the Advisory Committee tended automatically to become a campaign designed to muster support for the enlarged city district plan, climaxed by an intensive "informative petition" effort.

The work of the Petition Committee and its approximately 375 volunteer workers began during the week of May 24 and lasted for eight days.

The "Tally of Informative Petitions and Votes" (Exhibit 4) shows that of 9,073 people actually contacted by canvassers, 8,072 signed the informative petition.

The Opposition Campaign

Prior to the week of May 24, proponents of the enlarged city district plan were aware of opposition only to the extent that about sixty people in Painted Post appeared to be grumbling over the possibility of losing their Painted Post High School in the merger of the districts. These same people, who were known by name, had been the core of a move to form a centralization of Painted Post (Erwin 1) with the other Erwin and Lindley common school districts. Their plan for the solution of their own building shortages had been tabled by the State Department of Education. Their plan was felt by many, within as well as outside Painted Post, to be unsatisfactory from a whole area point of view.

The three leading persons identified with this Painted Post group were Dr. Robert B. Randels, a research physicist at the Corning Glass Works, Mr. Allen, a local business man, and Mr. Miller, owner and publisher of the weekly newspaper, the *Corning News*.

While the Harvard Staff was conducting the study, and during the presentation of recommendations, some of these persons attended many of the study area meetings held, asked many questions, and pressed various objections and criticisms. It was observed, however, that others in the various audiences had generally seemed unfavorable to the activities of this leadership, and on several occasions one or two citizens commented to members of the Harvard group on their "unrepresentative" actions and questions.

From March 20 to May 22 there was no information on the activities of this group. Members of the Advisory Committee felt that the Painted Post opponents to the plan had given up.

During the week of May 24, however, a letter (Exhibit 5) criticizing certain aspects of the Harvard Study appeared in the daily newspaper, the *Corning Leader*, which has a circulation of about 18,000. Proponents of the reorganization decided to ignore Dr. Randels' letter.

After the announcement of the success of the informative petition campaign, the *Corning News,* the weekly paper (1,200 circulation, according to certificate filed in the Post Office) came out on June 3 with a front-page spread questioning the honesty of the Harvard figures. (See Exhibit 6.) This was the first time that the *Corning News* had concerned itself with the school question.

The Advisory Committee decided to ignore the *News,* since, "the weekly paper operates under a policy of being against everything the *Leader* is favorable to."

It became known by the proponents of the plan that the editor of the *News* was being joined by Dr. Randels, and by a "few" other people in the Painted Post group who were known to oppose consolidation.

Attempts were made to discuss the issues with some members of the opposition; three informal home meetings were held to which were invited about a dozen of the known opponents. The atmosphere of these meetings was considered "cool" by observers.

On June 7, it was learned that six people in East Corning, Corning 1, intended to oppose the plan as a group. They had circulated a counter petition and had raised 151 signatures. Members of the Advisory Committee talked with the East Corning group, and with the group's representatives, on two occasions during the week of June 7. (See Exhibit 7.)

On June 15 and June 17, the *Elmira Advertiser,* the morning paper for the region with an estimated circulation of 18,000, carried two articles. (See Exhibits 8 and 9.) This paper had not printed any copy since March 15 on the school problems of Corning.

Also on June 17, the *Corning News* came out with another in its series of articles opposing the plan. (See Exhibit 10.)

On June 18, the *Corning Leader* reported on the mass meeting held in East Corning the previous night. (See Exhibit 11.) A day later, a "Citizens Committee Opposing School Consolidation," none of whose names were mentioned or known, sent through the mails a printed flier presenting arguments against the one-school-district plan. (See Exhibit 12.)

As this sudden and high-powered opposition campaign unfolded, following the climactic "informative petition" effort which had gained the signatures of 88 per cent of the voters in the area, the leadership of the proponent campaign increasingly wondered what to do.

The editor of the *Corning Leader* wrote and printed two editorials, one on June 15 and one on June 20, in an effort to minimize the effect of opposition moves. (See Exhibits 13 and 14.)

On June 19, the *Leader* carried a letter to the editor (Exhibit 15) from Mr. M. M. Cammen, one of the leading proponents of the reorganization, commenting on his reaction to receipt of the flier mailed by the "Citizens Committee Opposing School Consolidation."

The Voters' Decision

The day of the vote, June 22, was hot and humid until mid-afternoon when a heavy thunderstorm and rain felled many trees in the area; parts of the area were without electricity for four hours.

The carefully planned agenda for the meeting which preceded the opening of the polls was not, however, thwarted in any way. Of the estimated 400 people present at the New State Armory at opening time, 10 A.M., about 375 were known to be proponents of the reorganization. In the first show of strength, the nomination and election of a permanent chairman of the meetings, the proponents' candidate — the editor of the *Corning Leader* — was elected by loud acclaim.

The polls were open for twelve hours, from 10 A.M. to 10 P.M., June 22. Members of the opposition were asked to participate in the supervision of the polls and in the counting of the votes. The *Corning Leader's* report of the results of the vote is shown in Exhibit 16.

On July 1, 1954, the State Department of Education made the district reorganization final.

After the public relations consultants had completed their assignment, they received letters from three men, Messrs. Parsons, Shopoff, and Reed (Exhibit 17), all of whom had been very active throughout the phase just completed. Mr. Parsons, a member of the Corning 9 school board, and one of the original proponents of the study was elected president of the new Enlarged City District school board on July 2. Mr. Shopoff had been chairman of the Brochures Committee. Mr. Reed had been chairman of the Petitions Committee.

EXHIBIT 1 Memorandum by the Advisory Committee

April 15, 1954

MEMORANDUM

According to the resolution passed by the Advisory Committee on March 25, 1954, the following points were resolved:

> "To study the recommendations of the Harvard Study Group;
> To explain them to other citizens of the area;
> To make known our opinion of their merits; and, in any case,
> To take steps necessary to bring the question to a vote. . . ."

We now present for your consideration a tentative program of public education on the matter of the proposed enlarged city district plan as described in the Center's final report. It has been designed in the spirit of the Advisory Committee's resolution. This proposed program attempts to suggest ways and means the Advisory Committee can proceed to offer to the citizen of the area a balanced, fair-minded report of the recommendations of the Center's study of school problems as related to district structure. It is a plan which is educational in character and intent; its purpose is to assist the Advisory Committee in disseminating the report, in taking to the people the recommendations and the reasons behind these recommendations as developed in the Center's study.

This proposed program of public education has been designed to begin on April 12, 1954, and to continue for about five weeks, until about the end of the week of May 10, 1954. It is assumed that this program will be carried on by members of the Advisory Committee and by others they wish to involve from the area.

I. The Advisory Committee has *voted to distribute 500 copies of the final report* in the manner described in the *Minutes* of the March 25th meeting. These copies have been delivered as follows:

Reports

Mr. Clowe	61
Mr. Gregg	64
Mr. Severn	66
Dr. Phillips	2
Mr. Schoonover	25
Mrs. Palinkas	25
Mr. Freeman	25
Mr. Smith	232
	500

II. At the April 12th Steering Committee meeting *it was voted to recommend to the Advisory Committee creation of a Public Relations Committee.*

Personnel:

To consist of a General Chairman, eight sub-chairmen, and as many members as chairman and sub-chairmen may deem desirable.

To prepare and cause to be distributed publicity describing the Harvard plan.

Possible sub-committees:

A. *Speaker's Bureau.* To arrange for speakers or panels to discuss report before groups throughout the area. (Suggest that one person at least be designated as a desirable leader for each of the seven sub-areas.)

B. *Home Meetings.* To arrange for meetings in homes: these meetings could be morning coffee hours, afternoon teas, or brief evening get-togethers. The hostess could present the findings of the Harvard Plan and lead a discussion of the issues. (Assistance could be provided by the Speakers Bureau in many instances.)

C. *Brochure Sub-committee.* To prepare material which could be disseminated at selected times: sub-committee should consist of approximately five to seven people. (Some material for consideration by this committee has already been developed.)

D. *Poster Sub-committee.* To prepare posters which can be placed throughout the area at selected times. First poster has already been prepared and invites everyone to read the report.)

E. *Resolutions and Endorsements Sub-committee.* To prepare resolutions and seek endorsements for the plan.

F. *Volunteer and Assistance Sub-committee.* To assist in distribution of materials.

G. *Radio and Press Sub-committees.* To prepare and assist in presenting radio programs and press releases on the Plan and activities of the other committees.

III. At the April 12th Steering Committee meeting *it was voted to recommend to the Advisory Committee creation of a Petition Committee.*

Personnel:

To consist of a General Chairman, three sub-chairmen, and leaders from each of the 61 districts from which petitions must be obtained and such other members as the chairman and sub-chairmen may consider desirable.

Purpose (General):

To arrange for the printing, circulation, and collection of petitions.

Sub-chairmen to be selected to head up activities pertaining to obtaining voting lists, printing, test areas, and handling of petitions.

SCHOOL CONFERENCE COMMITTEE

In connection with the proposed program of public information and education on the recommendations and essential contents of the report by the Center for Field Studies, an important question to consider is the place of the schools in this program. Several needs and opportunities emerge in this respect, including:

1. Insuring an early and full opportunity for all of the personnel of the various public school systems in the area to study, consider, and discuss the report and its findings. Surely the personnel of the public schools should be among the first and best informed on this problem.

2. Discussion by the public education personnel in the area of various questions on policies concerning their roles individually and as groups, in relation to both the students and other members of the community during the period of public attention and discussion on this question. . . .

3. Consideration of the responsibility of the public schools to provide leadership in inculcating in the students, particularly in the more advanced grades, the principle of studying the problem and any findings on the problem before taking a position on the issue involved. . . .

Clearly if the schools are to assist in bringing to bear the principles of education in the forthcoming public consideration of this issue, study and discussion by school administrators, teachers, and other personnel is the logical starting point.

EXHIBIT 2 Memorandum by Eugene L. Belisle

April 12, 1954

MEMORANDUM

To: Steering Committee

Re: *Regarding a Time Schedule for Action on the Greater Corning School Problem*

A number of different time schedules must be considered as *possible* for completing the steps involved in bring the question of a single over-all school district to a final vote. From the possible time schedules, there is a need to select *one* which seems most logical and feasible in the light of all circumstances.

In undertaking this, the first question is: Who is to decide on this time schedule?

The answer is clear. Power and responsibility to decide is divided. It lies in Corning; it lies in Albany.

Decisions made in Corning as to timing successive sequences are dependent upon decisions made in Albany as to timing of certain other steps. Possibly the greatest single risk of an unsatisfactory outcome of the process would lie in the inability to proceed from the outset on the basis of an understanding on at least a preferred time-table, together with a strictly limited set of alternative time-tables to which the schedule might be shifted if some shift is dictated in the course of the effort.

There is *no way* of specifying in advance an over-all time schedule unless it is based upon some kind of understanding between Corning and Albany.

The whole process of organization, education, publicity, and petitioning can be conducted with greatest effectiveness only if it is planned in relation to *specific goals for specific periods and dates.* Gains and achievements at one stage could be seriously jeopardized by either uncertainty or an unanticipated shift in subsequent steps.

The purpose of both decision-making centers — Corning and Albany — will best be achieved by mutual discussion of the problem and arrival at the closest understanding and agreement possible in the light of the responsibilities of each.

The next immediate task is, therefore, that of working out a basic time-table, agreed upon both in Corning and in Albany, together with further agreement on (1) alternatives to which this time-table may be shifted, (2) what these circumstances warranting shift would be, and (3) how the decision to shift would be made.

At the present time it is apparent that:

1. There are differences of opinion within the Advisory Board and Steering Committee as to what would be a *desirable* time schedule and final voting date. Expressions of opinion have ranged from those favoring an immediate effort to obtain signatures on the first petition and a final voting date as early as possible in June to those suggesting as much as a full year of educational activity before bringing the question to a vote. The Advisory Committee cannot proceed effectively until it has emerged with some clear view as to a time schedule which the Committee has defined as desirable.

2. However, even an agreement within the Advisory Board and Steering Committee as to a *desirable* schedule would *not* represent a *realistic* time schedule for planning purposes unless it were known whether this time schedule would be acceptable to those in decision-making positions within the State Department of Education in Albany. Without such an understanding the risks of committing money and effort to the schedule would be substantially increased.

3. Some implications as to a time schedule are present in the formal ruling of the State Department as to required steps and accomplishments before the matter could be brought to a vote. Other communications from members of the State Department which have not been issued as formal rulings have enlarged the formal requirements; but these statements interpreting the formal requirements have in some cases not been definitive enough to clarify all the possible implications as to timing. Nor is it entirely clear whether all the interpretations have the status of a formal and unchanging policy; in fact, some subsequent positions expressed from within the State Department have tended to modify the timing implications inherent in some earlier statements and interpretations. As a result, certain areas of uncertainty remain as to just what requirements are considered necessary by the State Department including both those that directly affect timing and those significant implications as to timing the various steps in the process.

The above is, of course, to be expected when those responsible for decisions are by virtue of that fact endeavoring to exercise caution, make wise decisions, and bring to bear advice based upon experience. It is not a criticism.

Under these circumstances, a procedure might well be for the Advisory Board and Steering Committee to work through to a time schedule which in the light of their knowledge of this particular area would seem to them desirable, realistic, and feasible *if* acceptable to the State Department. This tentative time-table might then be discussed with the State Department to determine its acceptability in the light of the State Department's views and responsibilities.

It might be pointed out that the effectuation of a well-informed voter decision on the question of a single over-all district for the Greater Corning Area represents, both by virtue of the relative newness of the enlarged city district act and by virtue of the characteristics of the area, a *new kind of problem.* Its solution might well call upon the respective resources of knowledge in *both* Corning and Albany.

Some but by no means all the experience with the formation of centralized districts which has been developed in Albany needs to be considered carefully by Corning leadership in planning action in the Corning situation; (conversely some of the factors and experience within the Greater Corning area which differentiate this area from previous centralizations may need special consideration by those in decision-making positions in Albany). There would appear to be dangers in either of the respective extremes of assuming (1) that because the Corning problem involves a city area and the new enlarged city district act, experience of centralizations involving other than cities and a different law has little or no applicability, or (2) that experience related to centralizations applies with virtually no modifications to the Corning problem.

In order to work through to a clear view of the problem in the terms suggested above, it may first be helpful to set down the successive steps in the process of bringing this question to a vote and to identify at the same time where the responsibility, power, or initiative for determining the tempo and dates for each of these steps lies.

STEPS IN PROCESS OF BRINGING QUESTION TO VOTE

1. Program of public information and education designed to insure widespread public understanding of recommendations and essential facts and reasoning in the report made by the Center for Field Studies. This step is dictated not by law or by administrative ruling but as a recognized prerequisite to exercise of informed and intelligent choice by the voters. It must therefore *precede* action designed to get the voters to take a position; in fact, education cannot take place if people are committed to a conclusion before knowing something about the findings of a study and how these findings were obtained.

The Advisory Board has wisely taken this position and has furthermore assumed the responsibility of sponsoring such an educational program without itself taking a position with respect to the recommendation presented as the conclusion of the study. The nature, timing, and duration of this program of public information and education are still to be decided; the responsibility for the decision rests with the Advisory Board.

The educational program does not need to be "completed" before proceeding with the second step, as indicated below.

2. A ruling has been made by the State Department of Education to the effect that a so-called "informative petition" bearing sufficient signatures of qualified voters to assure the Department of significant support for the enlarged city district will be a prerequisite to the "laying out" of the district as provided in 1526. Technically, the law leaves the step of laying out a district for possible vote under the act wholly at the discretion of the Commissioner; legally, he could proceed with this step without any evidence whatsoever of interest or support in this or any other area of school districts covered by the law. He has chosen to apply to this situation essentially the same "informative petition" step which has been traditionally applied in the case of centralizations under consideration; but one of the areas of uncertainty with respect to timing is related to whether the Department will consider the requirements of proportions of voter signatures to be identical with those developed to fit the somewhat different framework of centralizations.

Further clarification of the requirements as to the "informative petitions" on an enlarged city district question, and for this area specifically, *may have a very great bearing on what will be required for Step 1 (educational program) as to goals, necessary organization of resources and total duration; it will have a major bearing on when and in what manner Step 2 (informative petition) can start.* It will thereby significantly affect the timing of subsequent steps and the question of the feasible date on which to plan for the final voting.

Thus, although the requirements of the "informative petition" represent the discretionary exercise of responsibility lying within the State Department, the terms of these requirements have a major bearing on the way in which the Advisory Committee may undertake to fulfill its responsibilities to the voters with respect both to informing them and to bringing the matter to a final vote at a time deemed appropriate in the light of local circumstances.

3. Following the meeting of whatever requirements may be fixed for an "informative petition," and receipt of these petitions, the Commissioner will proceed to lay out the district, as provided in 1526. This step involves some considerations of timing. How much time would be felt necessary, by the Commissioner, to study the petitions and lay out the area? It would, of course, be necessary to have at least some estimate as to this time period, if we are to plan an over-all time schedule.

Besides this time question, is the question of the calendar date the Commissioner might decide upon to lay out the area. This decision could be one of the crucial factors affecting the outcome on the final voting date. The Advisory Committee might suggest to the Commissioner a preferred date for laying out the area, in the light of local conditions.

4. Can it be assumed that the completion and filing of the required 10 per cent petitions will follow closely the issuance of the formal order laying out the area? This would seem to be the logical decision. It would seem advantageous if the order laying out the area could be issued at a time which would permit fairly prompt steps toward obtaining the formal petition signatures, with the final voting date then to come at a time which would permit a final period of effective voter information and participation.

5. Following receipt of a formal petition meeting the legal requirements, the final voting date automatically falls within certain limits of time specified in the law. This date must not be more than 30 days after the filing of the petitions, and a minimum of 10 days' notice must be given. The meeting held on the prescribed date may be adjourned from time to time by a majority vote but no adjournment may be for more than 10 days.

SOME BASIC FACTORS AFFECTING THE CHOICE OF TIME SCHEDULES

Before presenting four alternative time schedules, a number of factors relating to the local situation and the conduct of a program relative to 1526 will be very briefly cited.

1. *Need for public information and education.* The Advisory Committee has already voted a resolution to disseminate the report of the Center for Field Studies. In the light of the spirit of this resolution, and in the light of analysis of various responses to the questionnaire which are significant as indices for gauging sentiments favorable and unfavorable to *change* of the kind and degree associated with the recommendations in the Harvard Report, it seems wise to assume that a substantial minority of voters in the area will be predisposed

to oppose these recommendations unless *extraordinary* efforts are made to induce a change of viewpoint.

This minority also appears to be sufficiently large to jeopardize the outcome of a vote unless many of them are won over in the process of education. It will not be enough to rally those who may be predisposed in favor of change.

Likewise, the weight of the undecided middle, the lukewarm, and the disinterested may and often does fall disproportionately on the side of opposition to change in the actual voting process on a question of this kind.

2. *Specific urban factors present.* This question involves *both* urban and rural areas. Pattern of organization and public educational activity for such an effort as this must be quite different to correspond to a whole series of differences in social and communication patterns in these two types of areas. Patterns followed in experience with centralizations are not necessarily adequate or appropriate to the Corning Area.

Examination of the following table suggests some of the special urban and urban-rural factors.

Area	*Percent of Persons 21 and over*	*Special Notes*
I	8%	rural, village and new subdivision
II	10%	rural, village
III	8%	" "
IV	10%	" "
Painted Post (V)	8%	not same as either rural or urban
Corning #13 (VI)	33%	urban, voting
Corning #9 (VII)	23%	urban, not voting

A great effort is indicated as being necessary in the urban areas, of a kind and degree of organization not like the kind and degree required for other areas. A so-called area (geographic) organization reaching to every individual block and street seems essential.

3. *Differences in level of interest and participation in public issues at different calendar periods.* A consideration of habits and attitudes of people toward participating in tasks of volunteer organization or paying attention to public issues during various months ahead is necessary; competing demands on their time and attention arising out of other calendared activities must be taken into account. Differences between urban and rural areas in these respects are pertinent. Any time schedule involving activity between the period of June 15 and Labor Day needs to be thought through quite carefully in these respects.

4. *Planning and timing of a two-peak effort:* (A) the informative petition; (B) the final vote. Unless the informative petition requirement is modified, this becomes a two-peak effort insofar as organization and publicity are concerned. There are many major differences involved in planning and developing a two-peak effort as compared with a one-peak drive.

The allocation of resources, the utilization of human resources — interest, attention, incentive — affect both leadership and volunteer worker availability and drive for successive goals.

The duration of the time interval between the two peaks of effort has a major bearing on how to plan the allocation of both money and human energy.

At present, legal conditions seem to require a minimum of two major drives for mobilization of social support. *The second peak should evoke the more ultimate power.* Yet the informative petition requirement as currently implied would demand a maximum effort too. If this requirement is not modified, problems of exhaustion and overconfidence will make it impossible to mobilize the same degree of energy on the second seemingly easier task. A skilful opposition can wait out the first peak of effort and then step in to capitalize on this overconfidence and exhaustion. It is only when the second peak is recognized from the outset as a more rigorous test than the one which must first be surmounted, that the first can develop both power and new reserves of strength to accomplish the second.

With the foregoing considerations in mind, we can now mention briefly pros and cons of several possible time schedules.

The suggestion of a schedule involving as long as a year of educational activity before coming to a vote will first be mentioned, inasmuch as it was put forward from within the Advisory Committee.

This plan would be inadvisable if any shorter period proves equally worthy. The history of studies of district reorganization of the area; pressing problems of population increase and urgency of decision by various school districts (i.e. Beaver Dams, South Corning, Coopers, Corning 13 high school); signs of strong sentiment for moving toward an earlier voting date — these considerations argue against this position.

The alternatives recommended for consideration are three:

1. one which would involve only a one-peak effort, and, therefore, the earliest voting date, possibly by the end of June;
2. one which would carry over the date of voting into the fall;
3. one which would place the date of voting somewhere between July 20 and August 15.

The three time schedules and the conditions and assumptions relating to them are as follows:

Alternative Time Schedule # 1

1. *April 15–May 1.* Obtain signatures on informative petition. (*N.B. Basic assumption underlying this timing of signature getting is that these signatures would represent only an evidence of desire to bring the issue to a vote, rather than a demonstration of majority support for the enlarged city district.* This assumption would involve a major shift in the policy of the State Department.)
2. *April 15 to about May 20.* An educational program, under the sponsorship of the Advisory Committee.
3. *About May 20.* A careful sampling of opinion in selected areas, both urban and rural, to gauge sentiment before taking the crucial step of filing the 10 per cent petition, *about May 20.* If, on the basis of these and other measures it is felt unwise to have the final vote before the end of June, it should be postponed to the fall, *not to July or August.* (The June period, in the event of such a shift, should be used as in alternative time schedule # 2.)
4. Assuming that the decision is made to proceed to a vote toward the end of June, a campaign or organization and publicity must be ready for unfolding by May 15. Leadership and workers in this effort must, of course, be wholly committed to support of the enlarged city district.

Inasmuch as the Advisory Committee must certainly have some members who are opposed to the recommended plan, no attempt should be made to use this Committee as the vehicle for Step 4 in this plan. It is suggested that when the Committee has fulfilled its resolution for assisting in *educating* the public, it suspend its regular meetings, but remain formally in being until after the final vote.

There might however, be certain special meetings to provide for solution of some problems on which both proponents and opponents of the enlarged city district might well agree (i.e. arrangements for fair provisions for voting by all voters in case the Commissioner desired the advice of a representative local body). No matter what the outcome of the vote, there will be need for the Advisory Committee which, despite differences of leaning, has worked together, to come together again and help lead community opinion.

Alternative Time Schedule # 2

1. *April 15–May 10.* Program of public information.
2. *April 20–April 30.* Development and conduct of "test petition" project.
3. *May 15–25.* Development of organizational and publicity (as differentiated from preceding educational) effort.
4. *June 1–15* (approximately). Start and finish mass "informative petition" campaign, if test petition results are favorable. Otherwise postpone, for further cumulation of publicity and organizational impacts. Steps 3 and 4 in this plan could easily be shifted two weeks or even later, if conditions made it prudent to do so.
5. *July–August.* Review, strengthen, revise organization. Analyze all sources of strength and weakness, support and opposition. Prepare for intensive efforts preceding final vote date. Occasional timely publicity. But no major organizational activity.
6. *Assumption:* The Commissioner would feel justified in issuing the order laying out the district *immediately after Labor Day.*
7. *Sept. 5–12.* Obtain 10 per cent petition signatures.
8. *Sept. 5–Oct. 5–10.* Conduct maximum second peak effort in organization, publicity, and vote winning.
9. *Oct. 5–10.* Voting date.

Alternative Time Schedule # 3

1. *April 15–May 10.* Educational program as in alternatives # 1 and # 2.
2. *May 15–30.* Development and conduct of intensive organizational and publicity effort, (requiring numerous earlier steps in planning and preparation).
3. *May 25–June 15.* Conduct of informative petition effort. File with Commissioner no later than June 10.
4. *Assumption:* The Commissioner would see fit to issue an order laying out the area sometime later in June or within the first few days of July.
5. *July 10.* Complete and file the 10 per cent petition.
6. *July 10 to voting date.* Second intensive organization and publicity effort.
7. *July 30–August 10.* Final vote date. (It is recommended that if under Alternative # 3 it becomes apparent *at any time before the end of June* that the final vote date will be forced later than August 10, the schedule be immediately revised to conform as closely as possible with Alternative # 2.)

EXHIBIT 3 Proposed Schedule of Education Program

Activity	*Week of April 12*	*19*	*26*	*May 3*	*10*
Steering Committee	12–Meets to develop plans for educational program and to recommend them to Advisory Committee; plan for first test petitions		29–Meets to review work of PR and Petition Committee; plan for joint school conference		
Advisory Committee	15–Meets to take up Steering Committee's agenda				13–Meets to plan to get informative petitions out
Public Relations Committee		19–Meets to organize assignments	27–Meets for brief review and planning period; sub-committee meetings	6–Meets to plan for school panels, for informative petition period	11–Meets to review and plan campaign for petition drive
Speaker's Bureau Sub-committee		22–Seven study area meetings	*All week* – Speaking engagements	*All week*–Speaking engagements	*All week*–Speaking engagements
Home Meetings Sub-committee			*All week*–Coffee hours, teas, evening get-togethers	*All week*–Coffee hours, teas, evening get-togethers	*All week*–Coffee hours, teas, evening get-togethers
Brochure Sub-committee	13–Meets to prepare basic brochure — an abstract of the report, in précis style — to be ready for the seven study area meetings	20–Meets to prepare school teaching unit on "Our Schools"; preparation of other materials for Speaker's Bureau and Home Meetings; preparation of special material for test petition drive; (three or four brochures)			

(Exhibit 3 — continued)

Activity	*Week of April 12*	*19*	*26*	*May 3*	*10*
Poster Sub-committee	13–Preparation of Poster #1	19–Distribution of Poster #1		3–Preparation of Poster #2	10–Distribution of Poster #2
Resolutions and Endorsements Sub-committee		19–Meets after PR Committee, planning		6–Meets after PR Committee, planning	
Volunteer and Assistance Sub-committee	15–Available ------→	------→	------→	------→	------→
Radio {report, special programs}	12–Report 15–Report	19–Report 22–Report	------→	------→	------→
Press {report, special articles}	12–Report 15–Report	19–Report 22–Report			
Petition Committee		21–Meets to plan for test petitions; Informative petitions, prepare voting lists; select personnel	26–Meets to review and progress plans; ready test petitions 29–Meets to prepare test petition workers	3–Review and analysis	
School Conference and Contest		20–Meets with Brochure Sub-committee	30–Joint study conference of area school personnel	7–Junior-Senior Social Studies conference	14–Student Essay Contest awards
Test Petition		Week — ?	28–31–Test Petition Project		

EXHIBIT 4 Corning Enlarged City School District: Tally of Informative Petitions, May 1954. Summary

Town	*Number of Signatures*	*Number of Refusals*	*Number not Contacted**	*Total Estimated Eligible*
Lindley	411	54	43	508
Campbell	120	5	8	133
Catlin	484	26	49	559
Caton	448	34	48	530
Corning	4369	565	585	5519
Dix	141	72	13	226
Erwin	1773	228	127	2128
Hornby	300	73	39	412
Orange	34	2	4	40
Sub-Total	8080	1059	916	10055
Less Caton #2	8	2	12	22
Less Dix #10	0	56	0	56
Totals	8072	1001	904	9977*

* Includes errors in estimated number eligible.

EXHIBIT 5 A "Letter to the Editor" Published in the *Corning Leader*

OBJECTS TO STUDY PROCEDURES

341 N. Hamilton
Painted Post, N. Y.
May 23, 1954.

To the Editor:

In view of the barrage of information now being directed toward the promotion of the Enlarged City School District, it is unlikely that any effective opposition will be organized. I must, however, once more raise an objection to the way in which this vital matter is being handled. In the first place, the Harvard group did not conduct a seminar type of study in which the local group would have arrived at its own conclusions independently of the final recommendations by Harvard. In the second place, the alternatives were not adequately presented in the study, there was not even a mention of the possibility of an intermediate district over a few centralizations. And now we are getting literature which misrepresents and distorts the situation.

There are many errors of omission and commission in the report and flyers. It is simply not true that serious study has been under way for eight years, in fact, even after a request by the annual meeting of Erwin District No. 1, a whole year went by with no study at all. It is not true that in 1953 there was no law permitting the consolidation of other districts with city districts. The enlarged district law went into effect on April 17, 1952, and before that in April 1951 a law passed in 1950 became effective which extended to city districts the general consolidation law which had been on the books for many years. (These earlier laws were not very attractive since they made no provision for extra state aid.)

The annual grant of $265,000 seems to be emphasized as a most attractive feature of the One District Plan. The state aid formula for centralization is based on pupil attendance and increases as the population increases; the Intermediate District plan also involves special grants of state monies, but the Harvard study did not include these factors in any of its "alternative plans." There is no evidence in the report to support the claim that curriculum under the one district plan would be better than in other reasonable reorganizations. There is no explanation of the change in attitude of the study committee from one of insistence that the Eight Million Dollar program of a year ago was too much to the present wholehearted approval of a Twelve Million Dollar program.

Why, if the Assembly plan of representation is so desirable, must we wait for special legislation when the existing Intermediate District law incorporates an equivalent system in large measure? Some of our nearby Central Districts (Campbell, Savona, Bradford) are taking steps to organize just such a district.

Why must we have a district which is larger than several of the counties of this state to solve our acute problems? There are many districts in the state with only one fourth or one third of the population of this area which maintain adequate to excellent programs and school plants at a reasonable cost.

I don't find answers in the report or the flyers.

Very truly yours,
Robert B. Randels

EXHIBIT 6 From the Corning News

Are All the Figures of the Harvard Group Honest?

Based on State Formulas They May Be Accurate But Deceiving

Announcement the Committee of Ninety plan to bring the question of a large consolidated city school district to a vote this month has caused surprise in the area. Many citizens who thought this revolutionary proposal would be discussed from all angles before it was brought up for final decision are perturbed by the apparent haste.

As one woman expressed her mind to the Corning News a few days ago: "I think this thing is being rushed too fast. Publicity has been given to only one side of this proposition, the recommendation of the Harvard group. This is too important a matter to be decided without full discussion of all aspects. A debt of $12.47 million to which an affirmative vote will virtually bind us, is too serious to decide by snap judgment. I do not want to bind our children to such a debt for the next 30 years, until I know more about the alternative proposals."

Will that woman and other citizens of the area have opportunity for further study before they vote? Apparently not. Proponents of one large, consolidated city district have expressed their determination to force an early vote. Over 7,000 signatures to a petition on the question have been secured. Those who want more time to think, appear to be unorganized and leaderless.

The last issue of this newspaper gave a general outline of the history of school expansion plans and the proposals of the Harvard Study Group. In our efforts to find the truth we have talked to some people who have been familiar with the history of efforts for both centralization and consolidation of area schools. People the writer has talked to are interested as sincerely in what is best for the real educational needs of the area, as the strongest advocates of a great consolidated city district.

Going back more than a year ago it should be remembered the State Education Department made a study of the Corning school situation with a view to forming a consolidated district. People who were on the original committee when that study was made, inform this newspaper that committee "threw up its hands" upon learning the study called for an area building program that would cost eight and one-half million dollars. Because that committee were convinced the amount was too large for the community to absorb it was decided to hire the Harvard group for a second study.

Yet, when the Harvard group recommended a building program of some four million dollars more, the Committee of Ninety endorsed it.

The book put out by the Harvard Study Group entitled, A Valley and a Decision, contains a large number of charts and figures to prove the contention of the group that one consolidated city district is best for all the people in the area. The figures look convincing. No one going over the different tables with a casual examination would be in any position to dispute those figures. Relying on those tables, alone, the reader is forced to conclude the group is right, that judged on a tax basis, one city, consolidated district would give the most education per dollar.

According to one table in the book a consolidated building program of $12.47 million would cost a tax rate of $38.38, based on assessed valuation. A city district including northside and southside with territory east, south and north of the city would require a tax rate of $37.09 a thousand. A central district for the northside of the city and contributing area would require a tax rate of $42.96. A city district for the southside and territory east and south would have the lowest $30 tax rate, and a central district for Painted Post with the territory west, north and south of that village would require a tax rate of $45.29 per thousand.

Anyone familiar with state aid to central districts would be puzzled by these latter figures. It is well known that the centralization law was passed precisely to give children residing in the poorer areas of the state equal educational privileges with those in city schools. There are central districts in the state where approximately ninety per cent of the educational cost, buildings, teachers and all, comes from outside the district.

Any citizen knowing these facts could not accept the figures of the Harvard group without some study between the lines. The state pays 80 per cent of transportation in a central district, none in a consolidated city district. That is a major item where many children are brought in from outlying areas.

The question arises: are the figures given by the Harvard group on a Painted Post central district strictly honest?

This question was submitted to a citizen of Painted Post who has made a careful study of centralization. This citizen stated the figures themselves have a basis in fact, but they do not give a truly honest picture. He stated further that the group arrived at its figures without any real study of centralization for the Painted Post area.

EXHIBIT 7 From the *Corning Leader*

East Corning School Board Seeks Removal of District From Enlarged City Setup

Trustees of the Town of Corning Common School District One (East Corning) were taking steps today to have their district removed from the Harvard-recommended enlarged city school district for the Greater Corning and Painted Post Area. Last week petitions filed in Albany asking the new district to be laid out included those from the East Corning District with 151 signatures against 123 refusals.

Martin H. Kozlowski, trustee and former clerk said that the action was taken at special meeting of the board Saturday night. The president of the board, William Wise, was not present.

As of Sunday night, Kozlowski said, 212 signatures of legal voters of the district had been secured on a petition asking the commissioner of education of the State of New York to allow District 1 "to remain in our present status." He said the signatures were secured by a committee of about six persons, based on six prime questions raised in opposition to the plan for an enlarged district.

The 212 signatures represent "more than a majority of the voters in our district," Kozlowski said. He noted that the Advisory Committee of Ninety had estimated the number of eligible voters at 300 for District 1, but suggested that the actual number was about 400.

As spokesman for the trustee group he said the six questions raised and approved by the group were as follows:

"1. Representation — our district will be giving up its rights of representation. Sixty-two districts, including East Corning, will be controlled by the School Board of City District No. 9 and not by the 62 districts. By control, we mean all school assets, including buildings, properties, taxes, also liabilities.

"2. No place in pamphlet circulated by advisory committee of 90 is there a mention of a school district assembly as suggested by the Harvard commission, to our knowledge.

"3. We question whether or not proposed enlarged city district could operate as efficiently as present system.

"4. We believe that our school district has met the standards of the state education department and believe we will be able to continue to meet this standard in the future.

"5. It is our understanding that the Harvard group established tax rate per thousand of assessed valuation would be $39.30. Our present tax rate which includes new building costs is $17.30 per thousand of assessed valuation, an increase of $21.08.

"6. We have reason to doubt that the number of people signing petitions, circulated by Advisory Committee of 90 are the majority and therefore have decided to circulate petitions in an effort to determine this," Kozlowski said the six points carried the signatures of Trustee Harold Tobey, himself and Fredrick J. Wilding who will replace William Wise as trustee on July 1.

Mr. Wise who is president of the board said today, however, that he was taking no position on the matter inasmuch as he was retiring from the office. He said, however, that he did not learn of the special meeting until Sunday.

There are three members on the East Corning school board. They are Mr. Wise whose term expires officially June 30, Harold Tobey and Martin Kozlowski who was named to fill the vacancy created by Raymond Troll who recently moved from the district. Mr. Wilding replaces Mr. Wise officially July 1.

EXHIBIT 8 From the *Elmira Advertiser*

Calls E. Corning Meeting

School Board Member Hits Harvard Proposal

CORNING — A public meeting is scheduled at the East Corning School on Goff Rd. at 8 p.m. Thursday for discussion of "objectionable features" of the plan for the proposed enlarged city school district.

The meeting has been arranged by a committee which includes Dr. Howard E. De Camp, member of the Board of Education of School District 13, and Mrs. De Camp.

Dr. De Camp last night issued a statement charging bias in the public presentation of the report of the Harvard Graduate School of Education which conducted a survey of area educational needs.

An election on the Harvard Plan, which would bring 61 area school districts into the enlarged city district, is to be held at the State Armory Tuesday, June 22, from 10 a.m. to 10 p.m.

Dr. De Camp's statement in part, follows:

"One of the most misunderstood and confusing issues that has confronted the voters of Corning in the past quarter of a century is the one now under consideration for correcting the present overcrowded condition within our school districts.

"The group of persons. . . . favoring the enlarged city district have made statements. . . . that have been biased.

"In every instance when asked questions regarding matters not in favor of the 'one district plan,' no reply has been given.

"There is need of a correction of several impossible statements that have been made by members of the Harvard study group.

"It was stated that all of the local boards of education, comprising Corning Northside, Corning Southside, Painted Post and South Corning, had voted unanimously to support the change.

"When the matter was voted on by District 13, Northside School Board, I stated I was going to vote against the proposition because it was impracticable, too expensive for the value received and not a good substitute for the plans already made by the school boards of each of the named districts for expansion to accommodate their needs.

"I stated I would not support any proposition affecting the City of Corning and the surrounding territory considered in the action until all four plans suggested by the Harvard study club had received equal explanation.

"Many of the voters of District 3 think that their board of education voted unanimously in favor of this change, regardless of their wishes. This should correct such an error.

"I feel that the voters should be consulted.

"The board members and the voters of the entire area realize that new buildings are needed. However, a large number of people feel that other, more economical and more practical means will accomplish the same results.

"May I ask these questions? To date, no satisfactory reply has been forthcoming:

"1. Why did a group of people, who formerly turned down an $8 million project, now favor a project of $12½ million?

"2. Why has there been such a rush to push the thing over before more information has been given on all four plans?

"3. How can people get information when the speakers sent to various meetings cannot give the answers?

"4. Why will voters be required to come to one central voting place? Why is it not possible for each district to vote in its own voting place?

"5. Who is to count the vote? Who will appoint the tellers? Could this be planned as a means of helping to put the thing over?

"6. What will be the cost of the supervising superintendent? At the present high salaries, it will probably be several times the price now. No mention has been made of the high cost of operation. This is not a factory proposition — we are spending the people's money.

"7. Do you know that a similar proposal was recently refused by the voters of Ithaca?

"8. Do you know that a like proposal was suggested in Waverly, and the school board wisely said, 'We will work out our own solution'?

"Tremendous pressure has been brought to gain (voters) support by stating that each year until 1970, our area would receive $265,000 as school aid to the building program. I asked a member of the Harvard group if he could guarantee such payments of public money by the state for any number of years. He admitted that the sum could not be promised for more than a year at a time.

"In the second place, such a sum would be only a drop in the bucket with a $12.47 million project.

"9. Do you know that no voter in the area controlled by the School

District 9 will have the right to vote on this proposition, which will cost them a large increase in school taxes? They must rely on the vote of their Board of Education.

"Go to the voting place and vote. Believe me, I have no axe to grind, but I hate to see deception. When voting, remember that you need to make payments on your home for many years to come.

"Do not accept a plan which in many cases may make those payments impossible. Your local boards have plans to provide the schools on a practical basis."

EXHIBIT 9 From the *Elmira Advertiser*

Verify Harvard Plan Vote Not Unanimous

CORNING — The statement of Dr. Howard E. De Camp, member of the Board of Education of School Dist. 13, that the Board did not vote unanimously in favor of the Harvard Plan for an enlarged city school district was verified yesterday by R. W. Shopoff, chairman of the brochure sub-committee of the Advisory Committee of 90.

The Advisory Committee of 90 was largely responsible for pushing to a head a proposal to bring 61 area districts into the city district generally designated as No. 9. The proposal, which will be the issue of an election at the State Armory Tuesday, resulted from a survey made by the Center for Field Studies of the Harvard Graduate School of Education.

Lewis A. Wilson, State Commissioner of Education, set the election date in response to petitions signed by more than 8,000 qualified voters in the Corning area school districts. A public meeting for discussion of the Harvard Plan and to prepare for the election is to be held at the East Corning School on Goff Rd. at 8 tonight.

Dr. De Camp's statement, which was published in The Advertiser Tuesday, also drew a letter from Frederick W. Parsons, member of the Board of Education of City Dist. 9 and one of the elected representatives of that district on the Committee of 90.

"It was stated" said Dr. De Camp, "that all of the local boards of education, comprising Corning Northside, Corning Southside, Painted Post and South Corning, had voted unanimously to support the change.

"When the matter was voted on by Dist. 13, Northside School Board, I stated I was going to vote against the proposition because it was impracticable, too expensive for the value received and not a good substitute for the plans already made by each of the named districts for expansion to accommodate their needs."

Under date of June 15, R. W. Shopoff wrote Dr. De Camp and sent a copy of his letter to the local office of the Advertiser.

"In one of the pamphlets prepared by the brochure sub-committee of the Advisory Committee of 90," Shopoff said, "we erroneously indicated unanimous approval of the enlarged city district plan by the District 13 School Board."

He said he had found that approval by the Dist. 13 Board was not unanimous — and that Dr. De Camp did not endorse the resolution approved by a majority of the Board. He added that he was not aware of the misstatement in the pamphlet until Tuesday morning.

"The error in the pamphlet," he continued, "was unintentional and was an oversight only. The sincere intent behind the pamphlets was to present the facts concerning our schools without distortion or misrepresentation. The error in your connection — or any other errors — is not an effort to mislead."

The Parsons letter to Dr. De Camp, a copy of which was sent

to The Advertiser from the writer's office in Painted Post, contained the following:

"I read with a great deal of interest the article in the Elmira Advertiser this morning in regard to the meeting at East Corning Thursday. In reading the parts of your letter that were published along with this article, I believe there is some misunderstanding in regard to the contract the advisory committee had with the Harvard Study Group.

"The Advisory Committee of 90 hired the Harvard Study Group and it was financed by the participation of, I believe, all but one of the 63 school districts.

"The committee decided that we needed outside help by experts who thoroughly knew the subject, could devote sufficient time to the study and were not prejudiced or influenced by the local situation.

"We, therefore, hired the Harvard Study Group from the graduate school of education which is probably the top-notch organization in this work in this country. We asked them to come into this area, study the problems in an absolutely independent way, talk with all the people in the area who were interested — and come up with a solution.

"We specifically instructed them to study every possible plan that seemed practical for this area. This they did and they are all outlined in their report.

"We also told them that, since they had probably devoted 10 times as much effort to this study as any of us could possibly do, we wanted their recommendations as to what plan they thought best and the reasons why.

"I have devoted the major portion of my time for over the last year to this school problem for this area and I firmly believe we are on the right track. It is a golden opportunity and I believe that most people, who devote thoughtful study to it, will agree."

EXHIBIT 10 From the *Corning News*

• A WEEKLY NEWSPAPER • • READ ALL THRU THE WEEK •

CORNING NEWS

COVERING CITY AND COUNTRY BY CAMERA

SIXTEENTH YEAR—NO. 24 THURSDAY, JUNE 17, 1954 16 Pages

Lines Are Drawn in School Consolidation Poll Tuesday

Around the Town

With amazing suddenness, the question of whether or not 62 school districts will be consolidated with Corning School District 9 will be decided June 22, 1954 at the Corning Armory. It leaves the writer somewhat bewildered to think and believe that so major a change in the life of many many people might possibly be brought about before the people with such swiftness and long before anyone has had an opportunity to think about the many ramifications involved. trict, including the people of the city of Corning, will have to go along with whatever assessment is placed on property by the assessor. It won't be long before the assessor, who is generally an elected official outside a city, will have to look to his political job and keep assessments down. What recourse has the City assessed person? None.

Another ramification is the question of whether the residents of City School District 9 have a right to vote. As matters stand now, they will not be allowed to vote on the question. Still on the vote of others

Opponents Hold Mass Meeting Tonight; All Voters Must Go To Armory Between 10 a.m. - 10 p.m.

Opponents of a big, consolidated city school system for the Corning area are suddenly coming to life. Two weeks ago indifference hung heavily in the air, opposition seemed non-existent. Today all that is changed and citizens who showed no interest one way or another a short time ago, are stirring both vocally and physically.

One evidence of this new interest by opponents of one big city school is an announcement a mass meeting will be held in the East Corning school this evening at eight o'clock. Another sign is the number of people who are engaging in discussion, for and against the Harvard Study Group plan.

One of the many ramifications has to do with taxes. Tax assessors of towns have long been known not to tax farms too highly. This is evident from the tax equalization as published by the Board of Supervisors each year. Still the people of the entire new district tax assessment might be raised $10.00 or $15.00 per thousand a year. Somewhat akin to taxation without representation.

Another ramification is the transportation problem. The cost and maintenance of buses

(Continued)

COMMUNICATION

June 14, 1954

Dear Editor:

WILL PAINTED POST VOTE ITSELF OFF THE MAP?

Your paper is not alone in believing that Painted Post will be no more if the people vote to scrap their high school for the Corning consolidated school.

WE WONDER:

What has happened to the old pride in the community Painted Posters once exhibited? Remember when they dedicated the Indian monument?

Why do they appear to be complacently accepting the consolidation plan instead of requesting an opportunity to choose one of the other 3 plans? Is it because they fought so long for more adequate buildings, for centralization, etc., that there is no fight left in them? Do they feel that since they must have more adequate facilities for their children, and that since seems to be the fastest way to get them now, that they might as well accept them, and give up hopes of having a school of their own?

Yes, Painted Posters fought to maintain their identity through maintaining their post office; but, could it be because of a very highly publicized scandal that they hesitate to fight to maintain their identity through their school? Do they know how much closer this school system can bring them to becoming a part of Corning than the post office deal ever could have?

Are many Painted Posters really convinced that their children will be better off under the consolidated school system, under the supervision of a Corning school board? Are they really convinced that the advantages this school will bring their children will offset the disadvantages? Have Painted Posters thought of the disadvantages this school will bring with it for their children?

Will Painted Posters resent bigger taxes, with smaller voice, or no voice, in the school management? Will they one day be crying, "Too much taxation with too little representation"?

Just an Onlooker,
Wondering.

Proponents are saying that this is the greatest thing that ever happened to the Corning area. They claim a single school system will wipe out all prejudices that have divided the city socially just as the river divided it geographically. They appear supremely confident the voters will overwhelmingly endorse the Harvard plan.

Opponents counter that the Harvard Group did not fulfill its assignment to give equal study to plans for centralization as well as consolidation. They say the Group should not have taken it upon themselves to try to influence the citizens one way or another. They say the local daily press has deliberately presented only the favorable side of consolidation. That the people are being "sold a bill of goods".

Opponents, too, are talking quite confidently this week. They say people have been badly misled and are just coming awake to the disadvantages of this big consolidated school. They are giving reasons.

One man who states the people have been misled is Robert Johnson, proprietor of the Ramblers Ret, Painted Post. Mr. Johnson appeared on a tape recorded radio program Sunday evening to ask some question of the Harvard Study Group representative, Mr. Halloway. Johnson asked Halloway what assurance outlying districts have that the building program will be completed, since the buildings will be voted a part at a time. He stated that taxpayers may decide their taxes are high enough when the building program is one-half or two-thirds completed.

Halloway admitted he was unable to answer. That is understandable. This is unanswerable. The proponents of the Harvard Study plan cannot give a guarantee how much or how little of the building program will be voted.

Much dissatisfaction is being expressed among residents of District No. 9, that they are completely disenfranchised. All they can do is talk. Some are expressing the belief this program, if voted, will not stand up in the courts. One attorney residing on the Southside stated this week it was his considered opinion the courts would overrule the legislature if a final test should come.

"It is inconceivable," this man said. "That one segment of the population can vote tax burdens upon another group of citizens who have no right to take part in the voting. This thing will never stand up in the courts, if the voters approve it."

This viewpoint seems to be shared quite generally by the legal profession in Corning. At least five attorneys have in-

(Continued)

SCHOOL CONSOLIDATION

formed The News one way or another that they plan to work, directly or indirectly against the consolidation.

Considerable resentment has been expressed by opponents for the provision that the voters from all over the wide area this plan covers will be compelled to travel to one point, the Corning Armory, to cast their ballots. Some express the opinion this is a deliberate move by the State Education Department to influence the vote in favor of consolidation. These citizens say it is a fact residents of rural areas are less inclined to favor revolutionary plans to take their self-rule over schools away from them. Schools are closer to them than to city residents. Yet, they are compelled by this consolidation act to travel long distances to vote.

A further disadvantage to rural residents is the fact farmers are exceedingly busy at this time of year and will not feel they can afford to take the time off from work to drive the many miles to the armory.

A fact that caused much surprise up to two weeks ago was the apparent indifference of Painted Post people as to what became of their school. But now the day of voting has drawn nearer many residents of the Post have started to wake up and be heard. Many have called the News office and asked for information about things they did not understand. Others have written in to congratulate this paper for printing both sides of the story. Both written and vocal expressions have come in like the following:

"Congratulations on your story in The Corning News on 'Goodbye Painted Post.' . . . I agree with you heartily in all of it. I just wish the people would wake up, wake up before it is too late. . . This school story reminds me of Russia. 'We have plans for you, take your choice, only your choice shall be this plan.' I know only your paper would print this."

How many Painted Posters feel like the letter writer quoted above? No one will know until the votes are counted next Tuesday night. No one will know even then, as far as that is concerned, for the voting will be by secret ballot and this IS America where the right to cast one's ballot without observance is still unabridged.

Many people out in the rural areas feel this consolidation plan is a scheme to take away their representation and force them into a big city district. A deal to make them pay for huge new city schools. Oddly enough many residents of the city take an opposite view, saying all the advantages lie with the rural residents. That tax assessments are much lower outside, the expense of bringing children into Corning on busses will be terrifically heavy and will place burdensome costs on real estate within the city.

Southsiders say they are being forced into something for which they have no power to vote for or against. Many Northsiders say they believe strongly in a program for uniting the entire city into a single district, but are frightened by the idea of trying to bring 61 districts into one school system with all the involved problems of transportation and administration.

The arguments will doubtless continue right up until ten o'clock next Tuesday when voting starts. It is to be hoped citizens will do something besides talking about it. They should get out in large numbers to vote on this proposition. The vote should reflect a clear majority of all the people who have a right to vote. Even then a majority opinion of all citizens in Corning and the surrounding area will be impossible to obtain. The residents south of the river in District No. 9 are helpless to express their opinion at the polls.

That is not American.

AROUND THE TOWN

and garages has not been gone into nor have the people been told of the expense. These are just a few questions which remain unanswered and which people have had too little time to think about.

Why all the hurry? London bridge isn't falling down and there are enough schools to permit a thorough study by the people. We urge the readers of this column to vote no, not with the idea of never trying to better the school system but with the idea of gaining more time to study and acquaint themselves with the entire situation. The people who are going to pay the bill should have something to say about what they are buying.

As for residents of School District 9, I would suggest that they petition their Board to go slow on the project. None of the members of that board were elected on the platform that they would support a consolidated school district. It's getting pretty close to misrepresentation rather than to representation.

The Common Council adopted a budget Monday night. It's about 15 days late since the charter provides that the budget shall be adopted at the May meeting. We recall Mayor Andrews telling us his program will be one of economy. The only economy in Mayor Andrews program is the economy some poor veterans are going to have to make in their budget at home to be able to pay the higher tax rate per thousand. Spendthrift governments will not stay in office too long.

Before the next column appears the vote on the school district will have been taken. Naming the Corning Armory as the only polling place is a disgrace. People will have to travel all the way from Lindley and Monterey to Corning to vote.

Disenfranchisement can take many many forms. We don't like the methods the proponents of this plan are using to put across their aims. We trust the people will vote it down.

EXHIBIT 11 From the *Corning Leader*

East Corning Meeting Opposes Enlarged School District by 2 Votes; Secrecy Move Is Blocked

A two-vote margin, 47 to 45, at a meeting in East Corning Thursday night gave support to a resolution urging citizens of the proposed enlarged city school district to vote against the plan in the election scheduled next Tuesday at the New York State Armory in Corning.

The resolution was passed at a public meeting of taxpayers of the proposed district, attended by about 110 persons, called by a committee of five who stated they felt only one side has been presented, and held at temporary school building on Goff Road in East Corning.

This is the first resolution that has been adopted opposing the plan since it was announced in April that efforts would be made to bring the plan to a vote in June. The Advisory Committee of Ninety, five school boards, including the three major districts involved in the plan, and many local civic organizations, have adopted resolutions favoring the plan by overwhelming votes.

Adoption of the resolution last night came after about two hours of heavy discussion and was offered by Dr. Robert B. Randels of Painted Post. Attorney Jacob Welch presided at the meeting and Miss Doris Burr was clerk.

The resolution states "Whereas it has been demonstrated that on at least one important matter in connection with the Tuesday vote, a member of the Committee of Ninety has stated that he learned at this meeting the falsity of one of the claims in the brochure, 'The Time For Action,' and whereas in the general discussion it was clear that there was about as much misinformation as information, be it resolved that we recommend that the citizens should vote 'No' in order to gain additional time in which to learn the answers (to questions posed) and to study carefully alternate plans."

Strong objection to the wording of the resolution was offered by Elwyn Jacobs, the member of the Committee of Ninety referred to in the resolution, who said it was "unfair play" to so word the resolution.

Jacobs told Dr. Randels and the group that he had stated plainly before the entire group that his interpretation of a paragraph in the brochure to the effect that no further action on any plan for combining the districts for at least one year, was incorrect, and that the correct interpretation was that no further action could be taken for at least one year on the specific plan being considered, but that action could be taken on other plans.

Jacobs observed that this point was minor and in no way amounted to a compromise of his backing of the enlarged district plan nor did it show that he did not understand the enlarged plan he and the Committee of Ninety recommended to the voters.

A resolution recommending

that no publicity be given the number of votes cast either for or against the "vote No" resolution was offered by Attorney Raymond Troll, former trustee of the East Corning school district which recently placed itself on record as being opposed to having their district included in the enlarged district.

Six questions posed by "a majority of the trustees of the East Corning School board," in a letter accompanying petitions recently circulated in opposition to that district's inclusion in the enlarged district, were the center of heaviest discussion.

The six questions (all previously published in full in The Corning Leader) suggest that (1) and (2) the present districts will give up their control of local affairs to the present Corning District 9 school board and that no steps have been taken to insure representation from other districts, (3) that the enlarged district may not operate as efficiently at the present set-up, (4) that present districts have proved their ability to handle their own problems effectively, (5) that the tax rate for East Corning would be raised materially under the enlarged district plan, and (6) that there is reason to doubt the number of persons who signed petitions favoring establishment of the enlarged district constitute a true majority of voters of East Corning.

F. Louis Janowsky, former trustee of the East Corning district, stated in opposing the enlarged district, that the District 9 board is in no way compelled by law to give up control of the enlarged district if the enlarged district plan is adopted. If the District 9 board intended to have representatives from other districts under the enlarged plan or an advisory assembly composed of representatives from outlying areas, why, he asked, were steps not taken to have the State Legislature pass a bill authorizing expansion of the District 9 board to provide more equal representation.

Couldn't Act Yet

It was pointed out that no such action would be considered by the Legislature until it had been determined whether the voters of the area would approve the enlarged district. No similar situation has come before the Legislature and thus there has been and is no need for such legislation until the enlarged district becomes an accomplished fact, it was stated.

Proponents of the plan stated that the District 9 board had publicly announced plans to expand its number from seven to nine and to seek advice from an advisory group made up of representatives from the entire area.

Ernest Cook of District 13 (Corning) said he questioned whether the cost would be prohibitive and was answered by Warren Stewart of Lindley who suggested that when the cost in taxes is divided by the number of children in a given family and by the number of days of schooling received each year, the expense is relatively minute.

East Corning District Still In School Plan

School officials, in response to numerous inquiries this morning, issued a statement this afternoon advising that last night's action at the East Corning School DID NOT eliminate that district from the enlarged city plan.

"People of Corning District One did not lose the right to vote on Tuesday by the action taken last night for the meeting held was one for the whole area and had no legal effect on anyone's right to vote," the statement noted.

Voting will be at the State Armory from 10 a. m. to 10 p. m. on Tuesday with residents of 60 districts, including East Corning, eligible to vote.

Kozlowski Speaks

Martin Kozlowski, East Corning school trustee, said he wanted to state for the record that his district was not opposed to educational advances but felt that action must be taken while local control is still effective, to insure that the plan ultimately adopted is the best plan available. His point was added to by Dr. Randels who suggested that the four plans offered by the Harvard University Center for Field Studies should have been given more consideration, together with other possible plans.

Mrs. H. E. DeCamp of Corning District 13, suggested that voters should have been allowed to choose from several possible plans in "a more democratic way."

Dr. Randels suggested that perhaps the proper method would be to combine a few districts rather than to make one large district. James Collins of Corning Manor pointed out that increased benefits could be derived from one district in that specialization could be offered, together with a wider selection of courses at the high school level.

Sees Equal Opportunity

Robert Shopoff of Painted Post suggested that under the one district plan, equal opportunity would be offered to all students in the entire enlarged district through an equal and more perfectly balanced curriculum.

It was suggested that because a district is allowed, by law, to bond itself for only 10 per cent of assessed valuations, that it might not be possible to raise the money necessary to build schools which might be needed. This was countered by a legal interpretation that the law provides that a two-thirds vote of the people of the district can override this 10 per cent law.

Harry Leach of Hornby injected a Robert Burns type humor into the discussion, but nonetheless emphasized the opposition of citizens of rural districts to an anticipated higher cost in school tax. In this he was supported strongly by Fred Rogers, also of Hornby, who stated that taxes in many cases had forced

Why Only One Area Voting Place Tuesday? Law Outlined By State

The question of "Why only one voting place" for next Tuesday's vote on the enlarged city school district was answered today in the release for publication of a letter from the State Education Department.

Under date of May 28th Dr. Kent W. Phillips, chairman of the Advisory Committee of Ninety, sent a telegram to the State Department requesting a ruling on the point in that he and the Committee felt more than one voting place should be permitted. The reply dated June 1 and sent by John P. Jehu, director of the Division of Law, follows:

"Answering your telegram of May 28, addressed to the Commissioner of Education, please be advised that voting in the area to be laid out by the Commissioner of Education for consolidation with the City School District must be held in one place. Section 1526 of the Education Law requires the Commissioner to 'fix a time and place for a special meeting of the qualified voters' within the area contained in the order of the commissioner. There would be no authority for the Commissioner of Education to call a meeting in several places. Signed, John P. Jehu.

farmers to give up their land. He said 2,000 acres in his area had been taken over by the state in default of tax.

Opposition to this point suggested that farmers were leaving their land for reasons other than the cost of tax and noted that one reason was in order to insure better schools for their children.

Criticism of the plan to hold voting in Tuesday's election in only one place, was answered by Mrs. Mathew Cammen of District 13 who said the Committee of Ninety had sought to have the election held at several locations about the area but that Commissioner of Education of the State of New York had ruled that the vote must be held in one place only.

Chairman Welch suggested that he found nothing in the law barring voting in several places and observed that the commissioners were known to make mistakes on occasions. This was resolved to a discussion whose interpretation of the law was correct.

A letter in answer to the petition forwarded to the commissioner of education by the East Corning group which opposed their inclusion in the enlarged district was read by Mr. Kozlowski. Addressed to Harold Tobey, president-elect of the East Corning board, the letter stated that inasmuch as action had already been taken by a majority of the voters in the enlarged district in favor of the plan, nothing could be done to remove any of the component districts at this time.

Mr. Kozlowski said he felt the East Corning group was being given "the run-around" by the state department.

A question of how the vote was to be taken and how eligibility was to be determined was raised. Mrs. Cammen, who will have charge of the election clerks Tuesday, said procedures to be followed would be similar to those in political elections. She said any citizen could challenge the right of any of the voters to cast a ballot and that records would be available to check this right.

Mrs. Cammen said voting conditions would be presided over by a rotating board of clerks and that more help was needed. She offered to accept at least five volunteers from the group present to help with the check of voters who present themselves Tuesday.

EXHIBIT 12 A Direct-Mail Flier

Mr. and Mrs. Voter:

Vote NO on the proposal to consolidate your school into one, huge city district!

If you approve this plan you are in effect writing a blank check, and meekly submitting to the most extravagant, wasteful branch of state government, the State Education Department. This department has taken upon itself the right to automatically compel expenditure of your money by increasing your taxes with no chance for protest. YOU are to be the guinea pigs of the State, the persons to try a new experiment in education.

The plan proposed, according to the booklet, "A Valley and a Decision", states that in the opinion of the authors, the plan will cost $12.47 million for the new buildings. Conservative analysts of the plan can readily see a possibility that more than $18 million may be spent. Why hasn't the cost of new personnel and administration been given you? Because that information might be a deciding factor against the plan.

Why did the State Commissioner of Education not exercise his privilege to call a meeting in each of the districts affected? Was it because he, or his advisors realized, psychologically, voters do not like to put themselves out? They do not like to lose the time from work, or to stand in the boiling sun waiting to go into a single polling place.

With all the cunning of a Machiavelli, the ruthless Education Department promises you Utopia, and can't even guess as to what the cost will be. Under the state aid proposed to be given, the amount received will not equal the interest on the capital expenditures for buildings. Who will have to pay the difference, the real cost of this investment?

You Will Pay the Tax Increase

You, Mr. and Mrs. Voter, will pay the tax increases amounting to from 200 to 400 per cent.

The plan as proposed will be a step backward. If you vote for this nefarious plan you will vote for taxation without representation. You will have no control of the system you are taxed to support, no check upon its costs. The buyers of new houses will find their mortgage payments increased so much many will lose their homes, the pensioner will be unbearably pinched, the family which went into the suburbs to escape high city taxes will find those taxes catching up with them and engulfing them.

Will the revolutionary Harvard Plan assure good, new school buildings to all sections? This is probably what will happen:

The two elementary schools already voted for Dist. No. 9, Corning will be built and YOU will help pay for them as well as help pay for existing debt on other Corning schools. A new junior high school will be built in the swampy area east of Fenderson Street Extension, Riverside. A new big high school is planned for the eastern section of Dist. No. 9. THEN, the planners of this Utopia are leading you to believe they will start building schools for YOU in the outer area districts.

But what will happen? By that time the cost of these new buildings will be added to your bill, your neighbor's bill including the property owners in Dist. No. 9. THEN they will start to realize what this $12.47 million plan is costing in dollars and cents. Do you think the people of Corning No. 9 will keep on voting more and more debt to pour more dollars on their taxbills after they get THEIR schools?

They Cannot Guarantee You a Building

You know what will happen. YOUR school plan will be voted down, and YOU are helpless to do anything about it. They have the big population. They can outvote you five to one, THEN.

Your only chance is to stop this NOW. Stop it before they get the power under this autocratic law to force THEIR will on YOU.

You have been told the State will aid in paying for the overall cost of the plan. What you haven't been told is that the cost of city schools and outlying schools built but not finally paid for have not been considered in the cost of this plan, to you. What will happen, city dwellers will be burdened with the cost of rural area schools, and rural residents will be unjustly taxed for debts on present city schools.

Mr. Farmer, Mr. Rural Resident, Mr. Painted Poster whose beloved high school they plan to liquidate; you are being taken for a ride. The starry-eyed planners who are trying to cram this consolidation down your throat think they can beat you by the advantage of distance. They think you will not take the trouble to travel to the single polling place.

Don't Let Distance Beat You

Their scheme is to make ALL you people in the farthest corners of this proposed, big district, travel into the center of Corning to vote. They believe you are lazy, that you will stay home rather than take the trouble to go to the Corning armory to vote against this consolidation scheme. You can fool them by voting anyway.

Remember: this plan is what the Harvard group SAY is best. Remember they have juggled figures of costs to make it look as if the scheme they recommend is best. They never have made an honest study of the advantages of centralization for many residents of the area. They are trying to deny you the right to learn the real facts of relative costs and advantages of centralization versus consolidation, by rushing this plan through.

The time to halt this rush is NOW. If you stay away from the voting place next Tuesday you will NEVER again get a chance to control your own school matters. You will ALWAYS have to travel to Corning to vote, even though state law provides presently a way for you t vote near at home in all kinds of elections school, town, state and national.

Last Chance For Home Rule

This is your last chance. If you throw it away you will literally throw away ALL control c school matters. Beat these schemers, plannin to deprive you of present rights you can retai by voting against consolidation. The plan c starry-eyed dreamers from Harvard who know little and care less about the real problems o ordinary folks, farmers, suburban residents, hon est, hard working citizens of Corning Northside Painted Post and all the areas affected by thi scheme.

You, too, want the best in educational ad vantages for your children. But you want to b sure what IS best, not accept the untested plan of autocrats telling you what to do. You wan to have time to think, to compare one plan witl another, to decide for yourselves what is BEST

DON'T be a GUINEA PIG! Don't buy gold brick planners from Harvard say will las 30 years, and find it is only plated. The gol from Albany may wear off in one, two or fiv years. No, they cannot GUARANTEE the stat will pay for 30 years. No group or individua is authorized to make a guarantee for the Stat and there is no assurance that a legislative guar antee this year will not be cancelled by nex year's legislature. Remember what happene when we went off the gold standard — it becam a crime to demand payment in gold or ever possess it.

Keep your independence. Hold to local, repre sentative government.

Vote, Vote, VOTE NO.

VOTE NO, on this consolidation scheme.

Remember, taxation without representation is tyranny!

Citizens Committee Opposing
School Consolidation

XHIBIT 13 From the Corning Leader

EDITORIAL

Keeping the School Issue in Perspective

Next Tuesday the voters of the Greater Corn-g and Painted Post Area, with the exception District Nine, vote on the enlarged city school strict plan. The State Law mandates to the hool Board the authority for participation by city school district in such a plan now before r people and thus the non-voting status in istrict Nine.

The next few days are of the utmost impor-nce not so much from the standpoint of the tual outcome of the voting but rather in the atter of keeping the activity of both the pro-nents and opponents on a high level. Educa-n of our children is something that must not generate to the level of gutter politics. It is t a political matter in which either party eks to wield influence. Rather it is something uch closer to our hearts and affects our very milies and the character of leadership we ight expect from the adults of tomorrow who e the children of today.

In a political campaign there is always the ssibility of last minute blasts by both sides ith intent to raise issues completely false, ien and unrelated to the subject before the ople. There is the appeal to emotions and e design to make statements easily answerable t for which the time has run out.

The matter facing our people this week is mething they have known about for several onths, yes several years. People within our mmunity have had honest differences of opin-n on the proposal and most of them have dis-ssed these differences. The facts have been ven in a forthright manner and not at the last minute. The plan recommended for action of the people has been presented and discussed since early March. More than 500 people have been engaged in a program designed to acquaint the people with the facts. These people have been honest and most sincere. They have worked untiringly because they felt that more adequate educational facilities and programs could become realities. It would be most discourteous and unfair to charge them with being dishonest or engaged in the practice of deception. They have had nothing to hide, they have sought to give all of the information at their command, they have welcomed questions about the program and have invited questions as long ago as March and April. They have been endeavoring to give honest answers to the questions proposed.

As far back as April 22 the target date of June 22 for a vote on the proposition of an enlarged city district was announced publicly.

From May 20 to May 27, some 9,139 people were contacted for signatures on petitions asking the commissioner to lay out the proposed district. Eight thousand and eighty people signed those petitions.

From late Monday, June 7, through 6 p.m. on June 8, 1358 people were contacted and signed petitions asking the commissioner to set a date for a vote on the proposition.

No attempt has been made to hide any information or keep from the people the facts that a vote would be taken on June 22nd. On the contrary since the recommendation was made on March 15th and proved to be generally the same as presented on two previous occasions, 1946 and 1952, the Advisory Committee decided to give the people the opportunity to vote on a definite program of action. One cannot say enough in praise for the Advisory Committee of Ninety and the months and months of time and study they have been giving to the problem that most of us ignored with the hope that the other fellow would take care of it.

We must at all times keep this issue in perspective. We must realize that it is a program not designed to help just one or two districts but rather the entire area. It would be most unfair to carry the view that we should not worry about the rest of the area just so long as the children in our particular district have new and adequate schools. Some of our distric are more favored than others; But aren't w all, basically, human beings who in our christia way of living desire to share our good fortun if necessary to see that the kid in the next bloc or the adjoining districts has the same equ opportunity for decent and adequate education facilities?

We do not seek to play on emotions. W merely plead for honest consideration of tl facts as they have been presented. The vote c Tuesday is not one being cast for any individu but rather a vote on a matter affecting the grea est investment we have — our children.

EXHIBIT 14 From the *Corning Leader*

EDITORIAL

Five Minutes Please!

The people of Greater Corning and Painted Post Area make an important decision on Tuesday. It is a decision in which everyone should want to participate. With the full realization that everyone has read, or had the opportunity to read, thousands of words on the proposal to create a single school district for this area, we asked for five more minutes of thought and discussion.

Last week we expressed the hope that the proponents and opponents of the enlarged city school district would keep the current discussion above the level of "gutter politics." It was our contention that school matters are above politics, that we should keep the matter in perspective and not resort to last minute statements designed only to confuse the issues and appeal to emotions. Our opinion has not changed but apparently the opponents of the plan do not see it that way. Instead they resort to the dis tribution of a pamphlet that offers not a singl factual argument against the plan but rathe seeks to slander the many conscientious citizen who have acted a little differently than th writers of the pamphlet. The conscientiou citizens have had a long standing interest i educational problems of the community and are and have maintained that interest by becomin fully acquainted with the facts of the preser program. The writers of the pamphlet in ques tion had the same opportunity but choose, in stead, to ignore the problems and studies. It i not surprising that they lacked the courage t sign their names to the pamphlet. The pamphle through its lack of constructive discussion o the program, through its failure to present an facts or reasons for opposing the plan befor the people, was actually insulting to the peopl to whom it was directed. The people of thi

›mmunity and area have a far greater level of telligence than the writers of the pamphlet ›parently think.

There are more pleasant aspects to the situa- ›n and so we'll discuss them in brief.

The single school district plan was proposed st in 1946 and from that time through 1951 as turned over in the minds of educators and dividuals but with a realization that it was lite a drastic change, little was accomplished ward bringing it to the people.

In 1951 Amory Houghton, Sr., chairman of e Board of Corning Glass Works, at a testi- onial dinner given CGW by the Community, ›inted to the need for a more realistic study ' our educational problems. A short time later mmittees were formed and the Citizen's Com- ittee, a year or so later, presented a report cognizing the advisability of the single district an. Although armed with extensive facts to bstantiate their findings this Citizen's Com- ittee, made up of the people of this area, felt ore expert studies and surveys were necessary. he Harvard Group was employed and on arch 15th of this year presented its recom- endation for a single school district. And so is not a plan new to the people of this area.

The recommendation of the single district plan as preceded, however, by full publication and scussion of three alternate plans — this took ace about a month prior to March 15th when e formal recommendation of the single district an was given to the Advisory Committee of inety.

On April 22 the Advisory Committee decided › bring the matter to a vote of the people.

On May 20 some 350 canvassers started out › secure names on petitions asking the creation ' the single district. Names were secured from ery district in the present plan. The total ached 8,080, or approximately 2000 more than ecessary and secured in one week's time.

On June 7 the committee sought the 800 names necessary to set a date for a vote and in a 24 hour period 1,358 names were secured.

Tomorrow, Tuesday, June 22nd, the decision will be made when the voting takes place at the State Armory. It should be pointed out here that the State Law requires a single voting place when the district is created. After the creation of the district voting on other matters such as new buildings, bond issues, election of members to the Board, can be done in several places throughout the area.

It would be foolish to review the entire program, the arguments for and against. They have been discussed at length by the people of this area and nothing has been held back. The proponents have been open and above board. The honest and sincere opponents of the plan have also been open and above board and have discussed the plan at every opportunity and should not be confused with those who lead the opposition but fear to come out in the open.

The decision to be made tomorrow is one that the people are entitled to make. They have waited years for the presentation of a program on which they could act. They have seen hundreds of their neighbors and friends involved in the formulation of the committees that have made this program possible. More than 8,000 have shown by the signing of petitions asking the creation of the district that they want to do something about meeting the educational needs of the area in an equal manner to all the children.

We hope the program will be approved.

We hope, however, that if approved or rejected it is by a vote of the greatest number of people possible. This is a decision for all of the people in the districts affected in the voting and we hope for the largest turn out of voters possible so that whatever the decision on it will have been made by all of the people.

The voting will be at the State Armory in Corning from 10 a.m. to 10 p.m.

EXHIBIT 15 From the Corning Leader

Letters to the Editor

ANONYMOUS PAMPHLETEERS IN SCHOOL ISSUE

129 Pritchard Avenue
Corning, New York
June 19, 1954

Editor
Corning Leader
Corning, New York
Dear Sir:

I have just received an anonymous pamphlet dealing with our local school problems. This pamphlet bears no return address—although it came through the mails — and it is signed only by "Citizens Committee Opposing School Consolidation."

In the pamphlet there is a vicious attack on the Commissioner of Education and on the Harvard Group who made a study of our school problems for the Advisory Committee of 90. In particular the pamphlet says "Remember: this plan is what the Harvard Group SAY is best. Remember they have juggled figures of costs to make it look as if the scheme they recommend is best." This is a clear accusation of dishonesty.

In this letter I'm not going to deal with the various errors, distortions, and outright lies in this pamphlet. What I'd like to discuss is the moral issue involved in anonymous personal attacks.

Whatever the writer, or writers, of this pamphlet may think of the Commissioner of Education, his name is Lewis Wilson, and his letters and orders in regard to our local school problem have been signed by him. He stands back of them, and takes full responsibility for them.

Whatever the writer, or writers, of this pamphlet may think of the Harvard group, the gentlemen from Harvard signed their report. They take full responsibility for it.

Contrast to this the people behind this pamphlet, — The "Citizens Committee Opposing School Consolidation." They feel free to accuse reputable citizens of dishonesty, yet they hide behind a veil of anonymity.

When I was a boy, I was once told "A man who is afraid to sign what he writes is either a liar or a knave — or both. Avoid him."

Unlike our anonymous pamphleteers, I am happy to sign my own name.

Matthew M. Cammen

EXHIBIT 16 From the *Corning Leader*

Enlarged City School District Proposal Approved by Voters of Area 1,943-1,898

District 9 Acceptance, State Order Required

The enlarged school district plan, joining 60 separate districts of the Greater Corning and Painted Post Area with Corning City School District Nine, was approved by a margin of 45 votes Tuesday and formal action to make the consolidation a fact is expected within a week to 10 days.

Still required to formally put the plan into effect is acceptance by the Board of Education of School District Nine, and an order by the state commissioner of education, Dr. Lewis A. Wilson. The District Nine Board of Education already has adopted a resolution setting forth its willingness to go along with the enlarged district plan if a favorable vote was recorded.

The actual vote, tabulated shortly before midnight at the State Armory, was 1,943 in favor of the plan and 1,898 against it. A total of 3,872 votes was cast with 31 votes declared void. Voided ballots included those marked in ink, others marked with a check mark instead of an "X," and ones on which erasures were used.

Dr. Robert Randels, who has been associated with a group opposing the recommended plan, said today that an appeal to set aside the meeting and the vote will be carried to Commissioner Wilson. He said he asked Francis E. Griffin, chief of the Bureau of Rural Administrative Services, in what direction an appeal should be taken and will follow the necessary steps outlined.

Dr. Randels added that he did not plan to request a recount of the vote, stating he had "no doubt about the validity of the count" and that he had "absolute confidence in the honesty of the mechanics of the vote."

Dr. Kent W. Phillips, chairman of the Advisory Committee of Ninety which conducted the lengthy study, today issued the following statement to "my fellow citizens of the Corning-Painted Post area:

"The day of decision was yesterday. The people spoke and the verdict was in favor of the one consolidated district by a very narrow margin. I had hoped for a clear-cut decision one way or another but that was not to be.

"During the long period of study and discussion in search of an ideal solution for our school problems, we have entered into every phase of every possible remedy existing with present permissive education laws. The only possible cure seemed to be with the enlarged city school district plan. This we accepted and worked for its adoption. We have never said we were presenting a plan that was ideal but it was the only plan available which would cover all the existing situations in this very complex area.

"I want to personally and as chairman of the Committee of Ninety, thank those persons who have given so much of their time and energy to this study and the educational program that was culminated in yesterday's vote. I want also to thank personally and as chairman of the Committee of Ninety the press and radio for their excellent coverage of all the findings of the study group.

"To my knowledge there never was any attempt to cover up any facts which might be unpleasant to anybody.

"To those who have opposed the plan, I salute you. You built up a wonderful organization in a short time.

"My only wish right now is that the proponents of the one enlarged city school district and those who have opposed the plan, unite forces in making the accepted plan work for the betterment of all the children of all the area with the least amount of friction and for the good of all.

"I am thankful we live in America where these things can and do happen."

Voting at the State Armory continued right up to the last second with the final vote cast by Mrs. Ruth Ripley of Beaver Valley. An announcement that the polls would close was given at 9:55 p.m. by George H. Bevan, who had been elected chairman for the conduct of the vote at a meeting at 10 Tuesday morning.

Twelve election inspectors first counted the total number of ballots to check against the total number registered and then began the actual count of "yes" and "no" on the ballots. Just before midnight the vote was announced.

About 50 persons were on hand to hear the final vote. A motion by Dr. Randels to delay adjournment of the meeting 15 minutes was ruled out of order by Chairman Bevan. The chairman said Dr. Randels did not offer any reason for the 15-minute delay and that the purpose of the meeting conducting the vote had been accomplished.

The vote was conducted without incident. An early morning throng of 500 persons provided the peak voting period which tapered off for the remainder of the day. Officials said the total number of votes undoubtedly was held down because of the intense heat and the flash storm which struck the area, leaving many sections without electricity.

The election was supervised for the Commissioner of Education by Dr. Arthur W. Schmidt, an assistant commissioner of education, and Mr. Griffin, chief of the Bureau of Rural Administration Services.

EXHIBIT 17 Three Letters

June 24, 1954

MEMORANDUM TO: Mr. William Perry

Dear Bill:

I understand that you would appreciate a memo from us on the procedure that was followed by the Advisory Committee to procure a favorable vote on the consolidation.

I will confine myself to trying to answer the one question as to why the vote was so close when all previous indications seemed to show that the consolidation would be carried by a very large majority.

As you well know, we had some real hurdles ahead of us when we looked at the picture last March. First, we had an extremely difficult and complicated product to sell — the consolidation of these 62 districts, and second, the State law made the selling extremely difficult.

The people who voted against this, as I would appraise it, did so largely on an emotional basis, and in many cases, a highly emotional basis. They were not interested in reports or facts or figures. Mostly they were mad.

There were many emotional appeals for voting against this and, as you well know, they were carefully fanned and nourished by a poisonous campaign of untruths and fear that was very well done from the opposition's standpoint.

There was fear of the unknown. "Why vote for something that was so vast and complicated that no one could satisfactorily explain it? Why part from all our long-established traditions and give up our boundaries, our representation and everything else? Why pay these enormous taxes that would come with this unknown monster, etc., etc., etc."

We had no emotional appeal to combat this. We talked of a better standard of education, but that seemed a little obscure. We dealt in facts and figures and all that goes out the window when people get excited.

As I have told you before, I would not have changed anything we did in any manner. I thought it was a marvelous job. The results of the signing of the petitions proved it where better than 8 out of 9 people approached, signed the petition and indicated they would vote favorably on the plan. If the law had provided that we could have voted, we will say, two days after the signing of the petitions, I feel confident we would have carried a vote on the basis of 3 to 1. We devoted all of our energies to building up to the high point for the petition campaign which, I believe, was the only thing we could have done.

At the time of the petitions we had no organized opposition. This developed soon after and grew in strength, I believe, every day right up to the date of voting. Personally, I do not know how you can combat a campaign such as the opposition used except by fighting fire with fire, and I would not have subscribed to this tactic on a school issue. We obviously overestimated our strength and we did not get out our vote to any such extent as did the opposition. I believe the opposition voted 90 per cent of their strength and we perhaps voted 50 per cent of our strength. However, there is no doubt, as the day of the voting drew near, we were losing strength at a much greater rate than we realized.

We might have resorted to some positive emotional appeals to strengthen our case for the voting, such as pictures of children and asking for a vote for their future and that sort of thing. We did not deal in anything of this nature, however, and I was loath to start it.

Personally, I am, of course, tremendously pleased that we received a favorable vote by any margin and we have no misgivings but what within six months or a year the people will see tangible results of the benefits of one district.

Sincerely yours,
F. W. Parsons

FWP:DC

June 24, 1954
MEMORANDUM TO: Mr. William Perry
SUBJECT: Review of Program for School Reorganization
March 15 to June 22, 1954.

Dear Bill:

In considering the above period, it is impossible to cover all phases and to evaluate all the decisions that were made during this time. However, the following points seemed important and might be of value.

1. *The Harvard Report*

This was a very essential factor and was invaluable to the people working on the program.

Its advantages included:

A. Good reference on population and building forecasts.

Its disadvantages included:

A. Too wordy.

B. Transportation could have been covered better to our advantage.

2. *Informing the Public*

In this stage, the persons of George Holloway and yourself was invaluable and did a great deal toward the success of the over-all program. However, local people should be used to sell the program through meetings and the press.

The best method of influencing the public and also educating them, is by personal contact with the voters by people who are respected citizens. This should be done, as we did, through small public meetings. I believe in the late stages we failed to have enough such meetings and failed to meet some of the questions head on. The home coffee hours were a good example of public meetings that were successful.

As far as brochures are concerned, no over-all brochure is necessary in a case where there is a complete report available such as the Harvard Report. The simple, four-page pamphlets are absolutely necessary and useful but will not completely sell the program.

3. *Petition Canvassers*

The canvassers were well prepared in the handling of the petition itself, but this large group could have been educated and indoctrinated to a much greater degree concerning the issue and questions presented by the issue.

4. *One of the weak points of the program* was the failure to convince, in a sufficient number, school administrators and teachers. This, of course, was a difficult phase to handle. Also, religious groups were disregarded in a great extent in the late phases, especially the Catholic vote.

5. *The turning point of the campaign* was Dr. DeCamp's announcement in the Elmira paper. This was not met with enough vigor by the proponents of the plan.

6. *State Law*

The State law is cumbersome and responsible for many of the problems presented. Certainly no public meeting is necessary for the voting. I would suggest the following improvements for the State law:

A. The following steps should be adhered to instead of the present ones:

1. Informative petition
2. Public hearing held by State Department
3. Layout of area
4. Vote

The last three points should follow the petition in not more than two weeks, with the effort to inform the public being used in the period prior to the petition.

B. Allow more voting places where the area requires it.

C. Clarify requirements for the qualified voter, particularly in the case of the renter and his spouse.

D. The best point of the law is the fact that no record is available of how the individual districts voted.

Sincerely yours,

R. W. Shopoff
RWS:DC

June 29, 1954

Mr. William L. Perry
16 Story Street
Cambridge, Massachusetts

Dear Bill:

Since I'm not yet recovered from my fright, I remember most clearly the things that stand out as mistakes.

Using good old hindsight for guidance, we made some serious errors. The insistence on keeping the campaign on a high plane, along with our sincere attempts at education of the public, are probably points in our favor, but we came too close to going gloriously down to defeat. In view of the ultimate benefits, we might have been justified to preclude defeat by any means. There was so much at stake with so little chance of another try that, faced with another such campaign, I would take off the gloves with those who think it shows weakness to do otherwise.

It is difficult at this stage to analyze results correctly or to evaluate impartially what we did that was right. Certainly a goodly number of people were sold on the merits of the plan, and that speaks well for those who composed, explained, and discussed the literature and the information therein contained. That it failed of deeper penetration or more widespread effect warrants serious consideration in any future campaigns where public support must be enlisted. It is clear that the opponents roused dangerous support with much less reason behind their cause.

It is apparent to me that our timing was badly off. If the vote could have been held the day after the informative petitions were completed, I believe there would have been little doubt as to the outcome. Confusion had not set in at that point. Our literature was excellent, people appeared receptive, the opposition had little to get its teeth into, future moves were outlined and our pace was unhurried.

Confusion started seriously with the 10% petitions. It was amplified by the rapidity of notices and legal moves, and the actions of Messrs. Randels, De Camp, Janowsky and Company until it approached a peak on June 22. These men almost succeeded due to the assistance of this very potent factor. That they may not have fully appreciated their advantage doesn't alter the fact it was there.

Our second error was in selling. We just didn't have enough people well enough informed to resist the last-minute scare program of the opposition. I believe we neglected three factors: (1) the great number of people "cold" to a subject of this nature who won't respond to the unemotional printed word, (2) the diversified interests throughout the area, and (3) the simple fact that half the people are below average intelligence. It's interesting to note that in an early meeting of the public relations committee my suggestions on (2) were politely received but not accepted. Of course I can't say truthfully they would have made any difference, but they might have. The opposition's approach along that line certainly produced results.

The implications of (1) and (3) are that we should have put out ABC editions, perhaps filled with cartoons and simple phrases that could be repeated over and over. It may hardly be fitting in a campaign for better education, unless we look at it objectively. I'm sure a good politician would do so.

One of the most interesting and really amazing developments in the campaign was the teamwork that rapidly grew among so many people who were strangers to each other at the start. That was really heart-warming. There were lasting friendships made, and I hope one William L. Perry can be so counted.

We'll do our best to see you at Wells Beach. I'd like to meet the understanding gal who took a chance with you.

With best regards,

O. W. Reed

31 Enter the Superintendent

"I DON'T start my job until July, and already I got problems! Nothing serious, Bill, but still something I've got to work out within the next week or less. Let me tell you about it, and then *you* tell *me* what to do."

Carl Lynch was talking about his new job, his first as a superintendent, which was to start July 1, 1952. The time was mid-May, 1952. The place was Carl's home; Bill Appleton had stopped in to congratulate Carl on getting his Ed.D. in June.

Carl is in his early thirties, a man who gives an impression of quiet thoughtfulness. This impression is strengthened by a slow, at times almost painfully deliberate, manner of speaking. He is married and has three children. After graduation from a small private liberal arts college in 1940, he became a science teacher in a small-town high school. Two years later he enlisted in the Navy, and was discharged in 1946 with the rank of lieutenant senior grade. He went back to his teaching job, from which he was promoted to principal of the high school in the fall of 1947. In the fall of 1949 he decided to utilize the G.I. Bill of Rights by going to graduate school for his Ed.D. The next three years he spent as a student and junior staff member in Fairmont University.

He obtained his superintendency job through the university placement office with excellent recommendations from the faculty and from the people with whom he had worked in the past.

"Well Bill," Carl continued, "since I got this job about a month ago, I've been spending quite a bit of time in Littleton, talking to the superintendent, the town manager, the board members (there are eight of them plus the mayor, who is chairman of the board), and people in the school system and around town. I've also been going to the board meetings — they meet every two weeks this time of year. After the last meeting I got to talking with John Mealer, one of the members of the board, who told me something I've been mulling over ever since.

"It seems the board members had put their heads together privately and decided to set up a new position, the supervisor of maintenance and transportation, and to put one of the board members in this position. They hadn't taken action on it yet because they wanted to talk to me first. Pete Garman, the guy who's going to get the job, has been acting as supervisor of transportation for four or five years now, the past two years with the consent of the board as a whole. Apparently they decided that the job needed doing, and Pete thought he could do it, so they just went ahead.

"I guess Sherman (the former superintendent of schools) didn't object, or if he did it didn't count. In fact, he was probably pretty relieved to get the transportation problems out of his hair. He had been superintendent for seven or eight years, and he had a budget fight on his hands all that time. He managed to break even — that is, he succeeded in getting the budget almost doubled in that time. Expenses have just about doubled too, you know. He had a lot of opposition from the city council, which holds the purse strings, and I guess it was pretty rough for him. They still have an extremely low budget, only about

$610,000 for an enrollment of 4,000 children and 160 teachers. The town itself has a population of about 24,000. Now he's had an offer of a job in a smaller town at about a $3,000 increase in pay, and I don't suppose he's exactly brokenhearted about moving on.

"He's a guy who's come up through the ranks. He started as a classroom teacher, became a junior high school principal, then high school principal, and finally superintendent, all in the same system. The town has a high school, two junior highs, and eleven elementary schools. Each school has its own principal, although only two of the elementary principals are supervising principals, the rest of them being teaching principals. Eventually several of the one- to four-room elementary schools should be closed. We have too many classrooms for our enrollment.

"Parochial schools are not much of a factor. There are two elementary schools with five or six hundred pupils, and maybe another two hundred go to the next town to the parochial high school there.

"This continuing budget problem has meant that the superintendent has had no time to carry out the educational supervision part of his job. I think that's one reason the board is so willing, eager in fact, to put on an administrative assistant. They want to free the superintendent so that he can be an educator, not *just* a business manager. So far there have been no administrative assistants to the superintendent. There is a darn good secretary, who is sort of a secretary-bookkeeper-business manager all rolled in one.

"This supervisor of maintenance and transportation is a natural spot for an administrative assistant. The school system owns twelve buses, and the combination of bad winters and a town that's scattered all over hell's half acre, with a lot of roads that are none too good, means a considerable maintenance problem. In addition to that, there are only three full-time custodians for the entire system, plus a plumber who is paid around $2,000 a year to be on call. There has been no coordination among the custodians at all. The one of the three who would otherwise be a natural as a supervisor is a lone wolf who doesn't get along with the others. Somebody, one of the board members, I guess, got the bright idea of adding supervision of the custodians to the transportation supervision that Pete was already doing and making a full-time salaried job of it. Obviously Pete's the logical one for the job.

"Pete's a retired army top sergeant and is a natural for it. He knows his way around machinery and is a demon for work. He seems to get along with the employees, although he's a blunt-speaking sort of guy. When he sees a janitor doing a job and thinks he knows how to do it better, he'll go over and tell him how it should be done. If the janitor wants to argue, though, Pete will listen to him and even change his mind at times. The bus drivers all seem to like him O.K., too. Of course, he's been a board member in the past, and he won't be now. He knows that and sees why, but it will be quite an adjustment for him even so.

"Maybe I just don't see it clearly enough yet, but my problem as I see it will be getting Pete to accept his change of status from a board member to an employee. Even as a board member he kind of took things in his own hands now and then. He's the kind of a guy who likes to do it all himself. For instance, one time he hired a bus driver and didn't even bother to tell Sherman about it. The first thing Sherman knew about it was when he saw a new name on the payroll. He found out how come, and then looked up Pete and really read the act to him, I guess. Pete saw his point and allowed as how he'd done wrong, so he can be brought around. At the same time, he's likely to do the same sort of thing again. You can't teach an old dog new tricks, and Pete's around sixty now. Incidentally, there's no compulsory retirement at sixty-five for this kind of job.

"Another thing he's done is to draw up the schedule for next year's school buses. He's figured out where the kids are and the best way of getting them from there to the nearest school. I guess he's done a good job of it, but I'm sure he must have forgotten something along the line. He's just looking at the transportation problem in a sort of a vacuum, and probably didn't consider all the other factors like building capacities, grade placements, and so forth. I've got to get together with him this summer about that and straighten it out somehow, I'm not just exactly sure how.

"I don't know whether he figured the parochial school kids in on this either. Littleton's been transporting them for years, but the state just told the towns last year that they can't do that any more without charging for it. The board argued that the buses weren't going out of their way to pick these children up or let them off, and that no extra buses had been put on for them. The state said it didn't make any difference, though. The town would have to charge them or stop carrying them just the same.

"One of the big arguments for having Pete in this job is that we can get him for less than the job is worth. He has his retirement pay, so we can get him for around $3,500! So far he has only been paid expenses, about $10 a week. Otherwise it would probably cost us closer to $5,000. That helps a lot. It makes a good way to get the job established, and then when Pete moves on (he's a drifter type who gets all excited about something and then drops it in a year or two) we can put in someone we really want and pay what the job is worth.

"There's no provision in the budget for this next year to cover this job, but I think we can do it by reallocating some maintenance money for the one year. We can put off some fence-building, blacktopping, painting, or the like, and do it that way. Eventually we should be more than repaid for the investment in improved services and therefore longer life for equipment.

"Well, that's how it stands now. I've already suggested to John Mealer that I should be the one to make the recommendation that the position be set up when the board meets next Wednesday night. He bought that one hundred per cent. He says that the board members know they shouldn't be doing this sort of job, that it should be done by the superintendent, and if I want to start carrying the ball it's fine with them. That means one less problem for me — which is good. Now, some time between now and Wednesday night I've got to figure out what I am going to recommend, and then I've got to figure out how to handle Pete in this job. It looks as though I really haven't any choice about whether or not there will be such a job, or who is going to fill it. I haven't any ideas about who could take it except Pete. That's all right, though. I like the idea of having an assistant and he should work out well enough."

32 *Extra Duties at Westmouth*

WESTMOUTH is an industrial and residential community of 70,000. It has one three-year high school (1954 enrollment, 1,900 pupils) with a staff of one hundred teachers, fifty of whom are men. The high school building itself is adequate but it is located in the most densely populated area of the city, and because it has no open land around it, the athletic fields are placed in the four opposite corners of the city. The community is moderately athletics-prone; the football, basketball, baseball, soccer, hockey, and track teams compete in regular league play, and each team has won at least one league championship in the past ten years. There has been no community pressure to "beef-up" varsity athletics; the local newspaper is a small one; and the football coach is still paid less than the superintendent. The band is directed by a full-time music master, and it has won many awards in statewide competition.

In 1952 with a change of membership the board began to show increasing interest in extracurricular activities, including intramural sports. At that time only 20 per cent of the entire student body of Westmouth High engaged in any form of extra activity, including the sports programs. The social clubs had decreased in numbers over the past six years, and the high school teachers felt that there had been a concomitant decrease in enthusiasm by those members who did attend the club meetings. The club meetings were held during the regular school day, in a period specially set aside for school activities. The pupils who did not attend the club meetings stayed in their homerooms for study periods, being monitored by one teacher who covered several rooms, or by individual room teachers who used the period for paper work. There were no organized intramural teams for boys in any sports, but one teacher supervised a series of interclass tag-football games in the fall. There was some unorganized softball for the boys in the spring. The girls had no varsity squads but played intramural tennis, badminton, and softball under the sponsorship of the girls' physical education instructor. Language and study clubs varied in strength and popularity, according to the age and enthusiasm of the individual teachers. The Spanish teachers, Miss Rose and Mr. Halloran, had a strong and enthusiastic club which ran regular meetings with Spanish films and exhibits. The last meeting of the French Club, on the other hand, had been held in the spring of 1950.

In the early forties there had been three quarterly publications at Westmouth: a short-story magazine, a school newspaper, and a poetry magazine. In 1952 there was one quarterly which combined news and literature. In 1952 this was taken over by Miss Reynolds, an English teacher. The faculty agreed that the first issue published under the direction of Miss Reynolds was a "high-quality product, almost as good as in the old days." While she was working on the second issue, Miss Reynolds complained to Mr. Dunning, head of the English Department, that her duties were too heavy to permit her to carry on with the paper. At her suggestion Mr. Dunning relieved her of homeroom duty by taking the students from her study class and distributing them among other teachers. This took one class hour daily from her schedule. At the same time, and without discussing the matter first with other members of the department, Dunning appointed Mr. Brown as business manager of the paper. Mr. Brown, new to the high school that year, took the job without protest.

In January, 1953, Mr. Harold Bottsford, chairman of the school board and a sponsor of many community cultural projects such as art exhibits, opera performances, symphonies, and symposia, expressed open dissatisfaction to the superintendent. At the conclusion of the first board meeting of the new year, Bottsford said: "Let's start this year off in a worthwhile fashion. Here we've just spent thousands of dollars and hundreds of hours to get the Westmouth Symphony Orchestra organized in this community. When was the last time we had a high school dramatic production or operetta, Mr. Superintendent?"

Superintendent Patterson was completely unprepared for the question and in some confusion he confessed that he didn't know "exactly."

"Four years ago," Bottsford told him. "And before that we had a cultural hiatus of some six years when the war was used as an excuse. This is disgraceful, Patterson. Our schools simply are not keeping up to the cultural level of the community at large. We're lagging, Patterson. Lagging badly."

Superintendent Patterson confessed that there had been some slippage in the area of school-produced culture, and said that he would confer with Mr. Nason, the principal of the high school.

"That's not enough," Bottsford said. "I think we have a right to have some action on this. Conferences don't beget culture, just more conferences."

"Well, I don't think we can hold Mr. Patterson solely responsible," Committeewoman O'Hara said. "We all know that he needs assistance, and that Mr. Nason is ready to retire."

"Well then get Dunning in on it," Bottsford said. "He's young and eager." The upshot of the meeting was that Bottsford made a motion, which was voted unanimously, to make a senior play mandatory. It was further moved and carried that the director of the school production, a teacher of English at the high school, be given a fee of $400 for salary and expenses, a raise of $100 over the fee which had been given in the past. It was also tacitly understood that Mr. Dunning would be the director.

In July, 1954, Mr. Dunning, formerly head of the English department, was unanimously appointed principal of the high school to succeed Mr. Nason, who retired a year earlier than he had planned. Mr. Nason would have reached his compulsory retirement age of sixty-five in the middle of the 1954–55 school year and had hoped to continue through that one more year, but he was prevailed upon to go in June, 1954, instead. In the fall Mr. Dunning appointed Miss Reynolds director of the senior play for that year, and as customary he approached Mr. Brown and other male members of the faculty to perform such duties as overseeing the printing of the tickets and the production of posters and publicity, and acting as ushers and ticket-takers both at the actual performance and at the dress rehearsal to be given for the children in the lower grades. (Men teachers were also regularly assigned to ushering and ticket-taking duties at the football stadium during the season, and about half of that number were used for basketball and again for baseball.) There as some rumbling in the teachers' room because of the request. Early in October Mortimer Peirce, who during his twenty-seven years in the system had become famed for his wit and independence, held forth at great length in the men teachers' room to the meek Mr. Brown and some of the younger teachers.

"You know what I told Sokey Dunning, don't you?" Peirce asked.

"What did you tell him, Mort?" Brown and the others asked.

"I said, 'Listen, Sokey, I'll usher or sell tickets or do anything you want, but I want my share of that director's fee.' I told him the same thing back when he was director. I don't think you'll see young Mortimer down at the hall on the big night."

"Well, it is part of our job," Brown volunteered.

Mortimer pretended to glance all around the room, opening and shutting the water closet door and glancing under the sofa. "Just checking to see if there were any ladies around," he informed them with a large smile. "Now listen to this, boys. Those women, mostly elementary teachers I admit, rammed through the single salary schedule.[1] How many kids do you have, Brownie?"

"Four."

"Sure, four. I've got three. One's at Chicago, and the girl's back east at Wellesley. Both on scholarship, but both like to wear decent clothes like any other youngsters. How many children has Miss Tidbit got?"

"Miss Tidbit" was Mr. Peirce's name for Miss Eleanor Reynolds, recently appointed head of the English Department.

"She hasn't any," Brown said. "She's an old maid."

"Right. Where do you work after school?"

"At Al Stern's florist shop."

"Sure you do. And Norman there works in a newspaper store, and Joe Carroll manages a bowling alley nights. It costs you people money to help run school activities after hours. Ever see any of these girls on duty, prefecting the lunchroom, patrolling the grounds during recess, or ushering at dances, games, or graduation exercises? You do, like heck!"

The upshot of the conference in the teachers' room was a memo composed by Mort Peirce, signed by most of the men teachers, and sent to Mr. Dunning. The tone of the memo was subdued but firm. It pointed out that the town had a single salary schedule with no distinctions as to sex, dependency, or grade level. It pointed out further that men were required to assume many of the prefecting duties which women did not take, and that this requirement had been originally based on the premise that women would handle the club activities.

The memorandum threatened no refusals to assume duties, but merely reminded Mr. Dunning of facts which presumably he knew well, and requested that he support the signers' request with the superintendent and board. Mr. Dunning read the memo, and sat down to ponder. He knew that three-quarters of his men teachers worked at outside jobs, and that extra duties after the regular school day in one sense put the men personally out of pocket. He decided to lay the matter before Superintendent Patterson with the recommendation that extra pay be awarded all teachers who rendered services to pupils beyond the regular school day and after-school sessions. Dunning had sensed some resentment toward him among the men teachers, a resentment which seemed to have begun with the old-timers like Mort Peirce and spread to the younger men. Even young Brown had been less enthusiastic lately.

---

[1] The present maximum salary was $4500, reached from a minmum of $3100 in seven $200 increments which were awarded automatically for each year of service. An increment of $200 above the schedule was awarded to teachers with a Master's degree. For each additional fifteen hours of graduate work beyond the Master's, a $150 super-maximum increment was awarded; with two such increments being the limit.

33 *Tolltown Entrance*

Dr. Irving Weinstein was waiting in the office of Assistant Superintendent of Tolltown Schools, Ray Carter. As Carter came in he said, "Hello, Dr. Weinstein, sorry to keep you waiting. I was tied up in a staff meeting."

"That's all right," Dr. Weinstein said with just a hint of impatience in his voice. "As a matter of fact, I'm probably early. I'll tell you, Mr. Carter, this business about Gerry's admission has me going."

"Well I've heard something about it," Carter admitted. "Suppose we hear the rest of it."

Dr. Weinstein leaned forward in his chair and launched into a rapid-fire narration. He had gone over to Hope School the day before to register his son Gerry in kindergarten. He had hoped to get the registration over quickly because he had an "important appointment downtown." "I was absolutely astounded when your Mr. Fuller, the principal, refused to register Gerry. Do you know why, Mr. Carter?"

Carter said, "Well, I suppose he was under the minimum age."

"He was five hours too young, sir. Five hours!" Dr. Weinstein left his chair and began to move about the office. He hadn't been able to believe it at first. Tolltown had a staff psychologist, reading and speech consultants, and guidance specialist services. Tolltown boasted of its modern schools. Yet the only factor that was taken into account in determining a child's readiness for school entrance was chronological age. "What do you think of that?" Dr. Weinstein asked.

"I know it doesn't always sound too fair," Carter admitted. "In fact there are borderline and exceptional cases where an arbitrary age limit might be downright unjust." Carter granted all this. Yet he tried to point out to Dr. Weinstein that a city of 50,000 with 7,000 children in the schools had to have a set policy on admissions. If the age standard were lowered, the line would still have to be drawn somewhere. There were, Carter admitted, certain groups which advocated psychological testing. Yet Carter and many others in the Tolltown schools felt that the factors involved in a child's readiness for school were so numerous and so complex that single prediction devices were almost useless.

"We use them every day down at the Community Clinic," Dr. Weinstein argued.

"I think that is slightly different. You also supplement them with extensive interviewing and observation by highly trained people. Here we would have to put our trust in one single testing instrument, or the results thereof. This would be like reliance upon black magic. Any more extensive analysis would be prohibitively expensive. We try to keep our specialists and our psychologist for the children who are in need of such services. Of course, once the child is in school, a trained teacher can observe him. But entrance is the problem."

"I suppose it is," Weinstein agreed. "But I think we are getting off the point a bit. There is the case of my child."

"Yes," Carter agreed. "And of the more than eight hundred other beginning pupils of Tolltown. That makes it a public relations matter. If we don't adopt a fixed and arbitrary standard, parents might conclude either of two things: that a child denied admission was so denied because we were incompetent; or that we were acting out of prejudice."

"Ridiculous," said Dr. Weinstein. "There is no element of prejudice involved. It's a question of denying my child, while children who are far less ready are taken in."

"But we don't know that," Carter pointed out.

"Oh, yes, we do," rejoined Dr. Weinstein. "I have proof right here."

He laid a manila folder on Carter's desk. "Here are the records on my son Gerry. I'm not asking you to take the word of a doting father. These are accurate records compiled by a trained man on my staff. As you probably know, I am Director of the Children's Medical Section at Community Clinic. I have worked with Gesell at Yale. I am able to judge. . . ."

"I know you are," Carter said. "As a matter of fact, you're probably better able to judge than either Principal Fuller or myself."

"Well," Dr. Weinstein said, "I'm not sure Mr. Fuller felt that way. Of course it was opening day and he was busy. At any rate, here are the records."

Carter glanced through the very complete records on Gerry Weinstein. The child was indeed only five hours too young. Dr. Weinstein had written a covering paragraph on this in which he stated that the consulting specialist, who had been called by Weinstein before Gerry's delivery, had recommended that labor not be induced as had been planned. "Actually," Weinstein commented, "if I hadn't provided the best obstetrical service at the birth of my son, Gerry might have been born earlier and there would be no problem. That's what points up the absurdity of this admission policy."

"I'm no expert in medical matters," Carter confessed, as he read through the developmental records on the child. The records showed that Gerry was 45 inches tall and weighed 47 pounds, and was taller and heavier than the average kindergarten child. Dr. Weinstein's observations showed that Gerry was socially well-adjusted and that he had many playmates in his neighborhood. There was the further fact that all of these children were entering kindergarten that year. Weinstein had included some data compiled by a staff psychologist at the Community Clinic. The psychologist had administered a lower form of the Binet to Gerry. The results showed that Gerry was considerably above his age average in intelligence as measured by that test. There were also anecdotal records and the results of a performance scale and a projective test. All the test results and descriptive material pointed to the conclusion that Gerry was an exceptional child.

"I've made this observation sort of a hobby," Dr. Weinstein explained. "I feel that I am qualified to recommend in the case of my son. I might add that we at the Clinic have often been called by you school people on just such matters. I feel Gerry could make the adjustment easily."

"Yes, I know," Carter said. "It certainly makes it awkward for us. There is no question that with the grouping policy in force at the Hope School Gerry would be put into a work group that suited his maturity level."

"Well I've given you the facts," Dr. Weinstein said. "The decision on admissions is up to you. If Gerry can't go to public school this year, I'll send him to a private kindergarten. I don't like to do that. I have gone on record among my colleagues as favoring the public schools. I have two older children in them. I feel that far too many people in my position send their children to private schools."

"I can tell you this," Carter said. "When you put Gerry back into our schools next year he will probably be pushed up to Grade One. The teachers will have a chance to observe him."

"That's all well and good," Dr. Weinstein said, "but it seems to me all the more reason to admit him this year to kindergarten. Meanwhile I will have been denied a year of public education for my child." He stood up.

"All I can say," Carter told him, "is that I will bring the matter before our superintendent, Dr. Creel. It is an unusual case."

"Very well," Dr. Weinstein said. "At least you admit that. Mr. Fuller wouldn't go even that far. I'll leave the records with you."

That afternoon Carter and Dr. Weeks, the Director of Guidance and Special Training in Tolltown, conferred with Dr. Creel. Carter described Dr. Weinstein's visit and showed the records to Dr. Weeks and Dr. Creel. Both men agreed that it was more than a matter of a parent who was temporarily irritated by an abrupt principal. Jake Fuller, principal of Hope School, was famous for his brusqueness with parents. "Still, I think it's more than that," Superintendent Creel said. "Here is a man who wants to change policy. He feels that we are doing a general injustice. And maybe we are."

"There is the other side of it," Carter pointed out. "Every elementary principal in the city has opposed kindergarten entrances which drag out over the year. It causes a raft of paper work. The elementary supervisor did recommend delayed entrances in her report two years ago, but the teachers opposed the recommendation and it wasn't put into effect. I met with them on the problem last year. They maintain that kindergarten is a difficult enough adjustment for the child who gets in on time for the regular orientation period. The existing rule is that children must be four-nine on October first, if they are entering a September class. Gerry will be only four-eight."

"I would say," Dr. Weeks interrupted, "that in this case the chronological cutting point is meaningless. It's a crime to keep him out."

"It's not meaningless to principals," Carter argued. "Especially to principals like Jake Fuller. It isn't meaningless to teachers, either."

"Let's review the other side of it," Dr. Creel said. "Tolltown is a system with a reputation. People are still attracted to the community because of the schools. We pay for the best in teachers, and we get them. We've increased our per-pupil cost because of added services. We've done it gradually, but we've done it. With all this, our city tax rate is low. It's just that schools get a sizable share of the tax dollar, and the citizens know we don't waste their money. Now we are getting into somewhat of a spot. We need buildings. This capital outlay is going to cost the taxpayers of this city some money. You know the community. These people think about how things are going to affect their children and their children's children. We can't soothe them by saying that it goes to bond, and that our operational budget will still be low. There's one group of people in this town who are going to balk. They send their lads out to private schools anyway. There is another group, and Weinstein is one of them, who beat the drum for us. They would support new buildings. I think we owe it to Dr. Weinstein to give him a hearing."

"It will mean making a special exception," Carter pointed out.

"Oh, I'm not worried about that. I make special exceptions every day. Rules and regulations are just one way to group a bunch of special exceptions."

"You really want to take it before the school board then?" Carter asked.

"That's right."

"I agree," Weeks said.

"All right," Carter said. "Before the board it goes."

Five days later Dr. Weinstein presented his case to the Tolltown School Board. He presented his documents and outlined the case substantially as he had to Carter. It was apparent to Carter that Dr. Weinstein made a favorable impression on the board. Mr. Andred Tobiason, the chairman spoke for the majority when he said, "Frankly the admission policy in this case seems to make no sense to us. How about you, Dr. Creel?"

"It doesn't make sense to me either," the superintendent admitted.

"The board realizes that entrance policy is complex," Tobiason continued. "But in fairness to Dr. Weinstein we hope that you will arrive at a reasoned conclusion. I leave that to you, naturally. But I think the whole matter warrants study."

"Agreed," said Superintendent Creel.

The next morning Carter, Weeks, Creel, and Miss Borro, the Supervisor of Elementary Education, met in the office of the Superintendent. "I'd like to make only a few suggestions," Creel said. "I want Mr. Carter to take charge of a study of entrance policy. I'd like him to suggest a committee of appropriate personnel to make this study. I think we have a mandate to study this specific case and possibly to recommend general changes. Furthermore, I think we owe it to Dr. Weinstein to reach some sort of conclusion in this particular case. I know it will put you in a time bind, Ray. And you others will have to make your recommendations to Ray, so that he will have a chance to take action on them. But I think we owe it to Dr. Weinstein to have an answer as soon as possible. I want Mr. Carter to map out a course of study for the committee, and I want him to set up a procedure. I don't care how it's done. I want all of you to start thinking of possible changes, and how these changes may be best implemented." Superintendent Creel looked at his watch. "I'm going to have to run," he announced. "Could you carry on from there, Ray?"

"Yes," Mr. Carter said.

34 *The Paperbacked Books*

The citizens of Dexter, a city situated in the rolling country west of the Mississippi, looked at their morning papers on April 21, 1954, and read an accusation that made some of the old-timers wonder if it were time to buckle on their guns again.

City Councillor Jess Black, the headlines stated, had declared in the April 20th meeting of the Council that the Lincoln High School Library and the Madison High School Library contained books which had either been written by Communists, or were Communist-inspired or favored the Communist point of view. The headline reported his demand that these books be plainly branded. A secondary headline indicated that Councillor Jerry Brown had gone even further and demanded that the books be burned publicly.

"It has been brought to my attention by thoroughly reputable observers," Councillor Black was reported as saying, "that the libraries of our two great high schools contain hundreds of books of which every fighting American patriot should be ashamed. They include books written by known Communists. I believe that without more ado there should be a thorough check of all the books in our school libraries, and that those volumes which would indoctrinate the youth of our city in the ways of Red Communism should be plainly branded for all to see."

Councillor Brown was quoted as saying, "We should go further, Mr. Mayor. We should burn these books at public ceremonies. We should make an issue of it so as to show to the whole world that we believe first in the United States of America and second in the right of the City of Dexter to keep clean the minds of its youth."

"Something else has also been brought to my attention which bears looking into," Councillor Black said. "A whole series of cheap paper-covered books has just been made available in these high schools' so-called 'lending libraries.' This Council has been bringing moral pressure to bear on the Prairie News Distributors for some months, to remove from the newsstands many objectionable comic books and paperbacks which we consider deleterious to young people. How do we know that some of these are not getting into our school libraries? Furthermore, it is reported to me that there are plans to place these paper-bound books even in the elementary schools. Mr. Mayor, I think we should find out whether anyone is letting into these libraries some of those books which we have been trying to get rid of as dangerous to boys and girls, and if so, who is responsible. I demand action on this!"

Readers of the *Dexter Herald* were accustomed to big headlines and the sensational treatment of even routine matters. But this was far from routine and aroused concern in several quarters.

It was very disturbing to George Fallon. He was curriculum chairman of the city's English and Speech Department. For ten years he had worked to establish an enrichment program in reading throughout the entire system, from the first-year classes right through the senior year in the high schools. During the past four or five years, his program had begun to bear fruit. Several teams of reading specialists from the state university had studied the program and expressed the view that it had stimulated in the children wider interests in their leisure reading and an improvement in the comprehension of books used in other school subjects. They also felt that, among other desirable results, the program had spurred a development of taste and judgment in literature, an eagerness to explore in books and magazines for information about other times, places, and cultures.

The program was now a success, but it had not been an easy road for George Fallon. At the beginning there were the usual objections to innovation. Some of the older teachers, especially, felt that he was disturbing the set-up of their classes needlessly. They had their own schedules; there was no place in them for new frills and no time to experiment unless vital procedures already in operation were to be sacrificed.

Fallon particularly remembered one meeting of the high school English teachers during the early planning stages of his program. The suggestion that perhaps not *everyone* in a class should be reading the *same* book at the same time and at the same speed was apparently upsetting to Miss Harriet Noble.

"I've been teaching English for twenty years," she said, her mouth tight. "I think in that time I have gained some experience in successful methods. These new suggestions would make things quite chaotic. There are the complications in the marking system and the standard requirements of state law which have to be taken into account. A class has to work as a unit — not as forty or more individuals each going his own way at his own sweet will. I certainly hope I never live to see the day when teachers in the Dexter high schools will be forced to adopt the procedure Mr. Fallon suggests."

It was also pointed out by another teacher, a man named Becker, that there was not enough time for the realization of the English program even under the present set-up. He felt that if time were to be taken away for "free reading" periods and special individual instruction as suggested by the Fallon program, the teachers would just have to throw up their hands and give up.

Fallon remembered the compromises, the delays; he remembered the discussions at P.T.A. meetings; and he recalled how taken by surprise he had been — how appalled, really — at the amount of emotion aroused in some people over what seemed to him a reasonable experiment, one which had every likelihood of success judging by research and experience in other systems.

But Fallon's program also had some support. The administration had been with him; the board authorized the first tentative steps. A small victory here, a successful trial there; a good public relations program which made the project clear and acceptable to parents and taxpayers; the strong enthusiasm of some members of the teaching force, and assurance to teachers like Miss Harriet Noble that nothing was going to be forced upon them — little by little the enrichment program was accepted. The program proved itself as it progressed, and its reputation spread. Visitors from other school systems came to observe and study. In time, even Miss Noble joined in the approbation.

Four months before the attack of Councillor Black, something new had been added to the program. The combined P.T.A.'s in the city conferred with George Fallon on how they could take positive action to combat the influence of certain offensive comic books which were observed to be getting wide circulation. After careful planning, they set up lending libraries of paperback books in all the junior high schools to offer recreational reading which would be attractive enough to compete with the objectionable comics. Jacob Blaustein, owner of Prairie News Distributors, and Joseph Hammond, editor of the *Dexter Herald*, cooperated with the plan. The News company discontinued forty comics which were judged offensive and agreed to supply the paper-bound books almost at cost to the P.T.A.'s for school use.

Within three months, the lending libraries had proved successful enough to be placed in the senior high schools also. By the first of April all these schools had them, and the books were carefully integrated into the reading-enrichment program.

George Fallon was acutely conscious of the support that good public relations had given to the development of this new aspect of his long-nurtured reading-enrichment program. The growth of the city, and of the public schools, had been rapid during the last seven years, and the budget situation was desperate. It was clear to everybody that the moderate program for expanding the plant, voted without serious opposition a decade back, was now hopelessly inadequate. Large sums of new money would be necessary. As a result, every department had to think twice before requesting new equipment; and most requests had to take substantial cuts. Hence, without the offer of the P.T.A. to raise the money for lending-library books, this venture would not have been possible.

Superintendent Hershey, too, was aware of the significance of good public relations between the schools, the P.T.A., and the general public. It had been clear in September, when the schools opened, that widespread public support would be necessary in order to finance an expanded building program planned for the current year.

By mid-fall a Dexter Citizens' Committee for the Schools had been launched with the aid of Editor Joseph Hammond. He had been able to enlist support from many of the community leaders — industrialists, bankers, lawyers, ministers — although meeting resistance from some.

This committee, working closely with the schools, undertook an experimental Public Forum on Education. The plan for the first Forum was to divide the meeting into several discussion sections dealing with different topics such as: New Methods of Teaching the Three R's; How We Train for Citizenship; Visual Aids in Dexter Schools; How the Community Can Use the School Plant; The Best in School Libraries; and so on.

Each section was to be led by a citizen-chairman; a teacher would introduce the subject, and then the current practice would be presented by an expert in the field. A question period would follow.

The first Public Forum, held in January, attracted nearly seven hundred people. The sessions seemed to be friendly, interesting, and fruitful, with a minimum of "fighting questions."

The *Dexter Herald* announced that it would carry as much reader comment as people wished to send in, favorable or otherwise, and letters poured in. On the second day after the Forum, the letters filled two full columns; on the third day, the *Herald* had to devote an entire page to letters. And many of the comments praised the reading-enrichment program. In fact, this aspect of the schools drew more commendations than any other.

The first Public Forum was such a success that another one had been planned for the first week in May. Questionnaires placed in the hands of every person attending the first Forum indicated that only twelve people did *not* want a second Forum; and there were hundreds of questions which the audience hoped to discuss at the next one.

Now, however, the headlines of April 21 would almost certainly alter the program plans for this next Forum.

To one person who read the *Herald* that morning, the development in the City Council meeting signaled a long-hoped-for opportunity. Mrs. Clement

Fisher, organizer of the Dexter Chapter of American Women-in-Arms, read the words of Councillor Black with approval. At last, the city was coming to its senses.

For some months she and the Women-in-Arms had been trying to get people to recognize that the Dexter public schools had knowingly or unknowingly become allied with movements committed to remaking American society. In Mrs. Fisher's opinion these groups had been enormously successful in penetrating the school systems of the country, and even here in Dexter. They were dominated by the followers of John Dewey — nurtured by the schools of education, particularly in the East — and they aimed toward a socialist or communist society to replace the American Way of Life. They proclaimed that the individualistic society of capitalism was doomed and must be replaced by collectivism and a planned economy, hastened by and through the schools. Mrs. Fisher intended to fight these subversive influences, particularly in the public school system.

Within twenty minutes of her reading of the newspaper account of the council meeting, Mrs. Fisher went into action. She called ten of her most active fellow members of Women-in-Arms; each of them would telephone ten other members and friends. An emergency meeting was called for three o'clock that afternoon, in the auditorium of one of the junior high schools. Mrs. Fisher was always able to obtain an auditorium for meetings.

On April 22 the *Dexter Herald* reported that the American Women-in-Arms had appointed a Vigilante Committee to go through all the books in all the school libraries and list the subversive titles. The list of titles would be printed and made available to the City Council and to any citizen desiring copies. The meeting went on record with a resolution affirming the purpose of the Women not to rest until every vestige of Red influence in the public education system of Dexter was thoroughly extirpated. There were several speeches, and the meeting ended with the singing of the national anthem, a salute to the flag, and a brief prayer by Mrs. Fisher.

The following day, the Dexter Citizens' Committee for the Schools bought a full-page ad in the *Herald* countering the accusations and charges made by the Women-in-Arms. It urged the community not to "join the book burners" and listed several instances of what it called false accusations throughout the country. These, the ad stated, were the methods of Communism itself. The ad also reminded people of the Second Public Forum on Education to be held on May 6 and invited them to attend.

On April 27 the Women-in-Arms placed an ad in the paper urging that the school administration of Dexter adopt a set of criteria against which every book in the public school libraries could be measured. Banned absolutely from any school library, the notice said, should be any books whose authors did not support "the principles of American constitutional government" or any books whose nature and content are not "consistent with the principles of American constitutional government." The Women-in-Arms had already formed a committee which had prepared a list of books and authors to be banned by these criteria. The list which followed included well-known names of men and women in the arts, sciences, and social sciences, many of whom would have been surprised to find themselves included in a list of "subversives."

With all this public furor, Superintendent Hershey considered at what point and in what way it might become wise or necessary for the school board and administration to enter the situation with some official statement or act. From his knowledge of the board's membership and convictions, including its past support of the reading-enrichment and lending-library programs, he hoped that there would be no immediate or substantial danger to the continuation of these programs. But a critical climate of public opinion might make headway, and there was always the factor of school board elections to take into account.

The next meeting of the board was to be held on May 5. Hershey wondered if he could count on the board's standing on the position that a book should be judged on its merits as to its suitability for inclusion in the school libraries. He thought the board members would probably favor some sort of review of the titles in the lending libraries, if only in order to forestall any public criticism that the board was unwilling to examine the charges. But he felt they would not succumb to pressure for censorship merely because of an author's affiliations.

But when Mr. Hershey thought about the future he was not so sanguine. Until a few months ago he would have dismissed Mrs. Fisher and her Women-in-Arms as a group whose general tone of hysteria, in his opinion, would discredit them. But recently, when undertaking to organize the Citizens' Committee for the Schools, he and Joe Hammond felt that the resistance they met indicated some crystallization of influential forces that were highly critical of the schools even though for quite different reasons. And now this new publicity was a sure sign that there must be some real school opposition brewing. Even school board members who "knew the right answers" could get jittery on a question such as this.

These thoughts were still revolving in the back of Superintendent Hershey's mind on Wednesday afternoon, April 28, when Mr. Stanford called him. Stanford, president of one of the older industries in Dexter, was a strong supporter of public schools and a member of the Executive Committee of the Citizens' Committee for the Schools.

"Just got back in town after being away all week," Stanford began. "Things are certainly bubbling. Look. I have a proposition for you. I'm down on the list for an informal talk before the Council of Women's Organizations tomorrow noon. It wasn't anything important. But I've just talked with Joe Hammond and Mrs. Faye. You'll be hearing from her in a few minutes. We're all agreed that you ought to take over that spot for tomorrow and say something about this whole business. The Forum is still too many days ahead to let it ride until then, and whatever statement the board may get around to making after its meeting next week isn't the same thing as having a chance to reach a key audience face-to-face. It will help at least to keep some of this stuff from spreading without any check."

"Well . . . ," began Hershey.

"Look, Dan," continued Stanford, "you just can't afford not to take it on for the sake of the schools. My talk can wait. I'll be out of town or something. You can kill two birds with one stone . . . get some sanity across to an audience which won't be too unreceptive. Of course, there'll be some of Mrs. Fisher's troupe there and probably a lot of others who are kind of nervous about the whole thing. At the same time, it'll give you a trial run on things to say and the kind of reactions you get. That'll come in handy for your board when they start figuring out what to do and how we ought to handle this thing at the Forum. Dan, you'll have to admit it makes sense."

"I guess you're right," Hershey agreed.

"You'll be hearing from Mrs. Faye any minute. And Dan, if there's anything that Joe or I can do in reading over or hearing whatever you plan to say, we're ready to be called on. But we know you can do the job that's called for. Best of luck."

35 English at Central Western

In early March of 1954, four representatives of the Parents' Advisory Council of the Central Western High School met with Central City School officials and other interested parties, for the purpose of working out modifications in the English courses at the high school. Central Western, with a student enrollment of 2620 and a faculty of one hundred teachers, was the largest high school in Central City. It also had the largest per cent of its graduates in college: 65 per cent of the 750 graduates in the class of 1953 were attending "institutions of higher learning."

The meeting was held in a classroom at Central Western High, and a number of events which were largely coincidental helped to create an undercurrent of tension.

First, there had just appeared in a national magazine an article which criticized all five high schools in Central City and singled out Central Western High School in particular for unfavorable comparison with two big-city high schools in the East. The article criticized the practice of awarding scholastic credit for what the author termed "activity classes" (school paper, school magazine, dramatic clubs) and classes which developed "social skills" rather than "training the intellect." It ridiculed the idea of 26 boys "horsing around in the cooking class."

The newspapers of Central City immediately began a series of interviews with school officials, leaders of the Parents' Advisory Council at Central Western, graduates of Central City schools, and candidates for local office.

Superintendent Karl Kendricks and Assistant Superintendent Russell Kline said that the article was "slanted, biased, and incomplete."

Dr. Ralph Nance, principal of Central Western High, said that the article did not take into account other aspects of the school program such as a total enrollment of 350 in Latin classes. "Why didn't the author mention them?" he asked.

The newspapers also quoted at length from an article written the previous fall by Mrs. Laura Trabert, a leader of the Parents' Advisory Council.[1] She had written: "The time has come to take a penetrating look at the needs of the better-than-average students, the group from which our leaders spring. It is time to think again more seriously of the intellectual growth of these youngsters rather than demanding that so much of their thinking be about their social problems."

The newspapers had run their series of interviews just prior to the meeting on the problem of English at Central Western. Subsequently Mrs. Trabert told the case writer that a number of pressure groups had offered to back her to the hilt on a showdown fight with the schools. School officials who had been con-

[1] Mrs. Trabert's article, which appeared in an alumnae magazine in the fall of 1953, was a general criticism of "progressive education." The article was, however, in no sense the cause of the present meeting. Before the article appeared, Mrs. Trabert had attended several meetings of the Parents' Advisory Council, a permanent organization at Central Western, and had suggested that the council members address themselves specifically to the problems of English teaching at the high school. Mrs. Trabert was usually viewed by the school officials as the spokesman of the parents' group.

tacted by newsmen expressed the feeling that perhaps the newsmen were trying to get them to fire counter-criticism at Mrs. Trabert and the Parents' Advisory Council. Both Mrs. Trabert and the school officials showed reluctance, however, to permit the matter to be expanded beyond the specific problem of English at Central Western.

When the meeting finally was held, almost thirty people attended. These included: an assistant superintendent and the director of instruction from the Central Office; the principal and the coordinator of curriculum at Central Western; three English teachers from that school; a representative from the English Department of the State University; the city-wide consultant in English; two newspaper reporters; a photographer; and a number of parents, including the four representatives of the Parents' Advisory Council.

Dr. Nance, as principal of Central Western, gave a brief history of the Parents' Advisory Council from the time it had formed English course study groups during the previous September to the present meeting where specific reports on courses in English were to be given. He finished by stating that the teachers and staff were open to suggestions on any course or sequence of courses which seemed practical and profitable, and that the school authorities were interested in the parents' statement as to "what basic skills it was most necessary to develop in high school students." He reported that on the basis of a previous conference the parents were satisfied with the curriculum guide in English up through Grade 10, and that the main cause of parent concern was the program of electives offered in the last two years at the high school.

In summary, Nance said that the parents would present their report on the basic skills necessary. The teachers would then present their report on the English course electives, first to see if the essential courses were there, and second to see if the sequence of courses was satisfactory. Nance then hoped that the groups could jointly settle additional problems, such as those of (1) testing and evaluating students' course work, (2) determining which student should take which course, (3) determining how the courses could best be arranged and taught.

Mrs. Trabert spoke first for the parents. She made it clear that the group was not only interested in the 5 per cent of the students at Central Western who went to Eastern colleges, but was equally concerned with the rest of the 65-per-cent total of Central Western graduates who went on to college. She stressed the fact that the Council represented no pressure group, although she added that they had been contacted by various groups.

Mrs. Trabert said, "Our feeling is that good students are not being sufficiently challenged by the high school program." She felt that too little was done for the exceptional child. She said that the parents' group felt that the K–12 curriculum guide was "splendid" up through the tenth grade. But she pointed out that her daughter and the other children in the last two years of high school were not benefiting by it.

She repeated suggestions made by the Advisory Council several months before: that for the children in the last two years of high school there should be devised an experimental course in English which would consolidate the teaching of literature and composition and stress "theme writing." Her group felt that the present system of electives left too much choice to the student who was not adequately prepared to make such a choice. (See Appendix A.) In their view, it would be necessary for students to take all of the electives in order to have a complete program; yet this would obviously be impossible, since carrying all of the English electives would leave no room for other courses. The Advisory

Council proposed a consolidation of literature and composition, in which the themes would be based on literature rather than on experience.

Mrs. Esterbrook, who was head of the English Department that year (senior teachers alternated as department heads, each one serving a year), said that the English teachers had completely reviewed the course syllabi and were ready to present a detailed report on the courses. Mrs. Esterbrook said that the courses were not as segmented as they appeared; that spelling, for example, was stressed just as much in literature classes as it was in composition classes. She then introduced another member of the English Department, Mr. Boyle, who was to discuss the courses in literature.

Mr. Boyle listed the one-semester literature courses as: "American Literature," "Eleventh Grade Literature," "Contemporary Literature," and "English Literature." "Eleventh Grade Literature" was a remedial course designed for those students who came out of tenth-grade English with specific disabilities in reading, either in the mechanics or in overly limited coverage.

"American Literature, on the other hand," continued Mr. Boyle, "is a fast-paced survey course which covers everything from Mather to Hemingway. The main value is in the collateral reading. Students are expected to read nine books a semester, selecting from a recommended list at least one novel, one volume of short stories, one full-length drama, one biography, one collection of essays, and one book of poetry."

The essentials of the course were comprehensive coverage in a survey text ("We take them from Cooper to *Citizen Tom Paine*") and wide and deep reading in selected outside books. "We want more out of them than just book reports. We have discussions and follow-ups." Almost all students took this American Literature course. (The low verbal group were given the course after they had been through the Eleventh Grade Literature remedial course.) The records showed that 510 out of a total of 800 in a class took the course.

"This is no University of Chicago great books program, but these are standard works that every student should know," Mr. Boyle continued. There was some latitude in title selection, depending on the teacher; he personally allowed little free choice in his course. He felt it was of primary importance for the students to understand how the author created character, how decisions came about, how the characters reacted in crisis situations, what attributes the author placed on people and events, and whether these were objective or subjective. The major theme was the nature of conflict, internal and external.

Mr. Boyle added: "I feel that vocabulary building is a tremendous factor in all courses. We devote much study to words, and their meanings to different people."

Mr. Harrison, one of the parents' group, asked: "How do you get the students' grades? Do you use only objective tests?"

"We use both," Boyle said, "objective tests and subjective essays. I prefer the essay in literature courses." His weighting of a student in the literature course was: 40 per cent collateral reading; 20 per cent spelling and quiz; 30 per cent material in survey text; and 10 per cent on the final examination. "There is no standard school-wide exam required." Most of the teachers indicated that they gave essay paragraph tests regularly.

The chairman then inquired whether the parents wanted to discuss specific courses at that point or get an overview of all courses. One parent said that he wanted to hear about all the courses to see if Mrs. Trabert's thesis was borne out. "The problem is how to get a consolidated two-year course, and get the burden off student choice."

One of the teachers stated: "There's too much being offered to telescope. The advantage of this system is that the student who is weak in literature gets added work there. If he's weak in grammar, he gets more composition."

Mr. Boyle then described "English Literature." "This is a survey course designed to whet the appetites of the students so that they will go further on their own. We use an anthology and collateral lists of reading. We take them through the standard English writers. We have weekly quizzes and recitations — most of them subjective, some objective. We try to have the students read analytically. I lecture and they take notes. I act out and dramatize the reading — you can't just sit up there and drone. If a teacher doesn't try to give them the feel of the thing, doesn't throw himself into it, what can it mean to a student? We cover three general fields: Prose, Poetry, and Drama. I try to get them to think critically about the issues and views of the period in which the piece was written. I give them a phrase taken from a writer of the time and try to get them to see how a person of that time would develop it into a paragraph." He said that this was also done in the "Drama" course. "We want them to understand how, and more important why, the writer developed his theme as he did. They write in this course too, but it is a prose analysis of a dramatic work."

Next, Mr. Hegburgh of the English Department described the "Eleventh Grade Composition" and the "College Composition" courses. "College Composition is not remedial, like Eleventh Grade Composition." He explained that Eleventh Grade Composition stressed the fundamentals of grammar, but stopped short of clauses and verbals. The routine was to write one day a week, to criticize the writing one day a week, and to study formal grammar two days a week. "The approach is usage rather than formal grammar, but both are considered." He added that the subject of the writing was not drawn from literature but from the creative ideas of the students themselves. The aim was student knowledge of grammatical form and student ability to write in a meaningful, critical way. One day a week was devoted to vocabulary building in sentences, using words which were new and difficult. The course was designed on the premise that certain students have certain specific weaknesses, and that these vary with the student.

"This same philosophy is carried into the College Preparatory Composition course. We offer this course for those going on to college. It is not primarily remedial, but it is custom-tailored to the individual. We stress letter writing, theme writing, and usage." Six hundred of a class of 800 take Eleventh Grade Composition, or College Preparatory Composition; 40 per cent of the senior class regularly elect English Literature.

Mr. Hegburgh stated further that College Preparatory Composition was "high-geared," with a great deal of paragraph writing. The average was five themes (150 word maximum) for the first six-week period of the course. "The grammar here is formal rather than colloquial. We mark on paragraph content, detail, comparison and contrast. In the second six-week period we take them into longer-length themes. The final has to be written under time pressure; they have to decide on the spot the organization and make-up of their final theme. Our central purpose is to get a notion of the individual's style, so that we can question him and correct it, if he needs help. The second six weeks we also teach précis writing and summary writing. The main thing in the third six-week period is an evaluation by the teachers of the students' term papers."

The remaining course descriptions were then presented. "Contemporary Literature" covered the modern literature of all countries — "the complete range." "Speech Two" and "Speech Three" dealt with (1) outlining, (2) extempore speaking, (3) formal delivery of a prepared speech. "Shakespeare" covered "four principal plays of Shakespeare" (these were not listed and presumably there could be some selection by teachers). "Drama" was a double course (two semesters) which took the students "from Aristophanes to Odets." The drama group also presented a one-act play. "Productions" consisted of work on the school newspaper and magazine, for which regular credit was given, but which could be taken only with signed permissions from parent and guidance counselor. "Creative Writing" was an eleventh-grade one-semester course in which the students produced original fiction, short stories and sketches, and poetry. "Journalism 1" and "Journalism 2" were "courses designed to acquaint students with newspaper and magazine production and to provide practice in gathering, writing, and compiling the news of the school for the production of the school newspaper and the school magazine." This was partly a classroom course and partly a direct production course on the newspaper and magazine.

When the teachers had completed their description of the English courses, the chairman asked for questions from the parents. Mrs. Trabert said: "I feel that the writing courses emphasize writing on contemporary problems too much. There should be more writing based on themes drawn from literature." One of the teachers replied that the courses sought an equal balance between both; that motivation was less of a problem when the students were writing about something of great interest to them. Mrs. Trabert again alluded to a "telescoped course" for the final two years. A teacher pointed out that one problem was building a course of this type which would meet the varying needs of the different students. He said that tenth-grade English (English 3 and English 4) were composite courses and, in his opinion, far from satisfactory.

Mrs. Preston, the city-wide English consultant who had directed the preparation of the curriculum guide, said that it had been her intent to have composite courses up through the tenth grade, and from that point on to have electives in specific subject areas which would do two things: (1) provide specific help to students who needed it in one area but not another; (2) allow the good students to deepen their preparation in given areas. She added: "There is no proof that either the consolidated or the specific elective course is superior to the other at this grade level. But electives seem to be recommended by most colleges in the country."

Doctor Novak, a professor of English at the State University, asked whether there were any courses concerned with "logic," "critical thinking," or the development of proof in factual writing. A teacher answered, "This is attempted in the composition courses, but it is not a major concern of the English department." Mrs. Esterbrook added: "The main effort is to get the students to realize that reading, writing, and speaking are all integrated. This is carried into other courses in history and social studies." The discussion chairman agreed adding: "It's all language. Spelling should be just as accurate in a paper submitted in history as in a paper prepared for English composition."

One of the parents suggested that the problem was a matter of degree not kind. "I don't see anything missing there; but still the children are having trouble. So there must be something wrong. Maybe they just aren't taking the right courses."

Mrs. Trabert said: "I feel that English is taught excellently at Central Western. The problem is: how are the children to get enough of it? Then there is the matter of testing. I wonder if Professor Novak would talk about the way students are tested in English at State."

Professor Novak replied that both objective and essay tests were used at the State University. A difference of opinion then arose as to how well or how badly Central Western graduates were doing in college English. There had been conflicting viewpoints on this question between the parents and the school officials.

Professor Novak was able to give some statistics on the achievements of Central Western graduates in English courses at the State University. Of last year's graduates, 100 had been taken directly into the regular first-year English grammar and composition sections; 11 had been put into advanced sections; and 17 were in what had come to be known as "dumbbell English." In literature, 8 per cent had grades of "A"; 25 per cent, "B"; 39 per cent, "C"; 13 per cent, "D"; 15 per cent, "failure." In composition the distribution was 5 per cent, "A"; 22 per cent, "B"; 37 per cent, "C"; 19 per cent, "D"; 17 per cent, "failure."

Principal Nance pointed out that the state college records had been compared with the high school records, and the students had ranked about the same at Central Western as they had at State. The "D" and "failure" students at State had never received grades above "C" at Central Western. Mrs. Trabert asked about the admission policies at State. Nance pointed out that students in the lower one-third of the classes at Central Western could be admitted to the State University. Mrs. Trabert challenged a school department announcement which had appeared that week in a local newspaper, and which had quoted officials as saying that 21 of 26 Central Western graduates then attending Yale were on the Dean's List. "I personally know a girl from Central Western, attending Smith, who is about to lose her scholarship because of trouble in English."

Mrs. Preston, the consultant, said: "No one says there are not exceptions. We have to plan our program here in terms of the general average."

At this point a parent stood up and said: "Central City public schools are doing an excellent job preparing students. I challenge Mrs. Trabert's view that leaders come from the college group. Good understanding among students leads to better grades." She finished by stating: "People who do not go to college are the backbone of the United States."

Dr. Nance then suggested, "Perhaps we might now profitably consider the course offerings, and see what may be omitted, added, or combined." Mrs. Trabert said: "Well, certainly I can't see anything missing. It's all here." The other parents nodded agreement.

"Well," the chairman pursued, "since we have the courses here, let's look at the sequence. Suppose we list all courses which you feel might be of benefit to college students." The list as finally drawn up was:

11th Grade

Course	
11th Grade Composition American Literature	Absolutely necessary in 11th grade
Contemporary Literature One Speech Course Shakespeare Drama Creative Writing	Necessary

12th Grade

Course	
English Literature College Preparatory Composition	Absolutely necessary in 12th grade

Mrs. Trabert pointed out that to take the other courses which were "necessary" might result in a student's carrying six difficult courses in one semester — "American Literature," "Eleventh Grade Composition," a modern language, a science, math, and history. Mr. Nance said: "The usual procedure is for a student to carry four prepared classes, and one class which requires no outside preparation. Some students take five without difficulty, and exceptionally able students take six."

Mrs. Trabert was asked if she felt that children should take all of the courses listed. "Definitely not, this would result in the high school doing college work," she responded. The discussion moderator said: "But you seemed to indicate a while ago that you felt that they were not adequately preparing the students for college.

"That's true," Mrs. Trabert answered. "Both are true simultaneously. What I'm proposing is that the work be telescoped, so that there are no gaps for some children." One of the teachers then said: "But if the time is exactly the same in both cases, something has to be left out." Mr. Boyle commented: "We don't have three-hour supervised study periods at night, as they do in some Eastern prep schools. The value of literature courses is in how many books the students actually read, not how many they hear the name of. I think the problem is one of counseling by teacher and parent to see that the students get what will most benefit them. I also feel that parents have some obligation in the matter of enforcing regular study in a day school. If tough English courses are necessary, I should be delighted to give them, but they are pointless unless the children are held to rigorous study schedules at home as well as in school."

"I'm not suggesting that children with a bent toward math be penalized by being forced to take the most difficult English courses," Mrs. Trabert said.

The principal noted that it was nearing the end of the session, and asked what the parents would propose.

Mr. George Rolland, of the Advisory Council, suggested a minimum course for all college-bound students:

11B	Eleventh Grade Composition
11A	American Literature
12B	College Preparatory English
12A	English Literature

School officials pointed out that this was the general pattern, except for students to whom speech courses were recommended. Mrs. Trabert said, "I still think a combined experimental course should be put in." One teacher again commented that this had been done in the tenth grade and that he was not satisfied with the results. The principal pointed out that it would create schedule difficulties for students who wanted other activities. The meeting was adjourned at this point.

After the meeting, interviews were held with the individuals involved in the discussion. The following is a summary of the views of various of the participants.

Dr. Nance, Principal of Western High School

Dr. Nance felt that the parents' group represented a small minority of wealthy citizens who were interested in the preparation of children for Eastern colleges.

"However, I am heartened by the progress in the meeting," he said. "Mrs. Trabert has a much more constructive interest in the schools and the curriculum than she had at the beginning of the meetings. I feel that perhaps an experimental course of the sort she outlined *will* be tried at Central Western."

When curriculum was challenged, he felt the parents should be involved in active planning sessions and committee work to give them a chance to be heard. He felt that the initial work should be free of official influence.

"Much of the early heat in the meeting was due to the unfortunate coincidence of the hatchet job done by that magazine coming at the same time as the meeting on curriculum. What is so amusing is that these teachers at Central Western have long been considered by other educators to be the most tradition-bound staff in the city. It's amazing that they should have been the ones to be accused of 'progressivism.'

"Morale is high among the staff, and I don't feel they will resent the administration's recommendations for an experimental course."

Superintendent Kendricks, Assistant Superintendents Kline and Wayne

The superintendency staff also deplored the unfortunate appearance of the article. The coincidence in timing, they felt, tended to give the impression that the city was up in arms over the school situation.

"This is definitely not the case," the superintendent said. "The staff welcomes parent participation in curriculum planning, and we look forward to it as a regular source to help in curriculum development."

He said that the division of instructional services of the school department had three procedures in the matter of citizen participation. First, the schools sought, by means of a public opinion poll every three years, to determine citizen satisfaction with the schools and the curriculum. Second, school officials attempted to get citizen groups together to consider and remedy any specific area of criticism as indicated by the poll. This second procedure entailed the formation of advisory groups, of which the Parents' Advisory Council at Central Western was an example. These groups set up specific committees to study and evaluate the curriculum.

The third feature of the system was the establishment of the position of Coordinator of Curriculum — one for each large junior and senior high school in the city. The coordinator had charge of the instructional program in his school; it was his responsibility to maintain liaison between the parent groups and the teaching staff, between the principal and the staff in instructional matters, and between the central staff and the teachers in subject areas.

The last opinion survey, of 1953, had showed that the parents were much more satisfied with the schools than they had been in 1950.

Assistant Superintendent Kline said he felt that the poll did show that English was the area of primary concern for most parents. (Appendix B) "Mrs. Trabert is not unrepresentative of many parents, but her argument is based on the difficulties of a minority of children who went to Eastern colleges."

Mr. Kline also said that he felt that the newspapers were doing their best to promote a controversy between the schools and the parents.

Mrs. Laura Trabert, Parents' Advisory Council

Mrs. Trabert denied emphatically that she was interested only in Eastern college students. She said she wanted her children to go to the Eastern university which she and her husband, and their families for generations, had attended, but that this did not warrant the school department's charge that she was interested in the preparation of these children only.

"However," she added, "I make no apology for being interested in college-bound students. This reverse-snobbism that masks under the name of 'democracy in education' irritates me. We have the right to see that our children get out of school what we, the parents, determine is important."

She said that she had conducted a survey among Central City girls attending her college in the East, and found that they were doing well in science and social studies and badly in English.

"One problem is the objective-type examinations given in high school. The children have forgotten how to think and reason. Another problem is that children in high school just do not like to read. There are other problems, too.

"Children must write about themes from literature. There is too much attempt to be original in their writing. Children at that age don't have the maturity to develop significant themes from their own experience. There is entirely too much sympathy for the less-favored group of children. This is fine, but it can be carried to extremes where everything might be hitched to mediocrity."

She expressed the view that the three-hour study period was no real defense. "My daughter puts from four to five hours in on her studies every evening." Her daughter had taken remedial reading, which had sent her rate up to 500 words and her comprehension way down. "This is where writing on themes from literature comes in. It aids comprehension. In addition, I view it in terms of realism. Writing on themes from literature is what is expected in college. High school supposedly prepares them for college. To be realistic, then, high school should give students practice in this."

She said that the members of the school staff had been cordial, and that she and many parents had been invited to attend earlier meetings on the curriculum. "But," she indicated, "the problem was that we were never given an opportunity to discuss; we had to listen to school department experts give prepared talks."

She felt that the curriculum guide was excellent through the tenth grade, but that little had been done for the last two years. Even were the guide to be carried through these two years, there was no assurance that an English teacher would actually follow it. "If your child gets one of the good teachers, wonderful! But if he gets a poor one. . . ."

It was pure coincidence, she indicated, that the writer from the national magazine had been visiting in Central City at the time of the December meeting of the Parents' Advisory Council. Some of the parents had felt that the school officials had monopolized the meeting.

"Perhaps," Mrs. Trabert said, "some of the article was based on parent complaints. I had lunch with the writer, but I didn't give him any of the derogatory information he printed."

With regard to the problem of fitting all of the English into a few courses of the survey type, Mrs. Trabert said she recognized that if time and assignment levels were held constant, some things were going to have to be omitted in the telescoped course she was advocating. She thought sampling parts of literature might do, but not if this sacrificed the unity of a whole work. She said there must be some basis for the selection of worthwhile books.

Mrs. Josephine Preston, Consultant in English

Mrs. Preston said that the curriculum guide represented a compromise among many different approaches to English teaching — scientific, linguistic, classical literary, rhetoric and grammar, and even some attention to the principles of logic. The approach to a knowledge of the structure of English was based on usage rather than formal grammar, and attention was given to the common errors which had been determined by studies in the field.

"I argued no specific approach with the teachers' committees. I tried to distribute research results to them which would help." The child-development studies in language of Davis, Smith, LaBrandte, McCarthy, and others had been "helpful." Mrs. Preston said that one teacher had incorporated some of the approach of the semanticists (the Lees, Hayakawa, Johnson). "The stress in the writing courses in college English is on expository writing. It progresses from simple, unselective reports in the early grades to attention to significant interpersonal situations in the later grades."

"I would have preferred more attention to writing on literary themes," Mrs. Preston continued, "but not of the type — 'Describe Cassius in twenty words or less.' This is asking children to do what Shakespeare couldn't. Any teacher who expects anything better than 'Cassius was a sneaky customer' is an optimist." Her preference was to assign students in the advanced English courses to writing on broad significant themes such as "Ambition in *Macbeth*." "This develops a notion of the universality of character traits. The source develops standards."

"I'm opposed to the granting of student credit for work on newspapers and magazines. This should be purely voluntary and extra," she said.

"One problem for literature," Mrs. Preston concluded, "is that students have such a mass of technical data to assimilate from science course readings and collateral reading. The old standard literary works are neglected. Students have fewer hours in the day free for reading because of extra work possibilities. And there is too much recreation. Yet I don't see this as only the fault of the school. I don't think the answer is to take *Bartlett's Quotations* and make the students memorize it. They already have too much phone-book knowledge. Frankly, I don't know what the answer is. At least I don't have any one answer which will satisfy every one. We should hear more from the college people on the constructive side."

Interviews with Teachers

The investigator also conducted several interviews with teachers of English at Central Western and other high schools of the city. Some of the teachers expressed the feeling that the administration was too sensitive to outside pressure, but qualified their comments by saying that they were not in a position to gauge how necessary this was. They felt that the experimental course was an admission of weakness, but on the other hand indicated that they would be watching the results of it with great interest. Their almost universal comment on the teaching of English at Central Western was: "How much more traditional and formal can you get?"

APPENDIX A Courses in English

Grade Level	*Course*
10B	* English 3
10A	* English 4 ** Library Assistant (¼ unit of credit)
11B	American Literature; 11th Grade Literature 11th Grade Comp. (remedial); Drama Journalism 1; ** *Angelus* Staff Speech 2; Everyday Speech 1 Creative Writing
11A	Contemporary Literature Shakespeare 11th Grade Composition Journalism 2 Speech 3; Everyday Speech 2
12B and 12A	English Literature 12th Grade Composition College Preparatory Composition ** *Spotlight* Staff

* Required Course.
** By signed permission blank.

APPENDIX B Excerpt from the Opinion Poll

Question: Are there any of these subjects you think the Central Public Schools are neglecting or not spending enough time on?
[Respondent was shown card listing nine general school subjects]
Responses (tabulated):

NUMBER OF CITIZENS BELIEVING CERTAIN SUBJECTS ARE NEGLECTED BY THE CENTRAL CITY PUBLIC SCHOOLS

Subject Believed Neglected	*Number of Persons Per Hundred*	
	Parents	*Non-Parents*
English	24	30
Mathematics	15	19
Social studies (geography, history)	13	12
Homemaking	7	7
Business and trade	7	9
Health	5	7
Foreign Languages	4	7
Sciences	3	3
Arts	3	2
None believed neglected	40	22
No opinion	12	29

SECTION FOUR

EDUCATIONAL ADMINISTRATION FROM A COMPARATIVE POINT OF VIEW

Educational Administration from a Comparative Point of View

ONE WAY of clarifying a view of educational administration and of cases in educational administration is by comparison with some other fields of administration. This does not mean that educational administration should copy these other fields; but the search for both similarities and differences — existing or desirable — may assist discriminative selection in thought and learning in this field. In this book we can present only a very limited discussion related primarily to business and industrial administration, which, however, may be sufficient for our purposes. Obviously the comparative study of administration is a major field in itself.

In the 1920's when the case method of teaching business administration was getting under way, the specialization of knowledge and function in business had already been standardized to some extent. Although the boundaries between the specializations were not precise, many leading functions of business, represented by executive roles and departmental structure, had been rather highly crystallized. The major specializations included various functions and kinds of knowledge and skill involved in such broad areas as production management and industrial engineering; finance management; the comptroller function (usually including expenditure control, credit control, accounting, and auditing); plant and equipment engineering; purchasing; and sales and advertising.

These and other rapidly growing specializations were found as major functions of industrial organizations — in the developing manuals, texts, and specialized research relating to industrial management, in the establishment of professorships and departments in schools of business administration, and in the organization of technical and professional societies. The conditions of specialization existing in the 1920's had evolved from around the middle of the nineteenth century, initially as a consequence of pragmatic processes of specialization and later of consciously rationalized "principles" of specialization. These patterns represented attempts to cope with the problems of utilizing increasing diversities of knowledge within ever-larger organizations which themselves involved a growing diversity of different kinds of jobs to be done. Specialization of function and knowledge on the executive level of business or industry reflected a transition from the stage at which such organizations could be said to be managed by a *manager* or *administrator*, under whatever title, to management by *an administration*

— a group or cluster of administrators with special responsibilities and, presumably, special knowledge.

Some Nineteenth-Century Developments in Administrative Structure

This transition had been gradually taking place since the beginning of the factory system. A division of major executive responsibilities between mill management and production on the one hand, and finance, purchasing, and sales on the other, was developing fairly strongly by 1825 in the cotton textile industry, which pioneered the industrial revolution from the beginning to at least the Civil War period. The rapid growth of very large mills, based on large steam-plant installations and the large-scale use of water power, further introduced into the managerial structure the roles of engineering specialists on the one hand and intermediate hierarchies of building superintendents and departmental foremen on the other. Shortly before 1850, specialized scientific and engineering knowledge pertaining to mechanics was advancing so rapidly as to give birth to a new kind of role — that of the consulting engineer, with Samuel Webber, a now forgotten but extraordinary figure, probably deserving the title of "the first consulting industrial engineer."

At about the same time, legal counsel began to play increasingly important roles, with advice which frequently included broad considerations of public policy. Specialists in such fields as transportation emerged, frequently serving a number of companies or associations of industry, then just beginning. The emergence of these specialists — or business "auxiliaries," in the term of Norman S. B. Gras,[1] a leading historian of business — was followed, almost immediately after the Civil War, by a very rapid extension of the range of specializations handled by auxiliaries, consultants, staff specialists, and new kinds of executives under various titles. The growth of both knowledge specializations and role specializations leaped forward as electricity, chemistry, microscopy, industrial plant design, engineering, and other fruits of native and continental science and technology ushered in the twentieth-century industrial era.

Yet, throughout this long development, it was not until about 1880, in this country, that the *specialization of function* in industrial organization was translated from a somewhat pragmatic process to a consciously rationalized and articulate application of the idea as a "principle." The principle was defined primarily as it had come to be defined in the dominant and highly esteemed physical sciences. During the years from about 1880 to 1914, the concept of *scientific management*, which became primarily associated with the name and work of Frederick W. Taylor, penetrated deeply into the thinking of industrial and business management and into the whole approach to the design and operation of organizational and administrative structure.

[1] N.S.B. Gras, *Shifts in Public Relations.* Bulletin of the Business Historical Society, Vol. 19, No. 4 (October, 1945).

Just as Taylor's central concept was the radical application of the scientific method to every aspect of factory organization and operation, the primary principles embraced in this concept might be identified as *specialization* on the one hand and *coordination* on the other. The application of the scientific method, in terms of observation, data gathering, analysis, measurement, test, hypothesis, and experiment, depended upon using and developing *specialists*. The findings then needed to be organized, applied, and coordinated. It might be further noted that, of these two principles, specialization sprang from science above and beyond the necessity for the division of responsibilities in organization, while coordination sprang exclusively from the necessities of the organization of human effort. The scientific specializations flowed into an order at the level of *applied* science and technology, through human organization; that order was the physical product.

Scientific management approached full tide during the 1920's, under the added impetus of "efficiency expert" efforts during World War I, the post-war depression, and the money-making years thereafter. Before considering the new kinds of thinking which have profoundly altered or reduced the Taylor concept of scientific management and the efficiency expert approach, we might look briefly at the status of educational administration during the period we have been discussing.

In 1880 when industry and many fields of business had already grown to such a size and diversity of scientific and functional specialization as to give rise to stated principles of management and administration, the great majority of school systems in the United States consisted of very small units of organization. They involved, for the most part, district school boards operating one small school with one or a few teachers. Somewhat fewer school systems were of a size to require a principal or teaching principal who might be said to constitute the first American public school administrator.

Using merely numbers of persons in the school organization (teachers and pupils) as a yardstick to measure the complexity of the task of administration, one might compare these school units with the very early factories, perhaps of the 1790 to 1810 period of the industrial revolution. Relatively few school systems in the 1880's were large enough to have *an administration*, in the sense in which this word has been used in discussing industry. Such administrations, consisting of a superintendent and several school principals, might therefore be roughly compared with those in the early-nineteenth-century factories, at the stage where the size of the organization gave rise to an administrative hierarchy composed of the head of the mill and the sub-heads of different mill units.

The crude parallel might be carried still further by reference to those school systems of 1880 or later date in which grammar and high schools were separated in terms of units of organization in different buildings. Overall size of school systems remained small, however, and relatively few began to approach the numbers of sub-administrators found in numerous industrial organizations, until city growth and the consolidation of previously independent districts gave rise to large school systems. Gradually, specialists were introduced in the form of supervisors, and, later, assistant superintendents, business assistants, and deputy superintendents. The emergence, largely in the twentieth century, of numerous new specialized functions in educational administration, such as guidance, research, and public relations, together with the increasing need for and use of consultants and "auxiliaries," further marks the continuing rough parallel. In contrast, the influx of numerous specialists into the administrative structure of industry was well advanced from 1850 on.

Perhaps a word of caution is in order here. Concern is sometimes felt by educators when any comparison is undertaken between educational administration and business and industrial administration. There is concern that such comparison may be used to draw inferences which may be inimical to concepts and standards desired for the field of educational administration in the light of its essential goals and functions. These, of course, differ significantly from those of business and industry. To allay any such concern, let us emphasize that the above parallel, at different historical periods, between certain developments in the respective fields has been drawn for very limited purposes.

The comparison suggests primarily the different historical periods at which size of organization, on the one hand, and creation of specialized roles based on knowledge specialization, on the other, have increased the variety of administrative roles within the respective kinds of organizations. Each has first exhibited *growth,* in which administration has shifted from the role of *an administrator* to *a hierarchy of administration,* and then has exhibited *evolution* to what, for want of better words, we will call *more complex qualitative structure,* reflecting the introduction of *specialized roles based upon specializations of knowledge* into the administrative structure. We will disregard, as not germane to the discussion, whether the distinction "growth *first, then* evolution" is a true one; it has been stated in this way here simply in order to sharpen the two kinds of change treated in the parallel. Both kinds of change affect the complexity of the administrative structure simply in terms of the number of administrative roles. We will also omit at this time any consideration of certain parallels as to ways in which the respective kinds of administrative structure were conceived and organized, in order to comprehend and relate numbers and differentiations of roles.

The Idea of Complexity in Organization and Administration

It is axiomatic that an increase in the number of persons in an administrative structure increases the complexity of relationships. But does this mean that increase in the complexity of an administrative structure is merely a consequence of its size in numbers? The answer is clearly "no." Comparison of two examples will perhaps illustrate the point, once an essential distinction has been made between the *number of persons* in an administrative structure and the *number of kinds of specialized knowledge* possessed by one or another person — knowledge which must be organized in such a way as to be available for use at any given point in the organization.

Suppose that there are two organizations employing the same number of people and served by administrations of the same size. One of the organizations is involved in digging a ditch with hand tools. Given this situation, *technical* problems in coordination — supplying shovels to the diggers, assigning areas of the ditch to one or another sub-administrator, organizing and distributing information on ways of reducing backache and blisters, scheduling the movement of trucks to remove the dirt, and so on — do not suggest themselves to us as highly complex problems, if we omit the human factors involved.

Of course, if we consider the improvements that might possibly be made in the ditchdigging process through improved communication, morale, motivation, and group productivity, we might draw on virtually unlimited resources of specialized knowledge in psychology, semantics, physiology, psychiatry, nutrition, social relations, political science, group behavior, and cybernetics — and make the whole operation an exceedingly advanced experiment in the creative organization of multiple human efforts. This situation could present major complexities in procuring, developing, communicating, coordinating, and using these resources of specialized knowledge about human factors, within the administrative group and between that group and all other members of the organization. But apart from this possibility, the problem of coordinating a manual ditchdigging operation appears to involve relatively simple and limited kinds of specialized technical knowledge that must be brought together and applied; the complexity of administration due to problems of "technical" coordination would be low.

Let us consider that the other organization of the same size is engaged in the production and distribution of a hypothetical hormone derivative involving the production of genetically controlled and disease-free strains of animals; properly timed surgical removal of the secreting glands under antiseptic conditions; precise controls over temperature and moisture at various stages of extraction, centrifuging, reduction, chemical purification, crystallizing, and various other refining processes; testing and control; temperature control in transit; and the destruction of distributed supplies after permissible use-dates have expired. By thus taking an extreme opposite from the previous example, as regards the magnitude and the diversities of specialized knowledge resources involved for *technical coordination* of the process, it becomes hardly necessary to labor the point.

Clearly the administration of this second organization is confronted with a vastly larger and more complex task of organizing and distributing the required information, supplies, services, and conditions (testing controls, for example) to the correct location in the organization at the right time. To assure the requisite conditions at every point at all times, the organization must be carefully designed as a kind of complete techni-social complex which, so to speak, *encloses* the entire product from the genetic origin to the refrigerated packaged product. We might even view the finished product as the resultant of *an interaction between certain basic biological and physical materials,* on the one hand, and *an enveloping organization of human beings and their scientific knowledge and skill,* on the other. *This organization constitutes a completely planned and interconnected series of controlling environments.*

The volume of technical communication required to devise, develop, maintain, and improve this total technical and social environment would be of an entirely different order from that in the ditchdigging operation. This volume would reflect the much greater diversity of specialized technical knowledge which the organization must use to perform its defined purpose.

Yet it must be remembered that in this second organization, as in the first, if there were to be attempts to draw heavily on specialized knowledge dealing with *human behavioral factors,* there would be virtually no limit to the complexity of the problem of administrative coordination. Thus complexity in administration is affected by the numbers of persons involved, by the diversity of specialized "technical" knowledge required to perform the ultimate function of the organization, and by the extent to which the administration seeks to draw upon and use knowledge pertaining to human behavior.

The distinction between technical knowledge needed and human behavioral knowledge needed is a difficult one to maintain. For it can be imagined that the first organization could be managed so that at least some ditches would be dug, after a fashion and no matter how slowly, under conditions of absymally poor morale and human relations; but it can scarcely be imagined that the second organization could produce many usable products under similar human conditions. Thus it is probably safe to say that, in the long run, advancing technical complexity in the function of an organization requires a larger use of resources of knowledge regarding human behavior; relatively greater efforts must be made to use such knowledge in order to assure human organization of a quality consistent with the maintenance of this more complex technical organization.

From this theoretical vantage point, we might now review the emergence of the case method in business administration training in the 1920's, against the background of the high development of specialization in business at that time. The strong and increasing emphasis on conscious specialization in business knowledge and function since the 1880's had resulted in a great growth of knowledge organized in terms of *systems, standards, and proved practices.* So heavy had this trend become that young administrators in training were emerging stuffed with other men's abstractions and generalizations about still other men's experience. Yet in accounting, production, control, and other fields, seemingly proved experience did not always fit even the *technical* conditions or requirements of given situations.

The case method initially emerged *within* the established specializations as a corrective to the oversimplified concepts and assumptions of scientific management. But the cases that were developed were still predominantly cases dealing with specialized functions of business, in terms of case specifications defined by professors in the various subjects, to be used in courses dealing with the specialized knowledge areas involved. Specialized cases were developed in accounting, in production management, in finance, in marketing, and so forth.

These cases tended to be guinea-pig problems. That is, they tested the ability to differentiate between the specific problem at hand and other specific problems from earlier experience (or generalizations about them), and to work through to solutions fitting the particular case. Obtaining cases meant, of course, obtaining data on concrete situations involving the special problem or function in a business organization. Human factors were present and were usually included in the case reports to some extent.

But the prevailing *substantive orientation* of the whole structure of specialization, as carried over from business into the business schools, tended on the whole to subordinate the human factors and highlight the technical aspects of situations in the collection and use of these cases. The human elements of the cases appeared more as formal actors in the formal structure of the situation than as flesh and blood human beings.

It is significant, however, that the shift toward incorporating the clinical concept into the field of business administration was originally incubated and developed by and within the established framework of specializations of knowledge, teaching, and training, although it cannot be doubted that this movement strongly reflected an increased concern for the human factors also. Scientific management, it seemed, could not achieve its end by modeling itself on the patterns of the physical sciences alone; whether consciously or not, it was forced to adopt also the clinical model of medicine and the socially dynamic concepts of law.

The Impact of Human Factors on Older Structures of Specialization

While this development was taking place within the framework of the established business subjects, a major new development was just beginning to make itself felt in the thinking and practice of advanced management, both in industry and in schools of business. During and after World War I, particularly, the immediate, pressing, and obvious need for increased attention to the specific functions related to problems of personnel gave rapid rise to personnel departments and to new specializations in personnel administration and labor relations. The problem of relating these new "human behavior" specializations of administrative function to the existing structures of administrative specialization and organization has never been very satisfactorily solved, either theoretically or pragmatically.

Concurrently with the development of these new administrative specializations, there was being formulated a much larger and more novel concept of the human aspects of industrial organizations which presumably underlay the symptoms of need for personnel administration. This concept revolved around the idea and study of business and industrial organizations as bio-social systems; it inaugurated what was to become, in the 1940's and 1950's, a major new direction of thought. Early contributors include a number of names still too little known to the field of educational administration: for example, Mary Parker Follett, industrial engineer, whose thought, experience, and experiments in industry are reflected in her *Dynamic Administration;* Lawrence J. Henderson, eminent in chemistry, physiology, industrial sociology, and the philosophy of human sciences; Elton Mayo, pioneer in clinical research in industry through the famed "Hawthorne Experiment" at the Western Electric Company, and author of *The Social Problems of an Industrial Civilization;* and C. I. Barnard, former president of the New Jersey Bell Telephone Company, and author of *The Functions of the Executive.*

Thus theory, research, and practice in business management advanced, through the work of these and other contributors, to the stage of beginning to view those sciences which deal with human behavior as a primary and essential resource for the further development of business institutions. But to characterize the trend only in these terms would be to understate its nature and significance. For the major contributors to the new stream of development were beginning to think about administration as a skill in terms of knowledge from such fields as anthropology, sociology, psychology, psychiatry, physiology, and, above all, the study of human behavior in specific, "natural" social settings. This direction of thinking led subsequently to the development of cases and case methods whose primary focus was on administrative practices, including human relations skills.

The new trend produced some unexpected outcomes. The findings of the Hawthorne Experiment, for example, upset both the expectancies of the researchers and some basic beliefs of traditional scientific management. They dramatically underscored some of the unconscious biases which give rise to our notions as to "common sense" views of social cause and effect.

Unless an administrator really understands and behaves in terms of the implications of the past quarter-century's accumulated knowledge and thinking about the nature and dynamics of social organization and human behavior, his awareness of the human aspects of administration is archaic, no matter how up-to-date his technical knowledge may be.

A growing sense of the importance of administrative awareness of the human and social aspects of organization led to research and training with regard to human relations in administration, viewed as *interwoven with and underlying any apparent technical problem.*

A statement made in 1938 by Colonel L. Urwick, a leading British management engineer, seems even more pertinent today:

> . . . the emergence of new knowledge enforcing an increasing measure of specialization and hence of discrimination of function, has greatly out-

stripped our social inventiveness in devising organization patterns to take care of the new situation.[2]

One characteristic which an observer of business and industrial organization from the 1920's to the present might note would be a tendency for some of the power earlier concentrated at "the top" of the administrative and organizational structure to be redistributed at lower levels. This tended to occur in increasing numbers of organizations irrespective of the wishes of those in the highest seats of power in one or another organization. The redistribution of power to make decisions assumed a variety of forms, in which either of two types appeared to be predominant: (1) administrators at lower points in the hierarchy assumed decision-making functions previously concentrated at a higher point; (2) *groups* of administrators and other persons at lower points in the organization participated in decision-making.

In industry, these trends were revealed in multiple-management, foremen round-tables, greater autonomy at the branch plant level, "bottom-up" management, and many other combinations. In some cases, redistributions of power were achieved against vigorous opposition from seats of corporate administrative power. Social forces manifested through trade unions, government, and public opinion seemed to operate to restrain highly organized concentrations of administrative power from exercising earlier dominances. Under these conditions, even managements which opposed the new-fangled "human factors" increasingly took them into account as their power to maintain former organizational structure was reduced.

The patterns of organization of industry and of industrial managements and administrations no longer corresponded, as in the nineteenth century, to models in the minds of entrepreneurs, scientists, and engineers. Whether managements were willing or no, these models were being remolded into unpredictable future forms; but even willing managements found increasing difficulty in seeing what these might be. From a more general vantage point of the early 1950's, social forces appeared to be penetrating and modifying not only industrial organizations but virtually all other kinds of human institutions as well — in not too clearly predictable ways. Parenthetically, a similar trend might be noted in school administration, as evidenced by such developments as the autonomous school, staff-teacher-parent curriculum planning, and decentralization in city school systems.

As has been previously noted, the introduction into business and industrial organization of *a specialized major function* dealing with personnel administration raised new problems of administrative structure which have never been satisfactorily solved. Personnel administration is used here merely as a symbol of a variety of "human factor" functions which have arisen in business organization, largely since the 1920's, as major functions involving

[2] L. Urwick, "Scientific Principles and Organization," address delivered before the Institute of Management, September 15, 1938, New York, N.Y.

specialized knowledge and skills. One or more functions representing personnel relations, labor relations, public relations, and executive and foreman training are increasingly organized as among the perhaps six or seven *major* functional specializations of management. But how they are organized in relation to the much older standardizations (production, finance, sales) and to the over-all pattern and structure of relationship among these traditional major functions appears to be highly variable.

The variety of ways in which these "human factor" functions of management are conceived, established, and placed as functions in managerial structures, and related to the more traditional specializations of the structure, seems to be increasing rather than decreasing. The movement is away from rather than toward standardization of the "human factor" functions and their place in the administrative scheme. They appear to be modifying the concept and design of administrative structure *in the direction of greater amorphousness and indeterminacy.* Furthermore, the activities and functions which may be performed by the unit or units of administration constituting "human factor" specializations of function are increasingly broad, pervasive, and powerful. In many companies, "public and industrial relations" wears the halo.

The "human factor" function appears to be *reversing* the characteristics of the development of administration as these took shape under the impact of the older scientific specializations.

Administrative Deprivation in Public School Systems

In now turning to present-day educational administration, we find two conditions which may strike us as somewhat startling. The first of these conditions is the great discrepancy in the size of administrative units in relation to those for organizations of comparable numbers of human beings in industry. For example, let us take a company manufacturing brushes. Let us say that there are about 260 persons working together in the factory, excluding some branch sales office personnel. Approximately twenty-five members of the organization have responsibilities which include some authority over the actions of other persons, and perhaps ten more are primarily aides and assistants to these persons. Persons exercising "some authority" include subforemen and even lead-workers with some responsibility for supervising or coordinating the work of eight or ten fellow production workers.

Now let us look at a school involving the same number of persons. In most current educational thinking and practice, a 250-pupil elementary school would have one "administrator" (the principal), plus, of course, a portion of the time and attention of others on central administrative levels, plus perhaps a secretary. Let us say that there are, at the outside, three or four administrator "equivalents." Is education so simple — like ditchdigging — that it requires but little *administration?*

On the contrary, it seems to be quite complex even when ignorance attempts to oversimplify it. Is it as complex as business — in terms of both technical and social factors? Unless we assume that the three or four administrator equivalents for a 250-pupil elementary school can provide administration equal to the twenty-five or thirty in the industrial organization, we can only conclude that educational organization is less complex. Any other conclusion is unrealistic: To conclude that the three or four administrator units can comprehend and coordinate as many and complex specializations of knowledge and function as the twenty-five or thirty in the industrial organization implies differences in ability levels which would rarely, if ever, exist. If we assume that a 250-pupil school involves as complex a task in organization and administration as a brush manufacturing company, we must conclude that the former is grossly underadministered and must long since have broken down. There is obviously a major discrepancy somewhere.

A 250-pupil school would have about ten teachers. Should they be considered as part of the "administration" of schools? Let us attempt to define "administrator" in fairly elementary and irreducible terms. We might come out with some such definition as "one having some formal authority with respect to the behavior of other members of the organization." From this viewpoint, we might class teachers as administrators; so also the custodian. Without prejudice to our freedom to abandon this definition, let us see where it takes us.

By including the teachers and the custodian as part of the structure of administration, we have increased the total to about fifteen persons. The discrepancy between administrative units of our brush company and our elementary school is thus reduced from roughly 9:1 to roughly 2:1, assuming equal complexity in the two organizations and operations. But this discrepancy is still too great to stand. Some factor must still be missing from our thinking. What ways are there of assessing the possible complexity of the administration of school systems? What kind of range and structure of specializations of knowledge and function is involved in school administration?

Here we meet our second somewhat startling condition. We find virtually no agreed-upon ways of defining, organizing, and classifying the major administrative functions involved in operating a public school system, although certain titles — principal, supervisor, coordinator — are used very widely. This is in sharp contrast to industry during the fifty-year period up to about the mid-twenties. Furthermore, many of those functions that are most sharply defined and agreed upon in school administration are the ones that are carried over from business and industrial organization and administration — such as business management, transportation, some aspects of finance management, and plant maintenance. These are presumably subsidiary to the major function of school systems. It may be said that a large school system operates a really big business as a minor service auxiliary of its major function.

Although there are various goals in education which give rise to a variety of specialized administrative needs, educational administration is just beginning to grapple with the problem of how to describe and organize *functionally* the knowledge and services needed to meet its goals. For example: How should guidance be organized administratively? Is guidance something different from teaching? What teaches children? The teacher? The classroom? The peer environment? How should specialized knowledge and skills in guidance flow through the organization in order to be available at the right place and time to the particular individuals — pupil, teacher, parent, principal — who may need these resources? Many other questions lead into similar complexities.

The whole domain of knowledge which deals with man is thrown open as basic material out of which artifacts for education and its administration must be selected, developed, and organized. We are unable to escape the obvious: The function of education is to influence, presumably on the side of improvement, a natural process — the growth and development of human beings during very crucial years. The *technical* job of educational administration, apart from the administration of those functions in which knowledge is available from the field of business administration, is the designing, development, and maintenance of a *series of technical-social environments* (physical, social, psychological) *conducive to the development of children beyond what this would be if such an environment were not provided.* What more complex task has so far been defined by man than the construction and operation of such environments?

The difficulty in formulating a structure of specialized functions for educational administration is a reflection of this complexity. This does not mean that there are no designs that have utility, no designs that can be applied. But one need merely compare the continuing major functions of industrial administration with the major functions appearing in such a work as Sears [3] to realize the difficulties confronting educational administration. For we must assume major growth in both the volume of special knowledge and the numbers of persons involved in developing and maintaining educational environments, if our view of the function of educational administration is to be even approximately correct.

Let us assume that school staffs are now, say, one-half as large as they will need to be to maintain themselves as going organizations. How many school administrators would know now how to double their staffs and to use the additional personnel effectively? In how many school systems is the "administration," including all teachers and custodians, functioning at anything like the level which administrative knowledge and skill have today demonstrated as possible?

The tasks of educational administration are being increasingly clarified, as noted in Section Two. The items in such sets of definitions clearly exceed the knowledge-competence of any one administrator, or even of several taken together. These sets of tasks are tasks for a well-defined *unit of ad-*

[3] Jesse B. Sears, *The Nature of the Administrative Process* (New York: McGraw-Hill Book Co., 1950).

ministration, sufficient in number, quality, and specializations of knowledge and skill, to fulfill the "superintendency" function.

When administrative resources are basically inadequate for the achievement of an organization's goals, the organization must either break down or adapt itself to a more circumscribed set of goals as determined by administrative resources. Public school education has been administratively starved. Neither education nor society can escape the consequences.

It may be noted in passing that the limitation of the size of administrative units above the teaching level in school systems has been historically associated with the continuation of countless small school districts. According to our thesis, even these small school districts have been and are undermanned administratively, in comparison with business and industrial organizations of the same size. But these small districts, serving primarily village, small-town, and rural areas, have reflected, in their administrative structures, the attitudes of the communities they serve. These are predominantly the attitudes of the small independent proprietor of a business or farming enterprise. Such enterprises are also types of socio-economic organizations in which the complexity of organizational need has historically increased much more rapidly than the *size* of the organization or of its administrative or managerial resource units. The farmers, storekeepers, and other small proprietors in areas served by small school districts have had to cope with increased complexities in the operation of their enterprises: in agriculture, the introduction of scientific agronomy, plant genetics, and controlled breeding; in storekeeping, larger and more varied inventories and more elaborate systems of record-keeping; and in all small business, the problems stemming from the trend to greater specialization. And they have had to do this without the increased administrative resources that are available to their large-scale competitors. Under these conditions, the proprietor or manager has had to be a jack-of-all-trades and work interminable hours. It is not surprising that the superintendent or administrator of schools in the same areas would be expected to perform in a similar fashion.

This view of the requirements of school administration has carried over into those school systems which have grown large because of the industrialization of the community or the influx of population from metropolitan centers. Under such conditions, increase in administrative assistance has frequently lagged behind growth in the size of the school system, even against the inadequate yardstick of administration-organization ratios in systems which have appeared to overcome this lag.

Numerous small school districts have of course continued well past the stage at which consolidations have been *technically feasible* (automotive transportation and road improvement) and *educationally desirable* (increase in size sufficient to warrant introduction of specialists and to establish local school and classroom units representing improved physical and social environments for learning). The growth of consolidated districts and the reduction in numbers of archaically small school districts have lagged behind the massive shift of American society, during the last three-quarters of a century, from a predominantly village and rural society to an urban and metropolitan one.

There are now many signs that this gap is closing rapidly. District reorganizations and consolidations have been carried forward to a major extent in a number of states. The movement in this direction is certain to become powerful enough to reduce sharply the present proportion of school districts which represent obsolete hold-overs from a far different technological and social era. It is not pertinent to discuss here the many questions involved in district consolidations, the disadvantages of overly large consolidations, and the various concepts of *optimum size.* The clear trend is toward a substantial increase in the proportion of school systems standing between the extremes of size of the really big city system on the one hand and the isolated small school district on the other.

Turning once more to our basic premise, however, that, with some possible exceptions, school systems in general and irrespective of size are basically suffering from a deprivation of administrative resources, the *absolute* growth of the average size of administrative units resulting from consolidations (and population growth) does not and will not necessarily represent any reduction of this discrepancy. It will merely mean that a relatively larger proportion of school systems will reach that size at which their understaffing will become more easily comparable with administrations in *industry, large-scale merchandising, hospitals,* and some other kinds of organizations. This, however, may make it somewhat easier to confront society realistically with the question of whether education can be expected to fulfill its presumed functions when it is granted administrative resources *as if,* let us say, educational organization were only one-half as complex, in terms of *needed specializations of knowledge and function,* as the brush manufacturing company in our example.

Thus far, in commenting on the inadequacy of administrative resources, even from a quantitative point of view, to the size and functions of the organizations they serve, we have made no reference to administrative resources which are auxiliary to local school systems — such as state departments of education, professional and research agencies, institutions of higher learning, and foundations. However, even a cursory examination will leave little doubt that these auxiliary resources are also seriously underdeveloped relative to the various other fields of human activity already mentioned.

In agriculture, although the complexity of the managerial function historically increased much more rapidly than the size of the operating units and the managerial resources — indeed, partly because of this — major technical assistance has long since been organized as a governmental function, auxiliary to the individual farm enterprise. A huge interlocking structure of "administrative assistance" has been available to farmers through the U.S. Department of Agriculture, the state departments of agriculture, the federal land grant colleges, the state agricultural universities, the agricultural extension departments, and federal funds for the support of agricultural research, education, and training.

Similarly business and industrial organizations, both large and small, have had the major assistance of state and federal departments of commerce and industry, particularly with respect to commodity and labor market conditions, and more recently, numerous other kinds of technical knowledge and assistance.

But as far as education is concerned, the structure of assistance and auxiliary aids at state and federal levels, or via other resource units available to and serving local school systems, is relatively small and undeveloped in comparison.

The administrative deprivation in public school education underscores the concern which has been lately voiced by such men as Walter Lippmann. They have noted a relative decline in the proportion of national resources devoted to public education — a decline the more remarkable in that it has taken place over a half-century of national development toward a society demonstrably able to afford more luxuries. At the same time, it is clear that the tasks confronting education during the coming years are massive and critical ones. Administration, insofar as it embraces the notion of *creative leadership* (which would seem to be an essential ingredient), represents the *primary existing focal point of whatever means exist of remedying the situation.*

If administration is undernourished, the problem of overcoming the consequent starvation of the educational enterprise cannot but be a task for *administration* primarily. If administrators are incapable of leading a breakthrough of the circle of deprivation to enlarge the human resources of public school systems, it is extremely doubtful whether anyone else can do so. For presumably no one else is in any better position to *define the administrative needs.* Administrators must develop *the imaginative picture:* How many administrative personnel — of what competencies of specialized knowledge, and how organized as a highly interlocking unit of resources — are needed, with respect to a school-system organization of given size, in order to assure an improvement in the development of children passing through the resulting technical and social environments? Clear definition of both need and plan is a major condition for gaining the adherence of stronger social forces in the community and the society, in support of the implied goals and tasks.

However, there is a real question whether present educational administrative knowledge and thought are capable of developing the requisite imaginative pictures of the human components and relational design of administrations, let us say, of *twice the present size* in relation to enrollments in a given school system — which we are holding as a tentative yardstick. This problem is underscored by the amorphousness of thought with respect to definitions of the functions-and-structure of knowledge and activities involved in public school administration, together with the evidence in numerous school systems of inability to use effectively the specialized knowledge and personal resources which they possess. Somehow, it would appear, there may have to be something resembling a *leap* in knowledge-and-practice in educational administration, in such a way that the goals of development defined for this field may more nearly correspond to the implications of the idea of public education itself. Without increased understanding, is there any assurance that increased finances for schools will bring about educational achievement which is either corresponding or adequate to the survival problems of the society?

Fundamentally, the problem is one of administrative skill. Many systems include personnel who are either not competent or not used competently. Quality of school boards and citizen political behavior adversely affecting quality and quantity of school staffs must be viewed simply as conditions with which educational administration must deal. Coping with such situations is central to the function of educational administration. Educational administrators are confronted with the necessity of inventing and developing new and clearer conceptualizations of educational organization.

This task includes the design of administrative components and structures appropriate to educational organizations of varying sizes (pupil numbers), types (urban, suburban, regional-rural), patterns (grade organization, local school units, and curriculum concepts) and ways of characterizing school systems. Assuming a goal of administrative units much larger in size, with much greater diversification of knowledge and function and more intricate integration than now prevail in most school organizations, this implies the development both of general models and of projected administrative structures for specific school systems. To a considerable extent this is a task which calls for search into knowledge, critical analysis of experience, and rigorous thought. These are processes peculiarly associated with the idea of a *professional discipline*.

This task might be in many ways similar to the kind of tasks which the profession of medicine faced under the conditions created by larger populations and more massive wars, on the one hand, and the acceptance of germ theory and many new concepts in disease control and therapy, on the other. Such conditions called for the creation of medical-social units of organization, both large and rigorously controlled, first in hospitals, and subsequently in public health services. Conditions of need and opportunity brought about a situation demanding a virtual leap in the knowledge and thinking of the professional discipline of medicine. This thinking had to be directed toward a transition from the simpler concept of doctor and patient to the creation of administrative models for medical-social units of organization. The *realization* of the professionally defined models for hospital administration, however, confronted the medical profession with one problem quite different from that which today confronts educational administration. For although social forces outside the medical profession sometimes impeded and sometimes speeded progress toward more adequate medical social units, the medical profession was nowhere nearly as closely restricted by the conditions of nonprofessional society as is public educational administration.

The Professional and Public Roles of Educational Administration

In the educational field, the tasks of action which will be required to realize the administrative means that may be recognized as necessary, in the thinking of the professional discipline, involve problems in social relationship of a different order. The shaping of needs and models in educational administration through study and thought within the embryonic discipline cannot be isolated from the conditions of society to anything like the degree that has been true of the "private" field of industrial management or the "quasi-public" field of medical-hospital administration, during many of the most formative and growing years of these administrative systems. The "public" in public education dramatically signalizes the fact that administration in this field was originally incubated as a product of *nonprofessional social systems.* Only after the formal and constitutional creation of the school system did the special personnel of "teachers" and "administrators" emerge from the system and began to develop standards as new professions. Administrative development in public education has been and will continue to be essentially conditioned by the lay public controls within which a professional discipline must nonetheless mature in order to reach the underlying social goals for which public education was established.

The public school administrator is essentially a special kind of public administrator. Indeed, in a historical sense, the public school administrator emerged from the ranks of public servants (teachers), long before there emerged from the civil service the still-youthful profession of *public administration.* It might even be said, therefore, that the public school administrator was one of the first among the special types of administrators that have arisen to give professional status to certain public functions of our society.

The school administrator, like many other kinds of public administrators, must endeavor, at one and the same time, to think and act as a member of an admittedly young and relatively undeveloped professional discipline and as a pragmatist in the arena of political forces. He is in actual or potential competition with nonprofessional leaders and actors in the field of politics, with respect to the policy and the control of the public school system. To become too "professional," in one sense of the word, is to risk isolating not only himself, but perhaps the school organization also, from those currents of political behavior that ultimately sustain and determine the directions of educational policy. Under conditions of too great isolation, the pendulum may swing and the school system may in time be subjected to temporary capture by political forces reflecting public ignorance, anxiety, resentment at "loss of control to professionals," or even unvarnished political greed. These can be consequences of any concept of the professional role which implies professional control of public education.

To be, on the other hand, not "professional" enough is to sacrifice possibilities of educational progress to ephemeral shifts of public opinion or to the self-serving methods of persons or groups who seek to control the school institution in order to control the social mind. The fact that a school board may be the legitimate governing body for a school system does not permit the school administrator to sit with folded hands if, as in some instances, school board members connive in selling jobs in the system or otherwise playing purely predatory or parasitical roles. To overlook such practices is to deny professional behavior. The school administrator who becomes so politically "realistic" as to have no "professional" standards, even though not fully realizable by him, in any given real situation at any given time, has in effect become nothing more than a subservient politician.

A degree of tension between the dictates of "professional outlook" and "realistic political outlook" is inherent in the concept of a *professional discipline of public (school) administration.* Yet too great a degree of differentiation and tension between these concepts — which can only be synthesized or resolved relatively, in successive situational acts and decisions — leaves the administrator vulnerable to unproductive behavior. It is along a thin and ever-shifting line that the public school administrator must move toward the goals for public education and its administration, as these are advanced and defined according to the standards of a professional discipline, in the face of conditions determined by the social and political forces of American society in general and of his community in particular.

It is in the balancing — or, better, the *serial synthesizing,* through successive acts, decisions, and handling of situations — of the "professional" and the "public" or political roles (which are never synthesized *wholly* satisfactorily at any given time) that the greatest problems confront the administrator as a person and as a special kind of actor on the social scene. For this dilemma, always holding the potential of too great an accentuation of either the "professional" or the "public" role, may result in a personally rending or paralyzing conflict between the two. It is this condition which ultimately imposes upon the educational administrator the necessity of resolving the dilemma through his own growth *as a person.* In order to do this, he must become capable of recognizing the dilemma of roles and of achieving his self-fulfillment and life satisfaction in the unceasing but never completed work of *reducing* the dilemma. The reduction of the dilemma involves the transformation of social forces in both the school system and its community context in such a way as to yield a higher integration between the two.

It is for these reasons also that educational administration as a field can never be viewed as fully subject to the kind of organization of knowledge characteristic of nonhuman areas of experience. This would be true even under conditions of a hypothetical advance of "scientific" knowledge about human society to a condition of near perfection. The supreme achievement of administrative "knowledge" is each administrator's own self-knowledge which *must* be as variable as the character and experience of each person who aspires to the professional discipline of administration.

It is not the "objective reality" of administrative situations alone which determines what may constitute "appropriate administrative behavior." Appropriate administrative behavior must at its most mature level, and beyond any guide or certainties that "objective knowledge" might suggest, be governed by each administrator's awareness of his own characteristics as a person and of the values which he desires and chooses as his personal governing values. The "same" situation may be *most appropriately* acted upon by one administrator in one way and by another in another — yet both courses of action may be consistent with the best dictates of "objective knowledge" and of equally mature awareness on the part of both administrators.

As stated in the approximate language of Floyd Reeves: "The purpose of a training program in administration is to assist the potential or practicing administrator in developing and exercising a philosophy and practice of administration that is both *internally consistent in terms of knowledge* and also *meaningful for him.*"

SECTION FIVE

STUDY OF CONCEPTS — A REPORT OF EXPERIENCE

Study of Concepts—A Report of Experience

THE SPECIAL and traditional function of a university has been to develop and transmit concepts in the forms of knowledge; in undertaking to teach administration it becomes the responsibility of the university to undertake the new task of developing and transmitting concepts in the form of behavioral skill.

The problem of whether and how to relate the study of concepts to the study of cases has given rise to varying schools of thought. To communicate the course which we have chosen, the reasons for it, and some of the results, it is of course necessary that we make at least some tentative definition of what we mean by concepts. We will offer a definition that is suggestive rather than precise, partly because the problem of clarifying what is meant by concepts is inherent in the approach we have used; individual students and the class of students together, in thinking about the specific concepts which particularly interest them and in thinking about the general notion of concepts, gradually evolve their own understanding of what they mean by concepts.

In a sense, concepts might be considered to refer to the key terms in any system of thought about a field of knowledge or experience — that is, the terms which constitute basic building blocks in organizing and relating that knowledge or experience. While this definition may suffice for the moment, it might be pointed out that the term "concepts" is used differently in different fields of knowledge; its use in philosophy, in psychology, and in other fields of study varies not only with the fields but also somewhat according to whether it is used as an operational term in a specific research project or as an attempted means of relating notions in different fields.

We have already noted some of the disadvantages of emphasizing a study of concepts too greatly dissociated from whatever basis of concrete experience there may be in the minds of those engaged in study. There is the danger of confusing an acquaintance with terms and a verbal facility in using them with the development of a kind of awareness and a way of thinking which fits the needs of administrative behavior. There are the difficulties associated with motivation for study on the basis of academic expectancies which may or may not yield significant learning for the student in terms of retention of the meanings and their transfer to use in pertinent situations.

Yet to the extent that a student acquires more and more concrete experience, he must find a way of organizing and relating this experience if it is to remain among his resources. To the extent that he does proceed to develop some mental organization of this experience he will develop patterns of thought revolving around various ideas. Under whatever name, these are — for him — significant concepts. The study of concepts is ultimately designed to assist him in formulating an effective organization of his own mental content of experience. The adequacy and appropriateness of such concepts is central to the problem of the validity and utility of the resulting organization.

Two Aspects of Conceptual Development

In the growth of more mature administrative behavior, there are two major elements which, in our judgment, depend upon some development of concepts *in terms of the needs of each student.* We have already stated some reasons for our stress upon the qualifying phrase in the preceding sentence. For we feel that a study of concepts not so designed may do more harm than good.

These functions are, respectively, (1) to enrich the conceptual resources of each student, in terms of variety, and (2) to assist him in the reordering of his conceptual system where he may possess an adequate variety of concepts but an inadequate organization of their functional use to himself in his administrative role. There is no priority of importance as between the two functions, in our view.

These functions correspond, as we see it, to two kinds of problems faced both by educational administrators in their work and by students in training within a program that revolves around activities which in themselves constitute test and practice of administrative behavior. As we have pointed out, persons of administrative orientation tend to be more interested in the situational approach to learning than in study at a highly abstract level. And in grappling with abstract formulations, they tend to refer these frequently to situations of the kind in which they know they must learn to act. Through case methods exposing them to a broad range of situations, through working as members of a team fulfilling a contractual obligation to a school system, through apprenticeship roles as assistants to practicing administrators, and through other methods of training which involve practice and skill, more experience tends to emerge than can be comprehended within the student's frame of thought. Indeed, one test of whether anything new or significant is being learned through such methods might be: Does the experience force the student to rethink, expand, and reorder his conceptual system?

The growth of experience, when accompanied by a growing recognition of problems of retaining, relating, and integrating this experience, results in a need and readiness for conceptual study. But the directions of need are different for every individual.

This condition might seem to call for purely individual programs of study based upon consultation between teacher and student. But in the program of which we are speaking, the students constitute some kind of group. The program involves them in a series of "common" experiences over a period of at least one year — case situation interactions, a seminar on administrative problems, a unit in social science studies, and, quite centrally, organization of their relationships around the *focal responsibility* of a contract study on behalf of a school system.

If these students reflect needs which provide a basis of motivation for study in directions and at levels which they have not earlier undertaken, it is not unsound to view many of these needs as resulting in part from *their common concerns.* The role of the teacher *vis à vis* each individual student is therefore viewed in a different way than if we were dealing with a course or seminar where members have no relationships as a specific group outside the meetings of that particular class.

Since this is a report of experience which lays no claim to the appropriateness of the specific methods to other situations and other groups of students, it is pertinent to point out something of the character of the student body involved. All the groups with whom we have worked have embraced students ranging in age from the early twenties to the late forties or even the early fifties, but with the majority between the ages of thirty and forty. In terms of experience in education (other than as students) they have ranged all the way from the very few with perhaps only two or three years of teaching experience to the several who were well advanced in their careers as educational administrators — superintendents of schools, administrators in central staffs, principals. The majority might perhaps be described as having recently moved into the administrative structure after perhaps seven to ten years of service as teachers. All have completed graduate studies to at least the extent of the master's degree and are candidates for the doctorate.

Given a student body of different range of age and experience, there might need to be some variation in the approach to concepts study, as in other aspects of the training program. Yet it does not seem to us that a less mature group should necessarily be viewed as incapable of playing a significant part in the discovery of their own motivations and needs for such study. A younger and less experienced group may, it is true, need more prior situational experience. It is our observation that, among the younger and less experienced, some do need to test the functional utility of concepts which they have acquired in formal education. Their abilities to verbalize these concepts have sometimes outrun their abilities to order and integrate them, in terms which are functional in either administrative situations or administrative behavior. Others among the younger and less experienced students may be relatively inarticulate when it comes to discussions; yet growth of a "feel" of what is involved in administrative situations and behavior may bring to light latent conceptual resources. Younger and less experienced students of either tendency may, it seems to us, need intensive discipline in acting in relation to situations before undertaking to widen and enrich their resources. For they cannot yet manage, in terms of administrative behavior, the conceptual abstractions which they have already ingested — a condition which leads to inarticulateness in some and over-verbalization in others.

Conversely, the concepts which the older and more experienced students consider significant for administration, and the frameworks in which these concepts are organized, may tend to be somewhat too narrow and too firmly set. Yet if, from the perspective of the teacher, there is a need to enrich conceptual resources and remold concepts into a more flexible and therefore potentially growing system, we consider it wise to avoid the creation of pressures in that direction. For it has already been pointed out in the "Overview" that case methods have inherent in them factors which can be devastating to the attitude of expertise. A poverty of conceptual resources inevitably erects barriers to perceptions of situations presented in the cases; these, in turn, hinder the student in imagining administrative action which might be appropriate, and in recognizing the possible consequences of a decision which represents "how he would act" in the given situation. Experienced administrators no less than novices tend to reach greater readiness for conceptual growth and change through intensive case and clinical approaches to training.

Developing Mental Frameworks to Comprehend Experience

Thus *intensification* of situational experience within the framework of a training program seems to yield, in almost all students, some recognized need for both enlarging and revising their mental patterns in order to comprehend and relate this *widening* of their experience. Since this seems to us also to make sense in terms of learning theory in general, particularly for students who are administratively oriented to begin with, we can only hope that our impressions about what may be at work in this kind of situation do not represent merely the operation of a self-fulfilling prophecy!

The first of the two major functions which in our view require the study of concepts has already been touched upon in mentioning the need for an *enlargement* of conceptual resources. We contrast this with the reordering or rearrangement of those concepts which a person may already possess. These distinctions are, to our minds, fairly significant. For when it comes to responding to the cues given by any particular student as to the directions of study in which he feels he wants to strike out, it seems to us that the teacher is cast, whether he would prefer it or no, in the role of having to decide which of the two needs the student may be trying to voice. Is his head full of miscellaneous fragments of the multiple concepts that lie behind any particular piece of information in the veritable chaos of today's specialized knowledge? Does his major immediate problem therefore consist in organizing a framework capable of comprehending the data? Or do his cues mean that he does not have a rich enough variety of conceptual resources to permit the construction of an adequate framework for the "new" experience which now no longer fits his earlier pattern and terms of thinking?

Unless a teacher is to abdicate his role, he must make some response to cues given by students when they are requested to consider and choose some conceptual study which will be meaningful to them. One student will come up with a firm choice. Another will vacillate. Another will have a very general area in mind which he wishes to explore a bit before defining his interest more closely. Another may have an eclectic number of concepts, all of which he wishes to pursue. Still another may seem to be confused. Each of these responses serves as a cue to which the teacher must respond.

Fortunately, in a role so precarious as that of having to respond to each student with respect to the direction in which he should go, we do not need to depend upon the verbal cues of that moment alone. Our response is conditioned by whatever perception we may have developed, as the result of various close contacts, regarding that student and his behavior; many of these perceptions come out of the joint staff-student contractual field study phase of the program. Nor can we forget that the student's exploration must essentially become a self-motivated and predominantly self-directed one — a means by which he may discover his own needs and search for resources adequate to deal with them. For we feel that if a student can arrive at even a single new realization that his exploration has become highly vital to him, the chances are improved that he may continue to recognize the potential significance of conceptual study for himself, as an administrator. Some vivid realization which stimulates continued attention in this direction would seem to be necessary before he leaves the university to become involved once more in the essential action-orientation of this role.

It might be objected that the above characteristics should be assumed to be prerequisites to the admission of an individual to a graduate university program. According to many, it is not the function of a university to teach students the value of continuing to learn; they are not supposed to be there unless they already know this. It is our observation, however, that the human products of the predominantly "classical academic" and "ordered scientific" climates of colleges and universities and also of public and private schools in this country, do not exhibit very strongly the characteristics of continuing to *learn* — however much they may be ready to acquire knowledge (traditionally defined), and particularly knowledge to which is attached the symbol of a graduate degree, which constitutes potential power and reward in present-day society. We have not observed any very significant differences in these respects as among those college graduates who enter administration and those who embark on other careers. (We sometimes wonder whether the attempt to inculcate the value and habit of continuing to learn is not nullified, in terms of behavioral results, by the very kind of word magic which, at commencement time, exhorts the degree recipients to respect the values of learning, and at the same time welcomes them into "the society of educated men.")

We would therefore settle, if need be, for one achievement of *insight into learning* by each student, in preference to all the display of conceptual virtuosity which many intelligent students can put on as a temporary achievement if the academic climate demands it. In general, however, the possibilities of student performance and achievement have seemed to us to exceed this minimum. And that is fortunate. The need for conceptual growth seems to us to require continuing professional development on the part of the educational administrator throughout his entire period of service. Whether this need is now felt by educational administrators is not the point; the conditions of this field and role would appear to enforce it with increasing rapidity.

We have purposely dwelt at some length upon the point of view and the feelings we hold with respect to the development of concepts study and our relationship to students in this connection. We have done so in order to avoid that kind of miscommunication about what "they" do and what "we" do which might follow from a terse statement about each of a series of successive steps adding up to a "method."

An Account of Procedure

In reporting the following series of steps and activities, we are simply giving an account of experience, and not a recommendation for the adoption elsewhere of the same procedure. We hope, however, that others may find the report of value to them in their search for ways to relate conceptual development and administrative skill.

Perhaps now, having endeavored to transmit some feelings as to the tentativeness of both our procedures and our impressions about this kind of experience, we may go on to a much more rapid presentation in terms of a sequence of activities.

As we have noted, we do not raise any questions or make any references to the study of concepts until after several weeks of case study and discussion, as a minimum. During this period, each of a series of cases ranging widely as to situation has been subjected to intensive use. The focus of attention is always on *this* case, *this* situation. There is no attempt on our part to produce "carry-over" or reference or learning from one case to another, and it is our observation that students rarely feel inclined to make reference to earlier cases in the discussion of later ones, at least for a long time. There is apparently enough within each case itself to command undivided attention. Experience is taking place certainly; what may be emerging out of the variety of this experience in the minds of different students, we are anything but certain. It is in such a setting that attention is first focused in what may seem to be quite a different direction — that of concepts. That is, up to this point — quite unlike the presentation in this book — the idea of "concepts" has received virtually no mention, except as the term may have been used or the notion discussed by someone in the course of a case discussion. The procedure is about as follows:

1. We remind the group of the name of this unit of study in the program and indicate that since the time thus far has been devoted exclusively to cases, it might be in order to consider the concepts parts of the course unit. We suggest that each student make it a point to *reflect* from time to time during the next several days on the cases and the case study experience thus far, *as a whole*. We indicate that at a designated session about a week hence we would like each student to bring in a list of eight or ten "concepts" (or "areas of conceptual study," or "areas considered from a conceptual point of view") which arise in his mind in the meantime as significant in the cases or in relation to administration more generally.

The list noted by each student need not be limited to concepts which he thinks are of major significance in terms of his own knowledge and thinking; his designation of concepts which he himself wishes to study and explore can be made later. His initial list may reflect his own interests and his own sense of concepts significant to himself, but essentially the first step embraces some notions he may have as to concepts which may be particularly significant for administrators — notions formed out of his reflections on cases and out of other experience he has had in administrative situations. It is explained that, at the session about a week hence, the range of concepts represented in the individual lists will be cumulated for everyone to see, without reference, however, to whose lists they came from. We ask each student to have a copy of his list for our information.

The question has always arisen: "What do you mean by concepts?" We answer that we hesitate to give any particular definition, since this term is used rather differently not only by different individuals but by users in different fields. We suggest that we wish to avoid prejudicing the students' selection of items for their lists, or confining them too narrowly in terms of any one definition. We point out that a part of the value of what we are attempting to do may lie in each student's becoming aware of what meaning he attaches to the term in comparison with the way others may use it. We do explain, however, usually in answer to further questions, that the term as most widely used seems not to consist of a *statement* about something (which must always embrace a minimum of two terms and announce a presumed relationship between them); it consists of merely a single term, though perhaps involving more than one word.

In this respect, as we see it, a concept differs from a *principle;* the latter is usually understood to refer to a statement about something, hence announces a presumed relationship between two terms, even if sometimes elided into what appears to be a phrase or even a single word. We point out that we can make such distinctions as the above only in terms of what appears to be most common usage within and between disciplines; for we are here clearly not talking about usage in the market place. Finally, again in answer to usual questions, we indicate that the term "idea" seems to us (to the extent that it is still used in scholarly or scientific disciplines) to be used so variably that it possesses even less commonality of concreteness and meaning than the term "concept," variously used though the latter may be. We indicate willingness to give some references which may help to clarify the differing ways in which the term is used within different disciplines. According to the interest which we sense as we respond to questions, we may either suggest some of these references at the time or await the re-emergence of the problem of definitions at the next or a later session.[1] All of the above usually consumes not more than fifteen to twenty minutes.

2. At the next session, a week later, we go through a process which some members of a university faculty might consider a ridiculous waste of time. We merely cumulate on the blackboard a master list of the concepts appearing on the students' individual lists. One student will start off by reading several terms from his list (or all, if he wants to); another adds some from his list; and so on until there are no new terms to be added. We list them on the board simply as they come. In the process, various students usually suggest new concepts not already on their own lists or the cumulated list. If this tendency starts to snowball, we point out that each student will have an opportunity to select his own focus of study and that the list already accumulated is sufficient for the present purpose. Words that are etymologically different are always listed by the instructor without question. If question does arise within the group, an interchange among students usually makes clear that the questioned term has sufficient difference in meaning from any other to warrant being listed. A few terms may be challenged by the class as inappropriate in a list of concepts, and accordingly be dropped or question-marked — a term such as "school buildings," for example. The class itself tends to avoid terms apparently thought of as referring to physical objects. Such terms as "whole child," "gifted child" and "retarded child" have been included in lists of concepts, but have been challenged by some. As the listing continues, the class shows an increasing desire to discuss, though not necessarily to challenge, new terms.

We shall take a moment here to suggest the kind of list likely to emerge from this process. It may total perhaps sixty to seventy terms; the process of

[1] C. Hempell, "Concept Formation," *International Encyclopedia of Social Sciences;* M. Sherif, "Some Social Psychological Aspects of Conceptual Functioning," and C. Kluckhohn, "The Special Character of Integration in an Individual Culture," in *Proceedings of the Stillwater Conference, Stillwater, Oklahoma* (New York: The Foundation for Integrated Education, 1950); W. E. Vinacke, "Concept Formation," Chap. 7 in *The Psychology of Thinking* (New York: McGraw-Hill Book Co., 1952); K. Schuessler and A. Strauss, "Socialization, Logical Reasoning and Concept Development in the Child," *American Sociological Review,* Vol. 16, No. 4 (August, 1951); K. Schuessler and A. Strauss, "A Study of Concept Learning by Scale Analysis," *American Sociological Review,* Vol. 15, No. 6 (December, 1950); K. Duncker; "On Problem Solving," *Psychological Monographs,* No. 270 (1945); N. S. Timasheff, "Definitions in the Social Sciences," *American Journal of Sociology,* Vol. 53, No. 3 (Nov., 1947); F. S. C. Northrop, *The Logic of the Sciences and the Humanities* (New York: Macmillan, 1946).

listing results in a non-ordered assortment (although sociometric study might show a pattern — as indeterminately affected by both students' and instructor's awareness of the presence of the sociometric observers). In our very limited experience, there has been a fairly high correspondence of terms submitted by groups of students in administration. Most of the terms are commonly associated with educational administration or are rather widely used in some of the social sciences; a few are more closely related to philosophy.

We list a selection of terms here simply to communicate more concretely:

Communications
Public relations
Personnel relations
Leadership
Role of public education in democracy
Academic freedom
Function of state *in re* education
Community participation
Progressive education
Traditional education
Span of control
Avoidance
Discipline
Delegation
Association
Conservation
Group dynamics
Coordination
Separation of church and state

Profession
Learning
Indoctrination
Culture
Responsibility
Education in international outlook
Experts
Community
Mores
Forecasting
Power
Authority
Democratic administration
Whole child
Curriculum
Religious prejudice
Controversial issues
Organization
Personality
Maturation

Value orientation
Status
Role
Emotive imputations
Child growth
Progress
Change
Emerging design
Tradition
Prognosis
Policy
Planning
Evaluation
Moral training
Social factors
Awareness
Equality of opportunity
Supervision
Subversion
Group
Reporting
Higher education

At the end of the session each student is asked to decide on one or more concepts or areas of concepts which he wishes to begin to explore, with the understanding that he is not committed at this point to more than two or three weeks of initial exploration. (We have experimented, not in the scientific sense, but in a tentative way, with an idea which involves asking each student to prepare his own "arrangement" of the accumulated list. The resulting schemes of arrangement are then examined and compared in one or more class sessions intervening between the above and the following session. We are too uncertain of the values involved in these experiments to warrant any exposition here of the products of these efforts and the processes of examination to which they are subjected. But we are continuing and refining these experiments as a result of our impressions that this step, at this particular stage in a university program of administrative training, may prove to be one of the most effective and also theoretically significant keys to the acceleration of conceptual development on the part of students.)

3. At the next session (perhaps more than one session may be needed) each student who is ready with his choice announces it. He is asked to talk for a minute or two about the area he has in mind for which the concept term represents merely a name or handle. Some students have a fairly definite meaning in mind. Others indicate that they have chosen a concept which they feel they know nothing about, in the sense of ever having studied or read anything revolving, specifically around that particular concept term; that is what they now wish to do.

The instructor asks each student if he wishes to go at it on his own or wants any suggestions as to readings. Most want suggestions; some indicate that they feel squared away without the instructor's help. In both cases, the instructor *may* ask one or two additional questions about the area in which the student is interested. This is almost always in order when a student wants suggestions. On the basis of his own acquaintance with various works, the instructor endeavors to suggest two or three books which a student might examine, though not necessarily read in detail, to see whether these are in the area or of the kind that primarily interests him. This probing by the student and his response to it may assist the instructor in being more helpful to him in his search. In suggesting a book, the instructor usually says a few words about it as a further trial balloon to see whether it seems to be one which the student perceives as within his interest.

When the instructor feels incapable of suggesting any initial reading in the student's field of interest, he refers the student to some other member of the faculty who may be better able to help him. Students who want to talk over their selection of possible initial readings with the instructor at more length make arrangements to do so. Most students are squared away by this time, however, and in the course of the session they usually decide on some readings to be done within the next few days. Occasionally, when a particular student's interest is being considered, other students may offer comments or suggestions for readings. Students frequently take notes on books or other sources of information mentioned from time to time in connection with the interests of other students.

It is explained to the group that although each one is pursuing his own interest, earlier groups have found it valuable to recognize the possible interest of others in the various readings. Each student will have opportunities to discuss with the group whatever values or findings from his study he feels have been significant to him or may be of significant interest to others. These opportunities will continue as long as time permits. Case study sessions and sessions on concepts come along in various frequencies, usually at least two or three of each in a row.

To facilitate opportunity for students to obtain maximum benefit from the concepts studies, the following procedural provisions are made:

1. A list of the initial concepts, together with the names of the students pursuing them, is supplied to each member of the class.

2. Each student, after reading any book, paper, or article, is expected to make out a card for a central file. He is also expected to prepare for the central file a very brief description of the general focus and content of the work; this is to consist of not more than two typewritten pages, and preferably not more than one. In addition to describing the work, the student is urged to add his comment as to whether he thinks others in administrative training ought to become familiar with it, and if so, why. Any subsequent reader of the same work is similarly urged to add his own comments.

This file of titles and general descriptions (not presumed to be of the order of careful *abstracts*) is designed as a utility to the students themselves. It is accumulated from year to year. Despite the lack of 100 per cent co-operation, the absence of any policing, and the relatively unsatisfactory facilities for access, it continues to grow and to be used by students as a mutual service.

3. When two or more members of the class select the same areas for examination and it develops that they are interested in the same aspects, it is suggested that they collaborate informally by pursuing different readings initially and exchanging ideas as to what works or findings emerge as most significant. Similarly, since several members are likely to select topics which they will recognize to be somewhat associated — "power" and "authority," for example; or "group dynamics," "social interaction," and perhaps "community participation"; or "personality," "maturation," and "awareness" — it is suggested that they cross-check to avoid duplication of readings at the outset. Finally, two students may come up with the same term — "communications," for example — when asked for their choice; but questions may clarify that one is interested primarily in the semantic aspects of communication, whereas the other is thinking about patterns of communication as found through research in industrial or other formal organizations. It is suggested that in their respective explorations they remain aware that they started with the same term and consult together on the problems of relationship between these differing meanings.

4. There are no requirements for any formal papers in connection with the study of concepts. Reports on work in progress at class sessions are to be largely governed by the students' own sense of what is significant.

5. Students are free to change the direction of their explorations. They are asked only to keep the instructor informed of these changes. He stands ready to consult with any student at any time on any aspect of his work in connection with this part of the program.

Choices and Processes of Study

This outline of procedure suggests fairly well the character of the activity. Some individual conversations take place between the instructor and almost every student at some point in the sequence of study, but not on a formally planned basis. Impromptu situations are plentiful enough to permit the instructor to initiate a move toward a conference with any student if he wishes to make such a move. Many students, of course, request opportunities to confer. Some seem to need conferences at the outset; others, after the period of initial exploration; and still others, at a point where their needs apparently revolve around the problem of integrating their study with their previous patterns of experience and thinking.

At any of the reporting sessions, several students may give their reports. One may present a summary comparing the views of several authors, or perhaps his own attempt to synthesize these views; another may wish to stress a particular work that sets familiar materials in a new light (as compared with his own previous thinking and his perceptions as to the outlook of others in the group). Sometimes the session is devoted primarily to the discussion of a problem of relationship that has emerged in the reports or discussions of several concepts.

The principal sharpenings of viewpoint are the ones that come as the students themselves highlight their experience and their directions of development toward new insights. As a result of the different readings, interest tends to mount with respect to certain areas and even with respect to certain books. The reading of certain books begins to spread. The choice of readings now seems to reflect a movement of the interests of more and more students in directions earlier chosen by few, if any. The books that are most widely read tend to be of three kinds: (1) ones which deal with gaps between two or more highly defined older disciplines; (2) ones which essentially represent efforts to develop philosophies capable of integrating various kinds of knowledge and thinking; and (3) ones which deal with problems of relationship within oneself and between oneself and others. This is not a universal or exclusive tendency, however. Reading still goes on in specific concept areas such as those appearing on the original lists, and such reading clearly represents the only interests in some cases.

The volume of reading done by students also varies widely. How much or how little is read is looked upon as a factor to be considered in relation to the individual student, his purpose in choosing what he is reading, and what he seems to be getting out of it. We are quite as much interested in his *reflecting* on what he reads (in contrast to thinking, in the more active sense of the term) and in his *assimilating* both his reading and other experience into some sort of unity. We are not interested in the oral and written verbalizations he can make which simply present the author's thesis in the author's words, unless he has previously impressed us as having "surface pick-up" tendencies or as being careless in his use of data. With some students we wish to avoid stimulating oral or verbal display. We satisfy ourselves with trying to take note of tendencies that seem to us unproductive, and with finding opportunities to confer with students exhibiting these tendencies.

We have seen three kinds of tendencies that strike us as unproductive, although tentative judgments are always relative to who the students are. (1) One or two students may show a strong leaning toward books almost on the "how to do it" level and be conspicuously nonparticipative in the general movement of reading and discussion. (2) One or two may be almost frenetic in their reading activity in terms of either volume or diversity. (3) Several may be going just slowly enough, in amount of reading accomplished, to prompt our attention. Our reaction to each of these tendencies could be considered only in terms of how we have tried to act in the individual case, under limited conditions of time for such conversations. (In a somewhat similar teaching situation, not in this institution, and with students training for careers in a different field, two or three students out of approximately two-hundred showed a proclivity to an extremely eclectic and continually shifting variety of readings, weighted toward works of esoteric character, as judged from the particular perspective of the instructor.)

Some Patterns of Reading

For purposes of illustration, we present here *some* of the concept areas which have been most chosen during the early stages of reading, together with some references.

In selecting examples to illustrate the process, we are purposely omitting those areas of concepts which revolve centrally around the social and behavioral sciences, for whose study provision is made in other units of the training program. In selecting concepts for study according to the procedure in the "cases and concepts" unit of the program just described, many students choose either to continue or to enlarge their understanding of concepts used in these fields and of the development of research and viewpoints in the behavioral sciences as now defined. Suggestions for readings in such areas are based in considerable part on bibliographies brought to the attention of the students by members of the instructional staff identified with the fields of political science, social psychology, and sociology. Similarly, many students in the program carry an elective in the field of human development, reflecting the resources and viewpoints of social and cultural anthropology.

For our purposes of illustration and indication of reading references, we therefore select a few representative conceptual areas, chosen by students, which lie somewhat *outside* the behavioral sciences in terms of current definitions.

1. *Administration.* Most students choosing this concept, or perhaps some such related term as "coordination," indicate that their interest lies in comparative study and in formulations about administration based on comparative experience. Readings include such works as:

Gulick, L., and L. Urwick. *Papers on the Science of Administration.* New York: Institute of Public Administration, Columbia University, 1937.

Mayo, E. *The Social Problems of an Industrial Civilization.* Boston: Division of Research, Harvard Business School, 1945.

Mooney, J. D., and A. C. Reilly. *Onward Industry.* New York: Harper and Brothers, 1931.

Taylor, F. W. *The Principles of Scientific Management.* New York: Harper and Brothers, 1923.

Urwick, L. *The Elements of Administration.* New York: Harper and Brothers, 1943.

It should be pointed out here that prior to enrollment each student is sent a list of suggested readings. This list includes:

Barnard, Chester I. *The Functions of the Executive.* Cambridge: Harvard University Press, 1938.

Dubin, Robert. *Human Relations in Administration.* New York: Prentice-Hall, 1951.

Homans, George. *The Human Group.* New York: Harcourt, Brace and Co., 1950.

Hoslett, Schuyler Dean (ed.). *Human Factors in Management.* Revised edition. New York: Harper and Brothers, 1951.

Metcalf, Henry C., and Lyndall Urwick (eds.). *Dynamic Administration: The Collected Papers of Mary Parker Follett.* New York: Harper and Brothers, 1942.

National Society for the Study of Education. *Changing Conceptions in Educational Administration.* Forty-fifth Yearbook of the Society, Part II. Chicago: University of Chicago Press, 1946.

Roethlisberger, Fritz J. *Management and Morale.* Cambridge: Harvard University Press, 1941.

Sears, Jesse B. *The Nature of the Administrative Process.* New York: McGraw-Hill Book Co., 1950.

Simon, Herbert A., Donald W. Smithburg, and Victor A. Thompson. *Public Administration.* New York: Alfred A. Knopf, 1950.

Whyte, William F. (ed.). *Industry and Society.* New York: McGraw-Hill Book Co., 1946.

Most students interested in the comparative study of administration tend to find many of their interests somewhat closely related to those of students who have selected "authority" or "power" as points of departure. Readings relating to the latter concepts tend to lie chiefly in political science, although some readings reflect the more recent interest in "power" defined as a sociological concept.

Students concentrating on "administration" also cross into the field of studies being followed primarily by those who are interested in such concepts as "status" and "role," as these terms are used in sociology and anthropology. They may also move into the same area as those who, in selecting "morale" as a topic, have indicated a primary interest in this concept in relation to *formal* organization. All these students tend to find a common ground of interest in research studies in industrial or other formal organizations, some of which are represented in works already cited (Roethlisberger, Mayo, Homans).

The above discussion of converging or crossing lines of interest is by no means exhaustive. Those pursuing the concept of "administration" also meet, in some areas, those pursuing the concepts of "communications" and "organization" — the latter in the special sense in which various students are interested, as next noted.

2. *Organization.* We here refer to the readings of students who indicate that their interests lie in the concept "organization," in the sense of its meaning in the sciences that deal with living organisms in general (not merely human societies), and perhaps even more broadly. Their readings, therefore, initially involve different areas from those explored by students who in selecting this term have expressed a primary interest in *human* social organization; students expressing this latter interest start reading in areas closely related to those of students who have designated concepts ranging from "community" to "group dynamics" and "interactions." These, as we have noted, involve readings in the social sciences, which are dealt with in other units of the program; such readings are based largely on bibliographical references supplied by our colleagues from these fields.

Readings pertaining to the concept of "organization" as applied more generally to living organisms include such works as:

Haskins, C. P. *Of Societies and Men.* New York: W. W. Norton and Co., 1951.

Pearse, I., and L. Crocker. *The Peckham Experiment, a Study in the Living Structure of Society.* New Haven: Yale University Press, 1945.

Redfield, R. *Levels of Integration in Biological and Social Systems.* Lancaster, Pa.: The Jaques Catell Press, 1942.

Zipf, G. K. *Human Behavior and the Principle of Least Effort.* Cambridge: Addison-Wesley Press, 1949.

Those who read in this area find themselves dealing with some works which draw heavily on concepts from fields being explored by students who have selected "personality," "child development," and also "planning" (see below). Again cross-readings ensue, together with conversations among those who have converged upon the same readings from different directions.

3. *Planning.* Students selecting this concept tend to be primarily interested in broadening their understanding of city and regional planning. These interests apparently become important in their thinking during the course of their contract study for a school system. Readings include:

Directive Committee for Regional Planning, Yale University. *The Case for Regional Planning.* New Haven: Yale University Press, 1947.

MacKaye, Benton. *The New Exploration.* New York: Harcourt, Brace and Co., 1928.

Mumford, L. *The Culture of the Cities.* New York: Harcourt, Brace and Co., 1938.

It should be noted here that various readings in urban and community sociology, urban demography, and urban political organization constitute recommended readings in conjunction with earlier social science study in

> the training program. Further study is given to these areas by students who select "planning." Readings pursued in connection with the concept of planning also tend to draw on studies of the particular region (New England) which stimulate interest because of their relevance to the local problems and tasks in which the students have been or are still involved.

Students pursuing the concept of "planning" also find themselves involved in cross-links with those students pursuing "administration" who have veered toward a particular interest in the concept of "forecasting"; the latter interest seems to lead primarily to economic and business forecasting, and thereby to concepts of "trend" and "cycle."

Some who start with "planning" develop an increasing interest in "ecology" (another concept not originally appearing on the accumulated list), particularly with reference to the relations between human societies, or mankind as a whole, and the physical environment. The direction and conjunction of the interests in "planning," "forecasting," and "ecology" lead to readings which reflect quite different perspectives, for example:

Dewey, E. R., and E. F. Dakin. *Cycles: The Science of Prediction.* New York: Henry Holt and Co., 1947.

Gutkind, E. A. *Community and Environment.* New York: Philosophical Library, 1954.

Osborn, F. A. *Our Plundered Planet.* Boston: Little, Brown and Co., 1948.

4. *Personality and Awareness.* Students selecting "personality" and "awareness" tend to speak of their interests in such similar terms that these concepts can be dealt with as a single area as regards the division of labor on initial readings.

> It might first be noted that the following books either appear on the list of readings suggested prior to enrollment or are otherwise recommended earlier:
>
> Lecky, P. *Self-Consistency.* New York: Island Press, 1951.
>
> Moreno, J. L. *Who Shall Survive?* New York: Beacon House, 1953.
>
> Riesman, D. *The Lonely Crowd.* New Haven: Yale University Press, 1950.

Among the readings indicated to be of value by those who have selected either of these two concepts are:

Alexander, F., and T. M. French. *Psychoanalytic Therapy.* New York: Ronald Press, 1946.

Allport, G. W. *The Nature of Personality: Selected Papers.* Cambridge: Addison-Wesley Press, 1950.

Cattell, R. B. *An Introduction to Personality.* London: Hutchinson's University Library, 1950.

Fromm, E. *Man for Himself.* New York: Rinehart, 1947.

Ghiselin, B. (ed.). *The Creative Process.* Berkeley: University of California Press, 1952.

Jersild, A. T. *In Search of Self.* New York: Teachers College, Columbia University, 1952.

Lowenfeld, V. *Creative and Mental Growth.* New York: Macmillan, 1952.

Mead, G. H. *Mind, Self and Society.* Chicago: University of Chicago Press, 1934.

Rogers, C. R., *Counseling and Psychotherapy.* Boston: Houghton Mifflin Co., 1942.

Sullivan, H. S. "Conceptions of Modern Psychiatry," reprinted from *Psychiatry: Journal of the Biology and Pathology of Interpersonal Relations,* Vol. 3, No. 1 (Feb., 1940) and Vol. 8, No. 2 (May, 1945).

Tead, O. *The Art of Leadership.* New York McGraw-Hill Book Co., 1935.

5. *Value Orientations.* The initial interests of those who select this concept tend to lie in either of two directions. Some students are interested primarily in inter-group and inter-cultural relations within communities and within the larger American society. These students at the outset find themselves most closely allied with students of problems or concepts in social relations. Others are primarily interested in the relationships between the value systems of the major cultural outlooks and societies in the world today. Readings in this area include such books as:

Margenau, H. "Remarks on Ethical Science," *Proceedings of the Stillwater Conference, Stillwater, Oklahoma.* New York: Foundation for Integrated Education, 1950.

Mumford, L. *The Condition of Man.* New York: Harcourt, Brace and Co., 1948.

——— *The Conduct of Life.* New York: Harcourt, Brace and Co., 1951.

Northrop, F. S. C. *The Meeting of East and West.* New York: The Macmillan Co., 1953.

Sorokin, P. A. *The Reconstruction of Humanity.* Boston: Beacon Press, 1948.

Toynbee, A. *Civilization on Trial.* New York: Oxford University Press, 1948.

Ulich, R. *Man and Reality — Three Dimensions of Human Experience.* New Haven: Edward W. Hazen Foundation, Hazen Pamphlet #21, 1948.

The shift in the reading interests of those selecting "value orientations" as their point of departure appears to move in the direction of philosophy. This is hardly unnatural in view of the nominal identity in the originally selected term and of the "vectors of value" emerging through the stochastic processes of the group as a whole.

Bibliography on Cases and Case Methods

In presenting the following selected bibliography of books and articles on case methods, we suggest that the first three listed may have immediate interest and value to teachers of educational administration, for the reasons given in each instance.

Andrews, Kenneth R. (ed.). *The Case Method of Teaching Human Relations and Administration.* Cambridge: Harvard University Press, 1953.

This work consists of a series of papers by various members of the Faculty of the Harvard Graduate School of Business Administration. It treats such special aspects of case methods as views of the teacher role, use of written case analyses, and examination in case courses, as well as theory and perspectives.

Hunt, Pearson. "The Case Method of Instruction," *Harvard Educational Review,* 21: 175–92 (Summer, 1951).

An article written to an audience in schools of professional education.

Stein, Harold. "Introduction," pp. ix–xlv in *Public Administration and Policy Development: A Case Book.* New York: Harcourt, Brace, 1952.

Presents a point of view and an experience from the field of public administration.

Berrien, F. K. *Comments and Cases on Human Relations.* New York: Harper and Brothers, 1951.

Boedecker, K. A. "Case Method of Instruction," *Collegiate News and Views,* 5: 1–6 (March, 1952).

Cabot, H., and J. A. Kahl. *Human Relations: Cases and Concepts in Concrete Social Science.* Cambridge: Harvard University Press, 1953.

Castore, G. F. "Attitudes of Students Toward the Case Method of Instruction in a Human Relations Course," *Journal of Educational Research,* 45: 201–13 (November, 1951).

Conant, J. B. *On Understanding Science.* New York: New American Library: 1951.

Culliton, J. W. "The Question That Has Not Been Asked, Cannot Be Answered," *Education for Professional Responsibility.* Pittsburgh: Carnegie Press, 1948, pp. 85–93.

Donham, W. B. "The Unfolding of Collegiate Business Training," *The Harvard Graduates' Magazine,* March, 1921, pp. 333–47.

——— *Education for Responsible Living.* Cambridge: Harvard University Press, 1944.

——— "Why Experiment? Case System in College Teaching, Social Sciences," *Journal of General Education*, January, 1949.

Dubin, R. *Human Relations in Administration: The Sociology of Organization with Readings and Cases.* New York: Prentice-Hall, 1951.

Glover, J. D., and R. M. Hower. *The Administrator: Cases in Human Relations in Business.* Chicago: Richard D. Irwin, 1950.

——— *Some Notes on the Use of "The Administrator: Cases in Human Relations in Business"* (pamphlet). Chicago: Richard D. Irwin, 1949.

Lee, I. J. *Customs and Crises in Communication.* New York: Harper and Brothers, 1954.

McNair, M. P. (with assistance of A. C. Hersum). *The Case Method at the Harvard Business School.* (Papers by present and past members of the faculty and staff.) New York: McGraw-Hill Book Co., 1954.

Smith, G. A. *Policy Formulation and Administration.* Chicago: Richard D. Irwin, 1951.

Stein, H. "Preparation of Case Studies: The Problem of Abundance," *American Political Science Review*, 45: 479–87 (June, 1951).

Alphabetical List of Cases

For tables showing the distribution of cases by *Substantive Elements* and by *Actors*, see page 48.

DATE DUE